SURVEYING
SUBJECTIVE
PHENOMENA

VOLUME 2

SURVEYING SUBJECTIVE PHENOMENA

VOLUME 2

CHARLES F. TURNER AND
ELIZABETH MARTIN, EDITORS

Panel on Survey Measurement of Subjective Phenomena
Committee on National Statistics
Commission on Behavioral and Social Sciences and Education
National Research Council

RUSSELL SAGE FOUNDATION   NEW YORK

THE RUSSELL SAGE FOUNDATION, one of the oldest of America's general purpose foundations, was established in 1907 by Mrs. Margaret Olivia Sage for "the improvement of social and living conditions in the United States." The Foundation seeks to fulfill this mandate by fostering the development and dissemination of knowledge about the political, social, and economic problems of America. It conducts research in the social sciences and public policy, and publishes books and pamphlets that derive from this research.

The Foundation provides support for individual scholars and collaborates with other granting agencies and academic institutions in studies of social problems. It maintains a professional staff of social scientists who engage in their own research as well as advise on Foundation programs and projects. The Foundation also conducts a Visiting Scholar Program and a Post-doctoral Fellowship Program.

The Board of Trustees is responsible for oversight and the general policies of the Foundation, while the immediate administrative direction of the program and staff is vested in the President, assisted by the officers and staff. The President bears final responsibility for the decision to publish a manuscript as a Russell Sage Foundation book. In reaching a judgment on the competence, accuracy, and objectivity of each study, the President is advised by the staff and a panel of special readers.

The conclusions and interpretations in Russell Sage Foundation publications are those of the authors and not of the Foundation, its Trustees, or its staff. Publication by the Foundation, therefore, does not imply endorsement of the contents of the study. It does signify that the manuscript has been reviewed by competent scholars in the field and that the Foundation finds it worthy of public consideration.

THE NATIONAL RESEARCH COUNCIL was established by the National Academy of Sciences in 1916 to associate the broad community of science and technology with the Academy's purposes of furthering knowledge and of advising the federal government. The Council operates in accordance with general policies determined by the Academy under the authority of its congressional charter of 1863, which establishes the Academy as a private, nonprofit, self-governing membership corporation. The Council has become the principal operating agency of both the National Academy of Sciences and the National Academy of Engineering in the conduct of their services to the government, the public, and the scientific and engineering communities. It is administered jointly by both Academies and the Institute of Medicine. The National Academy of Engineering and the Institute of Medicine were established in 1964 and 1970, respectively, under the charter of the National Academy of Sciences.

The project that is the subject of this report was approved by the Governing Board of the National Research Council, whose members are drawn from the Councils of the National Academy of Sciences, the National Academy of Engineering, and the Institute of Medicine. The members of the panel responsible for the report were chosen for their special competences and with regard for appropriate balance.

This report has been reviewed by a group other than the authors according to procedures approved by a Report Review Committee consisting of members of the National Academy of Sciences, the National Academy of Engineering, and the Institute of Medicine.

Library of Congress Catalog Number: 83-61131
Standard Book Number: 0-87154-883-6 (Volume 2)
0-87154-882-8 (Volume 1), 0-87154-881-X (set)

Panel on Survey Measurement of Subjective Phenomena

Contributors

BARBARA A. BAILAR, Bureau of the Census

JAMES R. BENIGER, Department of Sociology, Princeton University

CLIFFORD C. CLOGG, Departments of Sociology and Statistics, Pennsylvania State University

JEAN M. CONVERSE, Survey Research Center, University of Michigan

THERESA J. DeMAIO, National Research Council

OTIS DUDLEY DUNCAN, Department of Sociology, University of Arizona

JUDITH T. LESSLER, Research Triangle Institute, Research Triangle Park, North Carolina

MICHAEL B. MacKUEN, Department of Political Science, Washington University

CATHERINE MARSH, Social and Political Sciences Committee, Cambridge University

ELIZABETH MARTIN, National Research Council

J. G. TULIP MEEKS, Faculty of Economics and Politics, Cambridge University

SANDRA J. NEWMAN, Graduate Program in Public Policy Studies, Johns Hopkins University

STANLEY PRESSER, Survey Research Center, University of Michigan

NAOMI D. ROTHWELL, Bureau of the Census

HOWARD SCHUMAN, Department of Sociology and Institute for Social Research, University of Michigan

TOM W. SMITH, National Opinion Research Center, University of Chicago

CHARLES F. TURNER, National Research Council

Contents

CONTENTS

Contents

Volume 1

Preface

Surveys are a relatively recent invention. Their modern form evolved from the experiences of election polling in the 1930s and from breakthroughs made during the same decade in developing the statistical theory of sampling. The mating of sampling theory and systematic interview techniques made it theoretically possible to estimate the characteristics of very large populations by studying relatively small samples.

Although the speculative use of surveys to make election forecasts led to some early disappointments (most notably in the 1948 presidential election), the survey enterprise has expanded greatly in size and influence during the ensuing decades. Today tens of millions of Americans are surveyed annually, and a veritable avalanche of newspaper stories, television broadcasts, and government and scholarly publications report the results of those surveys. Business and government agencies routinely conduct surveys for a wide variety of purposes. And in the social sciences, surveys have become one of the most commonly used methods of empirical research.

The amazing growth of the survey enterprise since the 1930s has been accompanied by persistent concerns about the reliability, validity, and usefulness of survey data, voiced by persons both inside and outside the survey field. Such concerns provided the general impetus for our study.

The Panel on Survey Measurement of Subjective Phenomena was convened in January 1980 under the auspices of the Committee on National Statistics. The panel included social scientists, statisticians, and survey researchers from academic, government, and commercial survey organizations. Volume 1 of *Surveying Subjective Phenomena*, the main product of the panel's work, presents a broad review of many aspects of our topic. In its work, the panel was aided by the individual contributions of panel members and others who undertook special studies on topics related to its charge. Volume 2 contains the reports of those studies. All the chapters in this volume were reviewed by members of the panel (and in some cases by other reviewers) and were revised in light of those reviews. Final responsibility for these chapters rests, of course, with the authors.

We believe readers will find these chapters helpful in appreciating more fully many of the topics that are treated more summarily in Volume 1. We are indebted to the authors for their willingness to share their work with us (in several instances, work already in progress before the panel came into existence).

We are grateful to the National Science Foundation and the Russell Sage Foundation for the support they provided for this work. (The preface to Volume 1 contains a more complete catalog of the acknowledgments due to the many people and organizations who made this study possible.)

Charles F. Turner and Elizabeth Martin

PART I

MEASUREMENT OF SUBJECTIVE PHENOMENA IN THE SOCIAL SCIENCES

The idea that people can be asked direct questions as a way of measuring their attitudes, opinions, and other subjective states is fundamental to most survey research. Despite the fact that all the social sciences draw upon data gathered in this way, the survey method of direct measurement is viewed with skepticism and ambivalence by many social scientists. The first part of Volume 2 offers an historical perspective on the ways social scientists have approached the problem of measuring subjective phenomena.

In Chapter 1, Jean Converse traces the development of the attitude concept in psychology and sociology, and recounts the history of attitude measurement and scale construction during the 1930s and 1940s. This was a lively and active period, and Converse shows how several enduring characteristics of the survey enterprise have their roots in this period—among them, the cleavage between psychological and sociological approaches to measurement issues, and differences in the institutionalization of survey research in the commercial sphere, in academia, and in government.

In Chapter 2, J. G. Tulip Meeks considers a rather different perspective. Many economists argue that life conducts its own surveys, presenting an unending series of problems that people resolve and act upon, and that these actions can be taken as revealing underlying preferences and values. To explore this "indirect" approach, the panel commissioned Meeks to review how economists have come to terms with the inescapably subjective concept of *utility* that lies at the heart of much economic theory. The panel invited Meeks to prepare an historical and philosophical review "of the roots and role of the concept of utility in economic theory . . . [including] a discussion of the defining characteristics of the concept, and how it should be inferred or measured."

It is fascinating to contrast Meeks's description of the evolution of the concept of utility in economics with Converse's account of the development of the attitude concept in psychology and sociology. If one were to caricature the psychologists and sociologists as fools who rushed in, naming and measuring all sorts of attitudes and subjective states, then the economists would be angels so ethereal they feared to tread in this area. Indeed, some economists have been so deeply troubled by its problems of measurement that they have sought to purge the concept of utility from economic theory. Despite this divergence between the disciplines, many of the arguments of the economists will sound familiar to other social scientists. Thus Edgeworth in 1881 sounds remarkably like a contemporary survey researcher when he confesses that while "we cannot *count* the golden sands of life [or] *number* the 'innumerable smile[s]' of seas of love . . . but we seem capable of observing that there is here a *greater* there a *less*. . . ."

In Chapter 3 we turn from theoretical to practical concerns. In that chapter Stanley Presser reviews the use of survey measurements in research reported in leading social science journals. His review indicates that over the past 30 years surveys have become a major source of research data for the social sciences. Presser's findings also contain some disturbing news; his review indicates that the increased use of survey data during this period has not been accompanied by very much improvement in the way surveys are reported. Indeed, Presser finds that "Although there has been improvement in some areas, overall, fewer than half the articles reported anything about sampling methods, response rate, the wording of even a single question, year of the survey, or interviewer characteristics. These reporting levels are not markedly better than those of the much-criticized mass media. . . ." (page 105–106).

1

Attitude Measurement in Psychology and Sociology: The Early Years

Jean M. Converse

The Beginnings

The study of attitudes began to flourish in academic social psychology in the early 1920s, well before the advent of the new opinion polls of 1935, and attitudes became a key piece of the mosaic that later became survey research. In later years, survey research became omniverous, taking in everything it could get—opinions, facts, information, behavior, preferences, beliefs, experiences, measures of personality and even of physiology. But attitudes were the first content. The quantification of attitudes represented in part an effort to apply to subjective phenomena in social science some of the precision of measurement of physical science. The enterprise had little of the prestige of experimental psychology, however, and the experimentalists in fact thought that things had gone rather too far even by 1926, when they took a stand at their annual meeting:

Resolved that this meeting deplores the increasing practice of collecting administrative or supposedly scientific data by way of questionnaires; and that the meeting deplores especially the practice under which graduate students undertake research by sending questionnaires to professional psychologists. [Ruckmick, 1930:34]

Attitude measurement nevertheless persisted, not only by questionnaire but also by personal interview, direct observation, unobtrusive observation, personal documents, analysis of records, and content analysis. Whether individual respondents themselves could be relied upon to report the content of their subjective experience depended in good part upon whether one came to the study of attitudes from the discipline of sociology or psychology. Sociologists were more hopeful of finding *behaviors* to illuminate attitudes, while psychologists were more likely to trust to *opinions* as at least useful indicators. In time, the psychological perspective held more sway in the definition, but in these early years, attitudes were a rich and amorphous lot.

THE CONCEPT OF ATTITUDE

W. I. Thomas is credited with introducing the concept of attitude into social psychology in 1918 in his work (with Florian Znaniecki) *The Polish Peasant in Europe and America* (Zimmerman, 1925; G. Allport, 1935; Faris, 1931; Fleming, 1967).[1] Thomas's definition was a loose one, referring to a state of consciousness, a potential activity toward or away from some object of value. It was vague on a number of points (Thomas and Znaniecki, 1918:22-23), and definitions subsequently abounded (for example, Allport collected 16 in 1935). Classification of types of attitudes was also a busy enterprise (see Park and Burgess, 1924; Faris, 1925; Bernard, 1930; Kulp, 1934-35). In a sense the concept of attitude became a catchall, but it simultaneously stimulated much empirical work. Its utility probably proceeded much from what attitudes were *not*.

1. Attitudes were not instincts, from the study of which psychologists were withdrawing (Fearing, 1931; Rice, 1930b; LaPiere, 1938).[2] Attitudes were bred of continuous experience in the social world, not inherent in biological structure. As Stuart Rice (1930a:11) pointed out, "since human experience is infinitely varied, attitudes are regarded as variables and hence theoretically subject to measurement." They could be measured over space, over time, within individuals, across groups, and as Thomas and Znaniecki conceptualized, they could be used to analyze the interaction and integration between groups and individuals, culture and personality.

2. Attitudes were not merely ideas, beliefs, or ideologies—not merely an intellectual matter. The light cast by Freud, Jung, and Adler on the purportedly rational made such intellectual constructs seem simplistic in their

neglect of feelings and unconscious motivations. In Gordon Allport's discussion (1935:801), it was the influence of Freud that resurrected attitudes from the unconscious level that could not be studied and "endowed them with vitality . . . longing, hatred and love, with passion and prejudice . . . with the onrushing stream of unconscious life." Attitudes were closer to the nerve and the bone. And everyone had them.

3. Yet attitudes were not just feelings. They had some cognitive structure, but they had energy or "color" as well. They were a mix of the affective and cognitive, and as cognitions they could be reflected upon—and reported to or observed by inquiring social scientists.

4. They were not merely opinions. Attitudes had something of deep structure: they were somehow underlying. Not so deep, usually, as the unconscious, where they would animate rationalization, illusion, and neurotic adjustments and could not be fairly reported at all (although certainly that could happen to some attitudes and to some people). But they also were not as superficial as opinions, which might be too specific, transient, or intellectualized, without an integrative role in personality or behavior. For many researchers, opinions would serve as a verbal indicator of underlying attitudes, however.

5. Attitudes were not only behavior, but they had something important to do with behavior and human action. Some social scientists (especially sociologists) argued that behaviors should be considered the only meaningful indicators of underlying attitudes. The sociologist Read Bain could point in 1930 to a veritable grab bag of terms that were often used loosely, vaguely, or interchangeably: attitude, trait, opinion, wish, interest, disposition, desire, bias, preference, prejudice, will, sentiment, motive, objective, goal, idea, ideal, emotion, instinct (Bain, 1930:367). (He did not even mention such candidates as habit, belief, feeling, judgment, value, ideology, or stereotype.)[3] But it was not quite as chaotic as Bain contended. One emergent order was created as psychologists and sociologists pursued the study of attitudes in their different fashions.

Psychologists and sociologists gravitated to different styles of attitude study. This was not a perfect split; there was variability within each group. But psychologists started their study of attitudes with training in laboratory experimentation that made their inquiry more rigorous; sociologists brought to their inquiry a tradition in fieldwork that was still informal and intuitive. Representatives of the two groups took different paths to techniques of measurement, the subjects used, the setting in which studies were conducted, and the indicators of attitude that each group trusted more. Psychologists used questionnaire data that permitted quantification most often obtained from students: their classroom setting had some properties of the laboratory; they inquired into verbal measures, especially opinions, as indicators of attitude. Sociologists, for their part, placed more reliance on personal interviews and case history methods; they sought out subcultures in the noncollege-educated adult population; their setting of choice was the community rather than the classroom; and they sought behavioral indicators that could be observed directly or had been recorded publicly or even recounted personally at least as supplements to opinions.

Psychologists and Sociologists

PSYCHOLOGISTS' ATTITUDES

Questionnaires. The psychologists' enthusiasm and skill for a quantitative approach to attitudes came naturally. This was only a new variant on the tradition of mental measurement, which had burgeoned in psychology after the development of Binet's intelligence tests in 1905. Testing of mental characteristics and character traits had flourished in the various applied psychologies, especially the intelligence testing of army recruits in World War I, but also the testing of school children, vocational testing, testing of employee performance and (later) morale (Hart, 1923; Manson, 1925-26). Noting a decline in the measuring of intelligence and a new enthusiasm for attitude measurement, Gordon Allport (1935:828) had the impression that "militant testing, having won victories on one field of battle, has sought a new world to conquer." To move from mental tests to attitude questionnaires was a step that psychologists took rather easily, publishing in this period a great volume of attitude studies in such psychological journals as *Journal of Abnormal Psychology*, *Journal of Social Psychology*, *Psychological Bulletin*, *Psychological Review*, as well as in journals of personnel and industrial psychology.

Student Subjects. "That attitude studies have so frequently been limited to students is a misfortune that we shall have many occasions to lament," wrote Murphy, Murphy, and Newcomb (1937:905) in their revision of a 1931 review of the attitude literature. But in fact, that being said, they did not lament much. In their 1931 review, the Murphys had described 55 studies of attitude in some detail; only 5 dealt with respondents who were all members of the adult population outside the college community; 45 dealt exclusively with students. Gordon Allport, in his important 1935 review, summarized various studies without indicating that they were based exclusively on college students or school children. It should be noted that the subject matter of the great bulk of attitude research was not the college experience itself, for which students would have, of course, been essential. Students were being used most often as surrogates for people in general. And rather than being a source of widely acknowledged regret, it was assumed as a fact of research life[4] for a number of reasons, not the least of which was the lack of research funds. That subjects in the classroom helped provide for low-cost research almost goes without saying. These were indeed days when many social scientists who embarked on research did so at their own expense, or with mere pittances of support. Attitude studies of national scope were largely out of the question.

Some psychologists ventured out of the classroom in person or by mail (see Vetter and Green, 1932-33; Robinson, 1933; Schanck, 1934), but more stayed put and worked with a set of complex questionnaires and attitude changes, for which students were appropriate subjects. First, to use such instruments one needed people with the talent for attitudes—people who were literate, comprehending, articulate, self-conscious to some extent about their intellectual, political, and moral positions; in short, people who were trained in having attitudes. Many students were indeed learning in college about just that—having attitudes on war, peace, the church, prohibition, business and labor, and the like. With experts (or emerging experts) such as this, one did not have problems of translation, involving language itself, simplified wording, presenting less-intellectualized ideas, or using situations and concerns closer to the common experience.

Second, one needed people with time and tolerance, and students could be—gently—imposed upon.[5] Authority relations of the classroom helped ensure that most students would cooperate in the request for data, and the form as a rule was the entirely familiar paper-and-pencil test. It is surely no accident that when Samuel Stouffer and his colleagues conducted research with American soldiers of World War II, they used paper-and-pencil questionnaires in classroom style, rather than going to the bother and expense of using interviewers. This was the case not only because soldiers were already gathered in groups, but also because they routinely worked within a setting where time was controlled.

Laboratory Settings. With these simple resources psychologists were free to conduct quite *pure* tests of attitudes where they would be found in abundance—it was a little like doing epidemiological studies in hospitals—and where conditions resembled those of a laboratory, in the degree of control. A single investigator could manage the test, specifying the time, place, duration, number of people, and invariant wording of questions, without risk that respondents or interviewers would change things when they were out of the reach of the investigator. Psychologists wrote up their results in good experimental fashion, explaining the conditions under which the test was given, along with tests of reliability and such indications of validity as they could muster, providing at least a portion of the test questionnaire if not the entire instrument.

Opinions. The use of verbal indicators by psychologists meant in theory that underlying attitudes were to be inferred from the opinions gathered by questionnaire. In practice the opinions themselves were often of commanding interest, and many investigators used the two terms synonymously. Asking opinions directly represented an implicit confidence that respondents were capable of giving reasonably faithful accounts of their own opinions under the admittedly contrived conditions of a written questionnaire. Psychologists paid tribute indirectly to the essential validity of self-reports of the subjective realm and to their own instruments for studying it. Sociologists were more likely to doubt both assumptions.

SOCIOLOGISTS' ATTITUDES

Interviews and Case Histories. The quantitative side of sociology was at this time being tended for the most part by demographers and statisticians who worked with grouped data of the census and other governmental statistics, or ecologists who studied physical-cultural distributions. Sociologists interested in attitudes were not generally as well trained in quantitative techniques. They tended to work intuitively with interviews of an unstructured sort, without standardized questionnaires or standardized interview schedules, using life histories, written or recounted, letters, diaries, and personal documents on the qualitative side of life. Various sociologists urged the integration of the statistical and case history approach to data (Burgess, 1927-28, 1928, 1929; Rice, 1931a; K. Young, 1931a) so that insight could be stimulated by the qualitative material and hypotheses could be verified by statistical analysis, but real integration of the two methods required case studies in greater number and standardization than could usually be had (Lundberg, 1929).

Subcultures and Communities. Sociologists and their wing of social psychology also used students in the classroom for the study of attitudes, but more often than psychologists they sought out other groups as well. The disciplinary concerns of sociologists with groups, communities, social structure, status, and culture and personality directed them to try to learn the attitudes of various subcultures—immigrants, Orientals on the West Coast, hoboes, lumberjacks, ministers, delinquents, farmers—finding in the study of attitudes the link between the individual and the culture (Anderson, 1923; Clark, 1923-24; Thrasher, 1927; Zimmerman, 1925, 1927; Zimmerman and Anderson, 1927-28; Park, 1926; Bogardus, 1926b, 1928; Burgess, 1927-28, 1929; Carpenter and Katz, 1928; P. Young, 1928; Lynd and Lynd, 1929; Albig, 1930-31; Hayner, 1936). These were sometimes of interest precisely because they were not in the mainstream of middle-class American life. The fact that these people were generally less educated than the college student subjects of psychologists was undoubtedly a factor encouraging sociologists to intuit and interpret their subjects rather than to let them speak for themselves directly through questionnaires.

Real-World Settings. Social scientists interested in these communities and groups naturally had to go out in the world to find them. Carle C. Zimmerman, for his study of farmers' attitudes in 1925, selected a total of 345 Minnesota farmers from nine towns by setting out north, south, east, and west from the center of town and taking each farmer along the road until he had located a quarter of the number needed. He collected all kinds of data about farm conditions in the area as well as about individual farmers' experiences, verbal attitudes, farmers' own explanations of their views, and other people's insights into those farmers' situations. But he left us very little specific information about his procedures. He appears to have worked with informal interviewing that was structured enough to permit tabulations of all 345 farmers on certain issues and to analyze attitudes that had been bred of experience in contrast to those based on traditional ideology (Zimmerman, 1925; see also Garnett, 1927; Allen and Barton, 1934; Locke, 1934-35; Kirkpatrick and Boynton, 1936; Webb and Brown, 1938).

Richard LaPiere explored French and English racial attitudes by roaming widely in both countries. He ranged up and down the social ladder by choosing first-, second-, and third-class railroad cars and restaurants, striking up conversations where he could, and thus encountered more than 700 people altogether. When it seemed appropriate to do so, he inserted a question about reaction to Negroes into the conversation. In France, he asked a question about welcoming a Negro into one's home; only upper-class French people showed much evidence of prejudice. In England, he asked a different question, about allowing white and black children to play together. He apparently did so because he found racial antipathy so much more widespread and intense in England that the question used in France would have produced no variation; that is, it would have yielded an invariable "No" (LaPiere, 1928). These studies by Zimmerman and LaPiere were imaginative explorations, but they were not the stuff of laboratory conditions and they did not present scrupulous accounts of the procedures used —both being experimental norms important to psychologists.

Behaviors. Experiments comparing observed behaviors with expressed opinions were rare in either field at the time (Schanck, 1934; LaPiere,

1934),[6] and they remain costly and difficult still. But in general, sociologists were less likely than psychologists were to trust to professed opinions alone. But how to gather up behaviors? There were three techniques available. First, there was the stock of behaviors that had been recorded prior to and independent of a given study: votes cast, taxes paid, magazine articles published, churches joined, concerts attended, and so forth, on which statistical analysis could be conducted. Here there was little risk of the subjective difficulties of fallible memory or conscious deception, but the advantages of such "hard" data had the attendant disadvantage that the data could not be disaggregated into individual records. This severely limited the analytic possibilities (Lundberg, 1927; Ogburn and Talbot, 1929; Rice and Weaver, 1929; Bain, 1930; Rice, 1924, 1931b; Carpenter, 1932; Hart, 1933). Two other techniques, which were sometimes merged in practice, permitted the observation of individuals' behaviors: namely, the live "participant observation" mode conceptualized by Lindeman (1924) and practiced in the Chicago field studies such as Thrasher's study of gangs (1927), Anderson's of the hobo (1923), Zorbaugh's study of Chicago's North Side (1929); and the personal histories of behavior, which could be gathered by personal interview or by written documents (Bogardus, 1923-24a; Park, 1924a; Krueger, 1925). In both, the social scientist assumed much responsibility for interacting with or interpreting the individuals in the context of their personal history or their ongoing group life.

A SCALE FROM EACH SIDE OF THE AISLE

When in 1924 the psychologist Floyd H. Allport, made his clarion call to sociologists to repudiate "group mind" theories and explain group phenomena through a social psychology of the individual (F. H. Allport, 1923-24), the sociologist Emory S. Bogardus made something of a rejoinder in the *American Journal of Sociology*. If there was a "group" fallacy, there was also an "individual" one, Bogardus cautioned, and Allport risked it if he was bent on measuring individuals apart from their group relationships. Social psychology could not be based exclusively on the social behavior of individuals, argued Bogardus (1923-24b:704); it must study the "intersocial stimulation that occurs between members of groups, that is, of persons with both 'individual' and 'group' traits."

Bogardus was an early representative of the band of sociologists who wanted to incorporate into social psychology and later into survey research the "contextual effects" of individuals in their community settings and group memberships.[7] Floyd H. Allport took his degree at Harvard, with a strong background in experimental psychology, and proceeded later to Syracuse University. There, under his aegis, social psychology and attitude study flourished as he labored to put them on a new footing of scientific rigor (Katz, 1968). When *Public Opinion Quarterly* was founded in 1937, Allport wrote the lead piece of Volume 1, Number 1, "Toward a Science of Public Opinion."

Bogardus devised his scale of social distance, after a suggestion from Robert E. Park (1924b),[8] in the interest of understanding structural relations and status, cultural accommodations, and conflicts—mainline sociological concerns at the University of Chicago. It was a measure of attitude toward groups, but it was at least hypothetically behavioral in that the respondents were to explain what they would do, rather than what they believed or advocated as policy. The Allport scale, in contrast, focused on the measure of attitudes through opinions, especially political ones, which he related to measures of personality.

The Bogardus (1924-25) scale was simple in language and conception. People were to decide, on the basis of their "first feeling reaction," how they would respond to various groups, along a seven-point scale of nearness/distance. To which level of association would they admit Armenians, Chinese, French, Koreans, Negroes, Russians, Turks, and so forth?

1. To close kinship by marriage.

2. To my club as personal chums.

3. To my street as neighbors.

4. To employment in my occupation.

5. To citizenship in my country.

6. As visitors only to my country.

7. Would exclude from my country.

Bogardus set the categories himself in a logical order that he assumed was cumulative: at least in steps 1-5, an individual espousing the first, most intimate level would be expected to admit groups to the other four, less intimate levels.[9]

The task of recording social distance was doubtless more difficult than Bogardus imagined, requiring imaginative projection of one's own behavior to a long list of groups (he offered 39 in one discussion of the method, and many of these groups were surely unknown personally to the respondent [Bogardus, 1926b:212-213]). Eugene Hartley later demonstrated that students would register their attitude to wholly imaginary groups inserted into the list—the famous Wallonians, for example (Hartley, 1946). Compared with some of the complex opinion statements that would clutter questionnaires, Bogardus's scale itself was straightforward and clear, and the variable had analytic meaning, showing variability by age, sex, occupational group, and the like. Bogardus satisfied himself by much personal interviewing that the written "recording" or scale method reflected attitudes expressed in a much fuller form in person. In his study *Immigration and Race Attitudes* (1928), he collected data from 1,725 respondents from various parts of the country who took the social distance scale; 700 of these people were also interviewed.

The Allport/Hartman scale assumed much knowledge of political issues, and asked students to react to propositions on seven topics, including the League of Nations, the Ku Klux Klan, prohibition, and others. The scale was constructed from personal opinions written by 60 students; the opinions were sifted and selected, and then arranged independently by six judges (college teachers) in logical order from one extreme position to the other. The average rank assigned by the judges was the final rank order accorded to each statement. The scale was not designed to be cumulative; students were asked to select the one statement on each issue that best represented their own opinion.

The scales varied in their length and complexity. Attitudes toward President Coolidge, for example, were arrayed on a ten-point scale ranging from "Coolidge is perfectly fitted for the office of President," to "A man such as Coolidge is bound to bring with him a corrupt government." On other scales, the steps were veritable portmanteaux of propositions, as in these clusters from the five-step scale on attitudes toward the distribution of wealth. At one end was the following step:

> The wealth of this country is at present distributed fairly and wisely. Wage earners get a perfectly fair deal. The poor are necessarily poor because of low mentality and lack of ambition.

And so on through three other provisos within the same step. The step at the other end of the scale read as follows:

> Concentrated wealth gives great power which should belong to the government alone. The amassing of fortunes beyond a certain limit should be prohibited by law, and the money returned to the people. There should be very heavy income and inheritance taxes, rapidly approaching 100 percent for the greater fortunes. [Allport and Hartman, 1925:752]

Again, three more clauses completed this scale step.

When the scales were administered, students were also asked to indicate on a five-point scale the degree of certainty and levels of intensity with which they held these opinions (they proved to be virtually the same thing) —in what appears to be the first use of intensity measures in data analysis.[10] Allport and Hartman graphed the distributions of both the opinions and the intensity measures and concluded that the "atypical" groups on the ends of the opinion distributions held their views more strongly than did those in the middle,[11] and on other personality measures tended to resemble one another more than either resembled the middle ranks. This presaged the study of authoritarianism of the Left, as well as the Right, as Daniel Katz (1968) has noted. Both the Bogardus social distance scales and the Allport-Hartman scales occasioned much interest in certain sociological and psychological circles and were cited regularly in attitude studies and in reviews of the attitude literature.[12]

Not surprisingly, in the journal that Bogardus himself edited, *Sociology and Social Research* (originally the *Journal of Applied Sociology*), social distance studies flourished. Numerous articles by Bogardus and others treated the social distance measures of racial groups, religions, occupations, communities, and parents and children.[13] There were the beginnings of further analytic developments in the "sociometric" potentialities of the scale and in the concept of the "social distance margin," to express how discrepant two groups' attitudes were toward each other (see Shideler, 1928; Poole, 1928-29). But in this journal there were only the beginnings of data analysis. A good deal of the social distance work published here was data-free, impressionistic, or conceptual (Bogardus himself was quite given to writing essays on social distance), and the inquiry remained something of a regional speciality for sociologists. While the *American Journal of Sociology* (AJS) reviewed Bogardus's books with regularity, "social distance" was not a topic by which articles were catalogued in the first AJS index (1935) nor in the second (1947). When in a later index (1965), eight articles from the early period under discussion here (through 1935-36) were reclassified under "Social Distance," only one of these dealt with a Bogardus-type scale.

This was an article by Stuart C. Dodd (1935-36) on social distance measures taken in the Near East. Curiously, he acknowledged a debt to Thurstone methods of scale construction (which we discuss presently) but did not mention Bogardus, from whom the measure's substance and form were obviously derived. If contemporary readers can recover from the shock of proceeding in five-scale steps, designed to be equidistant, from the intimacy of marriage partner, to dinner guest, to acquaintance, to not enjoying the companionship of the group, to the sudden ferocity of wishing the entire group were killed off!—they will find the article quite contemporary in certain respects. Dodd's (1935-36:195) scale read:[14]

> If I wanted to marry, I would marry one of them.
> I would be willing to have . . . as a guest for a meal.
> I prefer to have . . . merely as an acquaintance to whom
>   one talks on meeting in the street.
> I do not enjoy the companionship of these people.
> I wish someone would kill all these individuals.

He offered some interesting hypotheses from his exploratory use of social distance measures. For example, he found religious groupings to generate greater social distance than nationalities or economic classes, and he had administered measures on all three types of groups to student subjects who themselves represented major categories within each. He suggested that cross-cultural indices of equality could be derived from social distance and offered some general predictions about how these measures would behave in highly stratified and in more open societies. Dodd did fail to herald the future in one critical respect. Lavish in his algebraic notation, he failed to present one jot of data in support of the notions he presented. But the article is nevertheless conceptuall·· interesting and suggests some of the analytic implications of the Bogardus-type measures of attitude that few, if any other, sociologists were making at the time.

Bogardus probably did not see those implications either. The scale was his most original contribution, but he himself saw it as a preliminary or superficial "recording," especially suitable for administration to groups, requiring the additional richness of the case history methods of sociology, notably interviewing (Bogardus, 1923-24a, 1928). Bogardus rather distrusted subjective measurement. He doubted that the great mass of people understood their own experience well enough to provide primary data. (See also Park, 1924c; Lindeman, 1924.) Without naming the authors, he commented that the Merriam and Gosnell (1924) study, *Non-Voting*, was probably bootless because nonvoters were being asked to explain why they did not get to the polls, and chances were slim that they really knew. He relied on the unstructured interview (in a very clinical mode stressing rapport and "mental release") and on the written life history to yield insight to the investigator (Bogardus, 1925-26). As to large-scale analysis, Bogardus went to the trouble of incorporating over 1,700 people from across the country into his *Race and Immigration Attitudes* study; and the Race Relations Survey had been an ambitious effort to reach many people. But he held no brief for a "statistical psychosis." By the "method of personal experience," one case might be "proportionally as vital as a million," he felt, if it brought something new to the researcher's mind that illuminated understanding of the whole (Bogardus, 1923-24a:298; 1926b:192).

When he joined his colleagues in a 1931 festschrift to W. I. Thomas, Bogardus's contribution, "Attitudes and the Mexican Immigrant," did not make use of the scale of social distance or of any systematic quantitative material. It was an essay of generalizations about how Mexicans adapted to American culture (Bogardus, 1931). In its nonquantitative emphasis, it was typical of most of the book by former students and collaborators of Thomas, such as Kimball Young, Burgess, Thrasher, Znaniecki, Steiner, and others. The editor, Kimball Young, explained that while the authors did not discount the statistical method, most had found that the material in their analysis of social process and social structure did not so far really lend itself to statistical treatment, and was indeed qualitative.

The polar choice for sociologists was still case histories versus statistics. Young pointed to other work in progress that was promising in the effort to "devise methods of treating certain aspects of social attitudes by statistical techniques" (Young, 1931b,vii), and he referred to the psychologists All-port, May, and Thurstone, and the sociologist Rice. But not to Bogardus. His social distance scale had the potential, in our view, for extending sociology Chicago-style into a more quantitative social psychology. (As Rose [1951] noted, Bogardus's conception that attitudes were a function of the social situation did not have the influence it might well have.) But Bogardus appears not to have had the aspiration himself. In any case, he did not play the role that Gosnell did in empirical political science or that Lazarsfeld did in quantitative analysis of subjective data among sociologists.[15]

The social distance measures persisted, however, and very probably influenced a good deal of hypothetical-behavior question writing in survey research, especially in race relations (Rose, 1951). But neither the quasi-behavioral nor the cumulative properties of his rather homely, merely logical scale sparked wide interest or appreciation by sociologists in this early period. The quantification of attitude study flourished with questionnaires and scales of opinion indicators in the hands of psychologists.[16]

Floyd Allport's study of attitudes flourished more vigorously than did Bogardus's brand in two ways. First, Allport and his students related opinion indicators to underlying attitudes, such as "institutional" attitudes (Katz and Allport, 1931); "public and private" attitudes (Schanck, 1932), from which Allport developed the concept of "pluralistic ignorance"; and the application of stereotype to race prejudice (Katz and Braly, 1933-34). These studies were genuine contributions to data analysis.

More important for our purposes, Allport's attitude scales flourished in their transformation by L. L. Thurstone, University of Chicago psychologist. Thurstone became aware of both the Bogardus and Allport endeavors, but when Allport corresponded with him seeking counsel on psychological measurement, Thurstone's interest was captivated. He credited Allport with pioneering studies that directly inspired his own work in scaling (Thurstone, 1952:300; Thurstone and Chave, 1929:19).

THURSTONE SCALES

Thurstone had been involved in psychophysical measurement—the stuff of discriminating differences in weights, shades of gray, changes in handwriting—and he had come to think of it as a pretty trivial enterprise. After all the hairsplitting, as he later wrote (Thurstone, 1931-32), he had never yet seen a psychologist who really cared a rap about any particular person's limen (threshold of discrimination). At any rate, Thurstone no longer cared.

Stimulated by the Allport work, the thought occurred to him, however, that the "new psychophysical toys" might be put to productive use after all.

The crux of his efforts was the search for a true metric, an attitude scale with units of equal value all along a favorable-to-unfavorable continuum. The most elegant application from his psychophysical repertoire would have been the method of *paired comparisons*, in which judges compared every opinion statement with every other one, and the measure of dispersion in the judgments was used to allocate statements to scale positions.[17] But this was a tedious business. In the scale that Thurstone and Chave devised for attitudes toward the church, they asked judges to assign a value to 130 statements, and had they used the method of paired comparisons, this would have required 8,385 separate judgments per judge—that is, $[n \ (n \ - \ 1)/2]$—and Thurstone and Chave (1929) used 300! Not only were the judgments an enormous chore, the various calculations to assign statements to scale position after the judges had done their work were a vast enterprise. Instead, for the church scale they used a simpler method for judging, and even at that the construction of the scale took the better part of a year, as Thurstone told Gordon Allport (Allport, 1930:21).[18]

This was the method of "equal-appearing intervals." Judges were asked to sort opinion statements into 11 piles that seemed to them to represent equal distances of favorability. The statements were propositions of this sort—130 strong, in this particular scale:

> I believe that church membership is almost essential to live life at its best.
> I believe in what the church teaches but with mental reservations.
> I think the church is a parasite on society. [Thurstone and Chave, 1929]

The scale value of each item was the mean value assigned by the 300 judges, modified by statistical criteria for detecting items that were *ambiguous* (high dispersion around the median) or *irrelevant* (judged not to measure the same dimension), both of which were dropped. The original list of statements was winnowed to a final list of 45 statements about the church; these constituted a "more or less uniformly graduated series of scale values" (four opinions for each of the 11 class intervals). Various other Thurstone-type scales were shorter, numbering statements in the 20s (Rundquist and Sletto, 1936). The scale was obviously not a full-interval scale—and it had other problems, which Thurstone and Chave recognized—but it was not just a conventional rank order. For within limits, items could be added or subtracted without changing the values of other items in the scale; in a conventional rank order, such changes risked changing the values of many other items.

The Thurstone invention had an enormous influence. In the late 1920s and early 1930s, there was a flurry of scale building in the Thurstone style, especially the equal-appearing interval scale; subjects included war, race, law, God, professional training of social workers, prohibition, the Germans, the U.S. Constitution, capital punishment, patriotism, censorship, Communism, birth control, Sunday observance, and many others (Droba, 1932). Bogardus revised his own scale in response to the Thurstone technique by enlisting judges to assess an enlarged set of statements (Bogardus, 1932-33).

The issue of whether attitudes should be studied through opinion indicators was not of great moment to Thurstone. He saw his scales as a verbal index of attitude, limited as any index was, no more a representation of a full and complex attitude than a measure of a man's height was a rendering of the "whole" man. Opinions were surely no certain clue to conduct, he noted, but if people should intentionally distort their attitudes, one would at least be measuring the attitude they were trying to make people believe they had. He also pointed to the fact that people could disguise their real attitudes by dissembling behavior just as they could disguise their real attitudes by faking opinions. And in any case, he contended, attitudes were of great interest in themselves, a proposition with which many academic psychologists obviously agreed (Thurstone, 1928a).

By the early 1930s, however, Thurstone himself had grown weary of the enterprise, as a line formed at his door asking for still more scales on still more attitudes, with few petitioners showing any interest in the basic theory of attitude measurement. He later recalled that early in the 1930s he picked up a dozen or more attitude scales that were in preparation and threw them in the wastebasket and thereafter discouraged any further work on the matter in his laboratory (Thurstone, 1952:300). Thurstone moved on to factor analysis, but his achievement in scaling commanded influence and prestige long after he himself had had enough, and it still remains a classic in attitude measurement (see Katz, 1937; McNemar, 1946; Green, 1954; Scott, 1968).

Attitude Scales and Interviews

CRITIQUES AND ADAPTATIONS

Three key figures in these early years, Stuart A. Rice, Samuel A. Stouffer, and Paul F. Lazarsfeld, crisscrossed the disciplinary boundaries between sociology and psychology, taking different paths in their explorations of subjective phenomena. The sociologists Rice and Stouffer had catholic tastes in research that drew them to consider quantitative measures being developed by psychologists, including the Thurstone scales. Lazarsfeld, whom we consider somewhat later, gravitated into sociological circles from training in psychology and experience in market research, both of which focused on individual respondents' subjective accounts. Another notable figure, Rensis Likert, pursued subjective realms in psychology, and constructed an adaptation of Thurstone scaling for his dissertation.

The Rice Critique. Rice's research interests were in politics, so that he is now often taken for a political scientist, although he obtained his degree in sociology at Columbia University under Franklin P. Giddings. (In the first few years of his career, he might have been mistaken for a psychologist as well; he wrote a questionnaire for the psychologist Henry T. Moore [Moore, 1925] and himself inquired into students' expectations about marriage and children [Rice, 1929].) While most of his research bore on political topics, it had a strong methodological slant. He did a retrospective study of attitude change in students who had heard William Jennings Bryan's lecture against evolution; he conducted an actual "panel" measurement of change in students' attitudes in the course of the 1924 election. In a nonverbal measure he studied students' visual stereotyping of people appearing in newspaper photographs. He isolated interviewer bias operating in attitudes toward prohibition when respondents' recorded views closely mirrored those of the interviewers. He compared legislators' attitudes obtained by questionnaires with those of their constituents as indicated by votes. (All the last-mentioned studies are collected in Rice [1928].)

Had he pursued these research interests, Rice might well have exerted some of the same kind of influence on quantitative sociology and survey research that Paul Lazarsfeld later did. But he grew wary of subjective data obtained by direct measurement. He turned his attention back to electoral statistics, on which he had done his dissertation (Rice, 1924) and advocated the study of behavioral patterns to infer attitudes—through voting records and other behaviors such as patterns of attendance at movies, lectures, sermons; participation in organizations; gate receipts for sports events; radio programming; and a host of such cultural indicators of "public attention" (Rice, 1930a).

Rice's critique of Thurstone scaling was trenchant not only on the judging process, but on the practice of measuring attitudes through opinions. As he wrote (Rice, 1930b:190), constructing scales and measuring attitudes with them was increasingly difficult:

> . . . once we leave the classroom, the discussion club, and the other small, comparatively infrequent and highly selected groups that enjoy having experiments tried upon them. Such groups already have developed ways of making their attitudes articulate. It is the more numerous work-a-day groupings of society about whose attitudes the social scientist is in the most need of information. Students may be required, good natured academicians may be cajoled, and sun-

dry needy persons may be paid to sort cards containing propositions into eleven piles. But it is difficult to imagine securing comparable judgments, or satisfactory measurements in the final application, from bricklayers, businessmen, Italian-Americans, nuns, stevedores, or seamstresses.

The validity of a scale was open to question unless a random sample of the group to be measured served as the judges constructing the scale.[19] Rice also raised the prospect that would surely haunt many a survey researcher in the throes of designing an interview schedule for a national sample:

> Perhaps the attitude scale like the other scales employed in science is valid only within the middle ranges of its phenomena—in other words, among persons whose intellectuality and knowledge are neither too great nor too small. [Rice, 1930b:185]

Most fundamental, he felt that continued devotion to Thurstone scaling risked a spurious accuracy, a more refined statistical treatment than the basic data really warranted, when their validity and representativeness were still in question.

The Stouffer Experiment. Stouffer found the Thurstone scales attractive enough to test their equivalence to the qualitative case histories congenial to the Chicago sociologists. The work linking the two methods was Stouffer's 1930 dissertation at Chicago (Stouffer, 1931). Students were asked to write an essay on their personal experiences and attitudes toward prohibition law and personal drinking, which a small set of academic judges then rated on a five-point scale of favorability toward prohibition. The judges agreed closely with each other, and also with a pair of judges who were active in pro- and antiprohibition politics, and the rating scores of the essays correlated highly with students' scores on a Thurstone-type scale on prohibition. So it all worked well. The results favored the scale over the case history, as Stouffer pointed out, for the scale could be administered in perhaps 15 minutes, and in the time it would take to analyze a handful of case histories, one could gather up several hundred indexes of attitudes. In another study, he recommended questionnaires over case histories for the same reason, although he valued certain uses of the case history. In a statement that Lazarsfeld mirrored in the 1940s on the uses of open-ended survey questions, Stouffer pointed to two uses for which life histories were indispensable: the initial formulation of direct questions and the interpretation of the meaning of relationships after their magnitudes had been determined statistically (Stouffer, 1931; Cavan, Hauser, and Stouffer, 1930-31; Lazarsfeld, 1944). Stouffer's test of a Thurstone scale was a limited one dealing with a narrow topic, and the subjects were the obliging student population. But the results within those limits certainly did commend the more quantifiable procedure on practical grounds.

The Likert Revision. In the early 1930s, Rensis Likert, too, explored Thurstone methods. His dissertation in 1932 addressed particularly the construction costs, and his alternative to Thurstone scaling was designed to make judges unnecessary. The method, called "summated rating," used scaled items such as these:

In the interest of permanent peace we should be willing to arbitrate absolutely all differences with other nations which we cannot readily settle by diplomacy.

Strongly Approve	Approve	Undecided	Disapprove	Strongly Disapprove
(5)	(4)	(3)	(2)	(1)

An American committing a crime in Shanghai should be tried by a Chinese judge.

Strongly Approve	Approve	Undecided	Disapprove	Strongly Disapprove
(5)	(4)	(3)	(2)	(1)

Negroes' homes should be segregated from those of white people.

Strongly Approve	Approve	Undecided	Disapprove	Strongly Disapprove
(1)	(2)	(3)	(4)	(5)

Should there be a national referendum on every war?

Yes	?	No
(4)	(3)	(2)

How much military training should we have?
1. We need universal compulsory military training.
2. We need Citizens' Military Training Camps and Reserve Officers' Training Corps but not universal military training.
3. We need some facilities for training reserve officers but not as much as at present.
4. We need only such military training as is required to maintain our regular army.
5. All military training should be abolished.
[Likert, 1932; Murphy and Likert, 1938:34-39]

Items on various topics were mingled in the questionnaire (no numbers were attached to the choices) and later were grouped according to the topic of the various scales. What has come to be called the Likert-type item (the strongly approve/strongly disapprove form) was, as the examples indicate, not the only form of question that he used.[20]

The Likert method was a psychometric measure. It bypassed judges by administering a battery of items to subjects and then analyzing their suitability for the scale by the criterion of internal consistency, familiar in psychometrics, which had not before been applied to attitude measurement (Rundquist and Sletto, 1936:5).[21] Likert obtained high correlations between his scales and the Thurstone scales, and generally higher reliabilities with fewer items (Likert, 1932; Likert, Roslow, and Murphy, 1934). The method came into widespread use, despite some later debate about its comparability to Thurstone (Ferguson, 1941; Edwards and Kenney, 1946). Hall (1934) used it in morale measures of unemployed men; Rundquist and Sletto (1936) adapted it to a study of personality. The Likert scale became a classic in the history of attitude measurement, and virtually any review of attitude literature after 1932 would include a reference to Likert's work as well as to Thurstone's.

There were various efforts in this period to simplify the Thurstone judging process and to mass-produce scales by finding all-purpose items (Seashore and Hevner, 1933; Remmers and Silance, 1934). But Likert's scale was an alternative that proved just as serviceable, while lacking the theoretical coherence and elegance of a Thurstone scale. This was, in fact, an important feature. In the construction of his scale, Likert initially made the items comparable for scoring by transforming the percentages obtained for each alternative into a "sigma" value of a normal distribution. He repaired to the simpler, arbitrary 1-to-5 scoring when he found that it yielded almost identical results. Scholars committed to the theory of scaling (Paul Lazarsfeld for one) later found little of pure scaling in a Likert scale, but it was indeed a scale in a practical sense, and it implicitly raised an important question for the practicalities of empirical research on a mass basis. Did one stay with measures of theoretical elegance and clarity if they were more costly and yet in practice no more illuminating of quantitative data than simpler tools were? The Likert scale argued no, and Likert's subsequent professional experiences made the same argument.

OUTSIDE THE CLASSROOM: INTERVIEWING IN INDUSTRIAL AND MARKET RESEARCH

At the same time that Thurstone scaling was generating much interest in academic social psychology, applied psychologists in industrial[22] and market research were working largely with other methods. In industrial psychology generally, interviewing alone or in conjunction with much simpler questionnaires was the leading edge of inquiry. J. David Houser's influential studies of employer and employee attitudes used unstructured interviews on the one hand and a "question blank" method on the other (Houser, 1927; Kornhauser and Sharp, 1932; Kornhauser, 1933; Likert and Willets, 1940). In the latter, the interviewer asked standardized questions and then coded the answer on the spot into categories, memorized in advance by the interviewers, which Houser deemed to be at equal intervals of feeling from hostility to enthusiasm. In response to a question about opportunities to learn on the job, for example, the interviewer was to listen attentively to an employee's response and then mentally convert it into one of these "type" responses, which had a numerical value:

5. The company certainly does encourage me and offers me every opportunity to develop and make progress. I'm sure I'm being given every chance I could be.
4. Yes, there are a number of pretty good chances ahead. . . .

And so on down to the lowest rank:

1. Don't think I'm getting along at all. I'm in a fierce rut. No chance to learn. There's no encouragement at all to try to learn or get ahead. [Houser, 1927:178]

One well could wonder why these fully detailed categories were not simply given to the respondents who could decide for themselves where their attitudes best fit. But Houser was concerned with the lack of communication between employees and employers, especially the latter's insensitivity to employees' attitudes and morale. The interviewing situation was to provide communication, as well as a mechanism for summarizing attitudes in quantitative fashion. In Houser's program, written questionnaires would not have been as appropriate or informative.

Interviewing in the case of the famous Hawthorne experiments of 1927-32 took on an unexpected therapeutic purpose, as it seemed to yield insight to respondents themselves as well as to investigators. After industrial output at Western Electric's Hawthorne Works in Chicago increased steadily under experimental conditions—even after the liberalized rest breaks and lunch hours were withdrawn—there were clues that styles of supervision might be an important factor. Participants in the experimental room expressed great pleasure at being out from under the pressures of harsh bosses at the regular plant. A program of interviewing was instituted to look into workers' attitudes about working conditions and about supervision in particular, and in the period 1930-32, half the plant personnel (over 21,000 people) were interviewed. The masses of data gathered were rather perplexing to analyze, but it was clear that the very free-flowing, nondirective interviewing yielded much information about the workers' attitudes toward the company and about their personal lives off the job, subjects which workers and supervisors were pleased to discuss (Pennock, 1930; Putnam, 1929-30; Mayo, 1929-30, 1933).[23]

While the Hawthorne studies made the most massive use of unstructured interviewing, other industrial psychologists studying attitudes of morale had research problems that commended the use of interviewing over the exclusive use of questionnaires or scaled measurements—when there was enough money. First, there was the matter of motivation and reward. While workers were, of course, not entirely free from pressure to cooperate in company research, investigators did need to work to elicit active cooperation. As the Hawthorne experiments demonstrated, if there was no danger of being identified or punished for unpopular opinions, it was clearly more satisfying to tell one's opinions to a sympathetic listener than to a piece of paper. Using an adaptation of Thurstone scales for measuring political attitudes, Beyle reported that the printed scale served several functions, one of which was to generate interest and comments beyond the scale itself. It got people talking about politics; they did not want to stick to the scale alone (Beyle, 1932).

Second, there was a question of control of the situation. Interviewers could answer questions, determine whether a question was understood, note problems, and smooth over difficulties posed by an ungainly question. Bingham and Moore (1931:Chapters 5-6) recommended that interviewing be used to supplement mass questionnaires when it was too expensive to use interviewers exclusively. Third, there were opportunity costs to consider. To measure an attitude toward a company in all its Thurstone precision might well take up much of the available time and yield information on just one attitude. Kornhauser and Sharp (1932) reported being asked repeatedly why they had not used Thurstone-type attitude scales in their studies at the Kimberly Clark Corporation. They used the informal but "guided" interview, based on a set of topics, and questionnaires of the "cruder, shot gun" approach because they learned more, although with less precision. And as we have seen, Likert's revision addressed the burdensome construction costs of using judges. When research was conducted out of the classroom or out of the industrial plant, interviewers were necessary, as well, simply for finding people. Leonard D. White's study of attitudes toward public employment, published in 1929 (it acknowledged the counsel of Charles E. Merriam and L. L. Thurstone), was somewhat closer to the classroom-questionnaire model in that respondents filled out questionnaires themselves under the supervision of an interviewer. A goodly portion of the data was obtained by employees assembled in groups, briefly "on loan" from their jobs (White, 1929). But the Charles Merriam and Harold Gosnell study, *Non-Voting*, published in 1924, relied more heavily on the interviewer, because all respondents were contacted individually, and there was certainly little prospect that mail questionnaires would be returned in any number by nonvoters. Interviewers carried a schedule of questions, but they were to let the respondent do as much of the talking as possible while interviewers checked off from a list of reasons those that the respondent volunteered. The investigators' effort to get comparable information from

23

expert opinion *without* interviewers was doomed: only one noble precinct committeeman out of 3,800 gave an elaborate analysis on paper of what he knew about nonvoting. Many of the others marked all the reasons on the list (about 20) and needless to say no quantitative analysis could be done comparing nonvoters' reasons with those seen by political leaders (Merriam and Gosnell, 1924).

Interviewers using well-designed schedules could enhance the analytic meaning of the data by exploring respondents' reasons, a strong theme in Lazarsfeld's early writing on market research. When Lazarsfeld migrated from psychology and applied mathematics at the University of Vienna to a disciplinary base in sociology at Columbia University, he traveled via experience in market research (contract work that he plied in both places to sustain small research organizations when modest foundation grants were not sufficient, and they never were). Lazarsfeld was not taken up with Thurstone scaling. But he brought into sociology a psychologist's interest in subjective phenomena and a willingness to trust analytically to expressed opinions as well as an interest in quantitative analysis.[24] His first American publications in 1934 and 1935 were addressed to the market-research and business community. He urged upon them the collection of subjective materials—especially respondents' own reasons for their reactions, opinions, decisions—and more analytic probing of these data for an analysis of motive. From Lazarsfeld's standpoint, advertisers and market researchers failed to exploit subjective materials under the misapprehension that people were not aware of their reasons for purchase or preference, or very quickly forgot them, or were embarrassed to confess what prompted them in the first place. In "The Art of Asking Why" and other articles, he argued that one could and should ask respondents their reasons, but should specify the frame of reference (such as attributes of the product, influences from others, or impulses of the respondent) rather than asking the diffuse and unilluminating "Why?" (Lazarsfeld, 1934, 1935; Kornhauser and Lazarsfeld, 1935).

Lazarsfeld's early writings on interviewing and question design assumed the good offices of expert interviewers—people who were highly trained, well-educated, closely conversant with the objectives of the study, and free to use their own judgment in deviating from the questionnaire script when that might better serve the analytic purpose. The Lazarsfeld model of interviewing was thus not an entirely apt one for mass measurement in broadscale or national surveys; indeed he encountered some difficulties with it himself when he tried to apply it to less expert interviewers used in the Sandusky, Ohio, election study of 1940 (Rossi, 1959; Lazarsfeld, Berelson, and Gaudet, 1944). But these articles were nevertheless of importance in pointing up the analytical possibilities that could be structured into the interview schedule, and the richness of subjective materials.

The Impact of the Polls

Until the advent of the public opinion polls of the mid-1930s, there were very few national data that tapped directly the attitudes of the American public, except in regard to their market preferences, and much of that stock was local and regional in any case. For example, among the 29 chapters of *Recent Social Trends* (the large report on the nation commissioned by President Hoover and published in 1933), the chapter bearing most closely on subjective data was "Changing Social Attitudes and Interests," by sociologist Hornell Hart. This tracked attitudes toward science, religion, sex, prohibition, disarmament, unemployment, and other issues over a quarter of a century (Hart, 1933). But whose attitudes had been changing? Hart detected change by analyzing over time the content of a substantial number of magazines and newspapers. But did these attitudes reflect the views of large sectors of the population, or perhaps just the views of that narrow segment of the literate public composed of editors and writers? There was of course no telling.

In 1934, the National Industrial Conference Board (NICB), a private industrial organization, took a different tack in *A Statistical Survey of Public Opinion*. After interviewing more than 100 editors for advice, NICB sent out a questionnaire to the editor of every newspaper and farm journal in the country. More than 12,000 editors, (of whom some 5,000 responded, were asked to assess public opinion in their own communities on 35 different issues. Did the people in their community approve of increasing the national debt, nationalizing the banks, having compulsory unemployment insurance, and the like? As ambitious as this effort was, it too provided only an indirect measure of national opinion (NICB, 1934, 1936). When Stouffer and Lazarsfeld (1937:65, 137) reported on their inquiry into the state of the family in the Depression, they felt keenly the lack of national attitude/opinion data and looked hopefully to the availability and expansion of Gallup poll results.

In these same years, direct large-scale surveys under federal auspices were being conducted with better approximations to national samples of the population. The studies dealt with health, housing, employment, delinquency, recreation, family budgets, consumption, and so forth (Jessen and Hutchins, 1936; Mangus, 1934; National Institute of Health, 1938; Williams and Zimmerman, 1935). But for the most part these federal projects were focused on factual matters and verged only a little on subjective realms.

It was the commercial opinion polls that provided the first opinion data of national scope. Polls came out of market research by two routes. First, from the Psychological Corporation, a profit-making consortium of academic psychologists at a large number of colleges and universities; with their students they provided some semblance of a national field staff. Under the direction of Henry C. Link, this network began to add some attitude questions to market surveys being conducted for business corporations (Link, 1947). Then in 1935-36, the famous trio of Gallup, Roper, and Crossley brought their own substantial experience in market research to opinion polling and election forecasting, thriving in their 1936 presidential forecast where the *Literary Digest* failed.

The new pollsters had a cluster of practical techniques: a short, standardized interview schedule with fixed questions that could be administered by people with little or no training; a national field staff scattered in communities throughout the country and contacted mostly by mail; quota sampling that was carried out by the interviewers; and funds to mount such a far-flung and expensive enterprise. The latter were provided by sales of the polling results to commercial journalism: *Fortune* magazine (Roper), the Hearst press (Crossley), and a syndicated column sold to metropolitan newspapers (Gallup). The pollsters carried from market research the technique of quota sampling, a procedure that came under growing criticism by social scientists as new developments in probability sampling were constructed in the 1940s. Social scientists, especially psychologists, were also critical of the superficial and high-speed approach to public opinion measurement—the single questions, the untrained interviewers, the journalistic treatment. But the pollsters were important indeed in sparking the interest of the general public and government officials in the principle of sampling itself and in its application to the sounding of national public opinion.

Almost immediately after the poll's success, a few social scientists with an interest in attitude measurement were invited into government work by officials sensitive to new currents in social psychology and in commercial polling. In 1936-37, the United States Department of Agriculture set up a small group of interviewers who traveled around the country soliciting the opinions and experiences of their constituent farmers (Dreis, 1951). In 1939, Rensis Likert became director of this first governmental polling organization. As U.S. involvement in World War II became imminent, Likert's survey organization expanded and conducted interviews in the whole civilian population, as well as with farmers. (President Roosevelt was also quick to see the uses of national polling, and privately he commissioned trend data from Hadley Cantril on American attitudes, especially toward intervention/isolation [see Cantril, 1967].) Other opinion research organizations grew up in federal fields as civilian and military opinion, attitudes, cooperation, and "morale" became of special concern to wartime administrators. For psychologists particularly, Likert's organization provided a channel into governmental survey research. A similar channel for sociologists developed in the Research Branch of the U.S. Army established to study soldiers' morale, under the direction of Samuel A. Stouffer. Paul Lazarsfeld, psychologist-becoming-sociologist, had no such organizational responsibility in government, but he was a consultant in both the civilian and military research organizations and brought the individual measurement of market researchers and academic psychologists to the sociologists' concern with group structure.

In the new wartime work, the earlier schools of attitude study, one psychological and one sociological, were no longer distinct, as methods were adapted to new situations. Although sociologists were dominant in Stouffer's research group in the army, the group used paper-and-pencil questionnaires administered in what amounted to classroom groups of servicemen who could be required to assemble for that purpose, as psychologists had done with college students (Stouffer, 1949). The psychologists, who were dominant in Likert's civilian agency, could not summon the adult population in classroom fashion, so they sent interviewers out to find them as sociologists had done in their early field studies. Both disciplinary groups converged in their hope of finding how attitudes were expressed in both opinions and behaviors, and what connections there were between the two. But the focus during wartime was nevertheless on the psychologists' interest in opinion, the verbal indicators of attitude, for three interrelated reasons. First, the method matched the content. The self-report of individual questionnaires and interviews lent itself readily to disclosure of subjective phenomena and quantitative analysis of the individual record. The sociologically inclined, on the other hand, did not find a unique instrument by which to observe or measure group behavior or social structure, nor a clearly defined content—a set of particular behaviors that were of commanding interest.[25] Second, opinion-attitude research was funded substantially by the federal government for the first time during the war, as it created new agencies to gather data on national morale. And this had been stimulated, in turn, by the third factor, the prior example of the polls. Social scientists had already developed an academic specialty of attitude measurement before the polls achieved such éclat at the expense of the *Literary Digest* in 1936. But its expansion to mass measurement in technique, organization, and funding was preceded and facilitated by the example, publicity, and obvious political uses of the commercial polls. In the creation of national subjective data, the pollsters truly got there first.

Summary and Conclusion

Attitude was a vague but useful concept that stimulated both psychologists and sociologists to do empirical work on subjective phenomena in the 1920s and 1930s. Proceeding from constraints and opportunities in their respective disciplines, researchers in the two fields took different paths. Psychologists, for example, trained in laboratory experiment and mental testing, specialized in classroom studies of attitude that permitted a rigorous approach to quantification but were limited to a narrow base of subjects. Sociologists, proceeding from a tradition of fieldwork, more often reached groups in the broader public, using a variety of methods yielding material of much richness but little rigor. (Neither group had financial or conceptual resources to undertake the study of attitudes on a national basis—probability sampling, for example, did not come into established practice until the 1940s.)

Emory S. Bogardus's social distance scales of hypothetical behavior offered, in principle, some of the advantages of both the psychological and the sociological approach to attitude study, but they did not have the impact on sociologists in the mainstream that Thurstone scales had on psychologists interested in attitude measurement. Stimulated by Floyd Allport's work, L. L. Thurstone set out to give to the measurement of attitude through opinion indicators a basis in theory and precision that he had been pursuing in laboratory measurement of psychophysical phenomena. The psychologists' conception of attitude prevailed because it was buttressed by the prestige of physical science and because sociologists failed to develop a unique method of measuring attitude in the community and social context. Sociologists who later took the lead in survey research, such as Stouffer and Lazarsfeld, were influenced by or actually trained in psychology.

Attitude scaling in the Thurstone mode involved a large set of items (20, 30, or even 40) on a single subject. It occasioned great interest and application in classroom studies, where students were more likely to have such complex and detailed attitudes and where administration of long scales was feasible. Outside the classroom Thurstone scaling had limited application. In industrial psychology and market research it was usually of more interest to learn at least a little about a number of attitudes (or opinions) than to learn a good deal about just one. Interviewing rather than paper-and-pencil questionnaires also offered a number of advantages in the study of attitudes outside the classroom. On a number of practical counts Thurstone scaling was rather too elegant for the task at hand with adult populations, and the tools of attitude measurement were somewhat rough-fashioned in both questionnaire and interview design.

The commercial opinion polls, which developed from market research, brought still simpler tools to the task as they settled for very short interviews (10 or 15 minutes, for example), largely untrained interviewers, and single opinion questions designed to cover a broad spectrum of attitude. Psychologists whose efforts were invested in making more precise measurement and analytic study of attitude took special umbrage at the high speed and superficial approach of the pollsters. But the pollsters had two interrelated resources that the social scientists did not: they offered national data bearing directly on opinion, which until their advent was essentially unavailable, and they were funded for work of this expensive scope. With these resources they quickly became of interest to some government officials. Social scientists were recruited into government attitude/opinion/morale work before and especially during World War II because opinion polling was seen to have obvious political and administrative utility. It was the commercial opinion polls that first made this utility evident.

Notes

1. In a brilliant elaboration of Gordon Allport's history of the concept of attitude, Donald Fleming, the intellectual historian, credits Thomas with cutting the link between a *motor* meaning for the term—as a state of physiological readiness (for danger, flight, attack, and so forth), which Darwin had meant—and a purely *mental* state without intrinsic physiological content. Fleming interprets the changes in the meaning of attitude as a pulling back by scientists from excesses of materialism. It implied a new concept of the individual as a thinking/feeling organism, adapting to the environment and integrating it through mental attitudes (Fleming, 1967).

2. Thomas and Znaniecki had distinguished between attitudes of temperament, which were innate, and those of character, which were acquired, but little attention was paid to the innate branch; it was attitudes that could change with personal experience and social interaction that were of much greater interest (Park, 1931).

3. The confusion was not surprising. Political scientists gathering in 1925 could agree after protracted debate only that *opinions* were not necessarily rational processes or conscious choices but should be sufficiently clear to "create a disposition to act" if circumstances were favorable (*American Political Science Association* 1925, cited by Rice, 1930b:177-181). And attitudes were a richer, more mysterious matter than that.

4. Sturges (1927) and Donald Young (1927) both explored student attitude change from the college experience itself, but Stuart Rice noted that Young's study of attitude change resulting from an academic class was almost unique (Rice, 1928:252). The Katz and Allport (1931) investigation of student attitudes bore directly on the impact of college experience and student culture. Theodore M. Newcomb's (1939) study of attitude change in the course of Bennington college experience (1939) was not started until the 1930s. In his 1932 presidential address to the American Psychological Association, Walter P. Miles noted the problem of student subjects and the fact that with adult surveys one could rarely do test-retest-reliability measures or even make the instruments long enough for correlations by halves or by odd-even tests of reliability. He observed that subjects representing the population at large "are not available in the compact and responsive groups that school and college classes provide. Doubtless this is in fact the chief reason why we regard adequate selection of adult subjects as treacherous. . . ." (Miles, 1933:106-107). He was hopeful that representative groups could be built up from clubs, lodges, and social groups of one sort and another that would be willing to serve the purposes of science if group goals were rewarded by the scientists. See, however, Rice's criticism on just that point (section on Attitude Scales and Interviews).

5. The Katz and Allport census of Syracuse University students' attitudes stressed consultation with student power groups and the voluntary cooperation of the student body. But classes were dismissed for 2 hours to enable students to take the questionnaire, and those who did not show were penalized by "double cuts" (Katz and Allport, 1931:2).

6. In a mail questionnaire, LaPiere asked a set of innkeepers whether they served Chinese guests, and almost all who answered said "no." But in fact they already had, for LaPiere and a Chinese couple had been duly served in almost all of the places to which he later sent the questionnaire. This was indeed a reversal of the expectation that people would not act as admirably as they said they would, for here the reigning racial discrimination was greater in word than in deed. LaPiere did not debunk questionnaire measurement; he thought it a valuable indicator of ideology to use in conjunction with measures of experience and behavior (LaPiere, 1934). Schanck (1932, 1934) discovered the existence of "public" and "private" issues in the course of intimate contact with small-town residents on such issues as card playing, baptism, prohibition, church unification. Schanck's interpretation noted that the integration of attitudes and consistency within the individual had been exaggerated in other attitude studies.

7. In the 1940s and 1950s and beyond, students and associates in Lazarsfeld's Bureau of Applied Social Research reflected this interest somewhat more than Lazarsfeld did himself (see Barton, 1969).

8. Park was importing the concept from Simmel; it was apparently first advanced by Tarde (see Poole, 1927-28).

9. He later had a set of judges evaluate statements to determine scale steps in a modification of Thurstone procedures (see note 10, below), and he revised the middle levels somewhat. He also changed the language that had focused so directly on immigration (Bogardus, 1932-33, 1936). There were several editions of the social distance scale.

10. An intensity measure appears in the psychological literature as early as 1898, (see Sumner, 1898).

11. Suchman and Guttman's (1947) work during World War II incorporated the same finding.

12. For works citing both sources, see Lundberg (1929), Bain (1930), Droba (1931-32; 1932), Katz and Allport (1931), Murphy and Murphy (1931), Bogardus (1936). For works citing one but not the other see Bogardus (1926b), D. Young (1927), Bain (1928), Rice (1928), K. Young (1931a), Schanck (1932), Droba (1933, 1933-34), G. Allport (1935); LaPiere and Farnsworth (1936), and a host of articles in psychology journals bearing on attitude measurement (see *Journal of Abnormal and Social Psychology, Journal of Social Psychology, Psychological Bulletin*) and sociology articles bearing on social distance in *Sociology and Social Research*.

13. See Bogardus (1926a, 1928-29, 1932-33); Shideler (1928); Poole (1928-29); Binnewies (1926, 1931-32); Bogardus (1932-33); Wilkinson (1929); Hendrickson and Zeligs (1934); Zeligs and Hendrickson (1933).

14. Judges' ratings would have been interesting cross-cultural comparisons in themselves. These were not the judgments only of firebrand student ideologues, as Dodd also used a panel of Beirut businessmen. Would students and businessmen in other cultures construct a comparable scale that positioned personal marriage at one pole and wishes for genocide at the other,

equidistant from a midpoint of speaking acquaintance? Dodd did not raise this cross-cultural comparison.

15. Bulmer's recent work reminds us that the so-called qualitative tradition at Chicago may have been overemphasized somewhat to the neglect of the quantitative tradition of Ogburn, Stouffer, Thurstone, Gosnell, and others, which was also very important at Chicago (see Bulmer, 1980, 1981).

16. Eugene Hartley's (1946) study of racial attitudes of students used Bogardus scales to explore personality characteristics of individuals rather than intergroup relations. (The work for *Problems in Prejudice* was conducted in 1938, although not published until 1946.) For psychologists generally, the Bogardus scale lacked psychometric legitimacy; it was merely ordinal, and its design was such that it could not be tested for reliability by any means except test-retest.

17. For example, if the number of judges who perceived that statement *A* was more favorable than *B* was the same as the number of judges perceiving that *B* was more favorable than *A*, then the two statements could not be discriminated and were given equal scale values. Differing proportions in the judgment yielded different scale positions (Thurstone, 1928b). G. T. Fechner originated the basic method of paired comparisons that Thurstone first applied to attitude measurement (Droba, 1932).

18. J. P. Guilford was applying the method of paired comparison at the same time as Thurstone. Guilford credited the Bogardus scale with being the only scale up to that time that tried to measure racial attitudes as a form of social distance, although a very rough one. Thurstone (1928c) published "An Experimental Study of Nationality Preferences" before Guilford (1931) published his study, "Racial Preferences of a Thousand American University Students."

19. Some experiments in this period seemed to vindicate the Thurstone judging process, since judges holding very different attitudes showed high agreement on the placement of statements (Ferguson, 1935; Hinckley, 1932). Later work has cast some doubt on the generality of those findings, however (Scott, 1968).

20. In the Negro scale, two items of hypothetical behavior like the Bogardus scale items were included, but these were exceptions to the general pattern of opinion on policy and political issues.

21. In *item analysis* the correlation of the item score to the total score was used as an index of the discriminating power of the item; a low correlation meant that the item did not capture enough of the single common factor that was in principle underlying all the items. In tests of *internal consistency*, an "undifferentiating" statement was one that would not discriminate between two groups that scored high and low, respectively, on the total score. Likert used the criterion of internal consistency in constructing his scales because it was less laborious to compute and had yielded, experimentally, results comparable to item analysis. (See Appendix B in Murphy and Likert, 1938:281-291.)

22. Uhrbrock's (1934) application of a Thurstone-type scale of morale to 4,430 employees is the most ambitious use we have found in industrial psychology.

23. Only as the program continued did researchers realize that the kind of conversational

interview they had been conducting and the personal material it generated was not their discovery, and indeed had a parallel in the clinical work of Janet, Freud, and Jung (see Mayo, 1933:Chapters 3-5).

24. In later years, Lazarsfeld grew somewhat more "sociological," showing more concern for community structure and group contexts, though never so much as some of his close associates. See Barton (1969), who refers to the "random sampling of individuals" as a "sociological meatgrinder." Barton reviews studies, conducted at the Bureau of Applied Social Research, designed to capture sociological contexts. Rossi (1972:101-102) has pointed to both the difficulty and paucity of studies making systematic comparisons across a number of local communities.

25. As Presser points out in Chapter 3 of this volume, the well-known surveys into voter and consumer behavior that developed later were actually based more squarely on self-report of attitudes than on recorded, observed, or even reported behaviors.

References

Albig, W. (1930-31) Opinions concerning unskilled Mexican immigrants. *Sociology and Social Research* 15:62-72.

Allen, R.A., and Barton, S.B. (1934) Those who go down to the docks. *Sociology and Social Research* 19:103-116.

Allport, F.H. (1923-24) The group fallacy in relation to social science. *American Journal of Sociology* 29:688-703.

Allport, F.H. (1937) Toward a science of public opinion. *Public Opinion Quarterly* 1:7-23.

Allport, F.H., and Hartman, D.A. (1925) The measurement and motivation of atypical opinion in a certain group. *American Political Science Review* 19:735-760.

Allport, G.W. (1930) Discussion of methods of studying social attitudes by S.A. Rice. Institute of Methods of Rural Sociological Research, U.S. Department of Agriculture, Bureau of Agricultural Economics. Dec. 31, 1929-Jan. 4, 1930, pp. 20-23.

Allport, G.W. (1935) Attitudes. In C. Murchison, ed., *A Handbook of Social Psychology*. Worcester, Mass.: Clark University Press.

American Political Science Association (1925) Round table on political statistics of the Second National Conference on the Science of Politics. *American Political Science Review* 19:104-162.

Anderson, N. (1923) *The Hobo: The Sociology of the Homeless Man*. Chicago: University of Chicago Press.

Bain, R. (1928) An attitude on attitude research. *American Journal of Sociology* 33:940-957.

Bain, R. (1930) Theory and measurement of attitudes and opinions. *Psychological Bulletin* 27:357-379.

Barton, A.H. (1969) *Personal Influence* revisited. In L. Bogart, ed., *Current Controveries in Marketing Research*. Chicago: Markham.

Bernard, L.L. (1930) Attitudes, social. In E.R.A. Seligman and A. Johnson, eds., *Encyclopedia of the Social Sciences*. New York: Macmillan.

Attitude Measurement: The Early Years

Beyle, H.C. (1932) A scale for the measurement of attitudes toward candidates for elective governmental office. *American Political Science Review* 26:527-544.

Bingham, W.V., and Moore, B.V. (1931) *How to Interview.* New York: Harper.

Binnewies, W.G. (1926) A method of studying rural social distance. *Journal of Applied Sociology* 10:239-242.

Binnewies, W.G. (1931-32) Measuring changes in opinion. *Sociology and Social Research* 16:143-148.

Bogardus, E.S. (1923-24a) Personal experiences and social research. *Journal of Applied Sociology* 8:294-303.

Bogardus, E.S. (1923-24b) Discussion. *American Journal of Sociology* 29:703-704.

Bogardus, E.S. (1924-25) Measuring social distance. *Journal of Applied Sociology* 9:299-308.

Bogardus, E.S. (1925-26) The social research interview. *Journal of Applied Sociology* 10:69-82.

Bogardus, E.S. (1926a) Social distance between groups. *Journal of Applied Sociology* 10:473-479.

Bogardus, E.S. (1926b) *The New Social Research.* Los Angeles: Jesse Ray Miller.

Bogardus, E.S. (1928) *Immigration and Race Attitudes.* Boston: D.C. Heath.

Bogardus, E.S. (1928-29) Occupational distance. *Sociology and Social Research* 13:73-81.

Bogardus, E.S. (1931) Attitudes and the Mexican immigrant. In K. Young, ed., *Social Attitudes.* New York: Henry Holt.

Bogardus, E.S. (1932-33) A social distance scale. *Sociology and Social Research* 17:265-271

Bogardus, E.S. (1936) *Introduction to Social Research.* Los Angeles: Suttonhouse.

Bulmer, M. (1980) The early institutional establishment of social science research: the Local Community Research Committee at the University of Chicago 1923-30. *Minerva* 8:51-110.

Bulmer, M. (1981) Quantification and Chicago social science in the 1920s: a neglected tradition. *Journal of the History of the Behavioral Sciences* 17:312-331.

Burgess, E.W. (1927-28) Statistics and case studies as methods of sociological research. *Sociology and Social Research* 12:99-120.

Burgess, E.W. (1928) What social case records should contain to be useful for sociological interpretation. *Social Forces* 6:524-532.

Burgess, E.W. (1929) Is prediction feasible in social work? An inquiry based upon a sociological study of parole records. *Social Forces* 7:533-545.

Cantril, H. (1967) *The Human Dimension: Experiences in Policy Research.* New Brunswick, N.J.: Rutgers University Press.

Carpenter, N. (1932) Attitude patterns in the home-buying family. *Social Forces* 11:76-81.

Carpenter, N., and Katz, D. (1928) The cultural adjustment of the Polish group in the city of Buffalo: an experiment in the technique of social investigation. *Social Forces* 6:76-85.

Cavan, R.S., Hauser, P.A., and Stouffer, S.A. (1930-31) Note on the statistical treatment of life history material. *Social Forces* 9:200-203.

Clark, W.W. (1923-24) The measurement of social attitudes. *Journal of Applied Sociology* 8:345-354.

Dodd, S.C. (1935-36) A social distance test in the Near East. *American Journal of Sociology* 41:194-204.

Dreis, T.A. (1951) The Department of Agriculture's sample interview survey as a tool of administration. Ph.D. dissertation. American University, Washington, D.C.

Droba, D.D. (1931-32) Methods used for measuring public opinion. *American Journal of Sociology* 37:410-423.

Droba, D.D. (1932) Methods for measuring attitudes. *Psychological Bulletin* 29:309-323.

Droba, D.D. (1933) The nature of attitude. *Journal of Social Psychology* 4:444-462.

Droba, D.D. (1933-34) Social attitudes. *American Journal of Sociology* 39:513-524.

Edwards, A.L., and Kenney, K.C. (1946) A comparison of the Thurstone and Likert techniques of attitude scale construction. *Journal of Applied Psychology* 30:72-83.

Faris, E. (1925) The concept of social attitudes. *Journal of Applied Sociology* 9:404-409.

Faris, E. (1931) The concept of social attitudes. In K. Young, ed., *Social Attitudes*. New York: Holt.

Fearing, F. (1931) The experimental study of attitude, meaning, and the processes antecedent to action by N. Ach and others in the Wurzburg laboratory. In S.A. Rice, ed., *Methods in Social Science: A Case Book*. Chicago: University of Chicago Press.

Ferguson, L. (1935) The influence of individual attitudes on construction of an attitude scale. *Journal of Social Psychology* 6:115-117.

Ferguson, L.W. (1941) A study of the Likert technique of attitude scale construction. *Journal of Social Psychology* 13:51-57.

Fleming, D. (1967) Attitude: the history of a concept. *Perspectives in American History* 1:287-365.

Garnett, W.E. (1927) *Rural Organizations in Relation to Rural Life in Virginia with Special Reference to Organizational Attitudes*. Bulletin 256. Blacksburg, Va.: Virginia Polytechnic Institute, Virginia Agricultural Experiment Station.

Green, B.F. (1954) Attitude measurement. In G. Lindzey, ed., *Handbook of Social Psychology*. Reading Mass.: Addison Wesley.

Guilford, J.P. (1931) Racial preferences of a thousand American university students. *Journal of Social Psychology* 2:179-202.

Hall, O.M. (1934) Attitudes and unemployment: a comparison of the opinions and attitudes of employed and unemployed men. *Archives of Psychology* 25(165).

Hart, H. (1923) Progress report on a test of social attitudes and interests. *University of Iowa Studies in Child Welfare* 2:7-40.

Hart, H. (1933) Changing social attitudes and interests. In President's Research Committee on Social Trends, *Recent Social Trends in the United States*. New York: McGraw-Hill.

Hartley, E.L. (1946) *Problems in Prejudice*. New York: King's Crown Press.

Hayner, N.S. (1936) *Hotel Life*. Chapel Hill: University of North Carolina Press.

Hendrickson, G., and Zeligs, R. (1934) Checking the social distance technique through personal interviews. *Sociology and Social Research* 18:420-430.

Hinckley, E.D. (1932) The influence of individual opinion on construction of an attitude scale. *Journal of Social Psychology* 3:283-295.

Houser, J.D. (1927) *What the Employers Think: Executives' Attitudes Toward Employees*. Cambridge: Harvard University Press.

Jessen, C.A., and Hutchins, H.C. (1936) *Youth Community Surveys*. Bulletin 1936, No. 18-VI. Washington, D.C.: Office of Education, Committee on Youth Problems.

Attitude Measurement: The Early Years

Katz, D. (1937) Attitude measurement as a method in social psychology. *Social Forces* 15:479-482.

Katz, D. (1968) Floyd H. Allport. In D.L. Sills, ed., *International Encyclopedia of the Social Sciences*. New York: Macmillan and The Free Press.

Katz, D., and Allport, F.H. (1931) *Students' Attitudes: A Report of the Syracuse University Reaction Study*. Syracuse, N.Y.: Craftsman Press.

Katz, D., and Braly, K. (1933-34) Racial stereotypes of 100 college students. *Journal of Abnormal and Social Psychology* 28:280-290.

Kirkpatrick, E.L., and Boynton, A.M. (1936) Rural young people face their own situation. *Rural Sociology* 1:151-163.

Kornhauser, A.W. (1933) The technique of measuring employee attitudes. *Personnel* 9:99-107.

Kornhauser, A.W., and Lazarsfeld, P.F. (1935) The techniques of market research from the standpoint of a psychologist. Institute of Management Series. *Institute of Management* 16:3-15, 19-21 (reprinted in P.F. Lazarsfeld and M. Rosenberg, eds., *The Language of Social Research*. Glencoe, Ill.: Free Press, 1955.)

Kornhauser, A.W., and Sharp, A.A. (1932) Employee attitudes. *The Personnel Journal* 10: 393-404.

Krueger, E.T. (1925) The technique of securing life history documents. *Journal of Applied Sociology* 9:290-298.

Kulp, D.H (1934-35) Concepts in attitude tests with special reference to social questions. *Sociology and Social Research* 19:218-224.

LaPiere, R.T. (1928) Race prejudice: France and England. *Social Forces* 7:102-111.

LaPiere, R.T. (1934) Attitudes vs. actions. *Social Forces* 13:230-237.

LaPiere, R.T. (1938) Sociological significance of measurable attitudes. *American Sociological Review* 3:175-182.

LaPiere, R.T., and Farnsworth, P.R. (1936) *Social Psychology*. New York: McGraw-Hill.

Lazarsfeld, P.F. (1934) The psychological aspects of market research. *Harvard Business Review* 12:54-71.

Lazarsfeld, P.F. (1935) The art of asking why: three principles underlying the formulation of questionnaires. *National Marketing Review* 1:32-43 (reprinted in Daniel Katz et al., eds., *Public Opinion and Propaganda*. New York: Dryden Press, 1954).

Lazarsfeld, P.F. (1944) The controversy over detailed interviews—an offer for negotiation. *Public Opinion Quarterly* 8:38-60.

Lazarsfeld, P.F., Berelson, B., and Gaudet, H. (1944) *The People's Choice*. New York: Duell, Sloan and Pearce.

Likert, R. (1932) A technique for the measurement of attitudes. *Archives of Psychology* No. 140.

Likert, R., and Willets, J.M. (1940) *Morale and Agency Management*. Hartford, Conn.: Life Insurance Sales Research Bureau.

Likert, R., Roslow, S., and Murphy, G. (1934) A simple and reliable method of scoring the Thurstone attitude scales. *Journal of Social Psychology* 5:228-238.

Lindeman, E.C. (1924) *Social Discovery*. New York: Republic.

Link, H.C. (1947) Some milestones in public opinion research. *International Journal of Opinion and Attitude Research* 1:36-46.

Locke, H.J. (1934-35) Unemployed men in Chicago shelters. *Sociology and Social Research* 19:420-428.

Lundberg, G.A. (1927) The demographic and economic basis of political radicalism and conservatism. *American Journal of Sociology* 32:719-732.

Lundberg, G.A. (1929) The measurement of attitudes. In Lundberg, *Social Research: A Study in Methods of Gathering Data.* New York: Longman, Green.

Lynd, R.S., and Lynd, H.M. (1929) *Middletown: A Study in Contemporary American Culture.* New York: Harcourt, Brace.

Mangus, A.R. (1934) Sampling in the field of rural relief. *Journal of the American Statistical Association* 29:410-415.

Manson, G.E. (1925-26) Bibliography on psychological tests and other objective measures in industrial personnel. *Journal of Personnel Research* 4:301-328.

Mayo, E. (1929-30) Changing methods in industry. *The Personnel Journal* 8:326-332.

Mayo, E. (1933) *The Human Problems of an Industrial Civilization.* New York: Macmillan.

McNemar, Q. (1946) Opinion attitude methodology. *Psychological Bulletin* 43:289-374.

Merriam, C.E., and Gosnell, H.F. (1924) *Non-Voting: Causes and Methods of Control.* Chicago: University of Chicago Press.

Miles, W.P. (1933) Age and human ability. *Psychological Review* 30:99-123.

Moore, H.T. (1925) Innate factors in radicalism and conservatism. *Journal of Abnormal and Social Psychology* 20:234-244.

Murphy, G., and Likert, R. (1938) *Public Opinion and the Individual.* New York: Harper.

Murphy, G., and Murphy, L. (1931) *Experimental Social Psychology.* New York: Harper.

Murphy, G., Murphy, L., and Newcomb, T.M. (1937) *Experimental Social Psychology* (Rev. Ed.). New York: Harper.

National Industrial Conference Board (1934) *A Statistical Survey of Public Opinion Regarding Current Economic and Social Problems as Reported by Newspaper Editors in August and September, 1934.* New York: NICB.

National Industrial Conference Board (1936) *A Statistical Survey of Public Opinion Regarding Current Economic and Social Problems as Reported by Newspaper Editors in the First Quarter of 1936.* New York: NICB.

National Institute of Health: U.S. Public Health Service (1938) *The National Health Survey 1935-36.* Preliminary Reports. Washington, D.C.

Newcomb, T.M. (1939) *Personality and Social Change.* New York: Holt, Rinehart, and Winston.

Ogburn, W.F., and Talbot, N.S. (1929) A measurement of the factors in the presidential election of 1928. *Social Forces* 8:175-183.

Park, R.E. (1924a) A race relations survey: suggestions for a study of the Oriental population of the Pacific Coast. *Journal of Applied Sociology* 8:195-205.

Park, R.E. (1924b) The concept of social distance. *Journal of Applied Sociology* 8:339-344.

Park, R.E. (1924c) Experience and race relations. *Journal of Applied Sociology* 9:18-24.

Park, R.E. (1926) Methods of a race survey. *Journal of Applied Sociology* 10:410-415.

Park, R.E. (1931) The sociological methods of William Graham Sumner and of William I. Thomas and Florian Znaniecki. In S.A. Rice, ed., *Methods in Social Science: A Case Book.* Chicago: University of Chicago Press.

Park, R.E., and Burgess, E.W. (1924) *Introduction to the Science of Sociology.* Chicago: University of Chicago Press.

Pennock, G.A. (1930) Industrial research at Hawthorne: an experimental investigation of rest periods, working conditions, and other influences. *The Personnel Journal* 8:296-313.

Poole, W.C. (1927-28) Distance in sociology. *American Journal of Sociology* 33:99-104.

Poole, W.C. (1928-29) The social distance margin reviewed. *Sociology and Social Research* 13:49-54.

Putnam, M.L. (1929-30) Improving employee relations: a plan which uses data obtained from employees. *The Personnel Journal* 8:314-325.

Remmers, H.H., and Silance, E.B. (1934) Generalized attitude scales. *Journal of Social Psychology* 5:298-311.

Rice, S.A. (1924) *Farmers and Workers in American Politics.* New York: Columbia University Press.

Rice, S.A. (1928) *Quantitative Methods in Politics.* New York: Knopf.

Rice, S.A. (1929) Undergraduate attitudes toward marriage and children. *Mental Hygiene* 13:788-793.

Rice, S.A. (1930a) Measurements of social attitudes and public opinion. Institute of Methods of Rural Sociological Research, U.S. Department of Agriculture, Bureau of Agricultural Economics Bulletin. Dec. 31, 1929-Jan. 4, 1930, pp. 11-20.

Rice, S.A. (1930b) Statistical studies of social attitudes and public opinion. In S.A. Rice, ed., *Statistics in Social Studies.* Philadelphia: University of Pennsylvania Press.

Rice, S.A. (1931a) Hypotheses and verifications in Clifford R. Shaw's studies of juvenile delinquency. In S.A. Rice, ed., *Methods in Social Science: A Case Book.* Chicago: University of Chicago Press.

Rice, S.A. (1931b) Behavioral alternatives as statistical data in studies by William F. Ogburn and Ernest W. Burgess. In S.A. Rice, ed., *Methods in Social Science: A Case Book.* Chicago: University of Chicago Press.

Rice, S.A., and Weaver, W.W. (1929) The verification of social measurements involving subjective classifications. *Social Forces* 8:16-28.

Robinson, E.S. (1933) Trends of the voter's mind. *Journal of Social Psychology* 3:265-284.

Rose, A.M. (1951) Discussion of Bogardus' paper, "Measuring changes in ethnic reactions." *American Sociological Review* 16:52-53.

Rossi, P.H. (1959) Four landmarks in voting research. In E. Burdick and A.J. Brodbeck, eds., *American Voting Behavior.* Glencoe, Ill.: Free Press.

Rossi, P.H. (1972) Community social indicators. In A. Campbell and P.E. Converse, eds., *The Human Meaning of Social Change.* New York: Russell Sage.

Ruckmick, C.A. (1930) The uses and abuses of the questionnaire procedure. *Journal of Applied Psychology* 14:32-41.

Rundquist, E.A., and Sletto, R.F. (1936) *Personality in the Depression: A Study in the Measurement of Attitudes.* Minneapolis: University of Minnesota.

Schanck, R.L. (1932) A study of a community and its groups and institutions conceived of as behaviors of individuals. *Psychological Monographs* 43(195).

Schanck, R.L. (1934) A study of change in institutional attitudes in a rural community. *Journal of Social Psychology* 5:121-128.

Scott, W.A. (1968) Attitude measurement. In G. Lindzey and E. Aronson, eds., *Handbook of Social Psychology*. 2nd ed. Reading, Mass.: Addison Wesley.

Seashore, R.H., and Hevner, K. (1933) A time-saving device for the construction of attitude scales. *Journal of Social Psychology* 4:366-372.

Shideler, E.F. (1928) The social distance margin. *Sociology and Social Research* 12:243-252.

Stouffer, S.A. (1931) Experimental comparison of a statistical and a case history technique of attitude research. *Publications of American Sociological Society* 25:154-156.

Stouffer, S.A., and Lazarsfeld, P.F. (1937) Research memorandum on the family in the Depression. *Social Science Research Council Bulletin* 29.

Stouffer, S.A., Suchman, E.H., DeVinney, L.C., Star, S.A., and Williams, R.M., Jr. (1949) *The American Soldier, Vol. 1: Adjustment During Army Life*. Stouffer, S.A., Lumsdaine, A.A., Lumsdaine, M.H., Williams R.M., Jr., Smith, M.B., Janis, I.L., Star, S.A., and Cottrell, L.S., Jr. (1949) *The American Soldier, Vol. 2: Combat and Its Aftermath*. Princeton: Princeton University Press.

Sturges, H.A. (1927) The theory of correlation applied in studies of changing attitudes. *American Journal of Sociology* 33:269-275.

Suchman, E.A., and Guttman, L. (1947) A solution to the problem of question "bias." *Public Opinion Quarterly* 11:445-455.

Sumner, F.B. (1898) Rating of certainty of belief of 25 propositions of 100 persons. *Psychological Review* 5:616-631.

Thomas, W.I., and Znaniecki, F. (1918) *The Polish Peasant in Europe and America*. Vol. 1. Chicago: University of Chicago Press.

Thrasher, F.M. (1927) *The Gang: A Study of 1313 Gangs in Chicago*. Chicago: University of Chicago Press.

Thurstone, L.L. (1928a) Attitudes can be measured. *American Journal of Sociology* 33:529-554.

Thurstone, L.L. (1928b) Measurement of opinion. *Journal of Abnormal and Social Psychology* 22:415-430.

Thurstone, L.L. (1928c) An experimental study of nationality preferences. *Journal of General Psychology* 1:405-423.

Thurstone, L.L. (1931-32) The measurement of attitudes. *Journal of Abnormal and Social Psychology* 26:249-269.

Thurstone, L.L. (1952) Autobiographical note. In E.G. Boring et al., eds., *A History of Psychology in Autobiography*. Vol. 4. Worcester, Mass.: Clark University Press.

Thurstone, L.L., and Chave, E.J. (1929) *The Measurement of Attitude*. Chicago: University of Chicago Press.

Uhrbrock, R.S. (1934) Attitudes of 4430 employees. *Journal of Social Psychology* 5:365-376.

Vetter, G.B., and Green, M. (1932-33) Personality and group factors in the making of atheists. *Journal of Abnormal and Social Psychology* 27:179-194.

Webb, J.N., and Brown, M. (1938) *Migrant Families*. Research Monograph 18. Works Progress Administration, Division of Social Research. Washington D.C.: U.S. Government Printing Office.

White, L.D. (1929) *The Prestige Value of Public Employment in Chicago.* Chicago: University of Chicago Press.

Wilkinson, F. (1929) Social distance between occupations. *Sociology and Social Research* 13:234-244.

Williams, F.M., and Zimmerman, C.C. (1935) *Studies of Family Living in the United States and Other Countries: Analysis of Material and Method.* U.S. Department of Agriculture, Misc. Publ. No. 223. Washington D.C.: U.S. Government Printing Office.

Young, D.R. (1927) Some effects of a course in American race problems on the race prejudices of 450 undergraduates at the University of Pennsylvania. *Journal of Abnormal and Social Psychology* 22:235-242.

Young, K. (1931a) Frederick M. Thrasher's study of gangs. In S.A. Rice, ed., *Methods in Social Science: A Case Book.* Chicago: University of Chicago Press.

Young, K. (1931b) *Social Attitudes.* New York: Holt.

Young, P.V. (1928) Occupational attitudes and values of Russian lumber workers. *Sociology and Social Research* 12:543-553.

Zeligs, R., and Hendrickson, G. (1933) Racial attitudes of 200 6th grade children. *Sociology and Social Research* 18:26-36.

Zimmerman, C.C. (1925) *Farmers' Marketing Attitudes.* Minneapolis: University of Minnesota.

Zimmerman, C.C. (1927) Types of farmers' attitudes. *Social Forces* 5:591-596.

Zimmerman, C.C., and Anderson, C.A. (1927-28) Attitudes of rural preachers regarding church union and science: a methodological study. *Journal of Applied Sociology* 12:144-150.

Zorbaugh, H.W. (1929) *The Gold Coast and the Slum: A Sociological Study of Chicago's Near North Side.* Chicago: University of Chicago Press.

Acknowledgments

This chapter is part of a forthcoming book, *Survey Research in the United States: Roots and Emergence 1890-1960* (University of California Press), work on which has been supported by grants from the National Science Foundation (SOC78–11409) and the Earhart Foundation. I should like to thank Martin Bulmer, Charles F. Cannell, Dorwin Cartwright, Otis Dudley Duncan, Stanley Presser, and Howard Schuman for their critical reading of an earlier draft.

2

Utility in Economics: A Survey of the Literature

J. G. Tulip Meeks

What *is* utility? To answer, "Happiness," is to invite the further question what happiness is. Is it pleasure, satisfaction, contentment, absence of suffering, freedom, self-fulfillment, a high quality of life, serving others, obedience to God? Or all or none or some of these? Is it a sensation—as a tickle is—or is it rather, as the philosopher Ryle (1954) suggested of pleasure, to do with putting your whole heart into what you are doing?

Economists have not on the whole been troubled by definitional questions of this sort in their extensive use of the concept of utility.[1] At first it was usual to follow Bentham and Mill in identifying utility with happiness, and this with "pleasure, and the absence of pain" (Mill, 1863/1968:6); but more recently it has become the convention, though with little discussion, to interpret utility in a broad sense as welfare.[2] There is some tendency to use the concept in a circular way:[3] Robinson (1962:48-49) insists that, in economists' hands, "*utility* is a metaphysical concept of impregnable circularity; *utility* is the quality in commodities that makes individuals want to buy them, and the fact that individuals want to buy commodities shows that they have *utility.*" And she adds that, so far as economics is concerned, what utility boils down to is just this: "*Utility* is a Good Thing; the aim and purpose of economic life is to get as much of it as possible. And, set out in a diagram [graph], it looks just like a measurable quantity."

But of course depicting utility on a graph does not mean it actually *can* be measured. Is it measurable in fact?[4] I think it is fair to say that economists have been more concerned with drawing out the implications of utility assumptions based on casual introspection or on an a priori concept of rationality than with attempting to measure utility in practice (although there has been some interest in devising possible measurement schemes).[5] This typical shelving of actual utility measurement is no doubt associated with the general awareness of problems of measurement and with recognition of limitations on the usefulness of such measures as might be contrived. On the question of utility measurement, then, the tale told by the economics literature is in the main a somewhat abstract story of restrictions and difficulties.

Bentham began bravely, and he was not claiming too much when he wrote: "I have planted the tree of utility. I have planted it deep and spread it wide." He argued that happiness increased with wealth, but at a diminishing rate—"the quantity of happiness produced by a particle of wealth (each particle being of the same magnitude) will be less and less at every particle" (1843:Vol. III, 229). In an early manuscript he also gave some guidance on how individual utility might actually be measured, suggesting that

> the degree of intensity possessed by that pleasure which is the faintest of any that can be distinguished to be pleasure, may be represented by unity. Such a degree of intensity is in every day's experience: according as any pleasures are perceived to be more and more intense, they may be represented by higher and higher numbers: but there is no fixing upon any particular degree of intensity as being the highest of which a pleasure is susceptible. [Bentham in Halévy, 1901:Vol. I, App. II, p. 398].

But Bentham's initial optimism about numerical representation of degrees of intensity of pleasure was qualified by his later remark that intensity "is not susceptible of precise expression: it *not* being susceptible of measurement" (1843:Vol. IV, 542). He was indeed acutely aware of some of the key problems in measuring utility. He distinguished four dimensions of pleasure and pain (intensity, duration, certainty and propinquity) and believed that sensibility to pleasure and pain might vary between individuals for a number of reasons (he suggested 32 factors that might influence it, including age, sex, education and firmness of mind.[6] He also explained more pointedly than many subsequent writers the obstacle to adding individual utilities to arrive at a social sum, writing that " 'tis in vain to talk of adding quantities which after the addition will continue distinct as they were before, one man's happiness will never be another man's happiness; a gain to one man is no gain to another: you might as well pretend to add 20 apples to 20 pears, which after you had done that could not be 40 of any one thing but 20 of each just as there was before" (Bentham in Halévy, 1901:Vol. III, 481).[7]

Aware though Bentham was of difficulties in comparison and summation, however, he nevertheless held that practical reasoning must abstract from them: "differences of character are inscrutable; and such is the diversity of circumstances, that they are never the same for two individuals. Unless we begin by dropping these two considerations, it will be impossible to announce any general proposition" (1802:103); and similarly, the "addibility of the happiness of different subjects . . . [although] when considered rigorously it may appear fictitious, is a postulatum without the allowance of which all political reasoning is at a stand" (Bentham in Halévy, 1901:Vol. III, 481). The justification Bentham offers for this practice of proceeding as if acknowledged difficulties in making interpersonal comparisons and additions of utility did not exist is in several ways reminiscent of that which Friedman (1953) provides for using unrealistic assumptions in 'positive' economics: that it is the only practicable procedure, abstraction from acknowledged complicating factors being necessary "for the sake of abbreviation"; and that the "fictitious form of speech" adopted, though it "may prove false or inexact in a given individual case", may yet "approach nearer the truth" than does any manageable alternative and will be capable of yielding conclusions that are not false, so that it can be defended for its "speculative truth and practical utility" (Bentham in Halévy, 1901:Vol. III, 481; Bentham, 1802:103). But there are peculiar snags in the way of testing conclusions directly in welfare economics, and it is not clear that Bentham's defense will do.[8] Stigler's 1950 survey of utility theory applauds Bentham's "awareness of the crucial problems" in his utility calculus and notes his "ingenuity in attempting to solve them" but comments that the "resort to a question-begging assumption . . . justified by the desirability . . . of its corollaries" in place of achieving interpersonal comparisons by calculation represents "a fundamental failure of his project to provide a scientific basis for social policy: the scientific basis was being justified by the policies to which it led" (Stigler, 1950:311, 309). For all that, it will emerge that Bentham's 'solution' is still, in effect, adopted by a number of writers of the present day.

In his survey, Stigler argues that Bentham's near contemporaries and immediate successors did little to follow up his approach. It might perhaps be added, however, that the younger Mill in his philosophical essay on "Utilitarianism" had hit on an idea that may have influenced one important later line of economic thinking when he tackled the question how pleasures of different kinds might be compared (whether there could be any basis for ranking "pleasures of the intellect", say, as having higher value than those of "mere sensation"). Mill's suggestion was that we must accept the "verdict of the only competent judges", going by the choices actually made between two kinds of pleasure by those who are "qualified by knowledge of both." Of two pleasures, then, "if there be one to which all or almost all who have experience of both give a decided preference . . . that is the more desirable pleasure" (1863/1968:7-10). In its application to the different qualities of happiness allegedly enjoyed by those of "higher faculties", this 'preference' procedure has been much criticized, both on empirical grounds and for implicit elitism. But the device also had a more fundamental application, to the quantitative measurement of utility; for Mill went on to argue that

> there needs be the less hesitation to accept this judgment respecting the quality of pleasures, since there is no other tribunal to be referred to even on the question of quantity. What means are there of determining which is the acutest of two pains, or the intensest of two pleasurable sensations, except the general suffrage of those who are familiar with both? Neither pains nor pleasures are homogeneous, and pain is always heterogeneous with pleasure. What is there to decide whether a particular pleasure is worth purchasing at the cost of a particular pain, except the feelings and judgment of the experienced? [Mill, 1863/1968: 10]

Stigler argues that, after Bentham, the next significant development in the economic treatment of utility came with the 'marginal revolution' in the latter part of the nineteenth century, usually associated with the names of Jevons, Walras, Menger and Marshall.[9] There is some debate over whether the emergence of this new approach to economics did amount to a revolution, an issue recently discussed by Deane; but it is certain that the changes were significant. "The so-called marginal revolution," explains Deane, "involved a wide-ranging transformation of the characteristic methodology of analytical economics by means of what was essentially a mathematical tool derived from the calculus" (1978:95). With the aid of the new tool, economists hoped to put economics on a par with the natural sciences; and the prime concept to which they applied it was utility. Thus Jevons (1871/1911:vii) wrote that "the nature of Wealth and Value is explained by the consideration of indefinitely small amounts of pleasure and pain, just as the Theory of Statics is made to rest upon the equality of indefinitely small amounts of energy." Combining Bentham's utility calculus with the differential calculus helped to resolve a puzzle that had been raised much earlier by Adam Smith—why water, for all its usefulness, should fetch next to nothing in the marketplace while merely decorative precious stones are worth a great deal. This was no longer perplexing if the relative price at which a good was exchanged depended not on the *total* utility to the consumer from possessing quantities of it (nor on the average utility of each unit to him) but rather on its *marginal* utility—the additional benefit to him from obtaining a tiny increase of that good, *given* the amount that he already had.[10] And when the same marginal approach was extended from the theory of exchange to the theory of production, economists were in a position to attempt a rigorous analysis of the conditions for using scarce resources with maximum efficiency, with consumers gaining the maximum utility possible from their income. This was perhaps the heyday of the concept of utility in economic thought.

But though the new approach was in some ways an advance, it had disadvantages too. Deane (1978:121, 118) comments that "on the debit side of the account was the way it narrowed the scope not only of value theory but of economic theory generally", for it "turned away from the macro problems posed by the classical economists to focus on the problem of analysing market prices in long-term competitive equilibrium."

And even so far as the analysis and interpretation of market prices was concerned, the proponents of the new marginal system were conscious of some difficulties. Bothersome doubts about the measurability of utility persisted. Menger seems to have been free from them; but Walras was eventually convinced that utility, "though a quantity, was unmeasurable" (Schumpeter, 1954:1055, n.1), although his writings had commonly implied the reverse . And Stigler (1950:317) reports a similar confusion in Jevons, who "with gallant inconsistency" suggested a monetary means of assessing utility after being so outspoken on the remoteness of any possibility of measurement as to say:

> There is no unit of . . . suffering, or enjoyment. . . . I have granted that we can hardly form the conception of a unit of pleasure or pain, so that the numerical expression of quantities of feeling seems to be out of the question. . . . I confess that it seems to me difficult even to imagine how such estimates and summations can be made with any approach to accuracy. Greatly though I admire the clear and precise notions of Bentham, I know not where his numerical data are to be found. [Jevons, 1871/1911:7,12; 1871:12]

Interpersonal comparisons of utility were held by Jevons to be impossible too, although he can be detected attempting to make them.[11]

Marshall was, on the whole, more optimistic about utility measurement, presenting a possible method of assessing it indirectly (akin to, but more sophisticated than, Jevons's), based on the idea of considering how much a consumer would pay to avoid being deprived of a commodity.[12] Although he later became a little more tentative, he felt initially that this method might also permit "extremely accurate" comparisons of pleasure and pain between different sets of people from within an income group, providing the sets were fairly broad (Marshall, 1890:152). But he too was aware of problems. In practice, the application of the method had to be limited: it might work reasonably well as an indicator of a consumer's utility from tea, for instance, but not for his utility from food in general, since the limiting price that could be extorted for the latter would be so great as to distort the value of the basic monetary measuring rod.[13] And the procedure could not be relied upon to reflect realized satisfactions, which it was allowed "might differ considerably" from desires—since some desires "especially those connected with emulation, are impulsive; many result from the force of habit; some are morbid and lead only to hurt; and many are based on expectations that are never fulfilled . . . [while some satisfactions] may even partly result from self-abnegation" (Marshall, 1890/1920:92, n. 1)[14]. Marshall also spotted a potential weakness in the theory that the marginal utility of a good to a consumer always diminishes as the quantity he has of it is increased[15], making the observations that "the more good music a man hears, the stronger is his taste for it likely to become" and that "the virtue of cleanliness and the vice of drunkenness alike grow on what they feed upon." He promptly fortified the doctrine, however, by tacking on to it the condition that no time must "be allowed for any alteration in the character or tastes of the man" to whom it is applied and by maintaining that, in the awkward cases, "our observations range over some period of time; and the man is not the same at the beginning as at the end of it" (1890/1920:94). Stigler suggests that the tendency apparent here (and given prominence in Kuhn's [1962] account of scientific revolutions) to reformulate the theory in the face of any threatening empirical test was fairly widespread among the marginalists at this time.[16]

There were also questions—raised by Marshall and pursued by Pigou—about the traditional view that the unfettered operation of a perfectly competitive system would maximize social utility. This will not be so if the private costs and benefits registered through the price mechanism fail to reflect social costs and benefits (as they do when, for instance, a factory faces no charge for polluting the air). And again, the traditional analysis concentrated on conditions for maximizing society's "economic" utility: could it safely be assumed that total utility would follow the same pattern? Pigou's (1932:20) answer was to judge it *likely* that "qualitative conclusions about the effect of an economic cause upon economic welfare will hold good also of the effect on total welfare" in the absence of any specific evidence to the contrary (a comfortable position challenged by Graaff [1957:6], who writes that "if we really do not know, we do not know—and there is no point in pretending that we have enough information for a probability judgement").[17] Following Pigou's concentration on them, issues of social welfare and discussion of interpersonal comparisons of utility became the subject of a distinct branch of economic study (welfare economics) which developed a structure of its own, relying, however, on the individual utility calculus explored in the theory of the consumer as a basic building block.[18]

In 1881, Edgeworth initiated what Stigler presents as perhaps the main advance in the orthodox utility theory of consumer demand—the generalization of the utility function to allow for the fact that the utility gained from a commodity was not always independent of consumption of other goods, as Jevons's and Walras's formulation of the function had assumed (for example, the utilities of bread and of butter would depend on each other, as would those of badminton rackets and shuttlecocks or of left and right shoes, while the utility of a power mower would affect that of a hand machine). It was some years before the main implications of this more general utility function were drawn out—in particular, the implication that demand curves (relating quantity bought to price) will not necessarily slope downwards (it becomes possible that demand for a good will increase, not fall, as its price rises: for instance, if the price of a staple food such as rice rises, then poor consumers, finding the purchasing power of their income reduced, may be driven to cut back on relatively expensive foods such as meat and replace them with rice in their diet, purchases of rice rising in consequence).[19] A related extension of the utility function, suggested by Fisher and Cunynghame in 1892, was to allow for the well-known fact that an individual's utility is often not independent of the consumption of other people. To quote Cunynghame (1892:37):

> Almost the whole value of strawberries in March, to those who like this tasteless mode of ostentation, is the fact that others cannot get them. As my landlady once remarked, "Surely, sir, you would not like anything so common and cheap as a fresh herring?" The demand for diamonds, rubies, and sapphires is another example of this.[20]

But, while this realization has been a thorn in the side of welfare economists, it was largely neglected in the development of the traditional theory of consumer demand.[21] The main area of interest in demand theory for several decades was thus that sparked off by the Edgeworthian advance, an area that, in the judgment of some modern specialists, yielded only a sparse crop from its subsequent cultivation—in effect, the result that demand curves may or may not slope downwards, plus the (unsurprising) observation that they normally will, with some a priori specification of the conditions under which they actually would. Stigler ends his survey by remarking on the "unfruitfulness of the ruling utility theory as a source of hypotheses in demand", despite "the long labors of a very large number of able economists" (1950:396). In 1947 Samuelson had reached much the same conclusion: having shown that the utility framework implies remarkably little for consumers' behavior, he asks how much economic theory would be changed if the implications there are were found to be "empirically untrue", and he answers, "I suspect, very little" (1947:117).

The gradual probing of these implications of the orthodox utility theory of consumer demand was accompanied by a persistent movement to reinterpret the foundations of utility theory itself, so as to present them on what it was thought would be a more secure and scientific basis. Samuelson sums up this evolution of the central utility notion when he writes that "the concept of utility may be said to have been undergoing throughout its entire history a purging out of objectionable, and sometimes unnecessary, connotations" (1947:90). The purging process was precipitated by the problems of measuring utility.

Again Edgeworth was the harbinger of later developments. Like Bentham, Mill, Jevons and Marshall, he was aware of some problems in measuring utility; but, again like them, he nevertheless "*believed* the utilitarian psychology" in his important early work (Keynes, 1926:260).[22] His *Mathematical Psychics* (1881) dealt with "the applicability and the application of mathematics to sociology" and pursued further the idea of placing the moral sciences on the same footing as the natural ones by developing "the calculus of *Feeling*", man being conceived in essence as a "pleasure machine" (1881:1, 15). Measurement of utility was to be conducted in terms of "intensity-time-number units" in order to arrive at a social sum of happiness; and Edgeworth was sanguine about the feasibility of assessing the second of these dimensions ("an affair of clockwork") and the third ("an affair of census"). "But the first dimension," he wrote, "where we leave the safe ground of the objective, equating to unity each *minimum sensibile*, presents indeed peculiar difficulties. *Atoms of pleasure* are not easy to distinguish and discern: more continuous than sand, more discrete than liquid; as it were nuclei of the just-perceivable, embedded in circumambient semi-consciousness." He went on to deal somewhat briskly with these "peculiar difficulties";[23] but the original solution to them that he presented pointed the way towards ordinal rather than cardinal measurement of utility (assessments just of more and less, and not of how much): "We cannot *count* the golden sands of life; we cannot *number* the 'innumerable smile' of seas of love; but we seem to be capable of observing that there is here a *greater*, there a *less*, multitude of pleasure-units, mass of happiness; and that is enough" (1881: 8-9).[24]

In his brief biography, Keynes suggests that Edgeworth later became uneasy about the viability of this hedonistic calculus and

> felt his foundations slipping away from him. . . . The atomic hypothesis which has worked so splendidly in physics breaks down in psychics. We are faced at every turn with the problems of organic unity, of discreteness, of discontinuity—the whole is not equal to the sum of the parts, comparisons of quantity fail us, small changes produce large effects, the assumptions of a uniform and homogeneous continuum are not satisfied. Thus the results of *Mathematical Psychics* turn out to be derivative, not fundamental, indexes, not measurements, first approximations at the best; and fallible indexes, dubious approximations at that, with much doubt added as to what, if anything, they are indexes or approximations of. No one was more conscious of all this than Edgeworth. . . . [He] knew he was skating on thin ice; and as life went on his love of skating and his distrust of the ice increased, by a malicious fate, *pari passu.* [Keynes, 1926:262-263]

The possibility of exploring ordinal measurement of utility was not taken up for some 15 years after the publication of *Mathematical Psychics*—and then not by Edgeworth but by Pareto (1909/1927). After initial allegiance to traditional utility theory, Pareto became impressed by the critics' stress on the lack of means to make cardinal measurements of utility and turned instead to an ordinal system resting not on numerical measurement and the addition of utilities but rather on ranking preferences for different sets of goods as higher, lower or equivalent ('indifferent'). He saw that such a system could still incorporate the concept of consumers seeking the maximum fulfillment of their desires, since, as Schumpeter (1954:1062) explains, "there are means of telling whether or not we are on the top of a hill without measuring the elevation of the place where we stand."[25] He saw that inferring the existence of an ordinal utility function (which he called an index function) from preference rankings depended on making certain assumptions about the consistency of choices.[26] And he saw that if a utility function *could* be inferred in this way, it would be arbitrary in the sense that in principle any of the infinite number of functions obtainable from the first by monotonic (order-preserving) transformation would do equally well.[27]

The Paretian system marked a change of emphasis from the Edgeworthian approach, as Pareto himself explained, hailing the shift in perspective as a further move towards making economics truly scientific. "The entire theory," he wrote,

> . . . rests only on a fact of experience, that is to say, on the determination of the

quantities of goods which constitute combinations which are equivalent for the individual. The theory of economic science thus acquires the rigor of rational mechanics; it deduces its results from experience, without the intervention of any metaphysical entity.

[Edgeworth] assumes the existence of utility (ophelimity) and from it he deduces the indifference curves; I instead consider as empirically given the curves of indifference, and I deduce from them all that is necessary for the theory of equilibrium, without having recourse to ophelimity." [Pareto, 1909/1927:160, 169n][28]

But Pareto was not wholly consistent in banishing the "metaphysical entity" of measurable utility from his work: it crept back, for instance, in the guise of diminishing marginal utility so that, as Robertson (1952:18-19) puts it in his delightful piece, "Utility and All That", Pareto was "beguiled . . . into measuring utility in [his] sleep."

The main elements of a theory that could eschew mention of utility were, however, now provided. It fell to Johnson, Slutsky, Allen and Hicks to develop them. These writers shared the belief that the concept of measurable utility was inessential in demand theory and should be eradicated. Slutsky (1915:1), for instance, wrote somewhat sweepingly that "we must make [economics] completely independent of psychological assumptions and philosophical hypotheses" (at a time when logical positivism was in vogue, this perhaps seemed more feasible than it does today); and Hicks (1939:Chapter 1, Sec. 4, 6) held the quantitative concept of utility to be an "unnecessary entity" in the theory of economic choice, to be eliminated on the principle of Occam's razor as "likely to obscure the vision", presenting his investigations in the light of "a purge, rejecting all concepts which are tainted by quantitative utility."

The favored strategy for purifying the theory was to concentrate on indifference curves (loci of sets of goods regarded as equivalent by the consumer), on the grounds that these are uniquely given by his preferences[29] whereas no single utility index is. It was by showing that a consumer's indifference map (together with given price ratios) could suffice to establish his point of maximum satisfaction that, "in line with the growing trend towards a more positive formulation of economic theory", Allen and Hicks in 1934 "succeeded in emptying the Marshallian demand curve of some of its classical heritage of armchair psychology" (Deane, 1978:122). Schumpeter (1954:1066) judges that their theory was "the first to be completely independent of the existence of an index function and completely free from any lingering shadows of even *marginal* utility."

But this was not the end of the story. Robertson, tongue in cheek, explains that

> in slitting the throat of diminishing utility Hicks and Allen did not leave us destitute: they gave us in its place a creature which every teacher of economics

now knows as the marginal rate of substitution. The consumer, it seems, must not go about burdened with the knowledge, or belief, that a little more beef or a little more beer would add so much to his satisfaction; but he *may* go about with the knowledge, or belief, that he would be ready to go without so much beef for so much extra beer, and likewise for any other two commodities you like to name [Robertson, 1952:18][30]

—a way of looking at things that might still be questioned. Perhaps, as Schumpeter (1954:1066) suggests, "it should have been clear from the first that things would not stop at indifference varieties and that they are after all but a midway house."[31] They posed some puzzles for interpreting the system in terms of choice: for instance, if presented with two 'indifferent' options, a consumer might reasonably choose to plump for one; but then 'being in a chosen position' could not automatically be identified, as had generally been supposed, with 'being in a preferred situation' where the latter phrase carries a connotation of regarding oneself as 'being better off'.[32] And the psychological assumptions on which they seemed to rest were no more immune from doubt than those of the theory they ousted. It is not clear "that people have preference fields . . . in their minds, or indifference curves on the brain, and that a person's behaviour is determined by reference to these internal maps" (Little, 1950/1957:31); and "from a practical standpoint we are not much better off when drawing purely imaginary indifference curves than we are when speaking of purely imaginary utility functions" (Schumpeter, 1954:1067).[33]

There was, then, yet a further stage in the trend towards eliminating reference to mental states—a move to ground the theory firmly on potentially observable behavior in the marketplace, on the display of actual choices. Such a movement harbors dangers for the incautious: there is the risk, described by Samuelson (1947:91), that eventually "behavior is explained in terms of preferences, which are in turn defined only by behavior. The result can very easily be circular. . . . Often nothing more is stated than the conclusion that people behave as they behave. . . ." But, holding that behavioral analysis of consumer demand *need* not be circular, Samuelson himself fostered its development, as the leading figure amongst those "logicians and behaviourists [who], having tasted the blood of cardinal utility, were spurred to fresh efforts of purgation, which have resulted . . . in the development of the doctrine of 'revealed preference'" (Robertson, 1952: 19).[34] The central idea of the new doctrine is that the consumer reveals his preference for one set of goods rather than another if, while in a position (given his income and the respective prices) to buy either set, he actually opts for the former; so that a picture of his preferences can be built up by studying his purchasing behavior as prices vary.

With this transition from "concealed indifference" to revealed preference, Samuelson originally claimed to have ousted even "vestigial traces of the utility concept" (1938:61),[35] and the campaign to eradicate "metaphysical entities" ground to a halt. Its conclusion was not altogether triumphal, however.[36] In the end, there were doubts whether the game was worth the candle. "Was it worth while," Robertson (1952:22) asks, "to go to such mountainous trouble to formalise in non-mental terms the behaviour of beings whom we have every reason to suppose to be equipped with minds?" Even Samuelson, who does maintain that the result of the prolonged purging process has been "a much less objectionable doctrine", also holds that the new theory is however "a less interesting one" (1947:90). And recently Sen (1980b:Sec. 10) has reinforced this view, arguing that, by "focussing only on predicting behaviour", revealed preference theory has "substantially ignored . . . the richness of human psychology, refusing to see anything in utility or happiness other than choice. . . . The delimitation of utility theory to one of silent choice—no questions asked as to what lies behind choice—stifles descriptive inquiry into human joys and sufferings."[37]

There was still some question, too, whether victory had really been won even for the description of consumer behavior.[38] And it is now clear that any attempt to gain decisive information about the consumer's welfare merely by observing his market choices runs into enormous snags. There is the difficulty that preferences are only 'revealed' in choice among goods actually available, so no information is gleaned by this means about which list of goods the consumer would choose to choose from.[39] There is the difficulty, familiar after Marshall, that tastes may change over time so that there is a possibility that preferences will have changed between sequential purchases.[40] And there is the difficulty that, if the chosen goods have some (even slight) degree of durability, then the mere order in which they happen to be bought need reveal nothing about preferences among them.[41] Moreover, even if preferences were adequately revealed in market behavior, questions arise over making them the basis of moral rules: will it do simply to identify an individual's welfare with his being in a preferred position? Robinson concludes that it will not:

> We are told . . . that since *utility* cannot be measured it is not an operational concept, and that 'revealed preference' should be put in its place. Observable market behaviour will show what an individual chooses. Preference is just what the individual under discussion prefers; there is no value judgement involved. Yet, as the argument goes on, it is clear that it is a Good Thing for the individual to have what he prefers. This, it may be held, is not a question of satisfaction, but freedom—we want him to have what he prefers so as to avoid having to restrain his behaviour.
>
> But drug-fiends should be cured: children should go to school. How do we

decide what preferences should be respected and what restrained unless we judge the preferences themselves? . . .

[And] when we admit the influence of society, of the Joneses, of advertisement, upon the individual's scale of preferences . . . we begin to doubt whether preferences are what we really prefer. [Robinson, 1962:50-51][42]

In view of the labor that had been spent in trying to purge utility functions from consumer theory, it may seem rather odd that there should follow an attempt to bring them back: yet this is so—in Schumpeter's (1954:1068) words, "the corpse shows signs of life."[43] It has become fairly common to interpret the 'chosen position' approach for expository purposes in terms of utility once more—treating the consumer *as if* he were maximizing a utility function—though in general the corresponding utility function will only be ordinally specified.[44] But such a function is far from unique: suppose the consumer's behavior 'reveals' that he prefers A to B and B to C, then this may be summarized in terms of utility by saying that option A is worth a utils,[45] B is worth b, and C, c, where a, b and c are *any* numbers such that $a > b > c$ (the utility function is defined only up to a monotonic transformation)—Pareto over again. Is it possible to go beyond this ordinal analysis by inferring further restrictions on individual utility functions?

On certain conditions, the answer is: yes. But the value of the resulting utility measures is limited, partly because several rival methods of cardinalization have been suggested, partly because of the restrictions implied in the respective conditions on which they rest and partly because the measurements are made, like those of temperature or time, from an arbitrary origin on an arbitrary scale (the utility function is still unique only up to a positive linear transformation).[46]

One method of cardinalization rests on the idea, reminiscent of Bentham and Edgeworth, that people's ability to detect very fine differences in utility is limited. If each individual has only a finite number of discrimination levels, where the gap between each level is the smallest utility change he can register, then counting how many discrimination levels lie between any alternatives open to him will yield a cardinal utility scale, unique but for constants of scale and 'origin'.[47] But a number of criticisms of this method have been voiced: one is that its empirical basis is open to question; and another is that the numbering system can be thrown out if a new commodity is introduced.[48]

A second cardinalization procedure, initially used by Fisher and then by Frisch, relies on assuming the utility derived from each of a pair of goods to be independent of that derived from the other (in other words, on assuming the goods to be neither complements nor competitors). Again this is sufficient to ensure that utility is measurable up to a linear transformation. The method has been strongly criticized by Samuelson on the grounds that the assumption of independence implies "arbitrary" and "dubious" restrictions on price-quantity behavior (1947:174-183). More recently there has been some relaxation of the independence axioms required.[49]

It is a third way of cardinalizing utility that looms largest in the literature, however: that presented by von Neumann and Morgenstern in the 1940s (on lines explored earlier by Ramsey[50]) and restricted to situations involving risk. They showed that, so long as an individual's choices under risk satisfy a defined set of postulates (including postulates of completeness and consistency), a cardinal utility function for him can be constructed. The method is based on considering a consumer's preferences between gaining a 'bundle' of goods (I) for certain and participating in a gamble which gives him, with stated probabilities, either a 'bundle' he prefers to I or one to which I is preferred. By taking account of how his preferences change as the probabilities vary, it is possible to assign utility numbers to the available options in such a way that they mirror his preferences (in the sense that his actual choices correspond to those choices he would make if he acted so as to maximize the mathematical expectation of these utility numbers, where the mathematical expectation of each alternative is—following Bernoulli and Ramsey—its utility weighted by its probability). As before, this procedure yields a utility function unique up to a linear transformation. This system stimulated a marked revival of interest in cardinal utility measurement and prompted experimental research; and the approach was reformulated in alternative ways whose merits have been much discussed.[51] Various examples appearing to cast doubt on some of the underlying postulates have been presented. Among them are the following: a mountaineer for whom danger is part of the charm of his sport will probably prefer that his chances of survival should be, say, 99 percent rather than only 80 percent but may also prefer their being 99 percent to their being 100 percent (this would violate a monotonicity property required of preferences by the method); secondly, preferences for outcomes such as avoiding death or maintaining a pure life may be so dominant in some individuals (perhaps, respectively, nonmountaineers and saints) that they would never be indifferent between a lottery involving such an outcome—implying some risk, however minute, of losing it—and the certainty of some fairly desirable alternative (this violates a continuity postulate); thirdly, one may prefer the certainty of a large monetary prize to some chance of an even larger one, and yet prefer a possibility of the latter prize to a somewhat greater possibility of the former one[52] (this can violate a transitivity property required of preferences); and, lastly, a gambler may get more pleasure from several 'games' than from just a single lottery representing equivalent probabilities (this violates a requirement of lottery equivalence). And there are at least two further difficulties of importance: one concerns the consumer's subjective interpretation of the probabilities involved in the lotteries he is offered; and the second arises since the utility function inferred by this method will reflect the individual's attitude to gambling (the extent to which he is risk-averse or enjoys taking a chance), strongly limiting its general applicability.[53]

Several schemes for achieving cardinal measures of individual utility now exist, then; and the von Neumann-Morgenstern method in particular had gained considerable prominence and been tried out in practical experiments. But each of the methods is subject to qualifications, and there are doubts about the relevance of the resulting utility functions beyond rather limited contexts. To sum up the position in Lancaster's words, ingenious though the cardinalization procedures are, "these ingenuities have not received universal acceptance" (1974:231).

Suppose, however, that one of the above techniques *is* employed to establish cardinal utility functions for various people, functions that might be used in a study of individual choice. Would the resulting measures do anything to solve the problem of *group* welfare? Even assuming a utilitarian framework of social decision to be agreed, the answer is: not in themselves. Since neither the 'origin' nor the unit of the utility scales is specified, how can the utilities of different people be compared? If I place a smaller utility figure on one outcome than you do, this need not mean (though it could) that I really value this less highly, but may simply reflect the fact that I am using a different measurement scale. Various 'normalization' procedures have been devised; but they can yield different results and so pose a further reconciliation problem;[54] and further, to treat 'normalized' values as final will be to ignore any differences in overall utility that *do* exist. It might be thought that a fair procedure is to assign the value 1 to each person's best option in a given situation and the value 0 to his worst, with values for intermediate options obtained from his utility function by interpolation. But, as Luce and Raiffa (1957:34) explain, "often . . . this seems to fail to capture one's intuitive idea of an interpersonal comparison of utility: in a gamble between a rich man and a poor one which involves money in the range of $-\$1$ to $+\$1$, it is hard to believe that a gain of $1 should have the same utility for each of them." And even if a notion of equivalent utilities is to be used, still, as Sen points out, other procedures have "comparable symmetry": for instance, one might preserve the use of 0 for the worst option but now assign the value 1 to the sum of the utilities from all the possibilities. "Neither system is noticeably less fair than the other (one assumes equal maximal utility for all and the other assumes equal average utility for all), but they will yield different bases of social choice" (Sen, 1970:98).[55] Whatever its value in the context of individual decision, then, ability to measure individual utility cardinally—origin and scale remaining arbitrary—is not much of an advance over ordinal measurement or the basic preference rankings from the perspective of social welfare (even if it be granted that the aim is to maximize the total utility sum).[56] Its role in social decision-making could improve, however, if there were agreement on how to make at least some interpersonal comparisons—an issue that has been a persistent concern of welfare economics.

While the study of consumer behavior had led to development of a logic of choice and to discussion of new techniques for measuring individual utility, an additional literature on the problem of comparing the utilities of different people in order to reach conclusions about social welfare had grown up. Bentham had put his finger on the difficulty of adding together the potential utility gains of different men, so as to determine what course of action would maximize happiness; and the 'marginal revolution' did not overcome it: Marshall's (1890/1920:130) guarded optimism over some utility comparisons (based on what he regarded as the "natural" assumption that "a shilling's worth of gratification to one Englishman might be taken as equivalent with a shilling's worth to another . . . 'until cause to the contrary were shown' ")[57] vied with Jevons's doubts:

> I see no means by which . . . [comparison of] the amount of feeling in one mind with that in another . . . can be accomplished. The susceptibility of one mind may, for what we know, be a thousand times greater than that of another. But, provided that the susceptibility was different in a like ratio in all directions, we should never be able to discover the difference. Every mind is thus inscrutable to every other mind, and no common denominator of feeling seems possible." [Jevons, 1871/1911:14]

And Edgeworth (1881:vii), in his anxiety to escape the possible egalitarian implications of the principle of diminishing marginal utility of income and wealth,[58] lent some support to the doubts by holding that at any rate it would not do, after all, simply to assume people to be equally efficient in deriving utility from a given situation; for he admitted that "sentients [might] differ in *Capacity for happiness*—under similar circumstances some classes of sentients experiencing on an average more pleasure (e.g. of imagination and sympathy) and less pain (e.g. of fatigue) than others."

However, at this point, as Schumpeter (1954:1071) has it, "Pareto enters again to save the situation."[59] Salvation was offered in the form of an argument that some 'scientific' welfare conclusions might be drawn even if interpersonal comparisons of utility were impossible, since there were situations in which a change would make at least one individual better off without making anyone else worse off, the change thus constituting (the argument ran) an unambiguous improvement in welfare.[60]

This Paretian criterion for a welfare improvement (someone better off, no one worse off) and an associated criterion of Pareto-optimality (no further possibilities of benefiting anyone without injuring someone else) had great appeal, with their apparent success in bypassing the problem area of inter-personal comparison; and they still play a significant role in welfare economics. Their influence was reinforced in the 1930s by Robbins's eloquent submission that comparing the satisfactions of different people could have "no place in pure science." Robbins maintained that, whereas doubts about a man's preferences might in general be resolved "in a purely scientific manner" either by asking him or by observing his behavior in the relevant context of choice, there is no scientific way of settling differences of opinion about the satisfactions of different people. How, for instance, could a Benthamite demonstrate to a Brahmin that the latter was in error in asserting: "I am ten times as capable of happiness as that untouchable over there"? Or again,

> suppose that we differed about the satisfaction derived by A from an income of 1,000 pounds, and the satisfaction derived by B from an income of twice that magnitude. Asking them would provide no solution. Supposing they differed. A might urge that he had more satisfaction than B at the margin. While B might urge that, on the contrary, he had more satisfaction than A. . . . *There is no means of testing the magnitude of A's satisfaction as compared with B's.* If we tested the state of their blood-streams, that would be a test of blood, not satisfaction. Introspection does not enable A to measure what is going on in B's mind, nor B to measure what is going on in A's. [Robbins, 1932/1935:139-140]

If nevertheless "in daily life we . . . continually assume that [interpersonal] comparison can be made", this is in virtue of a background assumption—in Western democracies, typically the familiar assumption that "men in similar circumstances are capable of equal satisfactions"—which is *not* factually based itself. Thus apparent 'comparisons' of satisfaction involve "an element of conventional valuation": they are "essentially normative", "judgments of value rather than judgments of fact" (1932/1935:140,139,vii).[61]

The view that interpersonal comparisons of utility were inadmissible as factual statements gained widespread acceptance, although there was some confusion over the expression of it—with a tendency to go beyond Robbins's thesis on the impossibility of making such comparisons on a "purely scientific" basis to the stronger claim that comparisons could not be made at all. This led Robertson (1952:37) to remark: "I am never quite sure whether one must not try to [compare the economic welfare enjoyed by different individuals] because it is impossible, and attempting the impossible is a wicked waste of time; or because, while perfectly possible, the process is held to involve making judgments about what is nice or nasty, and not simply about what is true or untrue." But the upshot was clear for economic science either way, as "anyway it is considered naughty and you must not do it."

This might seem to leave the Paretian criteria, created with the express purpose of avoiding interpersonal comparisons, triumphant; and to some extent so they were. But unease began to be felt about their supposed ethical neutrality. There are the doubts already met with about the neutrality of founding a system on individual preferences.[62] But further, to designate as an optimum the position that terminates a series of Paretian welfare improvements from an initial situation which may embody a most unsatisfactory distribution of income seems to involve "[sanctifying] the status quo" (Arrow, 1950:330).[63] And then there is the difficulty that Paretian assessments fail to tell us so much that we want to know. For one thing, there are in principle an infinite number of Pareto-optimal configurations of the economy and the Paretian criteria themselves afford no means of ranking them. For another, and perhaps more importantly, almost all actual changes in an economy involve changes in income distribution that amount to benefiting some at the expense of others;[64] and about such changes the Paretian system is necessarily silent.

It began to be allowed that interpersonal comparisons are the very stuff of feasible recommendations on economic policy and that ruling out the former is in practice tantamount to forswearing the latter. Harrod (1938:397) expressed himself forcefully on the issue: "if the incomparability of utility to different individuals is strictly pressed, not only are the prescriptions of [Pigou and the Marshallian tradition] ruled out, but all prescriptions whatever. The economist as an adviser is completely stultified, and, unless his speculations be regarded as of paramount aesthetic value, he had better be suppressed completely." The dominant belief at this time that interpersonal welfare comparisons *were* illegitimate in a scientific approach thus underpinned, in Dobb's telling phrase, the "condition of nihilism that the subject had reached on the eve of the Second World War" (1970:81).

One response to this state of affairs was to recommend a cautious return to the traditional assumption of equal capacities for happiness in given conditions. Rather as Bentham had argued that the "addibility of the happiness of different subjects . . . is a postulatum without the allowance of which all political reasoning is at a stand", so Harrod concluded that the refusal to make interpersonal utility comparisons was too damaging to the process of policy formation to be tolerated: "No," he continued in the speech just quoted, "some sort of postulate of equality has to be assumed. But it should be carefully framed and used with great caution, always subject to the proviso 'unless the contrary can be shown'." One possible basis for the 'equal capacity for satisfaction' assumption was spelled out by Pigou in his restatement of the doctrine in 1951, when he argued against the skeptics that the admission of innate differences in taste and temperament between individuals need not wreck the theory since, if such differences were randomly distributed, the equality postulate would still hold good for large groups randomly chosen or for "representative" men. He wrote:

> if we take random groups of people of the same race and brought up in the same country, we find that in many features that *are* comparable by objective tests they are on the average pretty much alike; and, indeed, for fundamental characters we need not limit ourselves to people of the same race and country. On this basis we are entitled, I submit, to infer by analogy that they are probably pretty much alike in other respects also. In all practical affairs we act on that supposition. We can not prove that it is true. But we do not need to do so. Nobody can prove that anybody besides himself exists, but, nevertheless, everybody is quite sure of it. We do not, in short, and there is no reason why we should, start from a *tabula rasa*, binding ourselves to hold every opinion which the natural man entertains to be guilty until it is proved innocent. The burden is the other way. To deny this is to wreck, not merely Welfare Economics, but the whole apparatus of practical thought. On the basis of analogy, observation and intercourse, interpersonal comparisons *can*, as I think, properly be made; and, moreover, unless we have a special reason to believe the contrary, a given amount of stuff may be presumed to yield a similar amount of satisfaction, not indeed as between *any* one man and any other, but as between representative members of groups of individuals such as the citizens of Birmingham and the citizens of Leeds. This is all that we need to allow this branch of Welfare Economics to function. [Pigou, 1951:292]

Another reaction to the apparent impasse reached in the 1930s in the search for acceptable techniques to measure community welfare was to ask whether better could not after all be done, without resort to the 'equal capacities' assumption; and for a time it seemed as if it might. For two new schools of thought rapidly developed, each trying independently, Scitovsky's helpful commentary explains, "to restore the economist to his position of policy maker without the necessity of assuming the equal ability of different people to enjoy life" (1951:307).

The first school came to be known as the 'new' welfare economics, though Scitovsky alleges that "despite their name, [new welfare economists] actually said little that was new." They began from a basic Paretian approach, but aimed to go beyond it by means of the idea that a change benefiting some but injuring others might still be judged to be an improvement if the gainers from it gained enough to be able to compensate the losers fully and yet still themselves be better off than before. This 'compensation test' was proposed by Kaldor (1939): shortly afterwards, Hicks (1940) proposed what proved to be the rather different test that, for a change to be an improvement in welfare, the prospective losers from it must not be able to improve on the position that threatens them by bribing the gainers into rejecting it. It did not take long for commentators to recognize, following Scitovsky, that if either test is used alone, we may be led into contradiction: using either criterion by itself, we may "have to say that general [economic welfare] was both greater at *A* than at *B* and greater at *B* than at *A*, which," Robertson wryly remarks, "does not seem a very sensible thing to say" (1952:31). A further step in the argument then suggests itself naturally: it was Scitovsky who took it (1941-42), arguing that what is needed is a double test—that (Kaldor element) it would be to the gainers' advantage to secure the change by bribing the losers into accepting it, and that (Hicks element) the losers would not benefit from bribing the gainers not to seek it. However, Samuelson went on to show that even this test could be inadequate, each limb of it attaching undue significance to comparison with the particular income distribution prevailing, respectively, before and after change; and compensation-based tests of social welfare failed to fulfill the early hopes of giving value-free guidance on the awkward cases in which some gain at others' expense.[65] "One of the baffling things about discussion in this subject," comments Dobb, "is that a new departure setting out with promise seems to end up by returning to the same point."

The approach faced other difficulties too.[66] Measurement of the gains and losses themselves was of course highly problematic. But also there were understandable qualms about making welfare judgments on the basis of merely hypothetical compensation. If compensation is actually paid in a situation satisfying, say, the Kaldor test, then some actually are left better off and none worse off, and the Paretian criterion would apply. But if it is not paid, "the plain man's difficulty . . . is that [the proposed procedure] seems to make what *does* happen to general [economic welfare] depend on what *might* happen, but doesn't, and very likely for practical reasons couldn't," says Robertson (1952:31), noting that, "in due course this instinctive objection has been skillfully formulated by the big guns." A key "big gun" was Little; and his heaviest fire was directed at the hapless Hicks. Kaldor had held, not that economic welfare would actually be higher if a change passed his test, but rather that it would be providing any adverse changes in distribution associated with the change were indeed corrected— this, however, being the sphere of the politicians. Other commentators had tended to speak cautiously only of improvements in potential welfare. But Hicks (1941:111), enlarging on a suggestion of Hotelling's (1938), had taken the view that, if changes satisfying his test were made, then "although we could not say that all the inhabitants of [the] community would necessarily be better off than they would have been if the community had been organized on some different principle, nevertheless there would be a strong probability that almost all of them would be better off after the lapse of a sufficient length of time." But this depended on the heroic assumption that redistributions of welfare accompanying the economic changes would be random, tending to cancel each other out; and, as Robertson (1952:35) reports, "Little pours a cold douche on this particular brand of optimism by one of his cheery reminders that particular persons are apt to die, so that to weigh their losses against the gains of the unborn involves making precisely those obnoxious inter-personal comparisons of [economic welfare] which it is the object of all these exercises to avoid."

Little's own approach was to say that, in order to arrive at an acceptable criterion for a beneficial change, "an estimate of the sign of the potential net monetary benefits" should be *combined* with "a judgment about the merits of a change in the distribution of utility." He thus "advanced as a sufficient condition for an improvement (assuming that everyone could not benefit from the change) that both the redistribution should be good (strictly, not bad) and either the gainers could compensate the losers, or the losers be unable profitably to bribe the gainers to oppose the change" (Little, 1979: 126). Little's criterion, then, explicitly involves a value judgment about distribution. This can be seen as an advantage: his test does have the virtue of making it plain that value judgments are so far inescapable in the field of social welfare. On the other hand, some have felt that, with the need for interpersonal comparisons asserting itself once again, we are not really much further forward: the question how to make those judgments remains. For this reason, Dobb (1970:106) complains that Little's position is "trivial and uninteresting" as a solution to the theoretical problems of social welfare analysis: "it turns out that Mr. Little is not offering us any special principle that we can use for ourselves on any occasion when the problem crops up"; and so he is accused of "bye-passing all the difficult problems involved in making [the] comparisons, instead of providing analytical machinery to aid them: assuming the problem already solved by intuition instead of affording reasons on which an answer can rest."[67] And a further question arises too: if we can make an intermediate judgment about alternative distributions of welfare satisfactorily, why shouldn't we be in a position to compare the before-and-after situations quite directly—output differences, distribution differences and all—especially since these situations will sometimes (in retrospective welfare judgments) be ones actually experienced while a situation of purely distributional change is not? Graaff (1957:89) thinks it "fair to remark that the introduction of an intermediate point . . . serves no useful purpose whatever . . . and may even be a hindrance."[68] Little's defense is that his criterion has the merit that it "uses less information" than direct comparisons (to which he is not opposed, when they are indeed possible), that the two-stage test is "not redundant, even when direct welfare comparisons are made", and that it has been found useful in practice and "is, in fact, the basis of much—even most—applied welfare economics" (1979:126-31).

But a final, more general criticism of the entire approach through compensation tests has been voiced by Williams, the philosopher, who challenges one of the fundamental assumptions, an assumption he sees as being part and parcel of the utilitarian tradition. This is the assumption of "substitutability of satisfactions", the supposition that everything that is valued can in principle be "cashed" in terms of the basic utility measure, so that the loss of something valued can always be made up by an appropriate degree of compensation (perhaps in the form of money or goods; or, more generally, in anything else from which the individual gains utility). Against this, Williams argues that:

one should face the fact that goods are not necessarily intersubstitutable and consider the case, for instance, of an intransigent landowner who, when his avenue of limes is to be destroyed for the motorway, asks for 1 penny compensation, since nothing can be had for compensation. That there must be something which constitutes compensation for a finite loss is just a dogma, one which is more familiar in the traditional version to the effect that every man has his price. [1973:144-45][69]

The second new school of thought sought to surmount problems of interpersonal comparison with the aid of a concept introduced by Bergson: the social welfare function. The social welfare function is, in Lancaster's phrase, "the analog, for society as a whole, of the utility function for the individual"; and he explains: "if we can . . . rank every configuration of the economy with respect to every other, where a 'configuration' includes distribution of output between persons as well as levels of output, we have a complete social welfare function" (1974:298-99).[70] Once equipped with such a function, the economist would be in a position simply to work out, for instance, which of the infinite number of Pareto optima is best; and, as Dobb remarks, "the welcome accorded to so convenient a *deus ex machina* is scarcely to be wondered at" (1970:111). But what is to be the source of the function to which the economist will refer? Unless this question can be answered adequately, then the social welfare function concept seems to be, as Dobb contends, "an elegant example of the kind of formalism, so much in vogue today, which greatly facilitates analysis by supposing crucial problems to be solved by some ingenious (but undisclosed) device, without providing any actual means for their solution" (1970:112).

One natural answer—that the social welfare function is to be constructed from individual preferences—immediately runs into snags, quite apart from those associated with these preferences themselves, and the monumental nature of the task. In the first place, it is apparent that the old difficulty of avoiding value judgments is again shifted rather than solved. "Should everybody's preferences be given equal weight, or, if not, on what principle should different weights be allotted to different people's preferences?" asks Scitovsky, continuing:

> Most people would probably feel instinctively that everybody should be given an equal vote; but let us remember that it was the same instinct that led earlier generations of economists to give equal weights to different people's satisfactions. Do we stand on surer ground when we give people equal votes than did the classical economists when they assumed that everybody has the same ability to enjoy life? I doubt it. But even if we did . . . [the procedure] would still involve a value judgement, which presumably would have to be made by the economist. It appears therefore that the introduction of the social welfare function has not really solved the economist's problem. It has indeed taken off his shoulders the responsibility for attaching weights to different people's satisfactions or welfare; but it has imposed upon him the new and very similiar responsibility of attaching weights to different people's opinions or preferences. [1951:312][71]

In the second place, in a famous argument, Arrow has shown that derivation of social valuations from individual preferences by reasonable democratic voting procedures can, like the initial compensation tests, give inconsistent results.[72] Unless the underlying preferences form what is known as a 'single-peaked' system, a voting paradox arises in choice among more than two options, for the result of the voting procedure may differ according to the order in which choices are put to the vote. Suppose, for example, following Black and Dobb, that there are three people voting on the policy options, 'Left', 'Right', and 'Center', one—a socialist—preferring Left to Center to Right, the second—a right-of-center moderate—preferring Center to Right to Left, and the third—a puzzle—preferring Right to Left to Center. Then there are 2:1 majorities for Left over Center and for Center over Right, so that it seems reasonable to require that Left be socially preferred to Right; and yet there is a majority for Right over Left. Right wins overall if the vote is taken first between Left and Center and then (Left winning) between Left and Right; but Left wins if the voting order is changed to Right versus Center (Center winning) and then Center versus Left; while Center wins the second round (over Right) if the prior choice is between the extremes. Dobb (1970:114-115) points to the third voter—"an unorthodox kind of extremist"—as the source of the trouble, and explains that all would be well if individual preference scales were "governed by some uni-dimensional attribute, capable of being represented in terms of 'more or less' or 'nearer to or further away', along a scale."[73] But it is widely felt that this 'single-peaked' property cannot be relied on in the complex preference orderings on which the social welfare function was to be based; and so the idea that community preferences can always be revealed through voting, so that the 'chosen position' device can simply be carried over from the analysis of individual welfare, may not get off the ground. Arrow concludes that "unless the trouble-breeding individual preference patterns can be ruled out by *a priori* assumption, both majority voting and the compensation principle must be regarded as unsatisfactory techniques for the determination of social preferences" (1950:330).[74]

The problem raised by Arrow can be circumvented, however, if the social welfare function is differently conceived as simply an individual expression of policy priorities.[75] But the value of the function can then be questioned. Dobb (1970:115-116) holds it to lack objective basis and argues this is a very damaging limitation: "we are left with a mere affirmation, lacking economic content and of uncertain provenance: a subjective judgement incapable of being argued about, defended or disputed—a mere formal device . . . for enabling an optimising theorem to retain an appearance of verisimilitude." He suggests that "the precise logical status of this new all-embracing value-judgement" is in doubt, and he judges that, the norm being so "curiously undefined (apart from the assurance that it will tell us all we want to know)", the new theory "is very much less substantial and viable than the now *démodé* Pigouvian Welfare Economics" which at least "was not averse to telling one what it was doing."

"So far, then, the outlook seems rather bleak," wrote Scitovsky (1951: 314), summing up the state of welfare economics in 1951; for "neither the new welfare economics nor the social welfare function has provided the economist with an answer to his dilemma."[76] The need remained for some acceptable way of comparing the welfare of different people.

Graaff's masterly study of the theoretical foundations of welfare economics, appearing 6 years later, still similarly conveyed a general atmosphere of gloom. Graaff seconds Robbins's interpretation of interpersonal comparisons of well-being, holding that, if economists say in shorthand fashion that such comparisons are impossible, they do not really mean this: "all that they mean is that [the comparisons] cannot be made without judgements of an essentially ethical nature" (1957:8). He traces the difficulties in then reaching agreement on social welfare conclusions—the fact that only rather paltry results follow from adopting the Pareto criterion for an improvement in welfare,[77] the limitations of compensation tests,[78] the risk of inconsistency that besets the attempt to employ the 'chosen position' device at the level of the community.[79] He notes that interest has consequently centered on the consideration of social welfare functions explicitly based on value judgments, judgments in the light of which gains and losses to different individuals can be measured, and suggests that progress might be made if it could be shown that propositions of interest held true "for a wide range of welfare functions, or on the basis of ethical propositions of a broad and commonly accepted kind" (1957:9). But it is very hard to gain acceptance for value judgments that go beyond the Paretian framework; and at the end of his study Graaff's conclusion is that there probably *isn't* enough common ground on ethical matters to get a worthwhile welfare economics going in this way, for "it does not seem to be realised how *detailed* the agreement on ends must be if a consistent theory of welfare economics is to be erected. There are an infinite number of policy combinations capable (in theory) of securing [an agreed end]. No two will have precisely similar effects on all the variables which influence welfare. How are we to choose between them?" Furthermore, broad consensus would be required on how far the utility of future generations is to be taken into account and on attitudes to uncertainty (whether to "prepare for the worst or gamble on the best"), basic matters on which Graaff holds it to be "extremely improbable that agreement . . . will ever be reached", leaving "the possibility of building a useful and interesting theory of welfare economics . . . exceedingly small" (1957:168-169).

The situation might initially seem more promising for the measurement of community welfare on Little's behavioral approach, also a product of the 1950s. He contends that "no one could 'deny' interpersonal comparisons in the sense that they deny that people make them . . . there is no doubt that we do compare differences in happiness as between different people; there is also no doubt that we compare different people's total happiness" (Little, 1950/1957:54). But what is more, according to Little and against Robbins and Graaff, these "interpersonal comparisons of satisfaction are empirical judgements about the real world, and are not, in any normal context, value judgements" (1950/1957:66).[80] This optimistic but controversial position stems from Little's commitment to the behavioral belief that minds are not, as Bentham and Jevons had thought, "inscrutable": "it is a mistake to suppose that another man's mind consists solely of feelings or images which one cannot ever experience, . . . which are, by definition, not open to inspection by anyone else . . . [rather] we use different men's behaviour, in a wide sense of the word, to compare their mental states." Thus,

> if we say of a man that he is always miserable [meaning, "that he has a disposition to be more miserable than men usually are"], basing our judgement on how he looks and behaves, and how we know we would feel if we looked and behaved like that, and on a wide knowledge of his character gathered by observing his behavior and words in a variety of situations, and on the opinions of all his friends who similarly know him well, then we would think it was just nonsense to say that he might really be deceiving everyone all the time and be the happiest of men. [Little, 1950/1957:54-55][81]

Yet this belief in our ability to make empirical judgments of the form 'A is happier than B' does not lead Little to think that the problem of deriving an agreed measure of utility for the whole community by reference to which

65

policy decisions might be made is thereby solved.[82] He argues that judgments about changes in community utility cannot readily be constructed by inference from interpersonal comparisons made in a limited sphere, largely because of the difficulty in establishing the extent of any secondary effects (for example, even if we are able to observe that $1 given to a poor man typically increases his happiness more than $1 given to a very wealthy one, doubts about the effect on overall welfare of large-scale redistribution from rich to poor could still arise even for a utilitarian, because of, for instance, the possible effect of redistribution on the total size of the community 'cake').[83] And he holds that access cannot be had to direct factual judgments of changes in the happiness of the whole community in the way that was possible for individuals, the chief factor inhibiting empirical assessment of community happiness being sheer weight of numbers: this puts an obstacle in the path of forming a behavioral conclusion for so large a canvas since "no individual can observe the whole community, and each will inevitably take different facts into account. The larger the group of people being considered, the greater the disagreement is likely to be. . . . But the group under consideration is normally a whole country. Evidently 'the happiness of the community' can only have the vaguest possible descriptive meaning in such cases" (1950/1957:75). But this phrase does, Little maintains, have a strong emotive significance so that, although some weak descriptive element may remain, "any statement about increases or decreases in the happiness of the community *is* a value judgement" (1950/1957:80, emphasis added).[84] In the upshot, then, the difference between Little and other contemporary commentators on this point is not perhaps very great after all.

During the last decade or so, however, the literature on assessing community welfare seems to show more gleams of light amidst the darkness than did the, largely gloomy, surveys of the 1950s—though if the gleams do herald a new dawn, it looks on the whole unlikely to be a utilitarian one.

One issue on which some economists are now more optimistic is the question of the 'scientific' admissibility of comparisons of the welfare of different people. Part of the change in attitude here is probably due to a greater postpositivist willingness to tolerate value judgments in scientific work. Robbins's perception of the role of interpersonal comparisons was colored by his belief that:

> economics deals with ascertainable facts; ethics with valuations and obligations. The two fields of enquiry are not on the same plane of discourse. Between the generalisations of positive and normative studies there is a logical gulf fixed which no ingenuity can disguise and no juxtaposition in space or time bridge over. [1932/1935:148]

But the "logical gulf" view is one that some philosophers now question;[85]

and many economists are correspondingly less apologetic about departing from the austere dictates of a purely positive economics.[86]

But further, if some fact/value distinction is retained, Little's suggestion that comparisons of happiness between individuals can after all be factual has been gaining ground and has been extended in various ways. Sen (1979a:184-185) judges that "things have changed a great deal since those bleak days" of the 1950s: "there have been many recent attempts to make systematic use of interpersonal comparisons of welfare," he reports, arguing that "at least three distinct descriptive interpretations [of interpersonal comparisons] can be distinguished" in the literature. One is the behaviorist approach adopted by Little and more recently explored by Waldner (1972). A second is the approach of "introspective welfare comparison", which "interprets interpersonal comparisons as personal statements, each reflecting a particular person's thoughts in answering a question of the kind: 'Do I feel I would be better off as person i in social state x rather than as person j in social state y?' They . . . describe a particular person's thoughts on the subject" (Sen, 1979a:186). A third approach, that of "introspective choice", resembles the second, but the thought experiment "of placing oneself in the position of another is not followed by the question, 'In which position do I feel I would be better off?' but by the query, 'Which position would I *choose*?'", a query that may be answered differently, as the difficulties in simply identifying welfare with choice or with preference show (1979a:187).[87] Here the description involved, then, is of hypothetical choices.

However, the scope for these descriptive interpretations of interpersonal welfare comparisons does not resolve the problem of reaching agreement on policy decisions (even supposing it to be accepted that the utilitarian principle is to be employed): for now, if several different descriptive interpretations are possible, the "central problem in the theory of interpersonal comparisons of welfare seems to be . . . not one of poverty, but of an embarrassment of riches" (Sen, 1979a:199, 184). If the comparisons made on the different bases yield different results, which is the policy maker to go by? But further, each of the descriptive approaches Sen identifies leaves the utilitarian with difficulties of application. There are the difficulties already discussed in advancing from limited pairwise comparisons to assessment of the whole community's happiness; but in addition disagreement can still arise from the basic comparisons themselves, in spite of their 'descriptive' character. In the case of the Little version of behaviorism, for instance, the association of certain behavior characteristics with particular mental states might be a matter of dispute. With the two introspective approaches, however, the situation is rather different: here there is no question of needing to resolve differences if our judgments are not the same, argues Sen; for "if person 1 thinks that i is happier than j and person 2 holds the opposite" each is simply making "a personal statement . . . on the results of placing himself in the positions of i and j . . . If you say that given the choice you would have preferred to live in Pompeii of A.D. 79 rather than in London of 1979, and I boringly express a preference for London of 1979, we can discuss whether we have considered the relevant facts (e.g., whether you have heard of Vesuvius), but there is no need to 'settle our differences'" (1979a:189). However, if one grants that there is no *descriptive* difference to resolve here, differing assessments of relative happiness in alternative circumstances being consistent with each other on the introspective approach, the difficulty remains that, when the feelings or preferences I describe differ markedly from yours, opposing policy prescriptions are liable to result: in a utilitarian calculation, for example, how are we to reach agreement on which course of action will most increase happiness? Thus on both introspective interpretations the problem of settling differences on the policy plane persists.

Little's general approach has also been extended in another way by J. L. Simon; and it might be thought that the conclusions of the 1950s were unduly negative in view of the latter's (1974) paper boldly entitled, "Interpersonal Welfare Comparisons Can Be Made—and Used for Redistribution Decisions." The opening claim that "there are no insuperable obstacles to making quantitative science-aided comparisons of the welfare effects of economic policies on different people" (1974:63), which Simon presents as contradicting standard economic analysis, is no doubt intended to make economists sit up and take notice; and it certainly had that effect on me. Simon's idea is to "suggest ways that the policy maker can systematically gain more information about Little's 'large canvas'" (1974:65), by taking into account data (based on wide samples) on suicide rates, homicide rates, variation in consumption, responses to questions about happiness, and other variables that might similarly be thought to have a bearing on how happy people actually are, the underlying rationale being familiar—that without such a procedure "we can get nowhere" (1974:78).

Some of Simon's suggestions are interesting. And there would be some plausibility in an argument to the effect that it may be better for policy makers to reach the decisions they have to make in the light of the relevant evidence available (strenuous efforts being made to increase its supply) than to neglect evidence altogether on the grounds that, being inevitably incomplete, it may mislead.[88] However, Simon goes much further than this. He maintains that "in principle, the definition (and hence the measurement) of 'utility' is no more difficult than the definition (and measurement) of 'chair'" (1974:67). And "the key to avoiding useless arguments about whether one person's enjoyment is 'really' greater than another's" turns out just to be "to remember that welfare is, scientifically, what we operationally define it to be"; so that the "way to scientifically settle an argument about relative satisfaction is to agree on some measures we are willing to let serve as proxies for our theoretical notions about utility, and then measure them" (1974:77). But this is surely to make too light of the complex problems welfare economists have explored: at this point they might well feel, with some disappointment, that the rabbit pulled out of the hat is not after all the flesh-and-blood rabbit apparently promised at the outset but is only a cardboard imitation. However useful the measurement of Simon's variables may be as an aid to policy formation, still as he himself allows "the proxies are not the same as utility" (1974:77):[89] one can imagine Robbins intervening here to say that if we test the movement of the proxies, that is a test of them, "not satisfaction." And on views less extreme than Robbins's, I think it would be generally acknowledged that such proxies at any rate will not give us the degree of information about community happiness that Little believes can be gleaned for individual utility from behavioral study. There is also the question how the possible repercussions of a process of income redistribution, noted by Little, are to be allowed for (a question that may add to other doubts about the reliability of questionnaire responses in this field: I may say that I would be "very happy" after a particular income rise, not realizing that the extra money will be associated with, say, an additional nuclear power station that I will deplore, loss of export earnings for a Third World country, a rise in prices, more hours of work for me, or more money still for the man who lives next door). Then further, what if we cannot reach agreement on what measures to take as proxies or on what indicator to use in 'calibrating' individual utility functions? Simon (1974:66) admits that his method "requires value judgments in the choices of proxy and aggregation algorithm" and that "ultimately values are in control." He does not see this as much of a threat to the acceptance of his measurability thesis, taking some intrusion of values to be inevitable but also being sanguine on the whole about the extent of consensus: for instance, he takes the view that "in a democratic society . . . in most cases all utility functions will be considered equal . . . [so in such a society] the issue of different utility functions for different people is not an important practical consideration" (1974: 77, 81). But this is simply to revert, without argument, to the old 'equal capacities' assumption that has traditionally been used to do the trick.

Simon is not alone among contemporary writers in making use of the assumption of equivalent individual utility functions.[90] To do so just because of the difficulty of managing without it in welfare economics—with the hope it will not lead too far astray—is to go straight back to Bentham again, whose justification for the postulate still seems to have some currency. Given the obstacles to testing welfare conclusions and the doubts there are over whether equivalence actually holds, there is perhaps a slightly greater ring of comfort in Pigou's assurance that there is no reason to doubt differences to be randomly distributed and hence no reason to doubt that, when we use the 'equal capacities' postulate, the answers will on average come out about right—though it would be a good deal more cheering to know for sure that they did. A related argument (voiced by Lerner but criticized by Friedman)[91] is that the 'equal capacities' assumption may be justified by our ignorance of the extent of (stemming from our inability to measure) actual differences in individual capacity to derive happiness from given conditions.

A further justification (on the face of it, a promising one) lies in the moral claim that we *ought* to treat people as equal in their capacity for happiness, this shared capacity being part of what constitutes their common humanity.[92] Lutz and Lux (1979:87) make interesting use of this line of thought in their humanist treatment of economics, eventually taking it a step further with the contention that feeling is not a 'capacity' at all, and hence not a capacity that can vary between individuals: all people feel—"there is no issue of how much"—and those with diminished mental 'capacities,' for instance, feel just as much as anyone else. Yet even if one accepts the equivalence of everyone's range of feelings of pleasure and pain, "how much" issues may after all remain important in this context; for the question is not simply whether individuals differ in the range of their feelings but rather whether they differ in the utility that they derive from equivalent circumstances. To hold that they do is not by any means necessarily to injure the interests of the disadvantaged. Sen (1973:16-18, 81) has suggested that, on a narrow utilitarian approach, there might indeed be this consequence but that, in an egalitarian framework, recognition of differing utility functions could well be to the benefit of the handicapped, being a possible ground for arguing that greater provision should be made for them than for luckier members of society.[93]

Differences in capacity to derive utility from given conditions are not, then, universally assumed away in economics. Two other possible ways forward have recently been suggested, both by Sen, who leads current work in this field. Each tends to dent the Benthamite plea that an equality assumption is indispensable to getting welfare economics off the ground. Both carry some suggestion that it might sometimes be well to make use of nonutilitarian systems for deriving prescriptions from utility data, while one explores the idea of moving away from utility comparisons themselves.

The first suggestion is that advantage be taken of cases "intermediate" between noncomparability and full comparability of the utility 'units' of different people. "The attack of Robbins . . . and others on interpersonal comparability does not distinguish between *some* comparability and *total* comparability of units," Sen (1970a:99-102) writes, "and the consequence has been the virtual elimination of distributional questions from the formal literature on welfare economics." Complete comparability is, however, "not merely a doubtful assumption, it is quite unnecessary." For instance, if we say that the sum total of Roman welfare went down when "Rome burnt while Nero played his fiddle", some comparability is being assumed (since otherwise we could not say that Nero's delight was insufficient to outweigh the suffering of all the rest); but we need not go so far as to assume "that every Roman's welfare units can be put into one-to-one correspondence with the welfare units of every other Roman." Or again, take denunciations of the existing inequality in the distribution of money income: without being sure of "the precise welfare functions of . . . individuals and the precise correspondence between the respective welfare units, . . . we could quite reasonably still assert that in every possible case within the permitted variations the sum-total [of individual welfare] is less than what could happen with a more equal distribution."[94]

In a more detailed example, Sen shows that, given a particular set of figures for the 'normalized' welfare levels three individuals gain from three mutually exclusive events, whether a unique best option will emerge depends on what limits (if any) can be set on the extent to which the normalized welfare levels of each individual may be "blown up" (multiplied). The example also illustrates (and Sen goes on to demonstrate mathematically) how ability to rank outcomes in terms of aggregate welfare is systematically extended as variability in the relative welfare units of different individuals is reduced; and Sen shows that it can be possible not only to identify a best option but also to achieve a complete ranking of outcomes without full comparability of units (Sen, 1970a:100-102, 108-115). This line of argument suggests that mild variations in utility units between people will only throw a spanner in the works of utilitarian calculation when the issue is in any case comparatively finely balanced; and that, where there is disagreement about interpersonal comparisons, it may at least be possible to pinpoint the stage at which this could begin to loom large enough to affect particular decisions. Sen's general stress that prescriptions can sometimes still be drawn even when utility information is incomplete has also helped to stimulate interest in nonutilitarian bases for social choice, since having access to a variety of decision procedures may be an aid in making the most of the limited information available: in particular, Sen argues that, while utilitarianism (taking maximizing social utility as the aim) comes into its own when comparison of individual gains and losses of utility is possible but the ranking of individual utility levels is not, a maximin or leximin procedure (concerned with benefiting the less favored) comes into its own when this situation is reversed.[95]

Sen's second suggestion of a direction in which welfare economics might progress is that more interest might be taken in a needs-based approach in which the subject of concern is each individual's "primary powers" or "basic capabilities", rather than his utility. If a cripple has more difficulty in deriving utility from any given level of income than others do and in fact derives less, it might seem reasonable—once concern extends beyond simply maximizing the global utility sum—to require that he be given more income (or at the least not less) so that some of the disparity in welfare level may be made up (or at any rate not made worse). (This is the gist of Sen's "Weak Equity Axiom", which he uses to criticize utilitarian social welfare procedure.)[96] On this argument, utilitarianism's exclusive focus on marginal utility is rejected and it becomes relevant to look also at each person's level of total utility; but still only utility information is used. More recently, however, Sen has gone on to reject reliance on utility comparisons alone, arguing that even if a person is well off in utility terms he may still be deprived in terms of his actual capabilities. What if the cripple has such a "jolly disposition", or such a "low aspiration level", that he is *not* at a disadvantage in terms of utility realized from a given level of income (1980a:217)? Doesn't he still need some special provision? And again, the utility focus could lead to more income being given "to people who are hard to please and who have to be deluged in champagne and buried in caviar to bring them to a normal level of utility, which you and I get from a sandwich and a beer" (1980a:214-215), a result whose appeal is distinctly questionable.[97] These problems are avoided, however (although Sen notes that other difficulties arise),[98] if interest centers not on simply experiencing utility but rather on "a person being able to do certain basic things . . . the ability to move about . . . the ability to meet one's nutritional requirements, the wherewithal to be clothed and sheltered, the power to participate in the social life of the community" and so on (1980a:218). In this way, it is possible to avoid some of the difficulties welfare economics faces if the traditional assumption of equal capacities for happiness in given circumstances is not made—but only by moving away from exclusive concern with utility data.

In concluding, two important applications of ideas of utility in economics should perhaps be mentioned. The first comes in an attempt to interpret national income statistics as indicators of community welfare or 'utility,' an attempt that stirs up a hornets' nest of problems. There is the Marshallian point that the market prices used in national income calculations would at best register only marginal, not total, utilities. And for market economies, all the difficulties already confronted in the putative transition from purchases to welfare—introduction of new products, changes in tastes over time, existence of durable goods capable of yielding their services at a distant date, morbidity of desires, disappointed expectations, the power of advertisement, the influence of fashion and the like—are writ large. Then there are Pigou's concerns with possible divergence between 'private' market valuations and social worth and between economic welfare and welfare overall, matters viewed with gloom by the present 'antigrowth' lobby who stress the statistics' misrecording of pollution and waste and their failure to reflect changes in the quality of life. There are perplexities over 'regrettable necessities' (if the threat of war grows, increased defense spending might be thought to bring benefit; and yet welfare might very well be higher when the risk of war is less but—with fewer missiles—national income, as conventionally measured, is lower). There is the fundamental problem of neglect of distributional changes in concentration on the income sum. And there are the complications that market prices will often be distorted by monopolistic pressures and that they will typically be influenced by the prevailing income distribution, so that the size of the national 'cake' will not be independent of how it is sliced up.[99]

It can hardly be pretended that a national income measure that shows a rise when more gasoline is burned up through traffic jams and a fall just because a housekeeper marries her boss is a perfect measure of national welfare;[100] and, so far as I know, no economist disputes its imperfection. The live issue is rather whether its deficiencies are so severe as to make it quite worthless as a guide to welfare or whether there is still something in it. Are we to say, with Maurice (1968:15), that although "the valuations . . . do not provide precise measures of changes . . . in welfare . . . nevertheless, the significance of the broad trends shown by the aggregates is often unmistakable?"[101] Or should we join Robinson, Morgenstern and Mishan in a much deeper skepticism? Robinson (1962:122) charges the national income concept with being "a mass of contradictions"[102] (she puts its appeal down to its concern with measurable money values, economists having "a bias in favour of the measurable like the tanner's bias in favour of leather"). Morgenstern holds the stress laid on changes in gross national product is often "outright absurd":

> One single scalar figure to express something as complicated as changes in the entirety of economic activity! It is as if the growth—physical and mental and in experience—of a human being were measured from childhood on to death by the changes of one simple number (and "accurate" to 1/10th or 1/100th of 1 percent or even better on top of it!). When economics reaches a more mature state, it will appear incredible that such "measurements" have been taken so seriously. . . . [They] not only neglect the distribution of changes . . . but they also record as positive (!) malfunctionings of the economy. . . . Global measurements of this kind belong to the Dark Ages. [Morgenstern, 1972:1185]

And Mishan (1967:219) takes the line that, as welfare indicators, national income statistics may actually be perverse, believing that "the continued pursuit of economic growth [as measured by conventional statistics] by Western societies is more likely on balance to reduce rather than increase social welfare." Something of a middle course is proposed by Graaff and by Little. They lend their weight to the general view that "those who have attempted definite welfare interpretations of index numbers [of social income] . . . have expected too much" (Graaff) and that "such indices cannot be treated as *measures* of welfare" (Little). But they are of the opinion that the figures still have a role to play, their significance however being, so to speak, in the eye of the beholder. Thus the income statistics would be seen as "useful bits of data" in their own right from which economists "need not . . . go on to draw welfare conclusions. That each man can be left to do for himself, according to his own lights, and making use of whatever other information is available to him" (Graaff, 1957:166); or again, in Little's (1950/1957:237) words, the indices would be "regarded as providing some evidence, which people may use to assist them to make welfare judgements, if they want to." Each of these three interpretations of the statistics (loosely speaking, the optimistic, pessimistic and compromise positions respectively) has its attractions; and the whole issue remains open.

The second application of ideas of utility measurement is in cost-benefit analysis. Again there is an attempt to capture the effect of change on aggregate welfare in a single monetary figure, although cost-benefit analysis of particular projects does make a sustained effort to impute appropriate financial values to 'social' gains and losses that do not enter into actual market trade. But once more a host of familiar difficulties beset the procedure. For instance, it would be usual to quantify noise nuisance to householders from a prospective new airport by estimating the likely loss in value of their property; but the result will then be sensitive to the existing income distribution—reflected in current house prices—with the nuisance to the occupant of a terraced cottage counting for much less than that to the owner of a detached villa. And the old assumption of the substitutability of satisfactions seems to be implicit: yet there may be losses that cannot be fully compensated—"what is the 'worth' in yen of the health of a Japanese living on the coast, endangered by eating the fish poisoned through industrial pollution?" asks Kornai (1979:90), arguing that "there are effects against the pecuniary expression of which common sense, or moral sense, or both, protest."[103]

Again, the question is whether the difficulties are so serious as to vitiate the whole approach; and there is no consensus. Optimists might point to the fact that cost-benefit analysis does at least bring into the reckoning factors that would be ignored altogether if projects were assessed simply by the yardstick of commercial accounting. But others might take the gloomier view that, by a spurious appearance of precision and by sanctifying factors with potential measurability, the technique does more harm than good. Williams, for example, protests strongly against the argument in contexts of this sort that although

> everything is imperfect . . . all the same, half a loaf is better than no bread, and it is better to do what we can with what we can, rather than relapse into unquantifiable intuition and unsystematic decision. This argument contains an illusion. For to exercise utilitarian methods on things which at least seem to respond to them . . . is, at least very often, to provide those things with prestige, to give

them an unjustifiably large role in the decision, and to dismiss to a greater distance those things which do not respond to the same methods. . . . To regard this as a matter of half a loaf is to pre-suppose both that the selective application of those techniques to some elements in the situation does not itself bias the result, and also that to take in a wider set of considerations will necessarily, in the long run, be a matter of more of the same; and often both these presuppositions are false. [Williams, 1973:148][104]

Kornai (1979:88, 89), however, though he too rejects the half-loaf, lives in more hope of nourishment from some of its crumbs. He has no doubt that the "heroic experiment [of] translating every favorable and unfavorable effect into the language of pecuniary terms" through cost-benefit analysis must be a failure, since "it is not justifiable to add up different effects with a plus or minus sign and thereby unify them. A physician would never think of expressing the general state of health of a patient by one single scalar indicator. He knows that good lungs are not a substitute for bad kidneys." But this prompts a more constructive thought—"the physician thinks about health as a 'vector' and not as a 'scalar'. Why cannot the economist also shift . . . to that way of thinking?"—and leads Kornai to the suggestion that monetary estimates of those gains and losses that lend themselves "naturally" to such representation could play a useful role within "a vector of suitable indicators", where additional components of the vector would be "measured in other, non-pecuniary units" (1979:90, 91).[105]

The current diversity of opinion on these two areas of applied welfare economics may perhaps mirror that on broader questions of measurement, comparison and possible summation of utilities in economics, where attitudes appear to range similarly from optimism to gloom; and Williams's "half a loaf" analogy seems to sum up the more general situation. To a starving man, no doubt half a loaf *is* better than no bread: should we then, notwithstanding all the difficulties in making them satisfactorily, still employ utility calculations? Or is the need for their use reduced by the existence of other methods of assessment, while the risk of coming to rely on them too much is, as Williams maintains, severe? Would it do to accept them as one source, among others, of merely suggestive information, taking pains to remind ourselves that they are no more than this? Here disagreement persists. But scarcely anyone now questions the incompleteness of the loaf.

Notes

1. Their very detailed utilitarian framework has also typically been narrower than philosophers'. Some recent work suggests the necessity of moving away from the usual act-utilitarian,

self-interest models of economic theory but also shows that the broader base can introduce considerable complication (see Olson, 1971; Matthews, 1981; Sen, 1977; and Collard, 1978).

2. See Sen (1970a:98, n. 16). Also see Schumpeter (1954:1057), who suggests the *economic* term 'utility' could all along have been recognized to be "purely formal" rather than hedonistic, implying nothing about "the nature of the desires or wants from which it starts." Schumpeter also points out that, if a psychological interpretation of utility *were* intended, economists should have been more alert to the work in experimental psychology on measuring sensations, initiated by Weber and Fechner (on this, see also Stigler [1950:375-77]).

3. A tendency that seems apparent when Becker, Landes and Michael (1977:1142) seek to extend "the analysis of marriage developed by Becker. . . . He assumes that persons marry when the utility expected from marriage exceeds the utility expected from remaining single. It is natural to assume further that couples separate when the utility expected from remaining married falls below the utility expected from divorcing and possibly remarrying."

4. Clearly, not if the concept is "metaphysical" in Robinson's sense.

5. For example, Marshall's "consumer's surplus" concept, and von Neumann's and Morgenstern's method of cardinalization.

6. See Stigler (1950:309). I have sometimes relied on this secondary source for information about the early writers. Georgescu-Roegen (1968) also covers this material.

7. The analogy is not altogether judicious, however, since it invites the response that 20 apples + 20 pears = 40 pieces of fruit.

8. Graaff (1957:3) writes that "in positive economics we can often simplify our assumptions as cavalierly as we please, being confident in the knowledge that their appropriateness will be tested when we come to apply the conclusions inherent in them to our observations of the world about us. In welfare economics we can entertain no such confidence. The result is that our assumptions must be scrutinized with care and thoroughness. Each must stand on its own feet. . . . [In positive economics] the proof of the pudding is indeed in the eating. The welfare cake, on the other hand, is so hard to taste that we must sample its ingredients before baking." Little (1950/1957:277) makes much the same point but draws a slightly different moral: "welfare economics is . . . likely to be useful if its factual assumptions are realistic enough . . . [but] the question whether they are realistic enough is very difficult to answer, because the conclusions of the theory cannot, in practice, be tested. Whether its conclusions, in any particular case, are to be accepted or rejected is thus . . . a matter of judgement or opinion. There is no question of proof."

9. But anticipated by Gossen in 1854: see Deane (1978:94); Stigler (1950:314-15); and Samuelson (1947:93).

10. This also implied, however, that market expenditure (price × quantity) data would not reveal the total utility gained from purchases of a commodity, since they neglect the extra utility to the consumer, over and above that represented by the price paid, on the *intra*marginal units. Marshall coined the term "consumer's surplus" to describe this 'hidden' gain: the large literature on consumer's surplus shows, however, that it is not an unambiguous concept and that it presents severe measurement problems of its own. (The idea of consumer's surplus was anticipated by Dupuit [see Schumpeter 1954:1061]).

11. See Stigler (1950:318).

12. See note 10.

13. See Schumpeter (1954:1061) and Robertson (1952:16).

14. Marshall holds, however, that since "to measure directly, or *per se*, either desires or the satisfaction which results from their fulfilment is impossible . . . we fall back on the measurement which economics supplies, of the motive or moving force to action: and we make it serve, with all its faults, [for] both. . . ." (1890/1920:92, n. 1)

15. There was also some haziness in the Benthamite idea of the diminishing marginal utility of income. As Little (1950/1957:11) notes, Marshall, unlike Bentham and (later) Pigou, applied the notion (less plausibly, in Little's view) to money income rather than to real income (income in terms of goods). In Marshall's (1890/1920:19) version, "a shilling is the measure of less pleasure, or satisfaction of any kind, to a rich man than to a poor one. A rich man in doubt whether to spend a shilling on a single cigar, is weighing against one another smaller pleasures than a poor man, who is doubting whether to spend a shilling on a supply of tobacco that will last him for a month. The clerk with 100 pounds a year will walk to business in a much heavier rain than the clerk with 300 pounds a year."

16. Stigler (1950:395). He cites another example: "when it was suggested that the marginal utility of the last yard of carpet necessary to cover a floor was greater than that of fewer yards, the theory was modified to make the covering of the entire floor the unit of utility analysis."

17. Graaff suggests that there may be two-way interaction between economic and other components of total welfare.

18. The rest of this chapter concentrates on these two areas of economics—the theory of the consumer, and welfare economics—in which the concept of utility has been prominent: this has not been the case in other areas, such as Keynesian macroeconomics.

19. A possibility that had occurred to Marshall, however (see Blaug, 1980:163).
Another result of Edgeworth's generalization was that the idea of the diminishing marginal utility of every good lost its central place.

20. In these circumstances, relative income, rather than absolute, may be the bearer of utility.
Some 'external' effects on a consumer's utility cut the other way from the Veblenesque factors of envy and emulation: "imagine what would happen to any one man's desire for a telephone if those of all his friends were permanently disconnected" (Graaff, 1957:43).

21. See Graaff (1957). Pigou saw the implication for welfare economics that consumer surpluses of different individuals might not be additive.

22. Similarly Schumpeter (1954:1060) judges that "in the beginning, utility, both total and marginal, was considered a psychic reality, a feeling that was evident from introspection, independent of any external observation hence . . . *not* to be inferred from those externally observable facts of behaviour in the market which were to be explained by it—and [until Marshall] a directly measurable quantity."

The argument immediately following owes much to Tony Cramp's lectures at Cambridge.

23. In an appendix entitled "On Hedonimetry," for instance, pursuing an analogy between the study of energy in physics and that of pleasure in psychics, Edgeworth imagines "an ideally perfect instrument, a psychophysical machine, continually registering the height of pleasure experienced by an individual" (Edgeworth, 1881:App. 3, 101).

24. Schumpeter (1954:1065) presents Edgeworth as happening on revolutionary ideas in this context (including the use of 'indifference curves' which was later to be important) despite being wedded in practice to the doctrine of cardinally measurable utility.

25. There may be difficulty, however, in determining whether that particular hill is the highest in the range.

26. Assumptions of the sort that led Myrdal (1929/1953:92) to condemn the utility theory of value for circularity: "the theory is claimed to be correct in the sense that anybody who acts in accordance with it acts as the theory claims he does." Samuelson (1947:90) suggests, however, more conservatively, that such 'rationality' assumptions may rather merely mark a dividing line between economics and sociology.

27. "If we can construct one utility surface, we can get another by squaring the amounts of utility, another by taking the logarithm of utility, etc." (Stigler, 1950:381).

28. Schumpeter (1954:1065-66) suggests that Fisher had priority in seeing the potential of such an approach, although he went on to suggest a possible method of measuring utility cardinally too.

29. On the usual assumptions of consistency, etcetera. The assumption that more is preferred to less is still involved and has been subject to criticism, particularly in its application to leisure (treated in effect as a 'good,' whereas work—at the margin—is associated with disutility) (see, for example, Robinson, 1962:87; and Scitovsky, 1976). On the idea that there are circumstances in which it would be rational to 'satisfice' rather than attempt to maximize, see Simon (1976).

30. Hicks's strict argument is not that the marginal utility concept is inadmissible but rather that it is one of the "unnecessary entities" that a theory is better off without.

31. He notes that as early as the turn of the century several writers had realized that even analysis in terms of indifference was not necessary for the theory of consumer demand.

32. See Little (1950/1957:23-24, especially n. 3). Little has also raised what Robertson calls the "pertinent" question, "How long must a person dither before he is pronounced indifferent?"
Edwards (1954) comments on the indifference concept from a psychologist's perspective.

33. See also Blaug (1980:165)

34. Little's behavioral approach has also been influential.

35. Again, in *Foundations*, Samuelson (1947:173) writes that "all empirical market behavior

is independent of the choice of a particular index of utility, or indeed of the choice of any measure of utility at all." He has subsequently wavered from his 1938 position. ("Concealed indifference" is Robertson's [1952:21] phrase.)

36. It could be argued that these qualifications reflect the wider background of the philosophical reaction against logical positivism, with increasing recognition that value judgments can have a place in scientific analysis.

37. Sen (1980b:Sec. 10; 1977) also argues persuasively that the dominant conception of the self-seeking, consistent consumer in economics is an unduly narrow one, failing in particular to take enough account of choices made out of commitment. See also Kenny (1965-66); and Scitovsky (1976).

38. Blaug (1980:168) suggests one limitation lies in the concern with choices only of the individual consumer, rather than with market demand.

Little (1950/1957:chapter 3) is very frank about the difficulties in his behavioral, choice-based approach (going so far as to admit that there are "formidable" arguments to the effect that "most individuals are liable to be very inconsistent"); but he suggests a way out of them by applying the analysis to "average individuals, or representative men." This is a solution of which Myrdal (1929/1953:95-96) would no doubt have been skeptical: he had earlier disputed the idea that rational (consistent) behavior is normal behavior, asking, "How do we know that 'irrational' deviations are distributed in such a way as to cancel out? May there not be a systematic bias?" Myrdal goes on to say that "it is now generally recognized that psychological phenomena are interrelated and tend to be cumulative, so that it is quite impossible that 'irrational impulses' should show a normal frequency distribution. We have therefore no reason to expect that the average type of behavior would approximate rational behavior if we aggregate a sufficiently large number of cases."

39. See Hicks (1974:14-15).

40. See Robinson (1962:51).

41. See Morgenstern (1972:1168).

42. She also points out that if revealed preference is to be used as a basis for social welfare decisions the situation is even worse, since my preferences may quite well be against your interests. See also Sen and Williams (1982).

43. The resurrected concept is not, however, quite the same as full-blooded Benthamite utility, associated with goods' ability to satisfy needs. As Little (1950/1957:20) writes, "utility was once thought of as a kind of reflection of satisfaction in the external world, a power in objects to cause satisfaction, but later it came to be thought of as a kind of reflection of satisfactions in logic."

44. Samuelson himself has had several changes of heart on this matter: see Robertson (1952:20); and Wong (1978). Some economists still oppose this reintroduction of ordinal utility, on the grounds that it may foster misinterpretation (see Luce and Raiffa, 1957:16).

Postulating the existence of a utility function again assumes the consumer displays some 'rational' consistency of choice: see, for example, Hahn and Hollis (1979, Introduction); Varian (1978:Ch. 3); and Houthakker's (1950) article. An assumption of continuity is also critical; lexicographic orderings that violate it may yield a complete preference ordering but be incapable of representation by a real-valued (utility) function (see Debreu, 1959:Ch. 4, Sec. 6; and his n. 2). (This issue is also discussed briefly in Luce and Suppes [1965:260-261]; and in Sen, [1970a:34-35]).

45. Utility units.

46. More strictly, an affine transformation: see Sen (1970a:105, n. 2).

47. See Sen (1970a:section 7.2), who gives references to the literature and provides a very useful short guide (on which I have sometimes relied) to modern treatments of utility measurement.

48. A third relates to one way of using the resulting measures of individual utility in social welfare decisions.

49. See Debreu (1960); Gorman (1968; and 1976, especially pp. 224-228); and Graaff (1957: 39). For some qualifications about the use of the cardinalization method that is based on these weaker independence axioms, see Sen (1970a:97).

50. Ramsey's 1926 contribution was little known until the mid-fifties (von Neumann and Morgenstern do not refer to it). His approach differs from that of von Neumann and Morgenstern in suggesting a joint method of assessing utilities and subjective probabilities, rather than proposing measurement of utility alone with probabilities objectively given (see, for example, Fishburn, 1970).

51. The approach has given rise to a very extensive literature, much of it appearing in publications in decision theory, statistics, mathematical psychology and operations research rather than in mainstream economics: I am grateful to referees for directing me to readings in these other areas. I do not attempt a full account of the technical literature here; for further details of it, see Savage (1954:Sec. 6); Fishburn (1964; 1970); Luce and Raiffa (1957:34-35); and a very comprehensive technical survey in Luce and Suppes (1965). For a broader sweep, with a psychologist's comments, see Edwards (1954); and for a critical perspective, see H.A. Simon (1959); and Fischhoff, Goitein, and Shapira (forthcoming). See also Graaff (1957:36-37); Little (1950/1957:34-35); Sen (1970a:95-98).

On an assumption implicit in the method, see Malinvaud (1952) and Samuelson (1952). Alternative axiomatic treatments are developed in, for example, Marschak (1950); Herstein and Milnor (1953); and DeGroot (1970). There have been some recent extensions of the approach to encompass adaptive utility, stochastic utility, unbounded utility functions, and multiple objectives (see e.g., Cyert and DeGroot, 1975; Becker, DeGroot, and Marschak, 1964; Fishburn, 1975; and Keeney and Raiffa, 1976). Among the empirical trials are the original attempt by Mosteller and Nogee (1951), and those of Davidson, Siegel and Suppes (1957), and Becker, DeGroot, and Marschak (1964).

52. The well-known Allais paradox turns on this: see Savage's (1954:101-103) interesting discussion; also Luce and Raiffa, (1957:25-26), and DeGroot (1970).

53. Both problems beset Mosteller and Nogee's early experiment. That of ensuring that the subjective probabilities assigned to alternatives by the participants coincide with the objective probabilities the experimenter records led to later experiments (for example, that of Davidson Siegel, and Suppes [1957]) being framed on the Ramsey model, aiming to determine subjective probabilities and utilities at the same time. (See also Little, 1950/1957:36; DeGroot, 1963; Hogarth, 1975). In Mosteller and Nogee's experiment, the problem of disentangling attitude to

gambling from the utility measures was especially acute, since participants had the option of rejecting each bet (some always did so under certain circumstances). Subsequent experiments tend instead to offer choices between bets, so that risk cannot be avoided altogether. Robertson, Little and Graaff particularly stress the 'attitude to gambling' difficulty, regarding it as severe. Sen (1970a:97), however, takes the view that the method can be appropriate in some circumstances (in which attitude to gambling *is* essentially involved, as for instance in Harsanyi [1955]) and argues that related problems of applicability beyond the context of estimation arise for the other methods of cardinalization. Champernowne (1969:Vol. 3, 30-38) investigates the possibility of achieving a partial separation of risk-aversion from utility, permitting partial observation of a cardinal utility scale. See also Arrow (1951; 1971) and Pratt (1964).

Summing up early experimental evidence, H.A. Simon (1959:258) noted that most experiments had "been limited to confronting subjects with alternative lottery tickets, at various odds, for small amounts of money"; and that, while the results here had been reasonably consistent with the axioms of the theory, they were much less so in the few extensions to more "realistic" choices that had been made. It is not clear how relevant utility functions estimated experimentally by this general method will be to questions about key commodities or an individual's whole income.

A weaker thesis about choices made under risk is expounded by Robertson (following Armstrong, 1948). He contends simply that making (rational) choices among lotteries implies ability to form *some* estimate of the relative differences in desirability of the various possibilities, though perhaps only a rough and ready one. (Some qualifications over the sense of 'rational' might have to be made, however; and the argument does not readily extend from risky situations to ones of complete uncertainty in which there is no basis for making probability judgments. See Keynes [1926:Vol. VIII, 344-349]; Champernowne [1969:Vol. 1, 39, and Vol. 3, 76]; and Meeks [1980]). Little (1950/1957:32) concurs in this weaker thesis, going on to argue that people do make rough comparisons of satisfaction ("it makes sense to say 'the satisfaction I get from coffee is *much* greater than the satisfaction I get from tea.' If someone asks 'how much greater?', I can reply, for instance, that the difference is greater than that between China and Indian tea") but that this does not amount to "measurement in the fullest sense" (see also Little, 1950/1957:33-34, 53).

54. In any case an additional problem can arise from the arbitrariness of the utility scale, even if the normalization procedure is agreed (see Sen 1970a:91-92).

55. Sen argues, however, that one procedure associated with 'discrimination level' cardinalization—that of assuming that each person's degree of discrimination is the same, so that the utility difference between adjacent discrimination levels is invariant between individuals—is both arbitrary and objectionable. Suppose that one man has only few discrimination levels but feels strongly about the difference between one and the next, while another distinguishes levels more finely but cares less about moves between adjacent pairs. Then, writes Sen (1970a:94), "it seems manifestly unfair to make the ethical assumption that the welfare significance of moving the first individual from what he regards as 'horrible' to what he finds as 'magnificent' is no more than moving the second individual from what he finds 'poor' to what strikes him as 'mediocre'." See also Hildreth (1953).

56. Graaff (1957:38, 40) goes so far as to say that "the whole matter [of the measurability of utility] is largely irrelevant as far as welfare theory is concerned", arguing that "exactly the same ethical judgements are required to pass from individual choices to social welfare whether or not such a thing or quantity as utility exists, whether or not it is measurable."

57. "Cause to the contrary" included, of course, difference in income. It also covered

differences in tastes; but the hope was to neutralize these by comparing groups sufficiently large for such differences to cancel out.

58. This interpretation is Robinson's (1962:66).

59. The quotation continues with "at least in part."

60. "Better off" can be interpreted in terms of increased command over goods and services only if individual welfare functions are assumed to be independent.

Pareto's criterion for a welfare improvement is designed to avoid the need for cardinal measurement of utility too.

61. Robbins (1932/1935:140-141) suggests that Westerners' assumption of equal capacity for happiness is not just speculative but is really believed by them to be *false*, although justifications of it on "grounds of convenience" or "by appeal to ultimate standards of obligation" may be offered (see also Robbins, 1938). Graaff (1957:166) calls the related assumption that all men are alike "wildly improbable."

62. Morgenstern (1972:1169-1170) raises further, related, doubts about the concept of Pareto optimality, asking whether in this construction interpersonal comparisons of utility "are . . . really avoided and if so, at what price? How does one find out whether there is improvement or diminution? . . . Either the individuals have to be questioned or the outside observer has to make the decision on the basis of the facts . . . If questioned, an individual may deny that he is better off, or assert that he is diminished if someone else receives an addition to his possessions. Neither of these statements need be true. They may be made to extract large compensatory amounts or to stop the other obtaining whatever is being offered. . . . [Or again, because of uncertainty] the individual may not be able to say truthfully whether he is better off or diminished. . . . he may not know his position fully. . . . [If] the observer has to decide what is the case: he has to state whether the total utility experienced by the first individual (to whom an addition of some particular good is made) is greater than before . . . and whether no other individual has been diminished in his utility by this operation. But as this is interpersonal comparison of utilities, it is precisely the notion that the Pareto optimum was designed to avoid!"

63. In addition, Sen (1970b, 1979c) has argued that the Paretian criteria can conflict with liberal values, a conflict with serious implications for related doctrines such as utilitarianism.

64. Hochman and Rogers (1969) have suggested that there could be some qualification if utility functions are interdependent in an appropriate way.

65. See Graaff (1957:87-88); and Dobb (1970:102-103).

66. Independence of utility functions was a typical assumption.

67. Dobb (1970:102, 107) allows, however, that Little's test is "unexceptionable" as a quite general statement and that it could be found useful in some practical situations.

68. See also Kennedy (1964:1016).

69. Williams similarly criticizes utilitarianism as a moral doctrine for its inability to pay due regard to commitments "which do not allow of trade-offs" and holds, for instance, that it cannot

give an adequate account of integrity. For another important critique of utilitarianism, see Rawls (1958:Sec. 7), who argues that a slave-owner's utility from owning slaves ought not to enter at all into an assessment of whether slavery is right or wrong, since his ownership is fundamentally unjust.

70. Emphasis omitted.

71. See also Graaff (1957:7), who argues that in welfare economics we have to be "interested in the welfare of the whole group, not just the majority."

72. In *Social Choice and Individual Values*, Arrow (1963:9) maintains that "interpersonal comparison of utilities has no meaning": resort to the democratic process on welfare questions would, then, offer a welcome method of decision, if it were feasible.

73. See also Black (1948).

74. See also Streeten's (1953) account of these debates.

75. An interpretation Bergson (1938) appears to favor.

76. He goes on to suggest, however, that "the situation is not quite so bad" since Arrow and others "have at least pointed the way along which constructive work in this field will have to be done."
77. See, for example, Graaff (1957:99).

78. Graaff (1957:84-90).

79. Graaff (1957:7).

80. Little (1950/1957:71) suggests that much the same is true of interpersonal comparisons of real income or welfare.

81. This is a considerably broader behavioral approach, then, than that of 'revealed preference', with its exclusive reliance on purchasing data. But, though the argument is appealing, there are still difficulties, particularly once one moves away from the more obvious extremes of misery and bliss. How is one to make allowances for the additional grins of the extrovert? Or for the fact that apparently happy behavior will sometimes be adopted for an ulterior purpose? (Pooh's 'hums' often reflected contentment or high spirits; but he also hummed in hope of deceiving the bees.) What overt behavior is to be looked for at the time of observation if Mill is right in thinking tranquillity and excitement complementary as contributors to pleasure, with happiness being found "not in a life of rapture; but moments of such, in an existence made up of few and transitory pains, many and various pleasures, with a decided predominance of the active over the passive, and having as the foundation of the whole, not to expect more from life than it is capable of bestowing"? (Mill, 1863/1968:12). See also Sen (1979a:185-186, 188), who notes the possible influence on Little of Ryle's philosophical approach, the comparative mildness of Little's position, and the questions that might arise on Little's version of behaviorism over the inference from observed behavior characteristics to mental states.

82. He points out that judgments of overall utility need not in any case be decisive if the basic utilitarian decision-criterion is questioned (Little, 1950/1957:53).

83. See Little (1950/1957:62-63, 71, 75).

84. This fits in with his attitude to compensation tests. Little also holds (1950/1957:71) that the statement "happiness could be increased by *shifting* money from A to B" is a value judgment.

85. See, for example, Hudson (1969). And on the arguments of philosophers of science such as Popper (1959/1968:420-425; 1972, Ch. 2, especially pp. 60-64, 70-71) and Kuhn (1962), Robbins's view of "facts" would be naive.

86. Myrdal (1958:1-2) goes so far as to say that "a 'disinterested social science' has never existed and, for logical reasons, cannot exist . . . our very concepts are value-loaded . . . scientific analysis . . . itself depends necessarily on value premises." For a different response to the philosophical debate, see Sen (1980b). See also Meeks (1980).

87. See some of the problems discussed above in connection with 'revealed preference.'

88. Compare, however, the positions, described later in this chapter, of Little and Graaff on the one hand with that of Williams on the other.

89. See Schwartz (1975).

90. See Mirrlees (1982).

91. In, respectively, *The Economics of Control*, Chapter 3, and *Essays in Positive Economics*, p. 310. Friedman's argument is itself criticized in Sen (1973:83-85).

92. See Sen (1973:81-82) and Williams (1962).

93. Sen, following Edgeworth, suggests that the traditional egalitarian interpretation of utilitarianism rests on an unwarranted assumption of equivalent utility functions, and writes that "fundamentally utilitarianism is very far from an egalitarian approach" (1973:18). (There may be some qualification, though, for the situation of partial comparability of utility units).

94. Taking a simple case in which secondary effects of the sort Little notes—for example, effects on the total income to be distributed—do not arise.

95. See, for example, Sen (1975). Hahn (1982) discusses the difficulties a utilitarian economist faces in applying his beliefs when his information is not certain: he also discusses complications introduced if utility attaches to means as well as ends and if one has preferences over alternative selves (for example, a preference not to be the cigarette-liking person one currently is).

96. Sen's 1973 book gives the stronger version; his more recent work, the qualified one.

97. Similarly argued in Sen (1978; 1979a).

98. Including new difficulties of definition and measurement (Sen, 1978:7).

99. See the much fuller discussions and the references to the literature in Beckerman (1968) and Sen (1979b). International comparison of national income statistics raises additional problems.

A sociologist has drawn my attention to the complementary literature suggesting that a person's income may not be the dominant factor in determining his satisfaction or the quality of his life (see, for instance, Campbell, Converse and Rodgers 1976).

100. The latter example (emphasizing the absence of housewives' services from national income accounts) is Pigou's, the former Morgenstern's (who also notes the anomaly of recording repairs after, say, hurricane damage as increasing gross national product).

101. This is an official publication of the U.K. Central Statistical Office.

102. In this welfare context.

103. There are many other difficulties: see Mishan (1972) and Layard (1972).

104. See also Williams (1972, final chapter).

105. Presumably there would still be some problems of measurement.

References and Bibliography

Allen, R.G.D., and Hicks, J.R. (1934) A reconsideration of the theory of value. *Economica* 1:196-219.

Armstrong, W.E. (1948) Uncertainty and the utility function. *Economic Journal* 58:1-10.

Arrow K.J. (1950) A difficulty in the concept of social welfare. *Journal of Political Economy* 58:328-346.

Arrow, K.J. (1951) Alternative approaches to the theory of choice in risk-taking situations. *Econometrica* 19:404-437.

Arrow, K.J. (1963) *Social Choice and Individual Values.* 2nd ed. New Haven, Conn.: Yale University Press.

Arrow, K.J. (1971) *Essays In the Theory of Risk-bearing.* Amsterdam: North Holland.

Becker, G.M., DeGroot, M.H., and Marschak, J. (1964) Measuring utility by a single-response sequential method. *Behavioral Science* 9:226-232.

Becker, G., Landes, E., and Michael, R. (1977) An economic analysis of marital instability. *Journal of Political Economy* 85:1141-1187.

Beckerman, W. (1968) *An Introduction to National Income Analysis.* London: Weidenfeld and Nicolson.

Bentham, J. (1802) In E. Dumont, *Theory of Legislation.* London: Trübner, 1871.

Bentham, J. (1843) *Works of Jeremy Bentham.* Edinburgh: Tait.

Bergson, A. (1938) A reformulation of certain aspects of welfare economics. *Quarterly Journal of Economics* 52:310-334.

Black, D. (1948) The rationale of group decision-making. *Journal of Political Economy* 56:23-34.

Blaug, M. (1980) *The Methodology of Economics.* Cambridge: Cambridge University Press.

Campbell, A., Converse, P.E., and Rodgers, W.L. (1976) *The Quality of American Life: Perceptions, Evaluations and Satisfaction.* New York: Russell Sage.

Champernowne, D.G. (1969) *Uncertainty and Estimation in Economics.* Vols. 1, 3. Edinburgh: Oliver and Boyd and Holden Day.

Collard, D. (1978) *Altruism and Economy: A Study in Non-selfish Economics.* Oxford: Martin Robertson.

Cunynghame, H. (1892) Some improvements in simple geometrical methods of treating exchange value, monopoly and rent. *Economic Journal* 2:35-52.

Cyert, R.M., and DeGroot, M.H. (1975) Adaptive utility. In R.H. Day, and T. Groves, eds., *Adaptive Economic Models.* New York: Academic Press.

Davidson, D., Siegel, S., and Suppes, P. (1957) *Decision-making: An Experimental Approach.* Palo Alto, Calif.: Stanford University Press.

Deane, P.M. (1978) *The Evolution of Economic Ideas.* Cambridge: Cambridge University Press.

Debreu, G. (1959) *Theory of Value: An Axiomatic Analysis of Economic Equilibrium.* New York: Wiley.

Debreu, G. (1960) Topological methods in cardinal utility theory. In K.J. Arrow, S. Karlin, and P. Suppes, eds., *Mathematical Methods in the Social Sciences 1959.* Palo Alto, Calif.: Stanford University Press.

DeGroot, M.H. (1963) Some comments on the experimental measurement of utility. *Behavioral Science* 8:146-149.

DeGroot, M.H. (1970) *Optimal Statistical Decisions.* New York: McGraw-Hill.

Dobb, M. (1970) *Welfare Economics and the Economics of Socialism: Towards a Commonsense Critique.* Cambridge: Cambridge University Press.

Edgeworth, F.Y. (1881) *Mathematical Psychics: An Essay on the Application of Mathematics to the Moral Sciences.* London: Kegan Paul.

Edwards, W. (1954) The theory of decision making. *Psychological Bulletin* 51:380-417.

Fischhoff, B., Goitein, B., and Shapira, Z. (Forthcoming) The experienced utility of expected utility approaches. In N.T. Feather, ed., *Expectancy, Incentive and Action.* Hillsdale, N.J.: Lawrence Erlbaum Associates.

Fishburn, P.C. (1964) *Decision and Value Theory.* New York: Wiley.

Fishburn, P.C. (1970) *Utility Theory for Decision Making.* New York: Wiley.

Fishburn, P.C. (1975) Unbounded expected utility. *Annals of Statistics* 3:884-896.

Fleming, M. (1952) A cardinal concept of welfare. *Quarterly Journal of Economics* 66:366-384.

Friedman, M. (1953) *Essays in Positive Economics.* Chicago: University of Chicago Press.

Friedman, M., and Savage, L.J. (1948) The utility analysis of choices involving risk. *Journal of Political Economy* 56:279-304.

Georgescu-Roegen, N. (1968) Utility. In D.L. Sills, ed., *International Encyclopedia of the Social Sciences.* Vol. 16. New York: Macmillan and The Free Press.

Gorman, W.M. (1968) The structure of utility functions. *Review of Economic Studies* 35:367-390.

Gorman, W.M. (1976) Tricks with utility functions. In M.J. Artis, and A.R. Nobay, eds., *Essays in Economic Analysis.* Cambridge: Cambridge University Press.

Graaff, J. de V. (1957) *Theoretical Welfare Economics*. Cambridge: Cambridge University Press.

Hahn, F.H. (1982) On some difficulties of a utilitarian economist. In A.K. Sen, and B. Williams, eds., *Utilitarianism and Beyond*. Cambridge: Cambridge University Press.

Hahn, F.H., and Hollis, M., eds. (1979) *Philosophy and Economic Theory*. Oxford: Oxford University Press.

Halévy, E. (1901) *La Formation du Radicalisme Philosophique*. Paris: Germer Bailliere.

Harrod, R.F. (1938) Scope and method of economics. *Economic Journal* 48:383-412.

Harsanyi, J.C. (1955) Cardinal welfare, individualistic ethics and interpersonal comparisons of utility. *Journal of Political Economy* 63:309-321.

Herstein, I.N., and Milnor, J. (1953) An axiomatic approach to measurable utility. *Econometrica* 21:291-297.

Hicks, J.R. (1939) *Value and Capital: An Enquiry into Some Fundamental Principles of Economic Theory*. Oxford: Oxford University Press.

Hicks, J.R. (1940) The valuation of social income. *Economica* 7:105-124.

Hicks, J.R. (1941) The rehabilitation of consumer's surplus. *Review of Economic Studies* 8:108-116.

Hicks, J.R. (1974) Preference and welfare. In A. Mitra, ed., *Economic Theory and Planning: Essays in Honour of A.K. Dasgupta*. Oxford: Oxford University Press.

Hildreth, C. (1953) Alternative conditions for social ordering. *Econometrica* 21:81-94.

Hochman, H.M., and Rogers, J.D. (1969) Pareto optimal redistribution. *American Economic Review* 59:542-557.

Hogarth, R.M. (1975) Cognitive processes and the assessment of subjective probability distributions. *Journal of the American Statistical Association* 70:271-289.

Hotelling, H. (1938) The general welfare in relation to the problems of taxation and of railway and utility rates. *Econometrica* 6:242-269.

Houthakker, H.S. (1950) Revealed preference and the utility function. *Economica* 17:159-174.

Hudson, W.D., ed. (1969) *The Is-Ought Question*. New York: Macmillan.

Jevons, W.S. (1871/1911) *Theory of Political Economy*. 1st ed., 1871; 4th ed., 1911. London: Macmillan.

Johnson, W.E. (1913) The pure theory of utility curves. *Economic Journal* 23:483-513.

Kaldor, N. (1939) Welfare propositions and interpersonal comparisons of utility. *Economic Journal* 49:549-552.

Keeney, R.L., and Raiffa, H. (1976) *Decisions with Multiple Objectives: Preferences and Value Tradeoffs*. New York: Wiley.

Kennedy, C. (1964) The welfare criteria that aren't. *Economic Journal* 74:541-547.

Kenny, A. (1965-66) Happiness. *Proceedings of the Aristotelian Society*. (Reprinted in J. Feinberg, ed., *Moral Concepts*. Oxford: Oxford University Press, 1969.)

Keynes, J.M. (1921) *A Treatise on Probability*. In D. Moggridge, ed., *The Collected Writings of John Maynard Keynes*. Vol. VIII, New York: Macmillan, 1973.

Keynes, J.M. (1926) Francis Ysidro Edgeworth, 1845-1926. *Economic Journal* 36:140-153. (Reprinted in D. Moggridge, ed., *The Collected Writings of John Maynard Keynes*. Vol. X, New York: Macmillan, 1972.)

Kornai, J. (1979) Appraisal of project appraisal. In M.J. Boskin, ed., *Economics and Human Welfare: Essays in Honour of Tibor Scitovsky.* New York: Academic Press.

Kuhn, T.S. (1962) *The Structure of Scientific Revolutions.* Chicago: University of Chicago Press.

Lancaster, K. (1974) *Introduction to Modern Microeconomics.* 2nd ed. Chicago: Rand McNally.

Layard, R., ed. (1972) *Cost-benefit Analysis.* Harmondsworth: Penguin.

Lerner, A.P. (1944) *The Economics of Control: Principles of Welfare Economics.* New York: Macmillan.

Little, I.M.D. (1950/1957) *A Critique of Welfare Economics.* 2nd ed., 1957. Oxford: Oxford University Press.

Little, I.M.D. (1952) Social choice and individual values. *Journal of Political Economy* 60: 422-432.

Little, I.M.D. (1979) Welfare criteria, distribution and cost-benefit analysis. In M.J. Boskin, ed., *Economics and Human Welfare.* New York: Academic Press.

Luce, R.D., and Raiffa, H. (1957) *Games and Decisions: Introduction and Critical Survey.* New York: Wiley.

Luce, R.D., and Suppes, P. (1965) Preference, utility and subjective probability. In R.D. Luce, R.R. Bush, and E. Galanter, eds., *Handbook of Mathematical Psychology.* Vol. 3. New York: Wiley.

Lutz, M.A., and Lux, K. (1979) *The Challenge of Humanistic Economics.* Menlo Park, Calif.: Benjamin/Cummings.

Malinvaud, E. (1952) Note on von Neumann-Morgerstern's strong independence axiom. *Econometrica* 20:679.

Marschak, J. (1950) Rational behaviour, uncertain prospects and measurable utility. *Econometrica* 18:111-141.

Marshall, A. (1890/1920) *Principles of Economics.* New York: Macmillan.

Matthews, R.C.O. (1981) Morality in the economic behaviour of the individual. *Manchester School* 49:289-309.

Maurice, R., ed. (1968) *National Accounts Statistics: Sources and Methods.* London: Her Majesty's Stationery Office.

Meeks, J.G.T. (1980) Philosophical Issues in Modern Economic Theory. Mimeo. Faculty of Economics and Politics, University of Cambridge.

Mill, J.S. (1863/1968) *Utilitarianism.* Everyman ed., 1968.

Mirrlees, J.A. (1982) The economic uses of utilitarianism. In A.K. Sen, and B. Williams, eds., *Utilitarianism and Beyond.* Cambridge: Cambridge University Press.

Mishan, E.J. (1967) *The Costs of Economic Growth.* Harmondsworth: Penguin.

Mishan, E.J. (1972) *Cost-benefit Analysis: An Informal Introduction.* London: Allen and Unwin.

Morgenstern, O. (1972) Thirteen critical points in contemporary economic theory: an interpretation. *Journal of Economic Literature* 10:1163-1189.

Mosteller, F., and Nogee, P. (1951) An experimental measurement of utility. *Journal of Political Economy* 59:371-404.

Myrdal, G. (1929/1953) *The Political Element in the Development of Economic Theory* (English ed., trans. P. Streeten). London: Routledge and Kegan Paul, 1953).

Myrdal, G. (1958) *Value in Social Theory: A Selection of Essays on Methodology*, (ed. P. Streeten). London: Routledge and Kegan Paul.

Olson, M. (1971) *The Logic of Collective Action: Public Goods and the Theory of Groups*. Cambridge, Mass.: Harvard University Press.

Pareto, V. (1909/1927) *Manuel d'Economie Politique*. 2nd ed. Paris: Giard, 1927. (English ed., trans. A.S. Schwier. New York: Macmillan, 1972.)

Pigou, A.C. (1903) Some remarks on utility. *Economic Journal* 13:58-68.

Pigou, A.C. (1932) *The Economics of Welfare*. 4th ed. New York: Macmillan.

Pigou, A.C. (1951) Some aspects of welfare economics. *American Economic Review* 41:287-302.

Popper, K. (1959/1968) *The Logic of Scientific Discovery*. London: Huchinson, 1959 (rev. ed., 1968).

Popper, K. (1972) *Objective Knowledge: An Evolutionary Approach*. Oxford: Oxford University Press.

Pratt, J.W. (1964) Risk aversion in the small and in the large. *Econometrica* 32:122-136.

Ramsey, F.P. (1926) Truth and probability. In Ramsey's *The Foundations of Mathematics and Other Logical Essays*, ed., R.B. Braithwaite. London: Kegan Paul, Trench and Trübner, 1931.

Rawls, J. (1958) Justice as fairness. *Philosophical Review* 67:164-194.

Robbins, L. (1932/1935) *An Essay on the Nature and Significance of Economic Science*. 2nd ed., 1935. New York: Macmillan.

Robbins, L. (1938) Interpersonal comparisons of utility. *Economic Journal* 48:635-644.

Robertson, D.H. (1952) *Utility and All That*. London: Allen and Unwin.

Robinson, J.V. (1962) *Economic Philosophy*. London: Watts.

Ryle, G. (1954) Pleasure. *Proceedings of the Aristotelian Society* Supplement 28:135-146. (Reprinted in J. Feinberg, ed., *Moral Concepts*. Oxford: Oxford University Press, 1969.)

Samuelson, P.A. (1938) A note on the pure theory of consumer's behaviour. *Economica* 5:61-71.

Samuelson, P.A. (1947) *Foundations of Economic Analysis*. Cambridge, Mass.: Harvard University Press.

Samuelson, P.A. (1952) Probability, utility and the independence axiom. *Econometrica* 20:670-678.

Savage, L.J. (1954) *The Foundations of Statistics*. New York: Wiley.

Schumpeter, J.A. (1954) *History of Economic Analysis*, ed. E.B. Schumpeter. Oxford: Oxford University Press.

Schwartz, T. (1975) On the utility of interpersonal comparisons. *Journal of Philosophy* 72:549-551.

Scitovsky, T. (1941-42) A note on welfare propositions in economics. *Review of Economic Studies* 9:77-88.

Scitovsky, T. (1951) The state of welfare economics. *American Economic Review* 41:303-315.

Scitovsky, T. (1976) *The Joyless Economy: An Inquiry into Human Satisfaction and Consumer Dissatisfaction*. Oxford: Oxford University Press.

Sen, A.K. (1970a) *Collective Choice and Social Welfare*. Edinburgh: Oliver and Boyd.

Sen, A.K. (1970b) The impossibility of a Paretian liberal. *Journal of Political Economy* 78:152-157.

Sen, A.K. (1973) *On Economic Inequality*. Oxford: Oxford University Press.

Sen, A.K. (1975) Rawls versus Bentham. In N. Daniels, ed., *Reading Rawls: Critical Studies of 'A Theory of Justice'*. Oxford: Basil Blackwell.

Sen, A.K. (1977) Rational fools: a critique of the behavioural foundations of economic theory. *Philosophy and Public Affairs* 6:317-344.

Sen, A.K. (1978) Ethical issues in income distribution: national and international. Paper presented in the Saltsjöbaden Symposium on the Past and Prospects of the Economic World Order.

Sen, A.K. (1979a) Interpersonal comparisons of welfare. In M.J. Boskin, ed., *Economics and Human Welfare*. New York: Academic Press.

Sen, A.K. (1979b) The welfare basis of real income comparison: a survey. *Journal of Economic Literature* 17:1-45.

Sen, A.K. (1979c) Utilitarianism and welfarism. *Journal of Philosophy* 76:463-489.

Sen, A.K. (1980a) Equality of what? In S. McMurrin, ed., *The Tanner Lectures on Human Values*. Cambridge: Cambridge University Press.

Sen, A.K. (1980b) Description as choice. *Oxford Economic Papers* 32:353-369.

Sen, A.K., and Williams, B., eds. (1982) *Utilitarianism and Beyond*. Cambridge: Cambridge University Press.

Simon, H.A. (1959) Theories of decision-making in economics and behavioral science. *American Economic Review* 49:253-283.

Simon, H.A. (1976) From substantive to procedural rationality. In S. Latsis, ed., *Method and Appraisal in Economics*. Cambridge: Cambridge University Press.

Simon, J.L. (1974) Interpersonal welfare comparisons can be made—and used for redistribution decisions. *Kyklos* 27:63-98.

Slutsky, E.E. (1915) Sulla teoria del bilancio del consumatore. *Giornale Degli Economisti* 51:1-26.

Stigler, G.J. (1950) The development of utility theory (I and II). *Journal of Political Economy* 58:307-327, 373-396.

Streeten, P. (1953) Recent controversies. Appendix to G. Myrdal, *The Political Element in the Development of Economic Theory*. (English ed., trans. P. Streeten. London: Routledge and Kegan Paul.)

Varian, H.R. (1978) *Microeconomic Analysis*. New York: W. W. Norton.

von Neumann, J., and Morgenstern, O. (1944/1947) *Theory of Games and Economic Behavior*. 2nd ed., 1947. Princeton: Princeton University Press

Waldner, I. (1972) The empirical meaningfulness of interpersonal utility comparisons. *Journal of Philosophy* 69:87-103.

Williams, B. (1962) The idea of equality. In P. Laslett, and W.E. Runciman, eds., *Philosophy, Politics and Society*. 2nd series. Oxford: Basil Blackwell.

Williams, B. (1972) *Morality: An Introduction to Ethics*. New York: Harper and Row.

Williams, B. (1973) A critique of utilitarianism. In J.J.C. Smart, and B. Williams, *Utilitarianism: For and Against.* Cambridge: Cambridge University Press.

Wong, S. (1978) *The Foundations of Paul Samuelson's Revealed Preference theory.* London: Routledge and Kegan Paul.

Acknowledgments

I am very grateful to Amartya Sen for his extensive criticisms and suggestions; and I would also like to thank Tony Cramp, Phyllis Deane, Otis Dudley Duncan, Baruch Fischhoff, Cathie Marsh, Geoff Meeks, Charles Turner and an anonymous reviewer for their helpful comments.

3

The Use of Survey Data
in Basic Research in the
Social Sciences

Stanley Presser

Few innovations in the social sciences rival the importance of the modern survey. Both survey practitioners and their critics have suggested that research questions, concepts, and findings have all been shaped by the survey method. It is probably no coincidence that the blossoming of empirical social science and the development of survey research occurred nearly simultaneously. Yet the precise nature of the survey's impact on the social sciences has received little systematic attention. Indeed, setting aside the question of influence, there is surprisingly little quantitative evidence simply about the extent and character of the survey's use. Despite an essentially universal awareness that surveys have come to play an increasingly central role in the social sciences, there are few studies of the matter. Other than a number of articles that briefly touch on the issue (drawn on in sections below), I have located only two—one in sociology (Alwin and Stephens, 1979) and one in political science (Wahlke, 1979)—that probe the subject in any detail.

The purpose of this chapter then is to describe the place of the survey in basic social science research during the past three decades. The chapter documents the degree to which there has been a growing use of surveys, describes some of the factors associated with this growth, examines the uses to which surveys have been put, and evaluates the ways in which surveys have been drawn upon.

Method

The body of research examined here is that contained in the American journals of four social science disciplines: economics, political science, social psychology, and sociology. Although these areas do not exhaust the work done in the social sciences, they account for a large part of it. The journal literature occupies a central place in each of the fields and can be sampled in straightforward fashion. Moreover, it seems unlikely that the character of social science research reported in journals differs greatly from that published in books. In the absence of evidence, of course, this point remains uncertain, but findings based on journals should be of considerable significance, since journal articles are a key means of disseminating scientific results.

The original plan for the study was to choose three nonspecialized journals in each discipline—the journal sponsored by the field's professional association, and two others of leading stature. Stature was assessed on the basis of studies of journal prestige and citation patterns. In economics this resulted in the selection of the *American Economic Review* (published by the American Economic Association), the *Journal of Political Economy*, and the *Review of Economics and Statistics*, all of which ranked in the top four in studies of economics journals (Hawkins, Ritter, and Walter 1973; Quandt, 1976). (The fourth journal, *Econometrica*, was excluded because of its more specialized nature.) In sociology, the journals chosen were the *American Sociological Review* (published by the American Sociological Association), the *American Journal of Sociology*, and *Social Forces*, the top-ranked journals in that field (Lin and Nelson, 1969; Glenn, 1971). In political science, the three leading general journals (Giles and Wright, 1975) were selected: *The American Political Science Review* (published by the American Political Science Association), *The Journal of Politics*, and the *American Journal of Political Science.*

The selection of three leading journals in social psychology presented a problem. The general journal of the American Psychological Association, the *American Psychologist*, covers all subfields in psychology, not just social psychology, and more importantly is not a research journal in the sense of *The American Political Science Review*, *American Sociological Review*, or

American Economic Review. The same problems hold for *Psychological Review* and *Psychological Bulletin.* The most appropriate choice is the American Psychological Association-sponsored *Journal of Personality and Social Psychology (JPSP),* which is the leading social psychology journal (Buss and McDermott, 1976). Partly because *JPSP* has had a quasi-monopolistic position in social psychology, and partly because it publishes about three times as many papers as the selected journals in the other three fields, no other social psychology journal was chosen. This means that the "social psychology" referred to throughout this paper is psychological social psychology.[1] Finally, one interdisciplinary journal, *Public Opinion Quarterly,* was included because of its emphasis on survey research.

The analysis of the research reported in these journals is based on a systematic coding of every article in each issue of the 11 journals during 6 years of publication. Research notes, comments and replies, symposia and special supplements, as well as speeches by association presidents, were omitted. The years are 1949, 1950, 1964, 1965, 1979, and 1980, during which time academic survey research grew from a budding young enterprise into a firmly established industry.[2]

Findings

For present purposes, a survey is defined as any data collection operation that gathers information from human respondents by means of a standardized questionnaire in which the interest is in aggregates rather than particular individuals. Applying this definition, neither the present study of journal articles nor an investigation of, say, the social security files qualifies as a survey, even though both may involve data collected by a standard procedure from a set of elements systematically sampled from a well-defined population. The present study would be excluded because the information was not collected from human respondents; the social security study would be excluded because the data were collected for administrative purposes concerning particular individuals. In addition, operations conducted as an integral part of laboratory experiments are not included as surveys, since it seems useful to distinguish between the two methodologies. The definition is silent, however, about the method of respondent selection and the mode of data collection. Thus, convenience samples as well as censuses, self-administered questionnaires as well as face-to-face interviews, may count as surveys.[3]

Table 3.1 details the frequency with which surveys have been reported in social science journals during the past 30 years.[4] Over time all fields except

TABLE 3.1

Percentage of Articles Using Survey Data,
by Field and Years

Field	Years		
	1949 – 50	1964 – 65	1979 – 80
Sociology	24.1	54.8	55.8
	(282)	(259)	(285)
Political Science	2.6	19.4	35.0
	(114)	(160)	(203)
Economics	5.7	32.9	28.7
	(141)	(155)	(317)
Social Psychology	22.0	14.6	21.0
	(59)	(233)	(377)
Public Opinion	43.0	55.7	90.6
Quarterly	(86)	(61)	(53)

NOTE: Figures in parentheses represent the base on which percentages were calculated.

social psychology have come to rely more heavily on surveys. Indeed, in both economics and political science, the survey has gone from being an unusual method in the late 1940s to one used in about one-third of all published studies in the late 1970s. In sociology, the survey appears to have been fairly common prior to 1950, accounting for almost one-quarter of the journal research, but there too survey use increased considerably, to over half of all investigations by the mid-1960s—a pattern similar to that reported by Sudman (1976) and Alwin and Stephens (1979). Only social psychology bucked the trend, its reliance on surveys remaining at about 20 percent throughout the period. This lack of increase in the use of surveys in social psychology may be due to that field's embracing "the laboratory/ experimental methodology as the true path to knowledge" (Helmreich, 1975:550-551). Survey data tend to be "correlational in nature and hence considered second-rate by the canons of social psychology's establishment" (Helmreich, 1975:555).[5]

The growing use of surveys has been associated with a number of other trends. As might be expected on the basis of a "diffusion of innovation" model, the proportion of survey articles that identified a first author as affiliated with a survey organization (for example, the National Opinion Research Center, the Bureau of Applied Social Research) has declined since the early years. Whereas 23 percent of the articles using survey data in the late 1940s were written by such researchers, this was true of between only

9 and 10 percent of the articles in 1964–65 and 1979–80. Interestingly, survey affiliations accounted for about the same proportion of authors of survey articles across the four disciplines, although the proportion was markedly higher for *Public Opinion Quarterly.*

In a related development, the incidence of secondary analysis also grew dramatically in the last 30 years. Articles reporting data that the authors had no hand in collecting were 30 percent of all survey articles in the early period, 38 percent in the middle period, and 52 percent in the most recent period. (Most of this increase is independent of the decline in survey affiliations.) Table 3.2 presents the levels of secondary analysis disaggregated by discipline. As can be seen there, the increase over time was a general one, again with the exception of social psychology, in which secondary analysis appears to be virtually unknown.

The growth of secondary analysis reflects one dimension of the changing origin of data used in academic survey reports. Taking all fields together, authors who conducted a survey independent of a survey organization were the largest single source of data in each time period, but their share dimin-

TABLE 3.2

Percentage of Secondary Analyses Among Articles Reporting Survey Data, by Field and Years

	Years		
Field	1949–50	1964–65	1979–80
Sociology	42.4	34.1	60.1
	(66)	(138)	(158)
Political Science	[33.3][a]	19.4	52.1
	(3)	(31)	(71)
Economics	[83.3][a]	89.8	93.7
	(6)	(49)	(79)
Social Psychology	0.0	0.0	2.6
	(13)	(33)	(77)
Public Opinion Quarterly	8.6	32.4	39.1
	(35)	(34)	(46)

NOTES: The few cases in which it was unclear whether the analysis was primary or secondary are excluded from this table. Figures in parentheses represent the base on which percentages were calculated.
[a]Figures in brackets are based on very small frequencies and may be unreliable.

97

TABLE 3.3

Source of Data in Articles Reporting Surveys, by Field and Years

Source	Sociology	Political Science	Economics	Social Psychology	Public Opinion Quarterly
			Field		
			1949 – 50 and 1964 – 65		
Authors	46.5%	67.6%	6.9%	91.3%	48.5%
Governments	35.0	17.6	70.7	0.0	4.4
ISR	4.5	2.9	12.1	4.3	2.9
Other	14.0	11.8	10.3	4.3	44.1
Total[a]	100%	100%	100%	100%	100%
(N)	(157)	(34)	(58)	(46)	(68)
			1979 – 80		
Authors	27.3%	38.5%	6.3%	92.0%	42.2%
Governments	34.3	3.1	64.6	0.0	2.2
ISR	7.0	40.0	12.7	4.0	17.8
Other	31.5	18.5	16.4	4.0	37.8
Total[a]	100%	100%	100%	100%	100%
(N)	(143)	(65)	(79)	(75)	(45)

NOTE: The periods 1949 – 50 and 1964 – 65 have been combined partly because the patterns are similar in both and partly because the number of cases in the earlier period is small.
[a]Some totals do not sum to exactly 100.0 percent due to rounding.

ished from somewhat less than half the surveys reported in the late 1940s and mid-1960s to about one-third in the late 1970s.[6] Governments (the United States government, in 9 of every 10 cases) accounted for the next largest share, between 26 and 29 percent of the surveys in each period. (The fraction of sample surveys as opposed to censuses in the governments' share increased from about one-third in 1949–50 to over one–half in 1979-80.) The only other single source representing more than a tiny proportion of the reported surveys was the University of Michigan's Institute for Social Research (ISR). Data from ISR surveys were used in about 5 percent of the articles in the first two periods and in almost 15 percent of those in the most recent period.

Table 3.3 shows these trends separately for each discipline. At one extreme, surveys in social psychology have been carried out almost exclusively by individual authors. At the other extreme, economists rarely conduct surveys as individuals; they instead draw most of their survey data from government studies. (In addition to the Population and Economic Censuses, those appearing most frequently were the Survey of Current Business, the Current Population Survey, and various surveys carried out by the Bureau of Labor Statistics.) Political science underwent a transformation from a discipline in which survey data were collected mainly by individual authors to one in which a plurality of surveys was carried out by the Institute for Social Research. In fact more than one-third of the political science articles using survey data in the most recent period drew on a single ISR study, the Election Survey. Finally, in terms of data sources, sociology was the most eclectic field. By the late 1970s the origin of survey data used in sociology was distributed about equally among individual authors, governments, and private organizations. Sociology authors and *Public Opinion Quarterly* authors were the only ones to make appreciable use of surveys carried out by private organizations other than ISR. In *Public Opinion Quarterly* these were mainly National Opinion Research Center (NORC) and commercial poll data. In sociology almost half of these "other" surveys were conducted by NORC, commercial polls, or the Detroit Area Study, with the rest spread over many different sources.

In summary, there has been a large increase in the use of survey data in all fields except social psychology. This growth has been accompanied by several overlapping changes. Compared with reports of surveys three decades ago, surveys reported in journals today are more likely to have been conducted by an organization rather than an individual, and less likely to have been analyzed by someone who either had a hand in the survey or had an affiliation with a survey organization. Thus the proportion of survey analysts removed from data collection operations has increased, a change commented on further in the Conclusions section of this chapter. What has not changed, however, are the immense differences between disciplines in the amount and kind of survey use. Discipline accounts for considerably more variation in these matters than does time. This should be true to an even greater extent for the content of surveys, to which we turn in the next section.

SURVEY CONTENT

Writing about the survey 30 years ago, Rensis Likert (1951:251) ventured: "It can safely be predicted that this research tool, fundamental to all the social sciences, will have an increasingly wide application in the years that lie ahead." Indeed, it is tempting, although misleading, to assume there are few social science topics that cannot be addressed by the survey method. How wide, then, has the scope of survey research actually been? This section assesses the sagacity of Likert's prediction of increasingly wide application by examining the range of subjects that surveys have been used to study.

99

Table 3.4 classifies separately by field and time period the main focus of investigations that utilized survey data.[7] Two considerations should be kept in mind in interpreting the table. First, many articles have more than one focus and so could have been classified under more than one heading. For this reason a secondary-focus variable was coded using the same categories as for the main focus. These data, which are not included in Table 3.4, show results very similar to those that are presented in the table. A number of ways in which the two distributions differ will be noted shortly. Second, the categories themselves overlap. For example, many studies of the determinants of vote choice could logically fit under "Attitudes and Behavior," but almost all of them were classed with "Elections and Voting," as that seemed to fit more accurately their major emphasis. This overlap between categories, however, will mask some of the similarities between disciplines (in the vote choice example, between political science and social psychology).

One of the more striking findings in Table 3.4 is the prominence accorded subjective phenomena as subjects of study. It comes as no surprise that in each time period, attitudes (broadly construed to include beliefs, ideology, happiness, self-esteem, and so on) were the main focus of approximately one-third to one-half of the *Public Opinion Quarterly* articles that used surveys. Yet almost the same pattern is found in both political science (see also Wahlke, 1979) and social psychology. Only in economics is an emphasis on attitudes not found, for even in sociology, attitudes were the main focus of roughly one-fifth of the survey articles.

There are undoubtedly many reasons for the central place of attitudes in survey research, but among the most important is the fit between the content and the method.[8] Attitudes refer to internal states and thus are accessible only through introspection. As is true for all subjective phenomena, their measurement must rely on self-report by individuals—precisely the strength of the survey method.

Measures of subjective phenomena are even more widespread in survey research than is suggested by the proportion of articles that dealt mainly with attitudes. Many of the articles whose main focus was on objective phenomena (those coded in the nonattitudinal categories of Table 3.4) also made use of measures of subjective matters. In psychology and political science, 97 and 83 percent, respectively, of the articles drawing on surveys included such measures. For sociology, the figure is 59 percent, and for economics, 15 percent. These differences between fields, which are essentially constant over time, also hold if independent and dependent variables are considered separately, although dependent variables were more likely than independent variables to be subjective in sociology and psychology. (In both economics and political science the proportion of independent variables that were subjective was similar to that for dependent variables.)

TABLE 3.4

Subjects of Survey Articles, by Field and Years

Subject	1949–1950	1964–1965	1979–1980
Political Science			
Elections and Voting	[0.0%]	19.4%	22.5%
Other political participation	[0.0]	3.2	11.3
Political attitudes and beliefs	[33.3]	32.3	29.6
ideology/socialization	[0.0]	3.2	15.5
Political elites	[33.3]	22.6	11.3
Other	[33.3]	19.4	9.8
Total N	(3)	(31)	(71)
Social Psychology			
Happiness/anomie/stress	[0.0%]	2.9%	7.6%
Self-esteem/self-conception/ego development	[15.4]	11.8	16.5
Personality	[15.4]	8.8	13.9
Attribution/impression formation	[0.0]	5.9	17.7
Attitudes and behavior/attitude change	[7.7]	5.9	6.3
Politics (see appendix)	[7.7]	2.9	3.8
Attitudes/beliefs/values (nonpolitical)	[30.8]	23.5	10.1
Other	[23.1]	38.2	24.0
Total N	(13)	(34)	(79)
Economics			
Labor force participation/income	[25.0%]	17.6%	42.2%
Occupations	[0.0]	5.9	2.2
Savings-prices-consumption	[75.0]	23.5	23.3
Business	[0.0]	23.5	7.8
Taxation-welfare-regulation	[0.0]	7.8	4.4
Other	[0.0]	21.6	20.0
Total N	(8)	(51)	(90)
Public Opinion Quarterly			
Elections and Voting	8.1%	17.6%	6.2%
Political attitudes & beliefs	10.8	29.4	12.5
Other "politics" categories	5.4	8.8	0.0
Mass media	5.4	2.9	10.4
Attitudes/beliefs/values (nonpolitical)	24.3	26.5	22.9
Methodology	40.5	0.0	45.8
Other	5.4	14.7	2.1
Total N	(37)	(34)	(48)

TABLE 3.4 (*continued*)

Subject	1949–1950	1964–1965	1979–1980
Sociology			
Political attitudes and beliefs	1.5%	4.2%	4.4%
Other "politics" categories	0.0	1.4	10.1
Labor force participation/income	4.5	0.7	8.8
Occupations	11.9	17.6	14.5
Population/organization/ecology/technology	17.9	14.8	13.2
The home (e.g., marriage-divorce-family)	22.4	6.3	6.9
Education	0.0	5.6	0.6
Race and ethnicity	6.0	3.5	2.5
Religion	1.5	6.3	5.0
Crime and deliquency	0.0	2.8	5.7
Health	1.5	2.8	3.1
Other leisure categories	4.5	5.6	4.4
Happiness/anomie/stress	0.0	2.8	3.8
Attitudes/beliefs/values (nonpolitical)	14.9	14.8	10.1
Methodology	7.5	3.5	1.9
Other	6.0	7.0	6.3
Total N	(67)	(142)	(159)

NOTE: The full set of codes is presented in the appendix. The "other" category in this table consists of all codes containing fewer than 3 cases, as well as those cases originally coded "other". Figures in brackets are based on very small frequencies and may be unreliable.

Although most survey research in political science, psychology, and *Public Opinion Quarterly* has made use of indicators of subjective phenomena, a broad range of subjects has been investigated by surveys in economics and sociology without resort to such measures. This is the case for issues related to work and earnings, which occupy an important place in both these fields, but especially in economics. (A number of the most recent labor force survey investigations in economics examined the influence of family factors such as marital status and fertility, and this was responsible for the one significant difference in the distributions of primary and secondary focus in economics. For 1979–80, about 7 percent of the survey reports in economics were secondarily concerned with the family.) The remaining articles in economics that used surveys are clustered mainly in the areas of savings, prices, consumption, business, and government intervention in the economy—topics that have usually been approached with objective measures and also topics that the field appears to monopolize.

Sociology is the discipline with the greatest diversity of subject matters. As Neil Smelser (1969:5) has written, "sociology, by comparison with some other sciences, lacks a single accepted conceptual framework."[9] In addition to areas it shares with other fields (attitudes, politics, work), survey articles in sociology have been concerned with issues as varied as those in religion, crime, health, leisure, and race and ethnicity. (Race and ethnicity studies are somewhat underestimated in Table 3.4; in each time period, between 8 and 11 percent of the articles coded elsewhere have race or ethnicity as a secondary focus.) Moreover, there is little evidence for Smelser's belief that over time sociology "will shed certain aspects of [its] frameworks and consolidate others" (1969:6). If any trend during the last 30 years emerges from Table 3.4, it is one of decreasing concentration in the topics studied. Indeed, sociology provides the only compelling support for Likert's expectation that the survey method would find increasingly wide application.

If the survey has not been used to study an increasingly diverse set of topics outside sociology, it has produced a common topic of inquiry across the social sciences. It is often said that the behavioral revolution in political science, in which survey research played a dominant role, transformed that field from the study of political institutions to the study of political behavior (Eulau, 1969). But the content of survey investigations in political science is characterized more accurately as the study of political attitudes. Similarly in social psychology, traditionally thought of as the study of the individual in a social setting, the questions examined with survey data are more aptly described as the study of attitudes in the individual. Even in economics, which has come to rely on survey research without a corresponding emphasis on attitudes, one of the unique contributions of the survey method (the study of economic expectations) involves attitudes. By fostering this communality of focus, the survey may have contributed to the integration of the social sciences. At the same time, however, it may have been responsible for a narrowness of focus.

SURVEY PROCEDURE

The growing importance of surveys in social science makes it vital to evaluate the manner in which they have been used. A normative judgment about the impact of survey research on the social sciences must depend partly upon an assessment of the appropriateness of the use of surveys. Of course, even if surveys have been used appropriately, researchers with differing orientations will arrive at different views of the survey's impact. But to the degree that surveys have been misused, their influence will have been harmful.

At a minimum, a thorough evaluation of survey use would analyze the fit between the questions investigated and the sampling procedure, method of data collection, and analysis strategy. Such a task applied to almost a thousand articles from multiple disciplines requires resources beyond those available to this writer. What can be undertaken is a description of the extent to which authors present the information that would be needed in a full-scale evaluation. Are details of survey operations included in the reports that draw on survey data? The answer to this question is important for two reasons. The absence of a statement about procedure makes evaluation impossible, and is consequently inconsistent with the nature of the scientific enterprise, which calls for disclosure of the method by which results are obtained. In addition, the absence of such information suggests an inattention to these matters, and inattention to fundamental aspects of a survey is likely to be accompanied by misuse.

Concern about the reporting of survey design has focused mainly on the mass media. Attempts to adopt a code calling for the inclusion of certain information in journalistic accounts of surveys have a long history (Lee, 1949-50; Hollander et al., 1971; American Association for Public Opinion Research, 1980). Curiously there have been no parallel efforts in academic publishing, although theoretically the need is just as great. Apparently some social scientists believe that scholarly survey practice makes a set of standards unnecessary. John Wahlke (1979:12), for example, writes that, "Most political behavior researchers pay careful attention to sampling methods, operationalization of concepts, measurement of variables, testing the validity of findings and inferences, and so on." But the reporting practices in political science, and elsewhere, call this into question.

According to the National Research Council's Committee on Information in the Behavioral Sciences (1967:44), "In the characteristic research report, details of potential significance are suppressed throughout. Raw data are excluded, along with details of the research design and know-how of sampling, instrumentation, and the like." This impressionistic judgment is sustained by results based on a sample of sociology articles analyzed by Alwin and Stephens (1979). They found that only a small minority of the articles reported information about matters such as response rate, question wording, and interviewer characteristics.[10] Rare is the researcher who would neglect to indicate the statistical procedures used to produce results (for example, factor analysis, ordinary least squares, log-linear analysis), yet it seems that many researchers routinely fail to describe the methodological procedures used to produce the data upon which their results are based.

This lack of reporting might be due to the use of surveys that are either well known or for which documentation is generally available. Authors may omit a response rate when discussing Current Population Survey (CPS) data because they assume most readers are aware that CPS response rates are in the high 90s. Likewise articles drawing on the National Opinion Research Center's General Social Survey or the Institute for Social Research's Election Survey may not include exact question wordings because they can be found in the widely distributed codebooks of the two studies. For this reason all results to be presented below are based exclusively on articles re-

TABLE 3.5

Percentage of Survey Articles Reporting Methods Information, by Field

Information and Years	Field				
	Sociology	Political Science	Economics	Social Psychology	Public Opinion Quarterly
Sampling method					
All years	59.4%	49.2%	3.9%	57.4%	63.0%
Question wording					
All years	46.5	44.4	2.9	50.4	54.8
Mode of date collection					
All years	47.0	66.6	17.6	78.2	72.6
Response rate					
1949–50 plus 1964–65	20.9	24.0	20.0	13.6	41.3
1979–80	51.3	36.8	4.2	22.5	63.0
Year of survey					
1949–50 plus 1964–65	36.7	56.0	60.0	22.7	56.5
1979–80	75.6	81.6	54.2	19.7	59.3
Interviewer characteristics[a]					
All years	16.3	40.0	0.0	60.0	38.7
Total N[a]					
1949–50 plus 1964–65	(139)	(25)	(10)	(44)	(46)
1979–80	(78)	(38)	(24)	(71)	(27)
All Years	(217)	(63)	(34)	(115)	(73)

NOTES: This table is restricted to articles using data collected by individuals independent of organizations. Variables not broken down by time period show only slight temporal change.

[a]Tabulation for interviewer characteristics is restricted to surveys conducted by personal interview or telephone interview. [N: 43 (Sociology), 20 (Political Science), 2 (Economics), 10 (Social Psychology), 31 *(Public Opinion Quarterly)*.]

porting data the authors themselves collected or that were collected by other individuals independent of organizations.

Table 3.5 demonstrates that the reporting problem is a general one in the social sciences, even in this limiting instance in which the information is most essential. (As expected, levels of reporting are even lower in the articles excluded from the table—-those based on data collected by survey research organizations.) Although there has been improvement in some areas, overall, fewer than half the articles reported anything about sampling method, response rate, the wording of even a single question, year of the survey, or interviewer characteristics. These reporting levels are not markedly better than those of the much-criticized mass media, despite the considerably greater space available in journals. Paletz et al. (1980:505) report that during the mid–1970s, 30 percent of the articles in the *New York Times* drawing on survey data reported exact question wordings and 43 percent, the dates of the survey. (The figures for the NBC and CBS evening news programs were lower, 5 percent and 30 percent, respectively.)

In the absence of methodological information about a survey, it is difficult to interpret an author's results. How is a reader to know if findings have meaning for any population other than an author's sample if there are no details of the method by which the sample was selected? How is a reader to understand a result for a variable called "political agility" or to make sense of an analysis using a variable labeled "class ethos" if the items used to measure these concepts are not indicated? (For further details of these particular examples, see Presser, 1980.) Much social science literature based on surveys is not far removed from Herbert Hyman's (1973:326) portrait of Lasswell's pioneering study, *Psychopathology and Politics*:

> In 1930 no one knew in what exact pool Lasswell had done his fishing and how he had drawn and caught the fish. No one could anchor his findings. They simply floated somewhere in the great sea of humanity and only through the accident of an "After-Thought Thirty Years Later" (Lasswell, 1960) do we obtain some vague clues to their social location. His little pool of cases was only a drop in the ocean of humanity. What if he had fished in other waters [or, I might add, with other bait]?

The situation is not entirely bleak, however, since a fair number of authors do report methodological details. Furthermore, some of these authors take to heart the Bureau of the Census's (1974:iv) admonition that one "should not be content simply to make information on errors available, but should do so in ways that will maximize the likelihood that users will be aware of this information, understand it, and take it into account in using the data." A perfect illustration may be found in a *Journal of Political Economy* article by Edwin Mansfield. In a "Data and Methods" appendix, Mansfield (1964:339) writes

> One possible bias should be noted. Only about half the firms that I contacted could give me the sort of information I needed here, and the fact that certain firms could give me such data may indicate that they are more likely to conform to the model. If this is the case, there would obviously be much more unexplained variation if all firms were included in equation (10).

Yet examples like this, as well as the literature on method effects (see Volume 1), underscore the dangers of the lack of attention to these factors that is characteristic of much social science work. Indeed, too frequently social science research based on surveys is, to paraphrase Samuel Butler, "The art of drawing sufficient conclusions from insufficient premises."

Conclusions

The increasingly central role of the survey in basic social science research appears beyond dispute. Two major features of that role, however, will undoubtedly provoke controversy.

The extensive concentration on attitudes in the surveys of all fields except economics will be seen by some in negative terms. Many other features of the social world have been, relatively speaking, slighted. It might seem difficult to quarrel with the argument that more survey research should be devoted to the study of environments, behaviors, experiences, groups, organizations, and social systems. But it is possible that the survey is not well suited to studying some of these topics. Moreover, it would be a mistake to see the emphasis on subjective phenomena as responsible for the limitations that mark the contribution of surveys to social science, or to expect a shift toward the study of objective phenomena to overcome these limits. Accurate measurement of objective phenomena frequently may be no easier to achieve than is accurate measurement in the subjective realm (Morgenstern, 1963). Moreover, indicators of subjective matters often have advantages over objective ones. As James Morgan (1967:252) notes,

> Frequently a single thing like age or education or liquid asset holdings is a proxy for more than one concept. . . . Age may represent a chronological age or a difference in the period of history in which the individual grew up. In looking at the demand for housing, family size represents both the need for more housing space and pressures to use the income for food and clothing instead. A high level of initial liquid assets represents both a capacity to spend more than one's income and the probability that this is a family that has resisted the temptation to spend. . . . Actually *the attitudinal questions which seem too imprecise at first, may be a closer approximation to an operationally defined variable than the demographic facts which are only proxies for something else* [emphasis added].

A more troubling feature of the use of surveys is the low level of attention paid to the way in which data are produced. One of the most interesting features of Henry Cooper's (1979) account of the biology experiments conducted during NASA's Viking exploration of the planet Mars was the scientists' constant resort to instrument failure or measurement error as explanations for the observations transmitted back to earth. Paradoxically, the absence of great physical distance between the survey researcher and his or her measuring device has been accompanied by a disregard of such matters.

For the most part this is not due to the growth of secondary analysis, which separates the roles of data analyst and data collector; the disregard is almost as great among primary analyses as among secondary analyses. It is also unlikely that the responsibility for the problem lies with journal editors who ask authors to cut methodological details for reasons of space; much of the missing information can be communicated in a few words. Two such details, date of the survey and response rate, are reported no more frequently than are details requiring lengthier exposition.

The problem is due partly to the way in which methodology has come to be thought of in the social sciences. Say "methodology" and most social scientists will think "statistics." In a recent issue of the *American Behavioral Scientist* devoted to "Social Science Methodology," for example, there is hardly a mention of data collection methods. Its articles are focused exclusively on methods of data analysis. Similarly, in the first 11 volumes of *Sociological Methodology* (1969–1980), fewer than 1 out of 10 articles deals with methods for extracting observations from the world as opposed to methods for extracting information from observations. And this emphasis on what is essentially applied statistics accurately reflects the type of work done by most social scientists who call themselves methodologists. The resulting attention to matters of data analysis has led to the realization that erroneous conclusions have been drawn from much past research (see, for example, Duncan, 1974). The lack of attention to data collection issues may have led to a similar level of erroneous conclusions in research based on surveys.

In purely quantitative terms, the growth in the use of surveys appears to have peaked in some fields (witness the leveling off for sociology in Table 3.1). But there is obviously room for change in the way surveys are used in the social sciences. Two such changes have been discussed here. It would seem appropriate to complement the extensive focus on attitudes with additional surveys of nonattitudinal subjects, not only to understand these other subjects in their own right, but also to increase our understanding of attitudes by placing them in context. Likewise an enhanced sensitivity to data collection issues is needed to complement the growing sophistication about statistical matters. In sum, as Angus Campbell and George Katona (1953:51) wrote nearly three decades ago, "there is reason to believe that the possibilities of the survey technique are still not fully realized, either in scope of applications or in precision of method."

Appendix
Subject Codes

POLITICS

01. Elections & Voting
02. Other Forms of Participation
03. Political Attitudes and Beliefs
04. Ideology; Structure
05. Socialization

Political Elites

06. Psychology and Sociology of Office-Seeking ("The Political Personality")
07. Decision Making
08. Administrative Behavior

WORK

Labor Force Participation

10. Micro Employment—Labor Force Participation Studies
11. Macro Employment
12. Micro Unemployment
13. Macro Unemployment
14. Wages, Salaries, & Earnings
18. Job Satisfaction
19. Unions

Occupations

15. Occupations & Labor Skills
16. Attainment & Mobility
17. Choices & Prestige

FINANCES

Income

20. Micro Income
21. Macro Income (e.g., Distribution)

Savings, Prices, Consumption

22. Micro Savings
23. Macro Savings
24. Micro Consumption
25. Macro Consumption
26. Prices; Cost of Living
27. Interest Rates
28. Economic Expectations

BUSINESS

30. Economic Development; Industrialization
31. Production
32. Productivity
33. Capital Utilization
34. Industry Structure
35. Foreign Trade
36. Economic Cycles

GOVERNMENT AND ECONOMY

40. Taxation—Public Finance
41. Social Welfare Programs
42. Regulation

POPULATION, ORGANIZATIONS, ECOLOGY, TECHNOLOGY

43. Population
44. Organizations
45. Ecology
46. Migration
47. Rural Life—Agriculture
48. Technology; R&D

HOME

50. Marriage
51. Divorce
52. Family Relations & Characteristics
53. Childhood & Youth
54. Family Background
55. Fertility

LEISURE

57. Friendship and Kinship
58. Recreation
59. Community Involvement (Nonpolitical), Social Participation
60. Education & Schooling; Intelligence
62. Race & Ethnicity
63. Religion
66. Deviance
68. Crime & Delinquency
70. The Arts
72. Science
74. Health & Medicine

76. Mass Media
78. Transportation

QUALITY OF LIFE

80. Happiness, Well-being
81. Anomie
82. Stress
83. Personality
85. Self-Esteem, Self-Conception, Ego Development

ATTITUDES

87. Attribution-Impression Formation
90. Attitudes, Beliefs, Values (Nonpolitical)
91. Attitude Change
92. Attitudes & Behavior

OTHER

98. Methodology
99. Other

Notes

1. In his paper, "The Three Faces of Social Psychology," James House (1977:163) says, "the label 'social psychology' is most commonly applied to, and probably most semantically appropriate for, the tradition of social psychology within psychology." According to House (1977: 162), research in the other two social psychologies, symbolic interactionism and psychological sociology, "usually appears in general sociology journals (e.g., the *American Sociological Review*) rather than in *Sociometry* or other specifically social psychological journals."

2. With two exceptions, the 11 journals span this entire period. The first exception is a partial one: prior to 1965 the *Journal of Personality and Social Psychology* (*JPSP*) was the *Journal of Abnormal and Social Psychology* (*JASP*). The apparent effect of this change, as assessed by comparing the 1964 *JASP* with the 1965 *JPSP*, was to increase slightly the proportion of articles using survey data. The second exception is that the *American Journal of Political Science*, formerly the *Midwest Journal of Political Science*, did not exist in 1949 and 1950. (The "Midwest" to "American" name change, which took place in 1973, did not signal any change in content.)

3. All results presented in this chapter have been examined excluding censuses, which account for 13 percent of the surveys. Although absolute levels of some variables change when only sample surveys are considered, in no case is a conclusion about a relationship altered appreciably. (One of the largest differences is in the extent of secondary analyses. The percentages of secondary analyses reported later for 1949–50, 1964–65, and 1979–80 are 30, 38, and 52, respectively. Excluding census data, the percentages are 16, 26, and 47.)

4. The proportions in Table 3.1 probably underestimate to a minor extent the number of articles drawing on surveys; this is because the few articles in which it was unclear whether the data source was a survey were counted as nonsurveys. For example, the authors of one *Journal of Political Economy* (1980;921) article write that "the data used for estimation consist of aggregate age-year-specific observations on female wage rates, female employment ratios, male income, and fertility rates", yet nowhere in the article do they indicate where these observations come from. Since even variables like the unemployment rate, whose measurement might be thought to require a survey, may be estimated from other sources (for example, reports of unemployment compensation or models of a "full-employment" economy), it seemed best not to treat such cases as survey articles. (Also not counted as survey articles were those studies that drew on surveys in a purely incidental fashion, for example, to illustrate a statistical technique.)

5. It is noteworthy that the frequency of survey use in the *Journal of Social Psychology* (*JSP*) is substantially higher than in *JPSP* (Fried, Gumpper, and Allen, 1973). Thus the likelihood of a social psychology article drawing on survey data (and therefore not conforming to the canons of the field) is inversely related to the journal's prestige. (According to Buss and McDermott (1976), *JPSP* ranked second in reputation and seventh in citations among psychologists, and *JSP* ranked fifty-sixth in reputation and twenty-eighth in citations.)

6. If an article reported data from more than one survey, only the first-mentioned primary survey was coded. In articles reporting only secondary analyses, the first-mentioned secondary survey was coded. Omitted from the figures in the text and also from Table 3.3 are articles in which the source of the survey data was not specified. This was true of 17 percent of the 1949–50 survey articles, 13 percent of the 1964–65 articles, and 9 percent of those in 1979–80. The similarity of this gradual decline to that for author-conducted surveys suggests the possibility that these missing data represent mainly author-collected data.

7. A caveat is in order here, since the data in Table 3.4 refer to the article, not necessarily the survey reported in the article. Check-coding of a random 1 out of 10 cases for the focus-of-investigation variable yielded 69 percent exact agreement.

8. A second explanation turns on the origins of the modern sample survey in commercial attitude research (both product-oriented and political in nature). These early uses may have put an imprint on the method that was not easily shaken. Another explanation invokes the methodological individualism that pervades much social science research. If "the ultimate constituents of the social world are individual people who act in light of their dispositions and understanding of their situation" (Watkins, 1968:270), then the individual-level study of attitudes is obviously of paramount importance.

9. Discussing a number of histories of sociology, Lazarsfeld (1970:62) writes, "Whatever picture these authors paint, they all agree that sociology has not developed around a positive subject matter, but as a residual activity, filling in the blank spots in an intellectual map"—a judgment Lazarsfeld appears to endorse.

10. Fienberg and Goodman (1974:70) reach a similar conclusion about one important government publication, *Social Indicators, 1973*: "While many of the charts in *Social Indicators, 1973* are based on sample data, few of the related Technical Notes give any details on sample design."

References

American Association for Public Opinion Research (1980) *Newsletter* Vol. 7, No. 2 (Devoted to a debate on the Principles and Procedures adopted by the National Council on Public Polls).

Alwin, D., and Stephens, S. (1979) The Use of Sample Surveys in the Social Sciences. Paper presented at the 145th National Meeting of the American Association for the Advancement of Science, Houston, Texas.

Bureau of the Census (1974) *Standards for Discussion and Presentation of Errors in Data.* Technical Paper No. 32. Washington, D.C.: Government Printing Office.

Buss, A., and McDermott, J. (1976) Ratings of psychology journals compared to objective measures of journal impact. *American Psychologist* 31:675-678.

Campbell, A., and Katona, G. (1953) The sample survey: a technique for social science research. In L. Festinger and D. Katz, eds., *Research Methods in the Behavioral Sciences.* New York: Dryden.

Cooper, H. (1979) *The Search for Life on Mars.* New York: Holt.

Duncan, O.D. (1974) Open forum. *ASA Footnotes* 2(9):2.

Eulau, H., ed. (1969) *Behavioralism in Political Science.* New York: Atherton Press.

Fienberg, S., and Goodman, L.A. (1974) Social indicators, 1973: statistical considerations. In R. Van Dusen, ed., *Social Indicators, 1973: A Review Symposium.* Washington, D.C.: Social Science Research Council.

Fried, S., Gumpper, D., and Allen, J.C. (1973) Ten years of social psychology: is there a growing commitment to field research? *American Psychologist* 28:155-156.

Giles, M., and Wright, G. (1975) Political scientists' evaluations of sixty-three journals. *PS* 8:254-256.

Glenn, N. (1971) American sociologists' evaluations of sixty-three journals. *American Sociologist* 6:298-303.

Hawkins, R., Ritter, L., and Walter, I. (1973) What economists think of their journals. *Journal of Political Economy* 81:1017-1032.

Helmreich, R. (1975) Applied social psychology: the unfulfilled promise. *Personality and Social Psychology Bulletin* 1:548-560.

Hollander, S., Nedzi, L., Field, M., and Meyer, P. (1971) Toward responsibility in reporting opinion surveys. (A Symposium) *Public Opinion Quarterly* 35:335-349.

House, J. (1977) The three faces of social psychology. *Sociometry* 40:161-177.

Hyman, H. (1973) Surveys in the study of political psychology. In J. Knutson, ed., *Handbook of Political Psychology.* San Francisco: Jossey-Bass.

Lazarsfeld, P. (1970) Sociology. In *Main Trends of Research in the Social and Human Sciences* (Part 1). The Hague: Mouton/UNESCO.

Lee, A. (1949/50) Implementation of opinion survey standards. *Public Opinion Quarterly* 13:645-652.

Likert, R. (1951) The sample interview survey as a tool of research and policy formation. In D. Lerner and D. Laswell, eds., *The Policy Sciences.* Stanford, Calif.: Stanford University Press.

Lin, N., and Nelson, C. (1969) Bibliographical reference patterns in core sociological journals, 1965-1966. *American Sociologist* 4:47-50.

Mansfield, E. (1964) Industrial research and development expenditures. *Journal of Political Economy* 72:319-340.

Morgan, J. (1967) Contributions of survey research to economics. In C. Glock, ed., *Survey Research in the Social Sciences*. New York: Russell Sage Foundation.

Morgenstern, O. (1963) *On the Accuracy of Economic Observations*. 2nd ed. Princeton, N.J.: Princeton University Press.

National Research Council, Committee on Information in the Behavioral Sciences (1967) *Communication Systems and Resources in the Behavioral Sciences*. Washington, D.C.: National Academy of Sciences.

Paletz, D., Short, J., Baker, H., Campbell, B., Cooper, R., and Oeslander, R. (1980) Polls in the media. *Public Opinion Quarterly* 44:495-513.

Presser, S. (1980) Comment on Nelson and on Baloyra. *American Political Science Review* 74:459-460.

Quandt, R. (1976) Some quantitative aspects of the economics journal literature. *Journal of Political Economy* 84:741-756.

Smelser, N. (1969) The optimum scope of sociology. In R. Bierstedt, ed., *Design for Sociology: Scope, Objectives and Methods*. Philadelphia: American Academy of Political and Social Science.

Sudman, S. (1976) Sample surveys. In A. Inkeles, J. Coleman, and N. Smelser, eds., *Annual Review of Sociology* (Vol. 2) Palo Alto, Calif: Annual Reviews.

Wahlke, J. (1979) Pre-behavioralism in political science. *American Political Science Review* 73:9-31.

Watkins, J.W.N. (1968) Methodological individualism and social tendencies. In M. Brodbeck, ed., *Readings in the Philosophy of the Social Sciences*. New York: Macmillan.

Acknowledgments

It is a pleasure to acknowledge the contributions made to this research by a number of individuals. Beth Fuchs and Nancy Fultz rendered indispensable help in the coding of almost 3,000 journal articles. Frank DiIorio expertly managed various computer tasks. Helpful reactions to an initial draft were received from Duane Alwin, Jean Converse, Terry DeMaio, Otis Dudley Duncan, Lynn Kahle, Cathie Marsh, Sara Nerlove, Howard Schuman, Tom Smith, and Charles Turner. The comments of Drs. Duncan, Marsh, and Turner were especially incisive. Finally, the late Frank Munger, Director of the University of North Carolina's Institute for Research in Social Science, provided the resources that made this research possible. Only the author is responsible for any errors.

PART II

QUASI-FACTS

Perhaps the most common distinction made among survey questions is the one between fact and opinion, where opinion includes attitudes, beliefs, values, preferences, and similar notions. Facts are often assumed to be straightforward (in terms of both their existence and measurement), while opinion is usually thought to be much less certain in either sense. Few doubt the value of surveys aimed at factual matters, but criticism of opinion surveys, or more broadly of surveys of subjective phenomena, extends to doubts about whether such reports are possible, meaningful, or worthwhile.

The criticism might be avoided by restricting surveys to factual information—giving up any attempt to measure the realm of the subjective. One reason that such a solution is unsatisfactory, of course, is that subjective phenomena are exactly what many researchers, policy makers, and members of the general public are interested in. But another reason is that the distinction between "hard fact" and "soft opinion" is much too simple; the types of fact that are straightforward are far fewer than is frequently recognized.

The authors of the chapters in this section discuss three standard areas of inquiry that cannot be neatly classified as either objective or subjective: unemployment, ethnicity, and housing conditions. Each of these areas has inherently subjective aspects at the level of measurement.

The point of the following discussions of what we have called quasi-facts is not to suggest that such measurements are of doubtful value. It is rather to indicate that much of what we need to learn about our society forces us to deal with phenomena that are subjective in part, if not in whole; and that the solution of simply ignoring the subjective realm is not a feasible one.

4

The Subjectivity of Ethnicity

Tom W. Smith

Basic background variables are commonly seen as concrete and objective factors. In fact they often have a large subjective component. Ethnicity is a prime example. First there is the difficult problem of defining what ethnicity is. It is most frequently seen as some form of a cultural heritage or identification that is defined by some combination of nationality, language, religion, and race (Isajiw, 1974). We will not even try to disentangle how one plucks "ethnicity" out of these and related factors. Are Jews from Poland Jews, Poles, Polish Jews, or Jewish Poles? If we look at Catholic and Protestant Germans, do we see two ethnic groups or one ethnic group broken down by religion? Are West Indian blacks in the United States blacks, West Indians, some combination, or Africans? Are Creoles and Amerindians of Mexico both Mexican, both Hispanic, or separate? Are people from Sicily Sicilians or Italians? Certainly we could promulgate a complex set of standards to objectively resolve these and a long string of related ambiguities, but while perhaps objective in the sense of being susceptible to consistent repetitive application by different enumerators, such standards would be based on arbitrary classifications that undermine a full sense of objectiveness.

This chapter concentrates on the narrower problem of nationality.[1] Most social scientists give more weight or emphasis to this factor in their conceptualization and/or classifications, and people usually express their ethnicity in what might be considered nationality groups. If we count nationality groups within multinational states as nationalities (for example, Serbs and Croatians), then almost all respondents respond to even vague terms such as "origin," "ancestry," or "descent" in terms of nationality. (The major exceptions are blacks, who will either respond in terms of their race or with a general reference to Africa.)

Attempts to determine nationality use three basic approaches: (1) the natal, (2) the behavioral, and (3) the subjective.[2] The natal approach identifies a respondent's nationality by determining a person's place of birth, the places of birth of his or her parents, grandparents, and so forth. The behavioral approach determines a respondent's nationality according to some practice, affiliation, or membership such as language spoken or voluntary group membership. The subjective approach simply asks respondents what nationality they consider themselves to be or where their ancestors came from.

The natal approach to ethnicity is typified by the traditional item used by the Bureau of the Census. It asks the places of birth of the respondent and his or her mother and father:

13a. WHERE WAS THIS PERSON BORN? If born in hospital, give State or country where mother lived. If born outside U.S., see instruction sheet: distinguish Northern Ireland from Ireland (Eire).

_____This State
   OR _____
           (Name of State or foreign country; or Puerto Rico, Guam, etc.)

14. WHAT COUNTRY WAS HIS FATHER BORN IN?
_____United States
   OR _____
           (Name of State or foreign country; or Puerto Rico, Guam, etc.)

15. WHAT COUNTRY WAS HIS MOTHER BORN IN?
_____United States
   OR _____
           (Name of State or foreign country; or Puerto Rico, Guam, etc.)

A variant of this approach, used by the Michigan Election Studies, asks parallel information about the respondent and his or her parents, but then inquires about the general ancestral origins of respondents who are third (or later) generation:

1. Where were you born? (IF UNITED STATES) Which state?
2. Were both your parents born in this country?

—If response to Q. 2 was "no":

2A. Which country was your father born in?

2B. Which country was your mother born in?

—If response to Q. 2 was "yes" or "don't know":

2C. Do you remember which country your family came from originally on your father's side?

2D. Do you remember which country your family came from originally on your mother's side?

This begins to shift from being an objective measure to a subjective or self-identification measure. Inquiring about "which country your family came from" does not measure the national origins of the respondent's ancestors as a whole, but rather elicits a single origin from among potentially several different ancestral lines. A strict (although obviously impractical) natal approach would inquire about the place of birth of all ancestors until all lines were traced back to a country of origin.

This shift from the objectivity of place of birth to the subjectivity of self-identification proceeds one step further in a standard Michigan Election Study question which asks: "In addition to being an American, what do you consider your *main* ethnic or nationality group?" This question emphasizes one's "main" background but does not make clear how this concept is to be operationalized. Furthermore, the question moves away from the place-of-birth definition by referring to "ethnic or nationality group" rather than to country of origin in a geopolitical sense. Similar in kind is the Current Population Survey (CPS) item asking: "What is _____'s origin or descent?" The CPS establishes no criteria and uses the somewhat less specific terms "origin" and "descent." Likewise, the 1980 Census asked: "What is this person's ancestry? IF UNCERTAIN ABOUT HOW TO REPORT ANCESTRY: SEE INSTRUCTION GUIDE. (For example, Afro-Amer., English, French, German, Honduran, Hungarian, Irish, Italian, Jamaican, Korean, Lebanese, Mexican, Nigerian, Polish, Ukrainian, Venezuelan, etc.)" The question uses the very vague term "ancestry" (although from its examples it makes clear that it is referring to nationality) and offers no criteria for determining ancestry. The instructions make the nationality reference explicit, stating, "Ancestry (or origin or descent) may be viewed as the nationality group, the lineage, or the country in which a person or person's parents or ancestors were born before their arrival in the United States." The instructions also set a general standard for handling multiple nationalities: "Persons who are of more than one origin and who cannot identify with a single group should print their multiple ancestry (for example, German-Irish)." The instructions also make explicit the subjective component in the question by telling the informant to "Print the ancestry group with which the person *identifies.*" In sum, by failing to collect detailed information on nativity and asking people to select an ancestry on the basis of identification, the 1980 Census has established a largely subjective measure of ethnicity.

Even more explicitly subjective is the General Social Survey (GSS) (Davis, Smith, and Stephenson, 1980) question that asks: "From what countries or part of the world did your ancestors come? IF MORE THAN ONE COUNTRY IS NAMED: Which of these countries do you feel closer to?" Not only is no criterion specified by which to choose between origins in the initial question, but in the followup question, people giving multiple origins are told to use a subjective standard—feeling closer to—rather than to choose a particular lineage or their most frequent origin.

Clearly the line between the natal and subjective approaches is often a fine one. In general one passes from the natal approach when one moves from asking information about the place of birth of specific persons (the respondent and his or her ancestors) to nonspecific information about one's background, descent, ethnicity, nationality, or origin.

More clearly separated from the natal or subjective approaches is the behavioral approach, which classifies a person according to some practice or affiliation such as language spoken or membership in certain voluntary associations. An example of the language approach comes from the 1970 Census, which inquires: "What language, other than English, was spoken in this person's home when he was a child?"[3] The affiliation approach is commonly used when a list sample is employed to select respondents. Under this method, membership in the association that the list represents becomes the definition of nationality. This might include congregations, mutual benefit societies, or other groups (for examples, see Vrga, 1971; Masuda, Matsumoto, and Meridith, 1970; Barton, 1975). Also included in this approach are lists based on such documents as baptismal and marriage registers (which frequently include persons who are not actually members of such congregations). Another hypothetical example would be a survey that asked a series of ethnic-orientation questions (such as foods eaten, music preferred, and so forth) and then assigned ethnicity according to the responses.

Each of these approaches has particular strengths and weaknesses. We can broadly evaluate them by considering how each handles three major problems in measuring ethnicity: (1) nonidentification, (2) multiple identification, and (3) misidentification. Ideally, an ethnic measure would maximize the number of identifications, simplify the handling of multiple nationalities, and minimize erroneous identifications. No approach (nor any combination) can avoid or solve these problems completely, since nonidentification and multiple identification are intrinsic to the subject, and misidentification results from the general and basic problem of measurement error aggravated by the complexity of categorizations and situations. The approaches do vary, however, in how well they deal with each of these problems.

A basic drawback of the two relatively objective approaches (natal and behavioral) is that they lead to a much higher rate of nonidentification than the subjective approach. Responses to the 1970 Census nativity question, for example, showed that only 4.7 percent of the population were immigrants, and 11.8 percent were native-born of foreign-born or mixed parentage. That leaves without any indication of ethnicity the 83.5 percent who were native-born of native-born parents. In theory one could extend the nativity question back until each ancestral line was traced to foreign shores, but this is impossible since the number of ancestors increases geometrically across generations, while knowledge declines in a similarly precipitous fashion. Approximately 56 percent of the adult population report that all four of their grandparents were native-born. For this large segment of the population, the place of birth of at least eight great-grandparents (and many more ancestors if all eight were not foreign-born) would have to be known in order to have complete information. This is well beyond the knowledge of most people.[4] Without complete information, identification could be made only by assuming that the missing data agreed with the available data or via some other imputation procedure.

The behavioral approach suffers even more seriously from nonidentification. The 1970 Census found that only 12 percent of the population did not report English as their native language, and the General Social Surveys find that only 3 percent of adults report membership in a "nationality group." Again, in theory one could extend this approach across generations, but the results would probably be even less fruitful than in the case of nativity.

Only the subjective approach succeeds in classifying a substantial majority of people. The GSS question elicited some ethnic identification from 86 percent of the population (during the period 1972–80), while in the 1976 Michigan Election Study, 89 percent of the white population mentioned an ethnicity. In sum, nonidentification is a general problem, and there remains a significant share of the population (10 to 15 percent) with no meaningful ethnic identification. The subjective questions do, however, minimize the problem by asking for a simple, summary identification, while the more objective approaches, by necessitating more voluminous and exact information than typical respondents possess, are able to come up with complete nativity data for only a minority of the population.

The performance of the strictly natal approach can be enhanced considerably, however, if it is modified to ask about the general ancestral origins of people of the third (or perhaps fourth) generation, as in the Michigan Election Study example cited above. In the 1972 Michigan Election Study, for instance, 62 percent of the third-generation white Americans were able to give both maternal and paternal ancestral origins, and 18 percent more were able to specify the origin of one lineage. This modification of the natal approach greatly reduces the problem of nonidentification, but only by abandoning a strictly natal approach for a hybrid of the natal and subjective.

Nonidentification can also be minimized by the use of a combination of approaches. While a simple subjective question identifies a high proportion of all possible identifiers (see Smith [1980] on the reason for nonidentification), a natal approach or hybrid approach can identify the national origins of an additional segment of the population. In the 1972–74 Michigan Election Studies, for example, the additional information from the hybrid approach reduced the portion of whites unidentified on the subjective question from 28 percent to 12 percent.

In sum, nonidentification is an intrinsic problem. Even given the best possible combination of approaches, 10 to 15 percent of Americans have no ethnic identification and no information on their national origins. The nonresponse problem can be minimized by combining a subjective question with a natal or hybrid natal-subjective item. As a single item the subjective approach is most useful; strictly natal and behavioral approaches identify a smaller proportion of people.

The second major problem in ethnic identification is just the opposite of nonidentification (that is, overidentification or multiple-identification). On the 1972–80 General Social Surveys, 35 percent of respondents named two or more countries when asked about their national origins. In addition, the 1980 GSS found that among those who named one ethnicity, 24 percent mentioned two or more nationalities for their parents. For these people the task is to try to sort out a main ethnicity or to otherwise handle the multiple identification. The natal approach generates a large and rich array of identifications, but contains no device to distill the data or select a main identification. Several solutions are available for handling multiple ethnicities on nativity questions:

1. Each combination could be treated as a separate group. Thus English and German as well as English-German would be groups. This would soon lead to so many combinations with minuscule numbers that most would have to be collapsed into a residual of other combinations.

2. A simple trichotomy of all-English, some English, and no English could be established, but this would obviously hamper interethnic comparisons.

3. A set of rules to choose a primary ethnicity could be devised. If, for example, a person reports one Danish and three Swedish grandparents, then it might be reasonable to code Swedish as the primary nationality. Unfortunately the difference is often less clear—such as choosing between parents with different nationalities (for example, one Irish and one Swiss) or between grandparents

with multiple ethnicities (for example, one Irish, one Irish-English, one Polish, and one Lithuanian). In the 1980 GSS, of those giving nationalities for both parents, 43.2 percent had parents with a single, common nationality; 8.7 percent had different mixtures of nationalities but one shared nationality; and 48.1 percent had different nationalities for their parents. Under these common circumstances the assigning of a primary nationality would be impossible or arbitrary.

The behavioral approach does not typically have much of a problem with overidentification (since it suffers so severely from nonidentification), but if it was extended across generations, it would have the same problem as the nativity question does. The subjective alternative either minimizes the problem of multiple identification by asking for a simple summary nationality, as the Michigan Election Study question does, or by asking people to choose between nationalities on some subjective ground. The GSS, for example, asks people giving two or more nationalities: "Which one of these countries do you feel closer to?" The 1980 Census instructions ask for the ancestry a person "identifies" with. These kinds of followups can greatly simplify the problem of ethnic identification. On the 1972–80 General Social Surveys, for example, 68.5 percent of those naming more than one nationality were able to name a primary ethnicity.

It can be fairly argued that complexity and detail are desirable attributes of an ethnic measure and that they should not be compressed away in analysis. Condensation, however, is often a practical necessity and may even be more meaningful than detailed information on the birthplaces of several generations of one's ancestors. Given that some simplification may be useful, the question becomes whether a genetic approach, such as nativity, or a subjective choice is more useful. Compare, for example, the approaches used in the Census and the GSS. In the 1970 Census, father's country of origin is used to determine a person's nationality when the parents have different nationalities. On the 1980 GSS we were able to compare the nationalities of parents with the summary nationality of the respondent. The standard GSS ethnicity question asked: "From what countries or part of the world did your ancestors come? IF MORE THAN ONE COUNTRY IS NAMED: which of these countries do you feel closer to?" As part of a supplement to the 1980 survey, respondents were asked the country of birth of their parents. For parents born in the United States respondents were asked: "What countries or parts of the world did your (mother's/father's) ancestors come from?" Up to two responses were coded for each parent.[5] We compared the summary nationality data from the standard GSS question with the parental nationality data. We looked at instances in which (1) different ethnicities were reported for the parents, (2) two different ethnicities were reported for the same parent, and (3) interparental and intra-parental combinations of differences occurred. We found that among the cases where one or more different nationalities were reported for the parents, 20.4 percent had no ethnic identifications, 5.9 percent chose an identification different from that of either parent,[6] 14.5 percent selected an ethnicity shared by their parents, 26.4 percent chose their mother's ethnicity, and 35.8 percent chose their father's ethnicity. Among those who chose only between their parents, 58 percent selected the paternal line while 42 percent chose the maternal. This evidence indicates that the census had some basis for favoring paternal lineage over maternal, but in more than 40 percent of the cases it results in the assignment of an ethnic identity with which a respondent does not actually identify.

Depending on the research purpose, a person may wish to use various methods for handling multiple identities. In a study of Italian assimilation, for example, it might be desirable to include initially all people with any Italian lineage whether or not they identify themselves as Italian. Similarly, studies of father-son mobility have focused on paternal origins (Featherman and Hauser, 1978:523-528). An investigation of the pattern of ethnic identification might compare various nativity combinations with subjective identification. If the researcher is looking for a main identification, then subjective identification is probably more reasonable than is reliance on some type of genetic weighting or arbitrary assignment.

Finally, there is the problem of misidentification. Some misidentification is inevitable, given the vagaries of memory, misunderstandings, errors of transference, and so forth. In the natal approach the special type of misidentification that occurs involves disparities between place of birth and nationality. A strict geopolitical reporting will lose all "stateless" nationalities, such as Serbian, Kurdish, Walloon, French Canadian, Armenian, or Lithuanian. Such reporting will also be influenced by the shift of boundaries and the creation and destruction of states. Polish nativity prior to World War I is only discernible in the U.S. censuses by subtracting from the Russians, Germans, and Austro-Hungarians those with Polish as a mother tongue. Likewise, accidents of place of birth, such as birthplaces of children of military personnel or of those in the diplomatic corps, will confound the situation. Behavioral identifications such as mother tongue do not create as many problems as does geopolitical reporting, although it is impossible to distinguish between nationalities speaking the same language (for example, Irish, English, and Scottish; or German and Austrian). On the other hand, identification by mother tongue can separate out such groups as French Canadians, the Flemings and the Walloons, or the Serbians and the Croatians. The subjective approach can avoid the stateless nationality and boundary problem as long as it does not rigidly structure itself in terms of geopolitical entities, but uses nationality groups as units instead. Likewise, accidents of place of birth will typically not confound the data, since the respondent will screen out such false evidence and report national identity instead. On the other hand, since the self-identification approach elicits an ethnicity from many more people than does the natal or behavioral approach, it includes many people with weak and nominal identification. As a result, it probably receives a higher proportion of labile responses than do the natal or behavioral approaches.

Thus, subjective identifications are likely to have lower test-retest reliability than the more objective measures. In addition, reliability would also tend to be lower since a person with multiple nationalities might switch his or her subjective identification depending on personal factors and social pressures (National Research Council, 1978).[7] Also, the subjective approach can lead to certain questionable or inappropriate classifications (similar to the birthplace of children of diplomats) such as the black Irishman who calls himself Spanish, or a person adopting a spouse's nationality.[8] In brief, by relying on the nation/state of birth, the natal approach will probably create more erroneous identifications than most behavioral approaches (for example, language) or the subjective approach, either of which would reduce mistakes due to geopolitical peculiarities and circumstances of birth. The subjective approach, however, may have lower test-retest reliability because it encompasses more weak identifiers.

The previous discussion shows that a strictly objective approach to the measurement of ethnicity and nationality is difficult because (1) many people lack sufficient information to supply complete data on ancestral national origins, (2) multiple nationalities create difficult problems for objective methods, (3) objective ways of handling multiple nationalities probably produce classifications that are less personally and sociologically meaningful than those of a subjective approach, and (4) emphasizing the country or place of birth distorts classifications because of multinational states, changed boundaries, national minorities, and other "accidents" of birth and geography. In sum, a solely objective approach to ethnicity or nationality would produce less information, take more effort, and result in less relevant data than an approach that incorporates a subjective element.

The limitations of the strictly natal approach are tacitly recognized by the fact that the standard ethnicity questions used by the government and academia (see page 119) all either implicitly or explicitly incorporate a subjective element (Lowry, 1980). The preferred approach will depend on the precise research objective, but generally a combination of all three methods would be desirable. Nativity questions provide important information on immigrant generations and heterogeneous lineage. A behavioral question such as that of language can clarify various ambiguous identities and provide evidence of the strength of the identification. A subjective approach will minimize nonidentification, handle multiple identifications in a simple and relevant fashion, and reduce some types of misidentifications. When used together, each method can both buttress data obtained by the others and add valuable additional information that is missed by them. In addition, by using all three methods along with other items on strength of identity, importance of identity, and behavioral consequences, we would be able to study the meaning, sources, and consequences of ethnicity.

In summary, the measurement of ethnicity and the narrower element of nationality involves a strong subjective aspect. This is apparent in most governmental and scholarly approaches. We have further found that if one is forced to rely on a quick and simple approach, a well-crafted subjective question is the best single indicator for most purposes. Even the preferred method—combining the behavioral, natal, and subjective approaches—depends in large part on a subjective element.

Notes

1. Schemes that use multiple variables to construct ethnic categories still collect the constituent parts as separate variables, so one is dealing with what usually are clearly distinguished components.

2. In addition to these, there are several other methods of identifying national origins, such as by surname or by physical characteristics. Neither these nor other techniques are generally reliable or commonly employed.

For example, the Current Population Survey (CPS) found that "among all persons with a Spanish surname in the United States in March 1971, only about two-thirds reported that they were of Spanish origin . . . among all persons in the United States who reported they were of Spanish origin, about two-thirds had a Spanish surname and one-third did not" (Bureau of the Census, 1975:2). On the difficulty of using surnames for classification in general, see American Council of Learned Societies (1932).

3. For problems with this item, see Bureau of the Census (1974).

4. Both because of mortality and associational patterns (that is, with each prior generation the ancestor is less likely to be alive during the respondent's lifetime, and, if alive, is likely to have less contact with the respondent), knowledge about ancestors quickly diminishes with each intervening generation. A National Opinion Research Center mobility study (Davis and Smith, 1980) found, for example, that while 98 percent of respondents knew their father's occupation, only 76 percent knew the occupation of their paternal grandfather. Knowledge about paternal great-grandfathers could be expected to decline as sharply. Schneider and Cottrell (1975:65-66) found that while 55 percent of their white, middle-class Chicago sample could give the first or last names of all four grandparents, only 14 percent could identify half

(four) of their great-grandparents. Among respondents with at least one native-born parent, paternal and/or maternal origin was unknown for 24 percent. Among the 76 percent with both a known maternal and paternal origin, few could probably successfully track all ancestral lines as a strict natal approach would require (see also Davis and Smith, 1980).

5. Only 20 percent of those with one nationality gave a second nationality, so the restriction to code only two nationalities per parent probably lost little information.

6. We looked at these odd cases in which a respondent reported an ethnicity different from that of either parent. Around a quarter were instances in which people expressed an ethnicity in different ways, such as Mexico versus Spain or England versus Canada. The other combinations are not readily explainable. They probably result from such factors as mixing references to natural and adopted parents, contradictions between place of birth and nationality, and coding or processing errors.

7. In 1973 and 1974, subsamples of the GSS were reinterviewed about 1 month later; 82 percent either selected an ethnicity or chose no identity both times. Among the consistent identifiers, 89 percent selected the same nationality. This gives 74 percent as consistently defining their ethnicity (or lack of same). This percentage tends to be lower than that for other demographics: 97 percent were consistent on region of residence at age 16, 92 percent on religious preference, 85 percent on father's education, 70 percent on community type at age 16, and 69 percent on number of siblings. The consistency was higher when collapsed ethnic groups were used. For example, using English versus non-English, 79 percent were consistent.

8. We assume that distortion from conscious attempts at racial/ethnic passing would be similar across approaches. A person wishing to be identified with a more prestigious nationality would presumably alter natal as well as subjective responses.

References

Abramson, J.J. (1975) The religioethnic factor and the American experience: another look at the three-generations hypothesis. *Ethnicity* 2:163-177.

American Council of Learned Societies (1932) Report of Committee on Linguistic and National Stocks in the Population of the United States. In *Annual Report of the American Historical Association for the Year 1931*. Washington, D.C.: Government Printing Office.

Barton, J.J. (1975) *Peasants and Strangers: Italians, Rumanians, and Slovaks in an American City, 1890-1950*. Cambridge, Mass.: Harvard University Press.

Bureau of the Census (1974) *Census of Population and Housing: 1970 Evaluation and Research Program, PHC(E)-9: Accuracy of Data for Selected Population Characteristics as Measured by Reinterviews*. Washington. D.C.: Government Printing Office.

Bureau of the Census (1975) *Comparison of Spanish Surname and Persons of Spanish Origin in the United States*. By Edward W. Fernandez. Technical Paper No. 38. Washington, D.C.: Government Printing Office.

Davis, J.A., and Smith, T.W. (1980) Looking backward: a national sample survey of ancestors and precessors, 1980-1850. *Historical Methods* 13:145-162.

Davis, J.A., Smith, T.W., and Stephenson, C.B. (1980) *General Social Surveys: 1972-1980: Cumulative Codebook*. Chicago: National Opinion Research Center.

Featherman, D.L., and Hauser, R.M. (1978) *Opportunity and Change*. New York: Academic Press.

Isajiw, W.W. (1974) Definitions of ethnicity. *Ethnicity* 1:111-124.

Lowry, I.S. (1980) The science and politics of ethnic enumeration. Paper presented to the American Association for the Advancement of Science, San Francisco, January.

Masuda, M., Matsumoto, G.H., and Meredith, G.M. (1970) Ethnic identity in three generations of Japanese-Americans. *Journal of Social Psychology* 81:199-207.

National Research Council (1978) *Counting the People in 1980: An Appraisal of Census Plans*. Washington D.C.: National Academy of Sciences.

Plax, M. (1972) On studying ethnicity. *Public Opinion Quarterly* 36:99-100.

Schneider, D.M., and Cottrell, C.B. (1975) *The American Kin Universe: A Genealogical Study*. Chicago: University of Chicago Press.

Smith, T.W. (1980) Ethnic measurement identification. *Ethnicity* 7:78-95.

Vrga, D.J. (1971) Serbians in America: the effects of status discrepancy on ethno-religious factualism. In O. Feinstein, ed., *Ethnic Groups in the City*. Lexington, Mass.: Heath.

Acknowledgments

This chapter draws on material used in Smith (1980). I would like to thank Theresa DeMaio, Otis Dudley Duncan, Baruch Fischhoff, Lester R. Frankel, William Kruskal, Stanley Lieberson, and Robert Parke for their comments.

5

Measuring Employment and Unemployment

Barbara A. Bailar and Naomi D. Rothwell

Whether a person is employed, unemployed, or out of the labor force may seem at first a factual item, and one that can easily be verified. There are people, however, for whom labor force status is an attitude that cannot be verified from records. Whether or not a person will be reported in statistical tabulations as employed, unemployed, or out of the labor force may depend on various factors such as the weather or the interviewer's skill; who responds for the person; the respondent's interest, mood, or perceptions about the purposes and uses of the interview; the time of day; who else is present; other things that happened that day; and the questions asked. The effects on labor force classification of some of these variables will be illustrated here after some facts about the Current Population Survey are described.

The Bureau of the Census conducts the Current Population Survey (CPS) monthly to estimate employment and unemployment. The survey, begun in 1940, has undergone a number of conceptual changes, which are described in the chapter on historical development of the 1979 report of the National Commission on Employment and Unemployment Statistics (1979:

20-27). In summary, the changes have been in response to efforts to employ more objective definitions than were used initially. At present the survey includes the civilian noninstitutional population 14 years of age and older, although data are published only for persons 16 years of age and over.

People are not asked whether they are employed or unemployed, nor do interviewers classify their respondents' employment status. Instead, respondents are asked a series of questions about their activities and, on the basis of their replies, are classified for the survey by computer "Employment Status Recodes." Some of the questions they are asked are shown in the Appendix to this chapter. The definitions applied to responses are shown in the following extract, and some examples indicate how and why people who are interviewed may not necessarily agree with the way their employment status is classified. Thus survey responses have been translated into definitions with which respondents, economists, statisticians, or sociologists might not agree, though the recent review by the National Commission on Employment and Unemployment Statistics (1979) cited earlier left most definitions unchanged. Here are the definitions:

Persons are considered to be employed if replies to survey questions show that during the week prior to the interview they

- worked[1] for at least 1 hour as paid employees or in their own business, profession, or farm;

OR

- worked 15 hours or more as unpaid workers in a family-operated enterprise;

OR

- did not work but had jobs or businesses from which they were temporarily absent because of illness, vacation, labor/management disputes, or other reasons.

Persons are considered to be unemployed if they:

- did not work but looked for work[2] during the last 4 weeks and were available to take a job last week (the week prior to the interview);

OR

- were laid off from work because of a strike or lockout.

As explained earlier, these rules or definitions are incorporated in a series of questions. All except two[3] of the questions are about a person's principal activities during the reference week, which is the week containing the twelfth day of the month. The survey is conducted during the week containing the nineteenth day.

To illustrate how survey responses are fit into the definitions and how respondent attitudes can affect replies to what are intended as factual questions, six cases are cited. None of the cases illustrates error. Although the ambiguity of the first three makes their classification uncertain, and the arbitrariness of the rules may make the classification of the last three appear inconsistent with common sense or with the respondent's self-classification, all six of the following cases are classified consistently with the survey rules or definitions that have just been described.

Case 1. Three young men play basketball with each other and occasionally talk about where they might find work. Sometimes when they see a newspaper they look at the "help wanted" section. Assume that all three were interviewed and asked the questions shown in note 2 on page 141 (see also the Appendix). One discouraged man does not consider the conversations or occasional glimpse in the paper "looking for work" and answers "No" to the first question. A more hopeful second man thinks he may find something in the newspaper and answers "Yes" to the first question about looking for work, but, unable to cite anything more specific, he replies "Nothing much" to the followup question about what he did to look for work. As a result of these replies, both are classified as "not in the labor force." The third man takes the conversations with his friend more seriously or has a better memory and mentions the conversations and looking at advertisements in the newspaper as evidence that he is looking for work. He is classified as unemployed.

Case 2. A woman worked part time but was interested in working full time, so she might answer the question about current status as "looking for work" (see Appendix). The place where she worked had no need for a full-time person in the position. The woman spent much of her time during the reference week looking for full-time work, though she did work 5 hours at her office. That should result in her being classified as employed. If, however, she reported at the beginning of the interview that she was looking for work, she could be misclassified as unemployed.

Case 3. A teenage girl posted a notice at a shopping center that she was available for babysitting, and she also distributed flyers to her neighbors at the beginning of the summer. She had some work and promises of future jobs, but during the reference week in the autumn, she had not worked as a babysitter. She would be counted as out of the labor force if the definition was applied literally, but there is some possibility that she might report a phone call in which she was promised work and, thereby, be considered unemployed.

To illustrate the point made earlier that arbitrariness of rules adopted to achieve objectivity can result in classifications with which many experts, as well as the respondents themselves, might disagree, the following cases are cited.

Case 4. A man looked for work for 5 months and was unsuccessful. He followed up on fewer and fewer job leads as time went by, since the leads did not seem to work out. During the 4 weeks preceding the survey week he had done nothing to look for work. He would be counted as out of the labor force, though he might consider himself as unemployed.

Case 5. A man looked for work by contacting employment agencies, answering advertisements, and following up on leads from friends for 3 of the 4 weeks preceding the interview week. The fourth week he took a fishing trip with his son. The week he was gone happened to be the reference week for the survey. Because he was not available for work that week, the definitions would classify him as out of the labor force.

Case 6. A woman worked as a volunteer for a large social work agency and did not seek other employment. Her activities took her over 40 hours a week, often including weekends and evenings. During the reference week she worked 45 hours at the agency. If the interviewer properly probed an indication that the work is voluntary rather than for pay and verified that status, the woman would be counted as out of the labor force, despite her long hours of work.

Before turning to a discussion of errors, defined as classifications that are not consistent with the survey rules, some perspective is supplied by a hypothetical contrast between a head of household, employed full time and salaried, and his daughter, a part-time student who spent a few hours last week (or was it the week before?) trying to sell cosmetics on commission without yet having collected any money for the effort. The contrast is between virtually error-free and clearly error-prone situations. Almost no interviewer, respondent, mode of interview, question wording or sequence, or other variation would affect the classification of the first person, but classification of the second is marginal and subject to influences of interviewer, respondent choice or mood, data collection method, or other variation. This contrast is provided in an effort to put boundaries around errors of classification that occur in CPS. The suggestion is that, for most people, classification of employment status is robust and reliable; yet for a few, who are probably the exceptions in the country as a whole but may not be exceptions in selected segments of the population, classification is intrinsically weak and uncertain.

How to allocate responsibility for errors or differences is also a problem. Early in the 1970s, 4 professional staff members of the Bureau of the Census interviewed a group of respondents whose labor force status was reported as having changed from the initial to the subsequent interview. Although skilled and knowledgeable, the staff members could not obtain sufficient information in some of the interviews for unequivocal determination of the facts. Consequently they were not able to identify errors in those cases. Moreover, the staff failed to agree among themselves about reasons for any errors or misclassifications they thought existed.

We turn now from examples that tax the classification system to the subject of observed and clear-cut errors in employment-status classification. A number of reasons for such errors have been identified, starting with interviewers' contributions to errors. Interviewers have the opportunity to affect data in various ways: by misunderstanding the concepts, by failing to obtain an interview, by omitting questions, by changing question wording, by misunderstanding responses, by contacting inappropriate respondents, or by fabricating the "facts."

Approximately 1,200 interviewers work on the Current Population Survey. These interviewers vary widely in their length of experience with the survey. About 30 percent leave the staff each year, so new interviewers are always in training. They are given intensive training for the first 3 months on the job, including home study exercises, classroom work, and observations by supervisory staff. Prior to each month's enumeration, all interviewers are given home study exercises.

In 1975, a mock interview project was carried out at the Bureau of the Census in which 225 interviewers were selected at three levels of experience. Of the 225 interviewers, 114 were experienced (most of them with more than 12 months' interviewing experience); 72 had just completed classroom training but had no CPS interviewing experience; and 39 had completed classroom training and had 2 to 3 months of CPS interviewing experience. The selected interviewers were asked to conduct mock, tape-recorded interviews with other staff members who followed five scripts prepared to cover a variety of labor force situations.[4] In analyzing the tape-recorded interviews, it was found that the interviewers' most common errors included failure to ask questions as worded, to probe, and to record accurately. The outcome of those and other errors indicated that, for the scripts used, 36 percent of the experienced interviewers, 67 percent of the inexperienced interviewers, and 61 percent of those with 2 or 3 months of experience made one or more errors that prevented labor force classification or resulted in misclassification (see Rustemeyer, 1977). Two-fifths of those tested with a script describing a woman army officer reported her occupation in a way that would incorrectly have included her in the civilian labor force. One-fifth of those tested with a script that described a student looking for a part-time job provided reports that would incorrectly have excluded her from the labor force. More than one-tenth submitted reports in which a volunteer worker would have been classified as employed rather than as not being in the labor force (see Daina and Rothwell, 1977). Turning attention to the illustrations provided earlier, it is clear that failure to ask the appropriate questions, to probe, or to listen carefully and to record replies accurately could have caused these misclassifications.

Interviewers depend on information from respondents, who also have many opportunities to affect the data. When one thinks of a respondent, it is common to picture a person responding for himself or herself. Yet in many surveys, including the CPS, this is not necessarily the case. An interviewer will interview one person for the entire household. Thus if an interviewer visits the household in the evening and interviews an adult male, that man will usually respond for all the people who live there. If the interviewer calls by telephone and a teenage girl answers, that girl may be the household respondent. Records show that the number of respondents who are "other relatives" of the primary householder increases when telephone interviews are conducted.

Examples of the effect of proxy responses can be drawn from among the cases cited earlier. The wife, parent, or roommate of one of the three young men who play basketball together and occasionally talk about where they might find work (case 1) honestly might not know whether he had looked for work or not. If the respondent was the son of the woman who was working part time but was looking for full time work (case 2), he might not know whether his mother had looked for full time work and whether she had worked at all during the reference week. The husband of the woman who worked over 40 hours a week as a volunteer (case 6) might report that she was working full time because that is how it seems to him.

Not all respondent contributions to error are attributable to proxy response. As suggested in note 1, page 141, there are understandable motivations for deliberate misreporting by some people. Genuine misunderstanding, deafness, boredom, lack of concentration, memory loss or error, and disorientation are among other causes of respondent error. Finally, respondent errors tend to increase as situations deviate from the simple, easily classified, and stereotypical to the complex or ambiguous.

Mode of interviewing and conditioning of interviewers and respondents as well as interactions between interviewers and respondents may also contribute to error. There is a rotation pattern in the Current Population Survey: households are in the sample for 4 consecutive months, are dropped out of the sample for 8 consecutive months, and then are in the sample again for 4 consecutive months. For the first and second monthly interviews during the first 4-month period, and for the first monthly interview of the second 4-month period, the interviewers are supposed to collect the data in a personal visit to the household; in remaining months, they may use the telephone. Repeated interviewing may affect expectations or attitudes of interviewers or respondents. The choice of telephone or personal interview may affect not only the reception of the interview and the way it is conducted, but also (as suggested earlier) the choice of a respondent, which in turn can affect the replies.

In a recent experimental study, the Methods Development Study, the effects of three different methodological factors on estimated unemployment rates were examined. One factor was the use of personal interviewing versus telephone interviewing to collect the data. A second factor was the choice of respondent. In a set of randomly selected households, persons were supposed to report for themselves; in another set of randomly selected households, any responsible person could report for all persons in the household; in a third set of randomly selected households, a specific person was predesignated as the household respondent. Finally, the third factor was the use of the same versus different interviewers in different months of the survey (Roman and Woltman, 1981). These experimental treatments could not be carried out in all cases. One notable departure is that households assigned to telephone interviews were always visted by a personal interviewer in the first month, because that is standard practice. Also, if a wife was designated as the respondent for a household in which there was no wife, any responsible person was substituted as a respondent. Differences in unemployment rates were observed when these three factors were systematically varied over 4 months of interviewing. The highest unemployment rate resulted when there was self-response, when the interviewers differed from month to month, and when telephoning occurred after the first month. The lowest unemployment rate resulted when any responsible household member was the respondent, when the interviewer was constant from month to month, and when telephoning occurred after the first month.

In the following tables, differences are expressed in the form of index numbers. These show the total number of unemployed persons classified in the category for all rotation groups divided by the average for all categories over all months in the sample. This average is then multiplied by 100. If an equal number of unemployed persons was found using each method, the indices for all methods would be 100. As can be seen in Table 5.1, for the unemployed interviewed by telephone and by a different interviewer about their own status, the index was 121.0. This means that the method gave an estimate about 20 percent higher than the average for all methods. Since all first-month interviews were conducted by personal interview, Table 5.1 contains data for personal interviews for month 1. Consequently, Table 5.2 shows data only for the second to fourth interviews in which all treatments were carried out, insofar as they were feasible.[5]

Even if these results were easier to understand than they are, much remains to be explained before they can shed light on the parent CPS

TABLE 5.1
Unemployment Rate Indices from Methods Development Survey
(Months 1–4)

Treatment Level Combinations				
Mode	Interviewer Assignment	Respondent Type	Unemployment Rate Index	Std. Error of Index
Personal visit[a]	Same for all interviews	Household	95.1	10.4
		Designated	105.6	10.0
		Self	105.1	8.7
Telephone[a]	Same for all interviews	Household	89.2	7.9
		Designated	100.5	7.8
		Self	101.4	8.4
Personal visit	Alternating[b]	Household	90.5	7.2
		Designated	90.1	6.7
		Self	88.6	8.0
Telephone	Alternating	Household	105.8	9.0
		Designated	107.0	9.9
		Self	121.0	11.2

[a]All first-month interviews were conducted by personal visit.
[b]Different interviewer was assigned in the second and fourth interviews than that in the initial and third interviews.

survey. First, CPS data shown in Table 5.3 are consistent with continuing observation that unemployment rates are higher in the first than in subsequent interviews. Results from the Methods Development Survey are summarized in Tables 5.1 and 5.2 for a rotation plan that called for four interviews in the selected households, conducted a month apart. The monthly reports that are summarized show that the lowest estimate of unemployment was reported in the initial interview, and estimates ascend in subsequent interviews. Since this is contrary to continuing survey results, it raises questions about the applicability of these research findings to the CPS.

Another result of interest from the Methods Development Survey suggests that mode of interview—whether personal or telephone—may have affected the interviewer before it could affect the respondent. Each interviewer employed all of the survey procedures and knew the study design at the outset. Although all respondents were interviewed in person at the beginning of the survey, estimates of unemployment rates for the group later interviewed by telephone were higher than estimates for the group that was later interviewed in person. There is other research indicating that

TABLE 5.2

Unemployment Rate Indices from Methods Development Survey
(Months 2–4 Only)

Treatment Level Combinations				
Mode	Interviewer Assignment	Respondent Type	Unemployment Rate Index	Std. Error of Index
Personal visit[a]	Same for all interviews	Household	95.4	10.2
		Designated	109.1	9.5
		Self	110.9	7.8
Telephone[a]	Same for all interviews	Household	91.4	6.3
		Designated	102.7	9.2
		Self	95.3	6.2
Personal visit	Alternating[b]	Household	91.9	5.7
		Designated	90.9	5.6
		Self	87.5	8.3
Telephone	Alternating	Household	98.8	8.2
		Designated	109.5	9.2
		Self	116.9	10.2

[a]All first-month interviews were conducted by personal visit.
[b]Different interviewer was assigned in the second and fourth interviews than that in the initial and third interviews.

interviewer anticipation can create what appears to be a questionnaire or respondent effect (see Bercini and Massey, 1979).

In addition to the sources of error so far described (interviewers, respondents, interactions between them, and mode of interview), the questionnaire itself can contribute to classification errors. The following example of how adding questions affected the classification of persons in the labor force illustrates a combined questionnaire and interviewer effect. The labor force supplement questions (24a–24e in the Appendix) are asked of persons in a part of the sample each month who are supposedly not in the labor force. In 1968–69, these questions were asked of persons in the sample for the first and fifth interviews; since 1970, they have been asked of persons in the sample for the fourth and eighth interviews. These questions, asked *after* the questions used to classify people as employed, unemployed, or out of the labor force, make a difference in the classification. In Table 5.3, the indices shown in boldface type are for the months in which the supplementary questions were asked. These rotation-group indices reflect the effect of repeated interviewing on estimates of the size of the labor force and of the employed and unemployed components.

TABLE 5.3

Rotation-Group Indices for CPS Employment and Unemployment Items for Two Time Periods, 1968–69 (T1) and 1970–72 (T2)

Population aged 16+	Time	| Rotation Group								Std. Error
		1	2	3	4	5	6	7	8	
Total civilian	T1	**102.3**	100.3	99.8	99.5	**100.8**	99.3	99.1	99.0	.3
labor force	T2	101.6	100.0	99.6	**100.3**	100.0	99.1	99.2	**100.0**	.2
Employed	T1	**101.6**	100.2	99.9	99.8	**100.4**	99.4	99.4	99.3	.3
	T2	101.1	100.0	99.7	**100.3**	99.9	99.4	99.5	**100.1**	.2
Unemployed	T1	**120.0**	101.5	96.4	92.8	**109.3**	96.5	92.6	91.0	2.4
	T2	109.2	100.3	98.1	**101.2**	102.3	96.7	94.1	**98.2**	1.2
Males										
Employed	T1	**100.9**	100.0	100.0	99.8	**100.2**	99.8	99.7	99.7	.3
	T2	100.7	99.9	99.8	**100.2**	99.9	99.7	99.7	**100.2**	.2
Unemployed	T1	**114.1**	102.6	98.0	95.6	**106.0**	97.7	93.4	92.6	3.5
	T2	105.4	101.4	99.9	**101.6**	100.3	98.0	95.6	**97.9**	1.6
Females										
Employed	T1	**104.2**	100.6	99.5	99.2	**101.4**	98.7	98.4	98.1	.6
	T2	102.7	100.0	99.4	**100.4**	100.2	98.6	98.6	**100.0**	.5
Unemployed	T1	**125.5**	100.2	94.6	90.5	**112.5**	95.1	91.8	89.5	2.8
	T2	113.8	99.0	95.9	**100.7**	104.4	95.2	92.2	**98.6**	1.5

NOTE: Std. Error is the standard error of the index. Indices in boldface are for months in which supplementary questions were asked.

As can be seen in Table 5.3, the index for the estimate of the unemployed was 120.0 for the first interview (1) in 1968–69, and dropped to 91.0 for the last interview (8) in that same period. Further examination shows that the index in 1968–69 (T1) for unemployed dropped at each subsequent interview through the fourth month. When the group of respondents was interviewed after an 8-month lapse, the index rose again, only to fall each month thereafter.

Though the phenomenon of rotation-group differences still exists in the second time period (T2), there is not as much variability in the indices as there was in the first time period. Asking probing questions of people not in the labor force added people to the labor force and, consequently, to the unemployed component of it. Even though interviewers are told not to change the recorded answers to earlier questions because of responses to probing questions about job seeking, it is obvious that they do.

Examination of rotation-group indices for the second time period, when the probing questions were asked in the months that originally produced the lowest estimates of unemployment, still shows a difference in the number of persons classified as employed or unemployed in the first month in the sample and in later months. Although the differences shown are beyond sampling error, the differential is reduced, and the indices in the months in which the questions were asked were increased.

Reporting-bias in panel surveys has also been observed in a variety of other surveys: on expenditure, levels of illness, and crime victimizations. From the studies of this problem, it is obvious that no single factor accounts for the difference. Memory effects, interviewers, respondents, interactions between respondents and interviewers, the mode, setting, and timing of the interview, the wording and sequencing of questions asked, changing response probabilities for different segments of the population—all can contribute to the phenomenon which, we have been told, is not limited to survey research.[6] Given such evidence confronting survey researchers, it becomes obvious that there is not always a clear-cut demarcation between "factual" and "attitude" questions. The so-called fact of labor force status that the CPS is designed to determine objectively nevertheless shares some kinds of errors, as well as indeterminacies and ambiguities, which are frequently thought to be associated only with attitude questions.

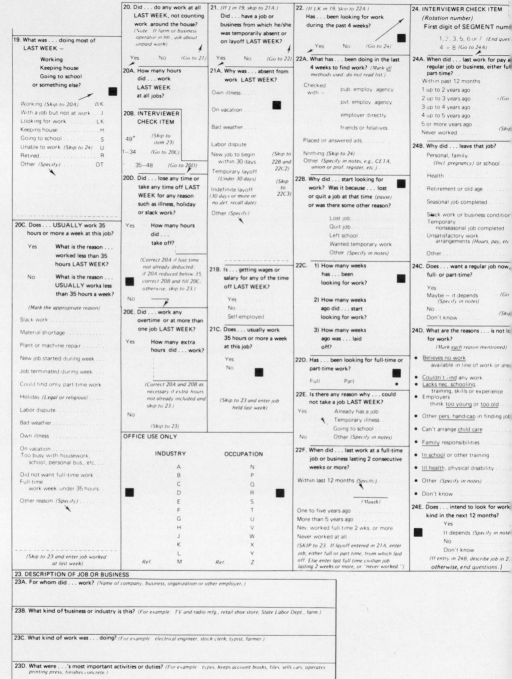

Appendix

19. What was . . . doing most of LAST WEEK —

Working
Keeping house
Going to school
or something else?

Working *(Skip to 20A)* . . . . WK
With a job but not at work . . J
Looking for work . . . . LK
Keeping house . . . . H
Going to school . . . . S
Unable to work *(Skip to 24)* . U
Retired . . . . R
Other *(Specify)* . . . . OT

20C. Does . . . USUALLY work 35 hours or more a week at this job?

Yes — What is the reason . . . worked less than 35 hours LAST WEEK?

No — What is the reason . . . USUALLY works less than 35 hours a week?

(Mark the appropriate reason)

Slack work . . . .
Material shortage . . . .
Plant or machine repair . . . .
New job started during week . . .
Job terminated during week . . .
Could find only part-time work . .
Holiday *(Legal or religious)* . . .
Labor dispute . . . .
Bad weather . . . .
Own illness . . . .
On vacation . . . .
Too busy with housework, school, personal bus., etc. . .
Did not want full-time work . . .
Full-time work week under 35 hours .
Other reason *(Specify)* . . . . . .

(Skip to 23 and enter job worked at last week)

---

20. Did . . . do any work at all LAST WEEK, not counting work around the house? *(Note: If farm or business operator in hh, ask about unpaid work)*

Yes   No *(Go to 21)*

20A. How many hours did . . . work LAST WEEK at all jobs?

20B. INTERVIEWER CHECK ITEM

49+ — *(Skip to item 23)*
1–34 — *(Go to 20C)*
35–48 — *(Go to 20D)*

20D. Did . . . lose any time or take any time off LAST WEEK for any reason such as illness, holiday or slack work?

Yes — How many hours did . . . take off?

(Correct 20A if lost time not already deducted; if 20A reduced below 35, correct 20B and fill 20C, otherwise, skip to 23.)

No

20E. Did . . . work any overtime or at more than one job LAST WEEK?

Yes — How many extra hours did . . . work?

(Correct 20A and 20B as necessary if extra hours not already included and skip to 23.)

No — *(Skip to 23)*

OFFICE USE ONLY

INDUSTRY	OCCUPATION
A	N
B	P
C	Q
D	R
E	S
F	T
G	U
H	V
J	W
K	X
L	Y
Ref. M	Ref. Z

---

21. *(If J in 19, skip to 21A.)* **Did . . . have a job or business from which he/she was temporarily absent or on layoff LAST WEEK?**

Yes   No *(Go to 22)*

21A. Why was . . . absent from work LAST WEEK?

Own illness . . . .
On vacation . . . .
Bad weather . . . .
Labor dispute . . . .
New job to begin within 30 days *(Skip to 22B and 22C2)*
Temporary layoff *(Under 30 days)* *(Skip to 22C3)*
Indefinite layoff *(30 days or more or no def. recall date)*
Other *(Specify)*

21B. Is . . . getting wages or salary for any of the time off LAST WEEK?

Yes
No
Self-employed

21C. Does . . . usually work 35 hours or more a week at this job?

Yes
No

(Skip to 23 and enter job held last week)

---

22. *(If LK in 19, Skip to 22A.)* **Has . . . been looking for work during the past 4 weeks?**

Yes   No *(Go to 24)*

22A. What has . . . been doing in the last 4 weeks to find work? *(Mark all methods used, do not read list.)*

Checked with —
pub. employ. agency
pvt. employ. agency
employer directly
friends or relatives
Placed or answered ads . . .
Nothing *(Skip to 24)*
Other *(Specify in notes, e.g., CETA, union or prof. register, etc.)* .

22B. Why did . . . start looking for work? Was it because . . . lost or quit a job at that time *(pause)* **or was there some other reason?**

Lost job . . . .
Quit job . . . .
Left school . . . .
Wanted temporary work . . .
Other *(Specify in notes)* . .

22C. 1) How many weeks has . . . been looking for work?

2) How many weeks ago did . . . start looking for work?

3) How many weeks ago was . . . laid off?

22D. Has . . . been looking for full-time or part-time work?

Full   Part

22E. Is there any reason why . . . could not take a job LAST WEEK?

Yes —
Already has a job
Temporary illness . . .
Going to school . . .

No —
Other *(Specify in notes)*

22F. When did . . . last work at a full-time job or business lasting 2 consecutive weeks or more?

Within last 12 months *(Specify)* .

_____
(Month)

One to five years ago . . . .
More than 5 years ago . . . .
Nev. worked full-time 2 wks. or more
Never worked at all . . . . . .

(SKIP to 23. If layoff entered in 21A, enter job, either full or part time, from which laid off. Else enter last full time civilian job lasting 2 weeks or more, or "never worked.")

---

24. INTERVIEWER CHECK ITEM
(Rotation number)
First digit of SEGMENT num

1, 2, 3, 5, 6 or 7 *(End ques*
4 or 8 *(Go to 24A)*

24A. When did . . . last work for pay a regular job or business, either full part-time?

Within past 12 months
1 up to 2 years ago
2 up to 3 years ago . . . *(Go*
3 up to 4 years ago .
4 up to 5 years ago . .
5 or more years ago . . . *(Skip*
Never worked . . . .

24B. Why did . . . leave that job?

Personal, family *(Incl. pregnancy)* or school . .
Health . . . .
Retirement or old age . . . . . .
Seasonal job completed . . . .
Slack work or business condition
Temporary nonseasonal job completed .
Unsatisfactory work arrangements *(Hours, pay, etc*
Other . . . .

24C. Does . . . want a regular job now, full- or part-time?

Yes . . . .
Maybe — it depends *(Go* *(Specify in notes)*
No . . . . *(Skip*
Don't know . . . . .

24D. What are the reasons . . . is not lo for work? *(Mark each reason mentioned)*

• Believes no work available in line of work or area
• Couldn't find any work . . .
• Lacks nec. schooling, training, skills or experience
• Employers think too young or too old . .
• Other pers. handicap in finding job
• Can't arrange child care . . .
• Family responsibilities . . . .
• In school or other training . .
• Ill health, physical disability . .
• Other *(Specify in notes)* . .
• Don't know . . . .

24E. Does . . . intend to look for work kind in the next 12 months?

Yes . . . . . .
It depends *(Specify in note*
No . . . .
Don't know . . . . .

(If entry in 24B, describe job in 2. otherwise, end questions.)

---

23. DESCRIPTION OF JOB OR BUSINESS

23A. For whom did . . . work? *(Name of company, business, organization or other employer.)*

23B. What kind of business or industry is this? *(For example: TV and radio mfg., retail shoe store, State Labor Dept., farm.)*

23C. What kind of work was . . . doing? *(For example: electrical engineer, stock clerk, typist, farmer.)*

23D. What were . . .'s most important activities or duties? *(For example: types, keeps account books, files, sells cars, operates printing press, finishes concrete.)*

continued on p.

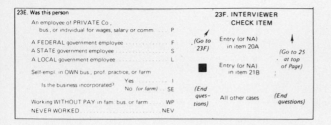

Notes

1. "Worked," while it appears to be a commonly understood status, may not always be. Although the concept is intended to be value-free, people engaged in illegal or immoral occupations or illegally employed in legal occupations may not describe themselves as working. Bookies, number writers, procurers or prostitutes, foreigners on student or visitor's visas, and others may either not consider their occupation to be "work" or may feel they have reason not to report working in an interview for a government-sponsored survey. Conversely, there are reasons why some people who are not working according to CPS definitions may be reported in some way that results in their classification as being "at work."

2. "Looked for work" classification depends on a "yes" reply to the question "Has . . . been looking for work during the past 4 weeks?" and a reply other than nothing to the following question: "What has . . . been doing in the last 4 weeks to find work?" and a reply to a question indicating that the person was available for work in the previous week.

3. While two of the three questions about looking for work refer to activities during the most recent 4 weeks, classification for all survey respondents rests on availability for work in the one previous week—the reference week.

4. Although the interviewers were sampled, the scripts could not be, so there is no evidence that they are typical or representative of situations that exist in reality.

5. Classification is according to the assignment of the specific treatment which could not always be carried out. For example, proxies are interviewed for people away from home or incompetent to be interviewed; personal visits are made to homes that have no telephones or in which telephones are not answered.

6. We are indebted to Lester Frankel for pointing out the following passage from Frederick Mosteller's discussion of nonsampling errors in panel studies in the *International Encyclopedia of Statistics* (Kruskal and Tanur, 1978:213): "Sample surveys are not alone in these 'first-time' effects. Doctors report that patients' blood pressures are higher when taken by a strange doctor. In the Peirce reaction time data, . . . the first day's average reaction time was about twice those of the other 23 days."

References

Bercini, D.H., and Massey, J.T. (1979) Asking for names before and after an initial interview in a telephone survey. *Proceedings of the American Statistical Association (Social Statistics Section)* 1979:136-140.

Daina, B., and Rothwell, N.D. (1977) Employment Status Recode Errors in the Mock Interview Project. Unpublished ms. Washington, D.C.: Bureau of the Census.

Kruskal, W.H., and Tanur, J., eds. (1978) *International Encyclopedia of Statistics*. New York: Free Press.

National Commission on Employment and Unemployment Statistics. (1979) *Counting the Labor Force*. Washington, D.C.: Government Printing Office.

Roman, A.M., and Woltman, H. (1981) The Methods Development Survey. Phase I, the Final Report: June 1978 to November 1979. Unpublished ms. Washington, D.C.: Bureau of the Census.

Rustemeyer, A. (1977) Measuring interviewer performance in mock interviews. *Proceedings of the American Statistical Association (Social Statistics Section)* 1977:341-346.

6

Housing Research: Conceptual and Measurement Issues

Sandra J. Newman

The impetus for all federal housing legislation and housing programs in this century has been the belief that housing plays an important role in promoting the health, safety, and well-being of the individual and the growth, wealth, and security of the nation. Since the 72nd Congress during the Great Depression, every successive Congress has enacted legislation or conducted studies dealing with housing (Bureau of the Census, 1957). Yet decades after the first federal intervention in the housing sector, long after the first recognition of improved housing as an important and legitimate goal of government policy, and after numerous large-scale population and sample surveys by the Census Bureau and many nongovernmental research organizations, the same basic issues that Census staff and advisory boards made an effort to address in the first Census of Housing in 1940 reappear each time the measurement of housing characteristics is attempted.

For convincing evidence of the apparent intractability of this problem, we need look no further than the history of the Census Bureau's measurement of housing condition. In the 1940 Census, housing condition was measured by the dwelling's "state of repair"; enumerators rated the structure as either needing "major" repairs or not. In 1950, this approach was replaced by another dichotomous classification of structures as either "dilapidated" or "not dilapidated." This dichotomy was refined in 1960 by further classifying those structures reported as "not dilapidated" as either "sound" or "deteriorating." Following the 1960 Census, the Bureau launched an unusually detailed and thorough evaluation of its approach to measuring housing condition. Its conclusion was unambiguous: the housing condition statistics are unreliable and inaccurate. Subsequent decennial censuses of housing have dropped all summary measures of housing condition.

In retrospect, it might have been more surprising if the Census Bureau had found that enumerators could provide consistent and accurate evaluations of structural condition. Enumerators received only 30 minutes of specific training on structural condition ratings, printed materials were general and often ambiguous, and payment on a per interview basis provided a built-in incentive to spend as little time as possible on each housing unit (Bureau of the Census, 1967; Aaron, 1972). In addition, the potentially biasing effects of the socioeconomic background of the enumerator and of environmental factors such as the socioeconomic or racial characteristics of the neighborhood or the tidiness and general upkeep of structures in the area were likely to create serious problems even under the best conditions. In contrast to subjective ratings, we might expect accuracy to be much greater for what seem to be purely objective measures or reports of fact, such as number of rooms in the dwelling unit, the age of the housing unit, the cost of the housing unit, the type of structure in which the dwelling unit is located (that is, single versus multi-unit, attached versus detached), the type of heating equipment used, the presence and characteristics of plumbing and kitchen facilities, and so forth. But here, too, the accumulated evidence suggests that there is often substantial variation between what is reported in a survey and what is considered the "correct" response.

There are two main problems affecting survey measurement in housing research: conceptual ambiguity and measurement error. Since the conceptual issues are fundamental and logically prior to the problems of measurement error, they will be discussed first.

Conceptual Issues:
What Should be Measured?

Part of the conceptual problem in housing research is the inherent complexity of the underlying concepts. Much of this complexity arises because housing denotes not only shelter, but also a range of housing services and a social and environmental setting. Thus, when a family purchases a house, they purchase a physical structure, housing systems (for example, electrical, plumbing, heating), an array of public services (for example, schools, police, fire protection), and a neighborhood characterized by many attributes including the demographics of the residents, a rate of crime, and physical appearance. From this notion of housing as a "bundle of services," it follows that measurement of only a subset of housing characteristics may not provide an accurate picture of the housing circumstances in which people live. Whether researchers are interested in housing characteristics per se or in housing characteristics as indicators of other states, the basic question remains the same: which components of the "housing bundle" should be measured?

Almost regardless of which components are measured, however, there is also a second problem of selecting empirical indicators that best represent each component. Key constructs such as "housing adequacy" and "housing quality," for example, are not based on completely explicit criteria and have no precise, quantifiable definitions of where "bad" ends and "good" begins. Even the construct of crowding, which has played a central role in housing and related research as well as in establishing eligibility of communities for a range of government assistance programs, is not conceptually clear. What determines whether an individual lives in a crowded housing situation? Do attributes of the household or of the housing unit count more than attributes of the area surrounding the unit? One recent study of residential crowding finds that the number of operational definitions of this concept is nearly equal to the substantial number of studies on the subject (Newman, 1981). More important, empirical testing of the substitutability of more than 30 alternative measures of crowding clearly indicates substantial differences among these measures.

This lack of clarity is not restricted only to housing constructs with a large subjective component. Even apparently more objective characteristics are often difficult to define and, ultimately, to measure. Determining whether a housing unit is vacant, for example, involves judgments regarding the length of time it has been unoccupied, whether it is being used for storage or business purposes, or whether it is undergoing major alterations (Bureau of the Census, 1957). In fact, determining whether a physical structure is a "housing unit" is not straightforward. The Census Bureau's approach involves specific stipulations regarding separate cooking facilities, direct access, and special treatment of institutional settings, tents, boats, caves, railroad cars, and other unusual habitats.

A third conceptual issue is whether housing constructs are more accurately assessed through attribute measures which are as objective as possible, or through subjective reports about those attributes. It has been argued, for example, that crowding is better measured by asking whether the occupants feel crowded than by counting people and rooms. Most indicators of the conditions in which people live ultimately rely on someone's judgment for defining standards of good and bad. Since many of these indicators are inherently subjective, relating most closely to an individual's experiences in that situation and to the individual's psychological makeup and socioeconomic background, only he or she may be able to provide an accurate assessment of whether the housing unit in question is crowded, has adequate heat and plumbing, and the like. This argument becomes more persuasive if we are interested in outcomes: the accumulated evidence clearly suggests that people's decisions about moving, for example, depend much more on how they perceive and evaluate their premove environment than on the relatively objective attributes of that environment (Newman, 1974; Newman and Duncan, 1979). Subjective indicators also have the attractive feature of self-adjustment over time. The same factors that bring obsolescence to standards for "objectified" indicators such as crowding and housing adequacy (for example, rising expectations and aspirations, and new technologies) are also expected to affect subjective indicators, eliminating the need for manipulation by researchers.

There are two basic types of criticism of subjective indicators (as suggested by Rodgers [1981]). First, there is concern about the credibility of answers. Do people really know how they feel? Do they give accurate reports of their feelings or are there deliberate or unconscious attempts to hide these feelings? Can people translate these feelings into points on a subjective rating scale? Second, these judgments are based on highly individual criteria, and they may even be so idiosyncratic that they defy logic and predictability. Thus they may be of limited use to policy makers.

Nowhere have these conceptual questions generated greater debate than in the search for a measure of housing quality.[1] What one observer has labeled the "plumbing approach toward housing adequacy" has always occupied a central place in all decennial Census studies: the absence or presence of complete, private plumbing facilities (Sternlieb, 1966; Tippett and Koons, 1977). Yet, while more than two-fifths of all housing units in the United States lacked some or all plumbing according to the 1940 Census, this proportion fell to 7 percent by 1970, and by 1975 was again cut in half (Bureau of the Census, 1977). The crucial point is that inadequate plumbing might have been a useful indicator of quality when it served to categorize such a large fraction of all housing units, because it almost certainly acted as a proxy for a wide range of other inadequacies in the housing bundle. (In fact there was some concern in the late 1940s that the plumbing indicators might be too inclusive, particularly for rural dwellings [Bureau of the Census, 1948].) The relative ease with which inadequate plumbing could be measured (compared with structural conditions) and its relationship to the health, safety, and welfare of the household (the factors that draw substantial consensus as components of any housing quality measure) made it all the more attractive. In later decades, however, the much greater prevalence of adequate plumbing facilities did not preclude the possibility of a host of other serious housing deficiencies. Thus, while plumbing may have once served well as a single proxy for housing quality, today it probably serves as an indicator of a more broadly based conception of quality for only the rural housing stock (Goedert and Goodman, 1977).

Decisions regarding what measures are most important to collect have similarly undergone dramatic change. As suggested earlier, this has occurred partly because housing quality is like a moving target: as housing conditions improve, Americans demand more and standards are raised (McGough, 1977). The major concern of those who prepared the second decennial Census of Housing in 1950 was to collect information on the availability of hot and cold running water and, if practicable, data on the presence or absence of kitchen sinks with drains in rural housing. The latter was suggested by the U.S. Department of Agriculture's representative on the advisory committee to the Census, who stated that ". . . kitchen sinks with drains is [*sic*] a critical factor in the determination of rural housing quality" (Bureau of the Census, 1948:4). The 1979–80 version of the Annual Housing Survey appears to have included everything except an item on kitchen sink drains; nearly 100 items on other housing characteristics and conditions were included in the interview schedule, which was designed to be administered to a household-reporter; additional data were to be collected by enumerator observation. Household-reporter items addressed a very wide range of characteristics, including whether wiring is concealed and whether there is an electric wall outlet in all rooms in the housing unit, the type of heating equipment in the housing unit, the number of times major housing systems (such as heating or plumbing) have broken down, and an array of subjective reports on neighborhood conditions and ratings of how bothersome they are. The inclusion of such a wide range of items is, in itself, an indication of the need to search for appropriate measures of housing attributes and constructs.

Indeed, there does not appear to be any single standard for physically and socially healthful housing accepted in the United States by law, by custom, or by experts (Schechter and Yentis, n.d.). Even the belief in a basic and direct relationship between housing and health, which has been the foundation for the "healthful living conditions" orientation of most housing indicators and standards, has been challenged. More complex, indirect relationships operating through social and economic factors have been proposed, suggesting the inaccuracy of solely housing-based measures of housing quality (Nicholls, Many, and Weinstein, 1974).

A good deal of analysis on the reliability, accuracy, and predictive validity of the Annual Housing Survey data is accumulating. What must be recognized, however, is that such analysis will be most illuminating only if the indicators included in the data set are accepted as reasonable measures of housing quality. But even the most sophisticated and rigorous analysis cannot answer more fundamental questions concerning the conceptual validity of these indicators.

Measurement Issues: How Accurate Are Reports of Housing Attributes?

Measurement problems would remain even if there were unanimous agreement on the concepts and attributes to be measured. The seemingly most objectively measurable attributes or observable facts involve some estimation or judgment by either respondent or interviewer. One clear example is the question on the number of rooms in the housing unit, which has been included in every decennial Census of Housing: there is enough variation in the design and layout of different units in the housing stock so that the count of rooms is not always straightforward.

This problem arises partly because directions or definitions to be used in answering questions are ambiguous. Sometimes no definitions are provided at all. An excellent example is the large number of questions included in surveys, over the years, that use the word "neighborhood." The absence of a definition in the interview schedules suggests that the researchers either did not care whether respondents used different frames of reference or assumed that everyone used the same frame of reference. Some recent work (Rodgers et al., 1975) in the Detroit metropolitan area indicates that, at least for that location, residents varied widely in the way they defined the size of "their neighborhoods." Respondents were asked to indicate which of six size categories best described their neighborhood. The categories and the distribution of responses were as follows:

1. "the 5 or 6 houses nearest to mine"   (8.0%)
2. "this immediate block"   (21.5%)
3. "2–5 blocks around here"   (21.2%)
4. "6–10 blocks around here"   (16.7%)
5. "about one square mile"   (20.7%)
6. "more than one square mile"   (11.9%)

Other studies, including the Annual Housing Survey, have provided a single definition to respondents prior to the battery of "neighborhood" questions, implicitly assuming that this frame of reference will be applied throughout the remainder of the schedule. It is questionable, however, whether an individual's divergent sense of neighborhood space can be changed so easily.

More frequently, problems arise in measuring what seems to be factual information about housing because respondents do not have the knowledge or expertise to answer questions, or cannot remember the details they are being asked to report. Although many of these characteristics are officially documented by local government departments, public utilities, or private companies, only the most well-endowed research budget could support the retrieval of this information for even a small sample of residents. A review of a large number of the Census Bureau's housing studies suggests that there is a limit to the type, amount, and detail of knowledge one can reasonably expect from a household member. These studies were undertaken to assess the accuracy of householders' responses to questions on shelter costs, utility costs, room size, house value, and age of structure. Highlights from the studies on the first three topics are illustrative of the range of relevant issues.

In the study of shelter costs, data obtained from homeowners with mortgages are compared with reports from their lenders, with the latter reports assumed to be the "true" or correct responses (Fronczek and Koons, 1976). Differences in reports on three measures of housing cost (that is, mortgage payments, taxes, and insurance) are significantly larger than those expected to result from sampling error alone, although they are smaller for monthly mortgage payments than for other payments. Fronczek and Koons speculate that a payment that is made 12 times a year, such as a mortgage payment, is probably easier to remember accurately; tax and insurance payments, however, are often embedded in the monthly mortgage bill, and homeowners may only see one or two summary statements of such payments during the year. A second study, analyzing the accuracy of real estate tax reports, suggests that respondents who pay higher tax bills are more likely to remember these payments accurately (Fronczek and Lay, 1977). The latter study shows that respondents who pay very low bills are more likely to report that they pay "nothing." Even if this reporting error largely represents an education effect, the measurement problem still remains, albeit for a subgroup of the population.

Reports of utility costs (that is, electricity and gas) from householders and their respective utility companies also indicate significant response error: homeowners are found to overstate their monthly electric bills by 43 percent and their monthly gas bills by 31 percent; for renters, the corresponding figures are 58 percent and 38 percent, respectively (Koons, 1979).

Thus, respondents find it difficult to recall specific amounts of expenditures that are low in visibility and not very substantial in amount. While response error without bias may have little significance in grouped data with relatively large intervals, the picture is less positive where precise, discrete measures of expenditures are required, such as for the analysis of microbehavior. For example, since utility costs constitute only one, relatively small component of total costs, reports of gross rents or shelter costs reported with grouped data would likely be unaffected by some response error. A much more significant problem would arise, however, if these individual component costs were disaggregated and analyzed in greater detail.

In the future, researchers might consider asking respondents to use some methods of voluntary record keeping, similar to the time and activity diaries that have been used in studies of the nonmarket economy, or the trip logs used in transportation research (Bureau of the Census, 1957). Prior to initiating new methodologies, however, it might be wise first to undertake careful analyses of the relationship between respondent characteristics and reporting errors (Benedik, 1977).

The absence of questions on the size of the respondent's dwelling and property in surveys of housing should not be attributed to oversight, but rather to difficulties in collecting such measures. Respondents cannot be expected to report attributes like square footages of their lot, house, and rooms, as every new researcher who tests such items discovers (Newman, 1981). Convincing reports of this fact have been made by Census staff who observed pretest interviews in which household respondents were asked to report the size of rooms in their housing units (Koons, 1976).[2] The observers found that respondents either had no concept of room size and therefore could not report it, or didn't know the size of their rooms, took a guess, and then changed their minds.

The 1980 Residential Energy Consumption Survey (sponsored by the U.S. Department of Energy and conducted by the Response Analysis Corporation) includes items on the square feet of living space and of the largest room in the respondent's housing unit. If the respondents do not know the answer to the first item, they can guess; if they cannot answer the latter, the interviewer can attempt to measure the room for, or with, the respondent.

It is not known whether any accuracy testing of this item is planned. Past experience would suggest that prospects are dim, but the apparent conceptual importance of a measure of actual living space argues for more testing. The Energy Survey offers one opportunity for such testing, but there is some concern that the wording of the question and the instructions to the interviewer imply that almost any answer is better than no answer at all. Other, less liberal approaches, perhaps using some mechanical devices such as telescopic tape measures, might be considered. Such devices are more precise than guesses by either observers or respondents and might be particularly useful for unevenly shaped lots and rooms.

In addition to concerns about the "art of asking questions," to which survey researchers in all subject areas must attend (the precision of the questions, their wording, the logic of the question sequence, and the like), much traditional housing research introduces an additional complexity to the process of data collection: the reliance on enumerators or observers to provide further information about housing characteristics.[3] Since enumerators are most often relied upon to report factual information about the house, property, or neighborhood, errors in these measures mean that these reports are really something less than "facts." There is substantial evidence that even under the best conditions, interenumerator reliability is low (Bureau of the Census, 1967). This conclusion is based on (1) numerous studies involving multiple enumerators rating a single dwelling (for example, Bureau of the Census, 1967; Coan, 1948; Koons, 1980); (2) comparisons of interrater reliability of "housing experts" and Census enumerators (Bureau of the Census, 1967); and, (3) interrater reliability using teams of experts (Bureau of the Census, 1967). Borderline and ambiguous cases exist for almost every variable and every unit to be observed, and the effects of the rater's background and extraneous environmental characteristics almost certainly bias results. Thus, the ratings ultimately assigned by enumerators are influenced by at least three major factors: the situation in which the rating takes place, the enumerator, and the rating instrument (including procedures, training, and so forth).

Again, ratings of "housing quality," either as a composite or as a series of distinct components, serve as a useful example of the problems that have been encountered. Early analysis of enumerator ratings indicates that in good neighborhoods enumerators apparently expect high-quality housing; when they find units below the level of the neighborhood, they apparently tend to rate less serious deficiencies as "major repairs." In contrast, many bad units in poor neighborhoods are not considered to be in need of major repair because the level of the neighborhood is so low (Bureau of the Census, 1948).

As recently as 1980, these same factors remained a primary concern in a test of a photograph-based technique conducted by the Census Bureau. This technique involved the use of a booklet of photographs depicting varying levels of quality in specific exterior characteristics of a physical structure. Enumerators were asked to compare each exterior characteristic observed in the field with the set of photographs representing different levels of "quality" for that characteristic. Enumerator instructions emphasized the importance of rating only the individual aspects of the structure being evaluated. Other aspects, such as trash in the street, the condition of neighborhood buildings, and the race or social status of the occupants, were to be ignored, as were the dollar value or rents of individual units in the structures being rated (Bureau of the Census, 1980). The instruction manual explicitly states: "You may find buildings which are in good condition in low income areas and buildings which are in poor condition in high income areas."

There also appears to be some tendency for enumerators to rate the condition of a particular structure relative to that observed at previously rated structures, rather than on the basis of the criteria set forth in the measurement instrument. On-site observers noticed that enumerators tended to compare physical characteristics across the structures that they rated rather than comparing each characteristic to its appropriate set of photographic references (D. Koons, personal communication, March, 1981).

Although the Census Bureau continues to be interested in new techniques for enumerator ratings of housing attributes, the Bureau no longer includes enumerator ratings of condition in the decennial Census of Housing. Nevertheless, most Census studies, as well as most household surveys, still rely upon enumerators for sample listings, which involve the determination of fundamental housing characteristics. These characteristics include whether a structure contains housing units; whether it is an institutional or noninstitutional residence; whether a housing unit is vacant, abandoned, fit for human habitation; and whether it is a single housing unit or a multiunit structure. The relative objectivity of these variables, supported by clear and detailed instructions, should result in minimal error. Of greater concern is the disposition of unclassifiable situations that simply cannot be anticipated. Precise descriptions of each situation along with its eventual resolution should be mandatory.

Special studies of housing stock characteristics rely on a much more intensive use of observer ratings and evaluations. The Experimental Housing Allowance Program evaluation, the Urban Homesteading Program evaluation, the evaluation of the physical condition of the public housing stock, the study of repair problems of new homes, and the study of home repair services for the elderly are all recent examples of large-scale survey studies that included housing observations by a field staff as a major component of the data collection. In contrast to the Census research cited earlier, each of these more recent studies used measurement instruments that were extremely detailed, employed individuals with considerable housing expertise, and involved lengthy and quite specific training. Whether these procedures produce stronger results remains unknown. The key question is, given the need for detailed audits of special housing characteristics and conditions that most household members simply cannot report, what feasible alternative methods are available? On the face of it, such highly detailed and specialized data collected by trained experts would appear to be less prone to measurement error, compared to the old "housing quality" ratings. But new methodological studies need to be undertaken if we are to learn whether this optimism is justified.

Notes

1. For the purposes of this chapter, "housing quality" is used generically to represent a whole family of terminology regarding housing standards, including "adequacy," "substandard," and the like.

2. The item tested was as follows (Koons, 1976):
About how wide and how long are the rooms in your house or apartment? (Measure from the center of one wall to the center of the opposite wall. Write your answers to the nearest foot. If more than 8 rooms, include the eight largest rooms. Identify each room, such as, living room, kitchen, bedroom, etc.)

Type of Room	Width (feet)	Length (feet)
1.		
. . .		
8.		

3. Traditional housing research denotes studies of the housing stock and change in the housing inventory (in contrast to quality-of-life studies, for example).

References

Aaron, H. (1972) *Shelter and Subsidies: Who Benefits from Federal Housing Policies.* Washington, D.C.: Brookings Institution.

Benedik, R. (1977) *Study of Yearly Real Estate Taxes for Single-Family Nonmortgaged Owner-Occupied Housing Units in the City of Austin, Texas: 1975-1976.* Unpublished memoradum. Washington, D.C.: Bureau of the Census.

Bureau of the Census (1948) *Measurng Housing Quality: Conclusions and ecommendations of the Interdepartmental Subcommittee on Housing Adequacy.* Washington, D.C.: Bureau of the Census.

Bureau of the Census (1957) *Intercensal Housing Surveys: Evaluation of Their Importance, Description of Concepts and Techniques Involved in Producing Reliable Results.* Washington, D.C.: Bureau of the Census.

Bureau of the Census (1967) *Measuring the Quality of Housing: An Appraisal of Census Statistics and Methods.* Working Paper No. 25. Washington, D.C.: Bureau of the Census.

Bureau of the Census (1977) *Annual Housing Survey: 1975, Part B, Indicators of Housing and Neighborhood Quality, Current Housing Reports.* Series H-150-75B. Washington, D.C.: Bureau of the Census.

Bureau of the Census (1980) *Training Instructions for the Pictorial Scale.* (Mimeographed) Washington, D.C.: Bureau of the Census.

Coan, C. (1948) *Measuring Quality of Housing in the l7th Decennial Census.* Unpublished memorandum. Washington, D.C.: Bureau of the Census.

Fronczek, P., and Koons, D. (1976) *Study of Homeowners' and Lenders' Responses for Monthly Mortgage Payments, Yearly Real Estate Taxes, and Yearly Property Insurance Payments.* (Mimeographed) Washington, D.C.: Bureau of the Census.

Fronczek, P., and Lay, C. (1977) *Preliminary Results of the Accuracy of Reports of Real Estate Taxes for Owner-Occupied Households.* Unpublished memorandum. Washington, D.C.: Bureau of the Census.

Goedert, J., and Goodman, J. (1977) *Indicators of the Quality of U.S. Housing.* Working Paper 249-2. Washington, D.C.: Urban Institute.

Koons, D. (1976) *Question on "Room Size" Included in First Content Pretest, May, 1966.* Unpublished memorandum. Washington, D.C.: Bureau of the Census.

Koons, D. (1979) *1977 Census of Oakland, California: Accuracy of Reports of Utility Costs for Occupied Households.* Unpublished memorandum. Washington, D.C.: Bureau of the Census.

Koons, D. (1980) *Analysis of the Reliability of a New Scale for Housing Quality by Schucany et al.* Unpublished memorandum. Washington, D.C.: Bureau of the Census.

McGough, D. (1977) *A Framework for Housing Policy.* Washington, D.C.: U.S. Department of Housing and Urban Development, Office of Policy Development and Research, May.

Newman, S.J. (1974) *The Residential Environment and the Desire to Move.* (Mimeographed) Ann Arbor, Mich.: Institute for Social Research.

Newman, S.J. (1981) *Residential Crowding: A Study of Definitions.* ISR Working Paper Series, No. 8028. Ann Arbor, Mich.: Institute for Social Research.

Newman, S.J., and Duncan, G. (1979) Residential problems, dissatisfaction, and mobility. *Journal of the American Planning Association* 45:154-166.

Nicholls, W., Many, F.V., and Weinstein, H. (1974) *Measures of Housing Condition Based on Administrative Records: Final Report of the San Francisco Housing Condition Study.* Berkeley: University of California (Survey Research Center), December.

Rodgers, W. (1981) Density, crowding, and satisfaction with the residential environment. *Social Indicators Research* 10:75-102

Rodgers, W., Marans, R., Nelson, S., Newman, S., and Worden, D. (1975) *The Quality of Life in the Detroit Metropolitan Area: Frequency Distributions.* Ann Arbor, Mich.: Institute for Social Research.

Schechter, H., and Yentis, D. (n.d.) *An Approach to the Measurement of Housing Quality.* (Mimeographed) Washington, D.C.: U.S. Department of Housing and Urban Development.

Sternlieb, G. (1966) *The Tenement Landlord.* New Brunswick, N.J.: Rutgers University, Urban Studies Center.

Tippett, J., and Koons, D. (1977) *Plumbing Facilities as Indicators of Housing Quality.* (Mimeographed) Washington, D.C.: Bureau of the Census, June 8.

Acknowledgments

The author would like to thank David Koons, chief, Research and Evaluation Branch, Housing Division, U.S. Bureau of the Census; and Duane McGough, director, Housing and Demographic Analysis Division, Office of Policy Development and Research, U.S. Department of Housing and Urban Development, for their generosity in sharing ideas and printed materials. Greg Duncan, Howard Schuman, and Linda Stafford of the Institute for Social Research and Jack Goodman of the Urban Institute also provided valuable suggestions for improving this chapter.

PART III

NONSAMPLING SOURCES OF VARIABILITY

Although commonly used standards of statistical inference take account of variability due to sampling, it is nonsampling factors inherent in the measurement process that sometimes account for the lion's share of the variability in survey measurements. The authors in this section demonstrate that we are still a long way from fully understanding and controlling nonsampling sources of variability.

In Chapter 7, Charles Turner reports several sets of anomalous survey findings that came to light serendipitously in the course of other investigations. These findings indicate that different survey organizations, asking the same (or almost the same) questions at the same time, can sometimes get very different results. Subsequent split-ballot experiments suggest that subtle and not-so-subtle variations in item context may account for some of these anomalies. Turner argues that such measurement problems are most likely to occur when surveys ask vague questions about topics that are remote from the everyday concerns of respondents.

Chapters 8 and 9 review specific nonsampling biases that have received a great deal of attention over the years from survey researchers and other social scientists. Philip Converse proposed in 1964 that much of what is measured in surveys consists of "nonattitudes"—answers hastily fabricated by respondents who have no real knowledge or feeling about an issue, but who try to give some sort of response to an interviewer's question. Converse's original formulation has been the subject of continuing controversy. Tom Smith reviews the literature on nonattitudes in Chapter 8, and finds that, despite a considerable amount of empirical work, it is still uncertain to what extent inconsistencies (from one interview to the next) in respondents' answers to a question reflect nonattitudes, true change, or a flawed and ambiguous survey question. He concludes that all three factors are important, and that different approaches and more powerful data analysis techniques are needed to disentangle the contribution of each.

Social desirability is another commonly acknowledged source of bias affecting survey data. The underlying notion is that respondents want to present themselves favorably, and so they answer survey questions in ways that will make them look good (or avoid making them look bad). Although this idea is pausible and there is evidence to support it, Theresa DeMaio's review of the literature on social desirability (Chapter 9) shows that much of the research in this area is flawed. Many of the problems are conceptual. One issue is whether social desirability bias should be treated as a personality tendency (due to a need for social approval, for example) or as a characteristic of survey items (reflecting the general desirability of the attitudes or behaviors in question), or as both. A second problem concerns the task of rating the desirability of traits or items. DeMaio finds that rating instructions are often vague and circular, and the items or traits to be rated are often ambiguous as well. As Smith found in the domain of nonattitudes, DeMaio finds that the research on social desirability has not yielded a clear understanding of the nature or magnitude of this source of survey bias.

The final chapter in this section examines differences over time and between survey organizations in the manner in which survey questions are asked. While question form may not seem as important as question content, there is no doubt that it does affect the answers obtained in surveys. In Chapter 10, Jean Converse and Howard Schuman document the procedural differences that have evolved between survey organizations over the last four decades. They argue that these variations in the manner of inquiry reflect not only the differing analytic styles of the organizations but also differing conceptions of the "reality" that surveys are meant to reflect.

7

Why Do Surveys Disagree? Some Preliminary Hypotheses and Some Disagreeable Examples

Charles F. Turner

Overview

This chapter reports a number of anomalies in the survey measurement of subjective phenomena. Initial examples are drawn from recent attempts to use survey measures as social indicators of phenomena such as the well-being of the population, public confidence in national institutions, and public support for science. Observed discrepancies between supposedly equivalent measures of the same phenomena indicate that survey measures of many subjective phenomena have large nonsampling variances that may contaminate both their univariate and multivariate response distributions. These nonsampling variances may confound attempts to measure population change in instances where complete survey replication is not performed. This is true because variation due to change in the population cannot be disentangled from variation due to changes in the measurement process itself.

Our present lack of systematic knowledge about the effects of factors, other than sampling, on the survey measurement of subjective phenomena often makes it difficult to predict which aspects of a survey must be replicated (and which can be ignored) to produce comparable measurements. This chapter reports results of several experiments involving systematic variations of survey contexts. While these experiments demonstrate the presence of some large effects due to experimental variations in survey context (for example, 14 percent fluctuations in the univariate response distributions), the unanticipated nature of many of these findings and the inconsistency of the results themselves testify dramatically to our inability to anticipate the impact of common variations in survey procedure.

While such problems are not rare, we nonetheless simultaneously observe many instances of apparently robust measurements of subjective phenomena. We suggest here that there may be organizing principles concerning the types of subjective measurements that are particularly vulnerable to nonsampling artifacts. A review of recent instances of replicated survey measurements provides modest but incomplete support for this approach.

The need for research on the components of measurement variability attributable to sources other than sampling is discussed. It is suggested that this research should involve coordinated methodological studies conducted across a number of survey organizations and should prompt a fundamental reconsideration of the psychological assumptions that underlie the practice of survey research.

AREA OF INQUIRY

Traditionally the term "subjective" has been used to denote those phenomena that are, in principle, directly observable only by subjects themselves. Phenomena of this sort include those commonly labeled attitudes, beliefs, and opinions. These may be conceptually distinguished from other phenomena which, although frequently measured by subjective means (that is, self-report), are theoretically amenable to objective (that is, independent) confirmation.[1]

For example, while we may measure age by asking respondents to report it, it would be theoretically possible to obtain independent evidence from other witnesses. For this reason we would not label chronological age, per se, as a subjective phenomenon. In theory, many other phenomena may also be measured independently of a subject's own report (for example, educational attainment, geographic mobility, fertility history, family structure, income, and so on). However, many important phenomena are inherently subjective and thus immune to independent verification. In particular, we have no direct knowledge of an individual's "attitudes," "beliefs," or "opinions."[2]

The present inquiry focuses upon survey measurements of such subjective phenomena.

USE OF SUBJECTIVE SOCIAL INDICATORS

Traditionally, national statistics have been the domain of demographers and economists. Inquiries made by the U.S. Bureau of the Census have generally been limited to assessments of the size and distribution of the population, and a variety of other phenomena that are, at least theoretically, amenable to independent corroboration, for example, age, income, educational attainment, and so forth.[3] This does not mean, of course, that subjectivity does not contaminate such assessments; the use of self-report inevitably raises this issue. However, the validity and reliability of survey estimates of such phenomena may be evaluated by using independent data (for instance, birth and earnings records) to estimate the magnitude and sources of error (and bias) introduced by the exclusive use of information supplied by subjects themselves. In contrast, the very concept of "true value" employed in such studies is difficult to conceptualize when one is discussing the measurement of subjective phenomena (Waksberg, 1975).

Our concern in the following pages centers upon examples of measurements that have been used in recent years as subjective social indicators. It would, however, be a gross oversimplification to distinguish between the "old objective" and the "new subjective" indicators. Some well-known measurements, such as the national unemployment index, contain fundamentally subjective elements.[4] Similarly, recent evaluations of the National Crime Surveys (Cowan, Murphy and Weiner, 1978; Gibson et al., 1978) point to the subjective components of crime victimization statistics.[5]

Nevertheless, in recent years national statistics have come to include an important and rapidly growing complement of statistics designed to measure explicitly subjective phenomena. For example, the Social Indicators program (Executive Office of the President 1973; U.S. Department of Commerce 1977; Bureau of the Census 1980) incorporates measurements of a wide range of subjective phenomena.[6] A recent volume of the *Social Indicators* series argues that such measures provide a

> . . . vitally needed supplement to traditional national statistics. The basic reason for including such subjective measures in this report despite the difficulties in their interpretation is that they offer a vital dimension in developing a comprehensive description of the condition of our society and the well being of its mem-

bers. The bulk of the information presented [in this report] relates to people's objective situation or condition—their jobs, their incomes, their health status, etc. The main purpose of the attitudinal measures is to provide some insight as to how people perceive certain aspects of these conditions. Such data are an essential source of information. . . . [U.S. Department of Commerce, 1977:XXVI]

For similar reasons, the National Science Board's recent series of reports (1973, 1975, 1977) on the state of science in the United States has incorporated a concluding chapter on public attitudes toward science and technology. Interest in this topic follows from the assumption that financial support, the imposition of legal constraints (for instance, regulation of recombinant DNA research), and the recruitment of young people into the scientific professions depend in part upon public perceptions of science.[7]

The increasing importance of measures of subjective phenomena in federal statistical programs is paralleled by a growing range of relevant research activities in the academic community. This work has included psychological studies of well-being (for example, Campbell, Converse, and Rodgers, 1976; Andrews and Withey, 1976; Bradburn, 1969; Staines and Quinn, 1979), investigations by sociologists of trends across time in sex role stereotyping and the tolerance of nonconformity (for example, Davis, 1975a; Duncan, 1979; Mason, Czajka, and Arber, 1976), and work by economists on the relationship of economic development to individual happiness (for example, Easterlin, 1974). In addition to such substantive work, considerable resources have begun to be invested in providing regularly replicated survey measurements to facilitate the study of social change (for example, the National Opinion Research Center's General Social Survey begun in 1972).[8] The wide dissemination of these rich data in the research community foreshadows the increasing use of such survey measures for scholarly research in the social sciences.[9]

COMPARABILITY OF SUBJECTIVE SOCIAL INDICATORS

Survey measurements of subjective phenomena are made by many organizations. In the United States, sources outside of the federal statistical system produced the majority of the subjective social indicator measurements reported in recent federal *Social Indicators* publications.

Use of data from a variety of sources inevitably raises questions of comparability. Despite one's hopes, comparability of measurement does not occur naturally. For example, in the natural sciences there has been a long history of concern with the difficult problem of ensuring the replicability of chemical and physical measurements. Early examples include the discovery of systematic variations in the observations of individual astronomers (see Boring, 1950). More recent work has included attempts to partition the variability in laboratory measurements in analytical chemistry into components representing the effects of different analytic procedures, measurable aspects of laboratory environments, interexperimenter differences, and differences between unmeasured attributes of laboratories that produce constant biases.

The experience in the natural sciences suggests that comparability of measurement is the result of careful standardization of research procedures, frequent calibration, and the continuous monitoring of performance. Equally clear is the fact that comparability is not easily achieved (Boffey, 1975), and thus published measurements of elemental physical constants sometimes reveal frightening discrepancies (see, for example, Hunter's [1977] plot of reported values for the thermal conductivity of copper, and data for other metals reported by Ho, Powell, and Liley [1974]). Such problems have led to the standardization of research procedures and the development of methods for collaborative tests among laboratories in such fields as analytical chemistry (Youden, 1975; Steiner, 1975). We will subsequently argue that problems of comparability in the survey measurement of subjective phenomena should prompt a consideration of parallel techniques by those interested in the development of more reliable subjective social indicators.

The Problem. The increased use of replicated time-series of subjective social indicators has spawned some disagreeable progeny. Most irritating has been the multiplication of instances in which supposedly comparable measurements have differed both substantially and significantly between surveys (see Turner and Krauss, 1978; Martin, 1983). Discrepancies of 15 percentage points have been observed between the univariate distributions of purportedly equivalent measurements of some subjective phenomena. Such large discrepancies prompt a number of questions. One would like to know, for example:

- What causes these measurements to disagree?
- Are these disagreements symptomatic of a larger problem or are they restricted to a few isolated cases?
- Are there any organizing principles which could identify indicators that are more (and less) likely to produce discrepant results?

In the following pages we review several examples drawn from current social indicators projects. We use these examples to illustrate the issues and to demonstrate the need for further research on the nonsampling components of variance in the survey measurement of subjective phenomena. We also propose some preliminary ideas concerning the types of subjective indicators that are particularly vulnerable to artifacts of measurement. We do so not in the hope of formulating final principles, but rather to provide initial hypotheses around which future research might be organized.

As a starting point, Turner and Krauss (1978:468) suggested that the vulnerability of measurement to nonsampling artifacts might be a function of the survey questions themselves and of the phenomena they intend to measure. In particular, it was hypothesized that vulnerability would be concentrated among survey questions that[10]

1. Were most amorphous in their meaning, for example, those seeking to assess "confidence," "trust," and so forth;
2. Were most ambiguous in their referents, for example, those inquiring about the "people running organized religion," and so forth;
3. Involved the most arbitrariness in the selection of a response category, for example, great deal versus some confidence; and
4. Dealt with topics that do not have a well-defined place in public discussions, for example, public evaluations of science.

While we argue in the conclusion to this chapter that these organizing principles are a reasonable place to begin, we do realize that they are at present overly general and are open to a wide range of interpretations. After considering some examples of problematic measurements, we attempt to show some ways in which these principles might be made sufficiently concrete to be tested in future research.

It should also be recognized that, when applied to most common measurements, the foregoing principles are often redundant. For example, questions about amorphous phenomena frequently and perhaps inevitably require arbitrary choices between response categories. At present we are unable to guess whether each of the foregoing characteristics of survey questions is equally important in determining a measurement's potential vulnerability to nonsampling artifacts. Indeed it is quite possible that it is the coincidence of two (or more) of these characteristics that induces vulnerability.

Readers will find no definitive answers in the following pages. The presently available evidence is too sparse and problematic to permit any confident disentanglements of the various effects. Methodological experiments will have to be embedded in future surveys to answer these questions. In the interim, we intend to illustrate the problems that are induced by the nonsampling components of the variance in survey measurements, to provide some insights into the sources of this variability, to document our considerable ignorance, to suggest the pressing need for research, to propose some avenues of inquiry, and to provide some examples of how one might proceed.

Examples

EXAMPLE I: DISAGREEMENTS ABOUT HAPPINESS

In the fall of 1977, we began an investigation of responses to national survey questions on personal "happiness." These questions have been incorporated in research attempting to define the nature of social well-being and to produce social indicators of life-satisfaction (for example, Gurin, Veroff, and Feld, 1960; Bradburn, 1969; Campbell, Converse and Rodgers, 1976). All of this work has gone beyond the notion that responses to a single question are ideal measures of subjective well-being. Nonetheless, responses to the simple question,

> Taken all together how would you say things are these days—would you say that you are very happy, pretty happy, or not too happy?

have been tracked from the year 1957.[11] And both the trends across time and differences between nations in response to this question have been analyzed by several authors (for example, Easterlin, 1974; Davis, 1975b; Campbell, Converse, and Rodgers, 1976; Andrews and Withey, 1976). Moreover, the responses to this "happiness question" have been used as a validity criterion in the development of more elaborate indices of life-satisfaction. Thus, responses to this question are of substantial importance and interest in their own right.

Figure 7.1 presents two independent series of happiness estimates derived from surveys conducted by the Survey Research Center (SRC) of the University of Michigan and the National Opinion Research Center (NORC) of the University of Chicago. It will be seen from this figure that there are not only discrepancies in estimates of absolute levels of happiness, but also that the (apparent) trends in the two series diverge. One series shows an apparent increase while the other series registers a decline in happiness.

We first noticed this "disagreeable" result in the fall of 1977, and it was the subject of preliminary discussions with an ad hoc working group which met to discuss discrepancies observed in the "confidence in institutions" series.[12] Subsequent examination of the two happiness series has caused us to doubt the validity of the comparison shown in Figure 7.1. Examination of the questionnaires used by NORC and SRC reveals a slight difference in question wording: the SRC version repeats "these days" after listing the response categories, while the NORC version does not (see caption to Figure 7.1 for exact wordings). Thus, it might be argued that the two questions were indicators of slightly different phenomena, although admittedly we might expect the trends across time to be parallel rather than divergent. On the other hand, it could be that the divergences are more apparent than

FIGURE 7.1

Trends in Self-Reported Happiness, 1971-73.

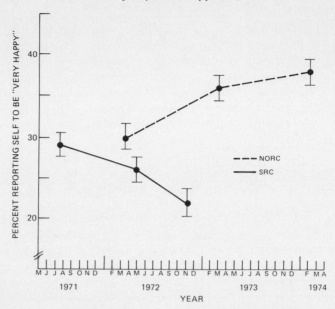

SOURCES: NORC, National Data Program for the Social Sciences: Codebook, 1972-74. SRC estimates from Campbell, Converse, and Rodgers (1976); survey dates from Campbell, Converse, and Rodgers (1976), Andrews and Withey (1976), and J. Varva (SRC, personal communication).
NOTE: Estimates are derived from sample surveys of noninstitutionalized population of the continental United States aged 18 and over. Error bars demark ±1 standard error around sample estimate.
QUESTIONS: "Taken all together, how would you say things are these days—would you say that you are very happy, pretty happy, or not too happy?" [NORC];
"Taking all things together, how would you say things are these days—would you say you're very happy, pretty happy, or not too happy these days?" [SRC]

real. For example, national happiness might have fluctuated rapidly between 1971 and 1973, and thus the data could be reliably monitoring month-to-month changes that were taking place in the national population.

While such arguments can be made, they are apologies rather than explanations. The NORC and SRC data have been treated as a unitary time-series by several authors, despite differences in wording (see, for example, Campbell, Converse, and Rodgers, 1976:26; Andrews and Withey, 1976: 319). Moreover, large month-to-month fluctuations in these indicators would preclude use of the (approximately) annual and biennial reporting schedules that have been the rule in the social indicators field.[13]

Despite their limitations, the data shown in Figure 7.1 prompted us to speculate about causes of the observed discrepancies. Our initial hypothesis followed from the fact that NORC altered its questionnaire in 1973 so that a question about marital happiness,

> Taking things all together, how would you describe your marriage? Would you say that your marriage is very happy, pretty happy, or not too happy?

immediately preceded the general-happiness question. In 1972 the general-happiness question followed questions asking about respondents' satisfaction with their financial situation and whether their financial situation had been "getting better, getting worse, or . . . stayed the same" in the last few years.

We hypothesized that insertion of this marital-happiness question created an artifactual response effect. Our initial examination of this hypothesis (see Table 7.1) indicated that:

- There was a high correlation (gamma = +0.75) between responses to the marital- and general-happiness questions;
- The marital-happiness question elicited a relatively high proportion (0.6) of "very happy" responses; and
- The increase in overall happiness between 1972 and 1973-74 in the NORC series occurred only among married persons (see Table 7.1).

This last finding[14] was particularly important because the hypothesized context effect could only have occurred for married individuals (unmarried persons could not, of course, be asked about the happiness of their marriages). On subsequent examination, we have also found that there was a

TABLE 7.1

Variation in Percentage of Married and Unmarried Respondents Reporting Themselves to Be "Very Happy" Between 1972 and 1974

| Sample | Year | | | X^2 for Temporal Change[a] | |
	1972[b]	1973	1974	1972 vs. 1973 vs. 1974[c]	1972 vs. 1973 + 1974[d]
Married	33.5%	42.7%	44.6%	22.0, $p < .001$	21.5, $p < .001$
Not married	17.9	20.0	19.6	0.4, *ns*	0.4, *ns*
Total	29.7	36.8	38.4	20.1, $p < .001$	19.6, $p < .001$

[a]Chi-square statistics were adjusted for design effects of NORC's clustered sample design by using a deflated sample size ($N' = 0.66N$) in computations. (Analysis of the intracluster correlations [median 1973-78 $r_i = 0.02$] for the happiness item indicates that this correction is not an unreasonable allowance.) This deflation in sample size makes it less likely for our tests to find significant differences between the results obtained by different surveys.
[b]1972 NORC General Social Survey did not include question on marital happiness.
[c]d.f. = 2.
[d]d.f. = 1.

significant alteration after 1972 in the association between responses to the general-happiness and financial-status questions. In later years, from 10 to 44 questions were interspersed between these items.[15]

While any comparison of the NORC and SRC happiness series admits to a plethora of alternative explanations (for example, wording effects, "house" effects, short-term temporal variations, and so on), the results of our initial explorations encouraged us to seek a better test for our hypothesis. We were fortunate to discover that a wealth of information on happiness was collected during this period. Between April 1973 and May 1974, NORC, with the support of the National Science Foundation (RANN division), conducted a series of pilot surveys to provide continuous monitoring of public opinion for policy makers in eight federal agencies. At intervals of approximately one month, NORC drew samples of the national population for interview. While the content of the surveys varied from month to month, the happiness item was included in every cycle of NORC's Continuous National Survey.

These data allow us to compare responses across time for two identically worded questions in surveys conducted by the same research organization. This comparison provides a control for both wording differences and any possible organizational idiosyncracies (for instance, variations in interviewer training). We obtained a copy of these data during February 1978 and set to work examining the plausibility of our context hypothesis for the misbehavior of the happiness time-series.

A graphic summary of our findings is presented in Figure 7.2. Specifically, we found that for unmarried individuals, yearly estimates derived from the NORC General Social Survey (GSS) and the monthly estimates from the NORC Continuous National Survey (CNS) were in general agreement. This is not to say that the estimates were identical. However, observed discrepancies were within the range expected on the basis of sampling error. In short, unmarried men and women responded to the happiness question in the same manner in the 1972, 1973, and 1974 General Social Surveys and the 12 cycles of the Continuous National Survey.

For the married respondents, a rather different result emerged. In particular, while the GSS happiness estimates exhibit a sharp rise between 1972 and 1973–74 (change = + 10 percentage points; Pearson χ^2 = 21.5, d.f. = 1, $p < .0001$), the monthly estimates derived from the Continuous National Survey evidence no similar trend. Moreover, the CNS happiness estimates are consistently below those of the GSS. Indeed, as Figure 7.2 shows, the GSS measurement in 1972 (when the marriage question was not included) provided a better prediction of the CNS estimates in 1973 and 1974 than did the actual GSS estimates in those years.

Although other hypotheses might be supported, we concluded that

FIGURE 7.2

Variations in Response to NORC "Happiness" Question for Married and Unmarried Respondents in the General Social Surveys (GSS) and Continuous National Surveys (CNS).

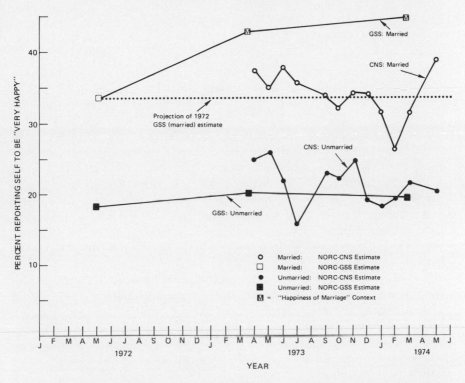

NOTE: Estimates are derived from samples of approximately 1,000 (GSS) and 440 (CNS) married respondents and 500 (GSS) and 220 (CNS) unmarried respondents.

1. The internal evidence of a temporal trend only for married GSS respondents; and,
2. The predictability of the 1973–74 CNS data from 1972 GSS data provide strong support for the hypothesis that a response effect arose from the insertion of the marital-happiness question into the 1973 and 1974 General Social Surveys.

Experimental Evidence. It was subsequently possible to test our conclusions experimentally. Four experiments using the happiness questions were conducted by the *Washington Post* poll, the General Social Survey of the National Opinion Research Center, the Survey Research Center, and the Opinion Research Corporation of Princeton, New Jersey. Each of these experiments manipulated the context in which the general-happiness question was asked.

The first three experiments (conducted by NORC, SRC, and the *Washington Post* poll) were similar in design. In one experimental condition in each of these experiments, the immediate context in which the general-happiness item was asked was "controlled" by asking it immediately after the question on marital happiness. In the other experimental condition, the context in which the general-happiness question was asked was uncontrolled; that is, it occurred after whatever other questions (varying from experiment to experiment) were contained in the questionnaire. So, for example, in the *Washington Post* survey, the general-happiness question followed a question on income in the uncontrolled context; in the SRC experiment, it followed a series of items on the gas shortage; and in the NORC experiment, it followed a series of five questions in which respondents were asked "how much satisfaction" they received from their cities or places of residence, hobbies, family life, friendships, health and physical condition.[16]

A parallel variation occurred serendipitously for the marital-happiness item in these experiments. In one experimental condition, it too followed these varying items, and in the other condition, it followed a fixed item: the general-happiness question.

As before, all samples were restricted to married respondents. Samples were drawn from the adult (aged 18 and over) population of the continental United States. The SRC and *Washington Post* experiments were done in telephone surveys using random-digit dialing to sample phone numbers. The NORC surveys were conducted as face-to-face interviews using a multistage area probability sample (see National Opinion Research Center [1980] for description of sample design).[17]

Figure 7.3 shows the proportion of respondents who said they were "very happy" in response to the marital- and general-happiness items for the controlled and uncontrolled contexts in each of the three experiments. Two important conclusions are evident to the eye in these plots:

1. When the survey context was controlled, all organizations obtained similar estimates of the proportion that was "very happy" for both the general-happiness and marital-happiness measurements.

2. However, when the measurement context was left uncontrolled, the general-happiness measurement showed considerable volatility, while the more specific question on marital happiness appeared to be unaffected.

More formally, we note that we can fit a model (see Table 7.2) to the data from the marital-happiness measurements which fits only the univariate response distribution for the marital-happiness measurement; the observed

FIGURE 7.3

Percentage of Respondents Saying that They Were "Very Happy" in Response to Questions on General Happiness and Marital Happiness.

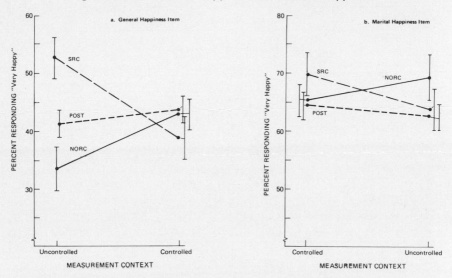

SOURCES: Data are from surveys conducted by the Survey Research Center, University of Michigan (SRC), the National Opinion Research Center (NORC), and by the George Fine Organization for the *Washington Post*. All samples were restricted to married respondents who had a telephone in their residence. See text for description of measurement contexts.

NOTE: Error bars demark ± 1 standard error for estimates.

variations across different measurement conditions and between different survey organizations are all within the range of sampling error (Likelihood-ratio chi-square: $L^2 = 10.8$, d.f. $= 10$, $p = .37$). In contrast, the general-happiness measurements show considerable variability in the uncontrolled context (the proportion saying "very happy" varies from 0.335 to 0.527), and require us to fit a three-way interaction term (Survey House by Context by Response) in order to obtain an adequate fit to the data obtained in this experiment.

We note that these results fit quite well the pattern originally hypothesized (the *general* question produced more labile measurements than the more *specific* item). It is also important to note that it would have been hard to predict in advance (and it is hard to understand after the fact) the direction and magnitude of the variations shown by the general-happiness measurement in the uncontrolled context. Thus, it is hard to intuit why SRC's measurements (which were made after respondents had been asked questions about the 1978–79 gas shortages) should produce an estimate of the proportion "very happy" that was so much higher than that of the *Washington Post* poll or the NORC experiment.[18] We do nonetheless note

TABLE 7.2
Test of Alternative Models for Behavior of Happiness Measurements

Model	Marginals Fit	d.f.	L^2	p
General-Happiness Measurements				
1. Stable measurements	{H} {CS}	10	28.0	.002
2. Context effect	{HC} {CS}	8	27.7	.001
3. Survey effect	{HS} {CS}	6	20.8	.002
4. Context and survey effects	{HS} {HC} {CS}	4	20.0	.001
5. Interaction effect	{HSC}	0	0.0	(n.a.)
Marital-Happiness Measurements				
1. Stable measurements	{H} {CS}	10	10.8	.37
2. Context effect	{HC} {CS}	8	10.7	.21
3. Survey effect	{HS} {CS}	6	5.9	.44
4. Context and survey effects	{HS} {HC} {CS}	4	5.5	.24
5. Interaction effect	{HSC}	0	0.0	(n.a.)

NOTE: Models were fit using procedures developed by Goodman (1971). L^2 values are likelihood-ratio chi-square statistics. Variables included in this analysis are
H = response to happiness question (three categories: very happy; pretty happy; not too happy). Respondents who did not answer this question (1 percent or less) were excluded from sample.
S = survey (three categories: NORC; SRC; *Washington Post*).
C = measurement context (two categories: controlled context; uncontrolled context).
n.a. = not applicable.

that since the three organizations' measurements agree in the controlled context, we can effectively rule out general organizational differences (so-called "house effects") in sampling, processing, and so forth, as an explanation for these discrepancies.

Reconciliation. While the first three experiments demonstrated the lability of general-happiness measurements, it remained to be demonstrated that any of the discrepancies that prompted our initial concerns could be accounted for by our hypothesis. This demonstration was achieved in a fourth experiment conducted for our panel in November 1980 by the Opinion Research Corporation. In this experiment, we made general-happiness measurements in contexts that replicated the low and high NORC General Social Survey measurements (see Figure 7.1).

In the negative (low) context, the general-happiness question followed three questions inquiring about the respondent's financial situation. These three questions were used in the 1973 NORC–GSS, and we had hypothesized that this context "depressed" respondents estimates of their happiness. The questions were:

We are interested in how people are getting along financially these days. So far as you and your family are concerned, would you say that you are pretty well satisfied with your present financial situation, more or less satisfied, or not at all satisfied?

During the last few years, has your financial situation been getting better, getting worse, or has it stayed the same?

Compared with American families in general, would you say your family income is—far below average, below average, average, above average, or far above average?

(As previously mentioned [see note 15], we were led to consider the financial-happiness questions as a likely contributor to the anomalies in the NORC-GSS series because the bivariate associations between responses to the financial questions and the general-happiness items showed a significant variation between 1972 and subsequent years.) In the positive ("high") context, the general-happiness question followed the marital-happiness item.

FIGURE 7.4

Proportion of Respondents Saying They Were "Very Happy" in Response to the General-Happiness Question in Different Measurement Contexts.

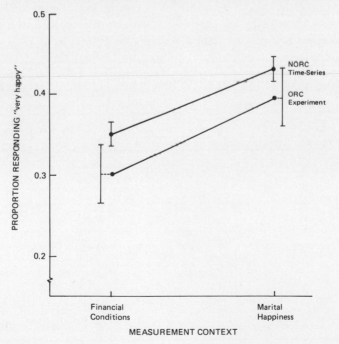

NOTE: Respondents are samples of married persons; error bars demark approximately ±1 standard error around the estimates.

These two sequences replicate those used in the 1972 and 1973 NORC measurements. We hypothesized that this context variation, when experimentally induced in the 1980 experiment, would produce results that would mimic the apparent change evidenced by the NORC–GSS series between 1972 and 1973.[19]

Figure 7.4 and Table 7.3 present the relevant results. It will be seen that (for married persons) 30 percent of respondents said they were "very happy" in the negative context, and 39 percent said so in the positive context. These results are similar in direction and magnitude to those observed in the NORC-GSS time-series. When we fit formal models to the experimental and actual data (see Table 7.4), we find that a model that posits only a unitary effect of measurement context is required to account for both the experimental data and the actual data. Our hypothesis that the measurement context, and not true change, accounts for the behavior of the NORC-GSS series was thus confirmed experimentally.

Conclusion. What do we learn from this example? Recalling the general hypotheses outlined in the overview section, we observe that:

1. The concept of "happiness" is notably amorphous.
2. The happiness question involved considerable arbitrariness in the choice of a response category, for example, what is the difference between being "very happy" versus "pretty happy"?
3. The question may be one to which individuals do not give considerable thought—at least as formulated in this item (that is, Am I happy?).

TABLE 7.3

Comparison of Results of ORC Experiment and 1972–73 NORC Measurements

Survey	Context	Response to General-Happiness Question				
		Very Happy	Pretty Happy	Not too Happy	Total	
ORC experiment, 1980	Marital	39%	51%	11%	100%	(358)
	Financial	30	52	18	100	(393)
NORC time-series, 1972–73	Marital	43	48	9	100	(1,073)
	Financial	35	52	14	100	(1,156)

NOTE: Includes only married respondents; "don't know"/"no answer" responses excluded. Numbers may not total 100 percent due to rounding.

TABLE 7.4

Fit of Alternative Models

Model	Marginals Constrained[a]	L^2	d.f.	p
1. No effects	{CS} {H}	39.9	6	.0005
2. House-year effect only	{CS} {HS}	31.5	4	.0002
3. Context effect only	{CS} {HC}	8.6	4	.07
4. Context and house-year effects	{CS} {HC} {HS}	0.4	2	> .5
5. Interaction effects	{CSH}	0.0	0	—

NOTE: Models were fit using procedures developed by Goodman (1971). L^2 values are likelihood ratio chi-square statistics.

[a]Variables included in this analysis are:

- H: Response to happiness question (three categories: very happy; pretty happy; not too happy). Respondents who did not answer this question were excluded from sample.
- S: Survey (two categories: NORC-General Social Surveys: 1972, 1973; ORC survey experiment, 1980. Note that Survey house is inextricably confounded with time, i.e., NORC = 1972–73 while ORC = 1980.
- C: Measurement Context (two categories: (1) financial conditions context; (2) marital happiness context.)

(We might add that happiness is not a state that is likely to be crystallized by public discussion.)

EXAMPLE II: DISAGREEMENTS ABOUT SCIENCE

Our next two examples (II and III) involve the measurement of public attitudes toward science and technology. These measurements were made in surveys commissioned by the National Science Board and conducted by the Opinion Research Corporation (ORC). The results of these surveys have been incorporated in the volumes *Science Indicators: 1972*, *Science Indicators: 1974*, and *Science Indicators: 1976*, published by the National Science Foundation.

Nonexperimental Evidence. Our interest in these surveys was first aroused by an observation[20] made during the analysis of the 1976 survey. In brief, the 1976 survey contained an anomaly that had potentially destructive implications for national science policy. It is thus a most appropriate illustration of the dangers inherent in our inadequate understanding of the error structure of the data employed as subjective social indicators.

The anomaly in the 1976 survey arose from an attempt to explore the meaning of public response to the following question about government spending for science:

Science and Technology can be directed toward solving problems in many different areas. In which of the areas listed on this card would you *most* like to have your taxes spent for science and technology? Please read me the numbers. [*Card*: 1. Reducing and controlling pollution; 2. Finding better birth control methods; 3. Weather control and prediction; 4. Space Exploration; 5. Improving health care; 6. Developing/Improving weapons for national defense; 7. Developing faster and safer public transportation for travel within and between cities; 8. Discovering new basic knowledge about man and nature; 9. Reducing crime; 10. Improving the safety of automobiles; 11. Finding new methods for preventing and treating drug addiction; 12. Improving education; 13. Developing/Improving methods of producing food.]

Please tell me the areas you would *least* like to have your taxes spent for science and technology. Again, please read me the numbers.

Data from the 1972 and 1974 Science Indicators surveys revealed that the public appeared to give relatively strong endorsement to funding science in order to reduce crime (59 percent in 1972 and 58 percent in 1974), to fight drug addiction (51 percent and 48 percent), and to improve education (41 percent and 48 percent), and relatively weak support to science spending for such purposes as the development of faster and safer mass transportation (23 percent and 26 percent), and discovering new basic knowledge (19 percent and 21 percent).

This ordering of public priorities contradicts many scientists' notions of where research could be useful, and it prompted an explicit study of this matter. In 1976 the Science Indicators survey added a question asking in what areas science and technology could (1) make a major contribution, and in what areas it could (2) make little or no contribution.[21] The same list of problem areas was used; these questions immediately preceded the questions on spending.

Surprisingly, neither an analysis of the relationship between the perceived usefulness of science and public endorsement of spending, nor the spending time-series appears in the 1976 report of the National Science Board. Instead, a footnote (National Science Board, 1977:180) observes that alterations in the content of the questions preceding the spending question precluded a valid comparison of the 1976 estimates to those obtained in previous years. Upon reviewing these estimates, the authors' reticence becomes very understandable. (See Figure 7.5 for plots of the more dramatic results.)

Table 7.5 presents all estimates derived from responses to the spending question in 1972, 1974, and 1976. These estimates show consistent and apparently precipitous declines in public support of spending for science and technology. In four instances, the declines (1972–76) exceeded 20 percentage points.

This "evidence" of a massive drop in public support is, however, incon-

FIGURE 7.5

Endorsement of Spending for Science and Technology in Four Areas.

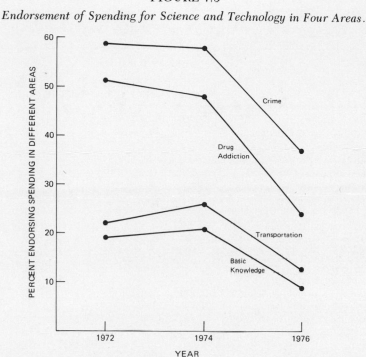

SOURCE: Science Indicators surveys, 1972-76. Sample size in each year was approximately 2,100.

sistent with other independent measurements. The NORC General Social Survey has included an item on spending since 1973. The NORC series shows virtually constant levels of public support for spending in related areas between 1973 and 1976 (see Table 7.6).

Because of the changes in the content of the survey questionnaire (and, perhaps, fearing the impact of such data), the National Science Board chose *not* to plot the time-series showing the declines in their measurements of public support for science spending. Instead, they argued that

> . . . the same [spending] question was used in the 1972 and 1974 surveys, but since it was not preceded in those years by the question about the capabilities of science and technology, the results are not strictly comparable to the 1976 results. [National Science Board, 1977:180]

Our own analysis of the NORC time-series indirectly supports this argument. However, this position contradicts the prevailing wisdom among survey researchers. In their comprehensive review of past methodological research on survey measurement, Sudman and Bradburn (1974:33) concluded

TABLE 7.5

Endorsement of Spending for Science and Technology as Estimated by Science Indicator Surveys in 1972, 1974, and 1976

Area	Percentage Endorsing Spending			Change	
	1972	1974	1976	1972–76	1974–76
Improving health care	65%	69%	57%	− 8	− 12
Reducing and controlling pollution	60	50	33	− 27	− 17
Reducing crime	59	58	37	− 22	− 21
Finding new methods for preventing and treating drug addiction	51	48	24	− 27	− 24
Improving education	41	48	33	− 8	− 15
Improving the safety of automobiles	38	29	15	− 23	− 14
Developing faster and safer public transportation for travel within and between cities	23	26	13	− 10	− 13
Finding better birth control methods	20	18	10	− 10	− 8
Discovering new basic knowledge about man and nature	19	21	9	− 10	− 12
Weather control and prediction	11	14	5	− 6	− 9
Space exploration	11	11	7	− 4	− 4
Developing or improving weapons for national defense	11	11	10	− 1	− 1
Average endorsement	34	34	21	− 13	− 13

NOTE: Estimates are for percentage selecting areas as ones in which they would most like to have taxes spent. See text for question wording.

that the available evidence (albeit evidence that was weak and fragmentary) indicated that

> . . . [the] position of a question [in the survey questionnaire] has by itself little biasing effect for behavioral items and a negligible effect for attitudinal items . . . [and] there do not appear to be any sizeable response effects associated with the placement of questions after related questions.

In the absence of experimental evidence upon the specific context effects postulated by the Board, it is difficult to assess the validity of these conflicting views.

Experimental Evidence. While we cannot directly test the claim made by the board, we have studied other evidence on context effects in the 1976 survey. This evidence arises because the Science Indicators surveys were amalgams consisting of several questionnaire sections sponsored by different organizations. The survey questions for the National Science Board's

TABLE 7.6

Evaluation of Government Spending Programs as Estimated by NORC General Social Surveys 1973–76

| Area | Percentage Saying Spending "About Right" or "Too Little" | | | Change | |
	1973	1974	1976	1973–76	1974–76
Improving and protecting the nation's health	95%	95%	95%	0	0
Improving and protecting the environment	92	92	90	− 2	− 2
Halting the rising crime rate	95	95	92	− 3	− 3
Dealing with drug addiction	94	93	92	− 2	− 1
Improving the nation's education system	91	91	90	− 1	− 1
Space exploration program	39	37	38	− 1	+ 1
The military, armaments, and defense	60	67	71	+11	+ 4
Average	81	81	81	0	0

NOTE: This question was not asked in the 1972 General Social Survey. Estimates are repercentaged to exclude "don't know" responses and no answers. Sample sizes in each year were approximately 1,500.
Question Wording: We are faced with many problems in this country, none of which can be solved easily or inexpensively. I'm going to name some of these problems, and for each one I'd like you to tell me whether you think we're spending too much money on it, too little money, or about the right amount. First _____ are we spending too much, too little, or about the right amount on _____?

1976 report were asked along with a melange of questions on hospitalization and medical expenditures, frequency of eating hamburgers, and the litter problem. As a partial control for context effects in these surveys, ORC administered two different versions of the survey; the order of questionnaire sections was rotated in the different versions. Also, for some multipart questions, the sequence of individual parts of a question was varied. Each version of the questionnaire was administered to (approximately) one-half of the sample.[22]

In both versions, the first item in the Science Indicators section asked respondents to assess the "prestige" or "general standing" of various occupations including "scientist" and "engineer." For the *Science Indicators* report, this question was of interest both because it was thought to be a surrogate measure of public attitudes toward science, and also because public perceptions of the prestige of scientific occupations influence the recruitment of talented young people into these professions.

For social scientists, the responses to such questions are important because they provide the basis for the well-known scalings of the socioeconomic status and occupational prestige (Duncan, 1961; Hall and Jones, 1950; Treiman, 1977). These scales have been central to much recent work on social and occupational stratification (for example, Blau and Duncan, 1967; Sewell and Hauser, 1975). It is thus of considerable interest to determine whether response to this question was affected by the context variation built into the Science Indicators survey. The survey question itself read:

> I am now going to read you a list of jobs and professions. For each one I mention, please choose the statement that best gives your own personal opinion of the prestige or general standing that such a job has.

The respondent was then shown a card containing the following responses: excellent, good, average, below average, and poor, and ratings were solicited for 10 occupations (see Table 7.7).

The variation in the context and administration of the "prestige" question was twofold. First, the list of occupations used in Form A was reversed in Form B (see Table 7.7). Second, the placement of this question in the survey varied. In Form A, this question was the very first question in the survey. The interviewer began:

> [STANDARD INTRODUCTION] Hello (Respondent's name), I am (interviewer's name) conducting a study for the Caravan Surveys of Opinion Research Corporation of Princeton, New Jersey. In this interview we would like to ask your opinion on a number of different subjects.

The interviewer then read the introduction to the National Science Board's questions:

> I am now going to ask you a group of questions that come from the National Science Foundation, which is a federal agency. They are preparing a report that will discuss public attitudes toward science and technology. Your participation in this survey will be very helpful to them, but it is entirely voluntary. No records will be kept that will allow your individual reply to be associated with you.

The item on the social standing of occupations immediately followed. In Form B, the survey began with the same standard introduction, but then asked a series of 38 questions[23] on litter,[24] hamburger makers,[25] and hospitalization and medical insurance.[26] After asking these questions, the interviewer read the NSF introduction and then asked the occupational-prestige question.

We did not anticipate finding a significant divergence in the results obtained from these two forms. Our findings, however, were striking. The relevant comparisons are presented in Table 7.7. For 8 of 10 occupations,

TABLE 7.7

*Variations Between Survey Forms in Percentage of Respondents
Rating Occupation's Prestige as "Excellent"
(rank orderings in parentheses)*

	Percentage "Excellent"				
Occupation	Form A	Form B	Discrepancy	X^2	p^a
1. Businessman	13.4% (10)	13.4% (10)	0.0	0.0	ns
2. Physician	47.6 (1)	56.4 (1)	− 8.8	17 8	.005
3. Scientist	46.8 (2)	49.5 (2)	− 2.7	8.4	ns
4. Congressman[b]	16.1 (9)	30.4 (7)	− 14.3	54.1	.0001
5. Lawyer	24.0 (6)	38.7 (3)	− 14.7	41.9	.0001
6. Architect	24.6 (5)	37.5 (5)	− 12.9	29.9	.0001
7. Minister	39.0 (3)	38.3 (4)	+ 0.7	9.3	ns
8. Engineer	25.5 (4)	34.0 (6)	− 8.5	18.9	.002
9. Banker	18.9 (7)	27.7 (8)	− 8.8	26.7	.0001
10. Accountant[c]	17.3 (8)	25.0 (9)	− 7.7	28.9	.0001

NOTES: Listing of occupations is in order used in Form A; the reverse order was used in Form B. Wording of occupational titles in table is identical to that used in questionnaire, except where noted otherwise.

Chi-square tests were performed across the entire response distribution (i.e., "excellent," "good," "average," "below average," "poor," and "no opinion" response); the degrees of freedom for the tests were 5. To conserve space only, the distributions for the response category "excellent" are shown; this category accounted for a majority of the variability across forms.

[a]Computed on assumption that sampling efficiency of clustered example was 66 percent that of equivalent simple random sample. See text note 22 for further discussion.
[b]Survey text: "U.S. Representative in Congress."
[c]Survey text: "Accountant for a large business."

prestige ratings are lower when the question is asked in the questionnaire's Form A. For 7 of the 10 occupations, this difference is 5 or more percentage points, and in 4 cases, it exceeds 10 percentage points. The sole exceptions to this general pattern occur for "Businessmen" and "Ministers"; there, the discrepancies are of trivial magnitude (0.0 percent and +0.7 percent).

Clearly, responses to this question were not identical in the two forms of the survey. Why this happened is unclear. One might speculate that survey respondents have an initial set against the use of extreme response categories (for example, excellent). This bias may diminish with practice in responding to survey questions. There is, however, some experimental evidence suggesting a modest trend in the opposite direction (Kraut, Wolfson, and Rothenberg, 1975). Alternatively, one might speculate that sequencing banal questions about beverage containers, litter, and hamburger makers immediately before questions about acute medical problems and experience with doctors and hospitals created a pro-science and pro-professional evaluation bias. The latter speculation may be plausible, especially since respondents were told that they were being asked to evaluate these professional occupations for "the National Science Foundation, which is a federal agency . . . [which is] preparing a report on public attitudes toward science and technology."

One could, of course, speculate endlessly about the causes of the observed anomaly. It is not our intention to interpret this context artifact; indeed, an interpretation would not be possible given the data at hand. Rather, we wish to know what these results tell us about our initial hypotheses. In this regard, we observe that:

1. The "prestige or general standing" of an occupation may not be a well-defined concept (particularly if the range of evaluated occupations is narrowly restricted, as in the present case).
2. The question requires an arbitrary choice between response categories (excellent vs. good vs. average vs. below average vs. poor).
3. The referents are imprecise, for example, does the "job" of businessman refer to the local grocer or the president of General Motors.
4. The *formal* rating task is one to which respondents probably give little thought in their everyday lives (although there is good reason to believe that informal ratings of jobs and occupations may be a constant and consequential part of the everyday life of most employed people).

On first impression, the foregoing results appear to be in conflict with the results of recent attempts to analyze and integrate occupational prestige data from surveys using disparate measurement methods (see, for example, Treiman's [1977] synthesis of measurements from 60 nations). On closer analysis, however, there is no inherent contradiction. Typically, attempts to integrate results from dissimilar studies of occupational prestige have relied upon the interstudy correlations as indices of agreement between the measurements. Since the prestige scales do not have substantively meaningful zero points, a general elevation or depression of scores in one study is not of concern, and it does not, in turn, affect the correlation coefficients.

If we, too, ignore the marginals and concentrate on the rankings of this restricted range of occupations, we also obtain a tolerable level of correlation between the two questionnaire forms (Spearman's rank correlation $\rho = +0.88$). Thus, the artifact in the present measurements could be finessed by avoiding undue concentration on the univariate response distributions. Unfortunately, it is the marginal distributions that have usually been reported in the *Science Indicators* publications.

EXAMPLE III: DISAGREEMENTS ABOUT PATTERNS OF ASSOCIATION

Our next examples concern a different sort of disagreement. In the preceding sections of this chapter, we have been concerned with whether or not the univariate response distributions obtained from different surveys were comparable, for example, did two surveys provide consistent estimates of the level of public support for spending on science and technology. In the present section, we are concerned with whether patterns of association between variables measured in different surveys can vary systematically. We wish to know whether we would come to the same conclusion about the association between education, for example, and a given attitude—regardless of the survey contexts in which the measurements were made.

In this area, the prevailing wisdom is that even with major wording changes, (not to mention context) the multivariate distribution of variables will generally be undisturbed, even though the marginal (univariate) distributions can vary substantially. As one recent review noted:

> The solution to this problem [of fluctuations in univariate distributions arising from changes in wording] advocated by . . . experienced survey investigators is to ignore single variable attitudinal results and concentrate on relationships. The assumption seems to be that single variable distributions vary for reasons that are artifactual, frivolous, or even quite meaningless, but that the ordering of respondents on items—and therefore associations among items—are largely immune to this problem. [Schuman and Duncan, 1974:234]

This point of view has recently been questioned, and some investigators have argued for caution in making the assumption that multivariate patterns of responses will be unaffected (see, for example, Schuman, 1974; Schuman and Duncan, 1974; Schuman and Presser, 1977; Duncan and Schuman, 1980.)

Some further information on this question can be gleaned from analysis of the *Science Indicators* data on occupations. In Figure 7.6 we plot responses to four items from the occupational prestige question by the educational level of the respondents. It will be seen from these results that the context effects observed in Table 7.7 are most pronounced for the highly educated. This, in turn, causes the bivariate patterns of association between respondents' educational level and their occupational ratings to vary systematically between Form A and Form B. Using ordinal measures of association, we observe modest (median gamma = 0.16) and generally significant positive correlations in Form A between educational level and the likelihood of

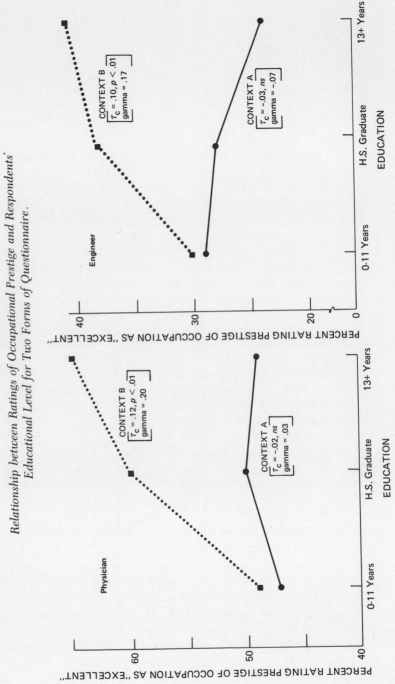

FIGURE 7.6

Relationship between Ratings of Occupational Prestige and Respondents' Educational Level for Two Forms of Questionnaire.

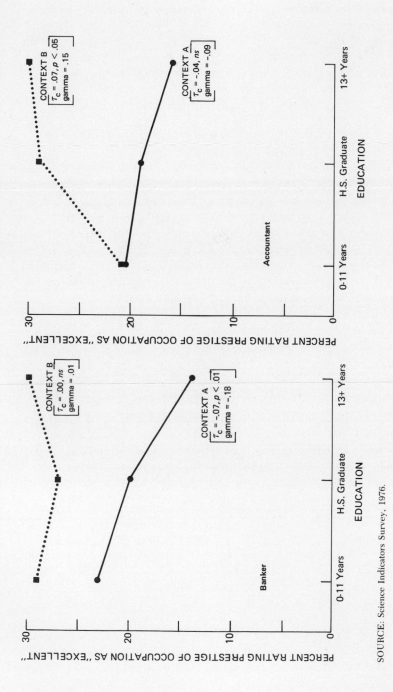

SOURCE: Science Indicators Survey, 1976.

rating the prestige of these occupations as "excellent." In contrast, the four correlations between prestige ratings and education are modestly negative in Form B of the questionnaire; in one instance (banker) this association is significantly negative (gamma = -0.18).[27] Thus, the conclusions one would reach about the relationship of respondents' education and their evaluation of occupations depend upon the survey context in which the questions were asked. Clearly, for these data the assumption that measurement artifacts are restricted to the univariate response distributions is unwarranted.

EXAMPLE IV: INCOMPLETE EXPLANATIONS: CONTEXT EFFECTS IN THE MEASUREMENT OF PUBLIC CONFIDENCE

In an earlier paper (Turner and Krauss, 1978), large and persistent discrepancies between Harris and NORC time-series on public confidence in the leaders of national institutions were analyzed. In that analysis, a variety of explanations for the discrepancies were investigated and discarded. These explanations included sampling variability, nonrepresentativeness of samples, the untoward effects of quota sampling, and temporal variation in public attitudes. It was concluded that the discrepancies between the Harris and NORC series, in their estimates of the level of and trends across time in public confidence, arose from the effects of large nonsampling errors in those series.

It was speculated that such nonsampling errors might arise, in part, because the questions used to measure public confidence were embedded in rather different survey contexts. These contexts varied both across survey organizations and within organizations across time. Particular attention was drawn to two instances of such contextual variation:

1. In 1976 the Harris questions on public confidence followed a series of negatively worded questions designed to measure political alienation.
2. The order in which particular institutions appeared in the confidence question varied, and in some years particular institutions were presented along with partial repetitions of the question.

It was hypothesized, in particular, that variations in use of the "alienation context" depressed the general level of confidence found by Harris in 1976, and that variations in use of a "people running" prefix accounted for the erratic behavior of NORC's estimates of confidence in organized religion. The latter effect was thought to occur because in some NORC surveys people responded to the prompt "How about the people running organized religion?" while in other surveys they were merely prompted with "organized religion."

To provide some experimental evidence upon the first hypothesis, NORC incorporated an experimental manipulation of survey context in the 1978 General Social Survey. Six "alienation" items were presented either immediately before or immediately after the confidence question. These items read:

> Now I want to read you some things some people have told us they have felt from time to time. Do you tend to feel or not . . .
> (1) The people running the country don't really care what happens to you.
> (2) The rich get richer and the poor get poorer.
> (3) What you think doesn't count much anymore.
> (4) You're left out of things going on around you.
> (5) Most people try to take advantage of people like yourself.
> (6) The people in Washington, D.C. are out of touch with the rest of the country.

It was hypothesized that exposure to these negatively worded alienation items would depress respondents' tendency to report a "great deal" of confidence in the leaders of the various institutions. The effects of this experimental manipulation are shown in Table 7.8.

What can one conclude from these results? Certain things seem clear. First, there is evidence that this variation in context *did* produce some significant variations in estimates of the proportion of the population having "a great deal" of confidence. In particular, for the institution that immediately followed the alienation items (major companies), the difference between contexts is − 7.4 percentage points. Smaller but still reliable differences were also found for two other institutions (Press: + 4.8 percent; and Scientific Community: − 5.2 percent). Curiously, while the alienation items generally reduced the frequency of the "great deal of confidence" response, a reverse effect was found for the press. When measured after a series of items focusing upon political alienation, measurements of confidence in the press rose.

A second conclusion we would draw from these results is that context, of the sort manipulated in this experiment, could provide only a partial explanation for the discrepancies observed between the 1976 Harris and NORC estimates. In that year, discrepancies of up to 16 percentage points were observed. In no instance did the experimental manipulation produce discrepancies of this magnitude. (We should note, however, that the NORC experimental manipulation did not fully duplicate the alienation context of the 1976 Harris survey;[28] this does introduce some uncertainty into comparisons of these experimental results to the actual survey measurements made in 1976.)

Patterns of Association. Preliminary examination of these data also revealed that the context manipulation had some significant effects upon the pattern of association between confidence and other variables. Using the three confidence items that showed significant shifts in their univariate dis-

TABLE 7.8

Effects of Experimental Manipulation of Question Context upon the Likelihood Respondents Would Express a "Great Deal of Confidence"

Institution[a]	Proportion Expressing a "Great Deal of Confidence"		Difference	X^2	p
	Neutral Context	Alienation Context			
Major companies	.264	.190	−.074	11.1	.0008
Organized religion	.329	.309	−.020	0.6	ns
Education	.294	.284	−.010	0.1	ns
Executive branch of the federal government	.126	.133	+.007	0.1	ns
Organized labor	.114	.117	+.003	0.0	ns
Press	.180	.228	+.048	5.0	.025
Medicine	.472	.456	−.016	0.3	ns
TV	.141	.139	−.002	0.0	ns
U.S. Supreme Court	.303	.285	−.015	0.5	ns
Scientific community	.421	.369	−.052	3.8	.05
Congress	.130	.136	+.006	0.1	ns
Military	.314	.299	−.015	0.3	ns
Banks and financial institutions	.351	.317	−.034	1.8	.18

NOTES: This analysis focuses attention upon the "great deal of confidence" category in accord with common reporting practices (e.g., *The Harris Survey*, Dec. 6, 1973; Sept. 30, 1974; Oct. 6, 1975; March 22, 1976; March 14, 1977; Jan. 5, 1978). We have eliminated missing data ("don't know," no answer, etc.) from the response distributions for each item.
[a]Institutions were presented to respondents in the same order as shown in table.
[b]Chi-square statistics have 1 degree of freedom and are corrected for continuity (Yates correction). Given that assignment to experimental conditions was fully random, the analysis treats the respondents (*N*s were approximately 1,500) as a universe and tests the hypothesis that the distribution of responses is independent of experimental condition.
Question: "I am going to name some institutions in this country. As far as the *people* running them are concerned, would you say you have a great deal of confidence, only some confidence, or hardly any confidence at all in them."

tributions, we examined the relationship of confidence to alienation and to respondents' educational level in order to determine whether there were significant context effects upon the multivariate response distributions. We found little evidence of such effects for education. Confidence in the press and major companies showed no significant association with education in either form of the questionnaire, while confidence in the scientific community had a virtually identical association with educational level (gamma = 0.30) in the two questionnaire forms.

Subsequently we examined the association between these confidence measures and three alienation items (1, 2, and 6) we thought to be most related to confidence in national institutions. Using log-linear techniques (Goodman, 1971, 1972) to model the response distribution of Alienation (A) by Confidence (C) by Questionnaire Context (Q), we found some evidence of context effects upon the multivariate distributions. In particular, using a model that was maximally constrained to fit the observed patterns of response but which excluded the three-way interaction term {CAQ}, we could not obtain an adequate fit to the data in two of nine instances ($p < .05$), and, we obtained a rather poor fit ($p < .20$) in two further instances. Table 7.9 provides details of these analyses. We report tests only for the maximally constrained noninteractive model ({CA} {CF} {FA}), since this is the appropriate comparison for testing the null hypothesis of no context effect upon the patterns of association.

Figure 7.7 presents the actual data for the instance in which this multivariate context effect is strongest. As this figure shows, we find a considerably stronger inverse association between alienation responses ("The rich get richer and the poor get poorer") and confidence in the people running "major companies" when the alienation item follows, rather than precedes, the confidence question (gamma = 0.62 vs. 0.39). An examination of the gamma coefficients shown in Table 7.9 reveals that this particular relationship holds true in seven of the nine other comparisons. The two exceptions involve reversals of trivial magnitude.

Conclusion. Although the experiment imperfectly replicated the actual context variation, we do nonetheless observe some significant effects upon both the univariate and multivariate response distributions. These effects, however, are neither so pervasive nor so overwhelming in magnitude as to provide a complete explanation for the discrepancies observed between the Harris and NORC confidence series. Clearly, many aspects of the behavior of these series remain to be understood, and other sources of nonsampling variation in these measurements will have to be investigated.

EXAMPLE V: AGREEMENTS ABOUT FERTILITY EXPECTATIONS

Lest the reader be misled by the preceding examples, we conclude by noting that all survey measurements of subjective phenomena are not equally vulnerable to artifactual biases. With this in mind, let us consider alternative estimates of the fertility expectations of American women.

TABLE 7.9

Test for Context Effects upon Patterns of Association Between Confidence and Alienation

Alienation Item	Confidence Item	Ordinal Association[c] (gamma)		Log-Linear Interaction Test[b]	
		Form X	Form Y	L^2	p
The people running the country don't really care what happens to you.	Major companies	.31	.32	0.0	ns
	Press	.16	.15	0.0	ns
	Science[a]	.18	.30	1.7	.20
The rich get richer and the poor get poorer.	Major companies	.39	.62	7.4	.01
	Press	.09	.13	0.0	ns
	Science[a]	.24	.22	0.1	ns
The people in Washington, D.C., are out of touch with the rest of the country.	Major companies	.21	.39	1.8	.18
	Press	.14	.15	0.9	ns
	Science[a]	.07	.27	4.0	.05

NOTES: Model fit to response distribution for Alienation (A) by Confidence (C) by Questionnaire context (Q) is maximally constrained nonsaturated model. In Goodman's notation, it is {CQ} {CA} {QA}. Failure to fit a model of this type to the data indicates an interaction, i.e., that the pattern of association between the variables was not independent of questionnaire context.
[a]Item read "Scientific Community."
[b]Test has 1 degree of freedom.
[c]Form X of the questionnaire presented the confidence questions prior to the alienation items; Form Y presented them in reverse sequence.

The U.S. Bureau of the Census conducts annual surveys of the birth expectations of American women. The data from such surveys are thought to be potentially useful in predicting fluctuations in the birth rate.[29] Clearly, the phenomenon being measured in such surveys is subjective. The "intention" or "expectation" of future pregnancy is not a datum subject to external verification. One must rely solely upon respondents' assessments of their own expectations or intentions.

Estimates from the Bureau of the Census's Current Population Survey (CPS) are shown in Figure 7.8 together with estimates derived from a related question on birth expectations asked in the 1972, 1975, 1976, and 1977 NORC General Social Survey. It should be noted that the latter estimates are based on modest-sized samples; on the average, there were fewer than 250 married women aged 18 to 39 in the GSS samples (versus approximately 4,000 for CPS samples). Thus, the standard errors for the GSS estimates are quite large (circa 4 percent).

Comparing the two sets of data we find that estimates of fertility expectations derived from NORC's General Social Survey are consistent with those derived from the Bureau of the Census's Current Population Surveys. In

FIGURE 7.7

Relationship of Confidence in Major Companies to Alienation Response for Two Forms of Questionnaire.

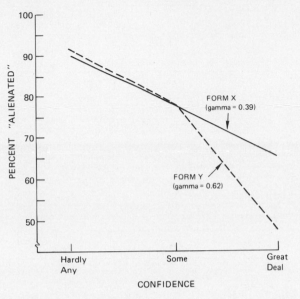

NOTE: In Form X, the confidence question precedes the alienation items; in Form Y, the alienation items precede the confidence question. The alienation item was: "The rich get richer and the poor get poorer."

only one instance (of eight) does the NORC-GSS estimate differ by more than 2 standard errors from the Census estimate.

The Lesson. The estimates of fertility expectations presented in Figure 7.8 differed in their measurement in several ways. The content of the questionnaires used to derive the estimates varied, the organizations conducting the surveys were different, and even the wording of the questions varied slightly.[30]

Because the comparison of these two series on birth expectations involved both wording and context differences, and since the measurements were made at different times of the year by different organizations, the consistency of these estimates is particularly impressive.

What lesson does this comparison teach us? In terms of our initial hypotheses, we note that:

1. The birth expectation question itself is relatively unambiguous in its meaning;
2. The response categories for the questions (for example, 0, 1, 2, 3 . . . children) have a clear meaning; and

191

FIGURE 7.8

Estimates of Fertility Expectations of American Women: Proportion of Women Expecting No Further Children in (a) All Future Years, and (b) Next 5 Years.

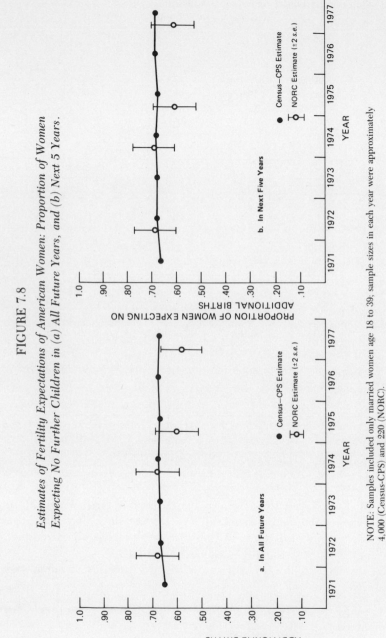

NOTE: Samples included only married women age 18 to 39; sample sizes in each year were approximately 4,000 (Census–CPS) and 220 (NORC).

3. The question deals with a topic to which most respondents (that is, married women of childbearing age) should have given considerable thought. This is particularly so since attitudes toward childbearing have behavioral consequences in the everyday life of the respondents, for example, for contraceptive behaviors.

Discussion and Conclusions

In addition to providing some preliminary hypotheses, we hope that the preceding evidence will focus attention upon intersurvey comparability in the measurement of subjective phenomena. The study of disagreeable data is not an end in itself, however. To be useful, it must stimulate the difficult process of ferreting out explanations for particular anomalies and deducing general principles—where they exist.

In this regard, we believe that the foregoing evidence allows one to dispose of three commonly heard apologia for inconsistencies in survey estimates of subjective phenomena. First, because of the range of examples presented here and elsewhere (for example, Cowan, Murphy, and Weiner, 1978; Gibson et al., 1978; Smith, 1978; Turner and Krauss, 1978), these discrepancies cannot be ascribed to the deficient practices of any particular survey research organization. Such a position would be both unfair and unfaithful to the observed facts. We and others have observed both discrepancies and consistencies in comparisons involving estimates made by a wide range of research organizations.

Second, both our own analyses and those recently undertaken by Duncan and Schuman (1980) and Schuman and Presser (1977) indicate that nonsampling artifacts in the survey measurement of subjective phenomena are not limited to univariate response distributions. Hence, it is not always safe to assume that analyses focusing upon multivariate patterns of association between variables will be resistant to the anomalies encountered in the analysis of univariate distributions.

Third, it appears that no single explanation is likely to be adequate to explain all the observed discrepancies. Experimental data upon artifacts in the confidence time-series suggest that context, for example, is only a partial explanation for the discrepancies in these time-series. Various other sources of error (for example, variations in fieldwork methodology, response rates, interviewer effects, and so on) need to be considered. Basic research in this area should be encouraged.

VULNERABLE INDICATORS

At the outset of this chapter, we hypothesized that indicators of some phenomena were more vulnerable to artifacts of measurement than others.

In particular, we speculated that measurement artifacts would be more likely to afflict estimates of phenomena that were amorphous in concept, that had little importance for the everyday life of respondents, that had ambiguous referents, and that involved relatively arbitrary choices between response categories.

Stated generally, the hypothesis is open to a wide range of interpretation. To make the hypothesis more concrete, we can begin by considering limiting cases. Certainly this hypothesis predicts that survey measurements of nonsubjective phenomena, such as chronological age and years of schooling, should be relatively invulnerable to artifacts of measurement (for instance, effects of variant question wordings, survey context, and so forth). This should be so, even when we rely upon subjects' self-reports. Davis (1976) has studied survey estimates of the sex, race, age, religion, and educational distribution of the population in 30 sample surveys conducted between 1952 and 1973 by SRC and Gallup. Davis reports that these estimates do, in fact, show considerable consistency with one another and with independent estimates made by NORC. (Of course, inadequacies of sample design and execution may still cause problems with demographic measurements; see Chapter 3, Section 3.2 of Volume 1.)

Similarly, expectations of childbearing—while clearly a subjective phenomena—should be less vulnerable to measurement artifacts under our hypothesis. This follows from the fact that childbearing is an unambiguous concept (although its expectation is admittedly open to intepretation); the response categories have a clear meaning; the referent is the respondent herself; and the question itself is directly relevant and has behavioral implications in the everyday life of respondents (married women of childbearing age). Our analysis of eight pairs of estimates of women's fertility expectations revealed a pattern of consistency that was within the range expected on the basis of sampling fluctuations.

The discrepancies observed in our Examples I through IV are also consistent with our preliminary hypotheses. In Table 7.10, we summarize these examples together with other comparisons made elsewhere (Turner and Krauss, 1978; Smith, 1978; Kalton, Collins, and Brook, 1978).[31]

This summary of 101 comparisons for 21 survey questions shows a rough correspondence with the typology of our preliminary hypotheses. Thus, we find relatively more significant discrepancies for the questions (1–14) at the top of the table. These questions involve measurements of rather amorphous concepts such as confidence in the people running institutions, and evaluations of occupational prestige, national spending, and contemporary driving standards. These same items also require a choice between relatively imprecise response categories, such as

1. great deal, only some, hardly any (confidence)

    2. too much, about right, too little (spending)
    3. excellent, above average, average, below average, poor (prestige)

In contrast, questions (15–21) about the legalization of marijuana, gun control, the death penalty, political party affiliation, and fertility yield relatively few discrepancies. The latter questions involve somewhat less amorphous topics and response categories, for example, support or nonsupport of legislation, the name of an actual political party, or an actual number of children expected.

One further difference between these two groups of questions is the (likely) salience of the topics for respondents. The latter group of questions inquire about topics that have been the subject of considerable public discussion (for example, capital punishment and the legalization of marijuana), or that are connected with specific behaviors that often have tangible behavioral components (for example, voting, party registration, and contraceptive practice). For this group of questions, only two significant discrepancies were observed in 19 comparisons. In contrast, the first group of items asked about topics which, we suspect, would not be subject to considerable public discussion as phrased in these questions (e.g., Do I have confidence in the people running organized religion? What is the prestige of accountants? Are we spending too much on science? etc.) More than one-half of the comparisons (42 of 82) involving this group of questions produced significant discrepancies.

While we believe that a case can and has been made for the general typology we hypothesized, Table 7.10 is not without its counterexamples. Voting for a woman president (Yes or No) is a concrete action and related to issues that have been the subject of considerable public discussion. Yet, in the one instance where a comparison was possible, there was a modest (4 percentage points) but reliable difference between estimates derived from independent surveys using this question. Thus, while the evidence is broadly compatible with our hypotheses, the correspondence between our typology and the available data is less than perfect.

Other recent evidence (not included in Table 7.10) seems to fit this typology of vulnerable indicators. For example, in an unpublished experiment, Duncan and Schuman found significant context-induced variations in responses to five (of seven) survey questions. These questions measured agreement with statements such as

- Public officials really care about what people like me think.
- Given enough time and money, almost all of man's important problems can be solved by science.

Respondents chose among four response categories: strongly agree, agree, disagree, strongly disagree.

TABLE 7.10

Examples of Discrepancies in Survey Measurements of Subjective Phenomena

Topic	Response Categories	Type of Comparison[a]	Number of Comparisons	"Significant" Discrepancies[b]
1. Confidence in people running national institutions	Great deal of confidence, only some confidence, hardly any confidence	Different houses[c] Context experiment[i]	27 13	18 3
2. Evaluation of amount of federal income tax	Too high, about right, too low	Context experiment[c]	1	1
3. General happiness	Very happy, pretty happy, not too happy	Different houses[d,i] Same house/different surveys[i,j]	2 2	1 1
4. Evaluation of prestige of occupations	Excellent, good, average, below average, poor	Context experiment[i]	10	7
5. Evaluation of contemporary driving standards	Lower than they used to be, higher than they used to be, about the same	Context experiment[f]	2	1
6. Evaluation of traffic noise	Becoming noisier, less noisy, or about the same	Context experiment[f]	2	1
7. Evaluation of need for nighttime truck deliveries to retail stores	Yes, no[g]	Context experiment[f]	2	1

Item	Response options	Method		
8. Evaluation of spending on national problems	Too much, about right, too little	Different houses[h]	10	5
9. Misanthropy I: people try to take advantage of you	Try to take advantage if they got a chance, try to be fair	Different houses[h]	2	0
10. Misanthropy II: most of time people try to be helpful	Try to be helpful, mostly just looking out for themselves	Different houses[h]	2	1
11. Misanthropy III: most people can be trusted	Can be trusted, can't be too careful in dealing with people	Different houses[h]	2	1
12. Courts' treatment of criminals	Deal too harshly or not harshly enough with criminals	Different houses[h]	1	0
13. Men or women better suited for politics	Men better suited, equally suited, women better suited	Different houses[h]	1	0
14. Vote for woman for president	Yes, no	Different houses[h]	1	1
15. Children safe bicycling in local area	Yes, no	Context experiment[f]	2	0
16. Law requiring police permit to purchase gun	Favor, oppose	Different houses[h]	3	0

TABLE 7.10 (continued)
Examples of Discrepancies in Survey Measurements of Subjective Phenomena

Topic	Response Categories	Type of Comparison[a]	Number of Comparisons	"Significant" Discrepancies[b]
17. Support for legaliza- tion of marijuana	Yes, no	Different houses[h]	1	0
18. Political party with which one identifies self	Republican, Democrat, Independent, other	Different houses[h]	3	1
19. Favor death penalty for murder	Yes, no	Different houses[h]	3	0
20. Ideal number of children for family	0,1,2,3 . . .	Different houses[h]	1	0
21. Expected number of children	0,1,2,3 . . .	Different houses[e, i]	8	1

NOTES: These examples were derived from comparisons cited in (Kalton, Collins, and Brook, 1978; Smith, 1978; Turner and Krauss, 1978; and Turner, 1981a). Only survey measurements of subjective phenomena are included; reports of behaviors (e.g., voting) and demographic estimates included in the foregoing sources were excluded. Comparisons involving variant question word- ings have been excluded—except where noted otherwise.

Appendixes F and G in Volume 1 present a more comprehensive list of (nonexperimental) intersurvey comparisons. Chapter 16 (Volume 2) present a separate assessment of the reliability and validity of 513 survey measurements of presidential popularity made during 1963–1980 by the Gallup Organization, Louis Harris and Associates, CBS/New York Times, NBC/AP, and the Roper Organization.

[a]All comparisons involve either (1) independent estimates made by different survey research organizations (different houses); (2) experiments involving the manipulation of the context in which survey questions were presented (context experiment); or (3) esti- mates derived from separate surveys conducted by the same survey research organization (same house/different surveys).

[b]Discrepancies are absolute differences estimated proportions of population giving a particular response in two surveys (or two

experimental conditions). Discrepancies have been terms "significant" if the observed discrepancy exceeded twice the sampling error for the difference between the proportions. Published statistics and/or standard errors from the source publications were used, if available. When data were derived from clustered samples and no published statistics were available, estimates were based on the formula for simple random samples, but the sample size was deflated ($N' = 0.66N$) to allow for sample design inefficiencies.

cTurner and Krauss (1978).

dComparison involves a modest difference in question wording.

eNote that all comparisons involve a subset of GSS sample that numbered less than 250 each year.

fKalton, Collins, and Brook (1978).

gSource does not quote explicit response categories; they are implied by text of question.

hSmith (1978).

iTurner (1981a) and present paper.

jComparisons were made by pooling data from two months of NORC Continuous National Survey closest to dates of General Social Surveys.

Similarly, studies of Census Bureau estimates of crime victimization (Cowan, Murphy, and Weiner, 1978; Gibson et al., 1978) have revealed that substantial variations have been induced by differences in survey contexts. Gibson and associates (1978) report that this measurement artifact produced a relative increase of 12 percent in the reported rate of property crime and 21 percent in the reported rate of personal crime. Examination of the National Crime Survey questionnaire suggests that these results may fit within the foregoing typology. The victimization questionnaire includes, for example, the following screening question:

Q. 42 Did anyone try to attack you in some other way? [other than attacks already mentioned]

The concept of "attempted" attack in this question is somewhat amorphous. (When, for example, does an accidental bump become a hostile blow?) Cowan, Murphy, and Weiner (1978:282) find that reported rates of "attempted assaults (without weapon)" showed significant variation across measurement contexts (Z of difference = 2.76) and that "attempted assault (with weapon)" showed a difference of borderline significance (Z = 1.83); however, Cowan, Murphy, and Weiner find that the reported rates for assaults "with injury" showed no significant variations across measurement contexts (Z = 0.17 and 0.27). This pattern of results suggests that the vulnerability of these reports to context effects decreased as the events in question became more unmistakably hostile and, we assume, more salient to the victims.[32]

AREAS FOR RESEARCH

The growing use of survey measurements of subjective phenomena in policymaking and social research make it important for us to understand the sources of variability that affect comparisons made across different surveys (and/or surveys conducted by different survey organizations). Intersurvey comparisons that rely exclusively upon sampling error computations can be dangerously misleading when the error structure of our survey estimates include large error and bias components contributed by nonsampling factors (for example, variations in fieldwork methods, interviewer training, response rates, questionnaire context, and so forth.). The preceding examples provide evidence of the untoward effects that can be induced by the nonsampling variances involved in such comparisons. A better understanding of the error structure of these measurements is needed.

A useful first step in a future research program might involve the testing of hypotheses concerning the types of indicators that are more (and less) vulnerable to such nonsampling errors. The results of such studies might be helpful in delimiting a domain of measurements that are robust. Relatively simple research designs might involve contemporaneous measurements made by a number of survey organizations. The extent to which the distribution of such derived estimates departs from what is expected on the basis of sampling error alone can provide some insight into the relative magnitudes of the nonsampling components of variance for different types of measurement.[33] If the preliminary hypotheses we have suggested are correct, we would expect some orderliness in these results.

To operationalize our preliminary hypotheses, we might consider some of the following procedures. Smith (1979a) studied the confidence question by asking respondents in the 1978 General Social Survey to describe what they thought this question meant. Respondents' answers were often sobering; for example, 34 percent of respondents could name no specific group that they thought was part of the "scientific community," and 2.3 percent of respondents thought that this term referred to their local community.

Similar probing of respondents' interpretation of other common survey questions might be done. The variability in respondents' interpretations might be taken as a measure of the degree to which questions are amorphous in concept or ambiguous in their referents. Our hypotheses would predict that larger nonsampling errors would be found for items that have greater variability in interpretation. Parallel procedures might be used to assess the extent to which response categories require respondents to make arbitrary choices. (See Bradburn and Sudman [1979:Chapter 10] and Hakel [1968] for relevant discussions.) The frequency with which respondents select an offered "don't know" category of response might also be a useful indicator of whether a particular topic has a well-defined place in public discussion.[34]

In addition to studies of contemporaneous measurements replicated across houses, planned experiments should be considered. Where specific measurement artifacts are thought to complicate the use of past data, experiments incorporated in future surveys may allow estimation of the magnitude of such artifacts and appropriate adjustments of past measurements (see Duncan and Schuman, 1980, for an example of such procedures). These experiments themselves might be contemporaneously replicated by several survey organizations to ensure the robustness of important measurements.

In addition to research involving the collection of new data, useful insights may also be derived by reconsidering data presently available in survey archives. For example, several organizations routinely use two alternative forms of the survey questionnaire in their amalgam studies (for example, the ORC Science Indicators study). Data from these studies would provide an inexpensive basis for post hoc experimental studies. Moreover, the advent of computer-assisted telephone interviewing (see

Chapter 2 of Volume 1; and Shure and Meeker, 1978) will provide the opportunity for easier experimentation with alternative questionnaire forms and wording in future research, and the possibility for more routine estimation of the interviewer component of the nonsampling variances in our measurements.

FUNDAMENTALS AND FUTURE DIRECTIONS

We would also suggest that there is a need for a reconsideration of the assumptions that underlie the practice of survey research.[35] The most fundamental phenomena of survey research are quintessentially social psychological in character.[36] They arise from a complex interpersonal exchange, they embody the subjectivities of both interviewer and interviewee, and they present their interpreter with an analytical challenge that requires a multitude of assumptions concerning, among other things, how respondents experience the reality of the interview situation, decode the "meaning" of survey questions, and respond to the social presence of the interviewer[37] and the demand characteristics of the interview.

The burden of the observed anomalies should prompt a reconsideration of the social psychological foundations of survey research. The foregoing examples are indicative of the deficient state of our present knowledge. We doubt any instant solutions exist, but it seems clear that complacency will not suffice.

Notes

1. In accord with traditional usage, we treat the *possibility* of independent verification (corroboration) as a litmus test for classifying phenomena as subjective or nonsubjective. This position assumes the existence of a nonsubjective (that is, "objective") reality whose properties are potentially discoverable through some consensual process. (We, of course, need not make such an assumption; see, for example, the writings of Bishop Berkeley or the radical skepticism of Descartes' first meditation.)

2. Observation of a subject's behavior can only provide an indirect measure of that subject's attitudes, beliefs, and so forth. Conceptually we can distinguish between behaviors and attitudes; in practice, experience affirms that an individual's behavior need not accord with his or her beliefs. Indeed, we should bear in mind that typical measurements of subjective states involve inferences made from subjects' behavior(s), that is, their verbal behavior in response to a question. Such response behaviors are used to infer the state and structure of subjective reality. However, as behaviors, such responses are only indirectly and assumptively linked with the inferred phenomenon (the subjective state of the individual). Among others, misreporting and measurement artifacts are common pitfalls in this inference process. The general topic of attitude-behavior inconsistency has itself received considerable attention in the social psychological literature (see, for example, the review by Schuman and Johnson [1976]).

3. See, for example, the work of the evaluation and research program of the Census Bureau or the valuable series of recent studies by Norman Bradburn, Seymour Sudman and their associates (1979) on response errors for "threatening questions" (for example, measures of the incidence of bankruptcy, drunkenness, and so forth).

4. For example, to be classified as "unemployed" in the Bureau of Labor Statistics index, workers must be both out of work and "looking for work." While the definition of the criterion "looking for work" is not left to the discretion of respondents, statements that a worker has "checked with friends or relatives" during the last 4 weeks meet the criterion. Persons without paid employment who are available for work and who have checked with friends are defined as "unemployed"; those who have not checked with friends or otherwise searched for a job are excluded from the unemployment tabulation and are not counted as part of the active labor force. See National Commission on Employment and Unemployment Statistics (1979:Chapter 4) for a further discussion of the subjective components of such measurements.

5. The meaning and interpretation of questions such as "Did anyone try to attack you . . . ?" are supplied by the respondents and may differ from respondent to respondent and across the contexts in which survey measurements are made (see Martin, 1978, 1981, 1983).

6. An independent review (Caplan and Barton, 1976) of the use of the first *Social Indicators* volume (1973) concluded that there was a need for federal statistical compendiums to "go beyond objective indicators and provide subjective measures of life experience and social well being."

7. In the board's words (1975:145):
   Public attitudes affect science and technology in many ways. Public opinion sets the general environment and climate for scientific research and technological development. It is influential in determining the broad directions of research and innovation, and through the political process, the allocation of resources for these activities. In addition, public attitudes toward scientists and engineers and their efforts affect the career choices of the young by influencing their decision to enter these fields.

8. Similarly, there was a unique, albeit short-lived, attempt to provide federal policy makers with easy access to an ongoing series of national surveys (NORC's Continuous National Survey). The latter project was funded by the RANN (Research Applied to National Needs) Division of the National Science Foundation (NSF) for the use of the Departments of Agriculture; Health, Education and Welfare; Housing and Urban Development; and Transportation; the Office of Management and Budget; the President's Commission on Gambling; and the NSF. For a history of this pioneering but ill-fated program, see, Rich (1975).

9. Parallel efforts are evident in Europe (see, for example, Abrams, 1973; OECD, 1974). In addition, the United Nation's report, *Toward a System of Social and Demographic Statistics*, voiced a concern for the inclusion of measures of subjective phenomena in the national statistics of member countries (United Nations, 1975:32).

10. Turner and Krauss (1978) hypothesize that
    . . . the degree of variability in indicator estimates derived from different surveys may be a function of an identifiable dimension of the indicator questions themselves. Thus, we know that sample surveys can show remarkable consistency in their estimates of the demographic characteristics of the population and that election predictions have been quite accurate in recent years. Furthermore, attitudes that have a relatively well-defined place in

public discussions, such as attitudes toward capital punishment, fertility expectations, and political party identification, also seem to yield rather consistent estimates in different surveys. However, there appears to be emerging some evidence that the most unstable indicators are those involving questions that are the most amorphous in their meaning (e.g., What is "confidence" or "trust"?), the most imprecise in their referents (e.g., Who are the people "in charge of running organized religion"?), and that involves the most arbitrariness in the selection of a response category (e.g., We know what it means to be "for" or "against" the death penalty, but what does it mean to have "a great deal of confidence" vs. "some confidence" or to be "very happy" vs. "pretty happy"?)

11. This question was first incorporated in a 1957 survey conducted by the Survey Research Center (see Gurin, Veroff, and Feld, 1960). A similar question, varying slightly in wording, has been asked by Gallup since 1946 (see Hastings and Southwick, 1974:400).

It should be noted that we report in this example (see Figure 7.1) only the disagreement that prompted our concerns. For a review of other measurements, see Smith (1979b).

12. The meeting was hosted by the Institute for Research in the Social Sciences, University of North Carolina, and was attended by J. Davis, O. D. Duncan, E. Martin, F. Munger, R. Parke, M. Schulman, H. Schuman, T. Smith, G. Taylor, and C. Turner. We first presented these data at the meetings of this working group. Subsequently, one member of the group conducted his own study of these data. He independently reached a conclusion similar to ours concerning the likely cause of the observed discrepancies (Smith, 1979b).

13. If large month-to-month fluctuations are taking place, then yearly or biennial measurements (taken in different months) are of little value in tracking annual changes.

14. The divergence in these trends is only suggestive, since analysis of the data indicates that a model positing only effects for year and marital status provides a tolerable fit for these data. An interaction term for the context effect (year × marital status × happiness) is not strictly required.

15. In particular, we found a significant interaction of survey Year (Y: 1972 vs. 1973–78) with responses to the Happiness (H response: very happy vs. pretty happy vs. not too happy) and Financial Status (F) questions. Analyzing data for the two financial-status questions separately, we found that models incorporating all two-way interactions (that is, {HY}, {HF}, {YF}) did not provide an adequate fit, and there was a decline in the rank correlations. The first financial-status question was "We are interested in how people are getting along these days. So far as you and your family are concerned, would you say that you are pretty well satisfied with your present financial situation, more or less satisfied, or not satisfied at all?" Using responses to this question, the likelihood ratio chi-square for the model was 11.8 with 4 degrees of freedom (p = .02). The rank correlation (gamma) declined from +0.47 (1972) to +0.40 (1973–78).

The second question was "During the last few years, has your financial situation been getting better, getting worse, or has it stayed the same?" Using responses to this question, the likelihood ratio chi-square for the model was 11.7 with 4 degrees of freedom (p = .02). The rank correlation (gamma) declined from +0.34 to +0.28.

Note that since the marital-happiness question was not asked in 1972, a parallel analysis of the bivariate associations between marital and general happiness was not possible.

16. Immediately *preceding* the experimental general-happiness and marital-happiness questions, respondents were asked the questions shown below:

SRC experiment

C74. Thinking ahead *3 or 4 years*, do you think you will be able to get all the gasoline you want, or will there be problems getting all the gas you want 3 or 4 years from now?

C75. Do you think that the price of gasoline will go up during the next 12 months, or will gasoline prices stay about the same as they are now?

IF answer to C75 was "go up":

   C75a. About how many cents per gallon do you think gasoline prices may increase during the next 12 months compared to now?

   C75b. If you were going to buy a new car or truck in the next year, would gasoline prices increasing by _____ (CENTS FROM C75a) per gallon affect your decision in any way?

   C75c. How would it affect your decision to buy a new car or truck?

C76. One government proposal has been to ration gasoline at 2 gallons per vehicle per day. You could obtain additional gasoline but you would pay a higher price for it. Would this rationing proposal affect your plans to buy or lease a car or truck in the next 12 months?

IF Answer to C76 was "would affect plans":

   C76a. In what ways would this affect your plans to buy or lease a car or truck in the next 12 months?

C77. There has been a lot of talk about our nation's ability to pay for the oil that we import from foreign countries. Do you believe this is a serious problem, or is it not very serious?

   C77a. Why do you say so?

Now we would like to ask a few questions about you (and your family living there).

D2. Are you currently married, separated, divorced, widowed, or have you never been married?

Washington Post Poll experiment

E. In what year were you born?

F. What religion were you brought up in—Protestant, Catholic, Jewish, or something else?

G. How would you describe the place where you live: Is it a large city, a suburb of a large city, a small town, or a rural area?

H. We'd like to know if the chief wage earner in your household is working now, unemployed, retired, or what?

I.   IF *Working*: What sort of work does he/she do?

   IF *Unemployed*: What sort of work did that wage earner do on his/her regular job?

J. What is your race? Are you white, black, hispanic or what?

K. If you added together the yearly income before taxes of all the members of your household last year in 1978, would the total be under $8,000; between $8,000 and $12,000; between $12,000 and $20,000; between $20,000 and $30,000; between $30,000 and $50,000, or would the total be over $50,000 [IF UNCERTAIN, ASK:] What would be your best guess?

   Now I would like to ask you one or two more qestions concerning your general feelings about life. . . .

NORC experiment

For each area of life I am going to name, tell me the number that shows how much *satisfaction* you get from that area. (READ ITEMS A–E. CIRCLE ONE CODE FOR EACH.)

A. The city or place you live in.

B. Your non-working activities—hobbies and so on.
C. Your family life.
D. Your friendships.
E. Your health and physical condition.

17. The data that we analyze in the following pages have been restricted to cases in which respondents reported that they had a telephone in their residence, in order to ensure comparability between the NORC sample and the samples used in the SRC and *Washington Post* experiments. (Approximately 3 percent of the NORC sample said they had a telephone but refused to supply a telephone number and thus the interviewer did not ascertain the exact location of the phone. On the assumption that most of these telephones were probably in the respondents' residences, these respondents were maintained in the sample we used for our analyses.) All data used in our analyses of these experiments are unweighted. Due to an error in the preliminary processing of the SRC data, six eligible respondents were eliminated from our tabulations. This error changes none of the SRC marginals by more than 1 percent.

Respondents were randomly assigned to experimental conditions in all experiments. In the SRC and *Washington Post* experiments, sample assignments were divided 50–50 between the two conditions; in the NORC experiment the division was 66–33. Selection of individual respondents within households was done by random selection from among all members of the households in the NORC and SRC surveys; in the *Washington Post* survey, selection was done from among those who were at home at the time of the initial contact.

18. The tabulations from the SRC experiment were independently confirmed by Howard Schuman, who also arranged for a subsequent hand-check of several questionnaires to ensure that the experimental conditions were not systematically miscoded or erroneously transcribed.

19. The experimental questions were introduced with the statement "These questions deal with several different topics—" followed by the inquiry:

X1. Are you currently married, separated, divorced, widowed, or have you never been married?

In the NORC-1972 replication, the respondents were then asked:

Y2. We are interested in how people are getting along financially these days. So far as you and your family are concerned, would you say that you are pretty well satisfied with your present financial situation, more or less satisfied, or not satisfied at all? (IF RESPONSE IS ANYTHING OTHER THAN THE RESPONSE CATEGORIES GIVEN, PROBE:) In general, (THEN REPEAT QUESTION).

Y3. During the last few years, has your financial situation been getting better, getting worse, or has it stayed the same? (IF RESPONSE IS ANYTHING OTHER THAN THE RESPONSE CATEGORIES GIVEN, PROBE:) In general, (THEN REPEAT QUESTION).

Y4. Compared with American families in general, would you say your family income is—far below average, below average, average, above average, or far above average? (IF THERE IS ANY DIFFICULTY ANSWERING, SAY:) Just your best guess.

Y5. Taken altogether, how would you say things are these days—would you say that you are very happy, pretty happy, or not too happy? (IF UNDECIDED, PROBE:) In general, how do you feel?

In the NORC-1973 replication, respondents were asked the marital status question X1, and then:

(IF "MARRIED" ON Q. X1, ASK):

X2. Taking things altogether, how would you describe your marriage? Would you say

that your marriage is very happy, pretty happy, or not too happy? (IF UNDECID-
ED, PROBE:) In general, how do you feel?

X3. Taken altogether, how would you say things are these days—would you say that
you are very happy, pretty happy, or not too happy? (IF UNDECIDED, PROBE:)
In general, how do you feel?

In addition to these conditions, approximately one-third of respondents were asked questions in a format designed to mimic the gas shortage context of the August 1979 SRC
measurements. These respondents were questioned as follows:

These questions deal with several different topics:

Z1. Do you think that the price of gasoline will go up during the next 12 months, or will
gasoline prices stay about the same as they are now?

Z2. There has been a lot of talk about our nation's ability to pay for the oil that we
import from foreign countries. Do you believe this is a serious problem, or is it not
very serious? Why do you say so?

Z3. Are you currently married, separated, divorced, widowed, or have you never been
married?

Z4. Taken altogether, how would you say things are these days—would you say that you
are very happy, pretty happy, or not too happpy? (IF UNDECIDED, PROBE:) In
general, how do you feel?

The results of this mimicry of the gas shortage context did not, however, provide results
comparable to those obtained by the August 1979 SRC experiment. We suspect that this
result may be due to both the incomplete context replication which was done and to the
general easing of the national gasoline shortage in the intervening period.

20. Communicated to us by Dr. Donald Buzzelli.

21. The question read: "This card lists a number of areas in which there are problems. In
your view, in which of these areas could science and technology make a major contribution
toward solving the problems? Please read me the numbers." [Card: same as spending question.] "In your view, in which areas could science and technology make little or no contribution? Please read me the numbers."

22. Selection of respondents to receive the different versions was performed as follows: The
survey itself used three separately generated national samples. In Sample 1: 60 sampling
points received Form A and 60 received Form B. For Sample 2, 30 sampling points received
Form A and 30 sampling points received Form B, and for Sample 3, 50 sampling points
received Form A and 50 received Form B. All forms were randomly assigned to sampling
points.

Randomization by sampling points rather than individual respondents causes some difficulties. In particular, we know that clustering of sampling points results in a departure of sample
efficiency from that of SRS designs; the extent of this departure is impossible to compute given
the presently available data. In the analysis of the confidence items, Turner and Krauss (1978:
461-462) found that the use of clusters of 15 as the unit for analysis produced a deflation of the
effective sampling size from 1,500 to 1,000 (using the level of intracluster correlation as a
deflator [Blalock, 1972:Chapter 20; Kish, 1965]). Whether that result holds here is unknown;
however, we would point out that analysis of the demographic characteristics revealed no
significant differences between the samples receiving the different versions of the questionnaire. (Note: Computations assume effective sample size to be deflated by 0.66—that is, N =
2,000 becomes N = 1,333.)

Variable	X^2	d.f.	p
Sex	0.0	1	ns
Education	4.9	9	ns
Age	8.5	8	.40
Income	13.2	11	.27
Religion	4.6	4	.35
Marital status	0.8	4	ns

23. This survey, the ORC Caravan, consisted of eight parts—each funded by different organizations. The Opinion Research Corporation treats each section of the questionnaire as the confidential property of the sponsoring organization. Thus, ORC has not been able to make available to us the actual questions used in each section. However, Dean Behrend and his staff have made available a summary of the content of each section and have been helpful in answering questions about survey administration. The following notes describing the content of survey sections are derived from summaries prepared by ORC staff.

24. (1) Seriousness of litter problem in United States; (2) who is responsible for problem; (3) degree of activity of eight organizations in fighting litter problem; (4) awareness and sponsor identification of antilitter advertising; (5) use of one-way or returnable packaging in purchase of beverages.

25. (1) Frequency of serving hamburgers in household; (2) how many cooked at one time; (3) ownership and usage of hamburger makers (electrical appliance); (4) purchase intention and brand intention for a hamburger maker.

26. (1) A series of questions on hospitalization insurance, family members covered, and so forth; (2) proportion of expenses paid by such coverages; (3) hospitalization incidence last year; (4) estimated cost of hospitalization.

27. Categorical analyses of the multivariate response distributions yields similar but weaker results. Treating the three categories of education (E) as an unordered classification, the patterns of response (R) to different forms (F) were only poorly fit by models that excluded the three-way interaction term {ERF}. In particular, models fitting only the marginals for the {ER} {FR} {EF} distributions produced the following fits to the data:

Occupation	L^2	P
Engineer	5.4	.07
Physician	4.3	.11
Accountant	5.0	.08
Banker	3.9	.14

In each case the degrees of freedom associated with the test of fit were 2; computations assumed that clustering effects diminished the effective sample size by one-third.

28. In particular, two questions that were interspersed between the alienation and confidence questions in the 1976 Harris survey were omitted from NORC's experimental context manipulation. These questions were (1) "Compared to 10 years ago, do you feel the quality of

life in America has improved, grown worse, or stayed the same?" (2) "Compared to 10 years ago, do you feel the leadership inside and outside of government has become better, worse, or stayed the same?" The questions about confidence in "the people running" national institutions followed these items in the original Harris survey.

29. Longitudinal studies indicate that these measures do predict subsequent fertility; see, for example, Wilson and Bumpass (1973); Freedman, Hermalin, and Chang (1975); Goldberg, Sharp, and Freedman. (1959).

30. The text of birth-expectations questions used by Census and NORC between 1972 and 1977, was as follows:

Organization	Years	Text
Census	1972–74	1. Do you expect to have any (more) children? 2. How many (more) do you expect to have? 3. How many (more) do you expect to have in the next 5 years?
	1975–77	1. Looking ahead, do you expect to have any (more) children? 2. How many (more) do you expect to have? 3. How many (more) do you expect to have in the next 5 years?
NORC	1972–77	1. Do you expect to have any (more) children? 2. How many (more)? 3. How many (more) in the next 5 years?

31. We have included only recent studies because the earlier literature was reviewed by Sudman and Bradburn (1974); their conclusions in some areas, however, are somewhat different from those that have emerged from later work.

32. A somewhat similar pattern was found for reports of thefts. Reports of larcenies of under $50, for example, evidenced significant context-induced variations ($Z = 3.07$), but those involving larger amounts of money and reports of auto thefts did not vary significantly between measurement contexts ($Z = 1.20$, larceny of $50 or more; 0.15, theft of car [Cowan, Murphy, and Weiner 1978:282).

33. In this regard, the procedures developed to assess analytical measurements made by different laboratories in the physical and chemical sciences may offer useful guidance (Youden, 1975; Steiner, 1975).

34. See Schuman and Presser (1978) for a thought-provoking discussion of the effects of offering a "don't know" alternative upon multivariate response patterns.

35. In this regard, we applaud those independent initiatives that have recently emerged (for example, Nisbett and Wilson, 1977; Wilson and Nisbett, 1978; Fischhoff, Slovic, and Lichtenstein, 1979).

36. I am grateful to O. D. Duncan for reminding me that just as the fundamental phenomena of survey research are psychological, so too they are fundamentally sociological. In his words, the topics we commonly survey largely

. . . have to do with political categories, economic sectors, institutional arrangements, or other social objects, entities, or systems. Hence, if most of the content of polls is subjective and hence psychological in one aspect, it is also true that most of the content is sociological (including, for simplicity, economic, political, cultural, etc. content under this heading). The statements are not contradictory, of course, but there is reason to suspect that survey work can go seriously astray when the productive tension between the two ways of looking at survey content is disregarded. Specifically, the survey researcher, whether interested in subjective or objective variables, does well to keep in mind the fact that interviewer and respondent are both fallible with respect to their supposed functions in making observations and reports. It appears that we have come to suppose an extraordinary proficiency on their part in carrying out cognitively complicated tasks. Perhaps some of the perceived deficiencies of survey data trace to exaggerated expectations of this kind. Secondly, however narrowly the research problem may be defined in terms of psychological material, the subject matter is inescapably thoroughly infused by sociocultural definitions and meanings. Quite often, in fact, the main causal variables accounting for the responses recorded in a survey actually are not observed in the survey itself but are to be found in the social milieu, narrowly or broadly construed, of the respondent. [Duncan, 1981:5]

37. In this regard, it is interesting to note that the average user of social survey data knows little or nothing about the interviewers who are the other half of the social interaction that produces these data. While few survey research organizations would fail to provide routine demographic information on respondents, similar information is seldom, if ever, provided about interviewers. Thus, by default, interviewers are treated by most analysts as anonymous and passive transducers of the subjective reality of respondents. It is, we think, a bit odd that as social scientists we often accept such a narrow view of the social realities involved in our own work.

References

Abrams, M. (1973) Subjective social indicators. In United Kingdom (Central Statistical Office), *Social Trends: 1973*. London: Her Majesty's Staionery Office.

Andrews, F., and Withey, S. (1976) *Social Indicators of Well-Being: American's Perceptions of Life Quality*. New York: Plenum Press.

Bailar, B., and Lanphier, C. M. (1977) *Development of Survey Methods to Assess Survey Practices: A Report of the American Statistical Association's Pilot Project on the Assessment of Survey Practices and Data Quality in Surveys of Human Populations*. Washington, D.C.: American Statistical Association.

Blalock, H. (1972) *Social Statistics*. 2nd ed. New York: McGraw-Hill.

Blau, P., and Duncan, O. D. (1967) *The American Occupational Structure*. New York: Wiley.

Boffey, P. (1975) Scientific data: 50 percent unusable; widespread defects in laboratory work found by National Bureau of Standards. *Chronicle of Higher Education* (Feb. 24, 1975):1.

Boring, E. G. (1950) *History of Experimental Psychology*. 2nd ed. New York: Prentice Hall.

Bradburn, N. (1969) *The Structure of Psychological Well Being*. Chicago: Aldine.

Bradburn, N., Sudman, S., and Associates (1979) *Improving Interview Method and Questionnaire Design*. San Francisco: Jossey-Bass.

Bureau of the Census (1980) *Social Indicators III*. Washington D.C.: Government Printing Office.

Campbell, A. (1981) Irregularities in survey data. In D. Johnston, ed., *Measurement of Subjective Phenomena*. Special Demographic Analyses, CDS80-3, U.S. Bureau of the Census. Washington D.C.: Government Printing Office.

Campbell, A., Converse, P., and Rodgers, W. (1976) *The Quality of American Life: Perceptions, Evaluations and Satisfaction*. New York: Russell Sage Foundation.

Caplan, N., and Barton, E. (1976) *Social Indicators 1973: A Study of the Relationship of the Power of Information and Utilization by Federal Executives*. Ann Arbor, Mich.: Institute for Social Research, University of Michigan.

Comptroller General of the U.S.A. (1978) *Better Guidance and Controls are Needed to Improve Federal Surveys of Attitudes and Opinions*. Washington, D.C.: General Accounting Office, Sept. 15.

Cowan, C., Murphy, L., and Weiner, J. (1978) Effects of Supplemental Questions on Victimization Rates from the National Crime Surveys. Paper presented at 138th Annual Meeting of the American Statistical Association, San Diego, Aug. 14-17.

Davis, J. (1975a) Communism, conformity, cohorts and categories: American tolerance in 1954 and 1972-3. *American Journal of Sociology* 81:491-513.

Davis, J. (1975b) Does Economic Growth Improve the Human Lot? Yes, Indeed, About .0005 per Year. Paper presented to International Conference on Subjective Indicators of the Quality of Life, Cambridge, England.

Davis, J. (1976) Background characteristics in the U.S. adult population 1952-1973: a survey-metric model. *Social Science Research* 5:349-383.

Duncan, O. D. (1961) A socioeconmic index for all occupations. In A. Reiss, ed., *Occupations and Social Status*. New York: Free Press.

Duncan, O. D. (1972) Federal statistics, non-federal statisticians. *Proceedings of the American Statistical Association (Social Statistics Section)* 1972:152.

Duncan, O. D. (1974) Developing social indicators. *Proceedings of the National Academy of Sciences* 71:5096-5102.

Duncan, O. D. (1979) Indicators of sex typing. *American Journal of Sociology* 85:251-260.

Duncan, O.D. (1981) Content of surveys. Unpublished ms. prepared for Panel on Survey Measurement of Subjective Phenomena, National Research Council, February 2.

Duncan, O. D., and Schuman, H. (1980) Effects of question wording and context: an experiment with religious indicators. *Journal of the American Statistical Association* 75:269-275.

Easterlin, R. (1974) Does economic growth improve the human lot? Some empirical evidence. In P. Davis and M. Reder, eds., *Nations and Households in Economic Growth*. New York: Academic Press.

Executive Office of the President (Office of Management and Budget). (1973) *Social Indicators: 1973*. Washington, D.C.: Government Printing Office.

Fischhoff, B., Slovic, P., and Lichtenstein, S. (1979) Knowing what you want to know;

measuring labile values. In T. Wallsten, ed., *Cognitive Processes in Choice and Decision Behavior*. Hillsdale, N.J.: Lawrence Erlbaum Associates.

Freedman, R., Hermalin, A., and Chang, M. (1975) Do statements about expected family size predict fertility? The case of Taiwan, 1967-1970. *Demography* 12:407-416.

Gibson, C., Shapiro, G., Murphy, L., and Stanko, G. (1978) Interaction of survey questions as it relates to interviewer-respondent bias. *Proceedings of the American Statistical Association (Survey Methods Section)* 1978:251-256.

Goldberg, D., Sharp, H., and Freedman, R. (1959) The stability and reliability of expected family size data. *Millbank Memorial Fund Quarterly* 37:369-385.

Goldfield, E., Turner, A., Cowan, C., and Scott, J. (1977) Privacy and confidentiality as factors in survey response. *Proceedings of the American Statistical Association (Social Statistics Section)* 1977:1-11.

Goodman, L. (1971) The analysis of multidimensional contingency tables: stepwise procedures and direct estimation methods for building models for multiple classifications. *Technometrics* 13:33-61.

Goodman, L. (1972) A general model for the analysis of surveys. *American Journal of Sociology* 77:1035-1086.

Gurin, G., Veroff, J., and Feld, S. (1960) *Americans View their Mental Health*. New York: Basic Books.

Hakel, M. (1968) How often is often? *American Psychologist* 23:533-534.

Hall, J., and Jones, D. (1950) The social grading of occupations. *British Journal of Sociology* 1:31-55.

Hastings, P., and Southwick, J. (1974) *Survey Data for Trend Analysis*. Williamstown, Mass.: Roper Public Opinion Research Center and Social Science Research Council.

Ho, C. Y., Powell, R. W., and Liley, P. E. (1974) Thermal conductivity of the elements: a comprehensive review. *Journal of Physical and Chemical Reference Data* 3(suppl. 1):1-244.

Hunter, J. S. (1977) Quality assessment of measurement methods. In National Research Council, *Environmental Monitoring*, Vol. 4a. Washington, D.C.: National Academy of Sciences.

Kalton, G., Collins, M., and Brook, L. (1978) Experiments in wording opinion questions. *Applied Statistics* 27:149-161.

Kish, L. (1965) *Survey Sampling*. 2nd ed. New York: Wiley.

Kraut, A., Wolfson, I., and Rothenberg, A. (1975) Some effects of position on opinion survey items. *Journal of Applied Psychology* 60:774-776.

Marsh, C. (1978) Opinion polls: social science or political manoeuvre. In J. Evans, J. Irvine, I. Miles, eds., *Demystifying Social Statistics*. London: Pluto Press.

Martin, E. (1978) Trends in victimization: problems of measurement. Paper presented at the 86th annual meeting of American Psychological Association, Toronto, Aug. 28-Sept. 1.

Martin, E. (1981) A twist on the Heisenberg principle: or how crime affects its measurement. *Social Indicators Research* 9:197-223.

Martin, E. (1983) Surveys as social indicators: problems in monitoring trends. In P. Rossi, J. Wright, and A. Anderson, eds., *Handbook of Survey Research*. New York: Academic Press.

Mason, K., Czajka, J., and Arber, S. (1976) Changes in U.S. women's sex role attitudes. *American Journal of Sociology* 41:573-598.

National Commission on Employment and Unemployment Statistics (1979) *Counting the Labor Force*. Washington, D.C.: Government Printing Office.

National Opinion Research Center (1980) *General Social Surveys, 1972-1980: Cumulative Codebook*. Chicago: National Opinion Research Center.

National Research Council (1979) *Privacy and Confidentiality as Factors in Survey Response*. Washington, D.C.: National Academy of Sciences.

National Science Board (1973) *Science Indicators: 1972*. Washington, D.C.: Government Printing Office.

National Science Board (1975) *Science Indicators: 1974*. Washington, D.C.: Government Printing Office.

National Science Board (1977) *Science Indicators: 1976*. Washington, D.C.: Government Printing Office.

Nisbett, R., and Wilson, T. (1977) Telling more than we can know: verbal reports on mental processes. *Psychological Review* 84:231-259.

OECD (Organisation for Economic Cooperation and Development) (1974) *Subjective Elements of Well-being*. Paris: OECD.

Rich, R. (1975) An Investigation of Information Gathering in Seven Federal Bureaucracies: A Case Study of the Continuous National Survey. Ph.D. dissertation, University of Chicago.

Schuman, H. (1974) Old Wine in New Bottles: Some Sources of Response Error in the Use of Attitude Surveys to Study Social Change. Paper prepared for Research Seminar in Quantitative Social Science, University of Surrey, April 1974.

Schuman, H., and Duncan, O. D. (1974) Questions about attitude survey questions. *Sociological Methodology: 1973-74*. San Francisco: Jossey-Bass.

Schuman, H., and Johnson, M. (1976) Attitudes and behavior. In A. Inkeles, ed., *Annual Review of Sociology* 2:161-207.

Schuman, H., and Presser, S. (1977) Question wording as an independent variable in survey analysis. *Sociological Methods and Research* 6:151-170.

Schuman, H., and Presser, S. (1978) The Assessment of "No Opinion" in Attitude Surveys. Paper presented at 73rd annual meeting, American Sociological Association, San Francisco, Sept. 4-8.

Sewell, W., and Hauser, R. (1975) *Education, Occupation, and Earnings*. New York: Academic Press.

Sheldon, E. (1971) Social reporting for the 1970's. In Presidential Commission on Federal Statistics, *Federal Statistics*, Vol. 2. Washington, D.C.: Government Printing Office.

Shure, G., and Meeker, R. (1978) A minicomputer system for multiperson computer-assisted interviewing. *Behavior Research Methods and Instrumentation* 10:196-202.

Smith, T.W. (1978) In search of house effects: a comparison of responses to various questions by different survey organizations. *Public Opinion Quarterly* 42:443-463.

Smith, T.W. (1979a) *Can We Have Confidence in Confidence? Revisited*. GSS Technical Report No. 10. Chicago: National Opinion Research Center.

Smith, T.W. (1979b) Happiness: time trends, seasonal variations, intersurvey differences, and other mysteries. *Social Psychology Quarterly* 42:18-30.

Staines, G., and Quinn, R. (1979) American workers evaluate the quality of their jobs. *Monthly Labor Review* 102:3-12.

Steiner, E. (1975) Planning and analysis of the results of collaborative tests. In W. Youden and E. Steiner, eds., *Statistical Manual of the Association of Official Analytical Chemists*. Washington, D.C.: Association of Official Analytical Chemists.

Sudman, S., and Bradburn, N. (1974) *Response Effects in Surveys*. Chicago: Aldine.

Treiman, D. (1977) *Occupational Prestige in Comparative Perspective*. New York: Academic Press.

Turner, C. F. (1981a) Surveys of subjective phenomena: a working paper. In D. Johnston, ed., *Measurement of Subjective Phenomena*. Special Demographic Analyses, CDS80-3, U.S. Bureau of the Census. Washington D.C.: Government Printing Office.

Turner, C. F. (1981b) Patterns of disagreement: a reply to Angus Campbell. In D. Johnston, ed., *Measurement of Subjective Phenomena*. Special Demographic Analyses, CDS80-3, U.S. Bureau of the Census. Washington D.C.: Government Printing Office.

Turner, C., and Krauss, E. (1978) Fallible indicators of the subjective state of the nation. *American Psychologist* 33:456-470.

United Kingdom (Central Statistical Office) (1970-) *Social Trends*. London: Her Majesty's Stationery Office (annual).

United Nations (Department of Economic and Social Affairs) (1975) *Toward a System of Social and Demographic Statistics*. New York: United Nations.

U.S. Department of Commerce (1977) *Social Indicators: 1976*. Office of Federal Statistical Policy and Standards. Washington, D.C.: Government Printing Office.

Waksberg, J. (1975) How good are survey statistics? *Proceedings of the American Statistical Association (Social Statistics Section)* 1975:26-27.

Wilson, F., and Bumpass, L. (1973) The prediction of fertility among Catholics: a longitudinal analysis. *Demography* 10:591-597.

Wilson, T., and Nisbett, R. (1978) The accuracy of verbal reports about the effects of stimuli on evaluations and behavior. *Social Psychology* 41:118-130.

Youden, W. (1975) Statistical techniques for collaborative tests. In W. Youden and E. Steiner, eds., *Statistical Manual of the Association of Official Analytical Chemists*. Washington, D.C.: Association of Official Analytical Chemists.

Acknowledgments

The author is grateful for the helpful comments provided by a number of people including Robert P. Abelson, Donald Buzzelli, Clifford Clogg, Otis Dudley Duncan, Sara Kiesler, Denis Johnston, Cathie Marsh, Elizabeth Martin, Naomi D. Rothwell, Howard Schuman, and Tom Smith. An early draft of this chapter was published as a working paper (Turner, 1981a); an exchange of views with Angus Campbell (1981; Turner, 1981b) doubtlessly strengthened this final product.

8

Nonattitudes: A Review and
Evaluation

Tom W. Smith

Studies of voting behavior and other political matters in the fifties developed a picture of the American electorate that was startlingly at odds with the basic assumption of a rational citizenry as formulated in classic democratic theory. John Q. Voter was found to have (1) low levels of conceptualization with a limited and distorted ideological comprehension of issues; (2) little information about procedural details of the government, the identity or party of officeholders, and topical issues of the moment; (3) minimal political participation, with voting being the only political activity engaged in by a notable number of people; (4) weakly related attitudes, with positions on related issues showing only low to moderate associations; and (5) low consistency in issue positions. In general, the low or defective levels of conceptualization, information, participation, attitude constraint, and consistency were seen as indicating a very underdeveloped level of political thought and weak or disorganized political attitudes.

In particular, inconsistency in attitudes over time was interpreted as indicating an abundance of nonattitudes.[1] That is, the data were interpreted to mean that on many issues many people (up to 80 percent in the extreme case) had no real position on a question and randomly chose a response in order to come up with an answer to the attitude question. This chapter reviews the literature on nonattitudes. It examines how the concept of nonattitudes compares with rival explanations of mass belief systems, evaluates the conceptual and empirical appropriateness of competing formulations, and then considers the implications of these findings for survey design and analysis in general.

Converse's Nonattitudes

In the Survey Research Center (SRC) national election panel for 1956, 1958, and 1960, Philip Converse (1964, 1970, 1974, 1975; Converse and Markus, 1979) finds low correlations between attitudes across waves of the survey (tau betas of .3 to .5 for two-year intervals). Two things—true change and measurement error—could cause this turnover in opinions. Converse rejects the true-change explanation since (1) the marginal shifts were minimal, indicating that the massive individual conversions must have almost perfectly balanced out to produce next-to-zero net change, (2) the four-year correlations were typically as high as the two-year correlations, indicating that time was not related to the switches (or at least not in a presupposed linear fashion), and (3) an alternative measurement error model better described the data. Converse finds that a "black-and-white" model with extreme but intriguing assumptions could fit the data. This model assumes that there was no true change. Looking at the 1956 and 1958 waves, Converse empirically distinguishes a group that changed sides and a consistent group. He supposes that all changers were people who had no true position on the issue and who were simply guessing or randomly selecting a position each time. The consistent group was made up of two distinct types, a random group without real attitudes who simply selected the same response twice by chance, and a group of people with real and unchanging attitudes. Converse reasoned that between the second and third waves (1958 to 1960), the group that changed sides from the first to the second wave (1956 to 1958) should show no correlation, since their responses were random. The group that was consistent in the first two waves would have a correlation that would be an average of its random subgroup (with zero correlation) and its consistent subgroup (with a perfect correlation). On one item (power and housing) Converse's black-and-white model almost perfectly predicted the actual correlations, and on the others the fit was close enough to suggest that a relatively minor third force of true change was also at work.

Converse further argues that the random change was a function of respondents who did not have any attitude, giving meaningless and essentially random or, at best, labile and ephemeral responses in order to hide their ignorance, give the interviewer the desired response, or otherwise fulfill the perceived obligation of supplying a substantive response. He does not see the measurement error as coming from the questions themselves in the sense of shoddy wording. He points out that the questions had a face comprehensibility, that the same question-writing team that successfully developed consistent (and therefore reliable) measures for other areas had probably not suddenly become incompetent in framing questions in the area of public policy, and that elites managed to have substantially high constraint "even when asked to respond to the very same simplistic issue items" (Converse and Markus, 1979:43).[2] Instead, he sees the measurement error coming from an interaction between the substance of the questions and nonattitudes toward these issues by a large segment of the mass public.

To this group of hidden nonattitudes Converse adds a second group of "self confessed" nonattitudes (1975:62). This group consists of respondents who did not take sides on an issue on one or more of the three waves. Self-confessions differ from hidden nonattitudes in that respondents did not feel compelled to manufacture a substantive response, but freely admitted they had no opinion. Except for this distinction, these groups are considered as similar blocks of nonattitude-holders by Converse.

As Converse (1964:245) sums it up:[3]

(L)arge portions of an electorate do not have meaningful beliefs even on issues that have formed the basis for intense political controversy among elites for substantial periods of time. Where any single dimension is concerned, very substantial portions of the public simply do not belong on the dimension at all. They should be set aside as not forming any part of that particular *issue public*.

Converse and colleagues (Dreyer, 1973; Asher, 1974b) also stipulate various attributes of people, questions, and issues that would lead to low consistency. These are outlined below:

Associates of High Consistency

1. Attributes of People
   A. High education[4]
   B. High partisan activity
   C. High political interest
   D. Political elite
   E. High ideological development
   F. High political attentiveness
   G. High attitude integration/constraint
   H. High political information

2. Attributes of the Question
   A. Nonideological
   B. Close to everyday life
   C. Coherent, nonshoddy wording
   D. Focus on socially visible group

3. Attributes of the Issue
   A. Crystallization
   B. Centrality (cognitive and motivational)
   C. Salience
   D. Importance
   E. Intensity

4. Other Indicators
   A. Low proportion of "don't know"
   B. High interitem reliability

In brief, this literature argues that certain types of people who are politically aware tend to have low levels of nonattitudes and more consistent attitudes. Also, questions that are simple to understand, concrete, and technically adequate tend to have less item-based measurement error, smaller numbers of people with nonattitudes, and therefore high consistency. Finally, issues that are salient and important to the public, central to their political thoughts, and crystallized show a high level of genuine attitudes and high consistency. Respondents' general political awareness, and the clarity and concreteness of the item influence the general propensity of the item to be consistent. On the individual level, however, consistent response essentially depends on whether a particular issue is salient and important to the respondent, crystallized in that person's thoughts, and occupying a position of centrality.[5] If an issue is crystallized and central to a particular individual's thoughts, then it will be consistent regardless of the fact that the respondent may be uneducated, uninformed, and/or apathetic and that the question is imperfect (Arrington, 1976).

Instrument Error

Converse's evaluation of the panel data and his conclusions about the prevalence of nonattitudes have been challenged by a number of investigators. They contend that instrument unreliability, rather than nonattitudes, was the cause of the low correlations. John C. Pierce and Douglas D. Rose

(1974) argue that the variation Converse studied was mainly fluctuations in responses. The underlying attitude was stable and the variation in responses reflected (1) temporal influences that (a) did "not raise the level of inconsistency over the threshold and (b) continue to reflect the basic underlying predisposition; and (2) instrument-related variations reflecting both the instrument's and the individual's inability to discriminate the individual's precise affect" (Pierce and Rose, 1974:629).

Similarly, Christopher H. Achen (1975:1229) reexamines the 1956–1958–1960 panel data and concludes, "Measurement error is primarily a fault of the instruments not the respondents" (see comments of Stephens, 1976; Arrington, 1976; Hunter and Coggin, 1976; and rebuttal of Achen, 1976). Recently, Robert S. Erikson subjected the panel data to yet another reanalysis and decided, "The evidence forces us to reject a literal interpretation of the black-and-white model" (1979:104). While differing in particulars, each of these and other evaluations find instrument error rather than nonattitudes to be the source of the measurement error and inconsistency. All of the instrument-error interpretations share Converse's dismissal of true change as an explanation for the inconsistency. The following section analyzes the nonattitude, instrument-error, and true-change explanations, and considers their plausibility.[6]

To evaluate the competing explanations, the following matters are considered: (1) how the concepts of attitudes and nonattitudes are used, (2) ancillary evidence for hidden nonattitudes, (3) whether item nonresponse is equivalent to self-confessed nonattitudes, (4) how hidden nonattitudes might be distributed, (5) whether hidden and self-confessed nonattitudes show a pattern of correlation, as Converse predicted, and (6) evidence of instrument error among the election panel questions.

CONCEPT

There does not seem to be any basic difference among the various authors about the definition of attitudes, and all would appear to be comfortable with Thurstone's characterizations of an attitude "as the intensity of positive or negative affect for or against a psychological object. A psychological object is any symbol, person, phrase, slogan, or idea toward which people differ as regards positive or negative affect" (Thurstone, 1946:39). Pierce and Rose, however, draw a sharp distinction between the underlying attitude itself and surface measurements of it. They contend that respondents' attitudes are generally inert, but the expressions of their attitudes (that is, their recorded responses) are quite variable. This response variation occurs because of "short-term, temporal influences, of which there are several types (psychological, social, physical) contributing to a dispersal of the response around the position of the real attitude" and "instrument related variations reflecting both the instrument's and the individual's inability to discriminate the individual's precise affect" (Pierce and Rose, 1974:629). They go on to argue that neither true change nor nonattitudes are indicated by temporal inconsistency, since this variability can be explained by response variation around meaningful and stable attitudes.

While the distinction made by Pierce and Rose between attitudes and responses is valid, they err in assuming a great disparity between the two with the former being real and stable and the latter being artificial and labile. Their two explanations for response variation—temporal instability and instrument error—undoubtedly cause variation, but there is little reason to believe that these are the only sources of variation. If we accept a sharp distinction between real and stable attitudes and mere responses, then observed variability is accepted as proof that responses are varying around underlying attitudes, and instrument- and observation-related errors like those above become accepted as sufficient explanations for the observed variation.

A second and related problem arises over the concept of nonattitudes. It is unclear just how vacuous responses have to be to qualify as nonattitudes. Converse seems to describe them as devoid of redeeming intellectual value. He variously categorizes them as "capricious constructions," "meaningless opinions that vary randomly," "no belief at all," "hastily fabricated affective judgments," "very ad hoc feelings," and "haphazardly chosen alternatives." This obviously includes responses from people who have no idea what the question refers to and from those who comprehend the topic but have no feeling about it. It would also apparently include those with no prior feelings about the issue but who comprehend it and take a position that truly reflects their spontaneous opinion. It is unsure whether the concept goes further to include people with some prior affect but with only weak or confused thoughts on the issue.

The vagueness and gradients of what does and does not constitute a nonattitude are in stark contrast to the black-and-white formulation that breaks respondents into heterogeneous groups—perfectly consistent attitude holders and randomly responding nonattitude-holders. We see, however, that it is not clear just where the line between nonattitudes and attitudes falls and that within both nonattitudes and attitudes there are different subgroups. Among other things, this suggests there is actually a continuum of attitudes/nonattitudes and the black-and-white model tends to obscure this by using rigidly distinct groups.

In the relationship of attitudes to responses and of nonattitudes to attitudes, there has been a tendency to establish sharp distinctions between categories where there are really only blurs. There is also a danger of having the definition of the problem and concepts preordain the conclusions. This has led in some cases to a simplified and restricted analysis of the structure of attitudes and errors.

Nonattitudes: A Review and Evaluation

ARE THERE HIDDEN NONATTITUDES?

In support of his conclusion that a great deal of hidden nonattitude is secreted away amongst the substantive responses, Converse relates personal interviewing experience in which respondents indicated either implicitly or explicitly that their responses were largely meaningless and were being supplied just as a courtesy to the interviewer or to avoid the appearance of ignorance (1974:650). While Converse's account is illustrative and anecdotal and not presented as real proof of nonattitudes, it does present one mechanism, interviewer evaluation, by which response could be systematically evaluated. General interview evaluations of such things as comprehension and cooperation are fairly common, and even evaluations of individual questions are occasionally done, but this author does not know of any literature analyzing these data and relating them to the issue of nonattitudes.

There are, however, other ancillary bodies of literature that do bear on the existence and prevalence of hidden nonattitudes. These include the literature on (1) nonresponse, (2) knowledge, (3) fictive questions, (4) validation, and (5) response error. Each of these has some relevance to the hidden-nonattitude hypothesis.

The "don't know" literature (Bogart, 1967; Crespi, 1948; Schettler, 1960; Erikson and Luttbeg, 1973; and Hennessey, 1975) agrees that a great many nonattitudes are disguised as opinion.[7] Apparently many people are loathe to reply "don't know" (DK), since it implies ignorance or indecision. While there is actually little hard data on this point, work by Schuman and Presser (1978) shows that when an explicit "don't know" response is offered, the proportion selecting it rises substantially, typically 20 to 25 percentage points. A similar experiment on the 1978 General Social Survey finds the percentage of DK on a self-ranking conservatism/liberalism scale was 4.7 percent when no DK was mentioned, and 22.4 percent when an explicit DK option was offered (Smith, unpublished research). In brief, the literature in general and empirical studies agrees that the level of "don't knows" reported in surveys substantially underestimates the true level of these responses.

The knowledge literature (Bogart, 1967; Markel, 1972; Ferber, 1956; Erikson, Luttbeg, and Tedin, 1980; Payne, 1951; Smith, 1970; Erskine, 1963a, 1963b, 1963c; Hyman, Wright, and Reed, 1975) finds that DKs are typically much higher on knowledge questions than on opinion questions. Ferber (1956), in an adult sample of Champaign Urbana, finds that between 60 and 80 percent were either uninformed (didn't know) or misinformed (gave wrong answer) about basic facts concerning four attitude items. Gallup (1978:1176), in a national sample, finds that while 96 percent had an opinion on the importance of a balanced budget, 25 percent did not know whether the budget was currently balanced, 8 percent wrongly thought that it was balanced, 40 percent knew it was unbalanced but didn't know by how much, 25 percent knew it was unbalanced but overestimated or underestimated the amount by 15 percent or more, and 3 percent knew it was unbalanced and knew the approximate level of the deficit (plus or minus 15 percent). This suggests that many people are either "guessing" their opinion or have such low levels of factual understanding that a "don't know" response rather than a substantive response to the opinion item might seem more appropriate.[8]

Ferber (1956) goes on to show that those unknowledgeable about an issue nevertheless frequently express opinions about it. The misinformed had opinions just as frequently as the informed did, while many of those either unable to define reference terms or not knowing a basic (but not necessarily essential) fact about an issue expressed an opinion (14 to 47 percent of those unable to define a term used in a question had an opinion, and 62 to 83 percent not knowing a basic fact had an opinion).

Gallup (1978) also finds that knowledge was lower for those who thought a balanced budget was an important issue. Among those who thought a balanced budget was very important, 65 percent knew it was unbalanced; among those who thought it was fairly important, 72 percent knew it was unbalanced, and among those who did not think it was important, 85 percent knew it was unbalanced. It almost seems that the less one knows about an issue, the more important (mysterious?) one considers the issue. The causal connection was probably more subtle than that, however. Perhaps those without affect toward or knowledge about budgets saw "importance" as the desirable or proper response.

It is tempting simply to take lack of correct knowledge as indicative of hidden nonattitudes among the opinionated but uninformed. Generally speaking, there is probably a positive correlation between knowledge and attitude holding. The association is not perfect, however. Presumably, to have an opinion on an issue requires a certain minimum of essential information. But specifying just what is essential is difficult. For example, to respond to a question on increasing the minimum wage, it would seem essential to know what the term "minimum wage" refers to. It might also seem important to have an idea of what the current minimum wage is, but actually this basic fact is not necessarily essential. Free market conservatives could say "no" without knowing the actual wage rate because they oppose a minimum wage in principle. Social welfare liberals, on the other hand, could say "yes" because they "know" the rate is too low (without knowing just what it actually is) or because they figure an increase in the minimum wage would redistribute income, which they favor. In fact, in an extreme case, staunch conservatives could reject an increase without even knowing what the "minimum wage" referred to if they knew only that it was a "socialist" program or that "increase" implied more government involvement. Of course, as mentioned in the discussion of fictive questions, in this extreme circumstance it may be fair to say that there is only an attitude toward government or spending and not one on the increase of the minimum wage. Despite the imperfect connection, knowledge does relate to the quality of attitudes, and a lack of knowledge may well indicate hidden nonattitudes.

In brief, the knowledge literature suggests that either nonattitudes or factually impoverished attitudes are common. Because of the imperfect relationship between knowledge and attitudes, it is impossible to tell whether unknowledgeable respondents are manufacturing attitudes (nonattitudes) or have true feelings but severely limited factual support for their feelings.

Other evidence on nonattitudes comes from the fictive-question literature. In student, community, and national samples people have often answered questions about fictitious or extremely obscure issues and subjects as if they were real and familiar (Kolson and Green, 1970; Ehrlich, 1964; Hartley, 1946; Bennett, 1975a; Schuman and Presser, 1980; Patterson, 1972; Gill, 1947; Bishop et al., 1980; and Ehrlich and Rinehart, 1965). Schuman and Presser (1980) find that on a question about two extremely obscure pieces of legislation, 26 to 31 percent of a national sample offered opinions. G.F. Bishop et al. (1980) find that 33 percent of a Cincinnati area sample took sides on a fictive piece of legislation. In other studies, student samples frequently rated fictional persons or ethnic groups and answered nonsensical questions. In all of these cases it was impossible (or nearly impossible in the case of extremely obscure references) to have a meaningful attitude about the object or issue at hand. Opinions represented either (1) mistaken identity in which a respondent honestly and unknowingly confused the false reference with a real object; (2) imputed meaning in which the respondent (a) thought the reference was real, (b) did not know what it referred to directly, but (c) imputed a meaning from clues in the question and general predispositions; and/or (3) disguised ignorance in which a respondent (a) thought the reference was real, (b) did not understand the import of the questions, so (c) the respondent blindly chose a response to avoid replying "don't know." While these three patterns are not rigorously distinct or exhaustive, they probably represent the three most common reasons for giving substantive responses to fictitious questions.

Schuman and Presser (1980), G.F. Bishop et al. (1980), and Hartley (1946) all show that many of the false answers result from imputation. Respondents read meaning into the question and answer in terms of some general predisposition toward the economy, the government, or tolerance. In one sense, when people rely on such a predisposition they are showing ideological or constrained attitudes, since they are using general attitudes to supply responses to specific questions. On the Monetary Control Act example of Schuman and Presser, many of the tricked respondents were applying something like the following syllogism: Major Premise: I support programs to curb inflation. Minor Premise: The Monetary Control Act is a program to curb inflation. Conclusion: I support the Monetary Control Act. The problem is that the minor premise that they imputed from the bill's name is wrong, since the Monetary Control Act in fact deals with bank regulations. Other qualitative evidence from this literature suggests that strict cases of mistaken identity (with real bills, people, or groups) are rare. Other respondents apparently chose an answer without any regard to the subject of the question, although they may have been influenced by the response categories in the form of positivity or playing-it-safe response effects (Kolson and Green, 1970).

The fictive-question literature shows a common tendency to overrespond to questions, to impute, or even conjure up answers. This is obviously similar to Converse's concept of hidden nonattitudes. There are some notable differences, however. Nonattitudes on the fictive questions are not distributed randomly, but are the result, in many instances, of imputations. Nonattitudes on the fictive questions can be correlated with other attitude items and would presumably show some consistency (correlated error in a sense) across time. In brief, the fictive-question literature suggests that hidden nonattitudes are fairly common, but that many of these nonattitudes are not random, as Converse's model supposes.

Next, data on validation provide evidence of a pattern of response distribution due to social desirability that is similar to the process that supposedly generates many nonattitudes. This literature indicates that good behaviors or conditions are overreported (voting, registration, having a library card), while bad attributes (bankruptcy, drunken driving) are underreported (Bell and Buchanan, 1966; Traugott and Katosh, 1979; Bradburn and Sudman, 1979; and DeMaio, chapter 9 in this volume). Of course, the items verifiable through record checks are distinctly different from attitudes since they are objective, concrete facts rather than personal feelings, yet it is reasonable to suppose that a similar desirability effect could cause people to give substantive responses (the good) and avoid disclosing nonattitudes (the bad). Of course this is not the only way that social desirability might interact with nonattitudes. Unpopular or impolite opinions (racist opinions held by a white being interviewed by a black, for example) might be transmuted into a *DK* as a "halfway" social-desirability effect. The relationships are outlined in Table 8.1 showing an attitude with three responses: Yes, DK, and No. Yes is assumed to be the undesirable substantive response, and No is the desirable substantive response.

In this example, outcomes 7 and 8 should be nil (except for something like recording error, for example, keypunching). Outcome 6 will be followed by those randomly choosing this substantive response plus those nonattitude-holders who grasp the question enough to perceive that this is

TABLE 8.1

Impact of Social Desirability on Opinions

True Opinion	Desirability of Opinion	Given Opinion	Characterization
Yes	Very undesirable	1. Yes	Nonconformist
		2. DK	False DK, "halfway" social desirability
		3. No	False conformist
DK	Somewhat undesirable	4. Yes	False nonconformist
		5. DK	Self-confessed nonattitude/ ambivalent
		6. No	False conformist
No	Desirable	7. Yes	False nonconformist
		8. DK	False DK
		9. No	Conformist

NOTE: Yes, DK, and No. Yes is assumed to be the undesirable substantive response, and No is the desirable substantive response.

the socially preferred response even though they have no opinion of the matter. Outcome 4 would presumably be taken only by the random nonattitude-holder, since if the issue was understood, one would then avoid covering up one's somewhat undesirable nonattitude by expressing an even more undesirable substantive opinion. (In effect the uncomprehending DK does not recognize that "yes" is less desirable than DK for this question. Not comprehending the question enough to recognize the undesirability of a "yes" response, the uncomprehending DK applies the general rule that it is more desirable to have an opinion than not to have one, and picks unreflectively between the two substantive positions.) In outcomes 2 and 3 the nonconformist hides this undesirable opinion by switching to either DK or "no."

The net impact would be that the observed number of "no's" would be greater than the true number, while the observed number of "yes's" would be lower than the true number. It is uncertain, however, whether the observed number of DKs would be higher or lower than the true number. The number of observed DKs would be reduced by the loss of respondents expressing an opinion to disguise their lack of opinion, but increased by the "halfway" social-desirability effect as those holding the undesirable position reduce social disapproval by opting for the relatively less undesirable DK position. Presumably if the number of people with a nonconformist position was substantial and the social-desirability effect was strong, then many would disguise their position by replying DK or "no." If the number of nonconformists was small and the social-desirability effect was slight, then few would change position to DK or "no." In the first case, the number of observed DKs might easily exceed the true number, while in the latter case the opposite would probably prevail. In sum, we see that the validation literature supports the notion that respondents will disguise their true state by giving more socially desirable responses, but at least where a strong social-desirability effect applies to the substantive responses it is uncertain whether the observed number of DKs would be higher or lower than the true number.

Finally, response effects such as context, balance, or response options may indicate the existence of nonattitudes. On one hand, these response errors represent instrument errors. It is commonly assumed in the survey literature that these factors cannot work their havoc or at least have a diminished impact if attitudes are crystallized (Converse, 1970:177; Payne, 1951:135, 179; Erikson, Luttbeg, and Tedin, 1980:29; Hovland, Harvey and Sherif, 1957; Schuman and Presser, 1981). Thus the evidence of these types of response errors may also indicate either weakly integrated, uncrystallized attitudes, or perhaps nonattitudes as we cross that hazy line. However, not all types of nonattitudes will be influenced by response effects. In the extreme case in which there is no comprehension, or comprehension but absolutely no affect, then a substantive-context effect would presumably have no impact, since the respondent answers each question independently by randomly picking a response. Nothing so substantive as a context effect would bother this person's selection process. In the case of an ad hoc affect just the opposite situation would apply. Presumably the context question might be a major factor in establishing a frame of reference that would in turn help to elicit the ad hoc affect on the subsequent related question (Stember, 1951-52). This divergent response of nonattitudes to response effects of course makes it hard to clearly relate these two features.

It could be that such things as context effects are created not by people with nonattitudes but because of measurement error in the subsequent question. Perhaps for a vague question, people rely more on the preceding question to help resolve the vagueness and supply an answer. If a measurement error is correlated with attributes of the respondent, then at least to some extent measurement error is no longer just instrument error but is partly respondent error. The distinction between nonattitude error and instrument error becomes hard to sustain. If a context effect or response set is greater for the less educated, this could be because the less educated are more likely to be nonattitude-holders. It could also be because the less educated are more likely to have their attitudes distorted (modified?) by extraneous influences. But even if we lean toward the second option, the question is whether the greater susceptibility of the less educated to response effects is completely unrelated to their attitudes. If they have less-crystallized attitudes or less integrated attitudes, then (1) their attitudes might be more susceptible to response effects, and (2) we have just about gotten back to nonattitudes as the cause of the response effect differential. If their attitude has the same quality as that of the better educated, but the less educated are more easily dissuaded because of some factor unrelated to the attitude in question, (such as inarticulateness, poor vocabulary, inattention, and so forth), then the measurement error is an interaction of instrument and respondent error, but nonattitudes have no role.

Traditionally, it was commonly supposed that most types of measurement error would be higher for the less educated, less politically involved, uninformed—in general, for those with less-crystallized attitudes. Unfortunately these expectations, while based on a reasonable theory, had very little empirical evidence to support them. In a recent work, Schuman and Presser (1981) find that more often than not response effects do not interact with these types of respondent attributes. When an interaction does occur, however, it is typically in the hypothesized direction. It is difficult from the evidence at hand to determine whether the occasional interactions are because of an attitude-related factor or because of more generalized factors not related to specific attitudes. The fact that Schuman and Presser find that counterargument questions tend to show interactions with education (with the less educated more influenced by the introduction of an explicit counter argument) does suggest that the magnitude of the response effect may be related to the quality of the attitude being measured. In sum, while traditional expectations suggest a relationship between response effects (such as context) and nonattitudes, the ambiguity of this relationship for different types of nonattitudes, the mixed empirical results, and the alternative explanations for the associations make it difficult to draw any definite connection between the two.

In reviewing ancillary evidence in support of Converse's concept of hidden nonattitudes, this author found various sources supporting the idea that a substantial number of substantive responses might really represent nonattitudes. The DK, fictive-question, and knowledge-question literature all indicate that people tend to give substantive responses even when they have little or no interest in a question, are only guessing at the meaning of a question, or lack knowledge about basic facts of a question. These pieces of evidence do not indicate that nonattitudes are the sole root of the problem, however.

The validation literature demonstrates that there may be a social-desirability effect similar to that supposed for nonattitudes working in related areas, but also suggests that DKs can include a nontrivial number of people who really have attitudes. The response-effect literature turns out to be too ambiguous in both theory and empirical results to shed much light on the matter. The net conclusion, however, must be that these various areas present substantial support for the notion of hidden nonattitudes while sometimes suggesting that nonattitudes may not be simply random and that there might be a continuum between nonattitudes; labile, unstructured attitudes; and crystallized attitudes, rather than any sharp separation.

ARE DKS NONATTITUDES?

Earlier in the discussion of DKs it was found that among substantive responses are hidden nonattitudes. This section examines whether among DKs ("self-confessed nonattitudes") there are attitude-holders. Researchers commonly distinguish between DKs that mean that the respondent has no position on the issue (a nonattitude case) and DKs that indicate the respondent cannot choose between the alternatives (an ambivalent case).[9] In the first case respondents have no place on the attitude continuum, but in the latter they are at the midpoint. Evidence on the relative size of these two categories suggests that both types are substantial. In their national survey on wind energy, Faulkenberry and Mason (1978) had interviewers code DK as being either a nonattitude or ambivalent. They that 45.2 percent of the DKs were ambivalent. Coombs and Coombs (1976), with a sample of Taiwanese women aged 20 to 40, find that based on an analysis of answers to a six-item abortion scale, "75.5 percent of all DK responses are scale dependent ('ambivalent') in the sense of being accounted for by admissible scale patterns" [p. 509]. Ehrlich (1964) finds in a sample of American college students that 80.4 percent who did not express substantive positions on issues selected an ambivalent nonresponse category over a nonattitude alernative. Dunnette, Uphoff, and Aylward (1956), in a sample from nine unions, report that nonresponse split 50/50 between ambivalent and nonattitude categories.

Actually, some of the most complete information comes from the SRC election studies. In the 1956 survey, 15 attitude questions were presented after the following introduction:

> Around election time people talk about different things that our government in Washington is doing or should be doing. Now I would like to talk to you about some of the things that our government might do. Of course, different things are important to different people, so we don't expect everyone to have an opinion about all of these.
>
> Q. 12. I would like you to look at this card as I read each question and tell me how you feel about the question. If you don't have an opinion, just tell me that; if you do have an opinion, choose one of the other answers.
>
> Q. 12a. "The government ought to cut taxes even if it means putting off some important things that need to be done." Now, would you say you have an opinion on this or not? (IF "YES"): Do you agree that the government *should* do this or do you think the government should *not* do it?

Nonattitudes: A Review and Evaluation

The card listed five categories: "agree strongly; agree but not very strongly; not sure, it depends; disagree but not very strongly; and disagree strongly." In addition to these five categories, responses were also coded as "no opinion" and as DK. Clearly the "not sure, it depends" response indicates an ambivalent answer. "No opinion" corresponds to not having an opinion. DK is a bit unclear; it appears to refer to the case in which people have an opinion but "don't know" what it is. These results show that an average of .605 of the nonsubstantive responses were nonattitudes, .342 were ambivalent, and .054 were the ambiguous DKs.

In the 1960 survey, eight attitude questions were coded in a similar format:

> Around election time people talk about different things that our government in Washington is doing or should be doing. Now I would like to talk to you about some of the things that our government might do. Of course, different things are important to different people, so we don't expect everyone to have an opinion about all of these.
>
> Q. 17 and 17A. "The government should leave things like electric power and housing for private businessmen to handle." Do you have any opinion on this or not. (If Yes) Do you think the government should leave things like this to private business.

The average results show fewer nonattitudes than do those in 1956 (.533), more ambivalent response (.408), and the same level of ambiguous DKs (.059).[10]

It is clear, however, from both sets of SRC data that ambivalent responses are common and may *on average* account for one-third to one-half of all nonsubstantive responses. In brief, the evidence indicates that a substantial share of nonresponse is ambivalent attitudes rather than nonattitudes.[11]

In addition, there are numerous other reasons why respondents might give DKs rather than the two commonly listed types. These include (1) concealing one's opinion out of a sense of privacy, (2) failing to assert one's opinion because of a lack of confidence, shyness, or related reasons, (3) trying to be inoffensive or polite (a halfway social-desirability effect), (4) attempting to avoid subsidiary questions and to rush completion of the interview (this strategy would not work if DKs were heavily probed), or (5) seizing a temporary expression of uncertainty while respondent collects thoughts and mulls over the issue. Virtually nothing is known about these DKs, but presumably some of the DKs customarily thought of as reflecting nonattitudes or ambivalence really stem from such unrelated causes as these. In sum, while numerous nonattitudes are disguised among definite responses, there are also among the DKs many that are not nonattitudes.

Converse is aware of the difference between nonattitudes and ambivalent responses (1970:179-180), but in his handling of the black-and-white model he treats all nonresponses as nonattitudes.[12] The undecided, however, do not fit the concept of nonattitudes since they are located on the affect continuum and do not behave like nonattitude-holders. According to the 1956–1958–1960 SRC panel data, the undecided group has notably more political involvement and education than the nonattitude group has.[13] Examination of the level of political activity (six-item scale), voting history, and interest in politics shows that in both 1956 and 1958 on both the power and housing and the school integration questions, the undecided group had distinctly more political involvement than did the nonattitude group. For example, in 1958, 16 percent of the nonattitude group on power and housing were very interested in politics, while 29 percent of the undecided group were. Similarly, only 4.3 percent of the nonattitude-holders were college educated, while 23.0 percent of the undecideds were. In brief, the undecided group is not only conceptually distinct, but differs from the nonattitude group in its political involvement and education.

In sum, DKs are not merely self-confessed nonattitudes, but contain a variety of attitudes, especially ambivalent responses. Because of this, DKs cannot be simply treated as off-scale nonattitudes and excluded, or placed in a middle category as ambivalent responses. DKs arise from complex causes and must be treated in a complex manner.

DISTRIBUTION OF HIDDEN NONATTITUDES

Converse states that hidden-nonattitude-holders will randomly choose between response categories with little or no regard for their substance. When Pierce and Rose (1974) showed that a random equiprobable distribution on nonattitudes was at variance with the observed distributions, Converse (1974) clarified his earlier remarks by noting that equiprobability was not a necessary attribute of randomness, and suggested a biased-coin model instead. A review of the literature on "random" responding found five models offered to explain the distribution of nonattitudelike responses. The equiprobability model has respondents distribute their responses equally among all categories. The playing-it-safe model has respondents favoring a middle or neutral response as the safest or least offensive response (Ferber, 1956; Rogers, Stuhler, and Koenig, 1967; Brim, 1955; Ehrlich, 1964; and Schuman and Presser, 1978). The positivity-response-set model suggests that respondents will favor a positive over a negative response (Berg and Rapaport, 1954; Kolson and Green, 1970; and Ehrlich, 1964). The social-desirability model has respondents trying to guess or impute the proper answer (Phillips and Clancy, 1972); that is, "proper" in the sense of the correct answer, the answer supplied by the majority, or the answer that the interviewer wants. Finally, the imputed-understanding model has respondents taking clues in the question to supply meaning and then answering the question according to a predisposition toward the perceived meaning (Hartley, 1946; Bishop, Hamilton, and McConahay, 1980; and Schuman and Presser, 1980).[14] In the equiprobable, playing-it-safe, and positivity-response-set models, the respondents need not have any understanding of the import of the question. In the social-desirability model they understand the question but have no affect toward it. In the imputed-understanding model they think they decipher the meaning and have an affect toward that imputed meaning.

The results make clear that various demonstrated effects are tendencies, not uniform, homogenous outcomes. Furthermore, each of these models is plausible and has some empirical support. The implications of each model for the distribution of hidden nonattitudes both cross-sectionally and longitudinally are quite different. The equiprobable model would produce a high rate of turnover that would be predictable in the aggregate. A biased-coin version of the positivity-response-set or middle-alternative models would produce less turnover but would still be known in the aggregate. If, however, we assume that some people consistently give the positive or safe response and that the remainder pick a response randomly using equal probabilities, the rate of turnover would be even less and would be hard to predict even in the aggregate. For the social desirability and imputed understanding models, there might be even less change if respondents interpreted the meaning or social-desirability clues consistently, as Schuman and Presser's (1981) work on obscure opinion suggests. Since each of these models probably operates to some extent, and their relative contributions vary across items, context, and other variables, it would be difficult to assess how nonattitude responses would be distributed and impossible to anticipate their distribution over multiple waves. Assumptions of random distribution, even a biased-coin effect, are too simplistic to describe most actual situations.

CORRELATES OF NONATTITUDES

Several tests have been made to see if the hidden and self-confessed nonattitudes behave as Converse and his colleagues argue, or whether the instrument-error explanation better fits the data. The three main tests are: (1) whether the nonattitude-holders show interitem attitude constraint, (2) whether the nonattitude-holders, have a background profile that is related to attitude holding, and (3) whether nonattitude-holders show temporal consistency. For the self-confessed nonattitude-holders, the tests check to see if this group behaves in a manner consistent with the nonattitude hypothesis. For the hidden-nonattitude-holder, the question is whether the black-and-white method of identifying this group (changing sides on the issue between time 1 and 2) actually specifies a group that behaves like nonattitude-holders.

In Converse's formulation, nonattitude-holders are concentrated among people with a low level of political involvement, little interest in political matters, and low level of education. In support for his position he notes that among "very limited sets of people . . . who had shown 'self starting' concern about particular controversies" on certain open-ended questions, the consistency correlations are substantially higher "beginning to approach levels of stability for party identification. . . ." (Converse, 1964:244-45). In later reanalysis, Converse looks at consistency within more general groups. He finds that the better educated were more consistent, but the differences were "quite trifling." He does find, however, that "partisan activists showed notably higher levels of stability in their responses to these issues over time than did persons less engaged in the political process" (1975:103–104). Achen (1975) and Erikson (1979), however, look at the association between consistency and such indicators as political concern, political interest, education, socioeconomic status (SES), voting, political activity, mass media attention, and political knowledge; they find no relationship.

We carried out a similar analysis of the 1956–1958–1960 panel data and came up with essentially the same conclusion as did Achen and Erikson. Because of the lack of details about the data that Converse used, it was not possible to attempt to replicate his findings, but many of the variables employed by Erikson and Achen which presumably overlapped with those that Converse used to specify his "partisan activists" were examined.

We also looked at related research that examined similar questions with alternative methods and different data sources. Grant and Patterson (1975) in a panel survey of Buffalo, New York, use three criteria to measure random responders (high intraperson variance to scale items, bidirectional change over time, and inconsistent responses to reversed items) and find that on three psychopolitical scales, nonattitudes correlated with low education, low political information, low income, and being black, but were unrelated to political interest (see also Patterson, 1972).

Asher (1974b) in an analysis of the 1956–1958–1960 election panel and the 1968 preelection and postelection surveys finds that consistency on political efficacy items was generally higher among those with more education and political interest. The opposite relationship appeared on the "no political power" item, however, and the other items showed mixed or qualified associations. Asher summarizes that "a partially successful attempt was made to attribute the low reliability to properties of the respondents rather than to deficiencies of the measuring instrument itself" (1974b:64).

Iyengar (1973), in a student sample using six social/political psychological scales, finds no consistent associations between social and political interest, political information, level of opinionation, grade point average, course grade, or age, and consistency. He does find that consistency is associated with scalability on the political efficacy scale. Those who tended to answer the efficacy scale in conformity with Guttman standards showed greater consistency in their scale scores over time. In effect, those who responded to the efficacy scale in a nonrandom manner were more consistent in their responses across time.

Smith (1980), in several small (200– to 300–case) national panels over a 6-week period, notes that education is the best predictor of consistency. He believes this was due to the better educated having greater reliability rather than greater stability. He does not relate reliability to instrument error versus nonattitudes, however.

Brown (1970), in a small, short-term study, finds no differences in consistency between people who are politically articulate and inarticulate.

Bishop, Hamilton, and McConahay (1980), in a small panel of suburban New Haven, find that the college educated are not significantly more consistent than are those without a college education over a 9- to 11-month interval.

Using a small subsample from SRC's 1972–1974–1976 panel, Judd and Milburn (1980) find that, correcting for measurement error, the stability of elite and nonelite groups (college graduates versus those having no college education) was the same. Finally, Hahn's (1970) analysis of a two-wave fluoridation survey in Detroit finds that "converters" (people who change sides on the issue) are less likely to have read about the issue, less interested in the issue, less likely to vote, less likely to vote on the fluoridation issue, but more likely to have a high or increasing level of discussion about the issue than is the consistent group. The differences are usually small and insignificant, however, and are less than the differences between converters and people who are ambivalent or indecisive (those with DKs at one or both times, respectively). Furthermore, Hahn accepts his data at face value as describing true differences between four accurately distinguished groups and does not infer that the converters are nonattitude-holders.

The net result of this comparison between over-time consistency and political and cognitive involvement is rather mixed. Evidence from the original SRC panel shows no relationship, while other relevant studies show mixed results. Overall, if we take inconsistency as indicative of nonattitudes, then we would expect a much more substantial and repetitive association. Two factors might explain these findings. First, we must assume that true change is a negligible factor, or at least is constant across groups. Trivial true change is assumed by both sides in the SRC panel data and is implicit in the Grant and Patterson (1975)[15] and Iyengar (1973) studies. Hahn (1970), however, makes just the opposite assumption—namely, that all the changes represent true change (and thus those who switch sides on the fluoridation issue are converters, while the black-and-white model counts them as nonattitude-holders). If there is an appreciable amount of true change and it differs between groups, we cannot separate the association between true change and these various attributes and have not even begun to determine if the measurement error resembles nonattitudes or instrument error.[16]

Second, it may be that most of the measures used do not really relate to nonattitudes. While Converse does argue that general measures are related to consistency, he also talks of specific "issue-publics." An individual is a member of some issue-publics but not all. It is only the fact that such general orientations as voting and political involvement are related to the number of issue-publics a person belongs to that explains the hypothesized relationship between consistency and these variables. Erikson (1979:109) acknowledges that it might be preferable to measure the level of interest toward the specific issue rather than to use global interest and involvement measures. He finds this unsatisfactory, however, stating that it would require that there be no association between general political sophistication and interest in a specific issue, and that interest levels be uncorrelated with one another across issues.

Schuman and Presser (1981) show, however, that general measures of intensity are usually poor substitutes for item-specific measures. Because of the disparity between the general and specific, we need to examine the correlates of consistency with more item-specific measures (for example, issue importance, knowledge about, or activity involving) before we can assess fully their connection. In national telephone panels, Schuman and Presser (1981) found that item-specific measures show that those who consider the issue more important are more consistent. Education shows an irregular association, sometimes playing an important role and other times apparently being unrelated to consistency. Similar results are reported by Goldenson (1979). In a student panel, he finds a positive association between issue intensity and consistency.

Because of the confounding of true change and time and the use of general and indirect measures of nonattitudes instead of issue-specific and more direct measures, it is impossible to conclude that nonattitudes are not prevalent among converters. However, the available data suggest that nonattitudes are not highly related to general cognitive and political indicators, and that either switching is not related to nonattitude holding, or that nonattitude holding is not the sole factor in switching, being mixed in with instrument error and true change.

In analyzing the 1956–1958–1980 panel data, we next looked at the association between the self-confessed nonattitudes (DKs) and these same background variables. Looking at people who gave one DK in 1956 or 1958 and those who gave DK both times to the power and housing question, we found that they had decidedly less political interest and lower education than respondents who were either consistent or who switched responses. While 52 percent of those who gave substantive responses engaged in no political activity, 67 percent of those with one DK and 75 percent of those with two DKs reported no activity. On education, 42 percent of those with substantive positions had less than a high school education, while 54 percent of those with one DK and 68 percent with two DKs had less than a high school education. Similar patterns appeared on voting, political interest, and political knowledge.

Looking at the general literature on DKs (for factors associated with DK, see Table 8.2), we find that there is definitely some correspondence between factors associated with attitude inconsistency (Converse's prime indicator of nonattitudes) and those associated with DK. Low education, low political interest and activity, and low information and unimportance of the issue are related to both. In general, the associations predicted for nonattitudes hold up more clearly and steadily for DKs than they do for the hidden nonattitudes. It is also apparent that some of the causes of high DK such as task difficulty and question form are not similarly related, and other attributes related to DKs have an unknown relationship to consistency and ultimately to nonattitudes. In sum, the factors associated with DK are generally similar to those predicted for nonattitudes.

A second test on Converse's hidden-nonattitude-holders compares the inter-item constraint for respondents who are inconsistent and consistent over time. Converse argues that inconsistent responses are random and should show no association with other attitudes. Pierce and Rose (1974) attempt this test, but because they operationalized inconsistency in a manner at odds with Converse's formulation, their findings are not relevant. Erikson does carry out this comparison successfully and concludes that "the evidence forces us to reject a literal interpretation of the black-and-white model" (1979:104). He overlooks two important patterns in his findings, however. First, there is a substantial difference in the associations for people who respond consistently and inconsistently.

Among consistent responders, the gammas average .60, but among changers the gammas are one-half as strong (.29). This is still nontrivial, but we should be equally impressed with the attenuation as with the residual. Second, by looking at all interrelations among the eight attitude items, Erikson includes variables that Converse admits do not fit his black-and-white model. Converse contends only that the power and housing question shows no true change. On the other questions, the changers include those with real attitudes at both times. This group would be expected to show attitude constraint across items. If we look at just the power and housing question, we see that the average gamma for consistent respondents (.52) is reduced by more than two-thirds if we use absolute values, or by almost four-fifths if we subtract associations that change signs (that is, reverse the initial relationship among consistent respondents).

TABLE 8.2
Characteristics Associated with High DKs

1. Characteristics of Respondent
   A. Low education[a]
   B. Low occupational prestige
   C. Low income
   D. Female
   E. Old[b]
   F. Low political activity
   G. Low political efficacy
   H. Housewives
   I. Member of general public rather than opinion leader

2. Characteristic of Interview
   A. Poor rapport
   B. No probing for substantive responses
   C. Telephone rather than personal

3. Characteristic of Issue
   A. Low media exposure about issue
   B. Low awareness of issue
   C. Low knowledge about issue
   D. Low personal involvement, low self-interest
   E. Low temporal consistency
   F. Low intensity

4. Characteristic of Question
   A. Dichotomy
   B. Task difficult (long explanation or future projection or requires thought or effort)
   C. Explicit DK option
   D. Language difficulty[c]
   E. Knowledge versus opinion

[a]With exception of Hyman and Wright (1979:28).
[b]Age is found to be related in many studies, although some suggest it might be a spurious association due to education. Gergen and Back (1966) argue that age is related to nonopinionation (DKs) as the elderly disengage from society. Glenn (1969), however, challenges this assertion and, with controls for education, race, and sex, finds there is no association between age and opinionation. Smith (1978), using the same controls as Glenn, finds that the association between DKs and age is reduced by these prior factors but does not diappear.
[c]Jean Converse (1976–77:521–23) finds little support for such an association, which contradicts early work cited in her article.

Since it is impossible to tell exactly how Erikson conducted his analysis or whether he precisely followed Converse's formulations, we carried out a parallel analysis. We examined respondents showing no changes from agree to disagree (or vice versa) between 1956 and 1958 and those with one or two changes but no DKs in 1956 and 1958. On the seven associations between power and housing and the other items, gammas for consistent respondents average .191 in 1956 and .196 in 1958. Among changers, it is .111 and .078, respectively. The difference between consistent and inconsistent respondents is even greater for the domestic items (for which there are fairly arguable face interrelationships). For the four domestic associations involving power and housing, the average gammas are: consistent respondents, .447 in 1956, .411 in 1958; and changers, .085 in 1956, .126 in 1958. This pattern is similar for the other domestic interrelationships and to Erikson's findings. It indicates that changers are much less constrained than are the stable. While they have some apparent constraint (and this varies from Converse's description of them as totally random), they show much less constraint than people who give consistent responses. It seems fair to argue that they have a much larger random component than do the consistent respondents.

It is possible that the stable cases have their interitem associations inflated by correlated error such as a response set. However, there is little evidence for this. Three of the five domestic items are framed in a liberal direction and two in a conservative direction. This reversal tends to negate the correlation-pumping impact of a response effect, and, moreover, the association between the two conservatively worded questions is not stronger than those in opposite directions.

A second explanation for the lower interitem association might be the idiosyncratic ideology perspective suggested by Lane (1962, 1973) to typify mass attitudes. He argues that attitudes are constrained, but neither by general liberalism nor by any other generalized belief system. Instead, attitudes are kept intact by personally meaningful belief systems which cannot be aggregated across individuals and thus do not show up in aggregate interitem correlations. In this case, for Lane's perspective to explain the differences in the observed attitude constraint, there would have to be an interaction between observed change and ideological type. For example, perhaps a general ideological framework leads to greater stability, while idiosyncratic ideology results in attitudes that are more changeable. This or some other causal connection would have to exist in order for changers to have just as many true attitudes but much less constraint. While possible, it seems unlikely unless we also accept the ideologically idiosyncratic as having much more labile attitudes on each specific issue, a condition that would not make them very different from nonattitude-holders.

Turning to DKs, we find a constraint pattern that is similar to that shown by changers. Erikson finds that among those with at least one nonresponse to at least one item, the gammas average .31, about the same as for the changers. We found that when there was a DK in either 1956 or 1958 and no change on the other variable, gammas average .144 (1956 and 1958) for the associations with the power and housing item and other domestic items. This is less than one-half the magnitude shown by the consistent respondents, but twice that shown by the changers (.071). Among those who had two tags of nonattitudes (either DKs on both variables or both variables changed), the associations are even lower, an average of .038 for the domestic power and housing associations in 1956 and 1958. These figures are similar for the other items. They indicate that people who switched from or to a DK had less constrained attitudes than did consistent respondents; but that this is not as indicative of lower constraint as inconsistencies were. It does suggest, barring Lane's interpretation, that DKs may indicate more random responses.

Another check on the association between DKs and attitude constraint comes from the opinion-floaters literature. Schuman and Presser (1978), Bishop and associates (1979a), and the 1978 General Social Survey (Davis and Smith, 1982) have used split-ballot experiments to compare questions with and without an explicit DK option. It was noted previously that the explicit DK version usually attracts around 20 to 25 percent more DK responses ("floaters") than does the implicit version. The impact of DKs on associations can be evaluated by comparing the associations between the implicit and explicit DK versions and other attitude items.

Schuman and Presser (1978) examine three hypotheses on the differences in associations between the forms. The traditional form-resistant hypothesis argues that while the response distributions would naturally vary, associations with other variables would be similar for both forms. Converse's hypothesis, on the other hand, argues that associations with other variables would be attenuated on the questions without an explicit DK, since that meant that more nonattitude-holders' random responses would slip into the substantive response categories, lowering inter-item correlations. Lastly, Schuman and Presser consider the counterintuitive explanation that the explicit DK form would have higher correlations. The results are sufficiently mixed to give strong support in particular cases to each hypothesis. As they conclude, "The number, nature, and size of substantively important interactions attributable to floating remain very much open" (1978).

Bishop et al. (1979a) also find a mixed outcome, with some associations increasing while others decline, but they conclude that "the dominant tendency is for floating to decrease the magnitude of the inter-item correlations" (1979a:301). In the 1978 GSS experiment with self-ranking on a liberal/conservative scale, the associations with seven of eight liberal/conservative attitude items are lower when floaters are included, but the decline averages a modest .025 (gamma). These results are equivocal enough to suggest that DKs not only do not indicate a complete lack of attitude constraint at prior or subsequent points in time, but also that floating DKs do not consistently have random, meaningless responses that automatically attenuate associations.

And finally, we come to the classic test for nonattitudes. Converse finds that on the power and housing question, those who changed sides between time 1 and time 2 show no association between their time 2 and time 3 answers. On other variables there are small associations between time 2 and time 3 responses for people who changed from time 1 to time 2, but the associations are weak enough to suggest to Converse that a small group of true changers were raising the associations above zero. While these facts have gone unchallenged, their interpretation has not. The instrument-error school also interprets these patterns as indicating random measurement error, as opposed to true change, but places the origin with the tools rather than with the raw materials.

A similar test of the impact of DKs on consistency can be carried out by looking at whether those with DKs at time 1 have any association between time 2 and time 3 responses. Achen (1975:1226) considers this and finds that "a respondent could describe himself as having no opinion at one of the time points and still give at the other two time points responses that were far from random." We find that this is true on the power and housing and school integration questions, but that the over-time correlations are weaker. For example, for those who in 1956 either agreed or disagreed with the power and housing question, the gamma between 1958 and 1960 is .371, while it is less than half (.182) for those giving DKs in 1956. Similarly, for school integration the respective gammas are .559 and .413.[17] Once again, this suggests that while expressing DKs does distinguish cases from substantive answers and indicates a presence of more random variation, DKs are not indicators of totally random responses, as the black-and-white model suggests.

It could of course be argued that at time 1 these were totally vacuous nonattitudes, but between time 1 and time 2 some had changed and adopted real attitudes on the questions. The lower associations would be explained by the fact that some had merely changed from self-confessed to hidden nonattitudes, and that these cases were attenuating the association between time 1 and time 2. This is a reasonable possibility, but one that neither Converse's black-and-white model nor the other three-wave models permit (except Dean and Moran, 1977). Both approaches exclude from analysis cases that were DK at any time. This results in a major loss of cases. For example, Achen (1975) reports reduction on attitudes of 30 to 50 percent, and Judd and Milburn (1980) have their case base reduced by 65 percent. This also precludes any true change between nonattitudes and holding real attitudes. The exclusion of this large group greatly restricts our understanding of the general process of attitude formation and change.[18]

Various tests of the hidden and self-confessed nonattitude groups often show differences in the expected direction, but not as extreme or regular as predicted. Responses of hidden-nonattitude-holders (changers) have weak and scattered associations with most general measures of political involvement and education, but show more notable associations with item-specific measures of interest. Changers show much less constraint than do consistent respondents, but their answers are associated with other policy items. Changers between time 1 and time 2 show weak or independent associations over subsequent waves. DK respondents are less politically involved and less educated, as expected. Their attitudes show lower constraint than the consistent respondents (although not as low as changers), and lower but not random associations over time. This may result from the contamination of nonattitude groups with attitude-holders (for example, true changers who give inconsistent responses at different times, or ambivalent people who say DK). It may also come from the fact that there is not a sharp dividing line between attitudes and nonattitudes. There is instead a continuum—from completely vacuous guesses at one end to crystallized, integrated opinions at the other. People tagged as nonattitude-holders because they switch answers or give a DK response at one time may have labile attitudes with low centrality, but still have some affect toward an issue. While they may lack a stable, fully-articulated, and meaningful position, they may well have certain leanings.

EVIDENCE OF INSTRUMENT ERROR

The instrument-error critics do not specify the source of the unreliability or how it might be corrected. Achen (1975:1221, 1222, 1226) talks generally about the "vagueness" of the questions and at one point subdivides that into question and response ambiguity. He also acknowledges that his statistical formulation counts all sources of "observation error" as part of measurement error. This includes such matters as level of measurement problems, clerical error, and interviewer effects. Erikson refers merely to "the general fallibility of the measuring instrument itself" (1979:91), and with equal generality, Pierce and Rose discuss "instrument-related variations reflecting both the instrument's and the individual's inability to discriminate the individual's precise affect" (1974:629).

These authors do not attempt an evaluation of individual items and offer neither specific nor general advice on how questions could be improved to reduce the instrument-related error. To a certain degree this is probably a prudent course, since it is a difficult and subjective task to evaluate the reliability of items merely by perusing the question and response categories. Except for obvious "basket cases", the reliability or "vagueness" of an item is often not readily apparent by simply reading it, and it is difficult to isolate instrument error from substantive error by face appraisal (for example, obscure issues might be thought vague by people not familiar with them). But despite the drawbacks of this approach, it is still worthwhile to subject the items to a face evaluation.

To start with the response categories first, since they are common to all questions, respondents are presented with a card with five ranked categories: agree strongly; agree but not very strongly; not sure, it depends; disagree but not very strongly; disagree strongly. There is naturally vagueness between any two adjoining points on this scale (as there would be on any scale), but the categories are well ordered and clear. Given our general state of knowledge about response categories, this scale seems satisfactorily standard.

Regarding the questions themselves, several are more problematic. Several suffer from concept vagueness. This vagueness usually comes from an attempt to frame general questions that cover some basic-issues domain such as isolationism, public/private ownership, or civil rights. The problem is that in trying to formulate a facet-free question that taps the broad issue rather than some particular specific example, one must frame the question in general terms. This unfortunately can also lead to a certain vagueness, and thus we begin to slide from substance-related difficulties into instrument-related problems. For example, people may have trouble with the isolationism question because they do not know and/or care anything about either foreign affairs or political issues in general, or they may run into difficulties because they cannot decide whether or not the question implies a strong anti-Communist policy. This is an intrinsic problem of asking general questions. The alternative is to ask several, more specific and concrete questions about the domain and determine one's general place on the underlying issue by scaling responses.

There is also a tendency to use vague or euphemistic action words and phrases: "to handle" power and housing, to have troops "help" against Communism: "to see to it that they (Negroes) do" get fair treatment. Probably the most problematic is the famous power and housing question, "The government should leave things like electric power and housing for private business to handle." It is double-barreled, and "to handle" is very vague. The isolationism question is also plagued with vague phrases: "This country would be better off if we just stayed home and did not concern ourselves with problems in other parts of the world." What does it mean to stay home and not concern ourselves? No military alliances, no foreign bases, no diplomatic overtures? What is a "problem"? Natural disasters, internal political turmoil, international disputes, the Korean invasion? Are "other parts of the world" a homogenous group? Are the Falkland Islands, England, and Canada all interchangeable? Other questions, such as those on foreign aid, federal aid for schools, and job opportunities are not vague, or double-barreled, and have no other obvious defects. In sum, there is face evidence that several items, and especially the power and housing question, may suffer from instrument unreliability.

Converse counterargues that since only those who switched sides on an issue were counted as inconsistent and thus as nonattitude-holders, it is doubtful that responses could vary so widely while still emanating from a meaningful and unchanged attitude on the issue. He is probably largely correct if we think in terms of response vagueness. There is not sufficient ambiguity in the response categories to permit many respondents with real attitudes to switch sides because they could not place themselves on the scale.

But question vagueness is another problem. Take again the power and housing question: "The government should leave things like electric power and housing for private businessmen to handle." Suppose some respondents believe in private ownership of utilities with a strong utility commission to protect consumers, and also believe in private construction and operation of housing, except for public housing for the poor. This would have been a common, mildly liberal position for the mid-fifties. Such respondents could have said "strongly agree," since in both cases they basically favor private ownership. But they might also have said "strongly disagree" because the question does not mention the liberal safeguards they favor. Both extreme positions are entirely reasonable, given the same attitude but two different interpretations of the question at different times.

While Converse's case is weakened by the apparent inadequacies of his central "power and housing" question, he does have a good example where instrument error is not the problem. On the 1972–1974–1976 panel, a feeling thermometer was asked about various public officials. For Edward "Ted" Kennedy, the correlations are .722 and .671 for two- and four-year periods, respectively. For Henry "Scoop" Jackson, the correlations are .445, and .343. Since the names were the only difference between the items, it is apparent that the variation must be accounted for by something other than instrument error. (Both correlations of course may be attenuated by simple random response error or other more complex errors, but we are interested in the relative difference that cannot readily be accounted for by an instrument-error differential.) True change is a possible explanation, and the decreasing correlations suggest that linear change was occurring. It is hard to imagine, however, that there was considerably more true change in reference to Jackson than to Kennedy. The more plausible explanation, which Converse offers, is that Jackson's ranking included considerably more nonattitudes at one or all three waves and that these responses attenuated the correlations over time.[19]

On one level the choice between the nonattitude and instrument-error explanations is crucial, since among other things it indicates what steps should be taken to remedy the situation. But both explanations posit forms of measurement error, and both argue that many ordinary or standard survey questions are heavily contaminated with error and are unreliable. An optimist might observe (making the standard assumption about the randomness of measurement error) that this merely attenuates relationships and therefore that correlations are really substantially stronger and social science models significantly better predictors than the tainted raw data indicate. Furthermore, the optimist might continue, if a three-wave model or other appropriate techniques were employed, the measurement error could be adjusted for and the true pattern of relationships revealed. Unfortunately, the underlying assumption that drives this optimism (that measurement error is purely random) is statistically convenient, but empirically dubious. The actual error structure, while undoubtedly containing a random element, is considerably more complex (although almost never actually known because of the complexity) and contains such intricacies as error correlated with true scores interacting with background variables (for example, a social-desirability effect specified by educational attainment). The upshot is that there is no quick, easy, and general solution to the problem of measurement error. Instead, considerable effort must be exercised to ferret it out, assess its nature and impact, and adjust for its distortions. This cannot be done either simply or completely, but through a combination of approaches it is possible to gain considerable useful information about the error structure (Smith and Stephenson, 1979; Jackson, 1979).

True Change

True change has been consistently rejected as an explanation for low consistency over time by both the nonattitude and instrument-error schools. The black-and-white model posits no true change, and the various stability correlations usually exceed .90 in the instrument-error models. Only Hagner and McIver (1980) propose true change as a significant source of response variation. In an unfortunately sketchy and problematic piece, they offer evidence from a national panel during the 1976 election campaign that real change is a source of response variation. While certain of their methods are unclear and their results are more equivocal than they realize, they do show that the Heise and the Wiley and Wiley techniques are much more suspect than is usually acknowledged. In 7 of 25 calculations, the stability coefficient exceeds 1.0. While this phenomenon occurs less often in the SRC data (in 6 of 36 instances in Erikson [1979:95]), other data sets find the explosion of stability coefficients even more common (in 16 of 32 instances in Smith and Stephenson, 1979). These anomalies result when the real data fail to meet the fairly stringent assumptions that are necessitated by the three-wave models. As Converse notes in regard to the 1972–1974–1976 panel data: "(A)ssumptions embedded in the calculations of the Heise or Wiley and Wiley type . . . are not entirely well met by the data" (1979:38; see also Jackson, 1979:413). Moreover, coefficients that exceed 1.0 are only the absurdly obvious consequences of modeled data being distorted by the deviations of the data from the assumptions. Other coefficients are distorted, but not exposed by being pushed over the 1.0 boundary.

In addition, there is some question of whether the model really distinguishes between measurement error and true change even when subsidiary assumptions (uncorrelated error, and so forth) are appropriate. The model assumes that true change is monotonically related to time. It assumes that as time increases, the stability correlations will decline. While this condition will frequently prevail, it is not a necessary attribute of true change. Cyclical change, such as business-cycle-related attitudes or perhaps presidential popularity, would not fit this model. Nor would a probably much more common type of change—what Kendall (1954) calls molecular change. Molecular change results from "personal, perhaps idiosyncratic" factors.[20] It is largely unrelated to societal-level events or to time. A person's attitude moves up and down or from pro to con to pro again based on such factors as mood and personal life events. True changes of this type that are essentially randomized over time will be counted as part of the error variance in the three-wave models (Smith and Stephenson, 1979:44-45). Because the three-wave models and other related approaches cannot actually separate true change and measurement error cleanly and simply, true change cannot be dismissed as a trivial factor in explaining inconsistency.

Implications

We believe that there is an appreciable amount of both instrument error and nonattitudes in many opinion questions. We also suspect that the nearly universal dismissal of true change as a force has probably been premature. What is needed is a two-pronged approach (1) to better sort out the relative roles of nonattitudes, instrument error, and true change, and (2) to minimize the measurement-error components. These two approaches are of course complementary, since presumably whatever we learn about the different types of error can in turn be used to segregate or reduce them. We will look at what might be done to deal with nonattitudes and instrument error and how true change can be distinguished.

From Converse's perspective, people without attitudes must stop giving random or labile responses to interviewers. Unfortunately, as Converse points out, respondents on the 1956–1958–1960 panel were in general encouraged to decline replying to questions that were not meaningful, and on particular questions were given an opportunity to say that they had no opinion (had not thought about the issue) or did not know where to place themselves on the issue. Despite this encouragement, Converse of course finds that many people with nonattitudes still slipped into the question and gave their random responses. It might be possible to reduce this problem further if the "no opinion" screener was made stronger (for example, "Please answer this question only if you've given this issue a lot of thought and have a firm opinion about it"). It is uncertain, however, how many would continue to offer nonattitudes, and the possibility exists that people with real attitudes will be driven from the question as one raises the barrier to nonattitudes (Presser, 1977:81). As an alternative, RePass (1971.391) suggests that open-ended questions be used since they "measure both affect and cognition. In using such questions, the researcher comes much closer to measuring an attitude which is on the respondent's mind (salient) at the time of the interview. . . ." Open-ended questions can quite clearly provide a better indication of the complexity and depth of attitudes, but by only relying on a substance-oriented open-ended question, information about salience and cognition are both hard to extract and imprecise. More promising would be an open-ended followup to plumb the depth and content of the initial response. Of course, certain attributes of open-ended questions, for example, low intercoder reliability and high cost, are known drawbacks of this approach.

Another promising approach is to ask the affect question of everyone, but to supplement the question by asking about related attitude dimensions such as knowledge, intensity, behavior, or centrality. George Gallup (1947), for example, proposes a "quintamensional design" that included five parts: (1) understanding or knowledge, (2) closed-ended affect, (3) open-ended affect, (4) reasons why, and (5) intensity. A similar approach is used by Faulkenberry and Mason (1978) in a study of wind energy. They asked interviewers to distinguish between nonopinions (or nonattitudes in Converse's parlance) and no opinions (undecided or ambivalent positions on an issue), and also included batteries on awareness, media exposure, and objective knowledge. Along these lines, Converse (1970:183) suggests that the level of information about the object in question should be measured. A related approach is followed by Goldenson (1979), who asked an intensity question along with an affect question about each item. He further suggests that a salience question might be asked with the others. Intensity and closely related concepts, importance and salience in particular, have been found to be important variables in explaining both substantive results and in discriminating between response styles and errors (Hennessey, 1970:104-107; Schuman and Presser, 1981; Jackman, 1977:162-164; and Kendall, 1954). While there is no general consensus on which variables should be included, there is evidence that several different dimensions play an important role.

The advantage of tapping the intensity, knowledge, salience, and other attitude dimensions, along with affect, is in the possibility of interrelating different dimensions. For example, to look at the affect consistency of only those people who really hold attitudes, we might exclude people whose responses indicate low intensity and low salience. This seems to be the best way to deal with the problem of nonattitudes. Of course it is not without drawbacks. People without any attitude toward an issue who nevertheless give a response out of fear of appearing ignorant might inflate the issue's intensity or salience in order not to appear shallow or uninformed.[21] Objective knowledge questions do minimize this problem, since guessing a wrong response will reveal a person's ignorance, but objective knowledge batteries cannot be used in lieu of intensity and salience indicators. Also, asking questions to measure several dimensions obviously takes much more time and effort than one question to cover a topic. All other things being equal, this would mean a tradeoff between asking only about affect on many issues, or asking about affect, intensity, salience, and knowledge on fewer issues. Finally, it will take careful development to design a set of questions that will give a good, accurate reading of all the relevant dimensions. Still, if we accept even part of Converse's argument about large segments of the population with nonattitudes, some attempt to distinguish such nonattitudes is clearly needed.

To most of Converse's critics, the need is not to screen out nonattitudes, but to improve the questions asked. Unfortunately the critics are silent about what specifically is wrong with the questions and thus do not offer remedies. Two fairly common approaches along these lines would be to improve wordings and response categories and use multi-indicator scales. SRC has apparently tried to follow the first approach, since their basic policy questions have undergone two basic transformations since the fifties. There is, however, little concrete empirical information on what, if any, improvements these changes have made toward reducing measurement error.[22] Multi-indicators have not been used extensively in the SRC national election surveys or in such sociological counterparts as the General Social Surveys. Scales are in common use, but repetitive parallel indicators needed for determining the equivalency reliability are rarely found[23] (Lehnen, 1971-72). Of course, as in the case with measuring various dimensions of a question, the more indicators one uses to measure a single issue, the fewer issues one will be able to measure, *ceteris paribus*. In addition, when putting together equivalency scales, we must be careful not to introduce more response error by inadvertently creating a response set or some other related error. It is also possible in part to assess the instrument reliability of old or improved questions by comparing the affect responses to the other dimensions outlined above. It is plausible, however, that items can be improved (or, in the case of SRC changes, have been improved), and any such improvement would be highly desirable.

In addition, more attention should be given to the role of true change as a cause of apparent inconsistencies. Once again the multidimensional approach should help by increasing our knowledge of the composition of attitudes. For example, someone who gives two different responses at two different times but also exhibits knowledge of the issue, and gives an informed explanation for the position each time, has probably undergone true change. Another direct approach is to ask for reconciliations when a different response is given (Smith and Stephenson, 1979). Statistical models such as three-wave techniques are generally inadequate solutions to the problem, however.

Finally, more attention should be given to considering when correlational measures of consistency (for example r) are the appropriate form or when changes in absolute position (for example, percentage with same response) are meaningful. As Weissberg (1976–77) has shown, these two definitions of consistency are not only theoretically different, but can create some large empirical differences as well. (See also Asher, 1974a, and Converse and Markus, 1979:44-45).

Two conclusions can be drawn from the preceding discussion. First, nonattitudes, instrument error, and molecular change are all contributors to the low consistency that Converse first sought to explain 20 years ago. The relative share of each factor probably varies widely across questions and among subgroups. Second, no simple statistical model such as the black-and-white or the Heise/Wiley and Wiley techniques can separate these elements. Instead, much more elaborate and multipronged approaches yielding no clear-cut summary adjustments will be needed to probe responses. Yet such an approach has a more meaningful reward. By probing individuals rather than aggregates, we will gain a much better understanding of the error structure of opinion questions, attitude change, and even of how the human mind works.

Notes

1. "Constraint" refers to interitem associations at one point in time. "Consistency/inconsistency" refers to across-time associations. Consistency covers the combined effects of measurement error (reliability) and true change (stability).

2. For the United States, Converse is referring to the 1958 study of congressional candidates. His point is made on weak ground since he has no panel data on this group and is inferring higher reliabilities from their higher level of constraint. Also, the questions asked of the elites were not identical to the cross-section items but were often notably different (see also Converse, 1964:228-229). Converse does, however, have panel data from France for both elites and the general population including some identical questions and cross-sectional elite/general samples with identical questions from Brazil.

3. For even more negative evaluations of public attitude formation, see Markel (1972:32) and Hennessey (1970:471).

4. Converse later (1975, 1980) downplays this association.

5. Modigliani and Gamson (1979) specify three hierarchical branchings that can lead to nonattitudes: inattention, nonassimilation, and disorientation.

6. Among two relevant but neutral studies, Bogart (1967) agrees with Converse that many people lack meaningful attitudes on many issues. He also agrees people may have complex attitudes that do not fit well into response categories, which is a point similar to ones raised by Pierce and Rose. Lehnen (1971-72) finds a correspondence between interitem reliability and the way that Converse found items ranked on consistency but did not choose between the nonattitude and shoddy question explanations. As he writes, "Such a pattern . . . suggests either a faulty measurement approach to some policy areas or the existence of attitudes among mass publics are not only unstable over the long run but may also suffer from instability over the short run" (Lehnen, 1971-72:590).

7. "Don't know" (DK) is used here as the generic term for nonsubstantive responses. The National Opinion Research Center and SRC tend to use this term, while the American Institute of Public Opinion favors "no opinion," and Harris uses "not sure" most frequently. DKs are also referred to as item nonresponse and nonsubstantive response.

8. There are several ways that opinion and knowledge questions can interact. The following table shows the basic association.

Issue Knowledge by Opinion

	Opinion	
Knowledge	Has One	Does Not Have One (Don't Know)
Correct	A[a]	B[b]
Don't Know	C[c]	D[d]
Incorrect	E[e]	F[f]

[a]In A, respondent is knowledgeable and has an opinion about the issue.
[b]In B, respondent is knowledgeable but does not have an opinion.
[c]In C, respondent is unsure about the facts but has an opinion.
[d]In D, respondent is unsure of both the facts and his or her position on the issue.
[e]In E, respondent is misinformed and opinionated.
[f]In F, respondent is misinformed and unopinionated.

If we take all responses as sincere, then the misinformed truly thought they knew the facts, and those with opinions took at least a minimally intelligent position on the issue. The problem is muddied, however, by the fact that we cannot assume sincerity, but must assume there is a predisposition for the uninformed to offer an opinion. There may also be a tendency for the consciously unknowledgeable to guess at the facts, but presumably the possibility of disclosing their ignorance by giving an incorrect response diminishes this. As a result, we assume that the consciously unknowledgeable will be more inclined to admit their ignorance by saying "don't know" than will the unopinionated. This being the case, we would expect a higher level of DKs on the knowledge questions than on the opinion questions and in part it would point to a quantity of nonattitudes hiding among the substantive attitude responses.

9. These are classified by various investigators as "nonopinion" versus "no opinion" (Faulkenberry and Mason, 1978); "item ambiguity" versus "scale dependent" (Coombs and Coombs, 1976); "ignorance" versus "ambivalence" or "uninformed indecision" (Schuman and Presser, 1978); "a lack of essential information" versus "a lack of decision" (Zeisel, 1968); and, in a slightly different context, as "apathetic" versus "ambivalent" (Goldenson, 1979).

10. The difference was smaller if only the eight items common to both surveys are compared (.573 nonattitudes in 1956 versus .533 in 1960).

11. There is, however, a type of ambivalent attitude that might be akin to a nonattitude. If an issue is salient to and understood by respondents, but the responsents are so torn by conflicting arguments and/or cross-cutting pressures that they do not know what they think about the issue or whether they favor one side or a middle course, they may be treated as off the continuum.

12. Converse's ambivalence about this group is shown when he repeatedly refers to 29 to 36 percent nonattitudes on the power and housing question, the range being the undecided category. In the black-and-white model, the "undecideds" are handled as having nonattitudes, or in application the 36 percent figure wins out (1974:651, 656).

13. The undecided group tends to have somewhat lower political involvement than the consistent group does, but is closer to them than to the nonattitude-holders. The small DK group tends to be between the nonattitude and undecided groups, but there are too few cases in this group for confident analysis.

14. Respondents forced to choose between equivalent alternatives are found not to randomize their responses, but to make choices that are correlated with their attitude toward the task being evaluated (Fischhoff, 1980; Slovic, 1975). The relevance of this research is problematic since it represents ambivalence situation rather than nonattitudes, and it posits some knowledge about (and a real attitude toward) the task under evaluation.

15. Grant and Patterson use across-time change as only one of three criteria to measure random responders, and their measure of bidirectional change on scale items also differs considerably from the simple criteria of switching sides on an issue.

16. If true change is an appreciable factor, then it becomes impossible to tell whether the measurement error behaves like nonattitudes, but it does argue that inconsistency over time is not an adequate way of separating nonattitudes from true attitudes.

17. Ambivalents had correlations betwixt agree/disagrees and nonattitudes. If they were switched from DKs to substantive responses they would lower both gammas slightly.

18. Panel attrition and initial nonresponse also reduce coverage, and the literature suggests that both of these losses would be disproportionately high among nonattitude-holders.

19. More generally, Converse (1964; Converse and Markus, 1979) explains that differences in consistency correlations are due to differing levels of salience and interest. On balance, this

seems a more plausible explanation for differences in consistency than do variations in instrument error.

20. Bennett (1975b:120) makes a similar argument. But see Wyckoff's (1980:121) comments.

21. Converse argues that such distortion would be less than in the measurement of affect itself (1970:183).

22. For some work of this type, see McPherson, Welch and Clark, (1977), and Asher (1974a).

23. In particular, we have in mind a series of items dispersed throughout the questionnaire for which it would be difficult or logically incongruent to answer in different ways. Examples would be (1) syllogistic triads, (2) reverse order agree/disagree's, and (3) parallel questions.

References

Achen, C.H. (1976) Communication. *American Political Science Review* 70:1231-1233.

Achen, C.H. (1975) Mass political attitudes and the survey response. *American Political Science Review* 69:1218-1231.

Arrington, T.S. (1976) Communication. *American Political Science Review* 70:1227-1231.

Asher, H.B. (1974a) The reliability of the political efficacy items. *Political Methodology* 1:45-71.

Asher, H.B. (1974b) Some consequences of measurement error in survey data. *American Journal of Political Science* 18:469-485.

Barton, A.H., and Parsons, R.W. (1977) Measuring belief system structure. *Public Opinion Quarterly* 41:159-180.

Bell, C.G., and Buchanan, W. (1966) Reliable and unreliable respondents: party registration and prestige pressure. *Western Political Quarterly* 19:37-43.

Bennett, W.L. (1975a) *The Political Mind and the Political Environment*. Lexington, Mass.: D.C. Heath.

Bennett, W.L. (1975b) Public opinion: problems of description and inference. In S. Welch and J. Comer, eds., *Public Opinion: Its Formation, Measurement, and Impact*. Palo Alto: Mayfield.

Bennett, W.L. (1977) The growth of knowledge in mass belief studies: an epistomological critique. *American Journal of Political Science* 21:465-500.

Berg, I.A., and Rapaport, G.M. (1954) Response bias in an unstructured questionnaire. *Journal of Psychology* 38:475-481.

Berger, P.K., and Sullivan, J.E. (1970) Instructional set, interview context, and the incidence of "don't know" responses. *Journal of Applied Psychology* 5:414-416.

Bishop, G.D., Hamilton, D.L., and McConahay, J.B. (1980) Attitudes and nonattitudes in belief systems of mass publics: a field study. *Journal of Social Psychology* 110:53-64.

Bishop, G.F., Oldendick, R.W., Tuchfarber, A.J., and Bennett, S.E. (1979a) Effects of

Nonattitudes: A Review and Evaluation

opinion filtering and opinion floating: evidence from a secondary analysis. *Political Methodology* 6:293-309.

Bishop, G.F., Tuchfarber, A.J., and Oldendick, R.W. (1978) Change in the structure of American political attitudes: the nagging question of question wording. *American Journal of Political Science* 22:250-269.

Bishop, G.F., Tuchfarber, A.J., Oldendick, R.W., and Bennett, S.E. (1979b) Questions about question wording: a rejoinder to revisiting mass belief systems revisited. *American Journal of Political Science* 23:187-192.

Bishop, G.F., Oldendick, R.W., Tuchfarber, A.J., and Bennett, S.E. (1980) Pseudo-opinions on public affairs. *Public Opinion Quarterly* 44:198-209.

Bogart, L. (1967) No opinion, don't know, and maybe no answer. *Public Opinion Quarterly* 31:331-349.

Bradburn, N.M., and Sudman, S. (1979) *Improving Interview Method and Questionnaire Design*. San Francisco: Jossey Bass.

Brim, O.G., Jr. (1955) Attitude content intensity and probability expectations. *American Sociological Review* 20:68-76.

Brown, S.R. (1970) Consistency and the persistence of ideology: some experimental results. *Public Opinion Quarterly* 34:60-68.

Converse, J.M. (1976-77) Predicting "No Opinion" in the polls. *Public Opinion Quarterly* 40:515-530.

Converse, P.E. (1964) The nature of belief systems in mass politics. In D.E. Apter, ed., *Ideology and Discontent*. Glencoe: Free Press.

Converse, P.E. (1970) Attitudes and non-attitudes: continuation of a dialogue. In E.R. Tufte, ed., *The Quantitative Analysis of Social Problems*. Reading, Mass.: Addison Wesley.

Converse, P.E. (1974) Comment: the status of nonattitudes. *American Political Science Review* 68:650-666.

Converse, P.E. (1975) Public opinion and voting behavior. In F.I. Greenstreet and N.W. Polsby, eds., *Nongovernmental Politics. Handbook of Political Science*, Vol. 4. Reading, Mass.: Addison Wesley.

Converse, P.E. (1980) Rejoinder to Judd and Milburn. *American Sociological Review* 45: 644-646.

Converse, P.E., and Markus, G.B. (1979) Plus a change . . . : The CPS Election Study panel. *American Political Science Review* 73:32-49.

Coombs, C.H., and Coombs, L.C. (1976) "Don't know": item ambiguity or respondent uncertainty? *Public Opinion Quarterly* 40:497-514.

Crespi, L.P. (1948) The interview effect in polling. *Public Opinion Quarterly* 12:99-111.

Davis, J.A., and Smith, T.W. (1982) *General Social Survey 1972-1982: Cumulative Codebook*. Chicago: National Opinion Research Center.

Dean, G., and Moran, T.W. (1977) Measuring mass political attitudes: change and unreliability. *Political Methodology* 4:383-413.

Dreyer, E.C. (1973) Change and stability in party identification. *Journal of Politics* 35:712-722.

Dunnette, M.D., Uphoff, W.H., and Aylward, M. (1956) The effect of lack of information on the undecided response in attitude surveys. *Journal of Applied Psychology* 40:150-153.

Ehrlich, H.J. (1964) Instrument error and the study of prejudice. *Social Forces* 43:197-206.

Ehrlich, H.L., and Rinehart, J.W. (1965) A brief report on the methodology of stereotype research. *Social Forces* 43:564-575.

Erikson, R.S. (1979) The SRC panel data and mass political attitudes. *British Journal of Political Science* 9:89-114.

Erikson, R.S., and Luttbeg, N.R. (1973) *American Public Opinion: Its Origins, Content, and Impact.* New York: Wiley.

Erikson, R.S., Luttbeg, N.R., and Tedin, K.L. (1980) *American Public Opinion: Its Origins, Content, and Impact.* 2nd ed. New York: Wiley.

Erskine, H.G. (1963a) Exposure to domestic knowledge. *Public Opinion Quarterly* 27:491-500.

Erskine, H.G. (1963b) Textbook knowledge. *Public Opinion Quarterly* 27:133-141.

Erskine, H.G. (1963c) Exposure to international information. *Public Opinion Quarterly* 27:658-662.

Faulkenberry, G.D., and Mason, R. (1978) Characteristics of nonopinion and no opinion response groups. *Public Opinion Quarterly* 42:533-543.

Ferber, R. (1956) The effects of respondent ignorance on survey results. *Journal of the American Statistical Association* 51:576-587.

Ferber, R. (1966) Item nonresponse in a consumer survey. *Public Opinion Quarterly* 30:399-415.

Fischhoff, B. (1980) Surveying poorly articulated values and opinions. Paper presented to the Panel on Survey Measurement of Subjective Phenomena, National Research Council-National Academy of Sciences, Washington, D.C., March.

Francis, J.D., and Busch, L. (1975) What we know about "I don't know." *Public Opinion Quarterly* 39:207-218.

Gallup, G.H. (1947) The quintamensional plan of question design. *Public Opinion Quarterly* 11:385-393.

Gallup, G.H. (1978) *The Gallup Poll: Public Opinion, 1972-1977.* Wilmington, Del.: Scholarly Resources.

Gergen, K., and Back, K. (1966) Communication in the interview and the disengaged respondent. *Public Opinion Quarterly* 30:385-398.

Gill, S. (1947) How do you stand on sin? *Tide* March:72.

Goldenson, D.R. (1979) The measurement of attitude intensity. Paper presented to the Midwest Association for Public Opinion Research, Chicago, November.

Glenn, N. (1969) Aging, disengagement, and opinionation. *Public Opinion Quarterly* 33:17-33.

Grant, L.V., and Patterson, J.W. (1975) Non-attitudes: the measurement problem and its consequences. *Political Methodology* 2:455-481.

Hagner, P.R., and McIver, J.P. (1980) Attitude stability and change in the 1976 election: a panel study. In J.C. Pierce and J.L. Sullivan, eds., *The Electorate Reconsidered.* Beverly Hills, Calif.: Sage.

Hahn, H. (1970) The political impact of shifting attitudes. *Public Opinion Quarterly* 51:730-742.

Hartley, E. (1946) *Problems in Prejudice.* New York: King's Crown Press.

Hennessey, B. (1970) A headnote on the existence and study of political attitudes. *Social Science Quarterly* 51:463-476.

Nonattitudes: A Review and Evaluation

Hennessey, B. (1975) *Public Opinion*. 3rd ed. North Scituate, Mass.: Duxbury Press.

Hovland, C.I., Harvey, O.J., and Sherif, M. (1957) Assimilation and contrast effects in reactions to communication and attitude change. *Journal of Abnormal and Social Psychology* 55:244-252.

Hunter, J.E., and Coggin, T.D. (1976) Communication. *American Political Science Review* 70:1226-1229.

Hyman, H.H., and Wright, C.R. (1979) *Education's Lasting Influence on Values*. Chicago: University of Chicago Press.

Hyman, H.H., Wright, C.R., and Reed, J.S. (1975) *The Enduring Effects of Education*. Chicago: University of Chicago Press.

Iyengar, S. (1973) The problem of response stability: some correlates and consequences. *American Journal of Political Science* 17:797-808.

Jackman, M.R. (1977) Prejudice, tolerance, and attitudes toward ethnic groups. *Social Science Research* 6:145-169.

Jackson, J.E. (1979) Statistical estimation of possible response bias in close-ended issue questions. *Political Methodology* 6:393-424.

Jennings, M.K., and Zeigler, H. (1970) The salience of American state politics. *American Political Science Review* 64:523-535.

Judd, C.M., and Milburn, M.A. (1980) The structure of attitude systems in the general public: comparison of a structural equation model. *American Sociological Review* 45:627-643.

Kendall, P. (1954) *Conflict and Mood: Factors Affecting Stability of Response*. Glencoe, Ill.: Free Press.

Kolson, K.L., and Green, J.J. (1970) Response set bias and political socialization research. *Social Science Quarterly* 51:527-538.

Lane, R.E. (1962) *Political Ideology*. New York: Free Press.

Lane, R.E. (1973) Patterns of political belief. In J.N. Knutson, ed., *Handbook of Political Psychology*. San Francisco: Jossey Bass.

Lehnen, R.G. (1971-72) Assessing reliability in sample surveys. *Public Opinion Quarterly* 35:578-592.

Markel, L. (1972) *What You Don't Know Can Hurt You: A Study of Public Opinion and Public Emotion*. Washington, D.C.: Public Affairs Press.

McPherson, J.M., Welch, S., and Clark, C. (1977) The stability and reliability of political efficacy: using path analysis to test alternative models. *American Political Science Review* 71:509-521.

Modigliani, A., and Gamson, W.A. (1979) Thinking about politics. *Political Behavior* 1:5-30.

Nie, N., and Andersen, K. (1974) Mass belief systems revisited: political change and attitude structure. *Journal of Politics* 36:540-590.

Nie, N.H., and Rabjohn, J.N. (1979) Revisiting mass belief systems revisited: or doing research is like watching a tennis match. *American Journal of Political Science* 23:139-175.

Nie, N.H., Verba, S., and Petrocik, J.R. (1976) *The Changing American Voter*. Cambridge, Mass.: Harvard University Press.

Olsen, M.E. (1965) Alienation and political opinions. *Public Opinion Quarterly* 29:200-212.

Patterson, J.W. (1972) *Non-Attitudes and the Measurement of Political Alienation*. Ph.D. dissertation. State University of New York at Buffalo.

Payne, S.L. (1951) *The Art of Asking Questions*. Princeton, N.J.: Princeton University Press.

Phillips, D.L., and Clancy K.J. (1972) Some effects of social desirability in survey studies. *American Journal of Sociology* 77:921-940.

Pierce, J.C., and Rose, D.D. (1974) Nonattitudes and American public opinion: the examination of a thesis. *American Political Science Review* 68:626-649.

Poulton, E.C. (1977) Quantitative subjective assessments are always biased, sometimes completely misleading. *British Journal of Psychology* 68:409-425.

Presser, S. (1977) *Survey Question Wording and Attitudes in the General Public*. Ph.D. dissertation. University of Michigan.

Presser, S., and Schuman, H. (1977) The measurement of a middle position in attitude surveys. Unpublished paper, November.

RePass, D.E. (1971) Issue salience and party choice. *American Political Science Review* 65:389-400.

Riesman, D., and Glazer, N. (1948-49) The meaning of public opinion. *Public Opinion Quarterly* 12:633-648.

Rogers, W.C., Stuhler, B., and Koenig, D. (1967) A comparison of informed and general public opinion on U.S. foreign policy. *Public Opinion Quarterly* 31:242-252.

Schettler, C. (1960) *Public Opinion in American Society*. New York: Harper.

Schuman, H., and Presser, S. (1978) The assessment of "no opinion" in attitude surveys. In K.F. Schuessler, ed., *Sociological Methodology: 1979*. San Francisco: Jossey Bass.

Schuman, H., and Presser, S. (1980) Public opinion and public ignorance: the fine line between attitudes and nonattitudes. *American Journal of Sociology* 85:1214-1225.

Schuman, H., and Presser, S. (1981) *Questions and Answers*. New York: Academic Press.

Sicinski, A. (1970) "Don't know" answers in cross-national surveys. *Public Opinion Quarterly* 34:726-729.

Slovic, P. (1975) Choice between equally valued alternatives. *Journal of Experimental Psychology: Human Perception and Performance* 1:280-287.

Smith, D.D. (1970) "Dark areas of ignorance" revisited: current knowledge about Asian affairs. *Social Science Quarterly* 51:668-673.

Smith, T.W. (1978) Age and social change: an analysis of the association between age cohorts and attitude change, 1972-1977. Paper presented to the Eastern Sociological Society, Philadelphia, April.

Smith, T.W. (1980) Inconsistent people. Unpublished ms. Chicago: National Opinion Research Center.

Smith, T.W., and Stephenson, C.B. (1979) An analysis of test/retest experiments on the 1972, 1973, 1974, and 1978 General Social Surveys. GSS Technical Report No. 14. Chicago: National Opinion Research Center.

Stember, H. (1951-52) Which respondents are reliable? *International Journal of Opinion and Attitude Research* 5:474-479.

Stephens, S.V. (1976) Communication. *American Political Science Review* 70:1224-1226.

Suchman, E.A. (1950) The intensity component in attitude and opinion research. In S.A. Stouffer et al., eds., *Measurement and Prediction. Studies in Social Psychology in World War II*, Vol. 4. Princeton, N.J.: Princeton University Press.

Sudman, S., and Bradburn, N.M. (1974) *Response Effects in Surveys: A Review and Synthesis*. National Opinion Research Center Monographs in Social Research. Chicago: Aldine.

Sullivan, J.L., Piereson, J.E., and Marcus, G.E. (1978) Ideological constraint in the mass public: a methodological critique and some new findings. *American Journal of Political Science* 22:233-249.

Sullivan, J.L., Piereson, J.E., Marcus, G.E., and Feldman, S. (1979) The more things change, the more they stay the same: the stability of mass belief systems. *American Journal of Political Science* 23:176-186.

Thurstone, L.L. (1946) Comment. *American Journal of Sociology* 52:39-40.

Traugott, M.W., and Katosh, J.B. (1979) Response validity in surveys of voting behavior. *Public Opinion Quarterly* 43:359-377.

Weissberg, R. (1976-77) Consensual attitudes and attitude structure. *Public Opinion Quarterly* 40:349-359.

Wyckoff, M.L. (1980) Belief system constraint and policy voting: a test of the unidimensional consistency model. *Political Behavior* 2:115-146.

Zeisel, H. (1968) *Say It With Figures*. 5th ed. New York: Harper and Row.

Acknowledgments

I would like to thank the following people for their comments on an earlier draft of this chapter: George F. Bishop, Philip Converse, Theresa DeMaio, William Kruskal, Howard Schuman, and D. Garth Taylor.

9

Social Desirability and Survey Measurement: A Review

Theresa J. DeMaio

Social desirability is generally considered to be a major source of response bias in survey research. Given the frequency with which it is mentioned as an explanation for particular results, definitions of the term are surprisingly rare and uninformative. Generally speaking, it refers to "a tendency to give a favorable picture of oneself" (Selltiz, Wrightsman, and Cook, 1976). A more specific definition (albeit somewhat circular) is included in the proceedings of a Health Survey Research Methods conference (U.S. Department of Health, Education, and Welfare, 1977b:47):

> . . . social desirability bias: answers which reflect an attempt to enhance some socially desirable characteristics or minimize the presence of some socially undesirable characteristics. Source of the expectations or values influencing answers can be the person himself (ego threatening), the perception of the interviewer, or society as a whole.

Explanations of the process by which respondents arrive at the socially desirable answers they provide to interviewers can also be found in the literature.

> Some questions call for the respondent to provide information on topics that have highly desirable answers, that is, answers that involve attributes considered

257

desirable to have, activities considered desirable to possess. If a respondent has a socially undesirable attitude or if he has engaged in socially undesirable behavior, he may face a conflict between a desire to conform to the definition of good respondent behavior, which says that one should tell the truth, and a desire to appear to the interviewer to be in the socially desirable category. It is frequently assumed that most respondents resolve this conflict in favor of biasing their answer in the direction of social desirability. [Sudman and Bradburn, 1974:9-10]

The behavior and opinions which . . . items describe have associated with them social norms reflecting the approval or disapproval that our society attributes to these behaviors and opinions. These norms apply to the reporting of one's own behavior and opinions as well as to the behavior and opinions themselves; these norms favor the reporting of approved behavior and opinions and the denial of disapproved ones. Social desirability response style may reflect conformity on items for which the social norms exist and are perceived; conformity on such items simply involves making responses approved by the social norms, i.e., socially desirable responses. [Stricker, 1963:320)

These explanations of social desirability, while not clearly defining the concept, explicitly share two elements—the notion that some things are good and others are bad, and the notion that respondents want to appear "good" and answer questions in such a manner as to be perceived that way.

Other issues are not so explicitly addressed; consequently, inconsistencies abound in discussions of the development of social desirability measures and their effect on survey responses. This chapter, in reviewing the social desirability literature, concentrates on elements of incongruity in the research. Three areas are of particular concern: (1) Does social desirability refer to a personality characteristic or an item characteristic? (2) What does "desirability" include? (3) Who sets the standards for determining desirability?

Personality or Item Characteristic?

A major source of ambiguity in the literature involves the nature of the concept of social desirability. Some authors approach it as a personality construct (for example, a need to conform to social standards) and measure the overall tendency of a person to respond in a desirable manner; others consider various behaviors or opinions to be more or less socially desirable and thus discuss social desirability in relation to particular items.

The earliest research on social desirability consisted of developing scales to measure people's tendency to present themselves in a favorable light. Three such scales, employing various interpretations of the concept, have been constructed.

Social Desirability

Edwards (1957), who was the pioneer in this area, considers both the personality characteristic and the item characteristic dimension of social desirability, while emphasizing the latter. He envisions the social desirability dimension as a continuum, ranging from highly socially desirable to highly socially undesirable, and passing through a neutral point. Using this notion he obtains social desirability scale values (SDSVs) for personality statements from the Minnesota Multiphasic Personality Inventory (MMPI) by asking groups of judges, usually groups of college students, to rate the statements on a nine-point scale according to the following instructions (Edwards, 1957:4):

> Indicate your own judgments of the desirability or undesirability of the traits which will be given to you by the examiner. . . . Remember that you are to judge the traits in terms of whether you consider them desirable or undesirable in others.

In replicating the procedure with various groups, primarily consisting of students (high school and college, day and evening, from various countries) but also including a group of male veterans hospitalized for neuropsychiatric disorders, he and other researchers find similar SDSV results. On this basis he asserts the uniformity of social desirability measurements regardless of age or sex and assumes that the instructions produce "judgments of social desirability which are made in terms of fairly general cultural norms of social desirability" (Edwards, 1957:15). These seem to be rather global assertions, given the restricted nature of the sample and the lack of specific criteria for making judgments of desirability or undesirability.

In subsequent research, different groups of judges were asked to rate the personality statements according to whether or not the statements accurately described the judges themselves. Results show that the probability that a person will endorse one of these statements in self-description has a high positive correlation (.83) with its social desirability scale value.

While emphasis on the social desirability scale value of various MMPI statements reflects concern with the item characteristic dimension of social desirability (SD), Edwards also recognizes the personality characteristic dimension. In this regard he asked 10 judges to provide socially desirable answers to a set of 150 MMPI items. The 79 items on which agreement was unanimous constitute the SD scale. A shortened version of the scale consists of the 39 items that show the greatest differentiation between a high group and a low group in terms of total SD scores (based on several administrations of the 79-item scale). The SD score assigned to an individual, which reflects that person's tendency to respond in a socially desirable direction, is calculated by summing the number of socially desirable responses given in self-description.

In order to establish the validity of this SD scale, Edwards observes the correlations between scores on the SD scale and scores on various MMPI subscales. Without presenting any evidence for his assertions, he declares that certain of these scales reflect socially desirable characteristics (for example, the Dominance, Responsibility, and Status scales) and others reflect socially undesirable characteristics (for example, the Dependency, Neuroticism, and Hostility scales). Because the correlations between the SD scale and the scales that reflect socially desirable characteristics are highly positive, and the correlations between the SD scale and scales that reflect socially undesirable characteristics are highly negative, he is satisfied that his scale is actually measuring social desirability.

The development of the Edwards SD scale was widely noted, and it sparked a debate within the field of psychology. Controversy focused in two areas: (1) the ability of the scale to measure social desirability as distinct from acquiescence (a tendency to adopt a response set and agree or disagree with items regardless of their content); and (2) the tendency of the scale to function as a mini-personality test rather than as a social desirability scale, because it correlates so highly with other MMPI scales.

The overlap between social desirability and acquiescence stems in part from the composition of the items comprising the scale. Rundquist (1966) cites considerable evidence that there is a lack of consistency between responses to pairs of items of similar content, depending on whether they are worded in a socially desirable or socially undesirable manner. Responses to socially undesirable (negative) items correlate more highly with each other than do responses to socially desirable (positive) items. Since 30 of the 39 items on Edwards' abbreviated scale are worded in a negative manner, Rundquist suggests that the high correlations Edwards uses to establish the validity of his scale are partially a result of the form of the statement rather than simply a reflection of socially desirable or undesirable content.

Other criticisms focus on the narrow conceptual distinction between social desirability and acquiescence. Since both can be considered aspects of conformity, Stricker (1963) posits that social desirability operates for items in which the norms are clear-cut, and acquiescence operates where the items are relatively neutral. Thus, a scale that includes both confounds the processes. Much work has been done in this area (Couch and Keniston, 1961; Edwards and Walker, 1961; Jackson and Messick, 1961; Stricker, 1963; Taylor, 1961), but since its emphasis is on personality measurement, it is not particularly relevant here.

The second major criticism of the SD scale is voiced by Crowne and Marlowe (1964), who cite its high correlation with other MMPI scales with skepticism, since the correlations suggest that social desirability accounts for a large part of personality. Crowne and Marlowe focus exclusively on the personality-characteristic dimension of social desirability, defining it as a need for social approval, and creating an alternative scale to measure that personality trait. The rationale in constructing the scale was to find behaviors that are culturally sanctioned and approved but which are unlikely to occur, and for which response in either a socially desirable or undesirable direction has minimal pathological implications. Since it is highly unlikely that individuals can honestly rate their own behavior in these areas in a desirable direction and since the consequences of not responding honestly are slight, scores to such a scale can be interpreted as indicating people's tendency to present themselves in a favorable light, or, as Crowne and Marlowe called it, their need for social approval.[1]

The scale was constructed by giving a list of 50 items from several personality inventories to 10 judges[2] who were instructed to "score each item in the socially desirable direction from the point of view of college students, using true and false as response categories" (Crowne and Marlowe, 1964: 22). Thus, no intermediate category is available for items that might be considered neither desirable nor undesirable. To ensure that socially undesirable responses would have minimal pathological implications, 10 other judges were asked to rate the same 50 items on a five-point scale, according to the degree of maladjustment implied by socially undesirable responses. Such responses to these items were rated as indicating significantly less maladjustment than socially undesirable responses to items in the Edwards SD scale. A third administration of the test items was conducted, using the original instructions, and the 33 items that significantly differentiated ($p < .05$) between high and low total desirability scores were included in the scale. Some of the scale items are from the MMPI, but none overlaps with items in the Edwards SD scale. Lower MMPI correlations with the Marlowe-Crowne scale than with the Edwards SD scale indicate the authors' success in fulfilling their original intention.

A third social desirability scale was developed more recently. Like the Marlowe-Crowne scale, it emphasizes the personality construct dimension; however, it uses general attitude and opinion statements rather than personality items to measure the dimension. Schuessler, Hittle, and Cardascia (1978) use a broader range of test populations as well as of item content to create a 16-item scale (RD16) to measure "responding desirably to attitude and opinion items." The scale items consist of "statements that people make about themselves, about others, and about life in general" (Schuessler, Hittle, and Cardascia, 1978:226). Judges (including both a student sample and a sample of randomly selected adults) were instructed to rate the social desirability or undesirability of approximately 200 statements on a nine-point scale, quite apart from whether they agreed or disagreed with the content. Eight pairs of oppositely keyed items from eight different content areas were selected to compose the final scale,[3] based on the stability in the ratings among various population subcategories (that is, race and education groups, since ratings of the items were relatively stable across age and sex). The authors present a reliability coefficient (KR–21 α) for the scale of .64, and limited validity information.

Hypotheses concerning the correlations between RD16 and other scales are only marginally supported. The correlation is stronger than expected with an acquiescence scale ($-.36$), indicating that RD16 is not as free from the effects of acquiescence as the authors had hoped. The negative relationship was anticipated by the authors, who assumed that socioeconomic status would be positively related to social desirability and negatively related to acquiescence. However, the magnitude of the relationship suggests that the scales are not measuring entirely distinct constructs. More problematic are the interpretations for the weaker-than-expected correlations with the Jackson Responding Desirably (JRD) scale (.55) and the Marlowe-Crowne (M–C) scale (.16). The former also measures a trait to respond desirably and is constructed in the same manner as is RD16, suggesting that its correlation with RD16 should be stronger. The Marlowe-Crowne scale is constructed using different procedures and a different rationale, but the correlation between two scales that purport to measure the same general concept is still quite low.

Two factors might be posited to account for these weak relationships. First, the reliability coefficients for all these scales are low (M–C = .72, JMA [Jackson and Messick Acquiescence] = .55, JRD = .63, RD16 = .64). Besides contributing to small correlations between social desirability scales (and high ones between social desirability and acquiescence scales), low reliability also indicates the lack of conceptual distinctiveness among the various scales.

The second factor is a difference in the type of items that compose the scales. The Schuessler, Hittle, and Cardascia RD16 scale consists of attitude and opinion items, while the other two (JRD and M–C) are basically composed of personality items. Perhaps the tendency to respond desirably differs from one domain to another. This explanation calls into focus the distinction between personality and item dimensions with which this section began. Although the literature reviewed here so far has dealt basically with one dimension or the other, the possibility of their interaction seems quite plausible, and in fact has been investigated in recent work.

Phillips and Clancy (1970) develop a personality characteristic measure of social desirability that differs from the previous measures in two ways: (1) they do not attempt to create a scale, establish reliability, and so on, but simply construct an index from answers given by survey respondents; (2) they explicitly attempt to combine the personality and item characteristic dimensions by using evaluations of individual items as components in the summary personality measure.

Social Desirability

The actual measurement of social desirability in their small telephone survey was accomplished by asking respondents to look at the numbers 1 through 9 on their telephone dials and rate the "desirability" of 22 mental health inventory items,[4] with higher numbers indicating higher desirability of an item. An average social desirability score was calculated for each respondent based on that person's desirability ratings of all 22 items.

In subsequent research, Phillips and Clancy (1972) expand their notion of social desirability and view it as both an item characteristic and a personality characteristic (which they call the need for social approval). The first refers to a person's measurement of the desirability of individual items— thus, ratings on this dimension by a single respondent might vary from one inventory item (for example, happiness) to another (for example, religiosity). The need for social approval measures a personality characteristic that is presumably insensitive to item content. Measuring each concept individually and not combining them in an arbitrary fashion allows Phillips and Clancy to determine how the item and personality dimensions of social desirability interrelate.

They address this in a study which also investigates how these dimensions relate to other items of general interest to investigators.[5] Need for social approval was measured by a shortened version of the Marlowe-Crowne scale; trait desirability is measured identically to the authors' original "desirability" measure, except that each trait is considered separately rather than being combined into a summary statistic.

The comparison of the two social desirability dimensions with each other shows that trait desirability ratings are generally independent of need for approval scores. That is, respondents who have high need for social approval do not rate the desirability of the various traits differently than do respondents with lower need for approval.

A critique of the Phillips and Clancy method for measuring social desirability is made by Gove and Geerken (1977). They also subscribe to the dual dimension idea (item desirability versus social approval), but feel that its measurement needs to be improved. Noting Phillips and Clancy's small sample sizes[6] and a confusing technique for measuring item desirability, Gove and Geerken base their work on personal interviews using a larger sample.[7] This allowed the respondents to rate item desirability with the visual assistance of a flash card containing verbal labels for each of seven points on a scale.[8] Measures of the need for social approval are obtained, as in Phillips and Clancy's research, using a shortened version of the Marlowe-Crowne scale. The research was conducted to investigate the effect of social desirability response bias (and also yeasaying/naysaying) on a substantive relationship of interest to investigators—specifically, the relationship between mental health and various demographic characteristics.

Gove and Geerken find that item desirability and need for social approval have independent, additive effects on reports of three mental health items (psychiatric symptoms, self-esteem, and positive affect). Their work thus substantiates Phillips and Clancy's finding that the two dimensions of social desirability are independently related to self-reported traits.

These investigations provide a start toward developing social desirability response effect models that specify the nature of the relationship between personality and item characteristic components. Further efforts might fruit-fully take an item-centered approach, hypothesizing that specific items will evoke a response consistent with social desirability as a function of their loading on social desirability and the respondent's need to respond in such a manner (see Volume 1, Section 6.1 for further discussion of this approach). Testing for the existence of such a function, if present, and then specifying its nature seem to be logical results of this endeavor. Such an undertaking would not be completed quickly or easily, but would be done with the intent of conducting valuable and necessary across-item analysis. This would seem particularly useful in comparing patterns of response to items that appear to have no normative element with response patterns for items that are controversial, or for which acceptability varies according to time or population subgroup.

What is "Desirability?"

The task of assessing the nature of the relationship between the personality and item components of social desirability presupposes a standard, commonly accepted definition of "desirability." Unfortunately there is no such precise definition, and in its absence, research has translated the term in a variety of ways—"acceptable" behavior, "desirable" behavior, a "need for social approval," and a "tendency to respond desirably," to name a few.

In addition to these differences in operational definitions, it is not clear whether respondents in the studies cited in the preceding section were sufficiently informed of what was expected of them to produce reliable measures of the operational definition used in the research. For example, the use of the term "social desirability" in the instructions given by Crowne and Marlowe to their judges (see page 261) allowed the judges to interject whatever meaning they ascribed to the term rather than respond in terms of need for social approval. Consistent ratings by the judges offer some evidence against idiosyncratic classification; however, since only two answer categories (true and false) were available and no neutral responses were allowed, consistent responses might be expected. Furthermore, the judges for the Schuessler, Hittle, and Cardascia RD16 scale were instructed to rate the desirability of attitude and opinion statements independently of their own attitudes toward the statements. This distinction seems somewhat tenuous, since it involves separating personal values from perceptions of what is generally desirable.[9] It would seem particularly difficult to judge the abstract desirability of items that elicit strong personal reactions. Even assuming that it is possible, what does it mean to rate the desirability of a statement such as "It is difficult to think clearly about right and wrong these days"? Does it mean to rate the statement according to whether it is desirable for me or for others? And how can my judgment of the statement be unrelated to whether or not I believe it? To the extent that the judges remain confused about exactly what they are expected to do, their ratings might measure something other than desirability.

Schuessler, Hittle, and Cardascia never define the personality trait that their scale measures, except as a tendency to respond desirably. They do explicitly state, however, that "individuals equal on approval needs may differ widely in tendency to respond desirably" (Schuessler, Hittle, and Cardascia, 1978:230). Their definition of the concept is obviously different from Marlowe and Crowne's, although theoretical differences are not specified, and we can reasonably wonder about the underlying basis for presenting both these scales as measures of social desirability. Anyone can ask people to rate a group of statements in terms of their desirability—beyond that, a precise definition of the term and an explicit substantive rationale for item inclusion (in the original set of statements) or selection (in the scale itself) are necessary in order to obtain comparable scales. The notion of social desirability is sufficiently ambiguous, in concept and definition, to allow different interpretations and operational definitions, resulting in scales that do not even purport to measure the same personality characteristic.

In their earlier work, Phillips and Clancy view social desirability as a personality characteristic and define it as "a tendency to say good rather than bad things about oneself" (1970:505). This definition introduces confusion between social desirability and the concept of self-esteem. Some of the good rather than bad things may be true, while others may be distortions. Some respondents may give certain answers because they think highly of themselves, while others may give the same answers because they want other people to think highly of them (whether or not they themselves do). The ambiguities arising from this definition (that is, the possibility that good self-descriptions may reflect true rather than socially desirable responses) are not addressed. In the actual administration of their survey instrument (see preceding section), respondents were provided with no criteria for judging the desirability of items, which makes it difficult to decipher the meaning of the ratings that were made.

Another example of an ambiguous definition of desirability is provided by

Sudman and Bradburn (1974). Using a staff of coders, the researchers themselves code the social desirability of the answer to each of a wide variety of survey questions. This approach does not allow for individual variability among respondents concerning the desirability of the question content. Social desirability is coded on a three-point scale: no possibility, some possibility, or a strong possibility of a socially desirable answer to each question. Unfortunately, the criteria for assigning each of the codes are not specified, although the authors note that

> . . . the ratings represent the coders' subjective impressions of the likelihood that one of the response categories to a question was distinctly more socially desirable than the others. In general, coders were instructed to be conservative and to code "strong possibility" only for questions that have figured prominently in concern over socially desirable answers. (Sudman and Bradburn, 1974:43)

In addition to being vague, these instructions also seem to go around in circles, leaving some question as to what the results of this exercise might mean.

In addition to being coded for social desirability, the questions are coded according to threat, as determined by the coders' subjective judgments "about the relative threat posed by each question to the respondent's self-esteem or the interviewer's appraisal of him" (Sudman and Bradburn, 1974:20).

In making a distinction between these two factors, Sudman and Bradburn are in a sense splitting hairs. Their definition of threat could easily be subsumed under the rubric of social desirability. A threat to the respondent's self-esteem or the interviewer's appraisal of that person is surely the force behind a respondent's tendency to present himself or herself in a more favorable light, which is one of the definitions of social desirability mentioned in the introduction to this chapter. Sudman and Bradburn make the distinction that the threat items are more likely to be personal items, while the social desirability items are more distant from the individual. In either case, response distortion is likely to be in a socially desirable direction. The confounding of the two variables is acknowledged by Sudman and Bradburn (1974:37):

> To a considerable extent, this variable [threat] may be confounded with social desirability, since admitting to behavior or opinions which lower the interviewer's esteem for the respondent would probably also be considered socially undesirable.

Although the coding scheme has been set up so that threat refers to the question and social desirability refers to the answer, they both refer to the same basic process of respondents answering questions untruthfully in order to present a more favorable image of themselves to an interviewer.

Social Desirability

As an aside to this point, Cannell and his associates (U.S. Department of Health, Education, and Welfare, 1977a, 1977c) include threat in their notion of social desirability. They describe the latter as including events that are perceived as embarrassing, sensitive in nature, threatening, or divergent from one's self-image, and which are likely to be either not reported at all or reported in a socially desirable direction.

Bradburn and his colleagues (1979), along with many of the other authors discussed thus far, adopt the concept of need for social approval to measure social desirability. The premise of the research of Bradburn and his associates provides an interesting variation from the others, however, and their reporting of the results suggests still another interpretation of "desirability." Drawing on work by Carol Stocking, they present an analysis using Marlowe-Crowne scores as a dependent rather than as an independent variable. Instead of viewing differences in behavior reports as response distortions grounded in respondents' need for social approval, they suggest that different levels of need for social approval are associated with differences in the way people think and act in the real world, which in turn are accurately reported in an interview. Since agreement with extreme statements (that is, always or never behaving in a particular way) characterizes people who score high on the Marlowe-Crowne scale, they may "tend to see the world in terms of absolutes and be more likely to have rigid standards for their own behavior (and that of others)" (p. 88). So, for instance, respondents who have a high need for social approval do not attend as many parties or participate in as many social activities as do people who have a low need for social approval. Differences in behavior reports of respondents with high and low need for social approval are noted consistently for the entire range of activities investigated (including attending parties),[10] not just for activities the authors consider to be proscribed by normative constraints (such as using marijuana or drinking to the point of intoxication). Thus Bradburn and his associates conclude that the Marlowe-Crowne scale is not a useful measure of a social desirability response effect.

Throughout the argument of Bradburn and his colleagues, however, reference is consistently made to "acceptable" rather than to "socially desirable" activities. Acceptable activities are not necessarily socially desirable; for instance, abortion may be acceptable these days, but that does not mean it is socially desirable. The use of these two terms as synonyms seems to confuse the notion of what is "common" with what is "good." The equating of these two terms, while it may be inadvertent, adds to the conceptual confusion in this area.

As a step toward resolving the inconsistencies that muddy these waters, it would be helpful if some kind of consistent and, it would be hoped, sound definition of "desirability" could be developed by researchers, which would outline specific elements to be taken into account in its measurement. The definitions could logically be dimension-specific; that is, separate tools would be necessary for the measurement of personality and item dimensions. In the personality area, research into the relationship between self-esteem and need for social approval might be undertaken to develop a measure of the tendency to respond positively (in a good-bad rather than a consistent-response-set sense).

Item desirability development might concentrate on the establishment of rules for determining whether the content of individual items reflects positive, or good, consequences. The many varied items included in surveys differ in several ways that make some more easily rated for desirability than others, as can be seen just by considering the items in the research described in this chapter. First, some of the statements are more open to ambiguity about their specific meaning than others. For example, while I might think that "Do you feel somewhat apart even among friends?" refers to an isolated, distant feeling (which would be considered undesirable), someone else might think it refers to a degree of individualism or independence (and view that as desirable). Or, another example—does the word *religiosity* mean belief in God, attending church, or something else? Other items, such as "visiting a doctor at least once a year," may require the respondent to impute a context in order to rate the desirability of the characteristic. I might rate the desirability of my visiting a doctor for an annual checkup one way; but from the point of view of someone I know who makes excessive visits to the doctor during the year, I might rate it quite differently. To take as a fourth example: "I'm the kind of person who seeks criticism" —seeking criticism might imply tolerance for criticism (desirable), but it might also suggest low self-esteem or masochism (undesirable). All these examples require respondents to impute meaning, either by interpreting the statements as written, or by adding context to provide enough information to assess them.

The second way that items may differ is in the extent to which they explicitly reflect good and bad. Mental health items such as "I have personal worries that get me down physically" or "I feel worthless at times" are easily recognized as having negative connotations, and such items as taking "a positive attitude toward myself" or feeling "proud because someone complimented you on something you had done" are obviously positive in tone. On the other hand, items such as rating the number of your friends or evaluating the frequency of your visits to a doctor are not loaded in the same way. Since the latter types of statements are not so obvious, the task of rating their desirability may be more difficult for respondents; the ratings would also seem to be subject to more individual variation among respondents. These distinctions between attributes of items are probably just two of many that could, and should, be made in the process of arriving at rules and measures of item desirability.

It should be noted that the large numbers and easy accessibility of mental health inventory items make them convenient subjects for social desirability research. Despite the frequent use of mental health inventory items in such work, research on item desirability could be more profitable if done in connection with other items that are used in more general survey research.

Who Sets the Standards of Desirability?

Even if a commonly applied definition of desirability were used in social desirability research, and even if measurements of desirability all meant the same thing, the comparability of responses would not be ensured. Three additional (and related) elements are involved in deciding whether an attitude or activity is "desirable" or "undesirable": (1) the frame of reference or standard that is applied (and against which a judgment is made), (2) the identity of the person making the judgment, and (3) the perspective from which the judgment is made. Unfortunately, variation exists on all three of these levels, introducing still another source of inconsistency in the study of social desirability.

The frame of reference is not specified explicitly in most of the empirical research, but is noted in some discussions of the topic. According to Stricker (1963), social norms provide the frame of reference, while the glossary definition cited at the beginning of this chapter (U.S. Department of Health, Education, and Welfare, 1977b) specifies the respondents themselves and the interviewer as sources of desirability standards. The latter additions open the issue up to a wide range of influences that prevent precise specification of the concept. Can we assume, for example, that what is perceived as desirable to the interviewer also coincides with social norms? If not, would research using these two different sources of standards be measuring the same phenomenon?

The second element, the source of the desirability judgment, is explicitly mentioned in research previously described. In some cases (Edwards, 1957; Schuessler, Hittle and Cardascia, 1978; Crowne and Marlowe, 1964; Phillips and Clancy, 1970, 1972), the respondent provides the ratings; in others (Sudman and Bradburn, 1974), the investigators do. The latter method has the disadvantage of not allowing for differences in the way various subpopulation groups view particular activities.

While the source of the desirability judgment is always either the respondent or the researcher, the perspective from which the judgment is made varies more widely. Whereas Phillips and Clancy obtained desirability ratings from the standpoint of the respondents themselves, the ratings used to develop the Marlowe-Crowne scale were requested from the point of view of college students. In other investigations (for example, Edwards, 1957; Schuessler, Hittle, and Cardascia, 1978), it is difficult to determine whether the perspective of the respondent or of people in general was requested. To the extent that differences in perspective influence ratings, the comparability of the results might be affected.

Differences in research design may also affect the comparability of the way similar concepts are measured. To the extent that uniformity is possible, however, it would seem helpful to adopt one perspective as a standard. The perspective that seems most flexible in accommodating subpopulation differences is that of the individual respondents. Perhaps future research might investigate both the extent to which these differences in perceptions of desirability exist and the reasons why they exist.

Substantive Results

Having discussed in detail the development of measures of social desirability, we now turn to some substantive results of this research.

Phillips and Clancy (1970) use their measure of social desirability in an attempt to investigate the usefulness of reference group theory as a basis for interpreting something as socially desirable (specifically, whether or not something is considered desirable depends on its prevalence among people of similar ethnic or socioeconomic background). In order to test this hypothesis, survey respondents were asked to complete the mental health inventory as it described themselves and to estimate the proportion of their friends and acquaintances who have a randomly chosen few of these symptoms, in addition to providing the desirability ratings.

Results of the survey indicate, not surprisingly, that people who rate symptoms as more undesirable report significantly fewer symptoms. This finding, which is similar to one Edwards reported earlier, does not provide concrete evidence of distortion resulting from social desirability bias (the truth about these respondents is unknown), but it suggests that people who consider these symptoms undesirable would be less likely to report them. Phillips and Clancy's (1970) hypothesis about the determinants of social desirability is partially supported; they report a significant X^2 but small (unspecified) correlation between symptom prevalence and social desirability, and conclude there are other determinants of desirability which they have not measured, such as "the individual's perception as to the societal assessment of the desirability of the various behaviors represented by these symptoms" (Phillips and Clancy, 1970:529). As this last statement indicates, the traditional meaning of the concept has not been measured by their research.

Social Desirability

In Phillips and Clancy's (1972) expansion of their previous work, they introduce the distinction between item desirability and need for social approval, and attempt to replicate, separately for each component, Edwards's original findings: that is, people who rate these items as desirable report them in self-description more often; people who have a high need for social approval also report them more often. Both hypotheses are confirmed. The relationship between item desirability and self-description is stronger than is the relationship between need for approval and self-description.

In an attempt to establish the direction of the link between respondents reportedly having a characteristic and their viewing that characteristic as desirable, a tendency toward "overclaiming" was measured. This was accomplished by including on the questionnaire several items that asked about engaging in activities that the respondent could not have done (for example, reading nonexistent books, watching nonexistent movies and television shows). Respondents were asked whether they had done these things and also were instructed to rate the desirability of being aware of the latest media releases (books, movies, and so forth). The results indicate that people who feel that being aware of the latest media releases is highly desirable are more than twice as likely to inaccurately report having read nonexistent books or seen nonexistent movies as people who rate such awareness as highly undesirable. Since, in this case, people could not possibly have accomplished the behaviors that might have led them to rate the related items as highly desirable, Phillips and Clancy conclude that this and other relationships go in the opposite direction, that is, that the desirability ratings are accurate and thus influence (inaccurate) reports of behavior.

Apropos of this validity check by Phillips and Clancy, Bradburn and his colleagues (1979) also investigate the possibility that self-reports of behaviors are accurate rather than being distortions resulting from social desirability bias. Their premise, as reported earlier, is much different, and their conclusion is also different. While Phillips and Clancy conclude that social desirability does produce distorted reports of behavior, Bradburn and his associates find that it does not.

It is especially notable that these divergent conclusions accompany differences in the conceptualization of social desirability. The former conclusion is based on the item-dependent desirability notion, and the latter is based on research involving the personality construct dimension.

A concept that incorporates both of these dimensions might hold that certain items are endorsed (artifactually) just because they are desirable, especially by those who need social approval. This position might be challenged on the basis that items are rated desirable only because they are true. Phillips and Clancy's results successfully counter this objection, but they do not clinch the social desirability argument because of a second argument: for those who need social approval, certain things are really true, including items high in "social desirability." The results of Bradburn and his colleagues, based on the personality construct component, support this argument, and thereby counter the original position. Thus, the two sets of results do not contradict each other as much as they argue against different aspects of a more universal concept of social desirability.

Although Phillips and Clancy make a distinction between two components of social desirability, their main concern seems to be with the item desirability notion. Besides the previously mentioned discussion of item desirability and "overclaiming," they also introduce an independent variable (gender) and observe the effect of item desirability, but not the effect of need for social approval, on the relationship between gender and responses to the items themselves. They find that differences between men and women in ratings of item desirability are not constant for all items, and that women are in general more likely to describe themselves as possessing desirable characteristics than men are. Phillips and Clancy also note that relationships between gender and self-reports of specific items are "specified" by how desirable the items are perceived to be. By this they mean that the magnitude of the original relationship is increased among those who see the item as highly desirable and is diminished or reversed among those who see it as less desirable. The independent effects of item desirability are found to be consistently stronger than the independent effects of gender.

Gove and Geerken's (1977) research expands the investigation of the relationship between desirability and other independent variables. Age is the demographic variable they find most strongly associated with both desirability measures. Education, occupation, and income show some significant differences; sex and race do not. In controlling for the response bias variables in the relationships between the various demographic items and the three mental health measures, Gove and Geerken find very few instances in which the outcomes are affected, and these are asserted to be the result of small variations in means among the subgroups. Their overall conclusion, then, is that social desirability (and also yeasaying/naysaying) does not constitute a form of systematic bias in substantive relationships, contrary to the implicit, but untested, assumption of most researchers.

The conclusions of Gove and Geerken are encouraging to researchers who have untested and thus unsubstantiated hopes that these forms of response bias do not affect their survey results. Much more work is necessary, however, to establish that the results can be replicated within the same subject area and in other areas as well.

Another example of the use of the Marlowe-Crowne scale to investigate the possibility of response bias is presented by Campbell, Converse, and Rodgers (1976) in *The Quality of American Life*. These authors divide a subset of the original scale items into two groups: an Assert Good subscale (that is, those items that measure a tendency to assert something good, but probably not true, in self-description) and a Deny Bad subscale (that is, items measuring a tendency to deny something bad, but probably true, in self-description). The correlations between the subscales and various global and domain-specific measures of satisfaction and dissatisfaction are examined for evidence of response distortion. Campbell, Converse, and Rodgers note that "edges of bias" are indicated by the magnitude of the correlations they observe. In general the Deny Bad subscale is more strongly associated than the Assert Good subscale with other measures, suggesting that concern about the accuracy of responses should be focused at the bottom rather than at the top of a scale such as the one they use. In terms of demographic characteristics, age and education tend to be associated with the tendency to give socially desirable responses, a finding similar to Gove and Geerken's. As age increases, correlations with both subscales increase. In contrast, the response bias associated with education is isolated in the Assert Good subscale. Overall, the authors conclude that the marginal nature of the response bias is indicated by the trivial differences between respondents' unadjusted scores and those adjusted for tendency to give socially desirable responses.

One of the more ambitious approaches to this topic was taken by Sudman and Bradburn (1974), who attempt to synthesize into summary statistics the results of a large body of research on response bias due to various factors such as faulty memory or attempts to enhance one's self-presentation. Through an elaborate (and sometimes questionable) procedure, Sudman and Bradburn calculate relative response effects by comparing differences in the proportions of various response categories relative to the dispersion in the sample as a whole. While they report a series of research findings about response effects resulting from social desirability, their results are not based on measures of social desirability as such, but (as described previously) on the impressions of coders. Their attempt to standardize the results of so many individual investigations may be subject to serious coding problems in other areas as well (for example, coding the interviewer's race). With this caveat stated, some of the results are presented.

Questions are divided according to content into behavioral and attitudinal items. The mean relative response effect for behavioral items with a strong possibility of a socially desirable answer is larger than that for items with little possibility, which is close to zero. For attitudinal items, the response effects are generally larger than they are for behavioral items, and the differences between the effects for different levels of socially desirable answers are smaller. The response effect for attitudinal items rated by coders as having little or no possibility of a socially desirable answer is actually larger than any of the effects for behavioral items. The magnitude of this effect is surprising and suggests that either the calculating formula does not accurately assess the effects of social desirability, or that other factors such as threat or saliency operate in conjunction with social desirability.

Attitude questions rated as highly threatening and as having a strong possibility of a socially desirable answer have much larger response effects than any other category of attitude items. Among behavioral items, the effects are most pronounced for items with a strong possibility of a socially desirable answer and which are somewhat or highly threatening.

In addition to exploring the relationship between social desirability and other question characteristics, Sudman and Bradburn have examined characteristics of the interview. Relative response effect measurements for attitudinal questions indicate more of a tendency to converge on a single (presumably desirable)[11] answer in personal interviews than in self-administered questionnaires. This is the case for all levels of social desirability, although the differences between the two modes of administration are greater for questions with a strong possibility of a socially desirable answer. Since personal contact between the respondent and the interviewer is present in the personal interview and absent in the self-administered questionnaire, this suggests that face-to-face interaction is an important factor in obtaining socially desirable responses.

Characteristics of interviewers interact with social desirability for attitudinal items (no behavioral data are presented). Response effects obtained by white interviewers (regardless of the race of the respondent) are larger than those obtained by black interviewers for items rated as having a strong possibility of a socially desirable answer, while the effect of interviewer's race is reversed for items with little possibility. Response effects obtained by male interviewers are larger than those obtained by female interviewers for items rated as having a strong possibility of a socially desirable answer, while the reverse is true for items with little possibility.

As with characteristics of interviewers, respondent characteristics also interact with social desirability for attitude items. Relative response effects are larger for women than for men for items with a strong possibility of a socially desirable answer, while the reverse is true for items with little such possibility. Response effects are larger for whites than for blacks for items with a strong possibility of a socially desirable answer, while the reverse is true for items with little such possibility. These results may be explained by the types of questions that have a strong possibility of a socially desirable answer, namely, racial, religious, ethnic, and to some extent sexual attitudes, as Sudman and Bradburn note. The predominance of these items in the "strong possibility" category is, as mentioned earlier, a function of the subjective impressions of the coders and the coding instructions.

Social Desirability

In general, Sudman and Bradburn conclude that task variables, of which social desirability is one, are more important sources of response effects than are interviewer or respondent characteristics. For social desirability response effects, however, characteristics of interviewers and respondents are important in producing differential responses.

With one exception (Sudman and Bradburn), all the research reported here deals with social desirability as a constant bias that does not vary according to the dynamics of the interview situation. Sudman and Bradburn's findings about the characteristics of the respondents who give and of the interviewers who receive socially desirable responses indicate the importance of this element. Some other work is relevant to this point. In a study concerning a specific population (welfare mothers), Weiss (1968) investigates the relationship of social desirability to rapport and social distance between interviewer and respondent. The questionnaire included both behavior and attitude items; the behaviors measured[12] had the positive feature that self-reports could be verified with actual behavior. The validation was accomplished through record checks, and overreports of these behaviors were attributed to social desirability (underreports were attributed to confusion). The attitudinal responses,[13] of course, could not be verified in the same way, and socially desirable responses were determined by the investigator.

Analysis of the behavior items reveals that, contrary to expectation, dissimilar pairs of respondents and interviewers (in terms of education, age, and socioeconomic status) did not receive more biased responses than did pairs of similar status. On the other hand, respondents who had the best rapport with interviewers (as rated by the interviewers on a five-point scale) gave the most biased responses. For the attitudinal items, both interviewer-respondent disparity and rapport had an effect on response bias (as measured by the Weiss's evaluation of desirable responses); for these items, however, status similarity was more strongly related to social desirability than was rapport.

Dohrenwend, Colombotos, and Dohrenwend (1968) deal with social distance between interviewer and respondent in a different way. Interviewers on a mental health survey were asked (after completion of the survey) about their preferences for interviewing certain types of respondents.[14] Interviewers who expressed at least one preference (out of a possible four) were identified as preferenced interviewers; those who did not express any preferences were identified as nonpreferenced interviewers. The purpose of the research was to investigate whether the preferences of interviewers were perceived by respondents and thus affected their responses. Dohrenwend, Colombotos, and Dohrenwend hypothesized that "unpreferred" respondents would underreport neuropsychiatric symptoms to a greater extent than would "preferred" respondents in order to present a more favorable image to interviewers, and so interviewers with preferences would obtain lower scores from unpreferred respondents than would interviewers without preferences. Since low-income blacks were less preferred than low-income whites, Dohrehwend et al. expected differences between levels of reported symptoms of low-income blacks interviewed by preferenced and nonpreferenced interviewers to be greater than differences for low-income whites, while both differences would be significant. The results show that for white respondents, only the low-income group reported significantly lower symptom scores to preferenced interviewers; among black respondents, however, the middle- and higher-income groups reported lower scores, while the lower-income group did not. The authors conclude that too much as well as too little social distance results in biased responses.

However, social desirability is not the only biasing mechanism that might be operating here. The authors "assume that the general tendency is for respondents to bias their answers to conform with what they believe to be the norms and expectations of the interviewer" (Dohrenwend, Colombotos, and Dohrenwend, 1968:410). It might also be plausible, for instance, that respondents from the "unpreferred" group who perceive these attitudes might give interviewers the answers they think the interviewers expect to hear from them, which might not be in a socially desirable direction. Although this possibility is not addressed by the authors, their results indicate that this might well be occurring.

Discussion

The literature reviewed here shows that conceptual ambiguities plague the notion of social desirability. Simply conceived, social desirability is a tendency on the part of respondents to give favorable impressions of themselves. The source of a respondent's notion of what are favorable expectations is ambiguous. Although this definition makes no explicit reference to the concept of norms, most research on the topic makes at least a passing reference to that concept in presenting conclusions relevant to social desirability bias.

Thus, the relationship between social desirability and norms seems like a logical place to begin a discussion of the conceptual problems. Norms refer to rules of conduct shared by participants in a society or in a social interaction, and are based on cultural values. They specify "what is appropriate or inappropriate, setting limits within which individuals may seek alternative ways to achieve their goals" (Broom and Selznick, 1968:54-55).

Thus, a wide range of activities is consistent with a basic set of values:

> [V]alues do not consist in "desires" but rather in the desirable, that is, what we not only want but feel it is right and proper to want for ourselves and for others. [Kluckhohn, 1962:289, cited in Broom and Selznick, 1968:54].

Given these definitions (of social desirability, norms, and values), it becomes apparent that some of the inconsistencies in the literature stem from a basic difference in the conceptualization of social desirability. Some researchers (for example, Phillips and Clancy) consider its relationship to basic values, which are fundamental and universal rather than specific. The existence of cultural values is taken to be a given for a society, and they are instilled in individual members of society by the socialization process. Thus, individual values are assumed to be in line with cultural values. Other researchers (for example, Sudman and Bradburn) view social desirability in terms of norms, that is, what is within the range of acceptable conduct that is in accordance with cultural values. Since the range has poorly specified boundaries, certain activities are more controversial than others.

The differences in these two views of social desirability are reflected in the types of items included in the research. Emphasis on values generally leads one to conduct research on reports of traits, which are abstract and relatively stable, while emphasis on norms entails investigating reports of behaviors, concrete units of activity. So, for example, Bradburn and his associates choose to focus on behaviors that are controversial, either because their acceptability varies for population subgroups or because they are at the limits of the acceptable range of behavior. Premarital sex and divorce are two more examples of behaviors that would fit into these categories. The items used by other researchers, on the other hand, relate to more value-oriented matters—absence of psychiatric symptoms, happiness, and so forth. Their desirability is generally considered to be high, rather than controversial, although some individuals might find this truer than others.

The mechanism for establishing standards against which to interpret respondents' answers also differs according to whether norms or values are viewed as the focal point of social desirability bias. Where norms are concerned, the pattern is for the investigators to establish what the norms are. A problem with this approach is the subjective nature of the assessment. The investigators might not be able to specify accurately what the norms are, if indeed there are norms for the specific behaviors being examined. A remote example of this is recorded in the work of Bradburn and his associates (1979). Although they are looking at the variable "threat," which they consider to be distinct from social desirability, their subjective assessment of a number of behaviors based on the amount of threat involved in each one turns out to be unsubstantiated by the amount of distortion in responses revealed by record checks of these behaviors. Specification of norms is also a problem; because norms have an elusive nature, they may vary for different geographic regions or different types of people (for instance, those of different ages, occupations, and genders), and they frequently cannot be defined until they are broken. What is the norm regarding abortion, for instance? It is legal, yet extremely controversial, and difficult to classify as far as normative behavior is concerned.

The means of establishing the desirability of value items is with the respondents themselves. Ratings of the "desirability" of various items are made by each individual, which allows for a more flexible assessment of the degree to which various characteristics are important to different people. Measurement in this instance, however, may be hampered by a lack of specificity in defining "desirable," so that no concrete standard is provided for respondents to use. Is it a question of whether I want to possess a certain characteristic, whether I think it would be good if I possessed that characteristic, or something else? These points of view are not necessarily identical, and their differences may be important to the ratings given by respondents.

This overview of the differences in ways of conceptualizing social desirability is somewhat simplified. All value-related traits are not measured by individual desirability ratings—such a procedure would add significantly to the length and cost of any survey. In other work (for example, Weiss, 1968), investigators make a judgment about what the desirable response is, as they do with behavior items.

Both sets of criteria have different measurement problems. In addition, the results of the two measurement techniques are different because they ask different questions. One branch of research emphasizes what is "desirable to me"—the desirability ratings provide an additional source of information and permit investigation of the relationship between individual values and survey self-reports. The other branch emphasizes what is "desirable to society"—investigators' judgments about acceptable or desirable responses permit research on survey self-reports as they are reflective of social norms and as they differ under various interviewing conditions. In neither case is the truth about the respondent's self-report known, so an exact specification of social desirability bias is impossible to measure. Even if it could be measured, however, it is not clear that the measurements would be comparable, because they reflect varying interpretations of the concept.

Another area in which interpretation of the concept differs is in the question of whether social desirability is a personality characteristic or an item characteristic. While this distinction has been made by several researchers who recognize them both, others focus their attention on one aspect or the other. No theory has been constructed to integrate both dimensions into an assessment of their relative importance. The findings of Phillips and Clancy (and of Gove and Geerken) that the two factors are independent suggest that people who have a high tendency to respond desirably do not necessarily agree on what is desirable. Given a choice of one dimension or the other, social desirability as an item characteristic seems to be more important, because even with information about a person's tendency to respond desirably, it would still be necessary to know how that person views various traits in order to evaluate his or her responses. The relationship between the two, however, merits much further study, including the development of models that incorporate both components.

Obviously the issues involved in specifying the meaning of social desirability are complex and could be discussed at even greater length without achieving a sense of closure on the subject. However, to the extent that our actions as well as our responses to survey questions are influenced by what we see as socially desirable, perhaps the problem is not as overwhelming as it appears to be.

Notes

1. Examples of the 33 items that were selected to comprise the scale are as follows (answers that indicate high need for approval are shown in parentheses):
   I'm always willing to admit it when I make a mistake (True).
   No matter who I'm talking to I'm always a good listener (True).
   There have been occasions when I took advantage of someone (False).

2. The judges were faculty members and graduate students in psychology.

3. Examples of the RD16 scale items include the following:
   One can always find friends if he tries.
   In general, I am satisfied with my lot in life.
   People will be honest with you as long as you are honest with them.

4. Examples of the items are:
   Are you the worrying type?
   I have personal worries that get me down physically.
   Every so often I feel hot all over.
   Do you feel somewhat apart even among friends?
   I'm bothered by acid (sour) stomach several times a week.

5. The items are both subjective and objective in nature. Desirability ratings and self-descriptions were obtained for the following items:
   Taking all things together, how would you say things are these days—would you say you're very happy, pretty happy, or not too happy these days?
   How religious would you say you are—very religious, somewhat religious, or not at all religious?

Thinking of people, including relatives, whom you consider really good friends—that is, people you feel free to talk with about personal things—how many such friends would you say you have?

Taking all things together, how would you describe your marriage? Would you say that your marriage was very happy, pretty happy, or not too happy?

If you went to a party and found that most of the people were of a racial or ethnic group different from your own, would you be very bothered, somewhat bothered, or not bothered at all?

True or false: I visit my doctor at least once a year.

6. Phillips and Clancy's 1970 work is based on 115 interviews representing adults who have telephones and live in areas with populations of more than 1 million people. Their second study (1972) involves a somewhat larger sample: 404 adults representing all households with a listed residential telephone in the New England and Middle Atlantic states.

7. The sample consists of 2,248 respondents residing in the 48 contiguous states.

8. The labels were "Extremely Desirable, Pretty Desirable, Only Somewhat Desirable, Neither Desirable nor Undesirable, Only Somewhat Undesirable, Pretty Undesirable, Extremely Undesirable."

9. It should be noted that in pilot work with college students, no differences in means and standard deviations were found between ratings from the standpoint of self and from the standpoint of others (Schuessler, personal communication, December 8, 1980).

10. In a national NORC (National Opinion Research Center) sample of 1,200 respondents.

11. Sudman and Bradburn hypothesize that social desirability would decrease response variability because responses would tend to converge on the socially desirable answer.

12. Voting and voter registration, children failing a subject in school, receipt of welfare.

13. The questions asked whether respondents' children will surely not be on welfare, whether they agree with teaching their children to live for today, whether at least one of their children will continue education past high school, and whether they have a party affiliation.

14. Preferences were revealed for respondents who were young, white, rich, and male.

References

Bradburn, N., Sudman, S., and Associates (1979) *Improving Interview Method and Questionnaire Design*. San Francisco: Jossey-Bass.

Broom, L., and Selznick, P. (1968) *Sociology: A Text with Adapted Readings*. 4th ed. New York: Harper and Row.

Campbell, A., Converse, P.E., and Rodgers, W.L. (1976) *The Quality of American Life: Perceptions, Evaluations, and Satisfactions*. New York: Russell Sage Foundation.

Couch, A., and Keniston, K. (1961) Agreeing response set and social desirability. *Journal of Abnormal and Social Psychology* 62:175-179.

Social Desirability

Crowne, D., and Marlowe, D. (1964) *The Approval Motive*. New York: John Wiley and Sons.

Dohrenwend, B.S., Colombotos, J., and Dohrenwend, B.P. (1968) Social distance and interviewer effects. *Public Opinion Quarterly* 32:410-422.

Edwards, A.L. (1957) *The Social Desirability Variable in Personality Assessment and Research*. New York: Dryden.

Edwards, A.L., and Walker, J.N. (1961) Social desirability and agreement response set. *Journal of Abnormal and Social Psychology* 62:180-183.

Gove, W.R., and Geerken, M.R.. (1977) Response bias in surveys of mental health: an empirical investigation. *American Journal of Sociology* 82:1289-1317.

Jackson, D.N., and Messick, S. (1961) Acquiescence and desirability as response determinants on the MMPI. *Educational and Psychological Measurement* 21:771-790.

Kluckhohn, C. (1962) *Culture and Behavior*. New York: The Free Press of Glencoe.

Messick, S. (1960) Dimensions of social desirability. *Journal of Consulting Psychology* 18:241-253.

Phillips, D.L., and Clancy, K.J. (1970) Response biases in field studies of mental illness. *American Sociological Review* 36:512-514.

Phillips, D.L., and Clancy, K.J. (1972) Some effects of "social desirability" in survey studies. *American Journal of Sociology* 77:921-940.

Rorer, L.G. (1965) The great response style myth. *Psychological Bulletin* 63:129-156.

Rundquist, E.A. (1966) Item and response characteristics in attitude and personality measurement: a reaction to L.G. Rorer's "The Great Response Style Myth." *Psychological Bulletin* 66:166-177.

Schuessler, K., Hittle, D., and Cardascia, J. (1978) Measuring responding desirably with attitude-opinion items. *Social Psychology* 41:224-235.

Selltiz, C., Wrightsman, L.S., and Cook, S.W. (1976) *Research Methods in Social Relations*. 3rd ed. New York: Holt, Rinehart, and Winston.

Stricker, L.S. (1963) Acquiescence and social desirability response styles, item characteristics, and conformity. *Psychological Reports* 12:319-341.

Sudman, S., and Bradburn, N. (1974) *Response Effects in Surveys*. Chicago: Aldine Publishing.

Taylor, J.B. (1961) The "yeasayer" and social desirability: a comment on the Couch and Keniston paper. *Journal of Abnormal and Social Psychology* 62:172.

U.S. Department of Health, Education, and Welfare (1977a) *A Summary of Research Studies of Interviewing Methodology: 1959-1970*. By Charles F. Cannell. Vital and Health Statistics Series 2, No. 69. Washington, D.C.: Government Printing Office.

U.S. Department of Health, Education, and Welfare (1977b) *Advances in Health Survey Research Methods: Proceedings of a National Invitational Conference*. NCHSR Research Proceedings Series. Washington, D.C.: Government Printing Office.

U.S. Department of Health, Education, and Welfare (1977c) *Experiments in Interviewing Techniques: Field Experiments in Health Reporting, 1971-1977* NCHSR Research Report Series. Ann Arbor, Mich.: Survey Research Center.

Weiss, C.H. (1968) Validity of welfare mothers' interview responses. *Public Opinion Quarterly* 32:622-633.

Acknowledgments

The author is especially grateful to Elizabeth Martin for her suggestions on an earlier version of this manuscript. Thanks are also extended to Robert Abelson, Catherine Marsh, Karl Schuessler, Howard Schuman, Carol Stocking, and Charles Turner for their helpful comments as reviewers.

10

The Manner of Inquiry: An *Analysis of Survey Question Form Across Organizations and Over Time*

Jean M. Converse and Howard Schuman

Nationwide sample polls and surveys have flourished in the United States for the last 40 years, and certain major survey organizations have been scrupulous in building a historical record of their work. The oldest and best-known survey, the Gallup Poll, has syndicated its questions and answers continuously since 1935 and has recently collected all its results in bound volumes (Gallup, 1972a).[1] The Harris Survey is of more recent vintage (1956), yet Harris and Associates has also begun to publish its syndicated findings in a permanent archive (Harris, 1971). Two academic organizations have been conducting surveys since the 1940s: the National Opinion Research Center (NORC), which was established in 1941 and has been an affiliate of the University of Chicago since 1947, and the Institute for Social Research (ISR), founded at the University of Michigan in 1946. The latter two organizations publish documentation of certain continuing studies.

The archives preserved by these four organizations are a valuable record of thousands and thousands of questions that have been asked of the American public. They permit us to examine in this chapter some recent professional practices in the American survey, to trace some of those practices over a period of four decades, and to characterize the question style of these four major survey organizations. To that end, we have selected a large sample of questions asked in the early 1970s by each of the four organizations (Gallup, Harris, ISR, and NORC) and another large sample of questions asked over time by two of the four surveys (Gallup and ISR). We have classified these questions, not by their subject matter or content, but by the way in which they were asked—their form.[2]

Classifying questions by their form does some real injury to the richness of these materials. Not only does it neglect subject matter; it also tears the question from its organic historical context and its analytic purposes. This is a problem that regularly confronts survey research itself. When we classify and assign numbers to respondents' opinions, feelings, and experiences in order to permit quantitative analysis, we make some rather heavy-handed and mechanical simplifications of living materials. Reducing the rich to the manageable inevitably involves some loss when one is trying to study survey respondents. This is no less true when one is trying to study surveys.

There is no elegant theory of survey questions, as anyone who has tried to write survey questions will testify. The construction of questions turns on practical matters that seem simple, but in fact are difficult because so little guidance from theory or evidence from experiments is available on the actual effects of asking a question one way or another. An example of these practical issues is the open versus the closed question. An open question is one that respondents answer in their own words rather than by choosing between or among stated alternatives: "What do you think is the most important problem facing the American government today?" A disadvantage is that respondents may tend to wander off into personal problems and long vignettes. A closed question gives the respondent a clear choice: "Which do you think is the more important problem facing the American government today, inflation or unemployment?" But those two alternatives may be too stark and simple, and may limit the response. Widening the alternatives to three or four is another possibility, especially for difficult issues, for example:

Abortion should never be permitted.

Abortion should be permitted only if the life and health of the woman is in danger.

Abortion should be permitted if, due to personal reasons, the woman should have difficulty in caring for the child.

Abortion should never be forbidden, since one should not require a woman to have a child she doesn't want.

But can respondents be asked to favor or oppose issues that are really quite complicated? Have they really thought about the issue in sufficient detail? It may be better to ask people first if they have any opinion at all, then let those who do not get "off the hook." Or perhaps one could ask how strongly they feel about their opinion. One may be able to get at these nuances by asking a scaled question:

> Do you agree that the government should loan Chrysler more money or do you think the government should not make another loan?
> 1. Agree strongly; government definitely should.
> 2. Agree but not very strongly.
> 3. Not sure; it depends.
> 4. Disagree but not very strongly.
> 5. Disagree strongly; government definitely should not.

But that may be too much to consider all at once. A three-way choice may be the way to ask certain questions, avoiding both the clutter of four or five choices and the spareness of the two-way choice, for example:

> During the last few years do you think our chances of staying out of war have been getting better, getting worse, or stayed the same?

With this choice people who really do not know much about the issue may prefer to select the safe middle alternative, rather than to admit their ignorance. For some issues, however (politics and voting, for example), people have to be for or against:

> Do you approve or disapprove of the job that Jimmy Carter has been doing as president?

For other issues, it may be better to let people say what they have in mind:

> What do you think is the most important problem facing the American government today?

Those who construct survey questionnaires must take all these issues into consideration. In order to investigate the role of question form in attitude surveys, we have classified sets of actual questions into broad categories, including a variety of subcategories. (The definitions of these categories appear in Appendix A, and the distribution of question types is presented in Appendix B.) We begin by explaining the sampling procedures used to select questions. We then discuss those question categories that we found of most interest or utility in characterizing the question style of survey organizations.

The Selection of Questions

We used two different kinds of sampling procedures in the selection of questions for study because the organizations themselves used two kinds of documentation. In the reference volumes for the two commercial polls, single questions are arranged chronologically and/or by general subject matter. For the Gallup polls, which were arranged chronologically, we randomly sampled approximately 200 questions from *The Gallup Poll: Public Opinion 1935–1971*, for each of four periods: 1941–42, 1951–52, 1961–62, and 1969–71. (For the last sample it was necessary to use three annual collections of Gallup questions to generate 200 unrepeated questions.) In each period we selected only the first chronological use of a question, eliminating all repeated uses. For the Harris Survey we used the same kind of procedure, using *The Harris Survey Yearbook of Public Opinion 1970* to sample approximately 200 questions for that year.

The two academic surveys document their questions in a different way. The Institute for Social Research (ISR) has published all the questionnaires used in the major continuing National Election Study (NES), and the National Opinion Research Center (NORC) has published all the questionnaires used in the General Social Survey (GSS).[3] From the ISR National Election Study, we selected six questionnaires conducted at the time of a presidential election: 1952, 1956, 1960, 1964, 1968, and 1972. We eliminated the first study of 1948, which was a small survey providing only about a dozen questions meeting our criteria (to be described), as well as the studies conducted at the time of congressional elections.[4]

From NORC we selected the first three questionnaires of the General Social Survey, which was instituted in 1972. NORC, like ISR, has conducted a great variety of studies since the 1940s, but we chose its General Social Survey as a practical matter because its documentation is readily available and because of its "general" nature. Its character is somewhat different, nevertheless, from the other surveys we examine in this chapter, because the study was designed to serve social indicator research and to provide replication of some questions appearing in previous national surveys between 1945 and 1971. But since more than 75 percent of the questions are either original with NORC or replicate other surveys not considered here, we concluded that we could meaningfully compare it with the other three polls.

We restricted questions to those asked of nationwide samples, excluding those asked of subgroups such as farmers, women, whites, and so forth. We also excluded questions of reported experience, such as, "Did you vote in the last election?" and questions measuring preferences among candidates. (Only Gallup and Harris have asked the latter with frequency.) Our sample is thus drawn from the population of published questions that measure opinion or attitude, plus measures of knowledge or information, interest or involvement, and strength or intensity[5] of opinion. These procedures yielded the following Ns:

Survey	1970s Sample	Historical Samples (including 1970s samples)
Gallup	218	880 (from 1941–42 to 1969–71)
Harris	207	—
ISR–NES	161	675 (six questionnaires, 1952–72)
NORC–GSS	242	—
Total	828	1,555

It should be noted that none of these four samples can be considered entirely representative of each organization's actual practice. In the case of the academic organizations, the long-term studies we have selected cannot be considered representative of question wording for NORC or ISR. In the case of the commercial organizations, neither published archive is a complete record of all the questions asked. *The Harris Survey Yearbook* presents "the bulk of the data obtained for the weekly Harris Survey" as well as results from six special studies in 1970 (Harris, 1971:xii). *The Gallup Poll* records all results that were published, but not every question that was asked (Gallup, 1972a:i–v).

Recent Practice in Four Organizations

A CERTAIN CONVERGENCE OF STYLES

The Closed Question. Across the four major survey groups, there is fair agreement in certain practices. The prototypic survey question of the 1970s is a closed question that poses a choice between two alternatives: either a choice between two rival arguments or, more often, a simple two-way formal choice between favoring or opposing a single proposition. For example, this question provides a substantive choice between two arguments:

> Recently there has been a lot of talk about women's rights. Some people feel that women should have an equal role with men in running business, industry, and government. Others feel that women's place is in the home. Where would you place yourself? [1972 Election Study, Form I, Q. G9]

The following question provides a formal choice of approving or disapproving a single proposition:

> Do you approve or disapprove of the way Richard Nixon is handling his job as President? [Gallup, 1972a:2275]

One effect of the dominance of this kind of question is that certain issues in question construction that once animated professional rivalry and debate (and, much more rarely, research) have been effectively tabled. The debate about open versus closed questions, which was very lively in the 1940s (Converse, 1984), has been stilled; the closed question predominates in all four organizations (Table 10.1). NORC–GSS asks no open questions at all; Harris, Gallup, and ISR–NES ask only a small minority.

There is a middle category, quasi-closed, in Table 10.1, which designates the kind of question that literally provides no alternatives, but in fact implies such a limited number of alternatives (of numbers, dates, or names) that answers to the questions could in fact be coded on the spot by the interviewer.[6] For example, for this question: "What do you think is the ideal number of children for a family to have?", a set of numbers is not usually supplied; it might sound foolish and take unnecessary time to read off the implied choices, "0, 1, 2, 3, . . ." and so on.[7] Gallup is the only poll that uses the quasi-closed question.

Both Gallup and the NES make some use of the fully open question (7 percent of the 1970s sample). Even this amount of open questioning is worth noting, for the coding of open questions is complicated, costly, and less reliable than is the coding of closed answers. The Harris Survey's use of open questions is a special case. While only 4 percent of our sample questions of 1970 are open, this may well be an underestimate. In the archive of Harris questions maintained at the Institute for Research in Social Science at the University of North Carolina, about 9 percent of the more than 12,000 questions of 1963–76 are open.[8] It is perhaps somewhat surprising to find commercial polls using these materials as frequently as the NES does, because they are commonly operating under the pressures of journalistic

TABLE 10.1
Proportion of Questions in Closed and Open Form

	Gallup 1969–71	Harris 1970	ISR 1972	NORC 1972–74
Closed	83%	96%	93%	99%
Quasi-closed	11	0	0	1
Open	7	4	7	0
N	(189)	(203)	(142)	(230)

NOTES: Only attitude/opinion questions are coded here; questions measuring knowledge, interest, and intensity are excluded. Due to rounding, percentages may not sum to 100.

288

publishing deadlines that would make postcoding of open materials more problematic.

Vanishing Forms. Three other question forms were not used frequently by these survey organizations in the 1970s: checklists of items, the choice of three or more arguments, and measures of strength or intensity of opinion. Checklists have come under occasional scrutiny, and the research findings suggest that while they stimulate recall more effectively than an open question on the same topic does, they may also limit recall to the items on the list, even when omitted items are obvious and likely choices (Lindzey, 1951; Jenkins, 1935:Chapter 15). Such lists have been used especially in assessing readership of magazines and viewing of television programs. The scant use of them observed in our four samples—there is no instance of more than a single checklist question in any of the recent surveys—is probably in part a result of our selection of questions that ruled out experiential questions on readership, radio and TV, health experiences, and the like.

The choice of multiple arguments (three or more), such as the previously mentioned abortion question, is rare in the polls. In two publications appearing 25 years apart, Gallup has testified to the difficulty of incorporating several arguments into a single question.[9] And it appears that only Gallup even tries, for 5 percent of the Gallup questions in the early 1970s provide multiple arguments, while the other three surveys present only 0 to 1 percent of their questions in this form.

Measures of intensity have inspired some enthusiasm, even in recent years (Hennessy, 1975:42), but across all four samples, the classic measure of intensity is conspicuous by its absence:

> How strongly do you feel about that issue—quite strongly or not so strongly?

It appears only once, in a single question asked by Gallup, supporting the judgment (Gallup, 1972b:106) that intensity questions are now used rarely:

> Questions put to respondents about "how strongly" they feel, "how important it is to them," "how much they care," etc. all yield added insights into the intensity of opinion held by the public. The fact, however, that they are used as seldom as they are in the regular polls, here and abroad, indicates that the added information gained does not compensate for the time and difficulties encountered by the survey interviewer.

Another question form, the Likert scale, has sometimes been considered a measurement of intensity, although the classification seems arguable. The scale, generally deemed to measure both opinion and intensity of opinion, gives respondents four or five choices of response, for example:

In general, women in our society have not been as successful as men—in business, politics, the leadership positions in our country. I'll read you some reasons people have offered to explain why this is so, including some things that other people don't agree with at all. For each, I'd like you to tell me whether you agree a great deal, agree somewhat, disagree somewhat, or disagree a great deal. . . . Men are born with more drive to be ambitious and successful than women, ... [1972 Election Study, Form II, Q. G12]

This is a genuine measurement of intensity for respondents who intend their answers that way: they "agree a great deal" because they indeed feel very strongly that "men are born with more drive . . . than women." But others may "agree a great deal" because they think the statement is really true—without necessarily feeling very strongly about the matter. Only a separate intensity measure would make that clear. In any case, Likert items of intensity are a minor enterprise in our samples, appearing only in the NES in nine questions.

SPECIALTIES OF THE HOUSE

The question styles of the four polls converge in the use of closed questions with a choice of two alternatives and in the virtual exclusion of questions providing checklists, multiple arguments, and measures of intensity. Beyond this, however, each survey has its own hallmarks, concentrating to some extent on one, two, or three kinds of questions. We coded 18 varieties of attitude/opinion questions, and the four surveys use from 11 to 16 of these forms. But they nevertheless specialize.

Gallup's Voting Model. Gallup shows a penchant for two-way questions of this kind (Gallup, 1972a:2243, 2211, 2186):

In general, do you favor or oppose the busing of Negro and white school children from one school district to another?

Everything considered, would you say that in general, you approve or disapprove of wiretapping?

A quarter of the recent Gallup questions are cast in this form. Ranking second in frequency is the direct question in which a yes/no alternative is implied rather than stated, as in:

Do you think college students should have a greater say in the running of colleges?

Altogether, Gallup provides over 60 percent of the 1970s questions in the form of single propositions that respondents are asked to favor or oppose, approve or disapprove, say "yes" or "no," and so forth. Gallup respondents are rarely asked to agree or disagree, however; Gallup apparently avoids this variant of the two-way choice, the very one that, as we shall see, Harris uses most frequently.

Of the four organizations here, the Gallup Poll has logged the longest experience in the writing of questions, and George Gallup, Sr., has written a good deal about his preferences and judgments. He has avoided three-way questions, feeling that the middle alternative is too attractive to respondents.[10] He has also rejected scales.

> Most attitude scales are, in fact, better suited to the classroom with students as captive subjects than to the face-to-face interviews undertaken by most survey organizations. [Gallup, 1972b:106]

He has favored the either/or choice because a primary goal has been to provide something of an informal voting booth in which the American public can register its ayes and nays before an official vote is taken by elected representatives. In response to this query from a magazine editor, reproduced in *The Sophisticated Poll Watchers' Guide* (Gallup, 1972b:89):

> On more than a few occasions I have found that I could not, were I asked, answer a poll with a "yes" or "no." More likely, my answer would be "yes, but" or "yes, if." I wonder whether pollsters can't or just don't want to measure nuances of feeling?

Gallup stated his belief that the either/or choice captures a political reality:

> At some point in the decision process, whether it be concerned with an important issue before Congress, a new law before the state legislature, or a school bond issue in Central City, the time comes for a simple "yes" or "no" vote. Fortunately, or unfortunately, there is no lever on a voting machine that permits the voter to register a "yes, if" or a "yes, but" vote. While discussion can and should proceed at length, the only way to determine majority opinion is by a simple count of noses. [Gallup, 1972b:90]

To this end Gallup specializes in single questions on an issue, with simple formal alternatives. He presents marginal results by total sample and major demographic subgroups, rather than analytic results that explore relationships. This general "voting" style of polling is not only efficient for prompt commercial distribution, it is consistent with Gallup's conception of his polling purpose.

Harris's Multiple Questions. The Harris style displays two hallmarks: the agree/disagree question and the four-point scale, each of which accounts for

20 to 22 percent of the 1970s sample. While Gallup asks the traditional question on presidential popularity with the approve/disapprove format, Harris asks that question and many others in this form:

> How would you rate the job President Nixon is doing as President—excellent, pretty good, only fair, or poor? [Harris, 1971:11]

Furthermore, the Harris Survey is singular in using fairly heavily the agree/ disagree form that the other three organizations tend to avoid and in linking questions on a particular topic in this way:

> Here are some statements which some people have made about 18 year olds having the vote. For each, tell me if you tend to agree or disagree:

> Until most people reach 21 years of age, they aren't mature enough to be given the vote.

> If young people are old enough to serve in the armed forces, they are old enough to vote. [Harris, 1971:268]

and so on with several others.

Harris frequently covers an issue with a range of different opinions. For example, in the 1970 sample, respondents are presented with 15 statements concerning the medical profession; for each they are to indicate whether the statement is completely justified, somewhat justified, or unjustified (Harris, 1971:197). The statements range from highly laudatory views of American medicine:

> It's all wrong that doctors are paid so little all those years they're being trained. Medical students and interns should earn a living wage.

> People have a higher regard for their doctor than anyone else they deal with. It is a recognition of his long and rigorous training.

to sharply cynical ones:

> The patient who gets sick on Wednesday afternoon or Sunday could die before they would get a doctor off the golf course.

> Doctors have the highest income of any group in the country. That shows how little they care about the Hippocratic oath.

More moderate statements appear as well:

> Big hospitals are not as cold-blooded as people think, but they need to be impersonal in order to function properly.

Without referring directly to Gallup, Harris (Louis Harris and Associates, l976:1) has recently expressed himself in direct opposition to his competitor's style:

> The way questions are put is a most sensitive and important area of polling. The best polls will not rely on a single question or even a few questions to obtain a true reading of public opinion. Experience has shown the people do not express their opinions in a neat package with a ribbon tied around it, but rather talk around their issues and preferences. Thus, a poll which asks 10 to 15 separate questions of the public is to be trusted much more than one that asks a single question.

One-third of Harris's 1970s questions appear in batteries of this kind bearing on a single issue.

Given this style of questioning, we might expect Harris's results to be analyzed in more detail. For example, the 15 questions on American medicine would lend themselves to at least a consistency check: Were there people in any number who subscribed to both statements of praise and blame for American doctors? Were the questions understood? Did a response set appear to be operating? To what degree did sets of items lie along a single dimension? Curiously, Harris reports these multiple questions as a set of single-question results, without availing himself of analysis that would illuminate relationships among the items in the series or among respondents. In both the *Yearbook* and in his commercial releases, he presents results much as Gallup does: overall findings, and percentages by major demographic groups (on occasion), almost always without further analysis.

By this evidence at least, it seems clear that commercial polls are not inherently limited to the presentation of marginal results by virtue of the kinds of questions they ask. Many Harris questions especially are perfectly appropriate to the more elaborate analysis that academic surveys typically undertake. The fact that neither Gallup nor Harris does such analysis may possibly reflect intellectual traditions and professional training, but it certainly reflects particular pressures on commercial polls—to publish results quickly, while they are still timely and interesting to the reading public, and to present them in a form that the nonprofessional audience will find meaningful and clear. The constraint is not intrinsic to the design of commercial questions themselves.

NORC-GSS's Two-Way, Three-Way, and Scaled Choices. The GSS shows about equal preference for three closed forms. The two-way form that we have seen as a Gallup favorite also bulks large in the General Social Survey: 29 percent of the attitude/opinion questions are of this form. The other two most common forms in the NORC-GSS study are those often used in the Harris Survey: 27 percent are three-way questions and 22 percent are scales.

Across the 18 types of attitude questions we coded, the GSS actually shows more similarity to both Harris and Gallup than the two commercial polls do to each other, using what is called the index of dissimilarity. This measure provides a simple comparison of two percentage distributions that ranges from 0 to 100 percent; if the distribution of question forms in two polls were exactly the same, the index of dissimilarity would be 0. As we see from Table 10.2, the dissimilarity between Gallup and Harris is .57, while NORC scores show a lower, more similar score in the .40s with respect to each of the commercial polls.

The degree of similarity of the GSS to the Gallup Poll reflects the force of replication in part. Fifteen percent of the GSS questions are replications of questions in our Gallup sample for the 1970s. Another factor has artificially enhanced the degree of similarity between the GSS and Harris: the decision not to include in GSS any open questions. This exclusion of open questions is not characteristic of NORC studies across the board, and it has the effect of increasing the similarity to the Harris sample. Seven percent of the GSS questions also appeared originally in the National Election Study. The NES is, however, something of an outlier, showing least similarity overall to any of the other polls (see Table 10.2).

ISR-NES and the Choice of Rival Arguments. As we have noted, the National Election Study shows a similarity to the Gallup Poll in using some open questions, but the NES hallmark is a closed question presenting rival arguments, for example:

> Sometimes a company has to lay off part of its labor force. Some people think that the first workers to be laid off should be women whose husbands have jobs. Others think that male and female employees should be treated the same. Which of these opinions do you agree with?

> As you may know Congress passed a bill that says that black people should have the right to go to any hotel or restaurant they can afford, just like anybody else. Some people feel that this is something the government in Washington

TABLE 10.2
*Index of Dissimilarity Between Survey
Question Forms*

	Gallup	Harris	NORC–GSS
Harris	.57	—	—
NORC–GSS	.44	.42	—
ISR–NES	.67	.56	.64

should support. Others feel that the government should stay out of this matter. [Election Study 1972, Forms I and II, Q. D3]

Such a choice of arguments addresses the possibility that respondents may tend to agree with a proposition unless presented with a genuine argument on the other side. This kind of balancing is of course complex because there may be any number of logical "opposites" to a given idea.

Close to half (45 percent) of the 1972 Election Study presents questions with two rival arguments, and the greater part of these also incorporate a seven-point scale, for example:[11]

Some people think that the use of marijuana should be made legal. Others think that the penalties for using marijuana should be set higher than they are now. Where would you place yourself on this scale, or haven't you thought much about it?

Make Use of Marijuana Legal					Set Penalties Higher Than They Are Now	
1	2	3	4	5	6	7

[Election Study 1972, Form I, Q. G3]

Of all the question forms we have observed, this 7-point scale would appear to be the most dependent on graphic presentation and thus on the personal-interviewing situation. (Respondents confronted with a "feeling thermometer scale" can conjure up the image of the familiar object. The Stapel scalometer, used by Gallup and NORC, is a 10-point scale, but it is more straightforward; see discussion on page 303.) A telephone interviewer, without visual aids, may be hard-pressed to explain such a rather complex question, involving a choice of two ideas and a scale placement of seven points. Yet this question form has become an important one for trend and panel measurement of the National Election Survey. If the NES undertakes large-scale telephone interviewing, the form may be modified.

It is important to note that all four samples represent questions used in the personal interviewing situation. No data were gathered by telephone. If all major surveys shift to telephone interviewing—of the four examined here, the two commercial polls made that shift in the late 1970s[12]—some of these distinctive house styles may fade. The telephone technique, with its premium on questions that can be transmitted without visual aids, may make survey question practice even more convergent across organizations than it is in the data here.

THE ACADEMIC/COMMERCIAL DIVIDE

Our examination of the "specialties of the house" of the different survey organizations does not support an assumption that we have often heard expressed informally in the profession—that there is a great divide, with commercial polls on one side and academic surveys on the other—at least not in the matter of question form. Neither is there a characteristic academic or commercial style in the use of filter questions or the level of language difficulty. Only in mean levels of expressed "no opinion" can the commercial and academic polls be distinguished.

Filter Questions. In the previous example from the NES, respondents are given a chance to say that they "haven't thought much about it," rather than be asked a set of questions about the legalization of marijuana. The 1972 ISR-NES asks another variant of the filter question as well:

> Some people feel that if black people are not getting fair treatment in jobs, the government in Washington ought to see to it that they do. Others feel that this is not the federal government's business. Have you had enough interest in this question to favor one side over the other? [Forms I and II, Q. D1.]

Only those claiming an interest are asked to specify which side they favor. Of the ISR-NES questions selected, 12 percent (19 questions) are designed to tap interest or knowledge; very few of these (2 questions) actually test the accuracy of information.

The Gallup Poll also filters respondents who show lack of interest or information about an issue. The typical filter question is of this kind: Have you heard or read about the recent invasion of Laos by South Vietnamese troops?

Those answering "yes" are then asked an opinion question about how they feel about that invasion; those saying "no" skip ahead to another issue. Thirteen percent of the Gallup 1970s sample questions concern knowledge or interest; close to half of them (12 of 28) assess the accuracy of the respondent's information, as in these examples (Gallup, 1972a:2210, 2284):

> Offhand, do you happen to recall about how much of every tax dollar is now spent for military and defense purposes?

> Can you tell me who the following men are and what they do?
> Edward Kennedy. . . .

Only the two polls, commercial Gallup and academic NES, display much concern for measuring interest or knowledge and then screening off the self-confessed uninformed on certain issues. Commercial Harris shows only one clear instance of screening in five questions measuring interest/knowledge, and academic NORC-GSS does not screen at all. (While in GSS questionnaires there are 12 items coded as knowledge/interest, 10 of them are actually vocabulary questions designed as measures of general intelligence, not of information about specific issues.) Either Harris and NORC rely on the uninformed or uninvolved to volunteer this fact, or they assume that invalid or unreliable opinion does not bulk large enough in the sample to materially affect results.

Level of Language Difficulty. There is no evidence of distinctive commercial or academic practice in the level of language difficulty used in questions (Table 10.3). In the 1940s and 1950s various formulas were devised for assessing the level of comprehension difficulty posed by samples of American prose. The "ease of reading" formula devised by Rudolf Flesch (1948; Chall and Dial, 1948) became the best known of these measures, and we have applied it to our samples of questions. The Flesch formula weights the average number of words per sentence and the total number of syllables, arraying most scores from 0 (most difficult) to 100 (easiest). The low scores represent language that will be comprehensible to college graduates; the high scores will be understood by those with lower grade school education. The standard level represents the reading level of the median educational attainment. In the 1970s, the median 12.1 years of school is represented by a Flesch score range of 50 to 60.

All four polls in the early 1970s show a mean score of standard or greater —that is, a level of reading difficulty that should be comprehensible to high school graduates and beyond (Table 10.3). The NES shows the easiest reading level by Flesch scoring, almost 73; and the Harris Survey, the most difficult, almost 59. It is worth noting that the similarity of the Gallup and GSS scores (both in the low 60s) cannot be attributed to any overlap in questions; only 29 of the 200 GSS questions measured by the Flesch formula are replication questions appearing in the Gallup sample, and excluding them does not significantly change the level of difficulty in the GSS

TABLE 10.3

Mean Level of Language Difficulty as Measured by Flesch "Ease of Reading" Scores (lower scores = more difficult language)

	Gallup 1969–71	Harris 1970	ISR-NES 1972	NORC-GSS 1972–74
Mean	62.1	58.7	72.7	63.6
s.d.	18.1	18.6	20.5	22.6
N	(206)	(196)	(157)	(200)

NOTES: Short probes numbering 1 to 3 words and questions in series numbering under 5 words were excluded from the count. All differences are significant at the .02 level or beyond, except those between NORC-GSS/Gallup. Values of *t* range from 0.7 (NORC/Gallup) to 6.7 (Harris/ISR).

questions.[13] In any case, the commercial and academic polls cannot be distinguished from each other by the level of language difficulty.

"No Opinion". We do find that the commercial and academic polls can be distinguished in mean levels of "no opinion" expressed on attitude/opinion questions (Table 10.4). The relatively high level of the commercial pair contrasts with the relatively low level of the academic pair, suggesting perhaps some meaningful difference by type of organization. We cannot be entirely certain, however, that we are tapping precisely the same kinds of answers in all four polls with our designation "no opinion." Harris, for example, typically uses a "not sure" category that we judge to be comparable to the "don't know" or "no opinion" most commonly used by the other polls (a view supported by documentation provided informally by Louis Harris and Associates).[14]

The one difference in procedure that we can identify suggests that the observed difference between academic and commercial surveys is, if anything, an underestimate. In the two academic surveys, figures for both "don't know" (DK) and "not ascertained" (NA) are presented—NA is generally a much smaller proportion of the total than is DK, and we have incorporated both into our total for "no opinion." The commercial polls, on the other hand, provide no NA category, meaning, perhaps, that NAs may simply be eliminated from the total sample on which the DK/NA percentage is calculated, a procedure that would systematically lower the commercial "no opinion" percentage. Given our lack of detailed information about these procedures, we assume that NA is in fact a trivial fraction of the commercial poll sample, just as we observe it to be in the academic data, and that treatment of it does not materially change DK levels. In any case, the discrepancies between academic and commercial "no opinion" levels

TABLE 10.4

*Percentage of "No Opinion" Responses on
Attitude/Opinion Questions*

	Gallup 1969–71	Harris 1970	ISR–NES 1972	NORC–GSS 1972
Mean	10.0	15.0	5.0	3.5
s.d.	7.0	8.4	3.9	2.7
N[a]	(138)	(182)	(77)	(210)

NOTE: All differences between means are significant from each other at the .002 level.
[a]The N includes attitude/opinion questions asked of everyone, excluding not only knowledge/interest questions, but also questions for which part of the sample has been filtered by prior questioning.

observed here seem unlikely to proceeed solely from different ways of defining and coding "no opinion" responses, and suggest broader issues in interviewing practice and question content.

We do have one piece of evidence suggesting that the observed difference is not just a matter of question content, from 18 questions of the GSS that are exact replications or close variants of questions asked by Gallup in the same 12-month period (see Table 10.5). In 16 of the 18 questions, the Gallup percentage of "no opinion" responses is slightly higher, and the mean difference between polls is significant ($p < .002$). When we focus on the 10 exact replications (Figure 10.1), we can see that 9 of the 10 "no opinion" percentages are higher when the question is administered by the Gallup Poll. In this modest bit of data, however, we cannot reproduce the overall discrepancy observed between Gallup and NORC (10 percent and 3.5 percent), much less claim any generality for the other academic/commercial pair for which we have no comparable questions. The finding remains merely suggestive.

CURRENT PRACTICE IN SUMMARY

In summary, then, the four surveys show similarity on five question forms:

1. Concentration on closed questions,
2. Substantial use of the two-way choice,
3. Minor use of multiple arguments,
4. Negligible use of checklists, and
5. Negligible use of intensity measures.

Even this degree of parallel practice somewhat overstates the case for similarity across all four polls or between academic and commercial types, for each survey shows a distinctive style, specializing in certain forms of question. Gallup favors the two-way formal choice between approve/disap-

TABLE 10.5

Mean Percentage of "No Opinion" Responses
on 18 Comparable Questions:
Gallup and NORC

	Gallup	NORC
Mean	7.7	4.2
s.d.	2.9	2.2
N	(18)	(18)

NOTES: The Gallup questions originally appear in issues of the monthly *Gallup Opinion Index 1971–73*. Difference between means is significant at $p < .002$, $t = 3.90$, d.f. = 34. If the comparison is restricted to the ten exact replications, the significance persists ($p < .02$).

FIGURE 10.1

Percentage of "No Opinion" Responses on 10 Questions Asked by Gallup, 1971-73 and NORC-GSS, 1972-74.

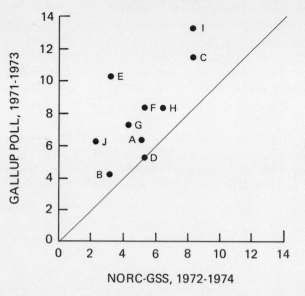

NOTE: The exact wording of the questions is as follows:

A. In general do you favor or oppose the busing of Negro and white school children from one district to another?

B. Would you favor or oppose a law which would require a person to obtain a police permit before he or she could buy a gun?

C. Are you in favor of the death penalty for persons convicted of murder?

D. If your party nominated a woman for President, would you vote for her if she were qualified for the job? [The Gallup question omits "were."]

E. What do you think is the ideal number of children for a family to have?

F. You will notice that the boxes on this card go from the highest position of "plus 5" for a country which you *like* very much, to the lowest position of "minus 5" for a country you *dislike* very much. How far up the scale or how far down the scale would you rate the following countries? Japan?

G. . . . Canada?

H. . . . China?

I. . . . Egypt?

J. Do you think the use of marijuana should be made legal or not?

prove, favor/oppose, and so forth, and single questions on a given issue; Harris favors agree/disagree questions and multiple viewpoints on a given issue; the GSS favors two-way, three-way, and scaled choices; and the NES favors a choice of two arguments or substantive ideas.

Commercial and academic polls can be grouped with respect to overall levels of "no opinion" responses, but not in the use of filter questions or in the level of language difficulty. In some ways the two kinds of survey enterprise obviously differ—modes and elaboration of analysis, presentation of results, perhaps even interviewing practice, and certainly the matter of journalistic deadlines—but there is little evidence from question characteristics by which to delineate an academic and a commercial style. We can in fact find somewhat more similarity across this conventional divide than we can on each side of it; still, in recent question-writing practice each organization shows considerable individuality.

Practice Over Time in the Gallup Poll and the National Election Study

A LIMITED SIMILARITY

When we consider two sources of survey practice over time, the Gallup Poll and the ISR National Election Study, we find that the two organizations have evolved in very different ways. Of the major characteristics summarized previously, in only one do both polls show a fair similarity over time—namely, in the persisting attention to questions measuring respondents' knowledge, interest, or the intensity underlying their opinions. In the 1970s Gallup and the NES devoted 12 to 13 percent of the total set of sampled questions to knowledge/interest questions, while the other two polls both showed a minimal interest in this kind of inquiry. This is fairly representative of Gallup and the NES; while the fraction fluctuates in both polls, it never falls below 5 percent of the selected questions (Table 10.6).

The two polls show a common research interest in allowing the self-confessed uninterested or ill-informed to screen themselves out of inquiry

TABLE 10.6
Proportion of Questions Measuring
Knowledge/Interest/Intensity

	Gallup			ISR National Election Study	
Year	Proportion	Total N	Year	Proportion	Total N
1941–42	5%	212	1952	6%	66
1951–52	21	230	1956	19	97
1961–62	8	220	1960	12	85
1969–71	13	218	1964	28	141
			1968	20	125
			1972	12	161

on a given topic. On other aspects of question form, however, they have few points of common practice. Such similarities as exist earlier in the organizations' histories disappear as each evolves a characteristic question style.

THE GALLUP STYLE

Analysis of Gallup questions over four decades of samples shows a characteristic style that emerges and persists. First we note a high stability in the general form of open and closed questions. Over the four decades, closed questions account for 79 to 83 percent of the sampled attitude/opinion questions (Table 10.7).

In the 1940s direct questions implying yes/no answers predominated. By the 1950s Gallup had turned to the two-way question as the dominant form, accounting for close to three-quarters of the sampled questions in the early 1950s and 1960s and well over half in the early 1970s (Table 10.8). Why Gallup shifted from the direct question to the two-way choice can only be conjectured, as he does not discuss the change in any materials known to us. But as there was considerable interest and debate in the 1940s and 1950s about question bias, we suspect that this change was a response to such criticism (Kornhauser, 1946; Link et al., 1947; Payne, 1950).

Minor Changes. Beyond the shift to the two-way question, the Gallup Poll shows a high stability in question form over the four decades sampled. Questions measuring intensity of opinion, for instance, are a negligible factor throughout the four samples, a single such measure appearing once in the 1940s and again in the 1970s sample.[15] The proportion of closed questions presenting a choice of ideas ranges narrowly from 6 to 10 percent in the four samples. The share of three-way alternatives is 8 percent in all three samples since the 1950s (Table 10.8).

In the early 1970s, we do find some increased use of two kinds of questions that Gallup has reported as rather difficult to use—multiple substan-

TABLE 10.7

*Proportion of Open and Closed Questions
in Gallup Samples*

	1941–42	1951–52	1961–62	1969–71
Closed	82%	79%	83%	83%
Quasi-closed	10	8	7	11
Open	8	13	10	7
N	(202)	(181)	(202)	(189)

NOTE: Knowledge, interest, and intensity questions are excluded from the table.

TABLE 10.8

Proportion of Specific Question Forms in Gallup Samples:
Closed Questions

	1941–42	1951–52	1961–62	1969–71
Single Idea (formal choice)				
Direct questions	64%	14%	10%	17%
Two-way questions	27	70	72	58
Three-way questions	1	8	8	8
Scales	0	1	1	7
Checklists	1	1	3	1
Choice of Ideas (substantive choice)	7	6	6	10
N	(165)	(143)	(167)	(156)

NOTES: See appendix A for definitions and examples of these categories. Table 10.8 incorporates categories 1–14. Due to rounding, percentages may not sum to 100.

tive arguments and scales. The use of scales rose in the 1970s to 7 percent of closed attitude/opinion questions (from 0 to 1 percent), and in this sample we find Gallup's first use of the Stapel scalometer, which presents the respondent with 10 points, 5 positive and 5 negative, on which to rate degrees of liking or disliking of, for example, institutions or public figures. Multiple arguments—three or more rival propositions—accounted for 6 percent of closed questions, a rise from 0 to 1 percent of previous samples (see Appendix B, Category 13). The fact that the increased use of these two question forms still represents minor proportions of the 1970s sample presumably reflects Gallup's judgment that multiple arguments and scales provide either the respondent or the polling organization with special problems.[16]

Language Difficulty. The stability of the Gallup style is also apparent in the level of language difficulty. The mean level of difficulty as measured by the Flesch formula always falls within the Flesch standard of 60 to 70 and across all four samples varies no more than three points, a difference that is not significant (Table 10.9).

It should be noted in conclusion that the stability we observe in Gallup question form is not a function of replicated questions. Within each decade sample, only the first chronological instance of a question is sampled; across samples, excluding replicated questions does not significantly change the distributions noted previously. Within the limits we have discussed, both the language and the form of the Gallup Poll questions show much similarity across all four decades since the early 1940s. The marked stability since the early 1950s provides sharp contrast, as we shall see, to the continuing evolution of question form in the ISR National Election Study since 1952.

TABLE 10.9

Mean Level of Difficulty in Gallup Samples Measured by Flesch "Ease-of-Reading" Scores (lower scores = more difficult language)

	1941–42	1951–52	1961–62	1969–71
Mean	65.5	65.4	62.6	62.1
s.d.	17.0	18.3	17.9	18.1
N	(212)	(229)	(220)	(206)

NOTE: Questions measuring only 1 to 3 words, such as very short probes and lists, and series of questions under 5 words are excluded from the count.

ISR NATIONAL ELECTION STUDY

In the National Election Study, practice over time shows a much more complex pattern; indeed, despite a fairly high incidence of replicated questions, question form in general reflects considerable experimentation and change. Only in the attention given to knowledge/interest questions and in the mean level of language difficulty can we find major question properties that are quite stable over the six studies of interest. The mean level of language difficulty varies only four points across the six questionnaires (Table 10.10). The mean Flesch scores of 68 to 72 are always higher and thus easier to read than the Gallup range of 62 to 65, although the difference between polls is significant ($p < .05$) only when that difference is six points or more.

TABLE 10.10

Level of Language Difficulty as Measured by Flesch "Ease-of-Reading" Scores in Six ISR National Election Studies (lower scores = more difficult language)

	1952	1956	1960	1964	1968	1972
Mean	69.0	68.2	69.8	72.0	68.4	72.7
s.d.	17.6	16.9	17.9	15.5	13.6	20.5
N	(46)	(94)	(76)	(120)	(101)	(157)

NOTES: All Ns are reduced by the exclusion of short probes numbering 1 to 3 words and questions in series under 5 words. The 1952 questionnaire N is reduced further by a set of questions for which documentation does not make entirely clear how much of the question language was left to the interviewer's discretion.

From one standpoint it is not surprising to find the level of language difficulty has been so stable: the collection of data for trend analysis has been a major feature of the NES; replications represent 20 to 59 percent of the questions selected in the six studies. From another perspective, however, that stability is somewhat unexpected, for across time there has been a persistent development of questions cast as rival arguments at the expense of both open questions and the closed questions of formal choice. The intellectual arguments of questions have thus become more complex, but not in a way that registers as more difficult to understand by the Flesch criteria.

Four Major Changes. The six election studies show a pattern of contrast between the two studies of 1956 and 1960 on one hand and the three studies from 1964 to 1972 on the other, with the first study, 1952, showing in certain respects least similarity to any subsequent questionnaire. In this evolution four changes are apparent: (1) the decline of the open question, (2) the development of the opinion filter, (3) the use of rival arguments replacing a single idea, and (4) the use of more elaborate scales.

In 1952 one-third of the selected questions were cast in open form, the greatest number of these asking for respondents' reasons for their own and others' opinions. After 1952 not only did the open question begin to decline generally, but the use of the "why" question was greatly restricted, appearing in only two to five questions in subsequent studies. This change was not simply a matter of closing up open questions and offering respondents a choice or checklist of reasons. Rather, the NES largely replaced these subjective open questions with other kinds of closed questions that could be used analytically to explore why respondents held the attitudes they did, especially measures of involvement in the election or interest in the issues. After 1952, in four of the five questionnaires, measures of interest bulked larger than open questions (see Table 10.11).

TABLE 10.11
Proportion of Questions in Three Categories in the ISR National Election Studies

	1952	1956	1960	1964	1968	1972
Attitude:						
Closed	61%	72%	66%	55%	67%	83%
Open	33	9	22	17	13	6
Knowledge/Interest/Intensity	6	19	12	28	20	12
N	(66)	(97)	(85)	(141)	(125)	(161)

NOTE: Due to rounding, percentages may not sum to 100.

The opinion filter made its first appearance in the NES in 1956 in a form that repeatedly emphasized that "no opinion" was a legitimate option, as in this example:

> . . . Of course, different things are important to different people, *so we don't expect everyone to have an opinion about all of these [questions].*
>
> I would like you to look at this card as I read each question and tell me how you feel about the question. *If you don't have an opinion, just tell me that;* if you do have an opinion, choose one of the other answers. . . .
>
> The government in Washington ought to see to it that everybody who wants to find work can find a job.
>
> *Now would you say you have an opinion on this or not?*
> [1956 Election Study, Q. 12B. (Emphasis added.)]

Respondents saying they had an opinion were then asked, "Do you agree that the government should do this or do you think the government should not do this?" This form of the filter persisted in the 1960 study, after which it was changed to conform to the new use of rival arguments.

The choice between rival substantive arguments replaced agree/disagree questions about single ideas in 1964, as in this example, which also incorporated a new filter question:

> In general, some people feel that the government in Washington should see to it that every person has a job and a good standard of living. Others think the government should just let each person get ahead on his own. Have you been interested enough in this to favor one side over the other? [1964 Preelection Study, Form II, Q. 18]

Those expressing no interest were skipped on, and others were then asked three questions. First, one on the issue itself:

> Do you think the government should see to it that every person has a job and a good standard of living or should it let each person get ahead on his own?

Then, an intensity question:

> Is your mind made up on this question or do you have some doubts about the best thing to do?

And finally a question about the parties' positions on the issue:

> Which party do you think is more likely to favor the government seeing to it that each person has a job and a good standard of living, the Democrats, the Republicans, or wouldn't there be any difference between them on this? [1964 Preelection Study, Form II, Q. 18a–18c]

The intensity question was an innovation of 1964 and virtually disappeared thereafter. (There were only four such questions in 1968 and none in 1972.) The choice between rival arguments ultimately dominated as the single more frequent question form (see Table 10.12), persisting through 1972 when it was used in conjunction with a seven-point scale, an example of which has been presented above.

The last major change, the use of more elaborate scales, appeared not only in the seven-point scale, but also in the device called a feeling thermometer. The thermometer was used to measure respondents' reactions to a fairly large number of groups, such as liberals, Catholics, Easterners, labor unions, and so forth, on a scale ranging from 100 degrees for a very warm or favorable reaction to 0 for a very unfavorable reaction, with midranges for neutral or indifferent feelings.[17] Scaled items were a substantial proportion of every questionnaire after 1952; this particular feeling thermometer required more sensitive discrimination than any other scale we found in our samples of survey questions.

PRACTICE OVER TIME: SUMMARY

The 1972 National Election Study fused into a single question series three different forms: the opinion filter, appearing first in 1956; rival arguments (substantive choices), which grew steadily from 1964 on; and scaled alternatives, which have played a prominent role in the NES since 1956. This complex question series accounts for a third of the entire questionnaire in

TABLE 10.12

Opinion/Attitude Questions in Specific Forms, ISR National Election Studies

	1964	1968	1972
Single Idea (formal choice)			
Direct question	3%	2%	6%
Two-way choice	16	30	20
Three-way choice	39	19	15
Scales	27	28	10
Checklists	0	0	0
Choice of Idea (substantive choice)	16	20	48[a]
N	(77)	(84)	(132)

NOTE: Due to rounding, percentages may not sum to 100.
[a]Includes scaled questions attached to propositions of substantive choice. If these scales are included with questions of formal choice, the total proportion for scales is 44, and for substantive choice questions, 14.
Opinion filters, measuring interest, are not included in this count. All opinion filters in these studies—which number 9, 11, and 14, respectively—also incorporate arguments of substantive balance.

1972, and neatly epitomizes the distance that has come to separate the NES and the Gallup Poll in recent years. Gallup has continued to rely on the choice between two formal alternatives, especially approve/disapprove, favor/oppose, and so forth, a subform that is seldom used in the National Election Study. Gallup has largely avoided scale items until a minor use in the 1970s; and the Gallup version of the opinion filter is distinct from that of the National Election Study, merely establishing that the respondent has some general acquaintance with a general topic. The degree of similarity between the two organizations that is observable in the 1950-60 period has effectively disappeared, as the NES has made increasing use of complex arguments and rather complex forms, while Gallup has continued the use of the single propositions as it did in the 1950s. This difference appears to reflect the persisting influence of George Gallup, Sr., who has been the major figure of his organization during the four decades in question, while a number of different social scientists have played some formative role over time in the National Election Study.[18]

The styles of the two organizations reflect in large part the analytical use to which each organization puts its data. Gallup's questions bearing on a single proposition are serviceable for the "straw votes" that especially interest him; the individual differentiation and complex comparisons permitted by scaled alternatives are not at all necessary when marginal results are of chief interest. The research interest of the NES is in the more complex analysis of relationships among variables. To this end, marginal results are of little consequence in themselves, except of course when they provide data for trend analysis. Scaled items can facilitate the study of the associations among questions and respondents.

Rival arguments, however, do not seem particularly appropriate to one mode of analysis or the other. Opinions for and against school busing, for example, can be reported with or without reference to the arguments used to justify the pro and con positions. The use of this form by the NES presumably reflects a certain chariness about possible question bias and a judgment that cognitive influences should be equalized by explicit references to two opposing arguments, lest respondents fail to share a common frame of reference or unwittingly slight an opposing point of view they might respect if they had thought of it. Gallup's own theory of polling does not require dealing with such possible subtleties. Gallup sees his respondent voting much as an elected representative ultimately will; neither nuanced reactions by the voter—the "yes but" reaction—nor counterpropositions by a bill's opponents have to be considered in the wording of the question. The various practices in question writing typical of the two organizations address not only different analytical purposes, but also a different conception of the reality that polling is to reflect. Whether they will persist under conditions of telephone interviewing is a question for the future.

Summary

This chapter compares the form of questions used recently by four major surveys and, for two of the studies, compares practice over time. For this purpose, samples of published questions were drawn from two commercial organizations, the Gallup Poll and the Harris Survey; and questionnaires were selected from two academic organizations, the General Social Survey of the National Opinion Research Center and the National Election Study of the Institute for Social Research. All questions were classified into a 21-category detailed code, the main categories of which are closed, quasi-closed, and open questions. Questions were also examined for their level of language difficulty, the percentage of "no opinion" responses, and other features.

In recent practice (in the early 1970s), all four surveys show major similarities. They use language of a level of difficulty within reach of the broad public. ISR's National Election Study shows the easiest level; the Harris Survey, the most difficult; but all four studies should be essentially within the range of comprehension of high school graduates. They also show similarity in their major use of closed questions and the two-way choice and in their minor use of multiple arguments, checklists, and measures of intensity. Each organization nevertheless shows a distinctive house style. Although academic and commercial organizations clearly make different use of their data, there is little evidence that question form itself shows distinctive academic and commercial styles.

In the long-lived Gallup Poll and the NES, which permit comparison over time, the differences are striking. The Gallup Poll shows great stability of question form. In the stock of questions selected in each of four decades, there is only one major shift, as Gallup turns from direct questions implying yes/no answers to those providing an explicit two-way choice (approve/disapprove, favor/oppose, etc). The NES shows considerable change in the course of six questionnaires at 4-year intervals (1952–72), as it diminishes the use of open questions in favor of scales and two-way questions presenting rival arguments. The permanence of the Gallup style doubtless reflects, among other things, the continuing influence of Gallup himself, while the change in the NES shows the varying interests of a larger group of analysts. The difference also reflects Gallup's theory of polling as a public referendum on legislative issues and the interest of the NES in more detailed and complex analysis.

Appendix A: Classification of Questions

Code Category	Example
I. Attitude/Opinion Questions	
A. Closed Questions	
Single idea (formal choice)	
Direct question	
1. (yes/no implied)	Do you think 1 year of service to the nation should be required of every able-bodied man over 18?
Two-way choices	
2. . . . or not?	Do you think 1 year of service to the nation should be required . . . or not?
3. Agree/disagree	Tell me if you agree or disagree: "All criminals convicted a second time should be denied parole."
4. Approve/disapprove, favor/ oppose, and other polar opposites	Do you favor or oppose capital punishment for persons convicted of murder?
5. Other two-way choices, short format[a]	Which do you think is the greatest threat, Russia or China?
6. Other two-way choices, long format[a]	Would you say that you are about average middle class, or that you are in the upper part of the middle class?
Three-way choices	Do you favor segregation, desegregation, or something in between?
7. Short format[a]	
8. Long format[a]	So far as you and your family are concerned, would you say that you are pretty well satisfied with your present financial situation, more or less satisfied, or not satisfied at all?
Checklists	
9. Four or more items listed (can choose any that apply)	Which of these magazines have you read in the past month . . . ?
Scales	
10. Likert-type (4 to 5 points, agree/disagree)	Would you say that you agree, strongly agree, disagree, or strongly disagree?
11. Other scales, 4 points or more	What kind of job do you think President Kennedy is doing as president: excellent, good, only fair, or poor?

Appendix A: Classification of Questions

Code Category	Example
Choice of ideas (substantive choice)	
12. Two rival arguments	Do you think white people should be allowed to keep blacks out of their neighborhoods, or should black people be allowed to buy any home they can afford?
13. Three or more arguments	Would you favor (1) immediate withdrawal from Vietnam, (2) a ceasefire for 3 months while withdrawal is being negotiated, (3) continued fighting at the present level, or (4) escalation of fighting and increased fighting?
14. Rival arguments with scaled choice	Where would you place yourself on this scale: (1) Women's place is in home . . . (7) Women should have an equal role with men.
B. Quasi-Closed Questions	
15. Answer in form of name, date, or number (possible to precode answers)	How many more months do you think the war will last?
C. Open Questions	
16. Open ended	How would you describe the kind of education your children are getting now?
17. Reasons and reasons why	What do you think is the main reason for the present increase in prices?
18. Probes	Can you tell me more about that?
II. Other Types of Questions	
19. Knowledge or information	Who is the secretary of state in the new cabinet?
20. Interest or involvement	Have you heard or read about the recent change of government in Mexico?
21. Intensity	Is this something you feel very strongly about, or not very strongly?

a"Long format" indicates that at least one alternative is phrased in five words or more; considered "short format" otherwise.

Appendix B: Distribution of Question Form

	Gallup Poll				ISR–NES						NORC–GSS	Harris
	1941–1942	1951–1952	1961–1962	1969–1971	1952	1956	1960	1964	1968	1972	1972–1974	1970
I. Attitude/Opinion												
A. Closed Questions												
Single idea (formal choice)												
Direct question	105	20	16	26	0	1	2	2	2	8	16	0
1. Yes/no implied												
Two-way choices												
2. . . . or not?	0	20	17	12	1	1	0	1	1	1	0	7
3. Agree/disagree	2	4	7	3	10	8	8	4	0	14	12	44
4. Approve/disapprove	27	44	61	48	0	0	0	1	0	1	66	10
5. Other two-way (short)	11	25	33	22	1	1	4	4	14	4	9	27
6. Other two-way (long)	5	7	3	5	7	2	0	2	10	7	2	10
Three-way choices												
7. Short format	2	11	12	11	13	20	25	28	15	17	57	35
8. Long format	0	1	2	1	3	5	2	2	1	3	4	4
Checklists												
9. 4 or more items	1	1	5	1	0	0	2	0	0	0	0	1
Scales												
10. Likert-type scale item	0	0	0	0	0	16	9	0	0	9	0	0
11. Other scales (4+ points)	0	1	1	11	0	16	2	21	24	4	50	41
Choice of ideas (substantive)												
12. Two rival arguments	12	8	8	6	5	0	2	12	15	18	8	13
13. Three or more arguments	0	1	2	10	0	0	0	0	2	1	4	1
14. Rival arguments (scaled)	0	0	0	0	0	0	0	0	0	45	0	0

B. Quasi-Closed Questions												
15. Answer: name, date, etc.	20	15	14	20	0	0	0	0	0	0	2	0
C. Open Questions												
16. Open-ended	12	21	20	12	7	4	9	16	11	7	0	2
17. Reasons why	4	2	0	1	12	3	5	4	3	2	0	7
18. Probes	1	0	1	0	3	2	5	4	2	1	0	0
II. Other Questions												
19. Knowledge or information	3	31	1	12	0	0	0	0	–6	2	10	3
20. Interest or involvement	7	17	17	16	4	18	10	24	15	17	2	2
21. Intensity	0	1	0	1	0	0	0	16	4	0	0	0
Totals	212	230	220	218	66	97	85	141	125	161	242	207

NOTE: Abbreviated labels are used in this table; see Appendix A for complete labels for coding categories.

Notes

1. Two additional volumes of *The Gallup Poll* have been published for 1972–75 and 1976–77.

2. For an earlier paper bearing in part on question content, see Converse (1976).

3. The Economic Behavior Program is the source of another continuing ISR study that dates from the 1940s. We judged that it would prove more specialized and less comparable to the General Social Survey and the commercial polls than the National Election Study.

4. The specific questionnaires used were the 1952 preelection; 1956 election; 1960 preelection; 1964 preelection, Form II; 1968 preelection; and 1972 preelection, Forms I and II. Twenty-six questions that were not an integral part of the National Election Study were excluded from the analysis of 1972 (Questions C1 through C26). In recent years the National Election Study has been conducted by the Center for Political Studies of ISR; it was developed within the Survey Research Center of ISR.

5. "Intensity" measures are defined as a particular type of "strength of opinion" measure by Schuman and Presser (1981). Here we do not distinguish between "intensity" and "strength" because other research we use does not.

6. This distinction does not necessarily separate the relative degrees of respondent effort required to answer, since quasi-closed questions can require just as much reflection as do open questions, but it does better estimate the relative length or discursiveness of most respondents' answers. Quasi-closed questions usually invite short answers, and the fully open questions impose no such implied limitation.

7. This example poses a basic issue of closed versus open questions, an issue of some concern in population research. If numbers are not specified, will all respondents assume that the ideal number of children can include zero children (Otis Dudley Duncan, personal communication, January 1981)?

8. Stanley Presser, when director of the archive at the Institute for Research in Social Science at University of North Carolina, kindly provided this information (personal communication, January 1981).

9. See Gallup (1947; 1972b:88):

> Probably the most difficult of all questions to word is the type that offers the respondent several alternatives. Not only is it hard to find alternatives that are mutually exclusive: it is equally difficult to find a series that covers the entire range of opinion. Added to this is the problem of wording each alternative in a way that doesn't give it special advantage. And finally, in any series of alternatives that ranges from one extreme of opinion to the other, the typical citizen has a strong inclination to choose one in the middle.

10. See note 9.

11. These seven-point graphic scales are not presented as measures of intensity. Respondents are asked to locate their own opinions with reference to the extremes of polar positions, not according to the intensity with which they hold these positions.

12. Neither the Harris Survey nor the Gallup Poll used telephone interviewing on any large-scale basis until 1977–78. Gallup currently conducts about half of its interviews by telephone (Barbara Winokur, Research Department, Louis Harris and Associates, Inc.; Merewyn McEldowney, operations manager, and Eileen McMurray, Research Department, The Gallup Organization, personal communications, February 1981).

13. The Flesch scores for the NORC-GSS sample are virtually unchanged by the exclusion of the Gallup replications: mean = 63.58; s.d. = 23.83; N = 171.

14. Ann Rosen, Coding Department, Louis Harris and Associates, Inc., personal communication, 1976.

15. Gallup's "quintamensional plan" of 1947 advocated intensity questions and four other types: filter or information, those eliciting an open or free answer, dichotomous questions bearing on a specific issue, and those requesting reasons why. In our samples, Gallup uses filter, open, and dichotomous questions with some frequency; he makes negligible use of reasons why or intensity measures (see note 9 and Gallup, 1947).

16. See note 9 and Gallup 1972b:106.

17. The thermometer device is not original with the National Election Study. Archibald Crossley suggested it to the *Literary Digest* in 1924 as a way of measuring interest in magazines (see Crossley, 1957). It was also used in the 1940s (see Katz, 1944).

18. Within the Institute for Social Research, at least eight different investigators have played leading roles in the design of various National Election Studies; as many as twice that number from outside the organization have had a hand in question design, especially in the most recent studies (Ann Robinson, National Election Study, personal communication, February 1981).

References

Chall, J.S., and Dial, H.E. (1948) Predicting listener understanding and interest in newscasts. *Educational Research Bulletin* 27:141-153ff.

Converse, J.M. (1976) Predicting no opinion in the polls. *Public Opinion Quarterly* 40:515-530.

Converse, J.M. (1984) Strong arguments and weak evidence: The open/closed questioning controversy of the 1940s. *Public Opinion Quarterly* 48:267-282.

Crossley, A.M. (1957) Early days of public opinion research. *Public Opinion Quarterly* 21:159-164.

Flesch, R. (1948) A new readability yardstick. *Journal of Applied Psychology* 32:221-233.

Gallup, G. (1947) The quintamensional plan of question design. *Public Opinion Quarterly* 11:385-393.

Gallup, G. (1972a) *The Gallup Poll: Public Opinion 1935-1971.* 3 vols. New York: Random House.

Gallup, G. (1972b) *The Sophisticated Poll Watcher's Guide*. Princeton, N.J.: Princeton University Press.

Harris, L. (1971) *The Harris Survey Yearbook of Public Opinion 1970: A Compendium of Current American Attitudes*. New York: Louis Harris and Associates, Inc.

Harris, L. (1976) Harris Survey Release, March 8, 1976.

Hennessy, B.C. (1975) *Public Opinion*. 3rd ed. North Scituate, Mass.: Duxbury Press.

Jenkins, J.G. (1935) *Psychology in Business and Industry*. New York: Wiley.

Katz, D. (1944) The measurement of intensity. In H. Cantril and Associates, *Gauging Public Opinion*. Princeton, N.J.: Princeton University Press.

Kornhauser, A. (1946) Are public opinion polls fair to organized labor? *Public Opinion Quarterly* 10:484-503.

Lindzey, G. (1951) To repeat—checklists can be dangerous. *Public Opinion Quarterly* 15: 355-358.

Link, H., Freiberg, A.D., Platten, J.H., and Clark, K.E. (1947) Is Dr. Kornhauser fair to organized pollers? *Public Opinion Quarterly* 11:198-212.

Payne, S. (1950) Thoughts about meaningless questions. *Public Opinion Quarterly* 14:687-696.

Schuman, H., and Presser, S. (1981) *Questions and Answers in Attitude Surveys: Experiments on Question Form, Wording, and Context*. New York: Academic Press.

Acknowledgments

This chapter is part of a larger investigation of the role of question form, wording, and context in attitude surveys. It describes the incidence of particular question variations in major academic and commercial surveys. The other main product of the research (Schuman and Presser, 1981) reports experimental studies of the effects of such variations on survey results. The project has been supported by grants from the National Science Foundation (SOC–76–15040) and the National Institute of Mental Health (MH–24266). The preparation of this chapter was also supported by a National Science Foundation grant (SES–78–11409). We would like to thank Otis Dudley Duncan, Stanley Presser, Tom W. Smith, Ann Robinson, Warren E. Miller, and James A. Davis for their helpful comments on an earlier draft.

PART IV

SOME STATISTICAL MODELS FOR ERROR AND STRUCTURE IN SURVEY DATA

The branch of statistical methods most relevant to the data collected in subjective suveys—methods for analyzing categorical data—was markedly underdeveloped until recently. In the last decade, however, there has been an impressive series of developments in this area (summarized in major textbooks by Bishop, Fienberg and Holland; Goodman; and Haberman). Dissemination of these new methods to survey practitioners—together with a heightened awareness of the need for such procedures—present the possibility of significant advances in the scientific use of subjective survey measurements.

In contrast to procedures such as factor analysis and Jöreskog's LISREL these new methods do *not* depend on the assumption of multivariate normality. That assumption infrequently holds for subjective survey measurements. The newer methods for the analysis of categorical data feature distributional specifications that are appropriate to such data.

The first two chapters (11 and 12) in this section use the apparatus of categorical analysis to explore two important models of particular relevance to subjective measurements. In Chapter 11, Clifford Clogg demonstrates the inadequacies of the linear model in analyzing response distributions that arise naturally in measuring subjective phenomena and then proceeds to explore new applications of association models and of the latent-class model developed over three decades ago by Paul Lazarsfeld. This treatment is then extended to develop a simultaneous latent-class model for across-group comparisons. In Chapter 12, Otis Dudley Duncan expands a discussion (begun in Volume 1) of the application to survey data of the promising measurement model originally suggested by Georg Rasch for the analysis of psychometric data.

In Chapter 13, Judith Lessler presents the results of a review of the statistical literature on measurement error in surveys. Drawing upon the traditional statistical approach, it summarizes the terminology and methods that have been used to deal with errors in survey measurements.

Sections 3.1–3.2 and 6.3–6.4 of Volume 1 may provide readers with a helpful introduction to these chapters.

11

Some Statistical Models for Analyzing Why Surveys Disagree

Clifford C. Clogg

Introduction

In order to understand why different surveys disagree in the measurement of subjective phenomena, it is necessary to consider the various contexts under which responses are elicited. Question wording, question placement (in relationship to other questions), the use of "filters," method used (telephone, mail, direct interview), interviewer quality, questionnaire length, and even time period are some of the possible contexts of interest. It is imperative that principles of experimental design be utilized in order to study context effects, involving at the very least the random assignment of contexts to individual respondents (see, for example, Cochran and Cox, 1957). (The proper design of a study that seeks to obtain valid inferences about context effects is not discussed in this chapter [for examples, see Duncan and Schuman, 1980; and Schuman and Presser, 1978]). It is also necessary to use scientific sampling procedures, so that context effects on responses can be assessed through the use of conventional statistical inference procedures, or possibly through the use of standard alternatives. (Among the "standard alternatives" to which we refer are the jackknife methods; see Fay, 1979; or Henry, 1981). This chapter has little to say about sampling schemes, but everything developed depends on the approximate validity of the conventional sampling theory implicitly assumed.

The primary focus of this chapter is on statistical models for analyzing context effects on responses, a topic that does not appear to have been studied nearly so much in the literature (but see Duncan and Schuman, 1980). Our central argument is that conventional techniques for studying measurement error, based largely on the linear model as amended by psychometric theory (Jöreskog and Sörbom, 1979) are entirely inappropriate. Recently developed methods for the study of qualitative data provide convincing alternatives to the conventional techniques. They permit the construction of a wide range of models that can yield sensitive insights into the sources of discrepancies among surveys. The models that we use are related to contingency table methods discussed by Bishop, Fienberg, and Holland (1975), Fienberg (1980), Goodman (1978), and Haberman (1978, 1979). While most of the models used here are identical to the ones surveyed in these very important sources, this chapter proposes some new models, or at least some new parameterizations of old ones.

Major subjects covered here are as follows: First, a deceptively simple example is analyzed from various points of view, indicating a wide range of models that can now be routinely utilized. The next section considers examples that demonstrate the failure of the linear model in analyzing response distributions that arise naturally in the measurement of subjective phenomena. Next is a discussion of the latent class model and analysis of some data within its basic framework of assumptions. The material included in that discussion is partly a survey of methods already developed, but the exposition nevertheless demonstrates the general utility of the latent class model. The section develops the "simultaneous latent class model" for across-group comparison and presents additional examples. Finally, there is brief discussion of a class of association models (Goodman, 1979; Clogg, 1982a) that appear to hold much promise for analyzing response distributions. (These methods are used frequently in the section on Testing Key Assumptions Used in Conventional Measurement-Error Models.) A nontechnical overview of the simple ideas that underlie this new approach is presented. Here the focus is on ordinal indicators, an ubiquitous form of data that is especially important in the measurement of subjective phenomena. The basic idea consists of making inferences about distances between response categories by assuming that the variable in question is associated with another "instrumental" variable in a specified manner.

Throughout this chapter a distinction is maintained between choosing the "best" of a variety of survey contexts and reconciling the differences actually observed among different survey contexts. The first issue relates to a question that we believe dominates present discussions of survey design: which of the many available survey formats gives the best results? The second issue pertains to how disparate results can be reconciled to yield consistent inferences about the subjective phenomenon in question. Models are required in order to address this latter issue, but even if a preferred model for reconciling response distributions can be formulated, this in itself need not provide any direction whatsoever regarding a proper answer to the first question. The example considered at length in the next section provides many possible ways to "reconcile" response distributions, but it provides less clear-cut guidance concerning the "correct" question format to be used.

An Example: Attitudes on Treatment of Criminals by the Courts

This section introduces a simple set of data that shows how two different survey contexts can lead to vastly different inferences about a subjective phenomenon. Various models are applied to the data; some of these models analyze possible sources of the discrepancy, and some effectively reconcile the discrepant distributions.

TABLE 11.1
Attitude Toward Treatment of Criminals by Courts
(from 1974 General Social Survey)

Response, R	Context (= Question Form)			
	A^a (count)	(c = 1) (%)	B^b (count)	(c = 2) (%)
1. Too harshly	42	5.6%	33	4.5%
2. About right	72	9.6	44	6.0
3. Not harshly enough	580	76.9[c]	436	59.7[c]
4. Don't know[d]	51	6.8	210	28.7
5. No answer	8	1.1	8	1.1
Total	753	100.0	731	100.0

[a]The question asked was, "In general, do you think the courts in this area deal too harshly or not harshly enough with criminals?" (National Opinion Research Center, 1978:80).
[b]The question asked was, "In general, do you think the courts in this area deal too harshly, or not harshly enough with criminals, or don't you have enough information about the courts to say?"
[c]Percentage adjusted to ensure that sum equals 100.0.
[d]For question form B, the "don't know" should in fact be replaced by "not enough information to say."

DATA

Table 11.1 classifies respondents in the 1974 General Social Survey (National Opinion Research Center, 1978) according to their attitude toward the court's the treatment of criminals. Two different questions were asked, each to approximately one-half of the respondents, and a randomization procedure was used to determine which respondents would be asked which question. (The procedure is often called "split balloting.") The exact wording of the two questions appears in the footnotes to Table 11.1. The first question appears to discourage the "don't know" (DK) response, while the second question appears to encourage the DK and, it can be noted, is somewhat similar to the "filter design" discussed by Schuman and Presser (1978). Mere inspection of the two percentage distributions reveals that context (question wording) has a definite impact. (In this chapter the term "context" is often synonomous with "question wording"; our models for analyzing effects of question wording can be used for detecting other survey or context effects on responses, so the more general term is used.) The first question leads to 77 percent in the "not harshly enough" category, while the second leads to 60 percent in the same (or similar) response category. The DK is 7 percent of the total in the first context, but 29 percent in the second. Subtle phenomenological nuances should be noted in comparing these distributions. The "about right" response is not presented as an alternative in either question wording: this response has to be volunteered by the respondent and properly coded by the interviewer. The DK response is really not the same for each question wording, since the second wording really elicits a "not enough information to say" response. The question asks for attitudes about the courts *in this area*, and it is unclear how respondents who felt they had knowledge about the courts in *some* area, or knowledge about the courts in general, might respond. While all of these linguistic problems are relevant for interpreting the differences observed, a model is required in order to examine how the two distributions actually differ, apart from sampling error.

TESTING FOR CONTEXT EFFECTS

Let C denote the context variable with categories $c = 1, 2$, and let R denote the response variable, with categories $r = 1, \ldots, 5$, including the DK and NA ("no answer") responses. The model of no context effects is the model that states that R is independent of C, or that the response distribution is homogeneous across contexts. This model can be described in a variety of ways: as an additive log-linear model for the expected counts; as the model that "fits" the marginals of R and the marginals of C (that is, the set $\{(R)\,(C)\}$ of fitted marginals would be the sufficient statistics capturing all relevant information in the data); or as a model that constrains all possible log-cross-ratios to be zero. This model is denoted as H_0, and the likelihood-ratio chi-square statistic L^2 associated with it is presented in Table 11.2.

To analyze the obviously significant departure from independence ($L^2 = 132.04$ on 4 d.f.), residual analysis is useful. Table 11.3 presents the estimated expected frequencies and the "adjusted residuals" (see Haberman [1978] for the definition of adjusted residuals). The adjusted residuals for the "not harshly enough" and the DK responses are exceptionally large, but the residuals for the "about right" response are quite large as well (± 2.54). The probability that a standard unit normal deviate exceeds 2.5 in absolute value is about .01. For H_0, five of the residuals are repeats of the other five, except for change in sign, and if the model were true, the expected number of residuals exceeding 2.5 in absolute value would be about $5 \times .01 = .05$. Thus, the finding of three adjusted residuals that exceed 2.5 is convincing evidence for the unacceptability of the model, and all three of these residuals indicate lack of fit. Context certainly affects the "too harshly" and the DK responses; it probably affects the "about right" response; it probably does not affect the other two responses. Most would therefore conclude that the slight change in question wording produced disastrous consequences. (It can be noted that the General Social Survey routinely used Question Form A in all years except 1974, when it was used for only half of the respondents.)

TABLE 11.2

Chi-Square Statistics for Some Models Applied to Table 11.1

Model	d.f.	L^2	Description of Model
H_0	4	132.04	Response independent of Context
H_1	3	1.50	Response independent of Context ignoring DKs
H_2	3	34.03	DK switch compensated by "not harshly enough" (Response 3)
H_3	3	12.85	DK switch compensated by responses 1, 2, or 3
H_4	15	18.13	Response category scores differ across Context; association model using schooling as an instrument
H_5	40	243.92	Independence of Response, Context, Political Views, Spending on Crime
H_6	21	37.19	Heterogenous 2–class model
H_7	15	17.54	Heterogenous 3–class model
H_8	30	27.76	Restricted 4–class model

TABLE 11.3

Observed Counts, Expected Counts, and Adjusted Residuals for Independence Model Applied to Table 11.1

Response	Question Form					
	A			B		
	Observed Counts	Expected Counts	Adjusted Residuals	Observed Counts	Expected Counts	Adjusted Residuals
Too harshly	42	38.06	0.94	33	36.94	−0.94
About right	72	58.86	2.54	44	57.14	−2.54
Not harshly enough	580	515.53	7.20	436	500.47	−7.20
Don't know	51	132.44	−11.11	210	128.56	11.11
No answer	8	8.12	−0.06	8	7.88	0.06

QUASI-INDEPENDENCE

It is instructive to begin an analysis of context effects by using quasi-independence models (Goodman, 1968). To do this, consider one possible parametric structure for the independence model just discussed. Let $v_{rc} = \log F_{rc}$ denote the log expected count in the r-th category of R and the c-th category of C (that is, the r-th response category and the c-th context). One way to parameterize the model is to define "effects," λ, λ^C, λ_1^R, λ_2^R, λ_3^R, λ_4^R, such that

$$v_{rc} = \lambda + \lambda_r^R + \lambda^C, \text{ for } r \le 4, c = 1, \tag{1.a}$$
$$v_{rc} = \lambda + \lambda_r^R - \lambda^C, \text{ for } r \le 4, c = 2, \tag{1.b}$$
$$v_{51} = \lambda + \lambda^C, \tag{1.c}$$
$$v_{52} = \lambda - \lambda^C. \tag{1.d}$$

The reader will note that Plackett's (1974) suggestions have been used to define the λ_r^R, while the more usual ANOVA-type definition has been retained for λ^C (Goodman, 1978:Chapter 4). Now consider a model in which a single parameter λ^{RC} is added to (1) by replacing the expressions for v_{4c} (the DK response for the c-th context) with

$$v^*_{41} = v_{41} - \lambda^{RC}, \tag{2.a}$$
$$v^*_{42} = v_{42} + \lambda^{RC}, \tag{2.b}$$

The model so obtained incorporates an inflation factor $(+\lambda^{RC})$ for the DK response for Question Form B, and an equal deflation factor $(-\lambda^{RC})$ for the DK response for Question Form A. The relationship between R and C is one of independence for all responses except the DK, and the model is equivalent to (a) a quasi-independence model for the 5 × 2 table "blanking out" the DKs in both groups, or to (b) the independence model applied to the 4 × 2 table obtained by deleting the DKs. By retaining the 5 × 2 table and using the parametric structure just discussed, however, more interesting results can be obtained. This model is denoted as H_1 in Table 11.2, and it yields the near-perfect fit of $L^2 = 1.50$ on 3 d.f. In other words, the response distributions are homogeneous once the DKs are ignored, and the DK response differential can be regarded as the sole "source" of the discrepancy between the two question wordings.

This elementary quasi-independence model should not be regarded as an adequate final solution to the problem, even though it does pinpoint the source of the discrepancy between the two distributions. The first form, after the DKs have been ignored, yields a response distribution that pertains to an estimated 93 percent of the population, while the second form, after the DKs have been ignored, yields a response distribution that pertains to only an estimated 79 percent of the population. That the percentage distributions within the respective *restricted* samples are homogeneous does not give, by itself, sufficient grounds for choosing one question form over the other. Moreover, the distributions are not as yet reconciled; the information in both tables has not been combined.

The parameter λ^{RC} was estimated at .857 with an estimated asymptotic standard deviation of .083, using Haberman's (1979) FREQ program and the appropriate model matrix. (On the model matrix, or "design matrix," strategy, see Ott [1977]; or Evers and Namboodiri, [1978]). If we assume that Form A discourages the DK while Form B encourages the DK, and if we assume that both do so to the same degree, then the parameters of H_1 are relevant for answering a potentially important question. If some "fair" question wording were used, neither discouraging nor encouraging the DK, what would the percentage of DKs actually be? To answer this question, we obtain the prediction of the DK response for each distribution, ignoring the inflation-deflation parameter λ^{RC}. This gives $F_{41}^* = 120$ and $F_{42}^* = 89$, and converting to percentages gives the common value of 14.6 percent for the DK response. (F_{41}^* is given as exp $[2.068 + .149 + 2.571]$ and F_{42}^* is given by exp $[2.068 - .149 + 2.571]$.) Thus, if the DK is somehow a measure of a "nonattitude," then the model says that a full 14.6 percent have no attitude toward the courts. The reconciled percentage distributions appear in Table 11.4, and it should be noted that the inferences obtained from this table are different from those obtained by using the raw percentage distributions in Table 11.1. The calculations producing Table 11.4 are not entirely trivial, since the imputed DK percent of 14.6 percent is lower than the average of the DK percentages in Table 11.4, equal to 17.8 percent. The calculations are indeed motivated by Clogg's (1978) method of "purging" and are related to certain of the "ratio indexes" presented by Goodman (1972) for the study of status inheritance in mobility tables. The smoothed

TABLE 11.4

Response Distribution of Table 11.1
"Purged" of the DK Deflation or
Inflation Factor of Model H_4

	Question Form	
Response	A	B
Too harshly	5.2%	5.2%
About right	8.1	8.1
Not harshly enough	71.0[a]	71.0[a]
Don't know	14.6	14.6
No answer	1.1	1.1
Total	100.0	100.0

[a]Adjusted upward to ensure sum = 100.0%.

distributions in Table 11.4, based on a model that was fitted to the data, represent one means by which the "true" distribution of R can be obtained.

The preceding results were obtained by assuming that the inflation factor for the DK response in the second context was equal in magnitude (but opposite in sign) to the deflation factor for the DK response in the first context. If it could be assumed that the inflation factor was actually g times as great as the deflation factor, for a *known* constant g, then the model could be modified by replacing λ^{RC} in equation (2.b) by $g\lambda^{RC}$. While this model would produce identical expected counts, the estimate of λ^{RC} would change, and the smoothed percentage distributions would also change. More generally, we could replace $-\lambda^{RC}$ in (2.a) by $-f\lambda^{RC}$ for some constant f, as well as replacing λ^{RC} in (2.b) by $g\lambda^{RC}$ to take account of any prior assumption about the degree of "discouragement" or "encouragement" of the DK. The case where $f = 0$, for example, would say that Form A is "honest," in a certain sense, and that Form B distorts the correct distribution by encouraging the DK from those who would actually prefer to respond otherwise. Other possibilities can be easily incorporated into the model.

MODELS FOR COMPENSATING SWITCHES

Next consider a model of "compensating switches," defined as follows. Replace v_{3c} and v_{4c} in (2) by

$$v_{31}^* = v_{31} + \lambda^{RC}, \tag{3.a}$$
$$v_{41}^* = v_{41} - \lambda^{RC}, \tag{3.b}$$
$$v_{32}^* = v_{32} - \lambda^{RC}, \tag{3.c}$$
$$v_{42}^* = v_{42} + \lambda^{RC}, \tag{3.d}$$

This model is designated as H_2 in Table 11.2. It states that the "not harshly enough" category is inflated by λ^{RC} and the DK is deflated by the same amount for the first question wording, while exactly the opposite is true of the second question wording. This model makes explicit the alleged sources of "switches" among response categories that must be taking place in Table 11.1, whereas H_1 discussed earlier makes no such assumption.

We find $L^2(H_2) = 34.03$, so this model can be rejected, but the difference $L^2(H_0) - L^2(H_2) = 98.01$ shows how important this kind of "switching" must actually be. Similar models might be relevant for other empirical situations, if hypotheses about switches could be formulated beforehand.

Now consider a model where the compensating switches are not restricted to just pairs of responses. Once again the v_{rc} of (1) are modified by incorporating a switching parameter λ^{RC} such that:

$$
\begin{aligned}
v^*_{11} &= v_{11} + .5\ \lambda^{RC}, \\
v^*_{12} &= v_{12} - .5\ \lambda^{RC}, \\
v^*_{21} &= v_{21} + .5\ \lambda^{RC}, \\
v^*_{22} &= v_{22} - .5\ \lambda^{RC}, \\
v^*_{31} &= v_{31} + \lambda^{RC}, \\
v^*_{32} &= v_{32} - \lambda^{RC}, \\
v^*_{41} &= v_{41} - \lambda^{RC}, \\
v^*_{42} &= v_{42} + \lambda^{RC}.
\end{aligned}
\tag{4}
$$

Note that for the first context $(c = 1)$, those discouraged from the DK are assumed to prefer equally well either Response 1 or Response 2 (with equal preferences for these responses) or Response 3. A corresponding statement pertains to those in the second context $(c = 2)$. This model is designated as H_3, and we have $L^2(H_3) = 12.85$ on 3 d.f., a marginally significant lack of fit.

Probably none of the compensating-switches models would be seriously considered for the data of Table 11.1 in view of the acceptable fit of H_1. But these models contain more structure than H_1, permitting more rigorous assessment of the context effects, and they are equally parsimonious. The models have been presented here solely as illustrative examples, but presumably such models could be applied successfully in other empirical situations. These models could be used to smooth percentage distributions, by applying the technique used earlier to produce Table 11.4.

USING GENERALIZED RESIDUALS

Haberman (1978) presents a general procedure for examining residuals; the procedure appears to have considerable utility in analyzing the sources of discrepancies between survey contexts. The adjusted residuals in Table 11.3 describe the deviations of each observed count from the estimated expected count under the independence model, and the procedure (used, for example, in the FREQ program) extends to any log-linear model. More general residuals can be defined by comparing $\sum_{r,c} a_{rc} f_{rc}$ with $\sum_{r,c} a_{rc} F_{rc}$, where the a_{rc} are sets of coefficients that determine which comparisons are of interest.

Suppose that model H_3 is considered, and suppose further that interest focuses on whether the sum of the first two responses in the first context compared with the sum of the first two responses in the second context is being fit adequately under the model. Here, $a_{11} = a_{21} = 1$, $a_{12} = a_{22} = -1$, and all other $a_{rc} = 0$; the sum $f_{11} + f_{21} - f_{12} - f_{22}$ is compared with $\hat{F}_{11} + \hat{F}_{21} - \hat{F}_{12} - \hat{F}_{22}$. With model H_3 the observed value of this contrast is 37, while the expected value is estimated at -5.09. Dividing $(37 + 5.09)$ by the estimated asymptotic standard deviation gives an adjusted residual of 3.30, which is quite significant. Thus, a major reason why the compensating-switches model H_3 failed is the inadequate prediction of $f_{11} + f_{21} - f_{12} - f_{22}$. Generalized residual analysis can be used in many similar ways to obtain a more sensitive analysis of a model's lack of fit, allowing the researcher to examine regions of the response distribution where anomalous predictions occur.

THE LOG-MULTIPLICATIVE ASSOCIATION MODEL

It will be appreciated that the data in Table 11.1 have thus far been approached without bringing ancillary data into the analysis. Such ancillary information might take the form of (a) test-retest data, (b) response distributions of the same variable R obtained under different contexts (for example, still other question wordings), (c) response distributions on similar variables (for example, the attitude toward government spending on crime), and (d) joint distributions of R with other variables. In this section, the strategy is to choose an "instrumental" variable with which R can be cross-classified, that is, the ancillary information is of type (d). The association models of Goodman (1979, 1981) or Clogg (1982a, 1982b) become relevant.

First, assume there is an underlying quantitative attitude on the treatment of criminals by the courts. Second, assume the DK response is somehow an indicator of a point on this underlying quantitative variable. In other words, the DK is not regarded here as a "nonattitude," which is unlike the interpretations implicitly used in preceding sections. Finally, assume the association between the attitude variable R (Response) and some objective criterion variable A can be specified in form. This specification entails the assumption that, while the A–R association can depend on the level of A (allowing curvilinearity), it does not depend on the level of R, once proper R-variable scores have been assigned. What is needed is a criterion variable that is associated with the response (attitude) in the assumed manner. The schooling variable (variable A) is chosen for this purpose, indexed by $i = 1, \ldots, 5$, corresponding to fewer than 12, 12, 13 to 15, 16, and 17 or more years of schooling, respectively.

For the cross-classification of A with R, let F_{ir} denote the expected counts, for $i = 1, \ldots, 5$, $r = 1, \ldots, 4$. (The NA response is deleted here.) Indexes of the association between A and R are the odds ratios θ_{ir} in 2×2 subtables formed by taking adjacent row and adjacent column categories of the 5×4 table, viz.,

$$\theta_{ir} = (F_{ir}F_{i+1,r+1})/(F_{i,r+1}F_{i+1,r}). \tag{5}$$

There will be $4 \times 3 = 12$ odds ratios for the 5×4 table, the number being identical to the degrees of freedom for the independence (null association) model. The log-multiplicative association model is defined by

$$\log \theta_{ir} = \phi \, (\mu_{i+1} - \mu_i) \, (\nu_{r+1} - \nu_r). \tag{6}$$

Letting c index the contexts (variable C) as before, the conditional association between A and R at each level c of C can be described by a conditional association model

$$\log \theta_{irc} = \phi_c(\mu_{i+1,c} - \mu_{i,c})(\nu_{r+1,c} - \nu_{r,c}). \tag{7}$$

For the data at hand, a somewhat more restrictive model will be considered, one that exploits certain assumptions to be made more explicit shortly. This model is

$$\log \theta_{irc} = \phi(\mu_{i+1} - \mu_i)(\nu_{r+1,c} - \nu_{r,c}). \tag{8}$$

The interpretation of the parameters is as follows. The quantity ϕ describes the overall association between A and R (schooling and the attitude), and is assumed to be the same for each context c. The quantities $(\mu_{i+1} - \mu_i)$ represent effects of A (schooling) on the association, which do not depend on context. That is, curvilinearity in the A–R association is permitted, but the same curvilinear relationship is expected regardless of context. The $\nu_{r,c}$ represent category scores for the response variable R, and they are allowed to differ across contexts. The differences $(\nu_{r+1,c} - \nu_{r,c})$ are assumed to account completely for any differences in the association between A and R, both across levels of A and across contexts. Defining distances $d_r^c = (\nu_{r+1,c} - \nu_{r,c})$, and letting $\phi_i = \phi(\mu_{i+1} - \mu_i)$, the model can be written more compactly as

$$\log \theta_{irc} = d_r^c \, \phi_i. \tag{9}$$

The different levels of association between A and R across contexts are assumed to arise entirely from the fact that the d_r^1 are different from the d_r^2. Thus, the assumption is that the distances among categories of R differ according to whether the first question wording or the second is used. For further details, see Clogg (1982a; 1982b); the model just discussed is an example of a "row and column effects conditional association model," as discussed in Clogg (1982a).

Using statistical methods discussed in Clogg (1982a), the model is found to have an L^2 of 18.18 on 15 d.f. (This model is denoted as H_4 in Table 11.2; to save space the three-way table used here is not presented.) The attitude variable scores (the $\hat{v}_{r,c}$) are presented in Table 11.5.

The results indicate one possible explanation for the different response distributions observed—an explanation that does not appear to be possible using other methods. For the first question wording, the DK response is virtually indistinguishable from the "not harshly enough" category (since $\hat{v}_{3,1} = \hat{v}_{4,1} = 0.29$); the distance between "not harshly enough" and "about right" is $(0.29 - 0.18)/(0.18 - 0.00) = 0.6$ of the distance between "too harsh" and "about right." It appears that the DKs under the first question wording were indistinguishable from the "not harshly enough" category, suggesting that the DKs as a group could be considered as holding the "not harshly enough" attitude. For the second question wording, the DK response is seen to lie between the "too harsh" and "about right" responses, although the DK is virtually indistinguishable from the "about right" category. Here the distance between "not harshly enough" and "about right" is $0.44/0.29 = 1.5$ times the distance between "about right" and "too harsh."

TABLE 11.5

Estimated Category Scores for the Attitude on the Court's Treatment of Criminals, Based on the Cross-Classification of Attitude by Schooling, by Context

Response	Question Wording	
	A	B
Too harsh	0.00[a]	0.00[a]
About right	.18	.29
Not harshly enough	.29	.73
Don't know	.29	.24

[a]The "too harsh" category was arbitrarily assigned the value 0.

TABLE 11.6

Estimated Category Intervals for the Attitude on the Court's Treatment of Criminals, Assuming Equality of Mean Scores for Each Context

Response	Question Wording	
	A	B
Too harsh	0.000[a]	−0.266
About right	0.183	0.025
Not harshly enough	0.290	0.464
Don't know	0.288	0.021
Mean	0.26[b]	0.26[b]

[a]The value of 0.000 is arbitrary.
[b]Calculations were carried out to more digits than are reported.

330

Thus, the DK response to the second question probably arose from persons who leaned toward the "about right" response.

While this interpretation speaks to the source of discrepancy between the contexts, explaining it in terms of different R category scores associated with each context, we have not as yet effectively reconciled the discrepant results. Since the motivation for the model has been built around the assumption that R is quantitative, it seems reasonable to effect such a reconciliation by considering the mean of R within each context. That is, let us assume that $\bar{R}_1$, the mean of R for the first context, is in fact equivalent to $\bar{R}_2$, the mean of R for the second context. $\bar{R}_1$ for the first context is estimated as 0.26, and so the scores $\hat{v}_{r,2}$ for the second context are shifted to ensure that their mean is also 0.26, preserving distances between scores. An elementary system of linear equations must be solved, and when this is done the scores presented in Table 11.6 are obtained. These results may be explained by noting, for example, that those who gave the "too harsh" response to the second question (the one that encourages the DK) are actually further to the left on the continuum than are those who elicited the same response to the first question. Suffice it to say that this appears plausible: those who provide the "too harsh" response when the DK is encouraged are presumably more "liberal" than those who elicit the "too harsh" response when the DK is discouraged.

There are other ways to estimate category scores, taking account of the fact that under the model, only ratios of category distances are identifiable. But a constraint on the means $(\bar{R}_1 = \bar{R}_2)$ represents a fruitful strategy for reconciling the disagreement among survey contexts.

The reader should carefully note the assumptions that were necessary to obtain the preceding results. To some these assumptions will appear quite strong, but in our view they are no more stringent—perhaps even less stringent—than those made in conventional measurement error models. The log-multiplicative model is employed frequently in the section on Testing Key Assumptions, and later a nontechnical exposition of its basic framework is presented.

LATENT CLASS MODELS AND BETWEEN-CONTEXT RESPONSE UNCERTAINTY

The approach considered in the preceding section used information in the form of an "instrumental" variable (schooling), resulting in a particular kind of association model. The context effects on response were studied by calibrating the "scale" of the response variable separately for each context, and the differing response distributions were reconciled by an elementary manipulation of model parameters. This section brings an entirely different set of models to bear on the problem, using "indicators" in conjunction with the response variable. The approach essentially consists of applying latent class models of the general kind considered by Goodman (1978:Chapters 8 and 10) and Clogg (1979b), using the maximum-likelihood latent-structure analysis (MLLSA) program (Clogg, 1977). Models of homogeneity and/or heterogeneity across groups (contexts) are relevant. The general procedures used here are discussed in the section on Simultaneous Latent-Class Analysis Across Groups.

The latent class model says that there exists a latent variable X, with classes $t = 1, \ldots, T$, which is defined so that the conditional association among indicators of X is nil. The general notation is presented on page 350, but for our purposes here we note that R (the response variable) will be included as one of the indicators. Table 11.7 presents a four-way cross-classification that will be studied. The four variables are Response, a trichotomous indicator (variable A) of liberal-moderate-conservative political views, a dichotomous item (variable B) asking whether the respondent believes spending on crime is too little or not too little, and Context (variable C). The suggestions of Clogg (1979b) are used to structure the latent variable for the situation encountered here, since two of the items are ordered. As before, the DK response is given special treatment, and the effects of question wording on the response distribution are isolated. Additionally, the response distributions are reconciled with each other.

At least 30 different latent class models were considered for the data in Table 11.7, but for the sake of brevity only a few of these are considered here. We let π_t^X denote the proportion in the tth latent class, for $t = 1, \ldots, T$, and we let $\pi_{rt}^{\bar{R}T}$ denote the conditional probability that R takes on level r when X is at level t, for $r = 1, \ldots, 4, t = 1, \ldots, T$. Model H_5 is the "one-class" latent structure, useful as a baseline, and equivalent to the model fitting the marginals $\{(A), (B), (C), (R)\}$. With $L^2(H_5)$ = 243.92, this model fails to fit, but it gives us a baseline index by which the improvement achieved from other models can be assessed. Model H_6 is the unrestricted two-class model, allowing the parameters to vary across groups. Its fit is unacceptable, with $L^2(H_6)$ = 37.19 on 21 d.f. (Some terminal parameter estimates were obtained for H_6, and the d.f. for the model reflects an adjustment for the terminal parameter estimates. See Goodman, 1978:chapter 10, for an analogous kind of adjustment.) Model H_7 is the heterogeneous three-class latent structure with some restrictions imposed. With $L^2(H_7)$ = 17.54 on 15 d.f. it can be concluded that a reasonable latent class model can be found.

Many other models were considered as well, and a model that was obtained through a combination of model search procedures and a priori restrictions is designated as H_8 in Table 11.2. With $L^2(H_8)$ = 27.76 on 30 d.f., this model is seen to perform rather well, and inspection of standardized residuals indicates that all counts in Table 11.7 are predicted successfully. The parameter estimates for this model are presented in Table 11.8, and

TABLE 11.7

Cross-Classification of Attitude Toward the Courts by Political Views and by the Attitude Toward Spending on Crime, for Each Question Wording

Responses on Crime and Courts	Question Form A[a]			Question Form B		
	Liberal[b]	Moderate	Conservative	Liberal	Moderate	Conservative
Spending on Crime Too Little[c]						
Courts too harsh	4	15	4	16	6	3
About right	12	19	8	9	6	6
Not harsh enough	90	174	130	79	114	85
Don't know	10	9	7	40	59	27
Spending on Crime Not Too Little[c]						
Courts too harsh	12	1	1	5	1	0
About right	12	10	5	7	5	5
Not harsh enough	32	50	55	33	38	41
Don't know	8	5	2	29	24	14

[a]See Table 11.1 for the questions.
[b]The question elicited seven responses, ranging from "extremely liberal" to "extremely conservative." The "extremely liberal," "liberal," and "slightly liberal" responses were condensed into a single "liberal" category, and a similar condensing procedure was used for the "conservative" category.
[c]The question asked was "Are we spending too much, too little or about the right amount on halting the rising crime rate?" The "too much" and "about right" responses were combined.

the reader should appreciate the fact that most parameter estimates have been constrained to be equal across contexts. (Of course the many 0–1 restrictions in the model are constraints as well.) The quantities in Table 11.8 are estimates of $\pi_{rt}^{\bar{R}X}$, $\pi_{it}^{\bar{A}X}$, $\pi_{jt}^{\bar{B}X}$, and π_{t}^{X}, respectively. The model posits varying degrees of response certainty or uncertainty with respect to the response variable, and a careful description of the model's implications is useful.

Let us first characterize the latent classes in the model. Class 1, consisting of 0.020 of the total in each context, is one that elicits the "too harshly" response ($r = 1$) with certainty ($\pi_{11}^{\bar{R}X} = 1$ for each group). However, in the first context this class is also perfectly associated with the "not too little" response on the B item (that is, response $j = 2$ for the crime-spending item). That is, $\pi_{21}^{\bar{B}X} = 1.0$, and in the several model specifications that we considered we could never find an estimate of $\pi_{21}^{\bar{B}X}$ that differed from 1.0. In the second context this same latent class is imperfectly associated with the same item, since $\hat{\pi}_{21}^{\bar{B}X} = 0.233$ for the second context. Several alternative specifications allowed for an equality constraint on $\hat{\pi}_{j1}^{\bar{B}X}$ across contexts, but this always led to an unacceptable increase in L^2 (usually 10 to 12). Thus, the second context appears to cause ambiguous response patterns for those who believe the spending on crime is "too little," whereas the first context produces an unambiguous response pattern for "liberals" given the question wording of the first context.

The second latent class includes those whose response uncertainty leads them to make a choice between "about right" and DK, since $\hat{\pi}_{22}^{\bar{R}X}$ is 0.479 and $\hat{\pi}_{42}^{\bar{R}X} = 0.521$ for each context. The proportion of respondents in this latent class is estimated at $\hat{\pi}_{2}^{X} = 0.091$. The third latent class consists of those who respond with certainty to the R item with a "not harshly enough" response, and we note that these persons are all politically conservative ($\pi_{32}^{\bar{A}X} = 1.0$). The proportion in this latent class is estimated at $\hat{\pi}_{3}^{X} = 0.121$.

The fourth latent class is one with complete response uncertainty and is somewhat analogous to the "unscalable" class in the Goodman scale model (Goodman, 1978:Chapter 9). We find the $\hat{\pi}_{r4}^{\bar{R}X}$ to be 0.051, 0.071, 0.854, 0.024 for the first context, and 0.031, 0.018, 0.636, 0.315 for the second context; these estimates isolate the context effect on response. The proportion of respondents in this class is estimated at 0.768 for each context. In the first context, the "not harshly enough" response was elicited from 85.4 percent of the members of this class, while in the second context this response was elicited from only 63.6 percent. Thus, the major effect of question wording on response is to influence the response patterns of a class of individuals who are extremely uncertain about their attitude toward the courts' treatment of criminals. It can be noted that the response distributions (for the R variable) are very different from each other within this latent class; for example, a model constraining $\hat{\pi}_{14}^{\bar{R}X}$ and $\hat{\pi}_{24}^{\bar{R}X}$ to be homo-

TABLE 11.8

Parameter Estimates for a Four-Class Restricted Latent Class Model Applied to Table 11.7

Latent Class	Context 1 (Form A)				Context 2 (Form B)			
	1	2	3	4	1	2	3	4
Response Distribution								
r = 1	1.0	0.0	0.0	0.051*	1.0	0.0	0.0	0.031*
2	0.0	0.479	0.0	0.071*	0.0	0.479	0.0	0.018*
3	0.0	0.0	1.0	0.854*	0.0	0.0	1.0	0.636*
4	0.0	0.521	0.0	0.024*	0.0	0.521	0.0	0.315*
A (political views) Distribution								
i = 1	1.0	0.498	0.0	0.305	1.0	0.498	0.0	0.305
2	0.0	0.257	0.0	0.494	0.0	0.257	0.0	0.494
3	0.0	0.245	1.0	0.201	0.0	0.245	1.0	0.201
B (crime spending) Distribution								
j = 1	0.0*	0.462	0.636	0.747	0.767*	0.462	0.636	0.747
2	1.0*	0.538	0.364	0.253	0.233*	0.538	0.364	0.253
Proportion in Latent Class	0.020	0.091	0.121	0.768	0.020	0.091	0.121	0.768

NOTE: Asterisks denote the parameters that are allowed to vary across contexts.

geneous across contexts leads to an $L^2 = 39.40$, for an increase of 11.24 on 2 d.f.

To summarize, the four-class model with many (but not all) parameters constrained to be homogeneous across groups produces the following interpretations. Only 2.0 percent of the respondents believe (with certainty) that the courts are too harsh; 9.1 percent hold an attitude that is almost equally likely to produce an "about right" or a DK response; only 12.1 percent can be said to believe (with certainty) that the courts are "not harsh enough." A full 76.8 percent of the respondents have uncertain beliefs, and their response patterns are affected markedly by the question wording used. The discrepancy between the contexts has thus been explained, and the effect of context was traced to a latent class of individuals with a high degree of response uncertainty. The reader should note the radically different interpretation of the data that is afforded by the latent-class framework. Of course, the results are all dependent on the ancillary information used to produce the above inferences. For example, there is no assurance that these inferences would be robust in the presence of additional indicators.

The latent-class model offers a fruitful strategy for analyzing why surveys disagree, and it is certainly a candidate model for analyzing survey measures of subjective phenomena in general. To use the model in an expedient way, it is necessary to modify existing methods to introduce models for the simultaneous estimation of latent-class structures across groups. This technique has been used to produce the results in Table 11.8, and in the section on Simultaneous Latent Class Analysis Across Groups, general procedures are outlined.

DISCUSSION

Several other examples are considered later in this chapter, but it is useful to elaborate the characteristics of the analysis just completed. The data are in a form that is certainly common enough in survey measurements of subjective phenomena: an ordered response classification was used; the possible number of response categories was rather small (three or four); the DK response had to be taken rather seriously (instead of employing standard "fixups" for missing data); and survey context (question wording) had a marked impact on the response distribution actually observed. This section began with the test for context effects, which was just the simple independence model for a two-way cross-classification. All of the other models and techniques were based on the independence model, whether conceived as a baseline from which other models should be constructed or conceived as a useful parametric structure from which convincing inferences could be drawn about context effects. Models of compensating switches were formulated, residuals and generalized residuals were discussed, and the "purged" percentage distribution of the response categories was obtained.

Two different contingency table models were applied in further analysis; each of these was based on the availability of ancillary information. The first approach consisted of the log-multiplicative association model, using information in the cross-classification of the attitude item with schooling to calibrate the scale of the attitude item. This analysis interpreted the context effects on response as the result of a "stretching" and/or "repositioning" of the points along the underlying continuum of the attitude. The second approach was based on the latent-class model. The preferred model within the latent-class framework posited deterministic relationships between response categories and values of a latent trait (or latent classification) for some individuals, and it posited stochastic relationships between response categories and two values of the latent trait. It was found that the context effects on the response distribution could be traced to a latent class of individuals possessing a high degree of response uncertainty. Response uncertainty, defined in probabilistic ways, is easily formulated with the latent-class framework of analysis.

At this step in the development of these methods, it would be specious to try to effect reconciliation among the disparate conclusions that each class of models produces. But it seems clear that these contingency-table models could each be appropriate in different survey situations. In our view, these methods are a clear improvement over the conventional measurement error methodology, principally because of the tremendous flexibility they offer.

Testing Key Assumptions Used in Conventional Measurement Error Models

The example considered at length in the preceding section illustrates how models for qualitative data can be used without violating distributional assumptions. Throughout the preceding section, multinomial, product-multinomial, or various restricted multinomial statistical distributions were assumed, and these correspond closely to the sampling distributions of the items used. No a priori assumptions regarding spacing of categories of the response variable were made, even though a conventional linear model approach would necessarily begin with such spacing assumptions. Special response categories (for example, the DK) were singled out for special treatment, using models that to our knowledge do not have counterparts in conventional measurement error models. When additional variables were brought into the analysis (for example, in the sections on Log-Multiplicative Association Model and on Latent Class Models and Between-Context Response Uncertainty), still no restrictive or unrealistic distributional assumptions were made. The argument has been that contingency table methods can be exploited with advantage in the analysis of survey measures of subjective phenomena, but we have not as yet presented specific reasons for preferring these methods to the usual psychometric methods based on the linear model. This section presents a preliminary analysis of key assumptions made in conventional measurement error models, using methods that are well suited for analyzing these assumptions. It shall be demonstrated rather forcefully how key assumptions of conventional measurement error models cannot be sustained when considering typical survey measures of subjective phenomena.

ARE FIRST AND SECOND MOMENTS ENOUGH?

Much empirical social research is built on the assumption that first and second moments (or means and variances) are a sufficient basis from which to study measures of subjective phenomena. Here we test this assumption by considering whether certain typical measures of subjective phenomena can be characterized by first and second moments in a satisfactory way.

Haberman (1978:Chapter 1) provides a variety of models for univariate (discrete or discretized) frequency distributions. For a response variable R, with classes $r = 1, \ldots, R$, let p_r denote the expected proportion in the r-th category, and let x_r denote the score assigned to the r-th category. For example, x_r might be the midpoint of the r-th category; it is assumed that R is interval-level with known intervals. A quadratic log-linear model

$$\log p_r = \beta_0 + \beta_1 x_r + \beta_2 x_r^2 \tag{10}$$

will be true whenever the distribution of R can be described in terms of first and second moments. The first and second sample moments will be fitted by the expected frequencies under this model. That is,

$$\sum_r x_r f_r = \sum_r x_r \hat{F}_r,$$

$$\sum_r x_r^2 f_r = \sum_r x_r^2 \hat{F}_r.$$

It is interesting to note that the univariate normal distribution says that p_r is proportional to $\exp[-(x_r - \mu)^2/2\sigma^2]$ when the number of categories becomes large. In this case the normal distribution is a quadratic log-linear model with

$$\beta_1 = \mu/\sigma^2, \tag{11a}$$
$$\beta_2 = -(2\sigma^2)^{-1}. \tag{11b}$$

Table 11.9 reports the fit of the quadratic log-linear model to 12 different frequency distributions from the 1977 General Social Survey. The categories are ordered for each item, with the number of categories ranging from 4 to 10. We assumed that $x_r = r$ to apply the models, involving the typical assumption of equal spacing. The degrees of freedom for the model is the number of categories minus 3. It is evident from the L^2 values that the quadratic log-linear model is unsuccessful for each of the 12 items, and the actual magnitudes of the L^2 values are alarmingly high. These items were selected with something approximating a random mechanism, and so it is all the more disturbing that the model fails for each item. We conclude that the population distributions from which these sample distributions were obtained cannot plausibly be described by first and second moments. This implies that the univariate normal distribution can be rejected as a statistical model for each of the response distributions in question, since the normal distribution can be described solely by first and second moments.

The cubic model was also considered for the univariate distributions, adding a term $\beta_3 x_r^3$ to the model in (10). Except for cases where a cubic model is tautological, which is the case for a four-category variable, the cubic model also fails to provide acceptable results. The addition of a cubic term to the model fits the third moment of the sampled distribution, and it would improve the fit if the response distributions were skewed (in a somewhat regular fashion). The response distributions cannot be described by first, second, and third moments, and so we conclude that higher-order moments are required in order to describe the distributions of typical measures of subjective phenomena.

Measurement-error models for univariate response distributions typically

TABLE 11.9

*Quadratic and Cubic Log-Linear Models Applied to 12
Ordinal Indicators (from 1977 General Social Survey)*

Item	Number of Categories	L^2 Quadratic Model	L^2 Cubic Model
Right to segregation	4	10.76	0.00
Opinion: premarital sex	4	70.63	0.00
Perceived income status	5	23.48	15.40
Satisfaction: health	7	75.60	56.06
Satisfaction: friends	7	81.25	36.89
Satisfaction: family	7	52.56	16.55
Satisfaction: hobbies	7	44.91	11.92
Satisfaction: home	7	78.29	73.57
Visits with relatives	7	134.36	103.92
Political party	7	115.58	110.23
Liberal-conservative	7	111.88	111.24
Rating of Egypt	10	109.58	97.13

begin with an assumption that the scores x_r are fallible measures of "true" values x_r^*, linked up by the equation

$$x_r = x_r^* + e_r. \tag{12}$$

Typically, x_r^* and e_r are assumed to be independent. If the e_r and the x_r^* are normally distributed, then x_r is normally distributed. Conversely, if x_r is not normally distributed, then either x_r^* or e_r, or both, are not normally distributed. In view of the dramatic departures of these data from the quadratic log-linear model, it must be concluded that the "true scores" and/or the "measurement error" are not normally distributed for typical survey measures of subjective phenomena. It should be noted that we are not criticizing normal-theory measurement error models solely on the grounds that the normality assumption is dubious (at best). Something much more fundamental is at stake: the assumption that first and second moments are a sufficient basis from which to attack the measurement error problem. Our results thus far indicate that this assumption cannot be sustained. Therefore, models that do not rely on first and second order moments, like those presented earlier in this paper, are all the more attractive.

THE ASSUMPTION OF EQUAL SPACING

Subjective phenomena are usually measured in social surveys through the mechanism of ordinal indicators. For example, approximately one-half of the 230 items in the General Social Survey are ordinal and also discrete in a meaningful sense of the term. If attention is restricted to items that actually measure subjective phenomena (excluding age, sex, education, and the like), perhaps two-thirds to three-fourths of these items are of the discrete, ordered variety. Typical category codes for the items to which we refer are: (1) very happy, (2) pretty happy, (3) not too happy; or (1) excellent, (2) good, (3) fair, (4) poor; or (1) far below average, (2) below average, (3) average, (4) above average, (5) far above average; or (1) a very great deal, (2) a great deal, (3) quite a bit, (4) a fair amount, (5) some, (6) a little, (7), none; or codes very similar in kind to these. Thus, much of the survey data now collected on subjective phenomena is of the Likert form (see Torgerson, 1958).

Social researchers confronted with ordinal indicators of subjective phenomena typically follow one of two different strategies. The first is the so-called nonparametric strategy, which utilizes methods for ranked data. While this approach has certain advantages in significance testing of routine null hypotheses, it can be criticized because it does not lend itself easily to partialing, and because it does not in fact correspond to any kind of "structural" model for data (in the modern sense of the term). The second strategy is to regard the ordinal variable as interval, assign arbitrary scores to the ranks, and then proceed as if the contrived variable so obtained was quantitative, or even continuous. This second strategy now appears to dominate research practice, and so it is worthwhile to consider a method through which the spacing assumptions implicit in this approach can be given direct consideration.

Table 11.10 is a cross-classification of the "happiness item" by schooling, by sex, taken from the 1977 General Social Survey. The happiness item is the response of interest here, and its categories $r = 1, 2, 3$ correspond to "not too happy," "pretty happy," and "very happy." This item will be recognized as perhaps the simplest of all ordinal indicators of a subjective phenomenon, and attention is directed toward the relative magnitudes of the intervals between adjacent categories. To maintain consistency with the Response-Context terminology used previously, we can regard sex as the Context variable, tacitly acknowledging the possibility that happiness item scores might be affected by Context. (In fact, we expect no effect of Context on the Response scores here, but if we were to find such an effect, the model to be considered shortly would be seriously jeopardized.) The schooling variable (variable A) plays the role of the "instrument," as in the section on the Log-Multiplicative Association Model, and we index its categories $i = 1, \ldots, 4$. A log-multiplicative association model (Goodman, 1979; Clogg, 1982) of special interest is

$$\log \theta_{ri(c)} = \phi_c \, (\mu_{r+1} - \mu_r) \, (\nu_{i+1,c} - \nu_{i,c}).   \tag{13}$$

In (13),

$$\theta_{ri(c)} = (F_{ric} \, F_{r+1, \, i+1, \, c})/(F_{r+1,i,c} \, F_{r,i+1,c}),$$

that is, the odds ratio in a 2×2 subtable formed from adjacent rows r and $r+1$ and adjacent columns i and $i+1$, for each context c. The ϕ_c define different overall levels of association between R and A for each context. The overall association in each conditional table is multiplied by a factor $\mu_{r+1} - \mu_r$, which reflects the distance between the rth and the $(r+1)$th response category. Note that these distances are constrained to be the same in each context. The $\nu_{i+1,c} - \nu_{i,c}$ denote schooling effects on the association, allowing the association to depend (curvilinearly) on the level of schooling, and allowing it to depend as well on the context. (Thus, males and females are allowed to have differing levels of R–A association across the levels of A, as well as different overall levels of association.) The assumptions thus far made are tantamount to saying that, subject to appropriate scores being assigned to the happiness item and the schooling instrument, the R–A association between the two items is described by "linear-by-linear" interaction within each context, in Haberman's (1974, 1979) terminology.

The model just discussed leads to a satisfactory fit of $L^2 = 6.15$ on 5 d.f., and rival models (see Clogg, 1982a) do not compete effectively with it. The

TABLE 11.10

*Cross-Classification of U.S. Sample
According to Their Reported Happiness and
Their Years of Schooling, by Sex (from 1977
General Social Survey)*

Reported Happiness	Years of School Completed			
	0–11	12	13–16	17+
Males				
Not too happy	40	21	14	3
Pretty happy	131	116	112	27
Very happy	82	61	55	27
Females				
Not too happy	62	26	12	3
Pretty happy	155	156	95	15
Very happy	87	127	76	15

estimates of the μ_r, $r = 1, 2, 3$, appear in Table 11.11. Note that the model says that the distance between "not too happy" and "pretty happy" is 3.0 times the distance between "pretty happy" and "very happy," that is,

$$(\hat{\mu}_2 - \hat{\mu}_1)/(\hat{\mu}_3 - \hat{\mu}_2) = 0.79/0.26 = 3.0.$$

Assuming that the preceding model is true, an explicit (conditional) test of the assumption of equal intervals can be constructed. Note that the response categories are equally spaced whenever $\mu_{r+1} - \mu_r = \delta$. Under the hypothesis of equal intervals, equation (13) can be rewritten as

$$\log \theta_{ri(c)} = \phi_c^* (\nu_{i+1,c} - \nu_{i,c}) ,$$

where $\phi_c^* = \phi_c \delta$, for $c = 1, 2$. This model is also easily tested, and it gives $L^2 = 11.64$ on 6 d.f. The difference $11.64 - 6.15 = 5.49$ would be re-

TABLE 11.11

*Category Scores for the Happiness
Variable in Table 11.10, Obtained from
the Conditional-Association Model with
Homogenous Row Effects and
Heterogeneous Column Effects*

Response	Category Score $\hat{\mu}_r$	$\hat{\mu}_{r+1} - \hat{\mu}_r$
Not to happy	1.35	
Pretty happy	2.14	0.79
Very happy	2.41	0.26

garded as a single-degree-of-freedom chi-square variate if the hypothesis of equal intervals were true. Since the descriptive level of significance is about 0.02 for such a statistic, we have considerable evidence that the hypothesis of equal spacing does not hold true. Thus, an assumption of equal intervals is not tenable for the happiness item, an item most would regard as the simplest possible survey measurement of a subjective phenomenon.

THE SPACING OF RESPONSE PATTERNS

Guttman scaling procedures have been an accepted part of social research methodology for nearly four decades. As noted in Chapter 6 of Volume 1, the Guttman model provides for a ranking of items (in terms of "desirability," for example) as well as a ranking of individuals according to their position on an underlying scale. A variety of statistical methods can be used to assess the conformity of the data to the Guttman model (Goodman, 1978:Chapter 9; Clogg and Sawyer, 1981; Lazarsfeld and Henry, 1968). To my knowledge, however, there have been no entirely convincing methods proposed through which scores can be assigned to the response patterns arising from the Guttman model. This statement is at least true for most of the several stochastic variants of the Guttman model, and stochastic models of some sort are necessary to account for the "response errors" usually encountered in empirical situations. This section presents one approach to the Guttman scaling problem that brings the spacing assumption into direct focus once again.

It should be noted that the Rasch model, discussed in some detail by Duncan in Chapter 12 of this volume, is one important stochastic generalization of Guttman's model. The Rasch model provides for a scoring of both the items and the individuals, but the Rasch model requires assumptions that may be difficult to satisfy in empirical situations. Our approach in this section is to avoid the assumptions of the Rasch model, invoking instead assumptions that we find to be somewhat weaker. Thus, scores for individuals will be obtained in a way that is different from those obtained from Rasch's model, and these scores are examined for their departures from the equal-interval assumption that regrettably still dominates practical applications of Guttman's model.

Table 11.12 cross-classifies a fivefold response item measuring the attitude toward legal abortion with a fourfold item (variable A, say) measuring the attitude toward premarital sex. The abortion-attitude variable was obtained by routine Guttman scalogram procedures applied to three items, and a full 11.3 percent ($= 155/1377$) were found to have "error response patterns." Goodman's (1978:Chapter 9) proportion "intrinsically unscalable" was 0.32, a value that indicates reasonable "scalability." It is difficult to determine the proper ordering of the error response patterns a priori, and it is equally difficult to justify the summated scale that is typically used with

Guttman procedures, especially when error response patterns occur. The premarital sex item can be regarded as an instrument, implying that the associational structure in Table 11.12 will be used to estimate scores for the response categories.

A log-multiplicative association model is of special interest here, as in earlier examples. Letting θ_{ri} refer to subtable odds ratios as before, the model is

$$\log \theta_{ri} = \theta(\mu_{r+1} - \mu_r)(\nu_{i+1} - \nu_i). \tag{14}$$

This model yields $L^2 = 5.55$ on 6 d.f. By way of comparison, the independence model yields $L^2 = 236.34$ on 12 d.f. The estimated scale scores appear in Table 11.13. If the five categories of the response are indexed by $r = 0, 1, 2, 3, 4$, with 0 denoting the error-response patterns, then the suggested ordering is 1, 0, 2, 3, 4. The error response patterns are estimated to indicate a position on the scale between the (1, 1, 1) and the (1, 1, 2) response patterns. The μ_r in Table 11.13 could be used to create an index of the abortion attitude, and the index so obtained can be defended in terms of the model used here to estimate distances. The reader should note that the estimates of μ_r in Table 11.13 are inconsistent with a hypothesis of

TABLE 11.12
Cross-Classification of Abortion Attitude, by Attitude on Premarital Sex (from 1977 General Social Survey)

Abortion-Attitude Response Patterns[b]		Premarital Sex[a]				Total
		1	2	3	4	
Error responses	0	44	11	38	62	155
(1,1,1)	1	59	41	147	293	540
(1,1,2)	2	23	11	13	27	74
(1,2,2)	3	27	8	16	27	78
(2,2,2)	4	258	57	105	110	530
Total		411	128	319	519	1,377

[a]The question was: "Do you think **premarital sex** is always wrong, almost always wrong, wrong only sometimes, or not wrong at all?" The responses are coded 1–4, respectively.
[b]The three abortion items were as follows: Should legal abortion be available to a woman: "if she is married and does not want any more children?" (NOMORE); "if the family has a very low income and cannot afford any more children?" (POOR); "if she is not married and does not want to marry the man?" (SINGLE). The Guttman-scale ordering for these items, based on inspection of the single-item marginals, was POOR–SINGLE–NOMORE; a response pattern for (1,1,2) corresponds to a "no" for NOMORE and a "yes" for both POOR and SINGLE.

equal intervals. Except for the difficulty in placing the error-response pattern ($r = 0$), the test of equal intervals could be easily obtained, using a more restrictive model like one of those discussed in the preceding section.

JOINT DISTRIBUTIONS OF ORDINAL INDICATORS: SPACING, RESPONSE CONSISTENCY, AND MULTIVARIATE NORMALITY

This section considers models for the joint distribution of ordinal indicators. The phenomenon of response consistency is addressed (see Duncan, 1979; Duncan, Sloane, and Brody 1982), and some indirect evidence about the plausibility of the multivariate normal distribution is presented. The spacing assumptions that would typically be made in analyzing joint distributions are also studied.

Table 11.14 is a cross-classification of three indicators of satisfaction with life taken from the 1977 General Social Survey. The items pertain to satisfaction with family, residence, and hobbies, and the category indexes are 1 (a fair amount, some, a little, or none), 2 (quite a bit), 3 (a great deal), and 4 (a very great deal). Although each item is a response, we use the symbols A, B, and C to refer to the items. We let i, j, and k index the categories of A, B, and C, respectively. To describe the data in Table 11.14, it is useful to consider partial odds ratios for each type of partial association. For the A–B partial association, these partial odds ratios would be

$$\theta_{ij(k)}^{AB} = (F_{ijk}F_{i+1, j+1, k}/(F_{i, j+1, k}F_{i+1, j, k}). \tag{15}$$

Similar partial odds ratios can be defined for the A–C and the B–C partial association.

The approach begins by assuming that each variable is a measure of an underlying continuum (satisfaction with residence, for example). Note that

TABLE 11.13
Estimated Scale Scores
for the Abortion-Attitude
Response Patterns

Abortion-Attitude Response Pattern	Scale Score[a]
0 Error	0.049
1 (1,1,1)	0.507
2 (1,1,2)	− 0.064
3 (1,2,2)	− 0.101
4 (2,2,2)	− 0.391

[a]Scores constrained to sum to zero.

345

TABLE 11.14

*Cross-Classification of U.S. Sample According
to Three Indicators of Satisfaction with Life
(from 1977 General Social Survey)*

$L =$	$R =$	$C = 1$	$C = 2$	$C = 3$	$C = 4$
1	1	76	14	15	4
1	2	32	17	7	3
1	3	64	23	28	15
1	4	41	11	27	16
2	1	15	2	7	4
2	2	27	20	9	5
2	3	57	31	24	15
2	4	27	9	22	16
3	1	13	6	13	5
3	2	12	13	10	6
3	3	46	32	75	20
3	4	54	26	58	55
4	1	7	6	7	6
4	2	7	2	3	6
4	3	12	11	31	15
4	4	52	36	80	101

NOTE: Variables L, R, and C refer to satisfaction with hobbies, family, and residence, respectively. Variable codes are 1 (a fair amount, some, a little, or none), 2 (quite a bit), 3 (a great deal), and 4 (a very great deal).

we are not assuming that each item is somehow a measure of a "common" factor. In terms of the partials, the general model can be written as

$$\log \theta_{ij(k)}^{AB} = \phi^{AB}(\mu_{i+1,1} - \mu_{i,1})(\nu_{j+1,1} - \nu_{j,1}), \tag{16.a}$$

$$\log \theta_{i(j)k}^{AC} = \phi^{AC}(\mu_{i+1,2} - \mu_{i,2})(\zeta_{k+1,1} - \zeta_{k,1}), \tag{16.b}$$

$$\log \theta_{(i)jk}^{BC} = \phi^{BC}(\mu_{j+1,2} - \nu_{j,2})(\zeta_{k+1,2} - \zeta_{k,2}), \tag{16.c}$$

The ϕ^{AB}, ϕ^{AC}, ϕ^{BC} refer to the overall partial association between A and B, between A and C, and between B and C, respectively. In (16.a), the $\mu_{i,1}$ are category scores for the A item, and the differences $\mu_{i+1,1} - \mu_{i,1}$ represent distances between adjacent scores; the $\nu_{j,1}$ are category scores for the B item, and the differences $\nu_{j+1,1} - \nu_{j,1}$ represent distances between adjacent scores. Subject to appropriate distances being assigned, then, the model is positing linear-by-linear partial association between A and B. Similar comments apply to the A–C and the B–C partial association equations, but the reader should note that the model of (16) allows the distances to vary across the type of partial being considered, that is, $(\mu_{i+1,1} - \mu_{i,1})$ is not constrained to equal $(\mu_{i+1,2} - \mu_{i,2})$.

Results of Goodman (1981) can be extended to relate the model of (16) to the trivariate normal distribution. If the three items follow a trivariate normal the model in (16) will hold true, and the parameters ϕ^{AB}, ϕ^{AC}, ϕ^{BC} can be linked up to the (partial) correlation coefficients that describe the (partial) association in the trivariate normal. Conversely, if the model in (16) does not hold true, then the trivariate normal distribution can be rejected as a suitable model for the joint distribution. Using statistical methods in Clogg (1982a), the model of (16) is found to yield $L^2 = 123.59$ on 54 d.f., a very unsatisfactory fit. We therefore conclude that the trivariate normal distribution can be rejected for these data; the partial association in Table 11.14 is more complicated than that described by the model. [Note that since the single items could not be described by the quadratic log-linear model (see Table 11.9) there is no real need to consider whether the joint distribution could be described by a trivariate normal. But the model of (16) might be expected to hold true even for some situations in which the trivariate normal fails.]

Inspection of residuals associated with the model of (16) indicates the source of the model's failure, and it also suggests a remedy. The consistent responses (where responses $[i,j,k]$ are $[1,1,1]$, $[2,2,2]$, $[3,3,3]$ or $[4,4,4]$) are not predicted well by the model, and this suggests "blanking out" these consistent response patterns. When this is done, much more acceptable results are obtained. Model (16) for the incomplete table yields $L^2 = 37.67$ on 34 d.f., which is certainly an acceptable fit. By way of comparison, the quasi-independence model applied to Table 11.14, blanking out consistent responses, gives $L^2 = 254.72$ on 50 d.f., and the model of no three-factor interaction, blanking out consistent responses, gives $L^2 = 21.93$ on 24 d.f.

In the model of (16), the distances between categories of the A item were allowed to vary across the type of partial being considered. It is natural to consider a model where the distances $(\mu_{i+1,1} - \mu_{i,1})$ are equal to the distances $(\mu_{i+1,2} - \mu_{i,2})$, and where the other distances for the B and C items are similarly constrained. When this is done, the model produces $L^2 = 49.31$ on 41 d.f., which is an acceptable fit. Thus, the model described by

$$\log \theta_{ij(k)}^{AB} = \phi^{AB}(\mu_{i+1} - \mu_i)(\nu_{j+1} - \nu_j) , \qquad (17.a)$$

$$\log \theta_{i(j)k}^{AC} = \phi^{AC}(\mu_{i+1} - \mu_i)(\zeta_{k+1} - \zeta_k) , \qquad (17.b)$$

$$\log \theta_{(i)jk}^{BC} = \phi^{BC}(\nu_{j+1} - \nu_j)(\zeta_{k+1} - \zeta_k) , \qquad (17.c)$$

is an acceptable description of the partial association in Table 11.14. (Note that this model is posited to hold only for the inconsistent response patterns.)

Next we consider the hypothesis of equal intervals, that is, the hypothesis where $\mu_{i+1} - \mu_i = \nu_{i+1} - \nu_i = \zeta_{i+1} - \zeta_i = \delta$. Note that as in the section on the Assumption of Equal Spacing, the assumption of equal intervals can be given explicit consideration in terms of a model, although the test of equal intervals is a conditional one [that is, the test assumes that the model of (17) is true]. This model yields $L^2 = 103.95$ on 47 d.f., implying that the assumption of equal intervals cannot be sustained. The difference in L^2 values, $103.95 - 49.31 = 54.64$, would be compared with the chi-square distribution on $47 - 41 = 6$ d.f. Conventional factor-analytic models applied to data like those in Table 11.14 would begin with an assumption of equal spacing, but we have just seen that this assumption cannot be supported. [See Andrews and McKennell (1980) for an analysis that does assume equal spacing of categories of similar items.]

The category scores estimated for the three items under the model of (17) appear in Table 11.15. No attempt was made to impose scale or location restrictions on these estimates, but nevertheless an anomalous result occurred for the estimated distance between the first and second responses to the family item (pertaining to "a fair amount, some, a little, or none" and "quite a bit" of satisfaction, respectively). The estimates indicate that the position of these two categories must be switched, and this is admittedly a perplexing result. In circumstances like these the model must be called into question, but as an expedient we might simply average the anomalous scores. The reader is referred to Clogg (1982b) for further comments on this result.

To summarize, the partial-association models applied to the data in Table 11.14 demonstrate the failure of assumptions that would be customarily used in a conventional linear model approach. Response consistency is a salient property of the data, and we suspect that similar kinds of response consistency are inherent in many survey designs where batteries of ordinal

TABLE 11.15

Parameter Estimates Under the Homogeneous Row-, Column-, and Layer-Effects Model Applied to Table 11.14 (with consistent response patterns deleted)

Parameters	Maximum-Likelihood Estimate						
Row Effects	−0.19		−1.11		−0.32		1.62
Differences		−0.92		0.78		1.95	
Column Effects	−1.09		−0.77		0.43		1.43
Differences		0.32		1.20		1.00	
Layer Effects	−0.92		−0.89		0.29		1.51
Differences		0.03		1.17		1.23	

indicators are used. This response consistency might be a pure artifact of, say, the order in which items appeared on the survey, or it might be due to "ideological" response patterns that actually characterize "latent" classes of individuals. Whatever the case, these results indicate that response consistency cannot be ignored, and yet it is ignored in conventional approaches. The assumption of multivariate normality cannot be sustained, and yet the statistical theory on which the factor models of Jöreskog and Sörbom (1979) are based depends on multivariate normality. Similarly, the assumption of equal intervals cannot be supported, and yet the usual approach to analyzing data like those in Table 11.14 assumes equal intervals.

Simultaneous Latent-Class Analysis Across Groups

This section defines the latent-class model used in the section on Latent Class Models and Between-Context Response Uncertainty and shows how to estimate latent-class models simultaneously across groups (or across contexts). Latent-class analysis has a long history, and important references include Lazarsfeld and Henry (1968), Goodman (1978:Chapters 8, 9, 10), Dayton and Macready (1980), and Haberman (1979:Chapter 10). A survey by Clogg (1981b) is useful for additional references, as is the work of Clogg and Sawyer (1981). A computer program called MLLSA (Clogg, 1977) appears to be the most general of the several programs now available, although Haberman's (1979) LAT program is also useful. We define the model for the case where there are two indicators; see Clogg (1981a) for examples where latent-class analysis is applied to the two-item situation. After defining the model, it is shown how to estimate models simultaneously across contexts (groups), and how to test for between-context heterogeneity. We let A and B denote the indicators of interest, and we let X denote the latent variable that is imperfectly measured by A and B. To be consistent with our earlier notation, X might be regarded as the "true" response variable of interest, and the actual response variable R might appear as one of the indicators.

THE MODEL

Let π_{ij} denote the expected proportion in the (i,j) cell of the contingency table cross-classifying A and B, with $i = 1, \ldots, I, j = 1, \ldots, J$. Suppose further that a latent variable X has T classes, indexed by $t = 1, \ldots, T$. Let π_{ijt}^{ABX} denote the expected proportion in the (i,j,t) cell of the $A \times B \times X$ indirectly observed table. If A and B are conditionally independent given the level t of X, then the following relationship will hold:

$$\pi_{ijt}^{ABX} = \pi_t^X \, \pi_{it}^{\bar{A}X} \, \pi_{jt}^{\bar{B}X}, \tag{18}$$

where π_t^X is the proportion in the tth class of X, where $\pi_{it}^{\bar{A}X}$ is the conditional probability that A takes on level i when X is at level t, and where $\pi_{jt}^{\bar{B}X}$ is the conditional probability that B takes on level j when X is at level t. Since

$$\pi_{ij} = \sum_{t=1}^{T} \pi_{ijt}^{ABX}, \tag{19}$$

we must have

$$\pi_{ij} = \sum_{t=1}^{T} \pi_t^X \, \pi_{it}^{\bar{A}X} \, \pi_{jt}^{\bar{B}X}. \tag{20}$$

Given A and B and the number of classes T of X, methods exist that provide maximum-likelihood estimates of the parameters on the right-hand-side of (20). Methods also exist for determining the identifiability of parameter estimates and for calculating the degrees of freedom from both identifiable and unidentifiable models. A large literature exists on the specific meanings that are ascribed to the parameters in (20). Suffice it to say that the classes of X can refer to the "true" (latent) classification of individuals, and items A and B imperfectly measure X (with error rates described by the conditional probabilities).

Restricted latent-class models impose restrictions on the parameters in (20). The MLLSA program, for example, allows a wide range of fixed restrictions ($\pi_1^x = 0.2$, $\pi_{12}^{\bar{A}X} = 1.0$, $\pi_{21}^{\bar{B}X} = 0.0$, etc.) as, well as equality restrictions ($\hat{\pi}_1^X = \hat{\pi}_2^X$; $\hat{\pi}_{12}^{\bar{A}X} = \hat{\pi}_{21}^{\bar{B}X}$; $\hat{\pi}_{11}^{\bar{A}X} = \hat{\pi}_{12}^{\bar{A}X}$; etc.). Using restrictions in a judicious fashion enables the researcher to specify a very wide range of scaling models, latent-variable path models, and related types of models involving observed indicators and latent variables. The case where two latent variables Y and Z are assumed to exist can also be handled, merely by letting X refer to the cross-classification of Y and Z. The X variable is assumed to be a mere classification, but restrictions of the kind considered by Clogg (1979b) indicate how an ordered latent variable can be considered. The reader is referred to sources already cited for some of the types of problems that can be considered in the latent-class framework. The analysis in the preceding section on Latent-Class Models and Between-Context Response Uncertainty indicates one means by which ideas of response uncertainty can be addressed in a latent-class framework.

SIMULTANEOUS LATENT-CLASS ANALYSIS

To our knowledge, latent-class models have not yet been considered for the case where two or more groups are under consideration. For example, the groups might refer to contexts, and the task might be to estimate a model simultaneously across groups. Clogg (1979a:Chapter 5; 1980a) and Tuch (1981) provide examples in which such a question becomes relevant. On analogous methods for the factor model, see Jöreskog and Sörbom (1979).

Let C denote the group (Context) variable, with classes $c = 1,2$. To consider a T-class latent structure simultaneously for each group, merely consider C as an explicit indicator, and change the number of latent classes from T to $2T$. The latent class model now becomes

$$\pi_{ijc} = \sum_{t=1}^{2T} \pi_t^X \pi_{it}^{\bar{A}X} \pi_{jt}^{\bar{B}X} \pi_{ct}^{\bar{C}X}, \qquad (21)$$

where we now impose the fixed restrictions $\pi_{lt}^{\bar{C}X} = 1.0$ for $t = 1, \ldots, T$, and $\pi_{1t}^{\bar{C}X} = 0.0$ for $t = T + 1, \ldots, 2T$. It is not difficult to show that

$$\sum_{t=1}^{T} \pi_t^X = \pi_{++1}, \qquad (22.\text{a})$$

$$\sum_{T+1}^{2T} \pi_t^X = \pi_{++2}, \qquad (22.\text{b})$$

given this specification, where $\pi_{++c} = \sum_{i,j} \pi_{ijc}$. Thus π_1^X/π_{++1} is the proportion of resondents in the first context in the first latent class, π_{T+1}^X/π_{++2} is the proportion of respondents in the second context in the first latent class, etc. The quantity $\pi_{11}^{\bar{A}X}$ is the conditional probability that A takes on level 1 for a member of the first latent class in the first context, while the quantity $\pi_{1,T+1}^{\bar{A}X}$ is the conditional probability that A takes on level 1 for a member of the first latent class in the second context. Similar interpretations follow for the other conditional probabilities in (21). The model (21) with the designated restrictions imposed is equivalent to a T-class latent structure applied separately to each context, and if no restrictions on π_t^X, $\pi_{it}^{\bar{A}X}$, $\pi_{jt}^{\bar{B}X}$ are imposed, the model is one of complete heterogeneity across contexts.

In the special case where $T = 1$, and hence $2T = 2$, we have the model that says A and B are conditionally independent given the level c of C. Since $\pi_{11}^{\bar{C}X} = 1.0$ (implying $\pi_{21}^{\bar{C}X} = 0.0$) and $\pi_{12}^{\bar{C}X} = 0.0$ (implying $\pi_{22}^{\bar{C}X} = 1.0$), (21) gives

$$\pi_{ij1} = \pi_1^X \pi_{i1}^{\bar{A}X} \pi_{j1}^{\bar{B}X}$$

and

$$\pi_{ij2} = \pi_2^X \pi_{i2}^{\bar{A}X} \pi_{j2}^{\bar{B}X}$$

showing that in this case

$$\pi_1^X = \pi_{++1},\ \pi_2^X = 1 - \pi_1^X = \pi_{++2}.$$

Finally, $\pi_{i1}^{\bar{A}X}$ would equal the marginal probability that A takes on level i in the first context, with similar comments applying to $\pi_{j1}^{\bar{B}X}$, $\pi_{i2}^{\bar{A}X}$, $\pi_{j2}^{\bar{B}X}$.

The preceding statements apply equally well to restricted latent-class models. Special applications of restricted latent-class models are discussed next.

TESTING FOR HETEROGENEOUS CONDITIONAL PROBABILITIES

Suppose a T-class latent structure were found for each context $c = 1,2$, using the simultaneous estimation discussed previously. Denote the model so obtained as model M_U, a hypothesis that the T-class model holds in each group. Suppose interest focuses on possible heterogeneity in the conditional probability that A takes on level i for the tth latent class. That is, a test of whether $\pi_{it}^{\bar{A}X} = \pi_{i,2t}^{\bar{A}X}$ is required. A model M_R can be estimated imposing the restriction $\hat{\pi}_{it}^{\bar{A}X} = \hat{\pi}_{i,2t}^{\bar{A}X}$, and the difference $L^2(M_R) - L^2(M_U)$ is a single degree-of-freedom chi-square test of the restriction, assuming M_U is true. A significant value of this statistic indicates heterogeneity; a nonsignificant value indicates M_U can be replaced by M_R, or homogeneity can be assumed. The MLLSA program allows for equality restrictions of the kind just discussed, providing a means by which this test can be carried out.

Suppose a restricted model M_R imposes d equality restrictions (across contexts). Then the main result is unchanged, that is, $L^2(M_R) - L^2(M_U) = L^2(M_R|M_U)$ is a d-degree-of-freedom test of the d restrictions. This procedure was used repeatedly to obtain the results reported in Table 11.8, and a judicious application of conventional model fitting procedures can lead the researcher to a variety of latent-class models with between context homogeneity and/or heterogeneity in the conditional probabilities.

A model of complete homogeneity in the conditional probabilities across contexts would be obtained by imposing the restrictions:

$$\hat{\pi}_{it}^{\bar{A}X} = \hat{\pi}_{i,2t}^{\bar{A}X},\ \text{for } i = 1, \ldots, I;\ t = 1, \ldots, T,$$

and

$$\hat{\pi}_{jt}^{\bar{B}X} = \hat{\pi}_{j,2t}^{\bar{B}X},\ \text{for } j = 1, \ldots, J;\ t = 1, \ldots, T.$$

Note that in analyzing Table 11.7, we found that most, but not all, conditional probabilities could be regarded as being homogeneous across contexts, and this led in part to the parsimonious explanation of context effects on responses.

TESTING FOR HETEROGENEOUS LATENT CLASS PROPORTIONS

It was noted earlier that π_t^X/π_{++1} is the proportion in the tth latent class for context 1, and π_{2t}^X/π_{++2} is the proportion in the tth latent class for context 2. To test whether the proportion in the tth latent class is the same in each context, the iterative procedure in MLLSA (see Goodman, 1978:chapter 10) can be modified. The likelihood equations for the simultaneous latent-class model will satisfy the constraints

$$\sum_{t=1}^{T} \hat{\pi}_t^X = \hat{\pi}_{++1} \cdot \tag{23.a}$$

$$\sum_{T+1}^{2T} \hat{\pi}_t^X = \hat{\pi}_{++2} \cdot \tag{23.b}$$

(in addition to others). The algorithm can be modified in straightforward ways to enforce the restriction $\hat{\pi}_t^X/\hat{\pi}_{++1} = \hat{\pi}_{2t}^X/\hat{\pi}_{++2}$, which is equivalent to imposing the restriction that the proportion in the tth latent class is constant across groups. Note that if $\hat{\pi}_{++1} = \hat{\pi}_{++2} = 0.5$, a restriction $\hat{\pi}_t^X = \hat{\pi}_{2t}^X$ suffices. Let the unrestricted model be denoted as M_U, and let the restricted model be denoted as M_U. Then $L^2(M_R|M_U) = L^2(M_R) - L^2(M_U)$ is a single-degree-of-freedom chi-square statistic which can be used to assess the across-context heterogeneity in the proportion in the tth latent class. Note in the analysis of Table 11.7, where a four-class model was considered for each context, it was found that the four latent-class proportions could be regarded as being homogeneous across groups.

In fact, an approximation to the preceding procedure was used to produce the results in Table 11.8. First the estimates of $\pi_1^X, \ldots, \pi_T^X, \pi_{T+1}^X, \ldots, \pi_{2T}^X$ were obtained for a model placing no restrictions on them (but placing the desired restrictions on the conditional probabilities). Then fixed restrictions were imposed by finding values $\tilde{\pi}_t^X, \tilde{\pi}_{2t}^X$ such that

$$\tilde{\pi}_t^X/\hat{\pi}_{++1} = \tilde{\pi}_{2t}^X/\hat{\pi}_{++2} = C_t,$$

or

$$\tilde{\pi}_t^X = C_t\hat{\pi}_{++1}, \ \tilde{\pi}_{2t}^X = C_t\hat{\pi}_{++2}.$$

353

While the $\bar{\pi}_t^X$, $\bar{\pi}_{2t}^X$ are not maximum-likelihood estimates under homogeneity, the actual maximum-likelihood estimates would produce lower values of L^2 than were actually obtained. Since the L^2 values for the model were acceptably small given this specification, there is no reason to worry about discrepancies between the $\bar{\pi}_t^X$, and the true $\hat{\pi}_t^X$.

In many empirical situations where strata (or contexts) are being used to simultaneously consider latent-class structures, the X-variable distribution corresponds to the true variable of interest. In our earlier analysis of Table 11.7, it was found that the latent variable possessed the same distribution in each survey context, and only the response uncertainty differed across contexts. In our view, it is advantageous to consider measurement error models built on the latent-class framework. A rich variety of models, each with its own probabilistic meaning, is offered by the approach. It might very well be that the "contexts" defined as the groups in the simultaneous latent-class model could be replaced by the "ulstrata" discussed in Chapter 12 of Volume 2, demonstrating an isomorphism between certain restricted latent-class models and Rasch models.

LATENT CLASS MODELS APPLIED TO TEST-RETEST DATA

The general techniques discussed in the four preceding sections will now be used to examine test-retest data. Table 11.16 presents a test-retest cross-classification of the happiness item for years 1974 and 1975. Only 227 subjects were in the retest for 1973, and only 209 subjects were in the retest for 1974. Some preliminary analysis is useful to determine whether the information in both years can be pooled. A test of homogeneity in the test marginals in 1973 and 1974 gives $L^2 = 2.05$ on 2 d.f., while a test of homogeneity in the retest marginals gives $L^2 = 0.02$ on 2 d.f. By viewing the data in terms of the consistent responses (three in number) plus the sum of the inconsistent responses, giving a fourfold classification for each year, a test of homogeneity gives $L^2 = 2.53$ on 3 d.f. Thus, the two years can probably be considered as giving essentially the same information, implying that certain of the restricted latent structures considered above might be suitable.

To formulate an appropriate model for test-retest data, where the items are discrete, strategies suggested by Bishop, Fienberg, and Holland (1975: 400) are used. A reasonable model might begin by positing the existence of three latent types who are consistently "very happy," "pretty happy," and "not too happy," respectively. A latent "very happy" class, for example, would be observed as "very happy" in both the test and the retest. An "intrinsically inconsistent" latent type will also be posited to exist, accounting for the inconsistent responses in Table 11.16. Within this latent class, responses will be random, depending only on the marginal distribution of the items within this class. Let R refer to the response item at the time of

TABLE 11.16

Test-Retest Contingency Tables for the Happiness Item
(from 1973 and 1974 General Social Surveys)

	1973 Retest			1974 Retest		
Test	Very Happy	Pretty Happy	Not Too Happy	Very Happy	Pretty Happy	Not Too Happy
Very happy	48	26	5	46	31	8
Pretty happy	22	88	14	20	68	12
Not too happy	4	6	14	1	12	11
Total			227			209

NOTE: These data were supplied by Tom W. Smith.

the test, let R' refer to the response item at the time of the retest, and let C be the year ($c = 1$ for 1973, $c = 2$ for 1974). Table 11.16 is thus the $R \times R' \times C$ ($3 \times 3 \times 2$) table of interest. A four-class model allowing complete heterogeneity across contexts can be written in terms of an eight-class model as

$$\pi_{rr'c} = \sum_{t=1}^{8} \pi_t^X \, \pi_{rt}^{\bar{R}X} \, \pi_{r't}^{\bar{R}'X} \, \pi_{ct}^{\bar{C}X} ,$$

where $\pi_{rr'c}$ is the expected proportion in cell (r, r', c) of the $3 \times 3 \times 2$ table, and where the parameters on the right-hand-side are the quantities discussed in the two sections above—The Model, and Simultaneous Latent Class Analysis. The restrictions are $\pi_{ii}^{\bar{R}X} = \pi_{i,2i}^{\bar{R}X} = 1.0$, for $\pi_{ii}^{\bar{R}'X} = \pi_{i,2i}^{\bar{R}'X} = 1.0$ for $i = 1, 2, 3$, and $\pi_{lt}^{\bar{C}X} = 1.0$ for $t \leqslant 4$, $\pi_{2t}^{\bar{C}X} = 1.0$ for $4 < t \leqslant 8$. It can be shown that this model is equivalent to a quasi-independence model "blanking out" the consistent responses, applied separately to each table. Table 11.17 provides L^2 values for this model (M_1) and several other models.

For baseline comparisons, the model of mutual independence is considered, model M_0 yielding $L^2(M_0) = 119.96$ on 12 d.f. The model M_1 gives $L^2(M_1) = 3.34$ on 2 d.f., an acceptable fit. Next model M_2 is considered, enforcing homogeneity in the test conditional probabilities for the intrinsically inconsistent latent class. That is, M_2 imposes the restrictions $\hat{\pi}_{r4}^{\bar{R}X} = \hat{\pi}_{r8}^{\bar{R}X}$ in the simultaneous model (where $t = 4$, $t = 8$ correspond to the intrinsically inconsistent latent classes for the first and second contexts). The model thus says that the test-response uncertainty is the same for the two years. We find $L^2(M_2) = 3.43$ on 4 d.f., and the test of the equality constraint is $L^2(M_2|M_1) = L^2(M_2) - L^2(M_1) = .09$. Thus, for members of the intrinsically inconsistent latent class, there was no change in the distribution of the R item.

355

TABLE 11.17
*Latent Class Models
Applied to Data in Table
11.16*

Model[a]	Degrees of Freedom	L^2
M_0	12	119.96
M_1	2	3.34
M_2	4	3.43
M_3	6	5.26
M_4	8	12.48
M_5	7	6.41
M_6	9	7.79
M_7	11	15.02

[a]See text for the description of models. M_1 is a quasi-independence model, but models M_2–M_7 are not.

Model M_3 imposes on M_2 the additional restriction of homogeneity in the retest conditional probabilities for the intrinsically inconsistent latent class. That is, $\hat{\pi}_{r'4}^{\bar{R}'X} = \hat{\pi}_{r'8}^{\bar{R}'X}$. This model says that the retest response uncertainty is the same for the two years. We find $L^2(M_3) = 5.26$ on 6 d.f., and the difference $L^2(M_3) = L^2(M_2) = 1.82$ demonstrates the suitability of the restriction. Thus, for members of the intrinsically inconsistent latent class, there was no change in the distribution of the R' item.

An interesting hypothesis (M_4) is obtained by restricting $\hat{\pi}_{r4}^{RX} = \hat{\pi}_{r8}^{RX} = \hat{\pi}_{r4}^{\bar{R}'X} = \hat{\pi}_{r4}^{\bar{R}'X}$, equivalent to the hypothesis that the test distribution and the retest distribution are homogeneous, and constant across contexts, for the intrinsically inconsistent. Such a condition might be expected to hold if the retest response is made without memory of the "test" response. We find $L^2(M_4) = 12.48$, and the difference $L^2(M_4) - L^2(M_3) = 7.23$ on 2 d.f. is statistically significant. Thus, for the intrinsically inconsistent latent class there appears to be a difference between the distribution of R and the distribution of R', owing perhaps to memory.

Model M_5 imposes the restriction that the proportion in the intrinsically inconsistent latent class is the same across contexts. That is, $\hat{\pi}_4^X/\hat{\pi}_{++1} = \hat{\pi}_8^X/\hat{\pi}_{++2}$. The test gives $L^2(M_5) = 6.41$, and comparing this value with $L^2(M_3)$ indicates that this homogeneity assumption can be sustained. Model M_6 constrains all latent-class proportions to be equal across contexts. With $L^2(M_6) = 7.79$ on 9 d.f. the model fits quite well, and so it can be concluded that (a) the latent-class proportions are constant across time, (b) the test distribution of the happiness item for the intrinsically inconsistent is constant over time, and (c) the retest distribution of the happiness item for the intrinsically inconsistent is constant over time. Model M_7 modifies M_6 in the same way that M_4 modified M_3, and with $L^2(M_7) - L^2(M_6) = 7.23$ on 2 d.f., the conclusion is that the R and the R' distributions are not identical for the intrinsically inconsistent. It can be noted that models M_6 and M_7 are almost as parsimonious as the null model M_0, but they fit the data remarkably well. Additionally, it should be emphasized that although the model of complete heterogeneity (M_1) is merely a reparameterization of the quasi-independence model, the models of homogeneity $(M_2 - M_7)$ are not equivalent to quasi-independence models.

Table 11.18 presents the parameter estimates for model M_6. The intrinsically inconsistent class possesses the test and retest response distributions in the first two columns of the table; for example., 29.1 percent give the "very happy" response on the test, but 7.5 percent fewer (21.6 percent) give the "very happy" response on the retest. Thus, there is an overall downward shift in the distribution, toward less happiness, which conceivably stems from memory of the first test. Since the retest distributions are constant over time, and since the test distributions are also constant over time, it is difficult to explain the difference between the retest and the test distributions without some kind of memory effect.

The estimated latent-class proportions appear in Part B of Table 11.18;

TABLE 11.18
*Parameter Estimates for Model M_6 Applied to
Data of Table 11.16*

A. Probability of Response for Intrinsically Inconsistent

Response	Test[a]	Retest[b]	Difference, Test-Retest
Very happy	.291	.216	+.075
Pretty happy	.622	.644	−.022
Not too happy	.087	.140	−.053

B. Latent-Class Proportions[c]

Very Happy	Pretty Happy	Not too Happy	Intrinsically Inconsistent
0.171	.077	.049	.704

[a]Estimates are $\hat{\pi}_{r4}^{\overline{R}X} = \hat{\pi}_{r8}^{\overline{R}X}$, $r = 1, 2, 3$.

[b]Estimates are $\hat{\pi}_{r'4}^{\overline{R}'X} = \hat{\pi}_{r'8}^{\overline{R}'X}$, $r' = 1, 2, 3$.

[c]Estimates are $\hat{\pi}_t^X/\hat{\pi}_{++1} = \hat{\pi}_{2t}^X/\hat{\pi}_{++2}$, $t = 1, 2, 3, 4$.

the "intrinsically very happy" are 17.1 percent, the "intrinsically pretty happy" are 7.7 percent, and the "intrinsically not too happy" are 4.9 percent of the total. The sum of these three quantities provides a measure of the proportion who are "latent-consistent," and this number is 29.6 percent. Thus, a full 70.4 percent of the population is estimated to have inconsistent response patterns intrinsically; they possess such extreme response uncertainty that it would be tendentious to speak of any fixed level of happiness for them. These deductions from the model are alarming, especially since conventional measures of reliability (consistency) would give a very different impression concerning how well happiness is measured by the trichotomous indicator. (The simple proportion consistent is 0.66 for 1973 and 0.60 for 1974, which might indicate reasonable reliability to some.)

LATENT-CLASS MODELS APPLIED TO THE STOUFFER-TOBY DATA ON ROLE CONFLICT

Duncan (in Chapter 12 of this volume) presents a Rasch analysis of data taken from Stouffer and Toby (1951). These data, or various forms of them, have been analyzed from many different perspectives over the past 30 years. Here the simultaneous latent-class model is applied, showing how a parsimonious description of the underlying structure in these classic data can be obtained.

Table 11.19 presents the data in a slightly different form from that used by Duncan. Four items (A, B, C, and D) are cross-classified for each of three randomly chosen groups. The groups were defined according to alterations in the question wording. The first group or form (Form A) pertained to a question wording in which Ego was the subject facing role conflict, while Forms B and C pertained to question wordings in which Friend and Smith were the subjects facing role conflict, respectively. For a fuller discussion of the data, see Duncan, Chapter 12.

Goodman (1978:chapter 10) began analysis of these items with the two-class unrestricted latent class model, although he considered only the Ego form. The simultaneous two-class model that was applied to all three forms was first estimated and tested. This model yields $L^2 = 21.16$ on 18 d.f., an acceptable fit. Next were considered several models that imposed across-group homogeneity in the model parameters. A model that was suggested from this procedure yielded $L^2 = 38.89$ on 35 d.f., and the parameter estimates under this model are presented in Table 11.20. Evidently, the only source of heterogeneity among the contexts (forms) is in the probability of responding "universalistic" or "particularistic" to the C item in the second (particularistic) latent class. And this heterogeneity exists only for the second group, with the first and third groups being entirely homogeneous with respect to all model parameters. The reader should compare these conclusions with those of Duncan in Chapter 12; in certain respects, these

TABLE 11.19
*Observed Cross-Classification of 648
Respondents: Tendency Toward
Universalistic (1) or Particularistic
(2) Values in Four Situations of Role
Conflict (A, B, C, D)*

Item				Observed Frequency		
A	B	C	D	Form A	Form B	Form C
1	1	1	1	42	37	35
1	1	1	2	23	31	17
1	1	2	1	6	6	9
1	1	2	2	25	15	26
1	2	1	1	6	5	3
1	2	1	2	24	29	27
1	2	2	1	7	6	3
1	2	2	2	38	25	32
2	1	1	1	1	2	3
2	1	1	2	4	4	5
2	1	2	1	1	3	2
2	1	2	2	6	4	5
2	2	1	1	2	3	0
2	2	1	2	9	23	20
2	2	2	1	2	3	3
2	2	2	2	20	20	26
Total				216	216	216

results provide a simpler explanation of the structure in the classic Stouffer-Toby data.

These results were obtained from the MLLSA program using restrictions like those discussed earlier in this section. Once again the latent class model has permitted a concise analysis of the effects of context (question wording) on responses.

Log-Multiplicative Association Model and Calibration of Ordinal Indicators

Two fundamentally different strategies have been used thus far in this chapter to analyze response distributions and the reasons why they differ across contexts. The latent-class framework represents one strategy. It involves the use of multiple indicators of the response, using the interactions among the indicators to characterize the latent variable assumed to produce these interactions. The interactions (2 factor, 3 factor, and so on) among the observed indicators are taken as given in this approach. A second strategy is

TABLE 11.20
Parameter Estimates for a
Simultaneous Latent Class Model
Applied to Data of Table 11.19

	Form A	Form B	Form C
	Conditional Probabilities		
$\hat{\pi} \, ^{\overline{A}X}_{11}$	.97	.97	.97
$\hat{\pi} \, ^{\overline{A}X}_{12}$	.64	.64	.64
$\hat{\pi} \, ^{\overline{B}X}_{11}$	.97	.97	.97
$\hat{\pi} \, ^{\overline{B}X}_{12}$	.28	.28	.28
$\hat{\pi} \, ^{\overline{C}X}_{11}$	.85	.85	.85
$\hat{\pi} \, ^{\overline{C}X}_{12}$	.38	.52*	.38
$\hat{\pi} \, ^{\overline{D}X}_{11}$	.72	.72	.72
$\hat{\pi} \, ^{\overline{D}X}_{12}$	.12	.12	.12
	Latent Class Probabilities		
$\hat{\pi} \, ^{X}_{1}$	.29	.29	.29
$\hat{\pi} \, ^{X}_{2}$	.71	.71	.71

NOTE: Asterisk denotes the only statistically significant heterogeneity in the model. All other parameters are restricted to be homogeneous across form.

represented by the association models. With this approach, the response variable is cross-classified with another variable, and the association is assumed to follow a certain specified form. To be precise, the model assumes that if appropriate category scores can be assigned to the ostensibly ordinal categories of the response, then the association will not depend on the level of the response. While the observed interaction (association) is also a given for this approach, the model in effect defines category scores in such a way that the "true" interaction (association) is simple in form. This section considers the association-model framework more formally, providing the rationale for the applications presented earlier.

Suppose that a discrete ordinal variable A with I categories is cross-classified with another discrete ordinal variable B with J categories. Let the expected frequencies be denoted by F_{ij}, for $i = 1, \ldots, I, j = 1, \ldots, J$. In terms of $\log F_{ij}$, the model can be written as

$$\log F_{ij} = \lambda + \lambda_i^A + \lambda_j^B + \phi \mu_i \nu_j. \tag{24}$$

Models for incomplete tables follow without difficulty, so for our purposes here we assume that (24) holds for all i and j. If the μ_i, ν_j are given constants, the model is identical to Haberman's (1979:Chapter 6) model of linear-by-linear interaction; the model is log-linear, and standard methods may be used to estimate the parameters (Bock and Yates, 1973; Haberman, 1979). The μ_i, ν_j refer to scores associated with categories i, j of A and B, respectively, and the product $\mu_i \nu_j$ defines a linear-by-linear interaction. Hence, ϕ is a parameter that describes the effect of linear-by-linear interaction on the log F_{ij}.

An alternative description of the model can be obtained by considering the subtable odds ratios,

$$\theta_{ij} = (F_{ij} F_{i+1, j+1})/F_{i, j+1} F_{i+1, j}),$$

for $i = 1, \ldots, I - 1$, $j = 1, \ldots, J - 1$. That is, θ_{ij} is the odds ratio measuring the association between A and B in the region of the table defined by adjacent row categories i and $i+1$ and adjacent column categories j and $j+1$. Upon direct substitution, we find

$$\log \theta_{ij} = \phi(\mu_{i+1} - \mu_i) (\nu_{j+1} - \nu_j). \tag{25}$$

Letting $d_i = \mu_{i+1} - \mu_i$ and $e_j = \nu_{j+1} - \nu_j$, the model can be written more compactly as

$$\log \theta_{ij} = \phi \, d_i e_j. \tag{26}$$

In (26), the quantity ϕ refers to the overall association between A and B, and d_i and e_j denote constants that multiply the overall association to produce the "local" association observed in each region of the table. If the μ_i, ν_j denote category scores, then the d_i, e_j refer to distances between adjacent category scores, implying that in this case the distances are solely responsible for producing the differences observed among the log θ_{ij}.

For example, consider a 3×3 table of counts, so that the basic set of odds ratios θ_{ij} consists of four numbers. These quantities can be displayed as follows under the model of (26):

$$
\begin{array}{ccc}
 & j = 1 & j = 2 \\
i = 1 & \phi d_1 e_1 & \phi d_1 e_2 \\
i = 2 & \phi d_2 e_1 & \phi d_2 e_2
\end{array}
$$

If we focus on the association in Column 1, the difference between log θ_{11} and log θ_{21} is $\phi e_1(d_1 - d_2)$, showing that the distances d_1 and d_2 account for the differences in association completely. Similar comments follow for column 2, row 1, and row 2 comparisons.

Now suppose that the μ_i, ν_j are not known, and must therefore be estimated from the data. The model is then a log-multiplicative model, and standard methods of estimation for log-linear models do not apply. Appropriate maximum-likelihood techniques have been presented by Goodman (1979).

Two different situations seem worthwhile to consider, and each of these has been used in this chapter. The first is the case in which one of the variables in the cross-classification is a response, and the other is an instrumental variable. If A is the response, for example, and B is the instrument, then the d_i refer once again to distances, but to be estimated from the data. The e_i do not necessarily have to represent distances for the B (instrumental) variable; they can be regarded as effects on the association in the following sense. Let $\phi_j = \phi e_j$, and note that the model can be rewritten as

$$\log \theta_{ij} = \phi_j d_i. \tag{27}$$

Here, the column-specific association is allowed to differ across columns, with ϕ_j denoting the column-specific association, but the d_i refer to distances as before. Thus, if interest focuses only on estimating the distances between categories of the row variable, it is not necessary to regard the e_j as distances between the column (instrumental) variable categories. "Curvilinearity" in the association across columns can thus be allowed, but the association across rows is assumed to be constant, influenced solely by the distance parameters d_i.

A second situation occurs when both A and B are regarded as response variables, and it is desirable to estimate the distances for each variable. Since much more is being requested of the model, it is not surprising that more stringent assumptions must be made. For the model to be used in this case, with distance parameters d_i and e_j both being relevant, it must be assumed that the true interactional structure is adequately described by linear-by-linear interaction, subject to the appropriate distances being assigned. Thus, ϕ would describe the "true" overall association in this case, and the distances d_i, e_j are assumed to be solely responsible for differentials in local association.

Extensions of the model to conditional and partial association are contained in Clogg (1982a). Note that a conditional association model (with context as the group variable) was used (section on Log-Multiplicative Association Model) to estimate distances of the response item, using schooling as the instrument. A conditional association model was also used (section on Assumption of Equal Spacing) to estimate category distances of the happiness item, using schooling as an instrument and sex as a group variable. An association model was used (section on Spacing of Response Patterns in a Guttman Model) to estimate the distances between scale types in a Guttman response distribution, and the premarital sex item was used as an instrument. If we had also wanted to estimate distances for the premarital sex item, stronger assumptions would have been required. Three response items were considered in a partial-association model (section on Joint Distributions of Ordinal Indicators), and to estimate distances for all three items a rather strong assumption of linear-by-linear partial interaction was necessary. Note that this example utilized models for incomplete tables, "blanking out" certain response patterns.

Given the basic model, a conditional test of equal intervals can be obtained easily. If the $d_i = \delta$ for all i, and $\phi^* = \phi\delta$, then the model of (26) becomes

$$\log \theta_{ij} = \phi^* e_j, \tag{28}$$

and a comparison of the fit of this restricted model with the fit of the model in (26) can be used to test the assumption of equal intervals. This and similar procedures have been used repeatedly in this chapter.

Conclusion

This chapter has been concerned with the problem of measurement error in the survey measurement of subjective phenomena. Recently developed contingency-table methods have been used throughout the work, indicating a range of models that can now be routinely considered. An example was considered that does not admit easy analysis with any kind of conventional linear model for measurement error, and yet scores of contingency-table models can be brought to bear on the problem. Latent-class analysis is now a technique that can be used in routine work with discrete measures of subjective phenomena, and the material on latent-class analysis across groups will be useful in many research situations. The log-multiplicative association model also appears to hold much promise, since it allows for the estimation of category scores for discrete ordinal variables. These methods also appear to lend themselves to the important task of explaining why different survey contexts lead to different conclusions about response distributions. The latent-class model explains context effects in terms of differences in "response uncertainty," and the association models explain context effects in terms of differences in response-category distances associated with each context. I do not know how fruitful these two different perspectives will ultimately prove to be. However, there appears to be good reason for at least considering these methods as alternatives to conventional measurement error models based on the linear model.

References

Andrews, F.M., and McKennell, A.C. (1980) Measures of self-reported well-being: their affective, cognitive, and other components. *Social Indicators Research* 8:127-155.

Bishop, Y.M.M., Fienberg, S.E., and Holland, P.W. (1975) *Discrete Multivariate Analysis: Theory and Practice.* Cambridge, Mass.: MIT Press.

Bock, R.D., and Yates, G. (1973) *MULTIQUAL: Log-Linear Analysis of Nominal or Ordinal Data by the Method of Maximum Likelihood.* Chicago: National Educational Resources.

Clogg, C.C. (1977) Unrestricted and Restricted Maximum Likelihood Latent Structure Analysis: A Manual for Users. Working Paper 1977-09. Population Issues Research Center, Pennsylvania State University, University Park.

Clogg, C.C. (1978) Adjustment of rates using multiplicative models. *Demography* 15:523-539.

Clogg, C.C. (1979a) *Measuring Underemployment: Demographic Indicators for the United States.* New York: Academic Press.

Clogg, C.C. (1979b) Some latent structure models for the analysis of Likert-type data. *Social Science Research* 8:287-301.

Clogg, C.C. (1980) Characterizing the class organization of labor market opportunity: a modified latent structure approach. *Sociological Methods and Research* 8:243-272.

Clogg, C.C. (1981a) Latent structure models of mobility. *American Journal of Sociology* 86:836-868.

Clogg, C.C. (1981b) New developments in latent structure analysis. In D.M. Jackson and E.F. Borgatta, eds., *Factor Analysis and Measurement in Sociological Research.* Beverly Hills, Calif.: Sage.

Clogg, C.C. (1982a) Some Models for the Analysis of Association in Multi-Way Cross-Classifications Having Ordered Categories. *Journal of the American Statistical Association* 77:803-815.

Clogg, C.C. (1982b) Using association models in sociological research: some examples. *American Journal of Sociology* 88:114-134.

Clogg, C.C., and Sawyer, D.O. (1981) A comparison of alternative models for analyzing the scalability of response patterns. S. Leinhardt, ed., *Sociological Methodology: 1981.* San Francisco: Jossey-Bass.

Cochran, W.G., and Cox, G.M. (1957) *Experimental Designs.* 2nd ed. New York: Wiley.

Dayton, C.M., and Macready, G.M. (1980) A scaling model with response errors and intrinsically unscalable respondents. *Psychometrika* 45:343-356.

Duncan, O.D. (1979) Indicators of sex typing: traditional and egalitarian, situational and ideological responses. *American Journal of Sociology* 85:252-260.

Duncan, O.D., and Schuman, H. (1980) Effects of question wording and context: an experiment with religious indicators. *Journal of the American Statistical Association* 75:269-275.

Duncan, O.D., Sloane, D.M., and Brody, C. (1982) Latent classes inferred from response-consistency effects. Pp. 19-64 in K.G. Jöreskog, ed., *Systems Under Indirect Observation.* Vol. 1. Amsterdam: North-Holland.

Evers, M., and Namboodiri, N.K. (1978) On the design matrix strategy in the analysis of categorical data. In K.F. Schuessler, ed., *Sociological Methodology: 1979.* San Francisco: Jossey-Bass.

Fay, R.E. (1979) Jackknifing Chi-square Test Statistics—Part I. An Application of Log-Linear Modeling of Data from the Current Population Survey. Unpublished ms. Statistical Research Division, Bureau of the Census.

Fienberg, S.E. (1980) *The Analysis of Cross Classified Categorical Data.* 2nd ed. Cambridge, Mass.: MIT Press.

Goodman, L.A. (1968) The analysis of cross-classified data: independence, quasi-independence, and interactions in contingency tables with or without missing entries. *Journal of the American Statistical Association* 63:1091-1131.

Goodman, L.A. (1972) Some multiplicative models for the analysis of cross-classified data. In *Proceedings of the Sixth Berkeley Symposium on Mathematical Statistics and Probability* 1: 649-696.

Goodman, L.A. (1978) *Analyzing Qualitative/Categorical Data.* Cambridge, Mass.: Abt Books.

Goodman, L.A. (1979) Simple models for the analysis of association in cross-classifications having ordered categories. *Journal of the American Statistical Association* 74:537-552.

Goodman, L.A. (1981) Association models and the bivariate normal for contingency tables having ordered categories. *Biometrika* 68:347-355.

Haberman, S.J. (1974) Log-linear models for frequency tables with ordered classifications. *Biometrics* 30:589-600.

Haberman, S.J. (1978) *Analysis of Qualitative Data.* Vol. 1: *Introductory Topics.* New York: Academic Press.

Haberman, S.J. (1979) *Analysis of Qualitative Data.* Vol. 2: *New Developments.* New York: Academic Press.

Henry, N.W. (1981) Jackknifing measures of association. *Sociological Methods and Research* 10:233-240.

Jöreskog, K.G., and Sörbom, S. (1979) *Advances in Factor Analysis and Structural Equation Models.* Cambridge, Mass.: Abt Books.

Lazarsfeld, P.F., and Henry, N.W. (1968) *Latent Structure Analysis.* Boston: Houghton-Mifflin.

National Opinion Research Center (1978) *General Social Surveys, 1972-1978: Cumulative Codebook.* Chicago: National Opinion Research Center.

Ott, L. (1977) *An Introduction to Statistical Methods and Data Analysis.* North Scituate, Mass.: Duxbury Press.

Plackett, R.L. (1974) *The Analysis of Categorical Data.* London: Griffin.

Schuman, H., and Presser, S. (1978) The assessment of "no opinion" in attitude surveys. In K.F. Schuessler, ed., *Sociological Methodology: 1979.* San Francisco: Jossey-Bass.

Stouffer, S.A., and Toby, J. (1951) Role conflict and personality. *American Journal of Sociology* 56:395-406.

Torgerson, W.S. (1958) *Theory and Methods of Scaling*. New York: Wiley.

Tuch, S.A. (1981) Analyzing recent trends in prejudice toward blacks: insights from latent class models. *American Journal of Sociology* 87:130-142.

Acknowledgments

This research was supported in part by Research Contract No. SES–7823759 from the Division of Economic and Social Sciences of the National Science Foundation. The author is indebted to Mu-Chian Chang for assistance in preparing some of the data used herein. For helpful comments, the writer is indebted to Otis Dudley Duncan, Shelby Haberman, Elizabeth Martin, James W. Shockey, Charles F. Turner, and a reviewer who prefers to remain anonymous.

12

Rasch Measurement: Further Examples and Discussion

Otis Dudley Duncan

This chapter continues the exposition in Section 6.4 of Volume 1, which should be read first. Reviews of work on Rasch models in psychometrics should also be consulted (Lumsden, 1976; Rasch, 1960/1980; Weiss and Davison, 1981; Wright, 1977), since it is assumed that the reader is acquainted with the rationale and motivation of Rasch's approach. Application of it to survey data has only begun, although educational psychologists report some work with attitude questionnaires (Andrich, 1978a; 1978d; Wright and Masters, 1982). An alternative approach to latent-trait models applicable in survey work is presented by Reiser (1981). Lazarsfeld and Henry (1968:223-225) give a brief statement on Rasch's ideas in reviewing latent-class and latent-structure models.

In the following sections, I describe a four-item scale measuring attitude toward the army; another four-item instrument, intended to measure universalism-particularism, that turns out to involve two dimensions; a two-dimensional set of four items pertaining to beliefs about effects of marijuana; results of an experiment on order and wording of questions, analysis of which is greatly facilitated by a Rasch model; and the extension of the model to items taking the form of the ordered trichotomy, with an illustration drawn from a classic panel study. All the examples illustrate serendipitous properties of data collected for purposes other than mine. The substance of some of the examples is related to themes developed by the panel in Volume 1, but in the interest of brevity I have not elaborated on these relationships or on the broader scientific significance of the empirical results I report.

A Four-Item Scale

The response distribution for four questions intended to measure "general attitudes toward the Army" is given in Table 12.1. These data are discussed by Stouffer (in Stouffer et al., 1950:17, 21-29) in relation to the Guttman scaling procedure and Lazarsfeld's latent-dichotomy model; by Lazarsfeld (in Stouffer et al., 1950:417-432) in relation to his latent-dichotomy model; and by Goodman (1978:376-383) in relation to various scaling models obtained by modifying the assumptions of the Guttman procedure. The questions are quoted below (Stouffer et al., 1950:17); letter designations for the items have been added, as have the codes for positive (1) and negative (0) responses that were used in dichotomizing responses:

A. In general, how well do you think the Army is run?
    _____ It is run very well (1)
    _____ It is run pretty well (1)
    _____ It is not run so well (0)
    _____ It is run very poorly (0)
    _____ Undecided (0)

B. Do you think when you are discharged you will go back to civilian life with a favorable or unfavorable attitude toward the Army?
    _____ Very favorable (1)
    _____ Fairly favorable (1)
    _____ About 50-50 (0)
    _____ Fairly unfavorable (0)
    _____ Very unfavorable (0)

C. In general, do you think you yourself have gotten a square deal in the Army?
    _____ Yes, in most ways I have (1)
    _____ In some ways yes, in other ways, no (0)
    _____ No, on the whole I haven't gotten a square deal (0)

D. Do you think the Army has tried its best to look out for the welfare of enlisted men?
    _____ Yes, it has tried its best (1)
    _____ It has tried some, but not enough (0)
    _____ It has hardly tried at all (0)

Rasch Measurement: Further Examples

It is well to note Stouffer's remark (Stouffer et al., 1950:21): "Responses are dichotomized, not as in scalogram procedure by choosing cutting points in such a way as to minimize scalogram error, but according to what seems, a priori, to be the manifest content of the response." The statement offers some reassurance, but in general, dichotomous items should be derived from questions with dichotomous response alternatives; ex post facto dichotomization introduces an uncontrolled element into the statistical model. But there is no way to grapple with that problem here.

The Rasch model for four dichotomous responses has four item parameters (although only three ratios of item parameters are identifiable or estimable) and one person parameter for each subject (respondent). Let a, b, c, d be the parameters for items A, B, C, and D, respectively, and let x_i be the person parameter (or value of the latent trait) for the ith respondent. Our procedure will be to derive from this model a log-linear parameterization for the four-way cross-classification of responses, Table 12.1. The approach taken here is elementary and heuristic; it slightly extends the original discussion of Rasch (1960/1980:171-172; 1966:93-96). For a rigorous and general derivation of the log-linear model for the multiitem case, see Tjur (1982).

The Rasch model can be stated in a variety of equivalent though apparently different ways. Here, it is convenient to state the basic postulate of the model in terms of the odds on a favorable response. The odds on responding favorably or positively to item A are simply ax_i for the ith respondent; the corresponding odds for the remaining items are bx_i, cx_i, and dx_i. The probabilities governing responses to the items are, therefore,

Item	Favorable	Unfavorable
A	$ax_i/(1 + ax_i)$	$1/(1 + ax_i)$
B	$bx_i/(1 + bx_i)$	$1/(1 + bx_i)$
C	$cx_i/(1 + cx_i)$	$1/(1 + cx_i)$
D	$dx_i/(1 + dx_i)$	$1/(1 + dx_i)$

The probabilities for the items considered jointly are generated from the foregoing expressions upon invoking the assumption of *local independence*: conditional on x_i, responses to A, B, C, D are mutually independent. (If x, which is of course unobserved, is conceived as continuous, then no two individuals will have exactly the same subject parameter. Hence, the assumption of local independence can also be stated in the form: responses to items are independent within, as well as between, respondents.) This assumption sometimes seems unnatural and arbitrary. On the contrary, it is implicitly used and inescapable in virtually all survey analysis. In studying the relationship of sex to labor force participation we take it for granted that we are investigating whether being male or female affects economic activity, not whether the *response* to "sex" affects the *response* to the labor force item. To be sure, the assumption that responses are independent, conditional on the "true" values of the variables under study, may be incorrect in some instances. But when we think that is so, we try to improve our survey design.

The assumption of local independence permits use of the multiplication rule for independent probabilities. The probability of response pattern 1 0 0 1 (positive on A and D, negative on B and C), for example, is

$$\frac{ax_i}{1 + ax_i} \quad \frac{1}{1 + bx_i} \quad \frac{1}{1 + cx_i} \quad \frac{dx_i}{1 + dx_i}$$

or

$$adx_i^2/\Delta_i$$

where

$$\Delta_i = (1 + ax_i) (1 + bx_i) (1 + cx_i) (1 + dx_i) .$$

The general formula for any of the 16 response patterns listed in the stub of Table 12.1 is

$$Pr\,(h_a h_b h_c h_d | x_i) = a^{h_a}\, b^{h_b}\, c^{h_c}\, d^{h_d}\, x_i^{\,t}\, /\Delta_i .$$

The notation is as follows: $h = 1$ if response is favorable and $h = 0$ if it is unfavorable; hence $(h_a h_b h_c h_d)$ is merely the response pattern. As an exponent, h determines whether the item parameter does or does not occur in the product, since $a^0 = 1$ and $a^1 = a$, and so on. And $t = h_a + h_b + h_c + h_d$, which appears as the power of x_i, is the number of items answered favorably. We now define the sample composition parameters or stratum parameters,

$$S_t = \sum_{i=1}^{n} (x_i^{\,t}/\Delta_i),\ 0 \leq t \leq 4 .$$

Each S is a complex combination of item and person (subject, respondent) parameters. It has no useful substantive interpretation. It is not a structural parameter; and from a statistical point of view it is just a nuisance that must be eliminated in order to estimate the item or person parameters in which we are interested. In the present example we have only one "stratum," so that there are just five sample composition parameters S_t ($0 \leq t \leq 4$). Each sample has a unique set of S's depending upon its composition (borrowing

TABLE 12.1

Cross-Classification of Dichotomized Responses
to Four Questions on Attitude Toward the Army,
for 1,000 Noncommissioned Officers,
October 1945

Item[a] A B C D	Count	Parameterization, Rasch Model	Estimate of Expected Count
1 1 1 1	75	$abc\ S_4$	75.0*
1 1 1 0	69	$abc\ S_3$	73.0
1 1 0 1	55	$ab\ S_3$	54.0
1 0 1 1	42	$ac\ S_3$	34.5
0 1 1 1	3	$bc\ S_3$	7.6
1 1 0 0	96	$ab\ S_2$	97.1
1 0 1 0	60	$ac\ S_2$	62.0
1 0 0 1	45	$a\ S_2$	45.9
0 1 1 0	16	$bc\ S_2$	13.6
0 1 0 1	8	$b\ S_2$	10.1
0 0 1 1	10	$c\ S_2$	6.4
1 0 0 0	199	$a\ S_1$	199.6
0 1 0 0	52	$b\ S_1$	43.8
0 0 1 0	25	$c\ S_1$	28.0
0 0 0 1	16	S_1	20.7
0 0 0 0	229	S_0	229.0*

SOURCE: Stouffer et al. (1950:22, table 1).
[a]1 = positive response; 0 = negative response. See text for question wording.
*Count fitted exactly under the model.

a term from demography) or distribution of values of *x*. Just as each individual has a unique x_i, each sample has its unique composition. The x_i are regarded as parameters. So any function of the sample collection of *x*'s, such as S_t, that aggregates the *x*'s into a scalar, may be said to define a sample parameter.

We may now write the basic formula of the log-linear model for the four-way contingency table:

$$F_{h_a h_b h_c h_d} = a^{h_a}\ b^{h_b}\ c^{h_c}\ d^{h_d}\ S_t\ ,$$

where *F* is the expected frequency in a sample of size *n* and its maximum-likelihood estimate (MLE) is $\hat{F}$. We can obtain the MLE in a way that is quite accessible to analysts who work with survey data using methods for contingency tables presented by Goodman (1978), Haberman (1978; 1979), and Fienberg (1980). In this presentation we do not consider the methods in the psychometric literature on the Rasch model (see, for example, Andersen, 1980) where the number of items is usually much greater than four, so that the contingency-table approach is cumbersome.

The next-to-last column in Table 12.1 makes fully explicit the parameterization of the four-way table derived from the Rasch model. In view of the fact that only ratios of item parameters can be estimated, we arbitrarily set $d = 1$. This has the effect of locating the origin of the scale for items. For a person with $x = 1$ (or $\log x = 0$), the probability of answering D favorably is just defined to be exactly ½.

The program FREQ (Haberman, 1979:Appendix), among others, can be used to fit the model to the data; it provides estimates of the parameters (in natural logarithmic form) and the estimated standard errors (SEs) thereof. The fit of the model to the data in Table 12.1 is judged acceptable in the light of the statistics L^2 (likelihood-ratio chi-square) $= 10.93$ and X^2 (Pearson's chi-square) $= 10.48$, d.f. $= 8$. (To compute d.f. we subtract from the number of cells, 16, the number of item parameters, 3, and the number of sample composition parameters, 5, to be estimated.) Estimates of item parameters (with SEs in parentheses) are $\log \hat{a}/d = 2.268$ (.126); $\log \hat{b}/d = 0.750$ (.114); $\log \hat{c}/d = .302$ (.115). (Recall that $d = 1$ by fiat; hence the circumflex pertains to the numerator of each of these ratios.)

As a matter of possible interest, we note that the model involving response-consistency effects (Duncan, 1979) described in Chapter 6 of Volume 1 (Section 6.3) is implied by the Rasch model and has 5 fewer d.f. The data in Table 12.1 yield $L^2 = 5.66$ for the response-consistency model, so it provides no significant improvement upon the Rasch model in the present instance. The difference in L^2 for the two models (here, $10.93 - 5.66 = 5.27$) with d.f. $= 5$ tests a hypothesis concerning partial associations. According to the Rasch model, the partial association for any pair of items, when one and only one of the other two items is answered favorably, is $S_3 S_1 / S_2^2$, estimated at 2.42 for these data. For example,

$$\hat{F}_{1110} \, \hat{F}_{0010} / \hat{F}_{1010} \, \hat{F}_{0110} = (73.0)(28.0)/(62.0)(13.6) = 2.42,$$

estimates the association (AB), net of C and D, when neither response pattern 1 1 1 1 nor 0 0 0 0 enters the odds ratio (AB). All six partial associations of this type are estimated to be 2.42. In the response-consistency model, there is no such constraint. The partial associations estimated from fitted counts under the response-consistency model range from 2.14 for (BD) to 3.35 for (AD), but this variation is no greater than one can reasonably attribute to chance, according to the test just cited.

In concluding this example we note two potentially serious qualifications of the results supporting the Rasch model. The first is that the dichotomizing of responses may have distorted the data in an unknown manner. The second is that no information is available concerning stability of item parameters across such factors as length of service, overseas service, or military grade. Only if item parameters are essentially invariant with respect to such stratifications of the noncommissioned-officer population could we be confident in the general applicability of the scale.

Multidimensional Structures: First Example

Stouffer and Toby (1951) present data pertaining to four dichotomous items constructed for a study of role conflict. Each response is coded as "universalistic" or "particularistic." (We do not go into the sociological meaning of these concepts or the plausibility of the question content as a measure of them.) The authors summarize results obtained in applying Guttman's scaling procedure and Lazarsfeld's latent-distance model to the four-way cross-classification of their items; the latent-distance results are given in more detail by Lazarsfeld and Henry (1968:142-148). Coleman (1957) studies the data further in a paper on multidimensional scale analysis. Goodman (1974, 1975, 1979) applies modifications of the Guttman and Lazarsfeld models, as well as various other models, to the data. Clogg (1981) uses these data to illustrate latent-class models constrained to have the same parameters in different groups.

The items are best described in the words of the original research report which are reproduced in Figure 12.1. (Note that the last two percentages in Figure 12.1 should be 52 and 71, rather than 51 and 70.) For one-third of the respondents the questions were in the form shown in Figure 12.1. For another third, the stories were rewritten so that the respondent's close friend, rather than the respondent himself or herself, faced the role conflict. The remaining third received a version of the questionnaire in which respondent and friend were replaced by Smith and Smith's friend, Johnson. Stouffer and Toby refer to these versions as forms A, B, and C, but we shall reserve the letters to designate the items and let the forms be called Ego, Friend, and Smith. The forms were interleaved and distributed to respondents at random.

Table 12.2 presents the four-way table pertaining to universalistic (code 1) versus particularistic (code 0) response for respondents completing each of the forms. For the time being, we shall regard the classification by Form simply as a three-category stratification of the total sample of 648 respondents.

Item parameters a, b, c, d pertain to items Car (A), Drama (B), Doctor (C), and Board (D), respectively. We postulate a latent "tendency for some individuals to have a predisposition or a personality bias toward one type of solution and for other individuals to have a predisposition toward another type of solution" (Stouffer and Toby, 1951:395). This variable has the value x_{ij} for the ith individual in the jth stratum. Hence, to state the basic postu-

FIGURE 12.1

Extract from original Stouffer and Toby research report.

Our data are based on a short pencil-and-paper questionnaire completed by 648 undergraduate students at Harvard and Radcliffe in February, 1950. No claim is made for the representativeness of the sample, since almost all were members of a single class, "Social Relations 1A."

Four little stories were presented, as follows:

1

You are riding in a car driven by a close friend, and he hits a pedestrian. You know he was going at least 35 miles an hour in a 20-mile-an-hour speed zone. There are no other witnesses. His lawyer says that if you testify under oath that the speed was only 20 miles an hour, it may save him from serious consequences.

What right has your friend to expect you to protect him?

Check one:
☐ My friend has a definite right as a friend to expect me to testify to the lower figure.
☐ He has some right as a friend to expect me to testify to the lower figure.
☐ He has no right as a friend to expect me to testify to the lower figure.

What do you think you'd probably do in view of the obligations of a sworn witness and the obligation to your friend?

Check one:
☐ Testify that he was going 20 miles an hour.
☐ Not testify that he was going 20 miles an hour.

2

You are a New York drama critic. A close friend of yours has sunk all his savings in a new Broadway play. You really think the play is no good.

What right does your friend have to expect you to go easy on his play in your review?

Check one:
☐ He has a definite right as a friend to expect me to go easy on his play in my review.
☐ He has some right as a friend to expect me to do this for him.
☐ He has no right as a friend to expect me to do this for him.

Would you go easy on his play in your review in view of your obligations to your readers and your obligation to your friend?

Check one:
☐ Yes
☐ No

3

You are a doctor for an insurance company. You examine a close friend who needs more insurance. You find that he is in pretty good shape, but you are doubtful on one or two minor points which are difficult to diagnose.

What right does your friend have to expect you to shade the doubts in his favor?

Check one:
☐ My friend would have a definite right as a friend to expect me to shade the doubts in his favor.
☐ He would have some right as a friend to expect me to shade the doubts in his favor.
☐ He would have no right as a friend to expect me to shade the doubts in his favor.

Would you shade the doubts in his favor in view of your obligations to the insurance company and your obligation to your friend?

Check one:
☐ Yes
☐ No

4

You have just come from a secret meeting of the board of directors of a company. You have a close friend who will be ruined unless he can get out of the market before the board's decision becomes known. You happen to be having dinner at that friend's home this same evening.

What right does your friend have to expect you to tip him off?

Check one:
☐ He has a definite right as a friend to expect me to tip him off.
☐ He has some right as a friend to expect me to tip him off.
☐ He has no right as a friend to expect me to tip him off.

Would you tip him off in view of your obligations to the company and your obligation to your friend?

Check one:
☐ Yes
☐ No

The problem is: Do the answers to these questions indicate the existence of a unidimensional scale, along which respondents can be ordered as to the degree to which they are likely to possess a trait or bias toward the particularistic solution of a dilemma? For simplicity, we label for a given item the response "My friend has a definite right . . ." as particularistic, the response "He has no right . . ." as universalistic. If he marks "He has some right . . ." we label the response particularistic if in the second part of the question he says he would favor the friend in action; universalistic if he says he would not favor the friend.

There was a considerable spread among the four items in the percentage giving particularistic responses:

Item 1 (car accident)............ 26
Item 2 (drama critic)............ 45
Item 3 (insurance doctor)........ 51
Item 4 (board of directors)....... 70

Such frequencies suggest the hypothesis of a distance or cumulative scale.

SOURCE: Stouffer and Toby (1951:396-397).

TABLE 12.2

Cross-Classification of Four Indicators of Universalism, by Form of Question Wording, Harvard-Radcliffe Undergraduates, 1950

Car (A)	Drama (B)	Doctor (C)	Board (D)	t	t'	Ego	Friend	Smith	Parameterization Model H_2
1	1	1	1	4	3	42	37	35	$ac\,T_{13j}$
1	1	1	0	3	2	23	31	17	$ac\,T_{12j}$
1	1	0	1	3	2	6	5	3	$a\,T_{12j}$
1	0	1	1	3	3	6	6	9	$ac\,T_{03j}$
0	1	1	1	3	2	1	2	3	$c\,T_{12j}$
1	1	0	0	2	1	24	29	27	$a\,T_{11j}$
1	0	1	0	2	2	25	15	26	$c\,T_{02j}$
1	0	0	1	2	2	7	6	3	T_{02j}
0	1	1	0	2	1	4	4	5	$c\,T_{11j}$
0	1	0	1	2	1	2	3	0	T_{11j}
0	0	1	1	2	2	1	3	2	$c\,T_{02j}$
1	0	0	0	1	1	38	25	32	$a\,T_{01j}$
0	1	0	0	1	0	9	23	20	T_{10j}
0	0	1	0	1	1	6	4	5	$c\,T_{01j}$
0	0	0	1	1	1	2	3	3	T_{01j}
0	0	0	0	0	0	20	20	26	T_{00j}
Total						216	216	216	

SOURCE: Stouffer and Toby (1951:Table 2).
[a]1 = universalistic response; 0 = particularistic response. See text for wording of questions and coding rules.

late of the Rasch model, the odds on a universalistic response to Car are ax_{ij}, and the odds on universalistic response are bx_{ij}, cx_{ij}, and dx_{ij} for Drama, Doctor, and Board, respectively. These odds correspond to probabilities of universalistic response of $ax_{ij}/(1 + ax_{ij})$, $bx_{ij}/(1 + bx_{ij})$, and so on. Invoking the assumption of local independence—that, conditional on x_{ij}, responses to the four items are stochastically independent—we have the following general formula for the joint probabilities:

$$Pr(h_a h_b h_c h_d | x_{ij}) = a^{h_a}\, b^{h_b}\, c^{h_c}\, d^{h_d}\, x_{ij}^t /\Delta_{ij}$$

in the notation of the preceding section, with

$$\Delta_{ij} = (1 + ax_{ij})\,(1 + bx_{ij})\,(1 + cx_{ij})\,(1 + dx_{ij}).$$

Corresponding to each probability is the expected frequency (F) of each response pattern, under the model, for a sample of size n in which the jth stratum has size n_j and $\sum_j n_j = n$; we have

$$F_{h_a h_b h_c h_d} = a^{h_a} b^{h_b} c^{h_c} d^{h_d} S_{tj} \, ,$$

where

$$S_{tj} = \sum_{i=1}^{n_j} (x_{ij}^t / \Delta_{ij}) \, .$$

This model, which will be called H_1, is just the model of the previous section generalized to apply in the case of two or more strata. Note that item parameters are constant across strata, but each stratum has a unique set of stratum-composition parameters, since it has a unique distribution of x, even if (as in the Stouffer-Toby study) the strata are random samples from the same population. H_1 has four item parameters and five stratum-composition parameters in each stratum, or a total of $4 + 5 \times 3 = 19$ parameters. However, we can only estimate ratios of item parameters, such as a/d, b/d, and c/d, so the count of functionally independent parameters is reduced to 18. There are 3×16 cells in Table 12.2. Hence H_1 has $48 - 18 = 30$ d.f. As before, we fit the model to the data with program FREQ. The fit is unsatisfactory in the light of the statistics $L^2 = 48.24$, $X^2 = 49.41$, d.f. $= 30$, both significant at $p < .02$. Other evidence to be presented shortly likewise leads us to call model H_1 into question for these data.

There are various possibilities to consider when the model fails to hold: (1) The wording changes may have altered the meanings of the questions, so that the assumption that parameters are constant across the Ego, Friend, and Smith strata is faulty. (2) The assumption of local independence may be unacceptable; perhaps respondents deliberately try to make the answers to the questions mutually consistent. (3) The items may be measuring more than one dimension. We next consider the third possibility and then carry out further analysis in the light of our decision concerning it.

In his examination of the Stouffer-Toby data, Coleman (1957) notes that, from the standpoint of Guttman scaling, the Drama item is involved in a relatively large number of nonscale-type responses. Coleman's reading (1957:259) of the content, moreover, "is that Item 2 contains a relatively large component of responsibility to self and a relatively small component of responsibility to a generalized other" by comparison with any of the other three items. How, then, should H_1 be modified if Drama measures a different latent variable—say, y_{ij}—from that measured by Car, Doctor, and Board, which we may call z_{ij}? Our odds on universalistic response are now az_{ij} for Car, by_{ij} for Drama, cz_{ij} for Doctor, and dz_{ij} for Board. (There is no assumption concerning a correlation or lack thereof between y and z.) We have

$$\Delta_{ij} = (1 + az_{ij}) (1 + by_{ij}) (1 + cz_{ij}) (1 + dz_{ij}) ,$$

and the general formula for the probability of a response pattern is

$$Pr(h_a h_b h_c h_d | y_{ij}, z_{ij}) = a^{h_a} b^{h_b} c^{h_c} d^{h_d} y_{ij}^{hb} z_{ij}^{t'} / \Delta_{ij} ,$$

where $t' = h_a + h_c + h_d$ and the other symbols are used in accordance with earlier definitions. We have a new set of stratum parameters, which appear in the parameterization shown in the final column of Table 12.2, defined by

$$T_{h_b \; t'j} = \sum_{i=1}^{n_j} (y_{ij}^{h_b} z_{ij}^{t'} / \Delta_{ij}) .$$

This model is identified as H_2. Looking at the configuration of item parameters and stratum composition parameters, we see that the expected counts

$$F_{h_a h_b h_c h_d} = a^{h_a} b^{h_b} c^{h_c} d^{h_d} T_{h_b t'j}$$

may be used to find ratios of parameters for the three items measuring z, to wit,

$$F_{1110} / F_{0111} = abc T_{12j} / bcd T_{12j} = abc/bcd = a/d$$

and

$$F_{1110} / F_{1101} = c/d.$$

But we cannot obtain b or the ratio b/d (or any other ratio involving b). We may nonetheless fit the log-linear model H_2 using FREQ. The model fits well: $L^2 = 19.36$, $X^2 = 20.46$, d.f. $= 22$. Moreover, H_2 fits significantly better than H_1: $L^2(H_1) - L^2(H_2) = 28.88$, d.f. $= 8$. It is difficult not to be persuaded that Coleman's argument is correct. The FREQ output gives the parameter estimates (with standard errors in parentheses) log $\hat{a}/d = 2.850$ (.188) and log $\hat{c}/d = 1.276$ (.160).

In view of these results we have no difficulty in accepting the Rasch model for the three items, Car, Doctor, and Board. But it is still of interest to investigate more specifically whether Form affects the item parameters. Such effects, if large, would have led to the rejection of H_2, but there remains the possibility of detecting Form effects not significantly registered in $L^2(H_2)$. We work henceforth with Table 12.3, the three-item response pattern by Form. The Rasch model leads to the parameterization given for model H_3 in this table. This parameterization includes the stratum parameters,

$$S_{t'j} = \sum_{i=1}^{n_j} (z_{ij}^{t'} / \Delta_{ij})$$

where

$$\Delta_{ij} = (1 + az_{ij})(1 + cz_{ij})(1 + dz_{ij})$$

and

$$t' = h_a + h_c + h_d$$

and joint probabilities of responses to the three items, given z_{ij}, are calculated in the fashion already illustrated. H_3 fits acceptably well: $L^2 = 11.69$, $X^2 = 12.75$, d.f. = 10, and only one of the adjusted residuals provided by FREQ is as large as 1.96 in absolute value. The last three columns of Table 12.3 show MLEs of expected frequencies under this model. From them we may estimate the ratio a/d as 47.1/2.7, 46.4/2.7, 40.4/2.3, 60.1/3.5, 53.8/3.1, or 56.9/3.3. These ratios differ because of rounding errors, but all of them approximate 17.3, the value obtained when more digits are retained in $\hat{F}$. Similarly, we estimate c/d from 47.1/13.2, 46.4/12.9, etc., and obtain 3.58. These are, of course, the same estimates we obtained under model H_2 for the four-item data.

TABLE 12.3

*Cross-Classification of Three Indicators of Universalism,
by Form of Question Wording*

Item				Parameter-	Count by Form					
				ization,	Observed			MLE of Expected		
Car	Doctor	Board		Model H_3	Ego	Friend	Smith	Ego	Friend	Smith
(A)	(C)	(D)	t'							
1	1	1	3	$ac\ S_{3j}$	48	43	44	48*	43*	44*
1	1	0	2	$ac\ S_{2j}$	48	46	43	47.1	46.4	40.4
1	0	1	2	$a\ S_{2j}$	13	11	6	13.2	12.9	11.3
0	1	1	2	$c\ S_{2j}$	2	5	5	2.7	2.7	2.3
1	0	0	1	$a\ S_{1j}$	62	54	59	60.1	53.8	56.9
0	1	0	1	$c\ S_{1j}$	10	8	10	12.4	11.1	11.8
0	0	1	1	S_{1j}	4	6	3	3.5	3.1	3.3
0	0	0	0	S_{0j}	29	43	46	29*	43*	46*
Total					216	216	216	216	216	216

SOURCE: Table 12.2.
*Count fitted exactly under the model.

For didactic purposes, we consider how H_3 could be modified if there were reason to distrust the conclusion that item parameters are invariant across Form. If we let a and c be the same on all three forms but have d for the third parameter for Ego, d' for Friend, and d'' for Smith, we keep the ratio of a to c constant across forms while the other two ratios vary. This model, H_4, fits well enough—$L^2 = 10.32$, $X^2 = 11.69$, d.f. $= 8$—but does not significantly improve upon H_3 inasmuch as $L^2(H^3) - L^2(H_4) = 1.37$, d.f. $= 2$. If we vary any two parameters across forms, all three ratios of parameters must differ by Form. The model so specified, H_5, is equivalent to treating Ego, Friend, and Smith as three populations each with its unique item parameters. We obtain $L^2 = 9.57$, $X^2 = 10.50$, d.f. $= 6$. The fit is acceptable. We see, however, that H_5 improves upon H_3 only to the extent of $L^2(H_3) - L^2(H_5) = 2.12$, d.f. $= 4$. Even with only 2 d.f., this improvement would not be significant. Hence it is not worthwhile to test separately for Form heterogeneity in a alone or c alone (actually, heterogeneity with respect to the two ratios involving a or the two ratios involving c).

But we have not quite finished with the issue of Form effects. Suppose the replacement of the Ego wording by the Friend wording makes each of the three items less likely to be answered in the universalistic direction. If each item parameter were multiplied by a constant to represent this effect, the comparisons we have made between models could never reveal the shift, because ratios of item parameters are unaffected by it. The effect would, however, be tantamount to an apparent shift of all person parameters by a constant factor. And that apparent shift, in turn, would be registered in a shift of the distribution of t' for one form relative to the other. The shift might not be adequately described, however, by the change in mean of t', inasmuch as t' is not linearly related to z. In the present problem, since assignment to Forms (Ego, Friend, and Smith) was at random, we expect no significant difference by Form in any of the moments of the distribution of t', assuming a common set of item-parameter ratios for all forms, unless Form itself (that is, the wording of the stories) has an effect. To check this possibility we aggregate Rows 2, 3, and 4, and also Rows 5, 6, and 7 of Table 12.3 to produce a 4×3 table, t' by Form. For the overall test of homogeneity of the distributions of t' we find $L^2 = 5.98$, d.f. $= 6$, a result which does not cast doubt on the hypothesis of no Form effect. However, for response pattern 0 0 0 in Ego, we have $f = 29$, $\hat{F} = 39.3$, and a significant adjusted residual, -2.23. With this cell deleted, we obtain $L^2 = 0.78$, d.f. $= 5$, for the hypothesis of quasi independence. There is some slight suggestion, therefore, that Stouffer and Toby (1951:398-399) were on the right track in remarking,

Experience with projective material has taught us to expect considerable differences when we ask, "What do you think about something?" from results if we asked, "What do you think somebody else would think about something?" Especially, when we are seeking by crude question-and-answer procedures to learn something about social norms, it is very important to know what, if any, differences are produced by such shifts imposed on the point of view of the respondents.

We are here using the adjusted residuals provided by FREQ in a heuristic fashion rather than to test prespecified hypotheses. For a more careful statement on interpretation of residuals, see Chapter 11 in this volume.

It will be noted that this result, which is the only evidence we have of a Form effect, pertains to one of the cells that does not enter into the fitting of any of our versions of the Rasch model. The reason that cell was excluded from the earlier calculations is that it pertains to the response pattern 0 0 0, and when all three items are answered in the same direction, the response pattern yields no information pertaining to item parameters or their invariance across groups.

Inasmuch as the Rasch model makes *no* assumption as to the form of the population distribution of the latent trait, the proportion of respondents answering with either of the completely consistent responses tells us nothing about the parameters of that distribution. However, in the present case, by virtue of the random assignment of forms of the questionnaire, we may assume that the three strata are random samples from the same population of z values, *if* Form does not affect the meaning of the items. Hence the relevance of the hypothesis that was just tested, albeit with a somewhat equivocal outcome in view of the scanning of residuals for a significant deviation from the hypothesis.

In concluding this example, we observe that the illustration brings out the clear distinction between (1) model failure due to multidimensionality, (2) Form effects on item parameters, implying that Form alters the meanings of questions, and (3) Form effects on all items alike. The latter can only be detected when the survey is appropriately designed with split ballots assigned at random. But the possibility of making such distinctions at all in a coherent fashion rests on the strong measurement model provided by Rasch.

Multidimensional Structures: Second Example

The Stouffer-Toby data illustrate a simple two-dimensional case in which three items measure one dimension and a fourth item measures a second dimension. We now consider illustrative data for which a plausible model includes one item that measures a composite of two dimensions, each of which is also measured by at least one other item in a set of four. (I avoid the term "multidimensional scale." A scale should measure one dimension. But a data structure may be multidimensional.)

Table 12.4 gives the four-way cross-classification of responses to the following questions from a 1972 Gallup Poll:

10. Please tell me whether you agree or disagree with each of the following statements:

    10A. For most people the use of marijuana is physically harmful.
    10B. For most people the use of marijuana is psychologically or mentally harmful.
    10C. For most people marijuana is physically addictive.
    10D. For most people the use of marijuana leads to the use of other drugs.

Information used to form strata includes the respondent's age at the time of the survey and the cross-classification of the respondent's view on the advisability of legalizing marijuana use by the respondent's experience in using marijuana (see footnotes to Table 12.4). For detailed analysis of these variables see B. Duncan (in press).

The models considered for the data in Table 12.4 are specified in Table 12.5. Like H_1 in the preceding section, M_1 postulates a single dimension measured by all four items. M_2 has two dimensions, one measured by items A and D, the other by B and C. (There are two other models of this type, but neither of them seems to be of interest for these data.) Each of models M_3, M_4, and M_5 has two dimensions, but in each case an ostensible third dimension is involved as a composite of the other two. Models M_6 and M_7 each have three dimensions, but none of the dimensions is composite. We see that if in M_6 we set $z = xy$, the constrained model is equivalent to M_4. Similarly, if in M_6 we set $y = xz$, we obtain M_5. And if in M_6 we set $x = yz$, M_3 is the resulting model. (But the letters x, y, and z in different models are not, in general, intended to denote the same latent traits.)

To illustrate the technique for deriving the parameterization of these models, consider M_5. The odds on positive response for the four items, respectively, are ax_i, bz_i, cx_iz_i, and dx_i. The response probabilities, accordingly, are

Item	Positive	Negative
A	$ax_i/(1 + ax_i)$	$1/(1 + ax_i)$
B	$bz_i/(1 + bz_i)$	$1/(1 + bz_i)$
C	$cx_iz_i/(1 + cx_iz_i)$	$1/(1 + cx_iz_i)$
D	$dx_i/(1 + dx_i)$	$1/(1 + dx_i)$

We obtain joint probabilities by multiplication (in the fashion already illustrated in earlier examples), and the expected frequencies are given by this formula:

$$F_{h_a h_b h_c h_d} = a^{h_a} b^{h_b} c^{h_c} d^{h_d} x_i^t z_i^u S_{tu}$$

where

$$t = h_a + h_c + h_d;$$
$$u = h_b + h_c ;$$

and

$$S_{tu} = \sum_{i=1}^{n} [x_i^t z_i^u / (1 + ax_i) (1 + bz_i) (1 + cx_iz_i) (1 + dx_i)] .$$

If there are two or more strata, latent traits x_{ij} and z_{ij} and stratum parameters S_{tuj} replace x_i z_i, and S_{tu}, respectively, for the jth stratum, and the summation is from $i = 1$ to $i = n_j$ for that stratum.

In carrying out model selection, we will look at pairs of models in which one model implies the other. Working out such implications is a little tricky, but is accomplished with the upper part of Table 12.5, following the rule, $M_g \Rightarrow M_g'$ if M_g' uses all the parameters in M_g (for the same cells) and one or more additional parameters. Applying this rule in regard to M_1 and M_2, for example, we note that six cells use an S_2 in M_1 and the same cells (and no others) in M_2 use an S_3 or else are fitted exactly; S_3 in M_1 is replaced by S_4 and S_5 in M_2 (and no other cells have these parameters); S_1 in M_1 is similarly replaced by S_1 and S_2 in M_2. All the item parameters in M_1 are used in M_2, the fitting of the omitted parameters (a in M_1 and a and b in M_2) being implicit. Inasmuch as the numbering of the sample composition parameters is arbitrary, we disregard discrepancies in subscripts, such as the use of S_3 in M_2 where S_2 is used in M_1. All that matters is that the same combination of cells is fitted in the two models. Inasmuch as this is true for all cells in comparing M_1 with M_2, we conclude that $M_1 \Rightarrow M_2$. Similarly, we find $M_2 \Rightarrow M_6$, $M_2 \Rightarrow M_7$, and each of M_3, M_4, and M_5 implies M_6.

For any model, d.f. can be calculated as number of cells without asterisks, minus number of parameters fitted (disregarding any parameter set equal to unity).

We first consider the Total column of Table 12.4. (Any model rejected for the total sample would not be acceptable on the basis of an analysis across strata, unless one is ready to treat the strata as distinct populations with different parameter values; even then, the model might not fit.) We find that M_1 and M_3 are unacceptable in terms of the chi-square statistics in Table 12.6. M_2 might be deemed acceptable, but a significant improvement in fit is obtained with M_6: $L^2(M_2) - L^2(M_6) = 8.65$, d.f. $= 2$. Yet M_6 itself is not preferred to M_5, for $L^2(M_5) - L^2(M_6) = 1.07$, d.f. $= 1$. A direct

TABLE 12.4

*Joint Distribution of Responses to Four Questions
on Effects of Marijuana, with Cross-Classification
by Birth Cohort and by Opinion on Legalization
by Prior Use of Marijuana, 1972*

Response Pattern[a]	Cohort[b]			Legalize by Use[c]				Total[d]	$\hat{F}(M_5)$
	1	2	3	1	2	3	4		
A B C D	18	90	616	0	13	19	692	724	*
A B C	3	6	7	0	0	0	16	16	16.2
A B D	7	23	40	0	7	9	54	70	71.3
A C D	1	1	9	1	1	0	9	11	*
B C D	3	16	29	0	1	2	44	47	46.8
A B	1	6	14	1	1	3	16	21	18.5
A C	1	1	3	0	0	0	3	3	3.0
A D	0	0	3	0	0	1	2	3	*
B C	0	0	2	1	0	1	0	2	*
B D	7	19	25	4	5	6	37	52	53.3
C D	1	2	7	0	0	0	10	10	8.7
A	2	3	2	3	2	1	1	7	8.0
B	5	21	28	12	5	15	21	53	*
C	0	0	1	0	0	1	0	1	2.3
D	2	11	11	5	1	4	14	24	23.0
- - - -	20	52	35	59	9	27	11	106	*

SOURCE: Unpublished tabulation from American Institute of Public Opinion (The Gallup Poll) Survey 846; data tape obtained from The Roper Center, Storrs, Conn.
[a]Letter entered if corresponding item was answered positively. A—physically harmful, B—psychologically harmful, C—physically addictive, D—leads to other drugs. Omits no opinion and missing data for any item.
[b]1:Age 18–20; 2:Age 21–29; 3:Age 30 and over. Missing data omitted.
[c]1:Yes, have tried, and Yes, legalize; 2:Yes, have tried, and No, not legalize; 3:No, not tried, and Yes, legalize; 4:No, No. Omits no opinion and missing data on either question.
[d]Differs slightly from total for cohorts because of missing data.
*Count fitted exactly under the model.

comparison of M_2 with M_5 is not appropriate, since neither implies the other, but the indirect comparison afforded by the foregoing results favors M_5. Similarly, results of indirect comparisons suggest that M_5 is preferred to M_7. We find that when either the cohort stratification or the stratification on use-by-legalization is employed, both M_5 and M_6 provide a satisfactory fit, but M_5 continues to be preferred on grounds of parsimony, inasmuch as $L^2(M_5) - L^2(M_6)$ is not significant. The fact that model M_5 is sustained in the tests involving stratifications is important. Such tests were not available in the previous examples, so that the acceptance of the preferred model in those cases must be quite provisional. Here, by contrast, we have introduced stratifications based on variables (cohort, use-by-legalization) that re-

TABLE 12.5
Models Fitted to Data in Table 12.4

Response Pattern	M_1	M_2	M_3	M_4	M_5	M_6	M_7
A B C D	*	*	*	*	*	*	*
A B C	$bc\,S_3$	$c\,S_4$	S_4	$b\,S_4$	$c\,S_4$	S_4	*
A B D	$bd\,S_3$	$d\,S_5$	*	*	$d\,S_3$	*	S_4
A C D	$cd\,S_3$	$cd\,S_5$	*	$d\,S_3$	*	*	$c\,S_4$
B C D	$bcd\,S_3$	$cd\,S_4$	$d\,S_4$	$bd\,S_4$	$cd\,S_4$	$d\,S_4$	*
A B	$b\,S_2$	S_3	S_2	$b\,S_3$	S_2	S_2	S_3
A C	$c\,S_2$	$c\,S_3$	S_3	S_2	$c\,S_3$	S_3	$c\,S_3$
A D	$d\,S_2$	*	$ad\,S_4$	*	*	*	*
B C	$bc\,S_2$	*	S_1	*	*	*	*
B D	$bd\,S_2$	$d\,S_3$	$d\,S_2$	$bd\,S_3$	$d\,S_2$	$d\,S_2$	S_2
C D	$cd\,S_2$	$cd\,S_3$	$d\,S_3$	$d\,S_2$	$cd\,S_3$	$d\,S_3$	$c\,S_2$
A	S_1	S_1	$a\,S_1$	S_1	S_1	S_1	*
B	$b\,S_1$	S_2	*	$b\,S_2$	*	*	S_1
C	$c\,S_1$	$c\,S_2$	*	*	$c\,S_2$	*	$c\,S_1$
D	$d\,S_1$	$d\,S_1$	$d\,S_1$	$d\,S_1$	$d\,S_1$	$d\,S_1$	*
- - - -	*	*	*	*	*	*	*

Item	Latent Traits Measured						
A	x	x	yz	x	x	x	x
B	x	y	z	xy	z	z	y
C	x	y	y	y	xz	y	y
D	x	x	yz	x	x	x	w

	Indentified Parameter Ratios[a]						
	b/a	d/a	a/bc	d/a	d/a	d/a	c/b
	c/a	c/b	d/bc	b/ac	c/ab		
	d/a						

[a]Parameters in denominators set to 1.0.
*Cell has a unique sample composition parameter and is fitted exactly under the model.

late substantially to responses concerning beliefs about effects of marijuana. The strata, therefore, must differ considerably in their distributions on the latent traits. Yet the model can be considered invariant across the strata. The importance of this kind of test in connection with Rasch's idea of "sample-free" measurement has been emphasized in a discussion by Andrich (1978c:459), although the test does not seem to have received much attention in most of the psychometric literature on Rasch measurement.

TABLE 12.6
*Statistics for Assessing Fit of Models
to Data in Table 12.4*

Model	d.f.	L^2	X^2
Total column			
M_1	8	26.85	23.04
M_2	5	9.20	7.03
M_3	4	36.38	28.21
M_4	4	6.72	7.43
M_5	4	1.62	1.46
M_6	3	0.55	0.55
M_7	3	8.85	6.71
Across cohorts			
M_5	16	12.68	12.66
M_6	11	9.75	10.10
Across use-by- legalization strata			
M_5	19 (22)[a]	20.83	16.25
M_6	11 (15)[a]	9.54	8.34

[a]Theoretical d.f. in parentheses are reduced to take
account of zeros fitted under the model owing to
sparse data.

The FREQ output for M_5 shows the parameter estimates (SEs in parentheses) $\log \hat{d}/a = 1.058$ (.171) and $\log \hat{c}/ab = -2.101$ (.291). The meaning
of these results may be a little more transparent if we express them in terms
of the so-called item-characteristic curves. Let p_A be the probability of
agreeing that marijuana is physically harmful, and similarly let p_B, p_C, p_D be
the probabilities of agreeing that it is psychologically harmful, that it is
physically addictive, and that it leads to other drugs. Our equations for A
and B merely serve to set the scales:

$$p_A = x/(1 + x) \; ;$$
$$p_B = z/(1 + z) \; .$$

The estimates for the other two items are

$$\hat{p}_D = 2.88\, x/(1 + 2.88\, x) \; ;$$
$$\hat{p}_C = .122\, xz/(1 + .112\, xz) \; .$$

From these equations it follows that when $x = 2.89$, $p_A = .743$, which is the univariate marginal proportion agreeing on A for the entire sample, and when $z = 5.99$, $p_B = .857$, the marginal for B. When $x = 1.56$, $\hat{p}_D = .818$, the marginal for D; and when $xz = 19.83$, $\hat{p}_C = .708$, the marginal for C. We have chosen values for the latent traits that correspond to the univariate marginal proportions merely for sake of illustration. Unfortunately, such illustrative calculations can tell us little about the population distributions of x and z. To estimate any parameters of the distributions would require quite a few more items to measure these latent traits.

Models like M_5 are somewhat suggestive of the models considered in so-called factor analysis of dichotomies. Muthén (1977) gives results of such an analysis for six items pertaining to respondents' approval of various grounds for abortion. He finds that items pertaining to mother's health, chance of a defect in the baby, and pregnancy as a result of rape load on the first factor (termed the "medical" factor), while the rape item, poverty of the family, woman being unmarried, and married woman wanting no more children, load on the second factor (termed the "social" factor). Only the rape item loads on both factors, therefore.

Muthén's model (1978), based on earlier work by Bock and Lieberman (1970) and Christofferson (1975), differs in at least two important ways from the models considered here, as does the model used by Reiser (1981): (1) Muthén postulates the normal ogive rather than the logistic as the form of the item-characteristic curve; (2) he allows items to differ in regard to the slopes as well as the intercepts of their item-characteristic curves. In fact, it is the slopes that assume the role of factor loadings. In the present work, all "factor loadings" (if that term is to be used) are either zero or unity. (The item parameters are not factor loadings nor are they analogous to them.) As in the basic Rasch model, an item either measures the latent trait or it does not (even if it measures something highly correlated with the latent trait). But the present formulation does allow the latent trait measured by an item to be represented as a composite of two or more latent traits. In addition to the differences in the model, the present approach and Muthén's differ considerably in regard to technique of estimation. Detailed comparisons of the two approaches are beyond the scope of this paper. But one thing should be made clear. With complex data there will often be more Rasch-type latent traits than there are Muthén-type factors. I do not believe it is fruitful to argue for either approach in general on the basis of this property of the models alone. It is a substantive question whether a Rasch-type latent trait or a Muthén-type factor is more nearly invariant across time and across populations, or fits more readily into an explanatory theory of attitude change. Up to now (mid-1981) so little use has been made of either approach in serious substantive inquiries that nothing can be said on these important scientific issues.

An Experiment in Survey Design

We consider next an experiment on the effects of order and wording of questions in the vein of the work described in Section 5.1 of Volume 1. In the 1971 survey of the Detroit Area Study, a sequence of questions was presented in reversed order on Forms A and B of the questionnaire (which were assigned at random):

> People have different ideas about how they think American life should be. I am going to read you some statements which represent some of these ideas. In each case please tell me whether you strongly agree, agree, disagree, or strongly disagree. (CARD 10)
>
> How about this one?
>
> A74/B80. Public officials really care about what people like me think. (CARD 10) Do you strongly agree, agree, disagree, or strongly disagree with that?
>
> A75/B79. So many other people vote in elections that it doesn't matter much whether I vote or not.
>
> A76/B78. People like me don't have any say about what the Government does.
>
> A77/B77. Sometimes politics and government seem so complicated that a person like me can't really understand what's going on.
>
> A78/B76. Voting is the only way that people like me can have any say about how the government runs things.
>
> A79/B75. Given enough time and money, almost all of man's important problems can be solved by science.
>
> A80/B74. I don't think public officials care much about what people like me think.

The analysis here is concerned only with questions 74 and 80, which were intended to be wording reversals of the same question. We henceforth denote the positive wording by A74 or B80 and the negative wording by A80R or B74R. A *pro* response is "strongly agree" or "agree" on A74/B80 and "strongly disagree" or "disagree" on A74R/B80R. A *con* response is "strongly disagree" or "disagree" on A74/B80 and "strongly agree" or "agree" on A80R/B74R. Dichotomizing responses in this manner followed upon failure to obtain helpful models with the original four-category format.

Table 12.7 shows the cross-classification of the two "public officials" items by Form for six classes of educational attainment. Later we use the education variable to test the Rasch model. To anticipate the conclusion, we find that the model is rejected by the Form A data though not by the Form B data. But for the time being, for didactic purposes, let us ignore the education classification and use only the two Total rows. We temporarily assume, for sake of illustration only, that the Rasch model applies to the two items on both forms. For clarity, the Total rows are repeated in Table 12.8, which

TABLE 12.7

*Cross-Classification of Responses to Two Questions
on Attitude toward Public Officials, for a Sample
of Respondents in the Detroit Metropolitan Area, 1971,
by Form of Questionnaire and Educational Attainment*

			"Public Officials"			
Form	Years of School Completed	Q. 74: Q. 80:	Pro Pro	Pro Con	Con Pro	Con Con
A	0–7		16	16	4	30
	8		20	10	8	27
	9–11		62	27	30	87
	12		114	25	54	108
	13–15		66	4	28	67
	16 or more		59	4	10	37
	Total		337	86	134	356
B	0–7		17	10	10	34
	8		12	5	14	30
	9–11		52	22	46	81
	12		141	45	41	101
	13–15		58	16	25	51
	16 or more		68	10	10	20
	Total		348	108	146	317

SOURCE: 1971 Detroit Area Study. See Duncan, Schuman, and
Duncan (1973) and Duncan (1975) for information on study design.

also shows the parameterization for the analysis. The parameters pertain to
the following model. For Question (Q.) A74 we state the basic postulate of
the Rasch model, a multiplicative expression for the odds on a *pro* response:

$$Pr(1 \mid x_{i1})/Pr(0 \mid x_{i1}) = c\, x_{i1}$$

where 1 stands for a *pro* response and 0 for a *con* response, x_{i1} is the value
of the latent trait for the ith individual responding to Form A, and c is the
item parameter for A74. For Q. B74R we have

$$Pr(1 \mid x_{i2})/Pr(0 \mid x_{i2}) = k_1 c\, x_{i2}$$

where x_{i2} is the person parameter, or value of the latent trait, for the ith
individual responding to Form B, and $k_1 c$ is the item parameter for B74R.
For Q. B80 we have

$$Pr(1 \mid x_{i2})/Pr(0 \mid x_{i2}) = k_2 c\, x_{i2}$$

and for Q. A80R we have

$$Pr(1 \mid x_{i1})/Pr(0 \mid x_{i1}) = k_1 k_2 k_{12} c \, x_{i1}$$

so that the factorial scheme for item parameters is the following:

	Order	
Wording	**First**	**Last**
Positive	c	$k_2 c$
	(Q. A74)	(Q. B80)
Negative	$k_1 c$	$k_1 k_2 k_{12} c$
	(Q. B74R)	(Q. A80R)

The effect of being asked last rather than first is k_2, the effect of negative rather than positive wording is k_1, and the interaction of the two is k_{12}.

Algebraic manipulation of the odds specified by the model yields explicit expressions for the probabilities of *pro* response; for A74 we obtain

$$Pr(1 \mid x_{i1}) = c \, x_{i1}/(1 + c \, x_{i1})$$

and for A80R,

$$Pr(1 \mid x_{i1}) = k_1 k_2 k_{12} c \, x_{i1}/(1 + k_1 k_2 k_{12} c \, x_{i1}) .$$

Hence, the joint probability of a *pro* response to both A74 and A80R is

$$k_1 k_2 k_{12} c^2 x_{1i}^2 / \Delta_{i1}$$

where

$$\Delta_{i1} = (1 + c \, x_{i1}) (1 + k_1 k_2 k_{12} c \, x_{i1}) .$$

Other joint probabilities are obtained in a similar manner. In the fashion already illustrated in this chapter, we obtain the parameterization shown in Table 12.8, where each expected count is given as a product of item parameters and one of the T's, which are stratum parameters, that is, mixtures of person and item parameters that depend upon the distribution of the latent trait within the stratum.

The number of parameters in Table 12.8 is so large that we have no degrees of freedom: there are 6 stratum parameters and 4 parameters pertaining to items, but only 8 observed frequencies. But if the latter are taken

TABLE 12.8
Q. 74 by Q. 80 by Form, with Parameterization
of the Model Used to Estimate
Order and Wording Effects

Sample counts		A80R	
A74		**Pro**	**Con**
Pro		337	86
Con		134	356

		B80	
B74R		**Pro**	**Con**
Pro		348	108
Con		146	317

Parameterization for expected counts		A80R	
A74		**Pro**	**Con**
Pro		$k_1 k_2 k_{12} c^2 T_{21}$	$c T_{11}$
Con		$k_1 k_2 k_{12} c\, T_{11}$	T_{01}

		B80	
B74R		**Pro**	**Con**
Pro		$k_1 k_2 c^2 T_{22}$	$k_1 c T_{12}$
Con		$k_2 c\, T_{12}$	T_{02}

SOURCE: Table 12.7.

to be estimates of expected frequencies, it is possible to estimate certain combinations of parameters, using only the 2 off-diagonal cells for each form. Thus, 86/134 estimates $c\, T_{11}/k_1 k_2 k_{12} c\, T_{11} = 1/k_1 k_2 k_{12}$ and 108/146 estimates k_1/k_2. If we assume no interaction of order and wording, that is, $k_{12} = 1$, we can solve for the main effects of wording and order:

$$\hat{k}_1 = [(108)(134)/(146)(86)]^{1/2} = 1.07$$

and

$$\hat{k}_2 = [(146)(134)/(108)(86)]^{1/2} = 1.45.$$

The estimated standard error of (natural) log $\hat{k}_1$ or log $\hat{k}_2$ is given (see, for example, Goodman, 1969) by

$$\tfrac{1}{2} \left(\tfrac{1}{108} + \tfrac{1}{146} + \tfrac{1}{134} + \tfrac{1}{86} \right)^{1/2} = .094 \, ,$$

so that log $\hat{k}_1$ is only .76 of its standard error while log $\hat{k}_2$ is 3.97 times as large as its standard error. Only the order effect is significant.

Apart from the applicability of the Rasch model (which we will shortly question) we see that the experimental design is inadequate for detecting interaction of order and wording effects. Suppose, however, that we had an experiment with four forms such that (in addition to Forms A and B) Form C has the positively worded question in both first and last positions and Form D the negatively worded question in both positions. We see that the cross-classification C74 by C80 has expected counts $c\ T_{13}$ and $k_2 c\ T_{13}$ in the *pro-con* and *con-pro* cells, respectively, while the cross-classification D74R by D80R has $k_1 c\ T_{14}$ and $k_1 k_2 k_{12} c\ T_{14}$ in those positions. (We assume that the ordering of the intervening five questions is immaterial and that the repetition of the very same wording does not compromise the assumption that Q. 74 and Q. 80 are answered independently by every respondent.) We can now estimate all the factors k_1, k_2, and k_{12} that appear in the factorial design and still have a degree of freedom to test the applicability of the Rasch model. With just three forms, say A, B, C, we can estimate the three factors and thus test for the order by wording interaction, but there is no test of the underlying Rasch model.

We turn now to the evaluation of that model for these data, making use of the stratification by education in Table 12.7. The setup for each of Forms A and B is the same as the one encountered in the presentation of the Rasch model in Volume 1, Section 6.4. The model implies independence for the 6×2 table, education by columns *pro-con* versus *con-pro*. For Form A we find $L^2 = 31.34$, d.f. = 5, so that the model is decisively rejected. Moreover, for the uniform-association model (Goodman, 1981), which postulates the same association between row and column variables for all pairs of adjacent rows of an ordered row classification, when (as here) there are only two columns, we obtain $L^2 = 4.66$, d.f. = 4, a quite satisfactory fit. From the expected counts under this model we estimate the ratio of the item parameter for A74 to the parameter for A80R as 2.89 for persons with fewer than 8 years of schooling. It decreases by a factor of .547 for each incremental step on the education scale, reaching a low of .142 for college graduates. Clearly these two items, A74 and A80R, are not measuring the same trait in the well-educated and the poorly educated strata. The story is quite different on Form B, where $L^2 = 9.57$, d.f. = 5, $.05 < p < .1$, for the hypothesis of independence in the 6×2 table and $L^2 = 8.55$, d.f. = 4, for the uniform-association model. There is no evidence here of a trend in ratios of item parameters across education groups, for the test of the hypothesis of no trend is given by $L^2 = 9.57 - 8.55 = 1.02$, d.f. $= 1$, $p > .3$.

One can only speculate about the cause of the model's failure on Form A. My speculation is this. The negative wording (A80R or B74R) is the "natural" one, inasmuch as the respondent will have heard many messages in dispraise of public officials, but few in praise of them; thus the negative wording "sounds right" to many respondents. Moreover, Q. 74 in the interview introduces a new response format, one not used hitherto in the first 73 items, namely the four Likert categories, strongly agree, agree, disagree, and strongly disagree. Respondents confronted with both a new task and an "unnatural" wording are simply confused, or some of them are. But by the time Q. 80 is reached, the use of the response categories has been learned, and the "unnatural" wording by itself is not an insuperable challenge. Even if we set aside the Form A data, however, we find that the marginals of B74R by B80 are not homogeneous. The McNemar test for symmetry gives

$$X^2 = (108 - 146)^2/(108 + 146) = 5.69, \text{ d.f. } = 1 \ .$$

The ratio $108/146 = .74$ estimates the ratio of the parameters for items B74R and B80. Conditional on any value of the latent variable (person parameter) the odds on a *pro* response to B74R are only three-fourths as high as the odds on a *pro* response to B80. The two items could be said to measure the same trait, albeit only on Form B, but they are not interchangeable items. Because the Rasch model applies only to the one form, we cannot say whether the cause of the discrepancy is order, wording, or both.

Ordered Polytomous Variables

In the final example we consider the extension of the Rasch model to items with more than two response categories, the order of which is presumed to be given a priori. For concreteness, we focus on the ordered trichotomy, although the same approach can be taken with any number of response categories. Our point of departure is the presentation of the Rasch model for rating scales by Wright and Masters (1982) and Andrich (1978a, 1978b, 1978c). But the notation and development are not the same here as in these sources.

Consider an item with ordered response categories A_0, A_1, and A_2. Our example concerns a question on "interest" in the 1948 election that was used in the Elmira panel study. Respondents were asked "if they had a great deal, some, or no interest in the campaign" (Lipset et al., 1954:1157).

(For other analyses of these data, see Kitt and Gleicher [1950]; Campbell and Clayton [1961].) The Rasch model specifies multiplicative expressions for the ratios of probabilities pertaining to adjacent response categories:

$$Pr(A_1 \mid x_i)/Pr(A_0 \mid x_i) = as_1 x_i$$
$$Pr(A_2 \mid x_i)/Pr(A_1 \mid x_i) = as_2 x_i .$$

Here we have one item parameter, a, pertaining to item A; two category parameters, s_1 and s_2, pertaining to the "steps" separating A_0 from A_1 and A_1 from A_2, respectively; and the person parameter x_i, the value of the latent trait—call it "disposition to pay attention to politics" if you like—for the ith individual. By multiplying the two equations we obtain

$$Pr(A_2 \mid x_i)/Pr(A_0 \mid x_i) = a^2 s_1 s_2 x_i^2$$

and, upon noting that

$$Pr(A_0 \mid x_i) + Pr(A_1 \mid x_i) + Pr(A_2 \mid x_i) = 1$$

we may solve for the three response probabilities:

$$Pr(A_0 \mid x_i) = 1/(1 + as_1 x_i + a^2 s_1 s_2 x_i^2)$$
$$Pr(A_1 \mid x_i) = as_1 x_i/(1 + as_1 x_i + a^2 s_1 s_2 x_i^2)$$
$$Pr(A_2 \mid x_i) = a^2 s_1 s_2 x_i^2/(1 + as_1 x_i + a^2 s_1 s_2 x_i^2) .$$

Now, suppose we have a second item B, with the same response categories as A but relabeled as B_0, B_1, B_2. We assume that s_1, s_2, and x_i are the same as for item A; only the item parameter, b, is different. Hence,

$$Pr(B_0 \mid x_i) = 1/(1 + bs_1 x_i + b^2 s_1 s_2 x_i^2)$$
$$Pr(B_1 \mid x_i) = bs_1 x_i/(1 + bs_1 x_i + b^2 s_1 s_2 x_i^2)$$
$$Pr(B_2 \mid x_i) = b^2 s_1 s_2 x_i^2/(1 + bs_1 x_i + b^2 s_1 s_2 x_i^2) .$$

In our example, Table 12.9, item B is in fact just item A, but asked (of the same respondents) on a different occasion.

Invoking the assumption of local independence, we obtain joint probabilities by multiplying the appropriate univariate probabilities for A and B. For example,

$$Pr(A_0, B_0 \mid x_i) = 1/\Delta_i ,$$

and

$$Pr(A_1, B_2 \mid x_i) = ab^2 s_1^2 s_2 x_i^3 / \Delta_i ,$$

where

$$\Delta_i = (1 + as_1x_i + a^2s_1s_2x_i^2)(1 + bs_1x_i + b^2s_1s_2x_i^2) .$$

Carrying out all nine of these multiplications and, for each of the resulting expressions, summing over i ($1 \leq i \leq n$) yields the formulas for expected frequencies shown in Table 12.10, where the U's are stratum parameters.

TABLE 12.9

Responses to Question on Interest in the Political Campaign in August and October, 1948, by Exposure to Party Propaganda: Elmira Panel Study

Exposure	Interest Level, August	Interest Level in October			Total
		Low	Medium	High	
		Observed Frequencies[b]			
Contacted[a]	Low	30	11	2	43
	Medium	10	30	29	69
	High	6	21	54	81
		46	62	85	193
Not contacted	Low	117	28	13	158
	Medium	48	107	52	207
	High	25	56	111	192
		190	191	176	557
		Fitted Frequencies Under G_1			
Contacted[a]	Low	30 *	9.4	3.8	43.2
	Medium	11.6	28.4	22.3	62.3
	High	5.8	27.7	54 *	87.5
		47.4	65.5	80.1	193.0
Not contacted	Low	117 *	33.9	14.3	165.2
	Medium	42.1	108.6	48.2	198.9
	High	22.1	59.8	111 *	192.9
		181.2	202.3	173.5	557.0

SOURCE: Lipset et al. (1954:Table 11).
[a]Visited by a party worker or received literature in the mail from one of the major parties.
[b]Reconstituted from whole percentages and, therefore, subject to rounding error.
*Cell count fitted exactly under the model.

TABLE 12.10

Parameterization for Expected Counts
under the Rasch Model in the Cross-Classification
of Two Trichotomous Responses with the Same
Ordered Categories, with Stratification by a Third Variable

Stratum	Response to Item A	Response to Item B		
		B_0	B_1	B_2
1	A_0	U_{01}	bs_1U_{11}	$b^2s_1s_2U_{21}$
	A_1	as_1U_{11}	$abs_1^2U_{21}$	$ab^2s_1^2s_2U_{31}$
	A_2	$a^2s_1s_2U_{21}$	$a^2bs_1^2s_2U_{31}$	$a^2b^2s_1^2s_2^2U_{41}$
2	A_0	U_{02}	bs_1U_{12}	$b^2s_1s_2U_{22}$
	A_1	as_1U_{12}	$abs_1^2U_{22}$	$ab^2s_1^2s_2U_{32}$
	A_2	$a^2s_1s_2U_{22}$	$a^2bs_1^2s_2U_{32}$	$a^2b^2s_1^2s_2^2U_{42}$

In this example we have two strata, according to whether respondents did or did not report exposure to party propaganda between the first and second interviews. (Stratum 1 or 2 is indexed by the second subscript of U.) The substantive issue in the research giving rise to Table 12.9 was, of course, whether exposure affects interest in the campaign. We consider that question after discussing properties of the model. For the moment consider a single population, such as the one represented by stratum 1. We note that $F_{10}/F_{01} = as_1U_{11}/bs_1U_{11} = a/b$ so that $a' = a/b$ can be computed from expected counts for this pair of cells. We also note that

$$a' = (F_{20}/F_{02})^{1/2} = F_{21}/F_{12}.$$

These expressions are constructed by choosing pairs of cells having the same stratum parameter. This strategy leads as well to a formula involving $s = s_2/s_1$:

$$F_{20}/F_{11} = (s_2/s_1)(a/b) = sa'$$

from which s may be obtained once a' is computed. There are 9 cells in the table; we must estimate the 5 stratum parameters $U_{01}, \ldots, U_{41}$, the item parameter a', and the category parameter s. Hence, the model has $9 - 5 - 1 - 1 = 2$ d.f. In fitting the model, cells involving U_{01} and U_{41} are fitted exactly, so that they may simply be omitted from the calculation. (The same is true of the middle cell when we are working with only one stratum, but not in models where several strata share item or category parameters.) In the computation it is expedient to replace a with a' and s_2 with s while setting $b = s_1 = 1.0$. We have shown the full parameterization in Table 12.10 to make the conceptual basis of the model explicit; but in applying it we must be satisfied to estimate only the two ratios a' and s. Maximum-likelihood estimates of expected counts and of these parameters and their standard errors are readily obtained with the program FREQ (Haberman, 1979:Appendix).

Inasmuch as the model for one stratum fits the three diagonal cells exactly, but does not fit either the row or the column marginals exactly, it is a stronger model than the familiar model of quasi-symmetry (QSym) for the 3×3 table, a model which does fit the marginals and has but one d.f. (For the 4×4 and larger tables the Rasch model no longer fits all the diagonal cells exactly, so that there are two ways in which it differs from QSym for these tables.) To obtain a parameterization for QSym, replace s_1 and s_2 in the probabilities pertaining to item B with $t_1 = s_1$ and $t_2 = s_2$. This is tantamount to assuming different response categories for the two items—if they are to be regarded as measuring the same latent trait—an awkward assumption if the categories are indeed nominally the same.

In the analysis of Table 12.9, we first consider G_1, the model just described, with the further specification that a' and s are the same in the two strata, although each stratum has its own U-parameters. Expected counts estimated under this model are shown in the lower half of Table 12.9. The fit is acceptable: $L^2(G_1) = 8.14$, d.f. $= 6$. We cannot improve the fit significantly by relaxing the assumption of invariance of parameters across strata. The model, G_2, keeping s the same in stratum 1 and stratum 2 but specifying two distinct item parameters, a'_1 and a'_2, yields $L^2(G_2) = 6.15$, d.f. $= 5$, so that $L^2(G_1) - L^2(G_2) = 1.99$, d.f. $= 1$, not significant. When both parameters, a' and s, differ by stratum, we have G_3, and again an acceptable fit, by $L^2(G_3) = 5.83$, d.f. $= 4$, but not a significantly better fit than that afforded by the original model, for $L^2(G_1) - L^2(G_3) = 2.31$, d.f. $= 2$. We note that G_3 simply treats the two strata as distinct populations, so that we are, in effect, testing the Rasch model within those populations. Hence, we may partition G_3 into $G_{3.1}$ and $G_{3.2}$, pertaining to the first and second strata, respectively. We obtain

$$L^2(G_3) = L^2(G_{3.1}) + L^2(G_{3.2}) = 3.42 + 2.41,$$

with d.f. $= 2 + 2 = 4$; thus the Rasch model is acceptable for each stratum considered separately. But G_1 is preferred to G_3 on grounds of parsimony, and the failure of G_3 to improve significantly upon G_1 is tantamount to a failure to detect an effect of exposure to propaganda. Such an effect would be registered either in a difference between strata in the values of the parameters a' and/or s, or in a failure of the model to hold in stratum 2 while it does obtain in stratum 1. If the model held in neither stratum, we should have to say that factors other than exposure were altering dispositions in such a way that the dispositions measured in October were no longer the same as those measured in August. Under G_1 we do have a shift in response distribution between August and October (in both strata) but we do not infer any change in the latent trait or disposition postulated by the Rasch model. The shift is entirely due to the item parameter a', which, we recall, measures the level of interest in August relative to the level in October. From the fitted counts in Table 12.9, we estimate a' as $59.8/48.2$ $= 1.241$ (agreeing, within errors of rounding, with calculations from other relevant pairs of cells). Or, in the FREQ output we find $\log a'$ estimated as 0.216, with standard error $.097$. The August response is, therefore, shifted upward (toward "high" interest) by comparison with the October response. In 1948, it would appear, presidential politics was less interesting in October than in August. That may, of course, have been an idiosyncratic feature of a presidential campaign in which most experts other than the incumbent himself were conceding victory to the challenger. But the point here is that we need not assume any change in the electorate's underlying distribution of dispositions to take an interest in politics. The change can, on the evidence presented, be attributed entirely to the political milieu (possibly including any change in the context of the question itself in the October interview, compared to the August interview). We cannot entirely rule out a change in dispositions, of course. But if much change in their distribution were occurring, we should not expect it to involve all respondents equally. With significant differential change, the fit of the data to the Rasch model would be impaired.

To comment on the other parameter, we estimate s as

$$(\hat{F}_{20}/\hat{F}_{11})/\hat{a}' = (22.1)(108.6)/1.241 = 0.164 ,$$

in agreement with the FREQ output, which shows $\log \hat{s} = -1.808$ (standard error $= .172$). We defined s as the ratio s_2/s_1, or the ratio of the size of the second step to the size of the first. With $\hat{s} = .164$, we infer that the distance from "medium" to "high" is only one-sixth (more or less, with due allowance for sampling error) of the distance from "low" to "medium" interest. That is, the increase in disposition to take an interest in political campaigns required to shift response from "medium" to "high" is much less than that required to shift response from "low" to "medium." Whether this spacing of the three adjectives is peculiar to the subject matter studied here or generalizes to other content would be an appropriate question for further research. For a different approach to the scaling of the response categories of polytomies, see Clogg (Chapter 11) in this volume.

Discussion

Over a third of a century ago, McNemar (1946) concluded his lengthy and largely negative review of "Opinion-Attitude Methodology" by holding out some hope that "progress in developing a science of attitudes and opinions" might yet be made, assuming "the success with which attitude and opinion variables are measured." He

> . . . stressed the basic need for reliability, validity, and uni-dimensionality for the instruments or devices used to classify or measure individuals with respect to their opinions or attitudes. Attitude scales can be so constructed as to attain satisfactory reliability. Unitary scales can be developed by the Guttman scaling technique. . . . [The] judicious use of factor analysis might help to bring some order out of chaos in certain areas, particularly that of morale and of liberalism-conservatism. [1946:367-368]

In the light of actual experience with scaling and factor analysis, one would be incautious in venturing another optimistic forecast based on the presumption that the right way to develop "unitary scales" is at last at hand. This chapter and its companion in Volume 1 (Section 6.4) make no promises except that it will be difficult to get out of our present "chaos in certain areas" with or without the aid of Rasch's ideas about measurement.

Without a rigorous model of measurement the difficulties will be the familiar ones: our inability to explain divergent behavior of ostensibly similar or related items, our lack of coherent understanding of response inconsistency, and our helplessness in the face of allegations that questions are "biased" or "mean different things to different people." With the measurement model, the difficulties will be in constructing items that really do measure the same thing, in deciding what and how many dimensions there are to multifaceted social issues or psychological states, and in designing survey questionnaires that are practical to administer—difficulties not created, but brought into focus, by the model. Whatever we have learned about how to construct unidimensional instruments in terms of the art of defining content themes, criticizing items, and interpreting scale values (see, for example, the text on scaling by Gorden [1977]) will not soon be rendered obsolete. Rather, we may hope to mobilize our wisdom more effectively. A measurement model is neither a substantive theory nor a substitute for one. It will be helpful in obtaining scientifically useful results only if it is applied to a problem the theory of which is correctly understood (Stinchcombe, 1972). The Rasch model defines a new level of aspiration and sets a new challenge for social measurement; it does not revoke the criteria scientists normally cite in deciding whether the right variables have been measured.

It follows that the case for the model does not stand or fall with success or failure in applying it in a particular substantive area. Whether it provides a constructive approach to the testing of ability and intellectual achievement (compare Goldstein, 1979, with Wright, 1977) is not at issue in assessing its worth for attitude measurement in the survey setting. Demonstrating its utility in that setting will require not only the completion of much more ambitious statistical exercises than those reported in this chapter. It will also require careful arguments establishing the relevance of such exercises to substantively significant problems. That is not going to be accomplished in a paragraph; so if I say more, I risk weakening my case. Yet I cannot forbear remarking how the Rasch measurement model reminds me of the earliest coherent formulation of the very concept of social attitude.

As Rokeach (1968:449) observes, "The sociological study of the Polish peasant by Thomas and Znaniecki (1918) is generally credited with being the first to propose that the study of social attitudes is the central task of social psychology, and it was the first to give systematic priority to this concept." In the famous "Methodological Note" to *The Polish Peasant in Europe and America*, Thomas and Znaniecki present their concept in the following language:

> By a social value we understand any datum having an empirical content accessible to the members of some group and a meaning with regard to which it is or may be an object of activity. . . . By attitude we understand a process of individual consciousness which determines real or possible activity of the individual in the social world. . . . The attitude is thus the individual counterpart of the social value; activity, in whatever form, is the bond between them. . . . An attitude may be treated as a social phenomenon as opposed to the "state of consciousness" of individual psychology; but it is individual, even if common to all members of a group, when we oppose it to a value. [1918:Vol 1:21, 22, 24]

The reader for whom this statement is opaque need not despair. I plan no exegesis of the quoted text nor am I interested in reviving a formulation later modified by its authors (Znaniecki, 1939; 1952). I only wish, by allusion to historically important work, to emphasize that the distinction between individual attitudes and the social objects they pertain to is crucial to a scientifically productive inquiry into attitude variation and change. Not that anyone would deny such an apparently banal declaration—but our general practice has *not* been to keep the two distinct aspects of subjective phenomena distinct. In all honesty, we have not known how. How, indeed, does the investigator separately measure the attitude and the "value" (social object) the better to understand the linkage between them and the ways in which they jointly produce individual and collective action? How to do it efficiently and predictably is something we have yet to learn. But a proper beginning is to be clear about what it is we want to do. At least for purposes of quantitative analysis, the goal is defined for us in the criterion called "specific objectivity" by Georg Rasch (1966:104-105), according to which "the comparison of any two subjects can be carried out in such a way that no other parameters are involved—neither the parameter of any other subject nor any of the stimulus parameters. Similarly, any two stimuli can be compared independently of all other parameters than those of the two stimuli."

We must be clear that Rasch does not pretend to supply the most general model one might want for the study of response structures—one flexible enough to accommodate the patterns that psychometricians have referred to as item-discriminating power, person sensitivity, guessing effects, and the like. Most data sets that readily come to hand, whether they originate in testing enterprises or in surveys, will exhibit complications of the kind suggested by these concepts (Reiser, 1981) and will, therefore, be too "messy" for the Rasch model to fit well. As long as we are content merely to find models sufficiently flexible to fit available data acceptably well, only by happenstance will we achieve what can be termed "measurement" in any reasonably rigorous sense of the term—the sense used by McNemar (1946), for example. Nor will we know whether Rasch measurement can be carried out in a deliberate way in surveys until we try very hard to do it.

That the effort is worth making is suggested by the hope Rasch's approach holds out for achieving "measurement" in the face of the complexities of human response—complexities recognized, to be sure, in other kinds of latent-trait models as well. Response is a probabilistic phenomenon, as is apparent from the wholesale occurrence of ostensibly inconsistent answers to different questions and from the fact that "dispositions" (including attitudes) are "weak predictors of behavior or events" (Rosenberg, 1979:248). Nevertheless, as the example from the Elmira panel study suggests, under favorable conditions we may actually be able to tell the difference between changes in dispositions and changes in the social entity (the election campaign, in that example) to which dispositions relate, thereby achieving the separation of measures of the two things that only Rasch's approach provides. If Rosenberg (1979:248) is correct, "that dispositions still remain the fundamental subject matter of social psychological research," we shall badly need the stern criterion formulated by Rasch.

References

Andersen, E.B. (1980) *Discrete Statistical Models with Social Science Applications.* Amsterdam: North-Holland.

Andrich, D. (1978a) Application of a psychometric rating model to ordered categories which are scored with successive integers. *Applied Psychological Measurement* 2:581-594.

Rasch Measurement: Further Examples

Andrich, D. (1978b) A rating formulation for ordered response categories. *Psychometrika* 43:561-573.

Andrich, D. (1978c) Relationships between the Thurstone and Rasch approaches to item scaling. *Applied Psychological Measurement* 2:449-460.

Andrich, D. (1978d) Scaling attitude items constructed and scored in the Likert tradition. *Educational and Psychological Measurement* 38:665-680.

Bock, R.D., and Lieberman, M. (1970) Fitting a response model for n dichotomously scored items. *Psychometrika* 35:179-197.

Campbell, D.T., and Clayton, K.N. (1961) Avoiding regression effects in panel studies of communication impact. *Studies in Public Communication* 3:99-118.

Christofferson, A. (1975) Factor analysis of dichotomized variables. *Psychometrika* 40:5-32.

Clogg, C.C. (1981) Latent class analysis across groups. Unpublished ms. Population Issues Research Office, Pennsylvania State University, University Park.

Coleman, J.S. (1957) Multidimensional scale analysis. *American Journal of Sociology* 63:253-263.

Duncan, B. (in press) Legalization of marijuana and year of birth: public opinion 1969 to 1980. In L. Brill and C. Winick, eds., *Yearbook of Substance Use and Abuse*, Vol. 3. New York: Human Sciences Press.

Duncan, O.D. (1975) Measuring social change via replication of surveys. In K.C. Land and S. Spilerman, eds., *Social Indicator Models*. New York: Russell Sage Foundation.

Duncan, O.D. (1979) Indicators of sex typing: traditional and egalitarian, situational and ideological responses. *American Journal of Sociology* 85:251-260.

Duncan, O.D., Schuman, H., and Duncan, B. (1973) *Social Change in a Metropolitan Community*. New York: Russell Sage Foundation.

Fienberg, S.E. (1980) *The Analysis of Cross-Classified Categorical Data*. 2nd ed. Cambridge, Mass.: MIT Press.

Goldstein, H. (1979) Consequences of using the Rasch model for educational assessment. *British Educational Research Journal* 5:211-220.

Goodman, L.A. (1969) How to ransack social mobility tables and other kinds of cross-classification tables. *American Journal of Sociology* 75:1-40.

Goodman, L.A. (1974) Exploratory latent structure analysis using both identifiable and unidentifiable models. *Biometrika* 61:215-230.

Goodman, L.A. (1975) A new model for scaling response patterns: an application of the quasi-independence concept. *Journal of the American Statistical Association* 70:755-768.

Goodman, L.A. (1978) *Analyzing Qualitative/Categorical Data*. Cambridge, Mass.: Abt Books.

Goodman, L.A. (1979) The analysis of qualitative variables using more parsimonious quasi-independence models, scaling models, and latent structures. In R.K. Merton, J.S. Coleman, and P.H. Rossi, eds., *Qualitative and Quantitative Social Research: Papers in Honor of Paul F. Lazarsfeld*. New York: Free Press.

Goodman, L.A. (1981) Three elementary views of log linear models for the analysis of cross-classifications having ordered categories. In S. Leinhardt, ed., *Sociological Methodology 1981*. San Francisco: Jossey-Bass.

Gorden, R.L. (1977) *Unidimensional Scaling of Social Variables*. New York: Free Press.

Haberman, S.J. (1978) *Analysis of Qualitative Data.* Vol 1: *Introductory Topics.* New York: Academic Press.

Haberman, S.J. (1979) *Analysis of Qualitative Data.* Vol 2: *New Developments.* New York: Academic Press.

Kitt, A.S., and Gleicher, D.B. (1950) Determinants of voting behavior. *Public Opinion Quarterly* 14:393-412.

Lazarsfeld, P.F., and Henry, N.W. (1968) *Latent Structure Analysis.* Boston: Houghton Mifflin.

Lipset, S.M., Lazarsfeld, P.F., Barton, A.H., and Linz, J. (1954) The psychology of voting: an analysis of political behavior. Ch. 30 in G. Lindzey, ed., *Handbook of Social Psychology,* Vol. II. Cambridge: Addison-Wesley.

Lumsden, J. (1976) Test theory. *Annual Review of Psychology* 27:251-280.

McNemar, Q. (1946) Opinion-attitude methodology. *Psychological Bulletin* 43:289-374.

Muthén, B. (1977) Statistical Methodology for Structural Equation Models Involving Latent Variables with Dichotomous Indicators. Ph.D. Dissertation, Uppsala University, Sweden.

Muthén, B. (1978) Contributions to factor analysis of dichotomous variables. *Psychometrika* 43:551-560.

Rasch, G. (1960/1980) *Probabilistic Models for Some Intelligence and Attainment Tests.* Copenhagen: Danmarks Paedogogiske Institut, 1960 (2nd ed., Chicago: University of Chicago Press, 1980).

Rasch, G. (1966) An individualistic approach to item analysis. In P.F. Lazarsfeld and N.W. Henry, eds., *Readings in Mathematical Social Science.* Chicago: Science Research Associates (Cambridge, Mass.: MIT Press, 1968).

Reiser, M. (1981) Latent trait modeling of attitude items. In G.W. Bohrnstedt and E.F. Borgatta, eds., *Social Measurement: Current Issues.* Beverly Hills, Calif.: Sage Publications.

Rokeach, M. (1968) The nature of attitudes. *International Encyclopedia of the Social Sciences* 1:449-458. New York: Macmillan.

Rosenberg, M. (1979) Disposition concepts in behavioral science. In R.K. Merton, J.S. Coleman, and P.H. Rossi, eds., *Qualitative and Quantitative Social Research: Papers in Honor of Paul F. Lazarsfeld.* New York: Free Press.

Stinchcombe, A.L. (1972) Theoretical domains and measurement: parts I and II. *Acta Sociologica* 16:3-12, 79-97.

Stouffer, S.A., Guttman, L., Suchman, E.A., Lazarsfeld, P.F., Star, S.A., and Clausen, J.A. (1950) *Measurement and Prediction.* Princeton, N.J.: Princeton University Press.

Stouffer, S.A., and Toby, J. (1951) Role conflict and personality. *American Journal of Sociology* 56:395-406.

Thomas, W.I., and Znaniecki, F. (1918) *The Polish Peasant in Europe and America.* Boston: Richard G. Badger. (2 volumes)

Tjur, T. (1982) A connection between Rasch's item analysis model and a multiplicative Poisson model, *Scandinavian Journal of Statistics* 9:23-30.

Weiss, D.J., and Davison, M.L. (1981) Test theory and methods. *Annual Review of Psychology* 32:629-658.

Wright, B.D. (1977) Solving measurement problems with the Rasch model. *Journal of Educational Measurement* 14:97-116.

Wright, B.D., and Masters, G.N. (1982) *Rating Scale Analysis: Rasch Measurement*. Chicago: MESA Press.

Znaniecki, F. (1939) Comment. In H. Blumer, *An Appraisal of Thomas and Znaniecki's The Polish Peasant in Europe and America*. Bulletin 44. New York: Social Science Research Council.

Znaniecki, F. (1952) *Cultural Sciences*. Urbana: University of Illinois Press.

Acknowledgments

This research was supported in part by National Science Foundation grant SOC77–27365. Robert P. Abelson, David Andrich, Clifford C. Clogg, Beverly Duncan, Leo A. Goodman, Ingeborg Heinrich, William Kruskal, Mark Reiser, Arthur L. Stinchcombe, and Benjamin D. Wright provided valuable suggestions. Charles Brody assisted with computations.

13

Measurement Error in Surveys

Judith T. Lessler

Introduction

This chapter summarizes the results of a taxonomy project established, in part, to review the literature on the terminology and methods used in dealing with errors in survey measurements. The project was entitled, *A Taxonomy of Survey Errors*[1] (Lessler, Kalsbeek, and Folsom, 1981), and focuses on four separate types of errors that can occur in surveys. The division into four categories of error corresponds to the four basic components of a survey:

1. Definition of a target population and construction of some means for identifying and accessing this population;
2. Specification of a sample design and selection of a sample;
3. Solicitation of a response from each member of sample; and
4. Measurement of the values for characteristics of interest in the survey.

If we define the total error of a survey statistic as the difference between its actual value for the full target population and the value estimated from the survey, then each of the preceding four components contributes to this total error. In the taxonomy project, these errors were referred to, respectively, as errors associated with the frame, sampling errors, errors due to nonresponse, and measurement errors.

Most of the treatment of survey errors in the literature has been in the context of a linear-models approach, which attempts to assess the contribution of various components of the survey design to the difference between the estimated population value and the actual value. Other candidates for error functions such as ratios, correlations, etc. have received less attention in the survey research literature. Likewise, this chapter is largely confined to the examination of linear-error models. Also note that, in this context, survey error is not entirely due to mistakes in the survey process. An obvious example of this is sampling error that arises from a deliberate decision to confine the survey to only a sample of the target population. In the same way, frame errors may result from a deliberate decision to use a readily available frame that covers only a portion of the target population because the expense and time required to construct a complete frame are not justified by the amount of error reduction that could be achieved with it.

Lessler, Kalsbeek, and Folsom (1981) present an extensive review of the literature of each of the four types of survey error (frame, sampling, nonresponse, and measurement). Summarizing the material on measurement errors in surveys, we will consider five topics: (1) the general nature of survey measurement, (2) the terminology used, (3) the mathematical models that have been developed for studying error in survey measurements, (4) the methods for quantifying these errors, and (5) the procedures that can be used in the survey to eliminate or reduce the effect of measurement errors. The appropriateness of these methods for surveys of subjective phenomena is indicated.

DEFINITION OF SURVEY MEASUREMENT

A survey is an attempt to gather information about a finite collection of objects. Dalenius (1974:63) gives an explicit definition of survey measurement, stating that it is a special case of scientific measurement in which

> [T]here exists a set $\{O\}$ of N objects and a set $\{Y\}$ of numbers; as a special case, $\{Y\}$ denotes the real numbers. Each object is assigned one and only one number; and two or more objects may be assigned the same number.

The meaning that can be attributed to the assigned numbers is generally recognized to vary with the level of measurement, with at least four levels being distinguished: nominal, ordinal, interval, and ratio (Lord and Novick 1968). The first two measurement levels are often referred to as categorical measurements; the latter two, as numeric or metric measurements.

The ability to define a measurement for the survey variables depends upon the nature of the variable. At least three different cases can be distinguished.

Case 1: The characteristic to be measured has a clear operational definition, and the measurement method adopted for the survey is that indicated by the operational definition. A characteristic is defined operationally if the definition of the characteristic defines or identifies the process to be carried out in obtaining values for that characteristic. For example, suppose one wishes to measure the length in inches of the elements of a population of line segments. The definition of the characteristic "length in inches" clearly indicates the process that one would go through to obtain the measurements. The measurement of the height and weight of school children in a survey would be covered by this case.

Case 2: In this case the characteristic to be measured can be operationally defined, but the process that one must go through to obtain the values is so difficult, cumbersome, or expensive that it is practically impossible to carry out in the context of a survey. In such a case, we devise a measurement process that is believed to give results close to those that could be obtained using the operational definition. An example would be asking children to report on their height and weight in a survey.

Case 3: In this case the characteristic to be measured has no clear operational definition. This case encompasses subjective phenomena such as attitudes, beliefs, and opinions. These are directly observable only by the subjects who possess these characteristics. Case 3 also covers certain qualities such as intelligence, kindness, and so on, that aim to describe complexes of behaviors and emotions. Operationally defined surrogate measures are used.

The foregoing classification is a simplification. The degree to which characteristics can be operationally defined varies along a continuum, and our willingness to accept a particular operational definition will depend upon the purposes of the survey. For example, consider measuring the weight of people. If we are interested in a general description of the distribution of weight among the adult population, attempting to control for whether or not the person drank a glass of water before weighing may be immaterial. However, if we are studying a group of infants in which weight gain is to be used to assess the general heartiness of the child or the success of some treatment program, whether or not the child drank an 8-ounce bottle of milk immediately prior to weighing could be an important consideration. Thus, whether or not a particular definition for a survey variable results in it being classified in Case 1, 2, or 3 depends upon the goals of the survey.

Each case requires different information to describe the errors that may be present in the survey measurements. In Case 1, where an operational definition is being carried out, we need only consider the reliability or precision of the measurement process. A completely reliable measurement method would be one that always gave the same result for repeated measurements on the same population element. A completely reliable measurement would be, by definition, the true value for that element. Thus, methods for assessing measurement error for Case 1 need only be concerned with how often the same answer for a specific element is arrived at.

In Case 2, we must consider both the validity of the measurement process and its reliability. An operational definition exists and is the criterion value that may be used to determine the validity of the survey measurement method. Thus, in Case 2 we generally are concerned with both the variability in measurements and net discrepancies between the average measurement and the true value.

In Case 3, the researcher is still concerned with the reliability and validity of the survey measurements. However, the researcher is severely hampered in assessing the validity because no generally agreed upon criterion values have been defined. So it is for subjective phenomena, which are, as the proposal for the study of survey measurement of subjective phenomena stated, "immune to third party verification."

Despite this immunity, requirements are placed upon the measurement of the Case-3-type characteristic. Namely, for subjective phenomena we would require that the measurement of the person's internal state be consistent with certain observable phenomena implied by the broader definition of the characteristic. For example, most of us would require that a "will-to-live" scale not assign very high values to persons who commit suicide soon after being interviewed. In addition, we require that measurements on one subjective characteristic be distinguishable from those for another, so that measurements of will to live are not perfectly correlated with, for example, happiness.

There is a rather vast literature in the social sciences on techniques that attempt to quantify how well a particular measurement process meets these two requirements. These methods include factor-analytic approaches for developing the measures, and statistical methods for assessing the validity, reliability, and invalidity of the resultant factor measurements (Heise and Bohrnstedt, 1970). Other methods include the multitrait-multimethod procedures developed by Campbell and Fiske (1959) and structural-equation models (Andrews and Crandall, 1976). They were beyond the scope of this author's taxonomy project, and are not included here.

The succeeding sections of this chapter deal with procedures that survey statisticians have developed for studying the effect of measurement error in Case 1 and Case 2. Advantages and difficulties in using these methods to study errors in measurements of subjective phenomena are indicated.

Measurement Error

Survey data are collected in a variety of ways, and the type of data collection determines the sources and the types of errors of measurement. Various researchers have attempted to formalize this idea, usually in the context of their attempt to define a measurement error.

Two approaches are used to define measurement error in a survey. One approach considers true values to exist independently of survey conditions; the other defines true values only in relation to survey conditions.

As an example of independently existing true values, consider a series of definitions given by Hansen et al. (1951). This article and its revision in the book by Hansen, Hurwitz, and Madow (1953) has had a strong and pervasive influence on all subsequent work by survey statisticians in the area of measurement/measurement error. Hansen et al. (1951:149) state that

> . . . the individual true value will be conceived of as a characteristic of the individual quite independent of the survey conditions . . . three criteria for definition of "true value" are (the first two essential, the third, useful but not essential):
>
> (1) The true value must be uniquely defined.
> (2) The true value must be defined in such a manner that the purposes of the survey are met. For example, a study of school children's intelligence would ordinarily not define the true value as a score assigned by the child's teacher on a given date although this might be perfectly satisfactory for some studies (if, for example, our purpose was to study intelligence as measured by teachers ratings).
> (3) Where it is possible to do so consistently with the first two criteria, the true value should be defined in terms of operations which can actually be carried through (even though these operations might be difficult or expensive to perform).

Hansen et al. (1951:153) describe an entity they call "essential survey conditions," which determine the errors in the measurement (responses); the essential survey conditions include the explicitly defined methods and the "conditions of a survey which arise implicitly as a necessary consequence of the explicitly specified conditions." Essential conditions also encompass the type of interviewer, quality of supervision, weather conditions, and time of year. Hansen et al. (1951:152) define the individual response (or measurement) error as:

> [*Individual response error.*] The difference between an individual observation and the true value for the individual.

They then introduce the idea of response variability in which they state that we could "consider interviewing each individual a large number of times under exactly the same [essential] conditions of the survey . . . to yield a population of responses for each individual" [p. 152].

They define the individual response bias as:

[*Individual response bias.*] The expected value of the response error for a particular individual. There will be a random component of variation around that expected value. The essential survey conditions determine both the expected value and the random component of variation. [pp. 152, 154]

Sukhatme and Sukhatme (1970:381) give a similar definition, defining

[*Observational or response error.*] The discrepancy between the survey value and the corresponding true value.

It may be preferable to use the word "discrepancy," as Sukhatme and Sukhatme do, rather than to use the word "difference," because in some cases using the mathematical difference to describe the degree of the discrepancy does not make sense. Such would be the case for categorical variables where the numbers assigned the categories are arbitrary. Ordinal variables also exhibit this difficulty.

Zarkovich, in his 1966 book on the quality of statistical data, takes the second approach to defining measurement error and does not allow the true value to be independent of the survey or measurement conditions. Zarkovich speaks of the adopted system of work described as:

[*Adopted system of work.*] The adopted system of work is composed of such factors as concepts and definitions, methods of collecting data, the units to be used in expressing the response, the tabulation program, the survey program, the wording of questions. . . . [1966:1]

Thus, the adopted system of work represents a complex system of concepts, definitions, procedures, and operations that constitute the survey. The true value is then defined as "the result that would be obtained in a particular survey if the adopted system of work is carried out correctly. It is an ideal result . . . obtained if the work is done in absolute conformity with the adopted system of work" (Zarkovich 1966:1).

Zarkovich then defines error as:

[*Error.*] The difference between the survey value or the results factually achieved and the corresponding true value, i.e., the value that would have been achieved if the adopted system of work had been carried out correctly. The bias is then defined as the net effect on population parameters of these individual errors. [1966:2, 3]

A similar approach is used by Deming (1960), who speaks of a "preferred survey technique" and the bias in the working technique that is actually adopted for the survey. Thus both Deming and Zarkovich distinguish two

410

sets of measurements—the preferred and the achieved. Measurement errors are present when these are not the same.

A later paper by Hansen, Hurwitz, and Pritzker (1967:50) distinguishes three sets of measurements:

1. The ideal goals are the set of statistics that would be produced if all the survey requirements had been precisely defined and rigorously met.
2. The defined goals are a more operationally feasible set of statistics that could be achieved if the actual specifications of the survey are carried out precisely and rigorously.
3. The expected values of the survey operations are a set of statistics which would be conceived of as the expected value of a set of survey statistics Y over a large number of independent replicates of the survey, all conducted under the same essential conditions.

They propose that the total mean square error of a survey estimate be decomposed into sampling and nonsampling variance components, a bias component due to the difference between the defined goals and the actual results, a relevance component that arises because of the difference between the defined goals and the ideal goals, and the interaction between the bias and relevance components.

Basically, some researchers—for example, Deming and Zarkovich—argue that survey statisticians should not be concerned with differences between the ideal and defined goals, even though these may be of great importance. Such differences are considered the purview of subject-matter specialists. Thus, in the context of the characteristics of Cases 1, 2, and 3 previously described, survey statisticians would confine their interest to Case 1 and Case 2 where agreed-upon operational definitions were available.

Others recognize the need to integrate the two activities (those of subject-matter specialists and survey statisticians) and have taken first steps toward doing so. Such an integration was called for by Hansen, Hurwitz, and Pritzker in 1967. The present study on surveys of subjective phenomena is a step toward integration.

Assessing the Extent of Errors of Measurement and Their Impact on Survey Estimates

There are many causes of measurement error. Questions may be designed poorly; respondents may not be able to recall the information requested;

respondents may not answer truthfully in an effort to save face; interviewers can make errors in asking questions and recording answers; interviewers' own expectations and biases may influence their interpretation and coding of respondents' answers; coders, keyers, and other data handlers may make errors. The list of error sources is almost endless.

Models for the effect of measurement error attempt to focus on either the most salient of the error sources or on those for which some opportunity exists for estimating the impact of the source. The measurement-error model is the means by which the researcher's recognition of a particular source of error as having a potential impact on the survey results is translated into components of the total error of survey estimates; it is a key to being able to assess the impact of an error source. The usefulness of a particular model depends upon on how well it reflects the process by which the various sources of error affect the results, and the degree to which the model provides information that facilitates modification of the survey method so as to control the error.

Models for the effect of measurement error on survey statistics are generally expressed as linear models that partition the effects of error sources on the total error by defining a series of bias, variance, and covariance components. They may be expressed either at the element level or the aggregate level. Kish (1965) presents such a general model. At the element level Kish gives:

$$y_i = Y_i + \sum_r B_r + \sum_r V_{ir}$$

where y_i = the measurement for the ith element; Y_i = the true value for the ith element; B_r = the constant bias due to the rth source of error; V_{ir} = the variable error of measurement for the ith element from the rth source.

At the population level, the mean square error of a sample estimate of the mean is expressed as

$$E(\bar{y} - \bar{Y}_{\text{TRUE}})^2 = (\sum_r B_r)^2 + \sum_r S_r^2/m_r = \text{MSE}(\bar{y}) .$$

The model can be adjusted to accommodate covariances that may exist, such as sampling covariances due to clustering, covariances between errors of measurements of a single characteristic, covariances between the measurements for several characteristics, and covariances between the true values and the measurement errors. This model is sufficiently general to accommodate most of the models that follow. To be useful in an actual survey, it must be made more specific. The following sections describe several types of models that have been used in the survey research literature. We first focus on models that consider only fixed bias, and then examine methods aimed at assessing the impact of measurement variability.

Measurement Error

General Procedures. The simplest models for the effect of measurement errors on survey estimates are those that consider fixed biases in either the individual measurements or in the estimates for the aggregate. Thus, the potential for variation in the measurement for a particular element of the population is ignored. In most cases this may be considered a simplifying assumption so that the procedures that follow can also be applied to measurements that exhibit variability. Specifically, for some fixed element of a finite target population, let Y_i = the measurement obtained for the ith target element, and X_i = the true (or preferred value) for the ith element. Then B_i, which is variously called the individual biases or element biases, is defined as $B_i = Y_i - X_i$. Net effects are usually discussed in terms of totals and means; however, the discussion can be generalized as follows:

Let

$\mathbf{X}$ = the vector of population true values.
$N \times 1$

$\mathbf{Y}$ = the vector of measurements for the target populations.
$N \times 1$

$\mathbf{B}$ = the vector of element biases.

$\mathbf{Y} = \mathbf{X} + \mathbf{B}$.

Now suppose the goal of the survey is to estimate some function of the population of true values. Thus, $f(\mathbf{X})$ = quantity to be estimated from the survey. Suppose that $g(\mathbf{y})$ = the sample estimate of $f(\mathbf{X})$ where $\mathbf{y}$ is the vector of measurements on the sample, and g is some function of these measurements, such as the sample mean. Then the mean square error of $g(\mathbf{y})$, MSE $[g(\mathbf{y})]$ is given by

$$\text{MSE } [g(\mathbf{y})] = E_s [g(\mathbf{y}) - f(\mathbf{X})]^2$$

where E_s = the expected value over all possible samples. Thus,

$$\text{MSE } [g(\mathbf{y})] = E_s[g(\mathbf{y}) - E_s g(\mathbf{y})]^2 + [E_s g(\mathbf{y}) - f(\mathbf{X})]^2 .$$

The cross-product term vanishes because the biases are fixed and do not vary from sample to sample (or from measurement to measurement for that matter).

Assuming that the sample design is one for which an unbiased estimation procedure can be produced, that is, $E_s g(\mathbf{y}) = f(\mathbf{Y})$ (there is no sampling bias), then

$$\text{MSE } [g(\mathbf{y})] = E_s [g(\mathbf{y}) - f(\mathbf{Y})]^2 + [f(\mathbf{Y}) - f(\mathbf{X})]^2$$
$$= \text{sampling variance of } g(\mathbf{y}) + \text{squared bias in } g(\mathbf{y}).$$

This simple model is applied in the literature to many sources of error, such as fixed biases introduced by the respondents or a systematic error in a measuring device.

Several methods are available for quantifying the effect of biased measurements. The first step is to examine the individual measurements or the aggregate estimates to determine whether or not any bias is present, that is, to detect the existence of biased measurements. The second step is to quantify the size of the bias or its impact upon the estimates. Usually researchers are not satisfied with merely detecting the existence of biased measurements. This is in contrast to the common practice when examining other types of error, such as nonresponse, where one commonly sees reports of overall response rates (a measure of the extent of nonresponse) and possibly reports of response rates for subgroups. Direct measures of the bias due to nonresponse are rarely given.

Bias can be detected by means of consistency studies. Zarkovich (1966) calls these post-hoc techniques, because they can be used after the survey is completed and/or the data are published. Three types of consistency studies are:

1. Comparisons of the survey data or estimates with some independent estimates or data from some external source;
2. Examination of the consistency of the data with known characteristics; and,
3. Internal consistency studies in which the data are examined to see if several measurements on the same unit are logically consistent or if equivalent questionnaire items give consistent results.

Note again the distinction between knowing that bias is present and being able to measure the actual value of the bias. In general, comparison of two pieces of information that should agree can indicate that biases are present in one of the two; however, measurement of the size of the bias requires assuming one source to be accurate.

Turner and Krauss (1978) compare data from several sources to search for the existence of bias in subjective social indicators. The authors use the method to examine whether or not certain differences in methods and populations under study could account for differences in estimates. They accept the hypothesis that significant "house" biases exist. (They call it house bias because they are looking at differences between the results of different organizations—houses—conducting the survey.) The authors are not, however, able to say what the magnitude of the bias is, because accurate criterion values were not available.

Consistency studies often deal with demographic data in which certain relationships among characteristics are assumed to exist. They include use of age and sex ratios to detect misreporting or underreporting of these characteristics; use of balancing equations in which the total of some characteristics in the survey should equal sums and differences of data from other sources; cohort survival techniques; and other procedures.

Internal-consistency studies are often used during the editing phase of a survey. These involve, for example, checking to see that the same person is not reported as male and hospitalized for a gynecological problem. Comparison of results from questions that presumably ask the same thing but are worded differently can indicate the presence of bias.

In order to measure the size of the bias, it is necessary to establish a criterion measurement to compare with the survey data. Any of the previously discussed procedures could be used to measure the size of the bias if one was willing to assume that the comparison data were accurate.

Field studies undertaken for a subsample of the units at a time close to the reference period of the survey are often used to measure the quality of the main survey. Two methods used are:

1. Record-check studies in which a source of records is checked for a subsample of elements included in the survey, and
2. Resurveys in which a subsample of the units is remeasured using more accurate methods.

The original measurements and the actual or preferred measurements for members of the subsample are paired. Sometimes discrepancy rates are calculated and used to indicate whether or not certain work should be redone, such as recoding a batch of questionnaires. Alternately, the size of the bias may be calculated as follows. If $g(\mathbf{y'})$ are the original measurements and $g(\mathbf{x'})$ the true values for members of the subsample, then

$$\text{Bias } [g(\mathbf{y})] = g(\mathbf{y'}) - g(\mathbf{x}).$$

Some researchers recommend that the quality of subjective phenomena be measured only in terms of the variability of the measurements. Sudman and Bradburn (1974) so recommend because there is no "objective external evidence against which to verify the response." Kish's general model indicates, however, that we need not necessarily follow Sudman and Bradburn's recommendation. There is more than one source of bias in the measurement of subjective phenomena. One is the bias inherent in the difference between what Hansen, Hurwitz, and Pritzker call the ideal goals and defined goals of the survey. This might be called the relevance bias and is the source for which criterion measures do not exist. However, the other sources of bias, such as those introduced by coders, interviewers, and ques-tion-wording effects, can be studied for subjective phenomena and do not require the true or ideal value as the criterion measure. These studies require only some criterion measure that can be assumed to be free of the source of bias that one wishes to study.

Typical record-check studies are of little use in measuring subjective phenomena, because the types of records used (such as administrative, bank, school, or medical records) are maintained for reasons other than a survey. Most often these will not contain measurements of a person's sub-jective state.

The measurements obtained in the resurvey may not be accurate, but may be closer to the true values than the original measurements were. This is the case when some more extensive measure of a subjective phenomenon such as an attitude scale with many items is used to validate a shorter scale that was used in a survey.

Such a situation would conform to a model proposed by Kish and Lansing (1954), which considers true values, respondent values, and values of inter-mediate accuracy.[2] The model may be summarized as follows: Let

Y_i = the respondent's value;
X_i = the true value; and
A_i = the intermediate value.

Then, let,

$Y_i - X_i = B_i$ = individual error of response;
$A_i - X_i$ = error of response in the improved measurement; and
$D_i = (Y_i - X_i) - (A_i - X_i) = Y_i - A_i$ = difference between the two errors.

The authors define

$\bar{B} = \bar{Y} - \bar{X}$ = the response bias;
$\bar{Z} - \bar{X}$ = the bias in the intermediate measure; and
$\bar{D} = \bar{Y} - \bar{A}$ = the difference between the two biases.

Also defined is a term called the mean square difference of the measure-ments:

$$\text{Mean square difference} = M_s(d) = E(Y_i - A_i)^2 .$$

The covariance between the differences in the two measurements and in-termediate values is

$$\text{Cov}(D,A) = E[(D - \bar{D})(A - \bar{A})]$$
$$= \text{Cov}(Y,A) - \text{Var}(A).$$

The preceding terms give rise to the basic equations for evaluating the effect of errors on the measurement process.

The increase in the total mean square error due to errors in measurement by the respondents is

$$\text{Var}(Y) + \bar{B}^2 - \text{Var}(X) = E(Y - X)^2 + 2\text{Cov}[(Y - X), Y].$$

Similarly, the increase in mean square error due to the lesser accuracy of the respondent values as opposed to the values of the intermediate measure is:

$$\text{Var}(Y) + \bar{D}^2 - \text{Var}(A) = \text{MS}(d) + 2\text{Cov}(D,A)$$
$$= E(Y - X)^2 + 2\text{Cov}[(Y - A), A].$$

Kish and Lansing (1954) give formulas for estimating the components of the error for a simple random sample design. Of note is that $\bar{D}^2$ is estimated by

$$\bar{D}^2 = (\bar{y} - \bar{a})^2 - \frac{1}{n}\{s^2(Y) + s^2(A) - 2\,\text{Cov}[Y,A]\}$$

where

$$s^2(Y) = \frac{1}{n-1} \sum_{i=1}^{n} (Y_i - \bar{y})^2;$$

$$s^2(A) = \frac{1}{n-1} \sum_{i=1}^{n} (A_i - \bar{a})^2;$$

and

$$\text{Cov}(Y,A) = \frac{1}{n-1} \sum_{i=1}^{n} (Y_i - \bar{y})(A_i - \bar{a}).$$

Because the estimate of the squared bias is a residual sample value, it can have negative values.

Measures of the effect of measurement bias other than the mean square error are given in the literature. In general, these are directed at looking beyond the effect of net bias on the mean square error of some overall statistic to detect whether or not biases may affect different subgroups of the target population differently. The aim of such analyses is to determine whether certain analytic statements comparing subgroups are adversely affected by measurement bias. The point is often made that if the bias in a measure is constant across comparison groups, then the comparisons are valid.

In a record-check study, Borus (1966) used a variety of measures to compare the "true" to the respondent values. These include:

1. Mean absolute deviation of the respondent values and the true values.
2. Mean percentage deviation measured as a percentage of the respondent values.
3. Pearson product-moment correlation between respondent values and true values.
4. The distribution of the absolute deviations.
5. The distribution of the percentage deviations measured as a percentage of the average of the two values, that is,

$$\frac{X_i - Y_i}{\frac{1}{2}(X_i + Y_i)}.$$

6. The distributions of the positive and negative deviations. Chi-squared tests of the equivalence of these distributions were done.
7. Finally, in an attempt to discover if certain subpopulations have more misreporting than others, he regressed the

$$\frac{\text{average response}}{\text{error per week}} = \frac{(\text{Actual value} - \text{Respondent value})}{\# \text{ weeks}}$$

on various characteristics of the respondents.

Each of these measures of the effect of bias could also be used in a resurvey that examined the quality of measurements of subjective phenomena. An intermediate criterion measure such as a more accurate scale would take the place of the true value.

In comparing Borus's six measures of the effect of bias, we can note that the net bias can be 0 even if the mean absolute deviation is not, so that this latter statistic may be preferable to net bias when subgroup comparisons are anticipated. The percentage deviation is a relative bias measure; however, the one in which the average of the true and respondent values is used in the denominator understates the effect of bias on the estimates. The correlation coefficient can be very high even though the net bias is high. This would occur if some relatively constant bias affects the results of each sample member. The distribution of the absolute errors indicates whether or not there is stability in the response error, that is, do they tend to cluster around some average error or are they widely dispersed? The distribution of positive and negative deviations and the test of significance indicates whether or not there is a net bias and whether or not there is a difference in the tendencies to underestimate or overestimate.

In medical and epidemiologic studies the effect of measurement errors is often assessed in terms of the sensitivity and specificity of the measurement process. These two statistics can be used for any type of dichotomous char-

TABLE 13.1
Relationship Between Actual and Measured Values

True Status	Status Measured by Procedure X		Totals
	1	0	
1	a	b	$a + b$
0	c	d	$c + d$
Totals	$a + c$	$b + d$	$n = a + b + c + d$

acteristic, although they are most often used to describe the quality of a diagnostic process. Table 13.1 shows the relationship between the true and measured status for a sample of size n. The sensitivity of the test (or measurement process) is defined as the proportion of those with the characteristic correctly measured as having the characteristic.

Using Table 13.1, we have

$$\text{Sensitivity} = \frac{a}{a + b} .$$

The specificity is the proportion of those without the characteristic correctly identified by procedure X, i.e.,

$$\text{Specificity} = \frac{d}{c + d} .$$

The net bias can be expressed as a function of the sensitivity and specificity of the measurement process, with

$$\bar{b} = \frac{c - b}{n}$$

$$\bar{b} = \frac{a + c}{n} - \left[\frac{(a + c) - n(1 - sp)}{n[s - (1 - sp)]} \right]$$

where s denotes sensitivity and sp denotes specificity. If a measurement process has high specificity and high sensitivity, the bias will be small. It is possible for the bias to be small when the sensitivity is small. This would occur when the number of false positives equals the number of false negatives, that is, $c = b$. In such a case, the procedure would be adequate for population measures but totally inappropriate for individual measures because individual biases exist even though there is no overall bias.

Procedures for Special Sources of Error. Each of the procedures we have described can be applied to study the effect of a particular source of error such as question wording, interview mode (telephone, personal, mail), and so forth, or the differential effect of measurement errors on certain subgroups of the population. In the former case, an experimental design is imbedded in the survey, with cases being randomly assigned to interview mode, question type, and so forth. Alternately, each element of the sample can be measured by each mode, question, and so forth, that is to be evaluated. In the latter case, detecting subgroup differences, applying the methods to the subgroups of the sample suffices because in most cases the subgroup members in a random sample of the overall population are a random sample of the subgroup. Thus, we could look at the effect of measurement bias on the MSE of estimates for blacks versus whites, the sensitivity or specificity of the measurements, or the correlation of true and measured values for different subgroups—whichever is appropriate.

For example, consider the measurement of panel bias. Panel biases are those occurring as a result of the attempt to survey the same sampling units repeatedly. There are three sources of panel bias:

1. *Reporting bias*: occurring when sample units in the survey are more likely to report in certain ways the longer they have been in the survey. The actual measurement does not change, just the reporting behavior. Thus, reporting bias will occur when measurement errors are a function of the number of times interviewed.
2. *Reactive effect*: occurring when presence in the sample and exposure to certain measurement techniques cause the characteristics to change within the sample units. Thus, the units in the sample are no longer representative of those in the population. An example is when people are asked if they used a public service of which they were previously unaware. The proportion of the sample using a service may increase over time because of the increased knowledge of the respondents. However, the proportion using the service in the rest of the population may not be changing.
3. *Differential nonresponse*: introducing bias when the probability of response is related to the values of the characteristics being measured. Changes over time in the probability of response for subgroups will cause estimates to change even when no real changes occur. This can occur even when the overall response rate remains the same.

Panels are used in two different ways in social research. The panel may be used to improve the statistical efficiency of a series of cross-sectional estimates, such as estimates of the unemployment rate. Alternately, the panel may be used to conduct a longitudinal study in which the emphasis is on tracking the behavior of individuals over time. In the first case, we are interested in controlling the efficiency of aggregate comparisons over time, such as changes in the employment rate; in the second, our interest lies in determining the components of aggregate changes, such as the proportion of employed who lost their jobs, the effect of attitudes on future job-seeking behavior, and so forth.

Bailar (1975) examines the effect of panel bias on a series of cross-sectional estimates from panel surveys. Bailar defines rotation group bias as

[*Rotation group bias.*] The effect of variation between responses at different times with repeated interviewing. [23]

This bias is detected by dividing the entire sample into subsamples, called rotation groups, and inducting these groups into the sample over time. Thus, for any particular time period, a reporting month for example, some people will be in their first interview, some their second, and so on, depending upon the total number of rotation groups.

The existence of rotation-group bias is detected by calculating the rotation-group index. This is defined by Bailar as follows:

[*Rotation group index.*] The index is computed by dividing the total number of persons in a given rotation group having the characteristic of interest by the average number of persons having the characteristic over all rotation groups, and then multiplying by 100. [23]

If all rotation groups had the same number of people with the characteristic, then the index would be 100.0 for each group. (In Bailar's study these indices range from 120 to 91.)

Bailar mathematically defines rotation-group bias using a model analogous to the general model presented previously (see section on "Assessing Bias: General Procedures").

Let $f_h(X)$ = population parameter being estimated for time period h, and $\hat{g}_h(y)$ = a ratio estimator for time period h for $f_n(X)$. Bailar gives $\hat{g}_h(y) = \sum\limits_{i=1}^{R} g_h[(y)_i]$ where $g_h[(y)_i]$ is the estimate for rotation group i.

Now,

$$E\{\hat{g}_h(y)\} = \sum_{i=1}^{R} E\{g_h[(y)_i]\}.$$

It is assumed that $\hat{g}_h(y)$ is unbiased except for rotation group biases, $a(i)$. Thus,

$$E\{\hat{g}_h(y)\} = f_h(X) + \sum_{i=1}^{R} a(i) .$$

This gives

$$a(i) = E\{g_h[(y)_i]\} - \tfrac{1}{R} f_h(X) .$$

Since the rotation group i is a subsample of entire sample,

$$E\{g_h[(\mathbf{y})_i]\} = \tfrac{1}{R} f_h[(\mathbf{Y})_i] \ .$$

Using an element-by-element model, let

$$Y(hij) = X(hj) + B(ji).$$

Assume that $f_h(\mathbf{X}) = \sum_j X_j(h)$, the total for some characteristic such as the total employed persons. This implies that

$$\begin{aligned}\tfrac{1}{R} f_h[(\mathbf{Y})_i] &= \tfrac{1}{R} \sum_j Y(hij) \\ &= \tfrac{1}{R} \sum_j X(hj) + \tfrac{1}{R} \sum_j B(ji).\end{aligned}$$

Thus,

$$\begin{aligned}a(i) &= \tfrac{1}{R} \sum_j B(ji) \\ &= \tfrac{1}{R} B(i);\end{aligned}$$

and the overall bias in the estimate is

$$\text{Bias} = \sum_i a(i) = \tfrac{1}{R} \sum_{i=1}^{R} B(i).$$

This is a good example of a source of bias that can be detected and measured without our being able to determine the true values. The rotation-group index will indicate that there is rotation-group bias, and a criterion measure that is free of rotation-group bias can be used in the resurvey.

Williams and Mallows (1970) present a model for systematic biases in panel surveys resulting from nonresponse. They consider the measurement of employment status in which the same sample is interviewed twice and the response rate changes for subgroups from time 1 to time 2.

Procedures for Adjusting for Effects of Bias in a Survey Measurement Process. Several methods have been developed for adjusting for bias in a survey measurement process. One entire class of procedures may be termed double-sampling procedures. In these procedures, more accurate data are collected for a subsample of the original sample. Instead of being used to estimate bias and/or mean square error of estimates from the original survey (as described in the previous sections), these data are used to correct estimates from the entire sample. The more accurate data are generally more difficult to collect so that the measurement process that provides accurate data is more expensive. Thus, the methods often focus on ways for determining the optimum allocation of the entire survey effort to the original sample and the subsample, given the cost of the accurate and inaccurate measurement methods.

Measurement Error

Frankel (1979) gives three methods for using what he calls "verification information." They are (1) substitution method, (2) ratio-adjustment method, and (3) regression-adjustment method. A fourth method for using resurvey data to adjust estimates is a difference estimator (Madow, 1965; Lessler, 1976). Tenebein (1970) gives a double-sample procedure for characteristics taking only 0,1 values.

A dual record system (Marks, Seltzer, and Krotki, 1974) is a method for adjusting for bias in reporting total number of events (originally developed by Chandrasekar and Deming, 1949). This method is not appropriate for subjective phenomena because it uses administrative records that count the number of events.

One source of bias in surveys is the reluctance of respondents to answer sensitive questions truthfully because they may wish to conceal from the interviewer their true status. *Randomized response* is a method that has been developed to compensate for reluctance to answer sensitive questions truthfully. The technique was introduced by Warner (1965) and involves using a randomizing device to conceal from the interviewer the exact meaning of the respondent's answer.

Suppose that we wish to estimate the proportion of people who had characteristic A, where A might be committing a crime during the past year. Two statements are provided to the respondent: (1) I have committed a crime in the past year, and (2) I have not committed a crime in the past year. The respondent is presented with a randomizing device that selects one of the two statements, and the respondent is to answer either "yes" or "no." Warner shows that if π = true proportion who have A, that is, who have committed a crime; p = probability the randomizing device selects statement 1; n = sample size; and n_1 = number that respond "yes"; then

$$\hat{\pi} = \frac{p - 1}{2p - 1} + \frac{n_1}{(2p - 1)n}$$

is an unbiased estimate of π (p not equal to one-half).

The variance of $\hat{\pi}$ is given by

$$V(\hat{\pi}) = \frac{\pi(1 - \pi)}{n} + \frac{p(1 - p)}{n(2p - 1)^2} . \tag{1}$$

This expression for the variance (from Greenberg et al., 1969) illustrates the effect of the uncertainty introduced by the randomizing device. The first term in (1) is the expression for the variance for a direct question about possession of characteristic A. The second component represents the increase in variance resulting from the randomizing device. However, the gain to be realized by using the randomizing device comes through reduction of the bias and the accompanying reduction in the mean square error of the estimate. Whether or not the mean square error is less than that of a direct question depends upon the values of p and the willingness of the respondent to answer truthfully under the two survey procedures.

There has been considerable theoretical development of the randomized response procedures since Warner's 1965 paper. In general, these methods have focused on ways to increase the statistical efficiency of the technique, new methods for constructing randomizing devices, and extensions of the methods to include the study of quantitative and multinomial data. Of particular usefulness is the unrelated-question randomized-response model (Greenberg et al., 1969), which has been shown to always be more efficient than the original Warner procedure (Dowling and Shachtman, 1975).

Randomized response is certainly applicable for the measurement of subjective phenomena. Imagine asking the respondents directly: Are you planning to commit a crime? or Do you hate your children? or Do you think this interview is useful?

ASSESSING THE IMPACT OF MEASUREMENT VARIABILITY

The notion of measurement variability has been around a long time. However, there is disagreement in the literature as to whether or not this variability can be studied by statistical methods. This disagreement centers around the nature of the process that generates response variability.

Survey measurements take place in a milieu composed of many factors. Some of these factors, such as the design of the sample and the questionnaire, are controlled to a high degree; others are controlled to a lesser degree, for example, interviewer actions that have been prescribed by the training and instructions; still others are minimally controlled, such as the respondent's mood, the political climate at the time of the interview, the respondent's reaction to characteristics of the interviewer such as age, race, sex, or social class. Hansen, Hurwitz, and Bershad (1961) call this whole complex of factors the "general conditions" of the survey. Hansen, Hurwitz, and Madow (1953) call the conditions that are subject to the control of the researcher the "essential survey conditions;" these are a subset of the general conditions.

Those who accept the idea of studying response variability by statistical methods assume that the uncontrollable factors in the survey milieu cause the measurements to behave like a random variable. In some cases this random variable is assumed to be independently normally distributed for different elements of the population (Pearson, 1902). Sometimes it is assumed that the measurements are stochastic without specifying a distribution (Raj, 1968; Cassel, Särndal, and Wretman, 1977). In 1953 Hansen, Hurwitz, and Madow posited a discrete distribution for the measurements over a distinct number of possible responses, each occurring with certain probabilities; however, later papers by Hansen and Hurwitz do not specify the nature of the distribution.

Some researchers reject the use of statistical models for response variability because they believe the models define quantities that are unmeasurable. Zarkovich (1966) describes this point of view. He argues that responses are unique. In discussing the factors that influence the response, Zarkovich accepts the fact that some factors are under the control of the researcher and that some factors have a random character, such as mood of respondent and interviewer, time of calling, interviewer-respondent interaction, respondent interest in the survey, and so forth. Other factors are seen to have a variable effect but not to behave in random fashion. The examples that Zarkovich gives are "(1) the quality of the enumerators selected, (2) the effects of the publicity campaign, and (3) special temporary features of the external circumstances, such as housing problems, psychological tensions created as a result of wars, a difficult economic or political situation, etc." (1966:44).

In addition, Zarkovich states that there are certain factors that produce a trend over time in responses, including (l) memory, because respondents will remember responses given in previous surveys, especially those responses that require careful consideration, (2) educational value of the survey for the respondent, and (3) reluctance to respond to another survey soon after a previous survey.

Thus, Zarkovich states that because of the joint action of these factors, we must conclude that successive responses are not random in character: "Each response must therefore be considered a product of particular circumstances and cannot be regarded as representative of the same population as the responses resulting from other trials" (1966:46). Basically, Zarkovich is saying that although each response may have a random component, it is impossible ever to measure that component.

There are three main views of response variability. Some researchers simply state that the measurements are a random variable with a mean and a variance (Sukhatme and Seth, 1952; Sukhatme and Sukhatme, 1970; Raj, 1968; Madow, 1965; Hartley and Rao, 1978; Biemer, 1978, 1979); others speak of the measurements as a random variable generated by a conceptual sequence of repeated independent trials of the measurement process (Hansen et al., 1951; Hansen, Hurwitz, and Madow 1953; Hansen, Hurwitz, and Bershad, 1961; Fellegi, 1964, 1974; Bailar and Dalenius, 1969; Koch, 1973; Nathan, 1973; Brackstone, Gosselin, and Garton 1975; Cochran, 1977; Koop, 1974); and still others do not allow for response variability at the element level (Zarkovich, 1966; Murthy, 1967).

In the literature, models for the effect of variable error are expressed either as mean-square-error-decomposition models or as mixed-linear models. Sometimes the net bias is assumed to be zero so that the models

425

deal only with variability; however, this is usually a simplifying assumption because the author(s) wishes to focus on the response variability in the particular paper. The mean-square-error-decomposition formulation and the linear-model formulation tend to merge as the various models focus on a particular source of error—often the interviewer. In such a specific case, both approaches can be expressed in terms of a linear model.

The big difference between the two approaches is that the decomposition approach usually has a term called the interaction variance (not always defined the same), and generally the linear-models approach omits this component.

Probably the most influential paper on the variance-decomposition approach is that by Hansen, Hurwitz, and Bershad (1961). That paper and the Mahalanobis (1946) technique of interpenetrating samples appear to have been the major influences upon succeeding work. Other researchers do not always have exactly the same model as that in the Hansen, Hurwitz, and Bershad paper, but they often have components with the same names and similar definitions. This has undoubtedly caused some confusion among readers.

The Hansen, Hurwitz, and Bershad model was expressed for 0,1 variables; however, it can be used for continuous data also. Trying to remain true to the original formulation of the model, one may express it as follows: Let X_i = true value for the ith element, and Y_{it} = measurement for the ith element at the tth trial:

$$E(Y_{it|i}) = E_{s|i}E_{t|s,i}(Y_{it}) = Y_i .$$ (2)

Hansen, Hurwitz, and Bershad define this expected value over all possible samples and all possible trials. The exact quote is "We can conceive of the possible repetitions of the measurements over all possible samples and trials under the general conditions represented by G, on one unit of the population, say the ith unit. Then the conditional expected value over all such possible measurements on this particular unit is $[E_i(Y_{it}) = Y_i]$" (1961: 361).

Hansen, Hurwitz, and Bershad do not specify the structure of $E(Y_{it|i})$ as is done in (2); however, it is hard to imagine that they can mean anything else. Equation (2) says that the expected value of Y_{it} given i over repetitions of the measurement process is the expected value over all possible samples that contain element i of the expected value over trials of the measurements given a sample that contains i. Some researchers have offered models in which new samples can be drawn at each trial (Bailar and Dalenius, 1969).

Hansen, Hurwitz, and Bershad do define the "conditional expected value for the ith unit over all possible repetitions of the survey for a fixed sample, s, as $[E_{is}Y_{it} = Y_{is}]$" (1961:362). These distinctions have implications with regard to the structure of the interaction-variance component, as we shall see later.

Assume a simple random sample of size n. Hansen, Hurwitz, and Bershad characterize the mean square error of $\bar{y}_t$ as follows:

$$
\begin{aligned}
\text{MSE}(\bar{y}_t) &= E[(\bar{y}_t - \bar{x})^2] \\
&= E\{(\bar{y}_t - \bar{Y})^2\] + (\bar{Y} - \bar{X})^2 \\
&= V(\bar{y}_t) + B^2.
\end{aligned}
$$

The variance of $\bar{y}_t$ is decomposed into components using

$$
\bar{y} = \frac{1}{n} \sum_{i=1}^{N} Y_i .
$$

Then

$$
\begin{aligned}
V(\bar{y}_t) &= E\{[(\bar{y}_t - \bar{y}) + (\bar{y} - \bar{Y})]^2\} \\
&= E\{(\bar{y}_t - \bar{y})^2 + (\bar{y} - \bar{Y})^2 + 2(\bar{y}_t - \bar{y})(\bar{y} - \bar{Y})\} .
\end{aligned}
$$

The three terms are, respectively, the response variance, the sampling variance, and the covariance between response and sampling deviations. The covariance component is not further characterized; however, the authors do state that it will be zero for a complete census and for repetitions using a fixed sample.

The response variance term is considered in more detail and is decomposed using the individual response deviation:

$$
d_{it} = Y_{it} - Y_i .
$$

Then, letting

$$
\sigma_d^2 = E\, d_{it}^2 \text{ and } \sigma_d^2 \rho = E\, d_{it} d_{i't} ,
$$

we have

$$
E(\bar{y}_t - \bar{y})^2 = \text{Var}\,(\bar{d}_t) = \frac{1}{n} \{\sigma_d^2 + (n - 1)\rho\sigma_d^2\} .
$$

The authors also define σ_d^2 in terms of the average of the variance of the individual response deviations over trials, such that,

$$
\sigma_d^2 = \frac{1}{N} \sum_{i=1}^{N} \text{Var}_t\,(d_{it}).
$$

Similarly,

$$
\rho\sigma_d^2 = \frac{1}{N(N-1)} \sum_{i \neq i'}^{N} \text{Cov}_t\,(d_{it}\, d_{i't}),
$$

although this is not explicitly defined by the authors. Other people do use this formulation (Raj, 1968; Tremblay, Singh, and Clavel 1976).

Two papers have examined the structure of the covariance between sampling and response deviations (Koch, 1973; Koop, 1974). Koch (1973) formulated his model for the multivariate case and unequal probability sampling. Koch defines a term called the interaction variance that is equivalent to the covariance between response and sampling deviations. He shows that this term is 0 if the expected measurement for a sample element does not depend upon the contents of the sample.

Koop (1974) defines a general model under various sample designs and estimation procedures and decomposes the total variance in terms of Y_{is}, the expected measurement for the ith unit given sample s. Koop shows that when Y_{is} is not equal to Y_i, the response variance can be broken down into four terms—a simple and correlated response variance resulting from the variance and covariance of the distribution of responses and a variance and covariance across all samples of the expected response for a particular sample. Koop calls these last two terms the interaction variance and covariance. This was partially realized in the Koch model in which he defined an interaction response variance that is equivalent to Koop's interaction covariance.

There is a great deal of variability in the literature in the terminology and approaches that are used to model response variability. The reader of a particular paper must be very careful to note the mathematical definition of various terms and not assume that terms that have the same or similar names have the same meaning. This is well illustrated by the two following models, which focus on the interviewer as the source of error.

Papers on the Census Bureau model describe experiments in which interviewers are randomly allocated sampling units. Assuming m units per interviewer, the assumption is made that the correlated response variance is 0 between interviewers. This gives (Bailey, Moore, and Bailar 1978)

$$V(\bar{y}_t) = \frac{1}{n} \{\sigma_d^2 + (\bar{m}-1)\rho\sigma_d^2\} + \frac{\sigma_s^2}{n} + \frac{2(n-1)}{n} \sigma_{rs} .$$

The term $\rho\sigma_d^2$ is called the within-interviewer correlated response variance. The model is derived by letting Y_{ij} = the measurement for the ith element obtained by the jth interviewer.

It is assumed that Y_{ij} is a random variable, and the preceding components of variance are derived by partitioning the variance using $E(Y_{ij|i})$, the conditional expected value over all measurements on the unit.

Murthy (1967) presents a mean-square-error-decomposition model in which he does not allow the measurements to be a random variable apart from the sample and measurement design. Murthy considers the survey to have two steps of randomization: (1) selection of a sample of population elements, s; and (2) selection of a sample of survey personnel, r. He defines X_i = true value for the ith element; and Y_{ij} = value obtained by the jth interviewer for the ith element. Y_{ij} is not a random variable.

Murthy decomposes the mean square error using conditional expected values. We will focus on the variance.

$$
\begin{aligned}
V(\bar{y}_{rs}) &= V_s[E_{r|s}(\bar{y}_{rs})] + E_s[V_{r|s}(\bar{y}_{rs})] \\
&= V_s(\bar{y}_{s.}) + E_s[E_{r|s}(\bar{y}_{rs} - \bar{y}_{s.})^2] \\
&= V_s(\bar{y}_{s.}) + E_r(\bar{y}_{.r} - \bar{Y})^2 + E_s\, E_{r|s}\, \{(\bar{y}_{rs} - \bar{y}_{s.}) - (\bar{y}_{.r} - \bar{Y})]^2\} \quad (3)
\end{aligned}
$$

Murthy calls the three components on the right of (3) sampling variance, the variance between survey personnel, and—the interaction between sampling and nonsampling errors! Murthy's interaction variance term is not equivalent to that of any of the authors mentioned in this discussion. In fact, for use of interviewers Koch (1971) gives a component of the sampling variance in his model that is very similar to Murthy's interaction variance component.

Murthy continues his derivation for a simple random sample of population elements and interviewers and arrives at a formula for the overall variance that is nearly identical to that given in the Census Bureau model, that is,

$$
V(\bar{y}_{rs}) = \frac{\sigma_s^2}{n} + \frac{\sigma_d^2}{n}\, \{1 + (m-1)\rho_c\}.
$$

These components are not defined the same, however, since in the Census models the response variance arises from the variability or random nature of individual responses, which Murthy's model does not allow. The individual response deviation in Murthy's model is due to the difference between the measurement for the jth interviewer, ith subject, and the average of this measurement across all interviewers.

Now let us look briefly at some of the linear-model formulations. Sukhatme and Sukhatme (1970) give such a model. Let

$$
Y_{ij} = X_i + \alpha_j + e_{ij}\,;
$$

where Y_{ij} = measurement obtained by the jth interviewer on the ith element; X_i = true value; α_j = bias of the jth interviewer in repeated observations on all the elements; e_{ij} = the random deviation of $X_i + \alpha_j$ from the reported value and is determined by the approach to the element and other random causes.

It is assumed that the e_{ij} are independently distributed with mean 0 and variance S_e^2.

Assuming a sample and measurement design with (1) a simple random sample of n elements from N, (2) a simple random sample of m interviewers from M, (3) subsamples randomly assigned to interviewers, Sukhatme and Sukhatme give

$$\text{Var}(\bar{y}) = S_X^2\left(\frac{1}{n} - \frac{1}{N}\right) + S_\alpha^2\left(\frac{1}{m} - \frac{1}{M}\right) + \frac{S_e^2}{n}.$$

The authors then derive the "correlation between responses obtained by the same interviewer." Ignoring the finite population correction, the variance for a single observation is $S_y^2 = S_X^2 + S_\alpha^2 + S_e^2$. The correlation ρ is defined as:

$$\rho\, S_y^2 \left(\tfrac{N-1}{N}\right) = E\left[\{y_{ij} - E(y_{ij})\}\,\{y_{i'j} - E(y_{i'j})\}\right]$$

$$= E\left\{E[\{y_{ij} - E(y_{ij})\}\,\{y_{i'j} - E(y_{i'j})\}|\,j]\right\}$$

$$= \frac{S_X^2}{N} + (1 - 1/_M)S_a^2.$$

$$\rho S_y^2 \cong S_\alpha^2, \text{ for large } N \text{ and } M.$$

This implies that

$$\rho = \frac{S_\alpha^2}{S_X^2 + S_\alpha^2 + S_e^2}.$$

This gives

$$V(\bar{y}) = \frac{S_y^2}{n}\left\{1 + \rho\left(\frac{n}{m} - 1\right)\right\},$$

a formulation similar to the Census formulation, but with slightly different interpretation of the components.

O'Muircheartaigh (1977) defines a very similar model and shows links to the Census Bureau model. He, however, defines ρ as

$$\rho = \frac{\sigma_\alpha^2}{\sigma_\alpha^2 + \sigma_e^2}.$$

These linear-model approaches to the structure of measurement errors give rise to statements, which are widespread in the literature, that the correlated response variance is always positive and arises from the biases of the interviewers. If we use the variance-decomposition approach, there is no restriction that ρ be nonnegative.

Measurement Error

Estimation of Response Variance Components. All of the preceding models require utilization of similar procedures in order to estimate the total variance and the components of variance. Three methods are used for making estimates of the total variance, including measurement variance and its components. These are (1) repetition, (2) replication, and (3) repetition/replication combinations.

"Repetition" refers to obtaining repeat measurements on the same population element. Under the assumption of independence between repeat measurements and the same general conditions inducing the random distribution of responses, this will allow an estimate of the simple response variance type components. "Replication" refers to the technique of interpenetrating samples developed by Mahalanobis. Under this method independent samples are drawn from the population of elements and are randomly assigned to enumerators. This method allows estimation of the total variance and the within-interviewer correlated response variance. There have been many clever ways developed for using these techniques.

All authors do not adhere to this distinction between repetition and replication. Hansen, Hurwitz, and Bershad (1961) call repeating the survey method the "replication method." This confusion in terminology has resulted in considerable misunderstanding. At several American Statistical Association meetings, I have heard people vehemently deny that the replication is required to measure interviewer effects. Others confidently assert that it is necessary. They are usually talking about different things— one group thinking that replication refers to repeat measurements on the same units, the other thinking that it refers to the use of the replicated or interpenetrated samples.

The basic fact about estimating the effect of measurement variability on survey statistics is that some type of experimental procedure must be introduced in the survey in order to allow estimation of the total variance.

Bias in the Usual Sample Estimates of Variance in the Presence of Measurement Variability. The usual sample estimate of the variance for a simple random sample of size n from a population of size N is

$$s_y^2 = \frac{1}{n}\left(\frac{1\,(N-n)}{N}\right)\sum_{i=1}^{n}\frac{(Y_{it}-\bar{y})^2}{n-1}.$$

This estimate is biased in the presence of measurement variability. Writing the total variance of the Hansen, Hurwitz, and Bershad (1961) model as

$$\text{Var}\{\bar{y}_t\} = \frac{1}{n}\left(\frac{N-n}{N}\right)\sigma_s^2 + \frac{1}{n}\{\sigma_d^2 + (n-1)\rho\sigma_d^2\} + \frac{2(n-1)}{n}\sigma_{rs};$$

it can be shown that bias $s_y^2 = -\rho\sigma^2 - 2\sigma_{rs}$.

Note that the bias in the usual estimate does not depend upon the size of the sample and is, therefore, not reduced by increasing the sample size. This was shown by Hansen, Hurwitz, and Bershad (1961) for 0,1 variables, by Cochran (1977) for the general case, and by Koop (1974) for unequal probability sampling and the Horvitz-Thompson estimator.

Use of Repeat Measurements. Repeat measurements can be used to estimate the measurement-variance components. In this method, more than one measurement is made upon the sample elements. Let

Y_{i1t} = measurement made in the original survey; and
Y_{i2t} = measurement made in the resurvey.

The repeat measurements can be made for the entire sample or for a subsample.

Consider the case of a simple random sample of n units from N and a resurvey of the entire sample. There are now two statistics available for estimating the measurement variance and its components. The first of these is the mean square of the element-by-element differences. This is termed the "gross difference rate" in some papers (Hansen, Hurwitz, and Pritzker, 1964; Bailar, 1968; Bailar and Dalenius, 1969). For a 0,1 variable it will be equivalent to the discrepancy rate that is often calculated during the quality-control activities of a survey (Lessler, 1976).

If we can assume that the repeat measurements are independent of the original measurements and that the Y_{it} have the same random distribution in the resurvey as they had in the original survey, then this statistic is an unbiased estimate of the simple measurement variance under the Hansen, Hurwitz, and Bershad model. We will call this statistic the mean square within elements (MSWE). Now,

$$\text{MSWE} = \frac{1}{2n} \sum_{i=1}^{n} (Y_{i1t} - Y_{j2t})^2.$$

$$\text{E(MSWE)} = \frac{1}{2n} E \sum_{i=1}^{n} \{[Y_{i1t} - E_t(Y_{i1t})] - [Y_{i2t} - E(Y_{i2t})]$$

$$- [E_t(Y_{i1t}) - E_t(Y_{i2t})]\}^2.$$

The assumption that the Y_{it} have the same distributions for the original and resurvey allows us to say $E_t(Y_{i1t}) = E_t(Y_{i2t}) = Y_i$. Thus,

$$\text{E(MSWE)} = \frac{1}{2n} E_s \{\sum_{i=1}^{n} E_t \{[(Y_{i1t} - Y_i) - (Y_{i2t} - Y_i)]^2\}\}$$

$$= \frac{1}{2n} E_s \{\sum_{i=1}^{n} E_t (Y_{i1t} - Y_i)^2 + E_t (Y_{i2t} - Y_i)^2$$

$$- 2 E_t (Y_{i1t} - Y_i) (Y_{i2t} - Y_i)\}.$$

Assuming independence between the original and resurvey makes the cross-product term 0 giving

$$E(MSWE) = \frac{1}{N} \sum_{i=1}^{N} E_t \, (Y_{i1t} - Y_i)^2.$$

This estimate is also unbiased for the variance-decomposition models presented by Koop (1974) and Koch (1973) under the same two assumptions.

Several research papers discuss the implications of the assumptions of lack of independence between the two surveys and changes in the distributions of the Y_{it}. Hansen, Hurwitz, and Pritzker (1964) discuss the effect of a positive correlation between the two measurements and the effect of the resurvey being an improved procedure relative to the original procedure. In each case, MSWE is an underestimate of the simple-response variance. Bailar and Dalenius (1969) discuss situations in which one can make various assumptions about the presence or absence of positive correlations between the two sets of measurements.

The MSWE is also used in the linear-models approach to investigating the effect of measurement errors. Assuming that n_{ij} observations are made on the ith element by the jth enumerator, Sukhatme and Seth (1952) show that the within-element mean square estimates s_e^2, which is the term in the linear-model formulation that is nearly equivalent to the simple response variance. In the case where the survey is repeated, $n_{ij} = 2$, and under the Sukhatme and Seth model

$$MSWE = \frac{1}{n} \sum_{j=1}^{k} \sum_{i=1}^{m} \frac{(Y_{ij1} - Y_{ij2})^2}{2}$$
$$= \frac{1}{2n} \sum_{j=1}^{k} \sum_{i=1}^{m} (e_{ij1} - e_{ij2})^2.$$

The second statistic available for the repeat survey is the difference between the two means: call this the squared mean difference (SMD), and we have

$$SMD = \frac{1}{2} (\bar{y}_{1t} - \bar{y}_{2t})^2 \, .$$

Under the assumption that

$$E_t(Y_{i1t}) = E_t(Y_{i2t}) = Y_i \, , \quad \bar{y}_1 = \bar{y}_2 \, ,$$

and

$$E(SMD) = \frac{1}{2} E\{(\bar{y}_{1t} - \bar{y})^2 + (\bar{y}_{2t} - \bar{y})^2 - 2(\bar{y}_{1t} - \bar{y})(\bar{y}_{2t} - \bar{y})\}.$$

Independence between the original and resurvey makes the expected value of the cross-product term 0, which gives

$$E(SMD) = MV = \frac{1}{n} \{\sigma_d^2 + (n-1) \rho\sigma_d^2\} .$$

This estimate is given by Hansen, Hurwitz, and Bershad (1961) and by Bailar and Dalenius (1969) in which the latter paper allows more than two repetition surveys each made by different agents and calculates the between-agent mean square.

As indicated in the previous section, the usual estimate of the sampling variance contains some portion of the measurement variance.

Use of Interpenetrated Samples. The use of interpenetrating samples to study the effect of measurement errors was first developed by Mahalanobis during the 1940s. It is used for measuring the total variance under the assumption that measurement errors are only correlated within interviewer assignments.

Under this method, independent samples are selected from the target population, and each sample is randomly assigned to an interviewer. Assuming k interviewers and m sample elements per interviewer, we have under the Hansen, Hurwitz, and Bershad model modified for interviewers (Bailey, Moore, and Bailar, 1978), the variance of the mean for a single interviewer is

$$Var(\bar{y}_j) = \frac{1}{m} \{\sigma_d^2 + (m-1) \rho\sigma_d^2\} + \frac{\sigma_s^2}{m} + \frac{2(m-1)}{m} \sigma_{RS} .$$

We have ignored the finite population correction factor in this formulation. The variance of the overall mean is

$$Var(\bar{y}) = \frac{1}{n} \{\sigma_d^2 + (m-1) \rho\sigma_d^2\} + \frac{\sigma_s^2}{n} + \frac{2(m-1)}{n} \sigma_{RS} .$$

The estimator that is used for the total variance is the between-interviewer mean square (BIMS) where

$$BIMS/M = \frac{1}{k(k-1)} \sum_{j=1}^{k} (\bar{y}_j - \bar{y})^2.$$

Thus,

$$E\{\frac{BIMS}{n}\} = \frac{1}{k} \{ \frac{1}{m} [\sigma_d^2 + (m-1) \rho\sigma_d^2]\} + \frac{\sigma_s^2}{km}$$
$$+ \frac{2(m-1)}{mk} \sigma_{RS} - \frac{1}{k^2(k-1)} \sum_{j \neq j'}^{k} E[\bar{y}_j - E(\bar{y}_{j'})] [\bar{y}_{j'} - E(\bar{y}_{j'})]$$
$$= V(\bar{y}) - C.$$

The term C is the covariance between the elements in two different samples. This latter term is given by several authors (Bailar and Dalenius 1969; Koop, 1974; Fellegi, 1974; Bailey, Moore, and Bailar 1978). In the last two papers it is further decomposed into two components, "the covariance of response deviations between elements in different interviewer assignments and the covariance between the response deviations in one interviewer's assignment and the sampling deviations in another interviewer assignment" (Bailey, Moore, and Bailar, 1978:17). Most researchers assume that this term is 0.

The between-interviewer mean square also estimates the total variance under the models given by Raj (1968) and Murthy (1967). It is also used in the linear models approach to formulating measurement errors, where the analysis is usually done in the context of an analysis of variance table (see Case I in the paper by Sukhatme and Seth, [1952]). Kish (1962) shows the results for the situation in which the sample size is not the same for each interviewer.

The BIMS and the sampling variance (within-interviewer mean square in the ANOVA terminology) can be used to estimate certain components of the overall variance.

Recall that the sampling variance has the following expected value:

$$E(s^2_{\bar{y}_{jl}}) = \sigma^2_s + \sigma^2_d (1-\rho) - 2\sigma_{RS} .$$

Assuming that C is 0, we get the following:

$$E\left(\frac{\text{BIMS} - s^2_{\bar{y}_{jt}}}{m}\right) = \sigma^2_d\rho + 2\sigma_{RS} . \tag{4}$$

Often the covariance between sampling and response deviations is assumed to be 0 so that (4) is an estimate of the correlated component of the measurement variance.

The method of interpenetrating samples can be extended to sample designs other than simple random sampling. Raj (1968) gives an example of a sample design in which the interviewers are allocated at random to primary sampling units (PSUs) that have been selected with probabilities proportional to size. Hartley and Rao (1978) and Biemer (1978) extend the method to complex multistage samples in which only the last units are selected with equal probability.

Combination Methods. It is not necessary to use only one of these two methods in a survey. They can be used in combination to allow estimation of additional components of error.

Sukhatme and Seth (1952) discuss a variety of sample and measurement designs that allow estimation of numerous components. They use a linear-models approach and allow multiple observations on the same population element. Fellegi (1964, 1974) describes a design that uses a combination of repeat measurements and interpenetration directed at estimating components of variance. A similar approach is used by Koch (1974) for a simple random sample and a cluster sample. In the latter case, repeat measurements are made on clusters of individuals and random assignment of clusters to interviewers is used.

METHODS TO ADJUST FOR RESPONSE ERRORS

Whereas earlier we dealt with procedures for adjusting for bias under fixed-bias models, these procedures can also be used in the context of measurement variability. Double-sampling schemes are employed in which a subsample of the original sample is selected and more accurate measurements obtained for members of the subsample either by means of record-check studies or more expensive interviews in which the accurate values can be obtained. Hansen, Hurwitz, and Madow (1953) present a ratio estimator using the double-sampling scheme; a regression estimator is discussed by Madow (1965); and difference estimators are discussed by Madow (1965), Lessler (1974, 1976), and Brackstone, Gosselin, and Garton (1975).

Consider the difference estimator. Let $\bar{y}_t$ = mean of the inaccurate values for the original sample of the size n; $\bar{y}_{st}$ = mean of the inaccurate values for a subsample of size n_1; and $\bar{x}_s$ = mean of the accurate values for the subsample.

Using these quantities, an unbiased estimate of the population mean is

$$\bar{w}_t = \bar{y}_t - (\bar{y}_{st} - \bar{x}_s).$$

Now the variance of $\bar{w}_t$, assuming the U.S. Census model and no interaction variance, is given by

$$\mathrm{Var}(\bar{w}_t) = \frac{n - n_1}{nn_1}\{\sigma_d^2 (1 - \rho)\} + \frac{n - n_1}{nn_1} \sigma_B^2 + \frac{1}{n} (\frac{N - n}{n}) \sigma_s^2 ;$$

where

$$\sigma_B^2 = \frac{1}{N - 1} \sum_{i=1}^{N} [(Y_i - X_i) - (\bar{Y} - \bar{X})]^2;$$

$$= \frac{1}{N - 1} \sum_{i=1}^{N} (B_i - \bar{B})^2.$$

This last component is the population variability of the element bias terms.

Note that the correlated response variance makes a negative contribution to the overall variance. This method may be adapted for use with interviews and in multistage designs (Lessler, 1974, 1977). Estimators for components are also given. The optimum allocation to the sample and subsample for various values of the components and alternate cost models is given in Kalsbeek and Lessler (1979).

All of the methods that have been developed to study response variability can be used for subjective phenomena. No criterion measures are necessary. In fact, given the nature of measurements of subjective phenomena that seem to be highly sensitive to the general conditions of the survey, it would seem that one should almost always adopt some method to assess response variability. Although most past studies have been limited to interviewers, coders, and other personnel, the methods can be adapted to study other sources of response variability. For example, respondents could be randomly assigned to questionnaire types that vary the context of questions, the wording, and so forth. It is imperative that social scientists begin to use some of these methods to assess and improve the quality of measurement if the measurements are to have any meaning for our understanding of our society.

Notes

1. Supported by National Science Foundation Grant No. SOC–780459.

2. Kish and Lansing develop their model for a study of the market value of houses. Some houses were measured by both a household respondent and an appraiser. The respondent values are assumed to be of lesser accuracy than the appraiser's values.

References

Anderson, R., Kasper, J., Frankel, M.R. (1979) *Total Survey Error*. San Francisco: Jossey-Bass.

Andrews, F.M., and Crandall, R. (1976) The validity of measures of self-reported well-being. *Social Indicators Research* 3:1-19.

Bailar, B.A. (1968) Recent research in reinterview procedures. *Journal of the American Statistical Association* 63:41-63.

Bailar, B.A. (1975) The effects of rotation group bias on estimates from panel surveys. *Journal of the American Statistical Association* 70:23-30.

Bailar, B.A., and Dalenius, T. (1969) Estimating the response variance components of the U.S. Bureau of the Census' survey model. *Sankhya: Series B*: 341-360.

Bailey, L., Moore, T.F., and Bailar, B. (1978) An interviewer variance study for the eight impact cities of the National Crime Survey cities sample. *Journal of the American Statistical Association* 73:16-23.

Biemer, P.P. (1978) *The Estimation of Non-sampling Variance Components in Sample Surveys*. Ph.D. dissertation, Texas A&M University.

Biemer, P.P. (1979) An Improved Procedure for Estimating the Components of Response Variance in Complex Surveys. Mimeo. Bureau of the Census, Statistical Research Division.

Borus, M.E. (1966) Response errors in survey reports of earning information. *Journal of the American Statistical Association* 61:729-738.

Brackstone, G.J., Gosselin, J.F., and Garton, B.E. (1975) Measurement of response errors in censuses and sample surveys. *Survey Methodology* 1:144-157.

Campbell, D., and Fiske, D.W. (1959) Convergent and discriminant validity by the multimethod-multitrait matrix. *Psychological Bulletin* 56:81-105.

Cassel, E.C., Särndal, C., Wretman, J.H. (1977) *Foundations of Inference in Survey Sampling*. New York: Wiley.

Chandrasekar, C., and Deming, W.E. (1949) On a method of estimating birth and death rates and the extent of registration. *Journal of the American Statistical Association* 44:101-115.

Cochran, W.G. (1977) *Sampling Techniques*. 3rd ed. New York: Wiley.

Copeland, K.T., Checkoway, H., Holbrook, R.H., and McMichael, A.J. (1976) Bias Due to Misclassification in the Estimate of Relative Risk in Epidemiologic Research. Paper presented to the Society for Epidemiologic Research, Toronto, Canada, June.

Dalenius, T. (1980) Discussion, session on taxonomy of survey errors. *Proceedings of the American Statistical Association (Survey Research Methods Section)* 1980:146-147.

Dalenius, T. (1974) *Ends and Means of Total Survey Design*. Stockholm: University of Stockholm.

Deming, W.E. (1960) *Sample Design in Business Research*. New York: Wiley.

Dowling, T.A., and Shachtman, R.H. (1975) On the relative efficiency of randomized response models. *Journal of the American Statistical Association* 70:84-86.

Fellegi, I.P. (1964) Response variance and its estimation. *Journal of the American Statistical Association* 59:1016-1041.

Fellegi, I.P. (1974) An improved method of estimating the correlated response variance. *Journal of the American Statistical Association* 69:496-501.

Frankel, M.R. (1979) Models for the use of verification information. In Ronald Anderson et al., *Total Survey Error*. San Francisco: Jossey-Bass.

Greenberg, B.C., Abdel-Latif, A.A., Simmons, W.R., and Horvitz, D.G. (1969) The unrelated question randomized response model: theoretical framework. *Journal of the American Statistical Association* 64:520.

Hansen, M.H., Hurwitz, W.N., and Bershad, M.A. (1961) Measurement errors in censuses and surveys. *Bulletin of the International Statistical Institute* 38:359-374.

Hansen, M.H., Hurwitz, W.N., and Madow, W.G. (1953) *Sample Survey Methods and Theory*. Vol. II, *Theory*. New York: Wiley.

Hansen, M.H., Hurwitz, W.N., Marks, E.S., and Mauldin, W.P. (1951) Response errors in surveys. *Journal of the American Statistical Association* 46:147-190.

Hansen, M.H., Hurwitz, W.N., and Pritzker, L. (1964) The estimation and interpretation of gross differences and the simple response variance. In *Contributions to Statistics*. Calcutta: Statistical Publishing Society.

Hansen, M.H., Hurwitz, W.N., and Pritzker, L. (1967) Standardization of procedures for the evaluation of data: measurement errors and statistical standards in the Bureau of the Census. *Bulletin of the International Statistical Institute, Sydney* 42:49-66.

Hartley, H.O., and Rao, J.N.K. (1978) The estimation of non-sampling variance components in sample surveys. In K. Namboodari, ed., *Survey Sampling and Measurement*. New York: Academic Press.

Heise, D.R., and Bohrnstedt, G.W. (1970) Validity, invalidity, and reliability. In E. Borgatta, ed., *Sociological Methodology: 1970*. San Francisco: Jossey-Bass.

Kalsbeek, W.D., and Lessler, J.T. (1979) Total survey design and procedures for controlling measurement errors. In DHEW Pub. No. (PHS) 79-3207. *Proceedings of the Second Biennial Conference on Health Survey Research Methods*.

Kish, L. (1962) Studies of interviewer variance for attitudinal variables. *Journal of the American Statistical Association* 57:92-115.

Kish, L. (1965) *Survey Sampling*. New York: Wiley.

Kish, L., and Lansing, J.B. (1954) Response errors in estimating the value of homes. *Journal of the American Statistical Association* 49:520-538.

Koch, G.G., (1971) A Response Error Model for a Simple Interviewer Structure Situation. Unpublished Technical Report No. 4. Project SU-618. Research Triangle Institute, Research Triangle Park, North Carolina. July.

Koch, G.G. (1973) An alternative approach to multivariate response error model for sample survey data with applications to estimators involving subclass means. *Journal of the American Statistical Association* 68;906-913.

Koop, J.C. (1974) Notes for a unified theory of estimation for sample surveys taking into account response errors. *Metrika* 21:19-39. Physica-Verlag, Wien.

Lessler, J.T. (1974) *A Double Sampling Scheme Model for Eliminating Measurement Process Bias and Estimating Measurement Errors in Surveys*. Mimeo Series No. 949. Chapel Hill, N.C.: University of North Carolina, Institute of Statistics.

Lessler, J.T. (1976) Survey designs which employ double sampling schemes for eliminating measurement process bias. *Proceedings of the American Statistical Association (Social Statistics Section)* 1976:520-525.

Lessler, J.T. (1977) Use of Error and Discrepancy Rates to Calculate the MSE of Survey Data. Paper presented at the American Public Health Association Annual Meeting.

Lessler, J.T., Kalsbeek, W.D., and Folsom, R.E. (1981) *A Taxonomy of Survey Errors, Final Report*. RTI Project 255U-1791-03F. Research Triangle Park, N.C.: Research Triangle Institute.

Lord, F.M., and Novick, M.R. (1968) *Statistical Theories of Mental Test Scores*. Reading, Mass.: Addison-Wesley.

Madow, W.G. (1965) On some aspects of response error measurement. *Proceedings of the American Statistical Association (Social Statistics Section)* 1965:182-192.

Mahalanobis, P.C. (1946) Recent experiments in statistical sampling in the Indian Statistical Institute. *Journal of the Royal Statistical Society* 109:327-378.

Marks, E.S., Seltzer, W., and Krotki, K.J. (1974) *Population Growth Estimation*. New York: Population Council.

Moser, C.A., and Kalton, G. (1972) *Survey Methods in Social Investigation*. 2nd ed. New York: Basic Books.

Murthy, M. (1967) *Sampling Theory and Methods*. Calcutta: Statistical Publishing Society.

Nathan, G. (1973) Response errors of estimators based on different samples. *Sankhya (Series C)* 35:205-220.

Neter, J., and Waksberg, J. (1964) A study of response errors in expenditures data from household surveys. *Journal of the American Statistical Association* 59:18-55.

Neter, J.E., Maynes, S., and Ramanathan, R. (1965) The effect of mismatching on the measurement of response errors. *Journal of the American Statistical Association* 60:1005.

O'Muircheartaigh, C.A. (1977) Response errors. In C.A. O'Muircheartaigh and C. Payne, eds., *The Analysis of Survey Data*. New York: Wiley.

O'Muircheartaigh, C.A. (1977) Statistical analysis in the context of survey research. In C.A. O'Muircheartaigh and C. Payne, eds., *The Analysis of Survey Data*. New York: Wiley.

Pearson, K. (1902) On the mathematical theory of errors of measurement. *Philosophical Transactions, Royal Society of London*, Series A, 198:235-299.

Raj, D. (1968) *Sampling Theory*. New York: McGraw-Hill.

Rogan, W.J., and Gladen, B. (1977) Estimating Prevalence With a Test. Mimeo. National Institute of Environmental Health Sciences, Research Triangle Park, N.C.

Sudman, S., and Bradburn, N. (1974) *Response Effects in Surveys*. Chicago: Aldine.

Sukhatme, P.V., and Seth, G.R. (1952) Non-sampling errors in surveys. *Journal of Indian Social and Agricultural Statistics* 4:5-41.

Sukhatme, P.V., and Sukhatme, B.V. (1970) *Sampling Theory of Surveys with Applications*. Ames, Iowa: Iowa State University Press.

Tenebein, A. (1970) A double sampling scheme for estimating from binomial data with misclassifications. *Journal of the American Statistical Association* 65:1350-1361.

Tremblay, V., Singh, M.P., and Clavel, L. (1976) Methodology of the labor force re-interview program. *Survey Methodology* 2:43-62.

Turner, C.F., and Krauss, E. (1978) Fallible indicators of the subjective state of the nation. *American Psychologist* 33:456-470.

Warner, S.L. (1965) A randomized response technique for eliminating evasive answer bias. *Journal of the American Statistical Association* 60:63-69.

Williams, W.H., and Mallows, C.L. (1970) Systematic biases in panel surveys. *Journal of the American Statistical Association* 65:1338-1349.

Zarkovich, S.S. (1966) *Quality of Statistical Data*. Rome: Food and Agriculture Organization of the United Nations.

PART V

PUTTING SURVEY MEASUREMENTS IN CONTEXT

It is common to interpret survey and poll results in the wider context of events and trends in society at large. Such interpretations are usually *ad hoc*, resting on a commentator's intuitions and insights about social change. Chapters 14 to 16, in contrast, illustrate ways that survey data might be supplemented by auxiliary data to illuminate historical trends and variations in public attitudes. Each of these chapters analyzes trends over time in subjective measurements of an aspect of public opinion and charts the interrelation between such subjective survey measurements and independent measurements of objective phenomena.

In Chapter 14, MacKuen tests the agenda-setting hypothesis that the amount of media coverage given to an issue influences public perceptions of its importance. In Chapter 15, Beniger focuses on trends in attitudes toward abortion, and brings to bear data on a variety of causal factors (including court decisions, media coverage of the issue, research findings on contraceptive methods, changes in contraceptive practices, and so on). In Chapter 16, MacKuen and Turner investigate fluctuations in presidential popularity, and demonstrate that analysis of inter-survey measurement reliability can be profitably embedded in a similar framework that takes account of the effects of media coverage and real-world events upon the public's assessment of its political leaders.

The final two chapters in this section take a somewhat different perspective. In Chapter 17, Martin introduces novel data on participation in popular culture (e.g., following sports) into a study of public opinion. Based on her exploratory analysis, Martin suggests that such data, which have not previously been exploited for their scientific value, have the potential to provide unique insights into the dynamics of public opinion formation.

Polls and surveys not only measure public opinion; when they are reported in the media they have the potential to influence it. In a sense, polls and surveys provide part of the context in which public opinion is formed. In Chapter 18, Marsh reviews the literature relating to what is probably the most controversial area in which polling effects have been posited—the influence of polls on political elections.

14

Reality, the Press, and Citizens' Political Agendas

Michael B. MacKuen

The independence of individuals in deciding what sorts of matters are politically important is an essential element in most democratic theory. After all, political decisions can only be made in subject areas that are in public view, and the ability to put matters on the political agenda is an important source of political power. An essential result of the last few years' examination of the empirical record, however, is a skepticism about the autonomy ordinary citizens exercise in matters of public affairs in general and, specifically, in choosing among political priorities. The importance of setting a democratic agenda has been clearly understood in the last three decades as the intellectual community has come to appreciate fully the implications of the cyclic nature of majority rule and, more generally, Arrow's impossibility theorem.[1] The fact that, except under restricted circumstances, the outcomes of public elections or referendums are subject to manipulation by those who control the substance and timing of presentation has pushed social scientists toward studying the factors that may set public agendas.[2]

This chapter reports on an examination (laid out in detail in MacKuen, 1981) of the factors involved in shaping the public's political agenda during the 1960s and 1970s. The essential purpose lies in contrasting two types of influences: those that can be interpreted as foundations for independent citizen evaluations and those that are more clearly subject to politically motivated manipulation. In the process of conducting the study, a secondary question was also addressed: whether it is possible at all to model public opinion dynamics as a consistent function of external stimuli. A demonstration that such a task is realizable provides some rebuttal to the argument that survey data do not measure anything real or reliable.

This analysis focuses on three sources of information upon which citizens may base their judgments about which political issues are most important. They are: (1) the objective conditions that individuals can experience in their local environments, (2) the editorial judgments of decision makers in the news media who determine how much news space various issues merit, and (3) those dramatic political events that may provoke individuals to reconsider their own views of what counts most in political life. Understanding the relative potency of these three elements will provide a partial description of the polity's power centers, and it also will paint a portrait of modern-day citizens and their political capabilities. If public response is limited to changes in objective conditions (say, in the economy, the level of warfare, or the crime rate), then it might be inferred that individuals make decisions on a self-interested evaluation of how their lives are affected. However, if it should appear that such factors are not related to changes in the public agenda, and that artificial sources of information (such as the press) dominate the public's judgment, then the skepticism about the appropriateness of a citizen-oriented policy-making system will be justified. To be sure, merely observing the historical relationship between public agendas and these three variables will neither completely describe the sources of political power nor measure the full range of citizen potential. The evidence from the contemporary United States to be presented herein, however, is meant to set some guides for future discussion.

Assessing the relative impact of these three factors requires a dynamic theoretical framework that explicitly introduces cross-time fluctuations, and it also demands an extensive array of data covering a wide range of political issues. For example, at any single moment, the correspondence between a newspaper's assignment of news space and a public's ranking of political issues enhances the plausibility of an agenda-setting effect, but it does not establish the newspaper as the prime-moving force. A strong counter-hypothesis suggests that both newspapers and the citizenry respond independently to a shared set of environmental conditions. The inference of agenda power may be spurious. Only a more fully specified estimation model, one that explicitly includes the major competing hypotheses, and an examination of the variables' joint movement over time will reduce this threat. A single-issue analysis, on the other hand, may be misleading because the effectiveness of the three factors may be expected to vary across issue domains; an examination of citizen concern with student unrest during the 1960s is less likely to find a role for objective conditions than is a study of inflation consciousness in the 1970s. Only a canvass of a fairly broad range of issues can produce statements that can even claim to be lawlike.

This chapter is divided into four sections. The first two outline the fundamental model of dynamics and then describe the data base available for analysis. The third presents a direct comparison of the "real world" and the "mediated" influences on the mass public's political agenda. Finally, an additional source, that of especially dramatic political events, is considered as a further complication.

The Elementary Dynamic Model

The following analyses, the technical matters of which are described in detail in MacKuen (1981:chapter 2),[3] are derived from confronting an elementary dynamic model with a broad array of data. The model, in its bare-bones form, posits that the public's concern with an issue at any given moment is a function of the contemporary informational environment (say, inflation rate, news coverage, and the occurrence of a presidential address) and another function of the past environments. While the form of these functions may be complex in theory, the data here are fit fairly well using an enormously simplified model. Contemporary influence is given a linear form, and previous history is added by simply applying exponentially decreasing weights (similar to the form associated with Koyck [1954]):

$$P_t = bE_t + d(bE_{t-1}) + d^2(bE_{t-2}) + \ldots + d^T(bE_{t-T}) , \qquad (1)$$

where P_t is public concern at time t; E_t, a measure of the informational environment at t; b, a scalar transformation; d, a number between 0.0 and 1.0 which, when raised to integral powers decreases exponentially; and T, some sufficiently large number. Additional impacts, that is, further E_t's, are added linearly to the model when appropriate (this assumes that public concern is an additive sum of different components, a clear simplification of what might be more complex interdependencies).

Although (1) is a useful nonlinear estimation equation, its interpretable properties are more apparent when it is expressed in another form. Because the past impact of experience is collected in the level of previous concern (P_{t-1}), the expression may be written:

$$P_t = bE_t + dP_{t-1} \qquad (2)$$

we may interpret $TC = (1/1 - d)$ as the *time constant* of the simple system defined by equation (2). This number, measured in time units, gives a sense of whether the process is relatively quick or sluggish. For example, the theoretical construction implies that about two-thirds of the overall impact of a causal influence will be felt in one time constant and that it will be absorbed mostly—a settling point of 95 percent—in three TCs. An empirical finding that a news story's effect on concern about civil rights had a TC of 3.27 (see the first row in Table 14.1 on page 465) suggests that the effect of any news story was concentrated in the first 3 months and that it had almost disappeared about 10 months later. This concept of measuring both immediate and enduring impacts over time is especially useful in comparing the overall impact of several variables, because it yields a term, here called "gain," which translates the instantaneous effect of the environment, b, into an equilibrium effect, $g = b(TC)$. In this example an immediate standardized impact of .12 gets translated into an eventual gain of .38 in public concern, because the effects of a long-distant past are added to those of the contemporary environment. In the same model (see the second row in Table 14.1), a larger momentary impact of .17 for transitory dramatic events yields a gain of only .30 because their effects do not persist as far into the future (the $TC = 1.79$, implying that the effect is mostly felt in 2 months). Thus, the explicit modeling of the variables' dynamic relations allows more comprehensive statements about comparative impacts than does ordinary cross-sectioned analysis. Statements about comparative dynamics and, more importantly for this analysis, about overall impacts fall straight out of the model.

The Data

The public opinion data base used here, generated from the Gallup organization's readings, covers the range of the American public's major issue concerns for the period 1963 through 1977. Some items (inflation, unemployment, and crime) were on the agenda, with changing degrees of emphasis, for almost the entire period; others (Vietnam, civil rights, energy, and the environment) had a briefer but still lengthy stand in the limelight, and one (campus unrest) was of very short duration. With the exceptions of Watergate and a vague concern about international problems prominent at the beginning of the period, this list covers the entire policy domain of almost two decades of public attentiveness.

The Gallup series, though, is flawed in three ways that limit the meaningfulness of conclusions. The first and most damaging is in the nature of the question itself. In the midst of a far-ranging questionnaire, respondents were asked, "What is the most important problem facing the country to-day?" Such a cursory inquiry into the individual's cognitions cannot be expected to elicit a particularly well thought out response, and probably represents for the ordinary respondent no more than a measure of what is on the tip of the tongue. This question does not provide as rich a picture of a cognitive structure as a more detailed and intensive probing would yield, and thus the results are weighted toward the most casual, superficial aspects of the public's political consciousness. On the other hand, the question's wording is, on its face value, just the sort of thing required and is probably the most that could be expected from a short item. Furthermore, public responsiveness to this particular question has an importance of its own, inasmuch as it is widely used by political elites as an indicator of public concern.

Less bothersome, at least at a first glance, is the fact that Gallup ordinarily asked for only one response to the question. Thus, the item indicates only what is at the top of each individual's importance ranking, with the subsequent ordering left untapped. Clearly there exist situations in which more than one issue domain is considered to be of first-rate importance to an individual, and he or she is unable to indicate the great importance of the marginally secondary item. If the analysis were limited to following only one person through time, it might falsely suggest that a particular issue domain had lapsed into unimportance because the individual did not mention it, when it had in fact only been superseded by an even more demanding concern. If the data were generated by a probabilistic model of individual response, in which the respondents are only more likely to mention their first concern but still have some (lesser) probability of mentioning the secondary item, then aggregations across individuals provide an indicator of the ordering for the public as a whole. Making such an assumption is not unreasonable, although it depends upon further assumptions of equal variance across individuals in the response-generating mechanism, or at least a variance independent of the individual's substantive concerns, and it may be that the interview situation is more likely to generate deterministic (or replicable) responses for the more politically involved who may be more sensitive to new or more esoteric issues. However, even though some noise may creep into the analyses, such confounding influences are not likely to pose major problems for proper inference.

Finally, and on the more technical side, the Gallup series presents irregularly spaced observations of the public's concern. Two potential problems arise: significant shifts in public opinion may have occurred during the periods of infrequent observations—this is surely the case during the early 1970s when the unemployment characteristic of the economy first captured public attention; in addition, the data will not permit modeling the autoregressive structure of the opinion measure, a condition that limits precision in determining the separate impacts of the three causal factors. Nevertheless, the historical record ought to yield some inkling of the way the process works.

On the media side a different sort of problem presents itself. The analysis requires a measure of the media intake for each respondent in the surveys during the relevant time period. This would ideally include a coding of the content of newspapers, magazines, and radio and television programs to which each respondent might pay attention. Clearly these data are not available, and a substitute must be generated to serve as an indicator of the media content each person is likely to have encountered. This requires an empirical measure that changes quantitatively in concert with the different media streams consumed by the respondent. Here again the virtues of aggregation suggest using a single measure of national media content; the idiosyncratic fluctuations in local, or source-specific, coverage will cancel out, leaving a single over-time component. The single national indicator strategy depends on assuming that cross-temporal variation of news coverage dominates cross-sectional variance.

The national newsmagazines (*Time, Newsweek,* and *U.S. News & World Report*) provide just such a record of national news coverage devoted to each political issue. The measure consists of a count of the number of articles presented each month from January 1960 through December 1977. (The counts were made on the references in *The Readers' Guide to Periodical Literature* and are, of course, subject to the vagaries of the indexing staff.) The counts were cumulated into month-long time slices in order to yield a sufficiently fine time gradient for measuring relatively quick processes, and yet wide enough to absorb some of the noise inherent in an indirect measure. In terms of validity it is worth noting that, while the newsmagazines' content represents only a small portion of the total news coverage and a raw number count is hardly a subtle measure of salience, the measure provides an indication of much more. The newsmagazines are by their nature encapsulations of the current week's news stories, and as such serve as summaries of a period's news to be found in any set of news sources. In addition, the magazine data measure coverage of *national* concerns without including the local clutter to be found in a small sampling of even the most prestigious of newspapers. Furthermore, with respect to the salience component, the editors of the magazines are forced to allocate limited space and editorial staff to a number of competing items and in doing so generate a measure that is more than a simple news-space survey in that it incorporates a natural salience component. This measure should not be interpreted as a simple mass of news coverage, but instead should be viewed as an indicator of the significance the news machine attributes to a particular political concern.

Again, the newsmagazine data are only an indicator of the general level of news coverage, and occasionally change with editorial currents peculiar to the magazine format. It is only by employing a fairly large weight of observations that this strategy can possibly get a fix on the amount of the actual coverage any one individual is likely to have digested.

The measures of the severity of objective conditions, again for reasons of practicality, are limited to indicators aggregated to the national level. For the personal impact of the Vietnam War, a preferred indicator would move with any given respondent's contact with the war experience or with those who were directly affected; the number here is a count of U.S. troop strength in Vietnam.[4] In terms of an individual's orientation to crime, personal-experience measures or at least locality-specific statistics would be desirable. Monthly measurements of this sort, however, are not readily available, and national crime statistics[5] take their place. Similarly, the economic variables are national aggregates of the rate of inflation and unemployment, and price levels of fuel.[6] Here, as well, the assumption is that cross-temporal variation will be fairly consistent for many different life experiences even if cross-sectional variation may be observed.

The third set of factors, the dramatic political events, has no naturally available measure, so their significance must be determined endogenously. The strategy used here (due to Erbring, 1975) consists of estimating the relative impact of each event in the context of the rest of the model. In detail: (1) the dates of potentially important events were taken from *The New York Times Index*; (2) the dynamics of all events in the subsequent series were constrained to be identical; and (3) the magnitude of the individual event spikes were then estimated simultaneously with the single dynamic coefficient and the parameters of the rest of the model. (Because this procedure is slightly out of the ordinary, the Appendix sketches out an example in some depth.)

The Press and the Objective Environment

An analysis of these data relating citizen concerns to changes in objective conditions, media coverage, and the timing of dramatic events evaluates the components' relative power. Because the data for event series are endogenously generated, this section presents a comparison between the effects of only the media and environment components. The estimates are presented issue by issue because the data show characteristic differences in the impact patterns, and the cross-issue comparisons yield further information about how the processes work. Only after the basic results are established are the event series added so as to complete the specification and slightly modify the substantive inference.

Thus the initial task requires discovering whether individuals' issue agendas are shaped by the media or reflect independent evaluations of the environment. The distinction here is between a passive "mediated-consciousness" model of the citizen in which the individual merely reacts to messages presented in (and potentially manipulated by) the press and a more active "life-space" model in which individuals independently translate their experiences into political consciousness. An analysis of the set of topics that are prima facie media issues presents an outline of the possible effects of the media coverage on the public. Making up this class of concerns are those for which objective conditions are sufficiently remote from the bulk of the population that citizens are not likely to be able to experience or understand the phenomenon in their daily lives. Included are civil rights, campus unrest, and the environment.

The most prominent of these items is, of course, the civil rights movement. While the issue dominated the early 1960s, it is implausible to argue that the severity of racism was directly felt by more than a small and obviously delineated portion of the population. In fact, it can be argued that the civil rights movement was the prototypical media issue insofar as its success can be attributed to the ability of its proponents to portray their cause to a potentially sympathetic but insulated audience. Clearly such motivations played a large part in the strategy of marches, demonstrations, and confrontation.

FIGURE 14.1

Actual and Predicted Public Concern with Race, 1962-77

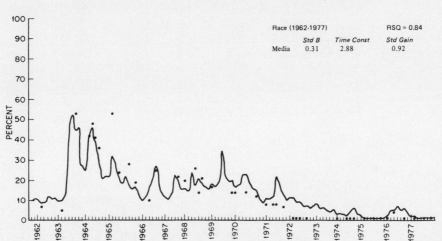

NOTES: Predictions (continuous line) were derived from model using media coverage alone; actual measurements (points) are percentage of answers mentioning this concern in response to Gallup survey question asking respondents to name "the most important problem facing the country today."

The estimation results[7] at the top of Figure 14.1 reveal a good fit, with 84 percent of the over-time variance accounted for by media coverage. The attractiveness of this correspondence is made more evident by the plot of predicted public concern against measured concern. The model does more than fit a mere trend line to the data. The media-based predictions (drawn in a solid line) fluctuate up and down frequently over time, and seem to capture similar movements in the target data (represented by dots). The dramatic surges associated with Selma in 1963, and the civil rights march and bill of 1964, and the subsequent declines are reflected in the model's operation. The sensitivity of the public to coverage is captured in the time constant of 2.88, indicating that two-thirds of the effect of the media was felt in the first 3 months. In all, the data are consistent with the notion that the public's concern about the racial question was largely determined by their vicarious experience through the media.

The second issue, which was perhaps even more characteristically a media creation, was that of campus unrest in 1969 and 1970. No sizable portion of the population could have directly experienced or felt threatened by student activities. Again (see Figure 14.2), there exists a high correspondence between the media-based predictions and the observable public reaction. The goodness-of-fit measure of .86 reflects the rise and fall of the issue during the spring of 1969 and of 1970. Public sensitivity in this case is particularly high, with most of the effect felt during the month of news coverage, and almost all of it lost by the next time period. Here, it can be fairly said, are seen the traces of a media issue in operation.

The third candidate for media-driven consciousness is the environment question. While all members of the public experience their environment by breathing air, drinking water, or simply looking about, it is not at all clear that they evaluate its quality day by day and translate their judgments into politicized cognitions (except, perhaps, in Los Angeles). We might argue more convincingly that public concern over the environment is keyed to ecological concerns portrayed in the media. However, the analysis reported in Figure 14.3 shows that media coverage accounts for practically no variance at all. The model itself looks reasonable, with a short enough time constant to indicate sensitivity, but the fit disappoints the mediated-consciousness prediction.

It should be noted from the graph in Figure 14.3 that concern over the environment fluctuates over an extremely narrow range, never exceeding 8 percent. Of course these observations of public concern are actually estimates from Gallup samples, and are subject to a sampling error of a couple of percentage points (as are all of these observations). Thus it is possible that the observed variation in public opinion, being so small in this case, represents an unusually large portion of sampling error and that the model is trying to account more for random variation than for true change. What-

FIGURE 14.2

Actual and Predicted Public Concern with Campus Unrest, 1968-72

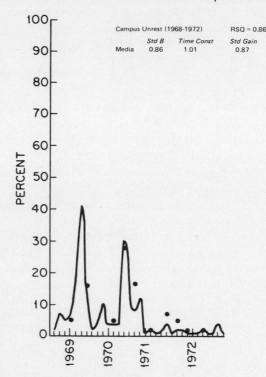

NOTES: Predictions (continuous line) were derived from model using media coverage alone. (See notes to Figure 14.1 regarding actual measurements.)

ever the case, either due to technical or theoretical limitations, a satisfactory fit does not obtain in this instance.

Thus, for two of the three cases—and the third's failure may be due to technical limitations—the level of public demand on the polity in a particular policy area is rather closely accounted for by the level of media coverage given that topic. But these are issues specifically selected to represent susceptibility to this pure media analysis. In order to assess more directly the ability of individuals to act as independent citizens, the analysis requires turning to a set of concerns in which real-life experiences might be expected to play a greater part: Vietnam, crime, unemployment, energy, and inflation.

The first of this set, the Vietnam War, moves only marginally away from media-dominance expectations. Most Americans were not directly affected by the war effort, or at least not in an obvious and personal way. However, during the height of American involvement, more than one-half million

FIGURE 14.3

Actual and Predicted Public Concern with Environment, 1970-77

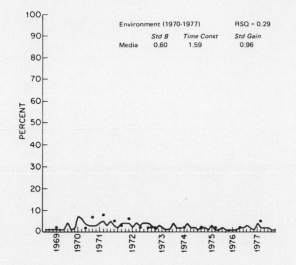

NOTES: Predictions (continuous line) were derived from model using media coverage alone. (See notes to Figure 14.1 regarding actual measurements.)

troops were in Vietnam, and it became commonplace for most citizens to have friends and relatives who had been involved directly in the war effort. In addition, millions more faced the possibility that they or their children would be drafted. Thus a large number of Americans had their lives (negatively) affected by the war effort; if they reacted to changes in their local environment, that number should vary with the intensity of the United States involvement. The results from Figure 14.4 expressly contradict such a prediction. Here the model attempts to predict popular concern about the war by troop strength in Vietnam. (Were the measure weighted by casualties, the result would be substantially the same.) Public concern mounted well before mobilization got into full swing, actually fell off as peak involvement was achieved, and then maintained a level of watchfulness well after Americans ceased to serve in the area. The poor performance of the life-space model is clearly reflected in the negative-fit coefficient, portraying the inability of the model to dominate a simple mean prediction. In a statistical sense, this means that the distribution of public concern about Vietnam cannot be said to be conditional on the extent of war activity.[8] It is clear that public opinion was not directly related to the objective condition of the war itself.

On the other hand, Figure 14.5 shows that media coverage accounts superbly for the variance. The model predicts the initial surge, the dropoff,

FIGURE 14.4

Actual and Predicted Public Concern with Vietnam, 1965-73

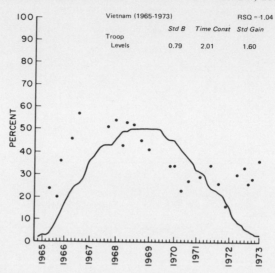

NOTES: Predictions (continuous line) were derived from model using only American troop levels in Vietnam. (See notes to Figure 14.1 regarding actual measurements.)

and the subsequent leveling and decline almost perfectly. The only lack of correspondence occurs during the intensive portrayal of the American evacuation. The media preoccupation with these last days did not translate into public concern; presumably these events were seen as an end to the entire matter rather than as a harbinger of further fighting.

When both the objective war-involvement measure and media coverage are introduced into the same equation, the analysis yields more nearly unbiased estimates of each's contribution (due to the fuller specification). The model reveals that the impact of the actual war level is in fact nil (that is, zero) at the point of optimal fit (not shown), leaving a pure media model determining war consciousness.

These basic outlines formed the basis from which Funkhouser (1973a) concluded that the public reacted solely to media coverage and not at all to changes in their actual environment. This finer-tuned analysis of the Vietnam data supports his conclusion; but the inference must be sensitive to the possibility that the phenomenon may be peculiar to one particular sort of issue, one in which the emotions of high politics might easily dominate ordinary life concerns. The final four issues represent much more mundane matters.

The next in the ordering of expected experiential impact is the crime problem. The rate of criminal acts, at least as reported, rose dramatically in

454

FIGURE 14.5

Actual and Predicted Public Concern with Vietnam, 1965-77

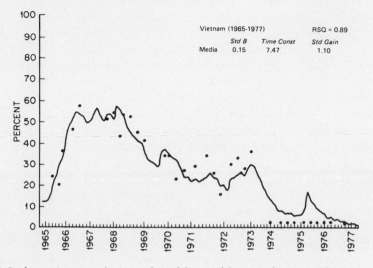

NOTES: Predictions (continuous line) were derived from model using media coverage alone. (See notes to Figure 14.1 regarding actual measurements.)

the 1960–77 period and became an object of much policy attention. While relatively few citizens actually become victims of crime, many more live in communities where crimes occur. When a crime, particularly of a violent nature, occurs in a neighborhood, word travels fast. The secondary involvement, while not necessarily reflecting an individual's personal experience, certainly falls into the category of life-space events. Crimes committed in the immediate neighborhood can be expected to provoke concern in the average citizen about personal safety. Thus, while only fractions of the population are victims, changes in the crime rate will likely bring the issue to the attention of entire neighborhoods, and thus affect the aggregated national concern with law and order. The evidence, however, gives little support to a notion of public sensitivity to criminal activity. Violent-crime change rates (which fit the target data considerably better than any other measure, particularly property crime) can only account for 15 percent of the variance in public concern and really do not produce a prediction sensitive to short-term fluctuations (that is, what might be an artificial long-term rise in reported crimes—artificial because the increase might be due to changes in reporting procedures—does not account for the mismatch here). On the other hand, media coverage by itself accounts for 44 percent of the variance. When these two inputs are joined together to obtain an unbiased set of coefficient estimates (see Figure 14.6), the media source truly dominates. The objective data provide only an additional 1 percent in predictive power, and the impact of the crime rate almost vanishes. As the media and environmental variables have different scales, this disappearance is most clearly evident in noting the standardized terms (which are not, by the way, interpretable as path coefficients), where the real world weighs in at a featherlike .007 and is dominated by media by a factor of more than 20 to 1. Again the conclusion is that the public's attention is directed by editorial judgments and not, at least in the aggregate, by awareness of the objective conditions.

The final three areas, however, provide the greatest hope of reversing this conclusion. They deal with aspects of a topic which, often derisively, is used to delineate the American character: economics. The first in line is unemployment, which affected sizable portions of the public; then energy, the shortage of which touched the nerves of many; and finally inflation, an impact felt universally.

In the first case, then, the life-space model predicts that the proportion concerned with unemployment should vary with the number of jobless Americans. At any given time, of course, only from 4 to 9 percent might actually be unemployed, but the affected proportion ranges considerably higher. A substantial number will have been out of work in the recent past; for example, if 10 percent are unemployed in March and 10 percent in April with, say, 5 percent hard-core, then 15 percent will have been directly affected in the immediate period. Others will have given up hope entirely, have had a family member or friend out of work, or begun to anticipate the

FIGURE 14.6

Actual and Predicted Public Concern with Crime, 1965-76

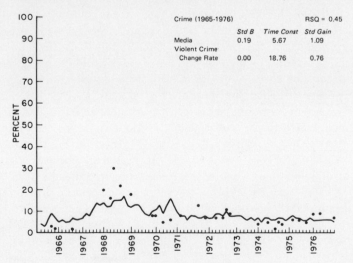

NOTES: Predictions (continuous line) were derived from model using both media coverage and violent crime change rate. (See notes to Figure 14.1 regarding actual measurements.)

possibility of being laid off in the near future. Mapping the jobless rate into public concern surprisingly produces a fit of only .35, disappointing in comparison with the media-only model's performance of .65 (a model which, however, is generated with an unbelievable time constant of 34 months, indicating no real sensitivity to short-term changes). At first glance it would seem that even unemployment falls into the media-power domain.

However, an inspection of the real-world model's fit (not shown) reveals a constant overprediction during the booming 1960s and an undershot for the 1970s recession. A rethinking of the nature of unemployment suggests that a portion of the work force will normally expect to be out of work for seasonal layoffs or for idiosyncratic reasons, and that the political impact would only be felt at levels above what is euphemistically called full employment. As a first approximation of the distinction, the analysis discounts a factor that people take to be business as usual (during the boom period the figure was around 3.8 percent) and uses upward deviations from this routine experience as the indicator of environmental impact.

This modification of the measure is handsomely rewarded by a rise in predictive power from .37 to a robust .80 for the environment alone. The result is depicted in Figure 14.7. When both inputs are jointly evaluated, the power of the media model (the theoretical value of which was on shaky ground in terms of its sensitivity parameter) evaporates into thin air. There is no improvement (.007) in fit due to the addition of media, and the impact coefficient for news coverage deviates only minutely from zero. In terms of unemployment, then, the public reacts hardly at all to the call of the media but is sensitive to changes in objective living conditions.

The second economic issue deals with the problem of energy. Much of the elite concern about an energy crisis was associated with projections of the future energy demands of an increasingly industrialized world and the anticipated difficulty in finding sufficient resources to satisfy that appetite. This aspect of the crisis may well be expected to have passed right over the head of average citizens and in any case had no direct or obvious impact on their daily life. However, during this period there were changes in the ready availability of energy which, while not directly due to future shortfalls, had been generated by conditions reflecting the overall phenomenon. In any case, such fluctuations could have been seen in the interpretative framework of the general crisis. To be sure, supplies of home heating fuel were threatened, and their prices rose dramatically in the 1970s. (Gasoline prices also rose, but their changes provided no predictive leverage, at least during this time period.) The life-space model clearly posits that citizens would have shown concern about energy in general when their fuel bills skyrocketed.

An evaluation of the comparison of this experiential input with the media's contribution may be found in Figure 14.8, which presents the results of a joint estimation of parameters for media and heating fuel. Here the fit

FIGURE 14.7

Actual and Predicted Public Concern with Employment, 1962-77

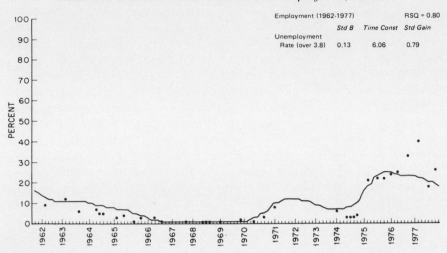

NOTES: Predictions (continuous line) were derived from model using only the unemployment rate (measured as deviation from "usual" level of 3.8 percentage). (See notes to Figure 14.1 regarding actual measurements.)

reaches .79 and, more important, comes in with standardized impact coefficients of .24 and .28 and standardized gain figures of .40 and .50 for media and environment, respectively. Thus there exists a solid case for substantial citizen responsiveness to objective life conditions although, unlike the unemployment item, here media coverage weighs in importantly as well.

The final item, inflation, promises the strongest candidacy for individual life evaluations. Here the phenomenon directly manifests itself to almost everyone on a daily basis. The public certainly reacted to the rate of inflation, producing a fit of .74 for a reasonably sensitive model. The media-only model comes in at .66, but with an extremely unlikely 67.57-month time constant. Putting the two components together yields a different and more properly evaluated model. As Figure 14.9 shows, the model can account for three-quarters of the variance with a model in which the public is sensitive to short-term fluctuations in each input. Moreover, the best comparative measures of impact, the standardized b's of .06 and .07, suggest that news coverage and objective conditions play about equal roles in shaping this aspect of the public's consciousness.

A close inspection of the tracking in Figure 14.9, however, reveals that while the large chunks of variation are fairly well represented, the timing of the predictions is sadly off in the late 1960s and early 1970s. This, of course, was the period when the issue first rose in prominence, and missing the

458

FIGURE 14.8

Actual and Predicted Public Concern with Energy, 1973-77

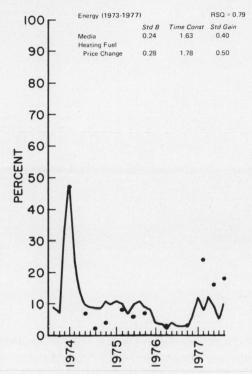

NOTES: Predictions (continuous line) were derived from model using media coverage and price changes for heating fuels. (See notes to Figure 14.1 regarding actual measurements.)

timing on its movement suggests a failure in the model. Partitioning the time period, though, captures a better sense of how these impact processes work.

The level of inflation, while widely noticed earlier, did not seriously begin to escalate until after 1972, when the price of Nixon's electoral strategy came due. Splitting the series into two eras, 1960–72 and 1973–77, yields a dramatic change in the estimated models. The second period (Figure 14.10) produces a model essentially similar to the overall picture of shared causality (the lower fit reflects the increased relative importance of underestimating the heights of concern in 1974, which the full model missed as well). The earlier period (see Figure 14.11) seems a distinctively different world. With inflation bubbling along at noticeable but hardly impressive levels, meaningful movement appears to have been largely determined by media coverage. The 1971 boost in inflation consciousness now is nicely accounted

FIGURE 14.9

Actual and Predicted Public Concern with Inflation, 1962-77

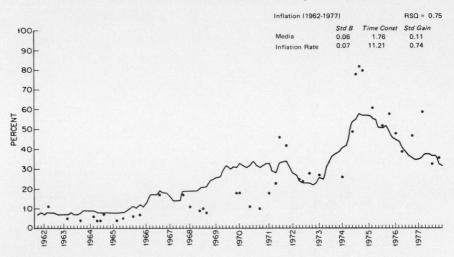

NOTES: Predictions (continuous line) were derived from model using media coverage and the inflation rate. (See notes to Figure 14.1 regarding actual measurements.)

for, and reveals itself as a media creation and not a reaction to the actual conditions.

This final exercise uncovers a clue to how the public reacts to the environment. From early 1967 through mid-1971 the rate of inflation was in fact moving downward well below previous levels. However, for whatever reasons, the Nixon administration reacted to financial community concern and, by playing the trump card of presidential power, made inflation a political issue. The public, taking their cues from the press, followed suit. It was not until after the price controls were dropped in 1973 and the Organization of Petroleum Exporting Countries' marketing strategy produced a real income drop that citizens began to react to fluctuations in their living environment.

Two inferences seem in order. First, even for economic issues it is possible for the public to be led by the media's representations. The press played a substantial role in forming energy and inflation (particularly early) consciousness. Thus there is nothing magic about economic criteria being easily or naturally handled by individuals. Second, and more important, it appears that for the public to react politically to its environment, substantial and dramatic changes must present themselves at both the symbolic and objective levels. Unemployment concern pretty well reflected fluctuations in the actual conditions, even without dramatic changes throughout the era. But the issue had been firmly placed onto the public agenda by the Depression years of the 1930s, with the result that individuals had long been at-

FIGURE 14.10

Actual and Predicted Public Concern with Inflation, 1973-77

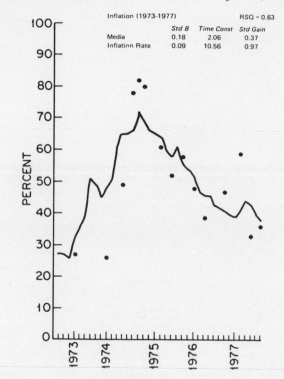

NOTES: Predictions (continuous line) were derived from model using media coverage and the inflation rate. (See notes to Figure 14.1 regarding actual measurements.)

tuned to the political implications of even modest changes in the unemployment rate. Inflation consciousness, on the other hand, was fairly insensitive to actual conditions until after the dramatic politicization in 1971 and 1972 was closely followed by a price explosion. Although such a clear case cannot be discerned for energy, both symbolic and actual changes being coincident, it is clear that the public did not react until events of major political proportions had occurred. This limited number of cases suggests that the public is able to translate into political terms their ordinary life observations only after having been sensitized by elite-generated symbolic presentations. An interpretative framework for political analysis must exist for experience to become consciousness. On the other hand, even during periods of real environmental change, individuals seem also, and independently, to follow the cues of the press.

The overall picture of citizen consciousness, then, is mixed. From the

FIGURE 14.11

Actual and Predicted Public Concern with Inflation, 1962-72

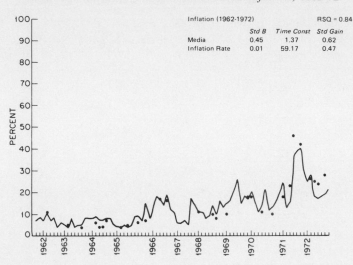

NOTES: Predictions (continuous line) were derived from model using media coverage and the inflation rate. (See notes to Figure 14.1 regarding actual measurements.)

comparative analysis of Vietnam and crime, and from the strong results for race and campus unrest, it is obvious that for a substantial portion of political issues, the public reacts wholly to the manifestation of elite representations in the press. On the other hand, the economic issues suggest that individuals are in fact *capable* of evaluating their local environment. The media do not by themselves set the public's agenda. The result, then, is a portrait of political man playing two parts. In the first, he seems to react to political events as a symbolic game in which he is merely a passive observer, though of course one with a rooting interest. In the second, he engages his full and active daily-life consciousness in assessing his environment when its nature is defined in understandably personal terms.

Dramatic Political Events

While these two distinctive sets of causal factors represent idealized extremes of citizens' capabilities, individuals are likely to pay attention to more complex stimuli. The first model, activated by media input, characterized the citizen as a basically passive receiver of the policy issues presented by the press. No allowance was made for the character of news content. The second formulation pretty well ignored public events and restricted the citizens' stimuli to changes in their personal scenes.

Clearly, between the extremes of passivity and autonomy lies an active-consciousness model in which citizens evaluate the significance of real-world events, even if these events do not actually impinge on their immediate life conditions. Citizens are not likely to limit their attention merely to those conditions that affect their daily lives and to ignore the play of events on the national stage. While an incident may occur at some geographical or social distance from any individual, he or she may see it as center-stage action in the commonly shared public arena. In order to provide a more nearly complete evaluation of how citizens form their agendas, the analytic model must consider the possibility that they may shape their judgments by also taking the measure of political events.

The idea, then, is to include a simultaneous measure of political-event impacts in the overall model. An independent rating of events of course does not exist, and their magnitudes must be estimated, as described in the Appendix. While the matter of the exact procedures used in developing the two series is a technical detail, it is important to understand the character of the events that are included. The series employed here reflect one central decision rule: the events included all possess the characteristic that they were sufficiently dramatic or accessible to have penetrated the indifference of the more casual observers of the political scene. This criterion excludes remote events even if they represented substantively important elite actions, such as ground-breaking legislation or court decisions. Passing the test are such events as political assassinations, the more massive civil rights and war-related demonstrations, the more dramatic urban riots, the oil embargo, the Tet Offensive, and all televised presidential addresses to the nation. The intention here is to include events of such a dramatic quality that their occurrence might make ordinary citizens take notice and begin to evaluate the political scene. (A list of the included events is presented in Table 14.A–1 at the end of this chapter.)

For several of the issue tests, the event array was divided into two sets because empirical experimentation suggested that two sorts of events could be demarcated. The first type, termed transitory, were events of the ordinary political sort. They were sometimes capable of attracting widespread attention, but their impact always proved short-lived. The second category of enduring events was made up of those with an effect that was long-lasting, presumably because they characteristically provided the stimulus for citizens not merely to notice an occurrence but also to rethink their fundamental views.

The inclusion of these event data into the model provides a noticeable change in predictive capability, even if all significant events are scored identically. Substantial improvements are revealed by comparing these results, portrayed in the second column of Table 14.2, with the first set of figures which represents the levels from the (previously described) media-environment analysis. At this intermediate stage, the event data are not rescored to fit the targets; the boost in fit can be attributed entirely to the timing of the series.

The final stage reevaluates the event data to reflect differential impacts. It combines the timing of each event and the opinion measurements after each event to calculate what the strength of the event must have been (see Appendix). The third column in Table 14.2 shows that this two-stage process of estimating event impacts produces a substantially better fit for all issues except Vietnam and employment, though for these some improvement results as well. The effect of events on public consciousness should not be thought trivial.

The parameter estimates, collected in Table 14.1, present the relative magnitudes of the sets of inputs and start to sketch a fuller picture of how the public forms its agenda. The inclusion of both ordinary and continuity-breaking events slightly alters the initial overview. The standardized-gain coefficients (the equilibrium effects normed to observable variations) show that the media impact diminishes considerably from the simpler model, while that for the environment remains fairly stable. For every case except the early inflation period, the contribution of events to consciousness dominates that of the amount of media coverage. For the economic issues (late inflation and employment) the coefficients for media drop to zero, which is to say that for these issues routinely generated news coverage (that not associated with spectacular events) carries little agenda-setting impact.

Now there are two ways to evaluate this array. First, from the viewpoint of inputs to the public as a whole, the picture remains essentially the same as that just presented. Aside from the purely economic issues, inflation and employment, the symbolic information represented in both events and media coverage dominates the available environmental measures and by itself accounts for the bulk of cross-temporal fluctuations. That is, for most issues, most of the time, individual agenda choices are only modestly affected by the objective environment. Citizens do not simply extrapolate their life experiences into these sorts of political judgments. In this sense it appears that an understanding of how these choices are made should concentrate on discovering how the symbolic environment is fashioned.

However, the portrait of the citizen is substantially altered. Individuals do not passively accept the weight of media coverage as a guide to their decisions, but instead evaluate political events and respond to them selectively and differentially. This is not to say that the press plays no role at all. Of course the character (and even occurrence) of public events is transmitted to the citizen by the press. Certainly the decision of how an event is to be depicted defines its nature and hence its impact, and in formulating that

TABLE 14.1
Standardized Impact Coefficients and Time Constants for Eight Issues

Issue/Input	Standardized B	Time Constant	Standardized Gain
Race			
Media	.12	3.27	.38
Event (transitory)	.17	1.79	.30
Event (enduring)	.16	17.73	2.86
Environment			
Media	.10	7.37	.77
Event (transitory)	.76	2.46	1.88
Vietnam			
Media	.15	6.39	.99
Event (transitory)	.15	1.67	.25
Event (enduring)	.10	5.51	.56
Crime			
Media	.08	8.82	.69
Environment	.01	15.53	.14
Event (enduring)	.41	7.82	3.17
Employment			
Media	.00	1.00	.00
Environment	.13	4.84	.61
Event (transitory)	.06	2.63	.17
Event (enduring)	.11	22.78	2.46
Energy			
Media	.14	1.00	.14
Environment	.40	1.00	.40
Event (transitory)	.35	3.79	1.34
Inflation (early)			
Media	.14	7.83	1.11
Environment	.00	1.00	.00
Event (transitory)	.28	1.61	.46
Inflation (late)			
Media	.00	1.00	.00
Environment	.07	14.33	.94
Event (transitory)	.17	3.56	.59
Event (enduring)	.07	8.78	.61

NOTES: These parameters are derived from estimates on the fully specified model for each substantive area. The standardized B's indicate the immediate impact of each variable on public concern about each issue (both normed for observed variation) while the standardized gains represent the full effect, both immediate and enduring. The time constant (in months) indicates the relative persistence of each immediate impact. The media, environment, (transitory) and (enduring) events rows provide the coefficients for news coverage, for the appropriate real-world conditions, and for the transitory and enduring events, respectively.

TABLE 14.2
R-Square Statistics for Event-Series Additions

Issue	Two Components	Unit Impulses	Evaluated Event Series
Race	.84	.89	.97
Environment	.29	.50	.57
Vietnam	.89	.90	.93
Crime	.45	.45	.87
Employment	.80	.81	.91
Energy	.74	.84	.95
Inflation (1961–73)	.84	.91	.93
Inflation (1973–77)	.63	.80	.87

NOTES: The R^2 statistics represent the fitting of increasingly complex models to the data. The two-component column represents models using only media coverage and environmental conditions (where relevant) in the predictive model. The unit-impulse series adds a variable with a set of equal spikes at the time selected for each dramatic event (and zeros otherwise). The final column represents results obtained by going on to the next step. The event-impacts were estimated from the data and used as additional variables. This column represents the fullest specification of the prediction equations.

definition the media managers clearly wield a heavy hand. However, the evidence clearly suggests that the bulk of the symbolic impact may more properly be attributed to the character of events and their portrayal, particularly the continuity-breaking ones, and not to the simple amount of news coverage allocated to the problems they represented.

Thus citizens' views of what is politically important derive most clearly from an active consideration of their environments, both local and distant, and do not merely reflect the editorial space allocations of the press. Nor does this mean that the public is in complete control of their sensitivities; one suspects that they are not. The meaning of events is clearly defined for the public, not by them. It should not be inferred that this active consciousness is intensely analytic or at all well considered; most citizens give only peripheral attention to the entire play of politics. Yet it is their understanding of the scene, not its repetitiveness, that forms their judgments.

Appendix

This appendix outlines the event-impact estimation strategy. The problem lies in estimating how much of an effect on public concern might be attributed to the occurrence of a given dramatic event when no independent measure of event magnitudes is available. Because the process is a little complicated, it might be best presented by way of an idealized example.

Reality, the Press, and Public Opinion

Take the data depicted in Fig. 14.A–1 as a portion of the predicted public concern for inflation based on the inflation rate and the amount of media coverage. There is clearly an increased level of concern immediately following the presidential address, which is probably due to its attention-getting potential. Fig. 14.A–2 illustrates the "residuals" from the predictions (of the rest of the model) showing a leftover bulge of 10 points 1 month after the event, and 2.5 points 3 months later. It can readily be seen that an event-impact of 20 points and a d term of .50 fit the data perfectly. After one period the prediction is: $0 + .50(20) = 10.0$; after three periods the prediction is only: $0 + .50^3(20) = 2.5$ [see Equation (1)]. Of course such perfect algebraic solutions do not generally obtain in the actual data. Thus while it is theoretically possible to estimate the impact with only two public opinion observations, having a number of subsequent readings is useful for grounding the estimates against sampling error and unspecified substantive disturbances.

In practice the procedure entails estimating a single dynamic coefficient (for all events) and a set of impact scalars (one for each event) that best fit the data, such as that portrayed in Fig. 14.A–3. Mechanically this amounts to introducing an additional variable, scored according to the estimated impact at the time of each event (with the persisting effects discounted by the dynamic parameter d^T in subsequent periods T time points removed). Of course at any point in time the remaining effects of several past events might still be felt, and these are merely summed up to produce an accumulated effect of all past-event history. For the distinction between "enduring" and "transitory" events, two separate series were introduced, each with a separate dynamic coefficient but with a set of individual impact estimates. It should be noted that these coefficients and event estimates are generated simultaneously with those that describe the rest of the model (and not in the step-wise process used as a heuristic above). The parameters for the whole model were estimated using a nonlinear, iterative least-squares approach which combined an extensive grid search with a steepest-descent gradient movement in order to find a maximum likelihood solution. For a more formal treatment, see MacKuen (1981).

The major inferential problem with this tactic lies in the possibility that sampling errors are inadvertently ascribed to the event estimates, and thus the variance of the model's disturbances will be underestimated. This difficulty would be most disturbing if the event estimates seemed to reflect sampling error rather than an intuitive notion of their importance. The estimates of the event-impacts used in this chapter (see Table 14.A–1) suggest that this is not likely to be a serious source of error. Most of the estimates appear to conform to commonplace expectations about their significance at the time. However, some of the disturbances must surely be "accounted for" by the impact estimates. These estimates thus must be taken as only rough approximations.

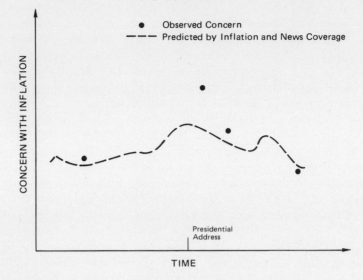

FIGURE 14.A-1
Idealized Tracking of Inflation Concern Over Time

● Observed Concern
--- Predicted by Inflation and News Coverage

CONCERN WITH INFLATION

Presidential
Address

TIME

FIGURE 14.A-2
Idealized Fit of Inferred Event and Dynamic Model to Observed Residuals

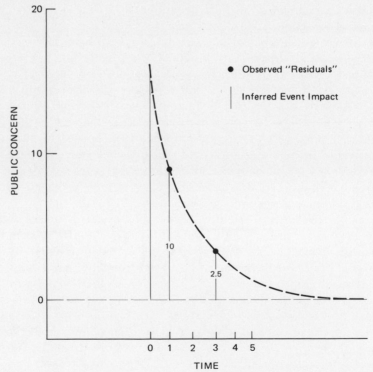

20

● Observed "Residuals"

| Inferred Event Impact

PUBLIC CONCERN

10

10

2.5

0

0   1   2   3   4   5

TIME

FIGURE 14.A-3

Fit of Several Events to Opinion Series

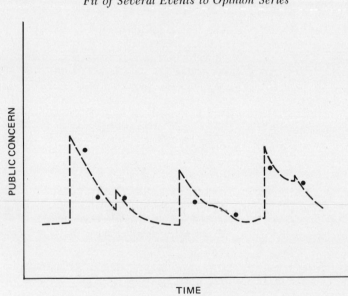

TABLE 14.A-1
Event Classification and Immediate Impacts

Transitory Impact	Enduring Impact	Event Description (Month-Year)
Race		
—	6	Birmingham (5–63)
0	—	JFK–TV, address on race (6–63)
—	32	Civil rights march on Washington (9–63)
12	—	1964 Civil rights bill passage (7–64)
26	—	LBJ–TV, Voting rights asked, Selma (3–65)
24	—	Watts (8–65)
—	10 [a]	Meredith shooting (6–66)
—	9	LBJ–TV, Detroit/Newark (7–67)
—	4	LBJ–TV, King assassination (4–68)
0	—	Nixon (RMN)–TV, address on busing (3–72)
Environment		
0	—	Santa Barbara oil spill (2–69)
0	—	Earth Day (4–70)
8 [a]	—	Oil spills (San Francisco, New Haven) (1–71)
0	—	Oil spill (St. Lawrence Seaway) (6–76)
15 [a]	—	Oil spills (*Argo Merchant*) (12–76)
Vietnam		
—	19	Tonkin Gulf (8–64)
0	—	LBJ–TV, bombing resumed (2–66)
4	—	Washington war protest (10–67)
8	—	LBJ–TV, Christmas from Vietnam (1–68)
0	—	Hue captured (Tet) (2–68)
0	—	Khe Sahn siege (4–68)
0	—	Saigon reached (2nd offensive) (5–68)
12 [a]	—	Democratic Convention (Chicago) (8–68)
—	11	1968 election campaign (10–68)
2	—	RMN–TV, policy address (5–69)
0	—	RMN–TV, withdrawal announced (11–69)
0	—	250,000 at Washington protest (12–69)
0	—	RMN–TV, troop cut announced (4–70)
0	—	Cambodian invasion (see below) (5–70)
—	10 [b]	RMN–TV, success of above (6–70)
0	—	RMN–TV, cease-fire call (10–70)
8	—	S. Vietnamese invade Laos (2–71)
4	—	RMN–TV, success of above (3–71)
25	—	500,000 at Washington protest (5–71)
4	—	Pentagon Papers release (7–71)
7	—	RMN–TV, offer secret negotiations (1–72)
9	—	N. Vietnamese cross DMZ (4–72)
17	—	RMN–TV, bombing of Haiphong (5–72)
—	4	1972 election campaign (9–72)
0	—	Kissinger, "peace at hand" (10–72)
3	—	RMN–TV, caution on expectations (11–72)
11	—	RMN–TV, resume full-scale bombing (12–72)
1	—	RMN–TV, cease-fire agreement (1–73)
0	—	RMN–TV, ground disengagement (3–73)

TABLE 14.A–1 *(continued)*

Transitory Impact	Enduring Impact	Event Description (Month-Year)
Crime		
0 [a]	—	J.F. Kennedy assassinated (11–63)
—	4	Watts (8–65)
—	29	Detroit/Newark riots (7–67)
—	2	M.L. King killed and riots (4–68)
—	12	R.F. Kennedy killed (6–68)
0	—	Democratic Convention (Chicago) (8–68)
—	6	1970 congressional campaign (10–76)
Employment		
0	—	JFK–TV, tax cut asked (9–63)
4	—	LBJ–TV, tax cut (2–64)
8	—	Ford (GRF)–TV, need to stimulate economy (1–75)
2	—	GRF–TV, tax cut (3–75)
2	—	GRF–TV, tax cut (10–75)
—	16 [a]	1976 election campaign (10–76)
Energy		
8	—	Oil embargo begins (10–73)
10	—	RMN–TV, energy crisis, (11–73)
9	—	RMN–TV, energy crisis, gas lines begin (12–73)
7	—	GRF–TV, energy crisis, (1–75)
0	—	GRF–TV, oil import fee, decontrol (5–75)
28	—	Carter (JEC)–TV, energy conservation (2–77)
16	—	JEC–TV, energy moral equivalent of war (5–77)
Inflation (early)		
0	—	RMN–TV, reject wage and price controls (6–69)
27	—	RMN–TV, announce controls (8–71)
25	—	RMN–TV, extend controls indefinitely (10–71)
Inflation (late)		
0	—	RMN–TV, meat-price ceiling (3–73)
0	—	RMN–TV, retail price controls (6–73)
13	—	RMN–TV, inflation general (7–74)
20	—	GRF–TV, inflation address Congress (8–74)
11	—	GRF address Congress inflation (9–74)
6	—	GRF–TV, Whip Inflation Now speech (10–74)
—	11 [a]	1976 election campaign (10–76)

NOTES: These impact estimates give a rough idea of each event's relative importance. They should not, however, be interpreted as precise measurements of individual impacts. In the event descriptions the initials of the respective presidents are used as abbreviations. The term TV marks a nationwide televised speech. Month and year of event are shown in parentheses.
[a] These estimates derive from few observations within a reachable time span and are not well fit. Their magnitudes are only vaguely approximated and are suggestive only.
[b] This effect surely represents a holdover from the Cambodian invasion itself, and the related protest.

Notes

1. See Arrow (1951). A summary of recent results and their implications can be found in Riker (1980).

2. An enormous research effort has followed these lines. For example, see McCombs and Shaw (1972); McLeod, Becker, and Byrnes (1974); Tipton, Haney, and Basehart (1975); Siune and Borre (1975); Bowers (1973); Williams and Larsen (1977); Palmgreen and Clarke (1977); Patterson and McClure (1976); Shaw and McCombs (1977); Erbring, Goldenberg, and Miller (1980); and particularly Funkhouser (1973a, 1973b).

3. The reader who is curious about the ways in which separate dynamics can be combined and efficiently estimated is referred to the more complete text of MacKuen (1981). This chapter is meant to be a summary of a rather complicated research endeavor and, as such, cannot provide as full a report on these matters as would otherwise be desirable.

4. Casualty counts by month proved unavailable for this analysis. Yearly counts indicate that the effect of weighting the troop-strength measure would be to make it more sharply peaked. That is to say that the line would go up more slowly until 1968 and then drop more steeply.

5. Here taken from the FBI's *Uniform Crime Reports for the United States* (Washington, D.C.: U.S. Department of Justice, 1961–77).

6. National Bureau of Economic Research data made available by the Department of Economics, University of Michigan, provided the inflation and unemployment series. The fuel prices come from U.S. Department of Labor's Bureau of Labor Statistics, *Retail Prices and Index for Fuels and Electricity* (Washington, D.C.: 1967–77). The rates for coal and heating fuel are combined.

7. The estimation strategy lies in simulating the model in the form of equation (14.2), iterating on the parameter values to obtain the maximum fit. This imitates the approach of Box and Jenkins (1976) and is reported more fully in MacKuen (1981).

8. The poorer fit in the ascent of the issue would cancel out a better prediction of its decline. See note 4 herein.

9. The analytic model does not use the means of the variables in that the mean does not seem to represent any natural phenomenon. Thus it can, and in this case does, obtain results which perform less well than that standard benchmark. The R^2 measure here uses that null model for comparison and hence the procedure yields a strange-looking fit coefficient. The error from the Vietnam model prediction is twice that from a mean prediction.

References

Arrow, K.J. (1951) *Social Choice and Individual Values*. New York: Wiley.

Becker, L., McCombs, M., and McLeod, J. (1975) The development of political cognitions. In S. Chaffee, ed., *Political Communication*. Beverly Hills, Calif.: Sage Publications.

Reality, the Press, and Public Opinion

Box, G.E.P., and Jenkins, J.M. (1976) *Time Series Analysis: Forecasting and Control.* San Francisco: Holden-Day.

Bowers, T. (1973) Newspaper political advertising and the agenda-setting function. *Journalism Quarterly* 50:552-556.

Erbring, L. (1975) *The Impact of Political Events on Mass Politics.* Ph.D. dissertation. University of Michigan, Ann Arbor.

Erbring, L., Goldenberg, E., and Miller, A. (1980) Front page news and real world cues: another look at agenda-setting by the media. *American Journal of Political Science* 24:16-49.

Funkhouser, G.R. (1973a) The issues of the sixties: an exploratory study in the dynamics of public opinion. *Public Opinion Quarterly* 37:62-75.

Funkhouser, G.R. (1973b) Trends in media coverage of the issues of the sixties. *Journalism Quarterly* 50:533-538.

Koyck, L.M. (1954) *Distributed Lags and Investment Analysis.* Amsterdam: North Holland Press.

McCombs, M., and Shaw, D. (1972) The agenda-setting function of the mass media. *Public Opinion Quarterly* 36:176-187.

MacKuen, M. (1981) Social communication and the mass policy agenda. In M. MacKuen and S.L. Coombs, *More Than News.* Beverly Hills, Calif.: Sage Publications.

McLeod, J., Becker, L., and Byrnes, J. (1974) Another look at the agenda-setting function of the press. *Communication Research* 1:131-166.

Palmgreen, P., and Clarke, P. (1977) Agenda-setting with local and national issues. *Communication Research* 4:435-452.

Patterson, T.E., and McClure, R.D. (1976) *The Unseeing Eye.* New York: Putnam's.

Riker, W.H. (1980) Implications from the disequilibrium of majority rule for the study of institutions. *American Political Science Review* 74:432-446.

Shaw, D., and McCombs, M. (1977) *The Emergence of American Political Issues.* St. Paul: West.

Siune, K., and Borre, O. (1975) Setting the agenda for a Danish election. *Journal of Communication* 25:15-22.

Tipton, L., Haney, R., and Basehart, J. (1975) Media agenda-setting in city and state election campaigns. *Journalism Quarterly* 52:15-22.

Williams, W., Jr., and Larsen, D. (1977) Agenda-setting in an off-election year. *Journalism Quarterly* 54:744-749.

15

Mass Media, Contraceptive Behavior, and Attitudes on Abortion:

Toward a Comprehensive Model of Subjective Social Change

James R. Beniger

Past work on monitoring subjective social change by means of objective indicators, usually survey measures of public attitudes and opinion, has tended to be narrowly focused. Virtually ignored is the broader context of news events, mass media reporting, and behavioral change that has long been known to influence subjective measures. At least three causal components that are necessary for a full understanding of subjective social change are usually overlooked. Those components are:

1. *The symbolic environment*, that is, the context in which public attitudes and opinions are formed and changed. This involves both discrete cultural events such as marketing decisions and elections, and also continuing problems and trends such as a rise in the crime rate or a movement to liberalize certain laws.
2. *Mass communication*, including news coverage by television, radio, newspapers, and periodicals, plus reflections of the more general cul-

ture found in books, movies, advertising, and other mass information-al sources. The mass media may report particular events, identify and interpret broader societal issues and trends, or present information not necessarily linked to the symbolic environment; in this latter sense media content itself constitutes an autonomous environment.

3. *Existential, perceptual, and behavioral factors*, which involve not only the so-called background variables (gender, race, ethnicity, age, region, religion, and so forth.), but also behavioral measures: characteristics of social networks, for example, or whether an individual has been unemployed, commutes to work, or is unable to finance a home. Age and marriage cohorts provide economical and convenient means by which to capture large complexes of existential influences.

Not all past efforts can be faulted for ignoring these three causal components of subjective social change. Social scientists have long been interested in describing the symbolic environment and mass communication independent of possible effects upon behavior. A classic example is the study by Dicey (1924) of the spread of collectivist ideas in England. In the 1930s, Lasswell initiated the use of content analysis of political propaganda (Lasswell and Blumenstock, 1939), an effort expanded at the Library of Congress during World War II (Lasswell et al., 1949). Survey research, still in its infancy, could not be an adequate monitor of opinion, Lasswell argued, without simultaneous monitoring of the "symbolic environment," a term he had coined earlier (Lasswell, 1935). Postwar studies that he began at Stanford's Hoover Institute produced the first trend analysis and cross-cultural comparisons of political symbols used in newspaper editorials (Lasswell, Lerner, and Pool, 1952; Pool et al., 1952). Recent interest in social indicators to parallel economic ones (Bauer, 1966; National Commission on Technology, 1966) has brought renewed calls for mass media content indicators to monitor changes in the symbolic elements of culture (Janowitz, 1976; Beniger, 1978). Trends in the labeling of editorial cartoons have been used to indicate the growth of a shared symbolic environment (Beniger, 1983).

Toward a Causal Model

The three components of subjective social change listed above might be seen as part of a larger causal model by which national changes and trends in subjective indicators can be monitored and explained. As shown in Figure 15.1, the symbolic environment, including news events, social problems, and trends, is considered exogenous. The mass media mediate this environment for the individual, with the environment also influencing perception and behavior directly without media intervention. Subjective

FIGURE 15.1

Causal Model of Subjective Social Change

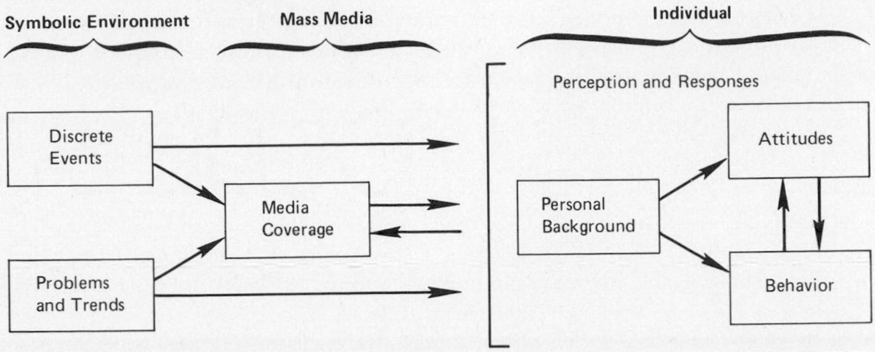

phenomena result, in this model, not only from environmental and mass media influences, but also through interaction of individual backgrounds, perceptions, and behavior.

To develop and test a causal model like that shown in Figure 15.1 would require data far more extensive than any currently collected. Proceeding toward a more comprehensive model of subjective social change despite lack of adequate data, however, can argue strongly for such data collection. This chapter attempts to develop piecemeal the various causal relationships shown in Figure 15.1 using data on a single, general topic—developments in birth control technology, contraceptive behavior, and attitudes toward abortion.

Data used in this effort come from a variety of sources. Attitudinal and behavioral measures are taken from the National Fertility Study (NFS) for 1965, 1970, and 1975, the National Opinion Research Center (NORC) General Social Surveys for 1972–78, and several Gallup polls dating from 1962. Measures of mass media coverage are constructed from the *Readers' Guide to Periodical Literature*, *New York Times Index*, *Television News Index*, and the *New York Times Information Bank*, which is a computerized index of articles published in the *New York Times* and some 60 other major newspapers and periodicals. Indicators of relevant events and trends are developed from these media sources as well as from data collected by the U.S. Center for Disease Control.

Variables considered in this analysis can be grouped under six general headings, each corresponding to one of the six blocks of the causal model shown in Figure 15.1. These are:

1. *Discrete events*, including U.S. Supreme Court decisions; congressional and other governmental hearings; statements of consumer advocates and public interest groups; announcements of new research findings; government adviso-

ries, warnings, and orders; and recalls, withdrawals, suspensions, and seizures of commercial products.

2. *Problems and trends*, that is, more general social changes, including legislative reforms of state abortion laws and trends in rates of legal abortions.
3. *Media coverage*—mass media content, including coverage of the above-mentioned events and trends by evening news broadcasts of the three major television networks and by major newspapers and national periodicals.
4. *Personal background*—variables, including years of formal education, which serve here as the most likely surrogate for exposure to health-related information in the news media, plus age, income, and religion.
5. *Attitudes* or attitudinal changes, specifically, changes in approval of abortion for various reasons, including danger to the health of the mother, the fact that the mother is not married, cannot afford another child, or does not want one, or cases of rape or likely serious birth defects.
6. *Behavior*, specifically, behavioral changes, including adoption of the birth control pill and intrauterine device (IUD) and discontinuation of these contraceptive means for health-related reasons.

These six categories of variables are used to address specific causal questions involving adverse publicity for the pill and IUD in the 1970s, discontinuation of these contraceptives, and changes in public attitudes toward abortion. For example, how closely does the volume of mass media reportage reflect actual events and trends? Are events and their coverage by the media related to behavioral changes? Do changes in behavior affect attitudes on related issues? How are both attitudinal and behavioral changes related to personal background variables, especially those reflecting media attention?

These and other causal questions are addressed in the next seven sections. Each section corresponds to certain of the more general causal relationships among the symbolic environment, mass communication, and individuals as represented by various arrows in Figure 15.1. The sections, named for the particular causal relationships they treat, are: Events, Trends, and Media Coverage; Media Coverage and Attitude Change; Discrete Events and Behavioral Change; Media Coverage and Behavioral Change; Individual Characteristics and Behavioral Change; Individual Characteristics and Attitude Change; and Behavior and Attitude Change.

The first two sections update earlier findings (Beniger, Watkins, and Ruz, 1979), the next two sections summarize work previously published (Jones, Beniger, and Westoff, 1980; Beniger, Westoff, and Jones, 1981), while the analyses in the final three sections are new to this volume. All of the findings, old and new, are brought together here by the explicit causal model shown in Figure 15.1 with which social changes and trends involving contraception and abortion might be monitored and explained. Specific sources of data and variables are further described as they are used.

To reiterate, no attempt is made to integrate the various findings into a single, conclusive test of a complex causal model of subjective social change. The data needed to accomplish this would necessarily include, among other variables, those linking individuals to particular media exposure. Lacking such data, the treatment here is intended simply as the best case that can be made, using existing limited resources, for a more comprehensive understanding of subjective social change.

Events, Trends, and Media Coverage

One difficulty in relating the volume of mass communication to events and trends in the symbolic environment is that media content and coverage usually rank among the better indicators of such phenomena. What is needed are separate measures, independent of media coverage, for assessing the national context in which public opinion is formulated and behavior is modified.

One such independent measure for assessing attitudes concerning abortion is the number of legal abortions performed in the United States. Legal abortions increased dramatically after 1967, when Colorado became the first of 17 states to reform abortion laws. The numbers of legal abortions have been compiled since 1969 by the Center for Disease Control; counts for 1963–69 are from Tietze (1970). Of course, the number of *illegal* abortions might also reflect and affect attitudes, but unfortunately even the better estimates—as for most behavior that is heavily proscribed—vary too widely to inspire confidence.

A plausible hypothesis is that mass media attention to the general topic of abortion will increase in relation to the number of legal abortions performed. Media coverage is here represented by two measures: the number of entries in the *Readers' Guide to Periodical Literature* listed under "abortion," and the column inches in the *New York Times Index* under the same heading. Unfortunately, television news broadcasts have not been indexed for much of the period.

The relationship between the number of legal abortions and the two indicators of media coverage of the more general topic is graphed in Figure 15.2. In order to remove possible distractions of arbitrary choices of units and scales, all three measures have been standardized by subtracting their means and dividing by their standard deviations. As revealed by Figure 15.2, legal abortions and media coverage of abortion in its various aspects are closely related.

The product-moment coefficient of correlation between abortions and *Readers' Guide* coverage is .63; the former is correlated .82 with *Times* coverage. The two media measures are themselves correlated .69, although if the *Times* coverage is lagged 2 years, the correlation increases to .78.

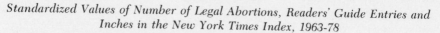

FIGURE 15.2

Standardized Values of Number of Legal Abortions, Readers' Guide Entries and Inches in the New York Times Index, 1963-78

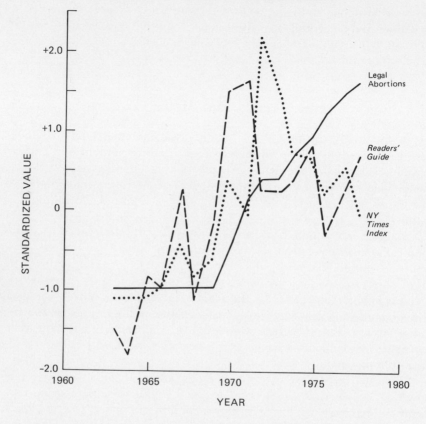

These statistics are not corrected for confounding due to autocorrelation, even though the Durbin-Watson *d* statistic indicates positive serial correlation, because the time series are in any case too short to permit more refined analysis. It seems better to take the correlations, including autocorrelation, as merely indicative of the temporal relationships clearly apparent in Figure 15.2.

Of course, the direction of causation between legal abortions and media attention to the general topic of abortion remains unspecified. It is likely that increasing numbers of legal abortions sustain media interest in the subject, but it is also plausible that media coverage might stimulate abortions, possibly by increasing public awareness and acceptance of the practice. In either event, the data support the initial hypothesis: media attention to abortion increases in relation to the number of legal abortions.

Media Coverage and Attitude Change

The dramatic increase in legal abortions after 1967, accompanied by increased attention to abortion in the mass media, is likely to have had an effect on public attitudes on the subject. One plausible hypothesis is that the accompanying increase in public discussion of abortion, coupled with the increased likelihood that abortion will affect one's social network, correlates with a liberalization of opinion as measured by repeated public surveys.

Unfortunately, several otherwise good data sets involving contraception are not early enough or frequent enough to provide time series for the period (1967–74) of most rapid change in attitudes toward abortion. The National Fertility Study was first conducted in 1965 and again in 1970, while the annual NORC General Social Surveys did not begin until 1972. The best time series is that of the Gallup Organization, which conducted nine polls between 1962 and 1974; these polls record disapproval of abortion under each of two specified circumstances: when a family does not have enough money to support a child, and at parental discretion (in the absence of financial and health problems). These Gallup polls can be compared with the two indicators of media coverage used in the previous section. The four time series, again standardized by subtracting their means and dividing by their standard deviations, are graphed in Figure 15.3. As hypothesized, the increasingly liberalized view of abortion after 1967 corresponds to increased media treatment of the topic during the same period.

The product-moment coefficient for the two Gallup measures is .98. The parental discretion series is correlated .51 with *Readers' Guide* coverage and .80 with that of the *New York Times*, while the financial item is correlated .73 with the former and .81 with the latter. The two Gallup items correlate .91 and .88, respectively, with the series on legal abortions as presented in the previous section. As in that section, the statistics reported here are not corrected for confounding due to autocorrelation. Again, the time series are too short to permit more refined analysis and are considered merely indicative of the temporal relationships clearly apparent in Figure 15.3.

Once again, the direction of causation between media coverage and attitudinal change remains unspecified. It is likely that increasing reportage tends to liberalize attitudes toward a previously sanctioned behavior, possibly by promoting at least the appearance that society at large is becoming more tolerant of that behavior. It is also plausible, however, that rapid changes in public opinion concerning abortion served to stimulate media interest in the subject. The meager time series data do not permit the type of cross-lagged analysis that might suggest resolution of the question. It is likely, however, that causation works in both directions (as indicated by the

FIGURE 15.3

Standardized Values of Percentage on Gallup Poll Disapproving of Abortion at Parental Discretion and Because Family Does Not Have Enough Money, with Reader's Guide Entries and Inches in the New York Times Index, 1963-78

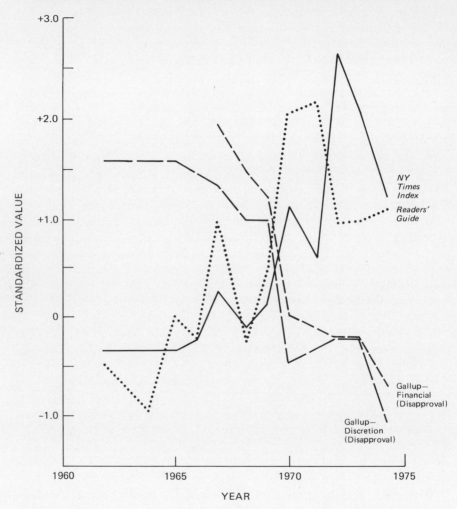

double arrows in Figure 15.1), so that media coverage and attitude change grow together—at least for a time—in a positive feedback relationship. In any event, the data that are available support the initial hypothesis: the increased media treatment of abortion after 1967 correlates with increasingly liberalized attitudes toward the behavior.

Discrete Events and Behavioral change

One major component of the causal model outlined in the opening section of this chapter was the symbolic environment, the external context in which a society's attitudes and behavior are established and changed. In terms of contraception, a series of events during the 1970–75 period—events resulting in unfavorable publicity for the pill and IUD—afford an unusual opportunity to test the effects of environment on behavior. These events include three congressional hearings and numerous public actions by the Food and Drug Administration (FDA).

Behavior that is likely to reflect the impact of such events is women's discontinued use of the pill and IUD during the same period. Rates of discontinuation for the two contraceptive technologies can be calculated using multiple increment/multiple decrement life table procedures on data from the 1975 National Fertility Study. These rates are graphed for the 72 months of 1970 through 1975 in Figures 15.4 and 15.5, along with 12 events that might have influenced discontinuation rates for the two contraceptives. Included are all events that either received coverage in news broadcasts of two or more television networks (as recorded by *Television News Index*) or coverage by one network plus one or more publications (as archived in the *New York Times Information Bank*).

The 12 events meeting these criteria are listed in Figures 15.4 and 15.5. Two of the events are not directly related to the pill or IUD, but concern adverse health effects of diethylstilbestrol (DES), used as a "morning after" birth control drug. Although DES should not be mistaken for the pill, it is likely that at least some people might confuse the two. Indeed, the NFS data suggest that less-educated respondents to the survey did have higher rates of pill discontinuation in conjunction with negative publicity about DES.

As can be seen in Figures 15.4 and 15.5, discontinuation rates do tend to increase following news events reflecting possibly adverse health effects for the two birth control technologies. For example, Figure 15.4 shows that within 8 months of October 1970, when the FDA recalled all sequential pills, pill discontinuation rates had risen by about 50 percent. The figure also reveals a sharp increase in rates following the appearance in February 1975 of an article in the *Journal of the American Medical Association* linking pill use to increased risk of stroke. Similarly for the IUD, Figure 15.5 shows that discontinuation rates rose sharply after suspension of Dalkon Shield sales in June 1974. After manufacturers withdrew this device from the market in January of the following year, IUD discontinuation rates more than doubled in a 6-month period.

A more rigorous test of the hypothesis that events reflecting adversely on the pill and IUD led to increased discontinuation of these contraceptives is

FIGURE 15.4

Percentage Probability of Pill Discontinuation, Based on 5-month Moving Average, and Seven National News Items That Might Have Increased Discontinuation Rates, 1970-75

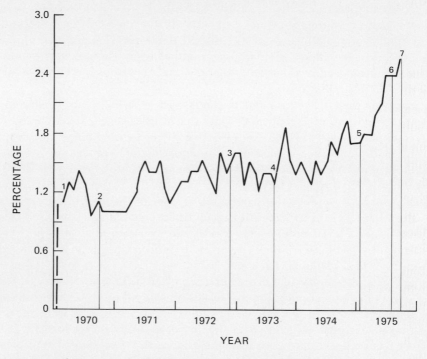

NOTES: National news events that might have increased discontinuation of the pill:
1. January, 1970: Senate subcommittee, chaired by Senator Gaylord Nelson, begins hearings on pill.
2. October, 1970: FDA takes C-Quens and Provest birth control pills off market; massive overdoses found to cause cancer in dogs.
3. December, 1972: Nader group urges FDA to control DES.
4. September, 1973: FDA orders physicians to warn patients on DES.
5. February, 1975: *Journal of the American Medical Association* reports that use of birth control pills can create greater risk of stroke.
6. August, 1975: FDA advises women over 40 to switch from birth control pills to avoid risk of heart attack.
7. October, 1975: FDA releases new package inserts for birth control pills, warning of possible risks from use.

given in Figure 15.6, which graphs the mean change in discontinuation rates as a function of time elapsed following events. As the figure shows, pill discontinuation rates rose for the first 3 months after the seven unfavorable events, on the average, and remained above the mean monthly rate (.09 percent) for another 2 months. Although discontinuation rates for the IUD actually fell in the month following the five events unfavorable to that contraceptive, the rates rose sharply in the next month; this suggests a 1-month

FIGURE 15.5

Percentage Probability of IUD Discontinuation, Based on 5-month Moving Average, and Five National News Items That Might Have Increased Discontinuation Rates, 1970-75

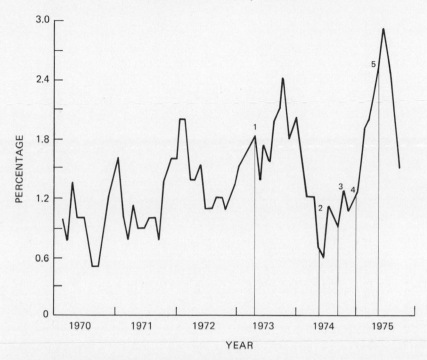

NOTES: National news events that might have increased discontinuation of the IUD:
1. May, 1973: FDA announces seizure of 9,000 Majzlin Spring IUD devices and recalls others because of possible complications; in House hearings, two doctors call IUD most dangerous contraceptive method.
2. June, 1974: Distribution and sale of Dalkon Shield suspended by FDA; wearers urged not to panic.
3. October, 1974: Experts advise FDA on health effects of Dalkon Shield; approve proposal to use standardized warning labels for IUDs.
4. January, 1975: Manufacturer of Dalkon Shield voluntarily withdraws device from market; Senate subcommittee opens hearings on possible dangers.
5. June, 1975: FDA proposes mandatory uniform labelling for IUDs to contain information on risks and contraindications to use.

lag in the effect of such events. The IUD discontinuation rate remained for another 2 months above the mean rate, -.5 percent (the negative number reflects a general tendency for discontinuation to diminish with length of use of the IUD). For both the pill and IUD, a peak in discontinuation followed 2 to 4 months after unfavorable news events.

Cumulative change in discontinuation following these events is graphed in Figure 15.7. Functions for both the pill and IUD approximate the familiar S-shaped curve common to logistic change. The cumulative mean

FIGURE 15.6

Mean Monthly Percentage Change in Pill and IUD Discontinuation Rates as a Function of Time Elapsed Following Selected News Events That Might Have Increased Discontinuation

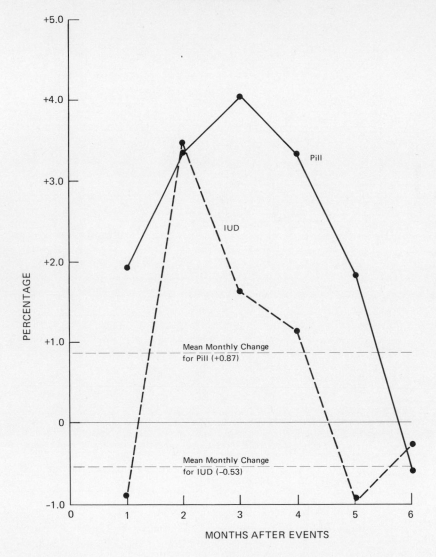

monthly change in pill discontinuation rises from 3.3 percent 1 month after a news event to 15.2 percent 4 months later. The increase in the IUD cumulative rate, by contrast, is not as sharp and less than half in total magnitude, rising from 1.0 percent at the first month to 7.2 percent after 4

FIGURE 15.7

Cumulative Percentage Change in Mean Monthly Pill and IUD Discontinuation Rates as a Function of Time Elapsed Following Selected News Events That Might Have Increased Discontinuation

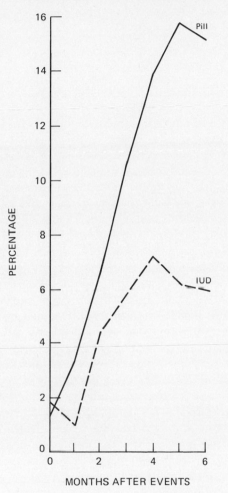

months. Both cumulative rates clearly peak 3 to 6 months after an unfavorable news event.

In summary, the data of this section, as graphed in Figures 15.4 through 15.7, lend considerable support to the initial hypothesis: a succession of events reflecting adversely on the pill and IUD during the period 1970–75 seems to have led to increased discontinuation of these contraceptives. On the average, this effect appeared to lag 1 to 2 months and to persist for 3 to

5 months following an event. Unlike the correlations of the previous two sections, the temporal ordering of relationships—from negative events to increases in discontinuation—is clearly established. It is possible, of course, that these relations are causally spurious, but they are about as plausible as might be established short of experimental design or at least some survey link to the influence of real events.

Media Coverage and Behavioral Change

In order to distinguish media treatment of the pill and IUD from reportage of specific news events, as analyzed in the previous section, *cumulative* media coverage is considered here. Cumulative coverage reflects a more general treatment of social problems and trends through feature stories and editorials. A plausible hypothesis is that more general media coverage of contraception is likely to have a more gradual and lasting effect on contraceptive behavior than do individual news events themselves.

Cumulative media coverage is measured by the number of articles in the *New York Times Information Bank* indexed under oral contraceptives (N = 54) and intrauterine devices (N = 61) for the period 1970–75. Recall that the *Information Bank* includes not only articles published in the *Times*, but also in some 60 other major newspapers and periodicals. A graph of the cumulative number of articles on oral contraceptives (not shown) approximates a linear function of time (the correlation with ordered months is .98). The graph of the cumulative number of articles on IUDs (also not shown), by contrast, increased much more rapidly near the end of the period, following the Dalkon Shield controversy early in 1974.

Comparison of these graphs of cumulative articles with those for discontinuation of the pill and IUD (Figures 15.4 and 15.5) suggests a difference in the media effects on the use of these two contraceptives: the discontinuation rate for the IUD is not related to cumulative media coverage, but the rate for the pill appears to be strikingly related. This can be shown by again standardizing measures. The resulting graphs, one of pill discontinuation rates and the other for cumulative articles on oral contraceptives, are superimposed in Figure 15.8. The latter series accounts for 34 percent of the variance in the former. Autocorrelation again confounds the picture, but again it seems better, given the small number of cases, to accept the results as merely suggestive, rather than to strain the data further with more refined estimation.

Because discontinuation of the pill increases over the period, a more direct link of this behavioral change to media coverage might be seen in the cumulative number of negative articles on oral contraceptives. Inspection of articles abstracted in the *Information Bank*, however, revealed that most

FIGURE 15.8

*Standardized Values of Probability of Pill Discontinuation, Based on 5-month
Moving Average, and Cumulative Number of News Items Dealing With Pill Use,
1970-75*

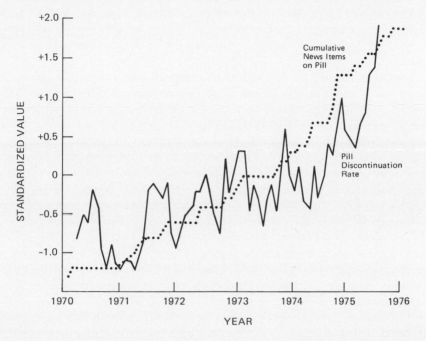

provided balanced accounts, with even the most positive articles relating
negative claims. The latter type of articles, positive only on balance, might
well serve to allay the fears of readers aware of earlier negative coverage,
but might equally well arouse suspicions among those not previously exposed to the controversy. Because of such confounding of positive and
negative influences, and because virtually every article had a prominent
negative component, it seemed arbitrary to single out predominantly negative coverage, and this was not done.

Based on the relationship in Figure 15.8, it seems reasonable to accept
the initial hypothesis, at least for the pill. That is, cumulative general media
coverage of oral contraceptives is likely to have had a gradual effect on
discontinuation of the pill, even apart from the effect of individual news
events themselves. As in the section on Media Coverage and Attitude
Change, the direction of causation between media coverage and social
change remains unspecified. Although it is likely that negative treatment of
contraception in the media tended to increase discontinuation, it is also
possible that this behavioral change served to stimulate media interest; the
small numbers of articles do not permit the type of cross-lagged analysis
that might suggest resolution of the question.

Individual Characteristics and Behavioral Change

One major component of the causal model outlined in the opening section of this chapter involved existential, perceptual, and behavioral factors, including the so-called personal background variables. Lacking survey items explicitly measuring attention to health-related information in the news media, the background variable most useful as a surrogate is years of education.

The National Fertility Study permits cross-tabulation of gross educational attainment categories (less than high school, high school, beyond high school) with discontinuation of the pill for the 5-year periods before each of the three surveys, namely 1960–65, 1965–70, and 1970–75. A plausible hypothesis, if education does indeed indicate attention to health-related information in the media, is that discontinuation rates will be higher for more-educated women, particularly during the period 1970–75 covered by the third NFS survey, when publicity for the pill and IUD was largely negative.

Table 15.1 presents pill discontinuation as a function of years of education separately for Catholics and non-Catholics, the most likely confounding factor. Because education is interesting merely as a surrogate for perception and response concerning adverse publicity for the pill, it is not necessary to control for every other variable that might further specify the effect attributed to education (and indeed the sample sizes do not permit consideration of additional variables).

For example, given that education is highly correlated with age and income, it is possible that these variables might partially account for the effect attributed here to education. This need not concern us, however, because the aim is merely to establish an independent role for personal background factors related to perception and response to information in the mass media. Whether such differential filtering is attributed to education, age, income, or some other variable correlated with these is a question outside the scope of this chapter.

As shown in Table 15.1, the percentages of pill users discontinuing use of that contraceptive are higher for more-educated women, both Catholic and non-Catholic, in all three time periods, but especially during the critical period 1970–75 when publicity was particularly adverse. Thus the data support the initial hypothesis that discontinuation rates are higher for more-educated women, particularly during the period of most negative publicity concerning the pill and IUD. This squares with the intuitive idea that the better educated will be more likely to assimilate complex information from the mass media, possibly through intermediaries like physicians and pharmacists, and to incorporate this information in their own behavior. The findings support an independent role for personal background factors in determining perception and response concerning the mass media, an im-

TABLE 15.1

*Discontinuation of the Pill by Catholics and Non-
Catholics During Three 5-Year Periods (Percentages)*

Religion and Education	1960 – 65	1965 – 70	1970 – 75
Catholics			
Less than high school	3.8	15.8	16.2
High school	4.6	23.5	24.1
More than high school	6.2	25.7	27.5
Non-Catholics			
Less than high school	6.0	24.1	24.9
High school	6.5	25.9	27.3
More than high school	8.6	27.9	30.0
Totals			
Catholic and Non-Catholic	6.2	25.0	27.1
Total N	3,720	4,960	3,367

portant element in the model of subjective social change as presented in Figure 15.1.

Individual Characteristics and Attitude Change

Of the seven sets of causal relationships examined in this chapter, none has been studied more extensively than that between personal background characteristics and attitudes. Since World War II this has been the central focus of what might be called the Lazarsfeldian tradition of survey research.

What this section intends to contribute to the tradition is consideration of both background and behavioral variables simultaneously in a model of attitude formation and change. One plausible hypothesis, if education indicates increased assimilation of mass media communication, is that this personal variable will help to account for the dramatic liberalization of attitudes toward abortion that occurred in the late 1960s and early 1970s. Such a result would further specify the relationship between media coverage of abortion and attitudinal change found in the section on Media Coverage and Attitude Change.

The three National Fertility Study surveys measured attitudes on abortion for six separate reasons: (1) danger to the mother, (2) the fact that the mother is unmarried, (3) inability to afford another child, (4) not wanting one, (5) cases of rape, and (6) cases of likely serious birth defects. These items can be combined in a seven-point Guttman scale locating each respondent's general position on abortion. The scale ranges from a value of 0, representing no approval of abortion for any of the six reasons, to a value of

6, for approval of abortion for all of the six reasons. Danger to the mother's health is the most widely accepted justification for abortion; that the mother wants no more children is the reason least often accepted. Because blacks were not sampled in all three surveys, the analyses here must be restricted to white women of childbearing age.

Table 15.2 presents the results of a stepwise regression of the six-point Guttman scale on six independent variables: age, education, income, religion (Roman Catholic or non-Catholic), pill usage, and pill discontinuation —separately for each of the three survey years 1965, 1970, and 1975. The latter three variables are dichotomous. As can be seen in Table 15.2, education and the two behavioral variables, pill usage and discontinuation, all rose in importance—relative to the background variables age, income, and religion—in explaining general acceptance of abortion. Education rose from third to first place in the stepwise regression equations between 1965 and 1975, while pill usage rose from fifth to fourth place, and discontinuation rose from sixth to third place during the same period.

These relationships are further specified in Table 15.3, which presents the constant terms, regression slopes, and standardized slopes for each of the three stepwise equations (because of the direction of the Guttman scale, negative coefficients indicate positive relationships to approval of abortion). As shown in Table 15.3, the effects of only three variables—education, pill usage, and discontinuation—increase monotonically in magnitude between 1965 and 1975. This result holds for both unstandardized and standardized regression slopes. The trends in slopes for the other three variables are either declining, relatively flat, or oscillating over the three surveys.

In other words (see Tables 15.2 and 15.3), more-educated respondents to

TABLE 15.2

Stepwise Regression of Guttman Scale Scores on Approval of Abortion for Various Reasons on Six Independent Variables, 1965, 1970, and 1975

Rank	1965	1970	1975
1	Religion	Religion	*Education*
2	Income	Income	Religion
3	*Education*	*Education*	*Pill discontinuation*
4	Age	*Pill discontinuation*	*Pill usage*
5	*Pill usage*	*Pill usage*	Income
6	*Pill discontinuation*	(Age)[*]	(Age)[*]
N	3,119	3,591	2,766
Multiple R^2	0.29	0.29	0.31
Value of F	49.3	56.0	49.2

[*]Not statistically significant at the 0.05 level.

the NFS surveys were more likely to approve of abortion for more reasons and to liberalize their views on abortion over the period 1965–75, that is, to increase the number of reasons for which they would approve of abortion. The same results hold for the two behavioral variables, pill usage and discontinuation. All three variables became increasingly better predictors of attitudes toward abortion during 1965–75, at least relative to three likely background predictors: age, income, and religion.

Thus the analysis here further specifies the correlation found in the section on Media Coverage and Attitude Change between increased media treatment of abortion after 1967 and increasingly liberalized attitudes toward the behavior. If increased reportage tends to liberalize attitudes toward abortion, possibly by promoting at least the appearance that society at large is becoming more tolerant of that behavior, this effect is likely to be stronger among the more educated, who are more likely to assimilate information from the mass media, and among contraceptive users, for whom the information is more salient, especially among those who discontinue use of contraception—thus making the question of abortion still more salient.

It remains possible, however, that causation works in both directions (as

TABLE 15.3

*Constant Terms, Regression Slopes (B) and
Standardized Slopes (B) for Six Independent
Variables in Stepwise Equations, 1965,
1970, and 1975*

	1965	1970	1975
Constant Term	5.17	5.72	5.93
Regression Slopes (*B*):			
Education	−0.05	−0.10	−0.22
Pill discontinuation	−0.26	−0.45	−0.47
Pill usage	−0.21	−0.44	−0.47
Religion	0.61	0.87	0.83
Income	−0.07	−0.08	−0.02
Age	−0.01	−0.01*	0.00*
Standardized Slopes (B):			
Education	−0.07	−0.11	−0.21
Pill discontinuation	−0.04	−0.09	−0.09
Pill usage	−0.05	−0.09	−0.10
Religion	0.19	0.19	0.19
Income	−0.19	−0.15	−0.07
Age	−0.09	−0.02*	0.02*

NOTES: Negative numbers indicate positive relationship to approval of abortion. Coefficients marked with an asterisk are not statistically significant at the 0.05 level.

indicated under Media Coverage and Attitude Change), with changes in attitudes among the educated opinion leaders serving to stimulate media interest. In any event, the data here support the initial hypothesis: education and pill usage and discontinuation serve to account for the dramatic liberalization of attitudes toward abortion that occurred in the late 1960s and early 1970s.

Behavior and Attitude Change

Individual attitudes and behavior constitute the highest levels of the model of subjective social change presented in Figure 15.1, that is, the levels farthest removed in the chain of causation leading from real events and trends through their coverage in the mass media to individual perception and response. Of all of the various components of the change model, behavior and attitudes are the two most likely to be linked through reciprocal causation, as indicated by the double arrows in Figure 15.1. That is, attitudinal and behavioral changes are likely to reinforce one another, so that the two grow together, at least up to a point, in a positive feedback relationship.

In terms of contraceptive behavior and attitudes toward abortion, there exist two opposite, ideal possibilities: at one extreme, it is possible that individuals either approve of birth control or oppose all types, contraception and abortion alike. In this case, one of contrasting attitudinal types, contraceptive behavior and support for abortion would be perfectly positively correlated. At the other extreme, just the opposite situation from the first but equally possible, contraception and abortion are viewed as alternative choices for controlling family size, so that women opposed to abortion will use the pill or IUD, while those unable or unwilling to use contraception will favor abortion. In this case, one of contrasting means of birth control, contraceptive behavior and support for abortion would be perfectly negatively correlated. There remains, of course, the intermediate possibility that the behavioral and attitudinal variables are uncorrelated.

Deciding which of the two ideal extremes more closely approximates the relationship between contraceptive behavior and attitudes toward abortion is possible using data from the National Fertility Study. If alternative means for controlling birth should be the predominant causal factor, women who discontinued use of contraceptives during 1960–75, the period covered by the NFS surveys, would be more likely to favor abortion than would women who continued contraception. This would be the case either because women who already approved of the abortion alternative found it easier to discontinue pill use, or because discontinuation forced them to liberalize their attitudes toward the alternative means of birth control (in other words, the causal direction is indeterminate). Conversely, if contrasting attitudinal types should be the predominant causal factor, women disapproving of abortion—and hence disinclined toward birth control in general —would be more likely to discontinue contraception under conditions of publicity about negative health effects. In the former case, discontinuation of contraception and approval of abortion would be positively correlated in the NFS data: the two variables would be negatively correlated in the latter case.

Table 15.4 presents data relevant to this question. Rates of disapproval of abortion for each of the six reasons are given for 1965, 1970, and 1975 for three categories of pill usage over the five years preceding each survey: uninterrupted usage, discontinuation, and nonusage. As the table shows, steady users far exceed nonusers in approval of abortion for all reasons in all years; women who have discontinued the pill much more closely resemble continuing users than they do nonusers. These relationships are similar for the IUD (not shown here).

The findings in Table 15.4 support the first of the two ideal extremes, that of contrasting attitudinal types. That is, women who discontinued use of the pill are somewhat more likely to favor abortion than are women who continued contraception, discontinuing users exceeded continuing users in approval of abortion for five of six reasons in 1965 and three of six reasons in 1970 and 1975. The relationship is more evident in Table 15.5, which averages support for the three most accepted reasons for abortion (danger to the mother's health, rape, and the possibility that the child might be born deformed) and for the three least accepted reasons for abortion (that the couple wants no more children, cannot afford the child, or is unmarried). In four of the six cases, approval of abortion is at least a full percentage point greater for those who discontinued the pill than for those who continued usage; approval among these two groups is 2 to 8 percentage points greater than for those who did not use the pill at all. Much the same relationships hold for the IUD (not shown here).

The importance of increasing pill usage and discontinuation in accounting for shifts in attitudes toward abortion is shown in Table 15.6. As the table reveals, mean approval of abortion for the three most accepted reasons increased from 65 to 84 percent between 1965 and 1975: 2.3 points (12.1 percent) of this 18.9 percentage-point shift can be attributed to increases in pill usage and discontinuation. Similarly for the three least accepted reasons for abortion, mean approval increased from 10.3 to 39.9 percent over the same 10-year period; 3.2 points (10.8 percent) of this 29.4 percentage-point shift can be attributed to increases in the two behavioral variables.

TABLE 15.4

Approval of Abortion by Pill Users, Discontinuers, and Nonusers,
for Six Different Reasons, 1965, 1970, and 1975 (Percentages)

Year and Group	Reason for Abortion						Percentage of Sample
	Endanger Mother's Health	Rape	Child Might Be Deformed	Mother Not Married	Cannot Afford Child	Want No More Children	
1965							
Discontinued pill	92.6	57.0	59.1	16.1	13.9	8.9	6.1
Uses pill	91.3	57.2	57.4	14.5	13.1	8.1	17.2
Total sample	88.7	54.0	52.4	12.6	11.0	7.3	100.0
Does not use pill	87.8	53.0	50.8	11.9	10.3	7.0	76.6
1970							
Discontinued pill	92.4	75.1	74.7	36.4	28.9	24.4	25.0
Uses pill	93.2	75.5	74.5	35.0	29.0	23.0	26.3
Total sample	90.3	72.1	70.6	32.6	25.3	21.6	100.0
Does not use pill	87.6	68.7	66.3	29.4	21.5	19.3	48.7
1975							
Discontinued pill	95.7	84.0	81.3	46.8	41.7	41.3	27.0
Uses pill	95.8	82.7	79.2	48.8	42.5	39.5	33.1
Total sample	94.2	80.0	77.7	44.5	38.1	37.3	100.0
Does not use pill	91.8	75.0	74.0	39.4	31.9	32.7	39.9

TABLE 15.5

Approval of Abortion by Pill Users,
Discontinuers, and Nonusers, for
Two Categories of Acceptance,
1965, 1970, and 1975
(Mean percentages)

Category 1: Three *Most* Accepted Reasons
(Danger to Mother's Health, Rape,
Child Might Be Deformed)

Group	1965	1970	1975
Discontinued pill	69.6	80.7	87.0
Uses pill	68.6	81.1	85.9
Total sample	65.0	77.7	84.0
Does not use pill	63.9	74.2	80.3

Category 2: Three *Least* Accepted Reasons
(Couple Wants No More Children,
Cannot Afford Child, Is Unmarried)

Group	1965	1970	1975
Discontinued pill	13.0	27.3	41.3
Uses pill	11.9	26.1	41.2
Total sample	10.3	24.0	39.9
Does not use pill	9.7	22.4	32.9

Thus analysis of the NFS survey data, as presented in Tables 15.4, 15.5, and 15.6, serves to explicate the relationships between behavior and attitudes in a general model of subjective social change. As hypothesized, contraceptive behavior would seem to help account for overall changes in attitudes toward abortion. Unfortunately, the causal direction remains indeterminate: it is impossible to tell whether women who already approved of abortion found it easier to discontinue the pill (because of the alternative means of birth control), or whether discontinuation for health reasons forced women to liberalize their attitudes toward abortion. It is likely that attitudinal and behavioral changes reinforced one another, as indicated in the model in Figure 15.1, through reciprocal causation and positive feedback. Whichever causal direction predominates, it is definitely not the case that women disapproving of abortion—and hence disinclined toward birth control in general—were more likely to discontinue contraception under conditions of publicity about negative health effects. The ideal type of alternative means of birth control must be rejected.

TABLE 15.6

Shifts in Approval of Abortion, 1965 – 75, for
Two Categories of Acceptance, Controlling for Changes in
Pill Usage and Discontinuation During the Same Period

	Three *Most* Accepted Reasons[a]	Three *Least* Accepted Reasons[b]
1965 mean approval	65.0%	10.3%
1975 mean approval	84.0%	39.9%
1965 – 75 shift in mean approval	18.9 percentage points	29.6 percentage points
1965 – 75 shift controlling for changes in pill usage and discontinuation	16.6 percentage points	26.4 percentage points
Difference, actual 1965 – 75 shift vs. shift controlling for changes in pill usage and discontinuation	2.3 percentage points	3.2 percentage points
Percentage 1965 – 75 shift due to changes in pill usage and discontinuation	12.1%	10.8%

[a]Danger to mother's health, rape, child might be deformed.

[b]Couple wants no more children, cannot afford one, unmarried.

Discussion and Summary

This chapter set out to establish a comprehensive model by which national changes and trends in subjective social indicators might be monitored and explained. The mass media are seen to be central to this model, intervening as they do between individuals and the symbolic environment. Subjective phenomena result not only from environmental and mass media influences, but also through interaction of individual perceptions, backgrounds, and behavior.

This model was tested for developments in birth control technology, contraceptive behavior, and attitudes toward abortion through piecemeal examination of its various causal relationships. Data were gleaned from a variety of sources, both time series of national surveys and indexes of the mass media. Although no attempt was made to integrate the various findings into a single model of social change, the findings nevertheless converge on a model something like that in Figure 15.1.

Mass Media, Contraception, and Abortion

Media attention to abortion was found to increase in relation to a series of real events, reforms of state laws, and a steady rise in the number of legal abortions. After 1967, the increased media treatment of abortion correlates with increasingly liberalized attitudes toward the behavior. A succession of events during 1970–75, including three congressional hearings and numerous public actions by the Food and Drug Administration, seems to have led to increased discontinuation of the pill and IUD. These effects appeared to lag 1 to 2 months and to persist for 3 to 5 months following an event. Even apart from the effect of individual news events, cumulative general media coverage is likely to have had a gradual effect on discontinuation rates, at least for the pill.

Discontinuation rates were also higher for more-educated women, particularly during the period of most negative publicity concerning the pill and IUD. This squares with the intuitive idea that the better educated are more likely to receive complex information from the media, possibly through intermediaries like physicians and pharmacists, and to incorporate this information into their own behavior. If increased reportage tends to liberalize attitudes toward abortion, possibly by promoting at least the appearance that society at large is becoming more tolerant of that behavior, this effect is likely to be stronger among the more educated, who are more likely to assimilate media information. In any event, education serves to account for at least part of the dramatic liberalization of attitudes toward abortion that occurred in the late 1960s and early 1970s. This finding clearly supports an independent role for personal background factors in determining perception and response concerning mass media.

It is likely that women who already approved of abortion found it easier to discontinue the pill, because abortion afforded an alternative means of birth control, and also that discontinuation of the pill for health reasons forced women to liberalize their attitudes toward abortion. At the same time, contraceptive behavior along with years of education, the surrogate for media perception and response, correlate with overall attitudes toward abortion. Such attitudinal and behavioral changes are likely to reinforce one another, so that the two grow together, at least up to a point, in a positive feedback relationship.

Within the limits of the available data, this is the best case that can be made for an integrated model like that shown in Figure 15.1. The data set required for a single, conclusive refinement of such a model has not yet been collected. It would necessarily include, among other variables, those linking individuals with particular media coverage. Because we do not yet have such information, this chapter is intended, above all else, as an argument for such a data collection effort. It would seem a necessary step toward the fuller understanding of national events and trends and subjective social change.

499

References

Bauer, R., ed. (1966) *Social Indicators*. Cambridge, Mass.: MIT Press.

Beniger, J.R. (1978) Media content as social indicators: the Greenfield Index of agenda-setting. *Communication Research* 5:437-453.

Beniger, J.R. (1983) Does television enhance the shared symbolic environment? Trends in labeling of editorial cartoons, 1948-1980. *American Sociological Review* 48:103-111.

Beniger, J.R., Watkins, S., and Ruz, J.E. (1979) Trends in the abortion issue as measured by events, media coverage and public opinion indicators. *Proceedings of the American Statistical Association (Social Statistics Section)* 1978:118-123.

Beniger, J.R., Westoff, C.F., and Jones, E. (1981) The effects of mass media reporting of events versus trends on discontinuation of the pill and IUD, 1970-1975. *Proceedings of the American Statistical Association (Social Statistics Section)* 1980:479-484.

Blake, J. (1977) The abortion decision: judicial review and public opinion. *In* E. Manier, W. Liu, and D. Salomon, eds., *Abortion, New Directions for Policy Studies*. Notre Dame, Ind.: University of Notre Dame Press.

Dicey, A.V. (1924) *Lectures on the Relation Between Law and Public Opinion in England During the Nineteenth Century*. London: Macmillan.

Janowitz, M. (1976) Content analysis and the study of sociopolitical change. *Journal of Communication* 26:10-21.

Jones, E.F., Beniger, J.R., and Westoff, C.F. (1980) Pill and IUD discontinuation in the United States, 1970-1975: the influence of the media. *Family Planning Perspectives* 12:293-300.

Lasswell, H.D. (1935) *World Politics and Personality Insecurity*. New York: McGraw-Hill.

Lasswell, H.D., and Blumenstock, D. (1939) *World Revolutionary Propaganda: A Chicago Study*. New York: Knopf.

Lasswell, H.D., Leites, N., et al. (1949) *Language of Politics: Studies in Quantitative Semantics*. New York: Stewart.

Lasswell, H.D., Lerner, D., and Pool, I. de Sola (1952) *The Comparative Study of Symbols*. Stanford: Stanford University Press.

National Commission on Technology, Automation, and Economic Progress (1966) *Technology and the American Economy*. Washington, D.C.: Government Printing Office.

Pool, I. de Sola et al. (1952) *The Prestige Papers*. Stanford: Stanford University Press.

Ryder, N.S. (1972) Time series of pill and IUD Use: United States, 1961-1970. *Studies in Family Planning* 3:233-240.

Tietze, C. (1970) United States: therapeutic abortions, 1963-1968. *Studies in Family Planning* 59:5-7.

Westoff, C.F. (1976) Trends in contraceptive practice: 1965-1973. *Family Planning Perspectives* 8:54-57.

Westoff, C.F., and Jones, E. (1975) Discontinuation of the pill and the IUD in the United States, 1960-1970. *Mount Sinai Journal of Medicine* 42:384-390.

16

The Popularity of Presidents: 1963–80

Michael B. MacKuen and Charles F. Turner

For four decades, polls have sought to measure the popularity of incumbent presidents, and the results of these polls have been widely reported in the media. It is claimed that "amidst the avalanche of polling data filling our newspapers and airwaves daily, none commands more attention than the periodic reports of presidential popularity (Orren, 1978:35)."[1] Anecdotes of President Lyndon Johnson bandying about poll reports of his popularity are well known, and it is widely believed that the behavior of politicians is influenced by the behavior of these popularity measurements. As Brody and Page (1975:136-137) observe,

> We can be confident that Presidents themselves are avid readers of the polls and view changes in the level of their popularity as feedback on the popularity of their actions. Lyndon Johnson was fond of quoting poll results to newsmen—at least in the early happy days of his administration. Both Johnson and Nixon earned reputations of eagerness to adapt their policies to the currents of public opinion. . . .
>
> Presidents, in short, have incentives to maximize their popularity; the polls provide information on how they are doing. Rises and falls in the polls after particular events may indicate what helps and what hurts and what corrective

actions should be taken. Popularity polls may therefore constitute part of a feedback system in which Presidents adjust their actions to public reactions.

More recently, commentators on the Carter presidency suggested that these measurements played an important role in some of that administration's more dramatic actions (see, for example, the account by Elizabeth Drew [1979] of President Carter's diagnosis of a "national malaise"; see also Converse [1979]). Indeed, one pundit was moved to write:

> Week after week we are treated to a succession of polls, each outbidding the other, with Carter Dropping, Carter Stabilizing, Carter Making Comeback, Carter Approaching Richard Nixon Lows. . . .
> [The corporate executives, editors and reporters who sponsor polls] believe that the noise they hear in the conch shell their pollsters hold up to their ears is the true, genuine, and unadulterated *vox populi*. So, unfortunately, do the politicans, including those in the White House.
> This explains the unbelievable events of the last couple of weeks in which a president, reacting to a bunch of percentages, hired and fired, made speeches, and did all manner of desperate things "to save his presidency," to use a phrase current among reporters. [Von Hoffman, 1979/1980:573]

The frequent reporting of these measurements was evidenced in the exploratory study of newspaper clippings that was reported in Chapter 2 of Volume 1. Reviewing American periodicals published in July of 1980, 40 reports of presidential-popularity polls were found (because of undercoverage in the sample, this figure considerably understates the actual frequency of such reports; see Appendix C of Volume 1). A review of national broadcasts of the evening news on the ABC, CBS, and NBC networks indicates that in the nonpresidential election years between 1973 and 1979, a monthly average of two to three nationally televised news stories were devoted to reports of such presidential-popularity readings.[2]

Presidential-popularity measurements, originated by the Gallup organization, extend back to at least 1941 (see Mueller, 1973:198). In later decades, four other survey organizations began publishing independent readings of presidential popularity. Louis Harris and Associates began reporting such measurements during the 1960s, and in the 1970s the Roper organization, the CBS News/*New York Times* (*NYT*) and NBC News/Associated Press (*AP*) polls initiated similar measurement programs.

The existence of a large body of measurements of the same subjective phenomenon made independently by five survey organizations presents a unique opportunity for assessing the reliability of subjective survey measurements. As noted in Chapter 5 of Volume 1, independent (and contemporaneous) replications of subjective survey measurements are not frequently made. Our search in other areas yielded only 120 instances since

1940 in which two survey organizations contemporaneously asked the same subjective question. Presidential popularity thus represents an unusual case, since we have 513 measurements of the same phenomena made independently by five survey organizations between 1963 and 1980. (As an indication of the scope of this enterprise, we would point out that more than 700,000 survey interviews were conducted to produce these measurements.)

Despite the political importance of presidential-popularity measurements, we are not aware of any previous attempt to systematically assess their interseries reliability. In the following pages we attempt that assessment, first by examining the extent to which the various series agree among themselves in their measurements of the level and variations across time in presidential popularity. Subsequently, we provide a separate evaluation of the extent to which the popularity data as a whole are responsive to factors that one might expect to affect the popularity of presidents. The latter exercise is not new in concept (see, for example, Mueller, 1973; Kernell, 1978; Monroe, 1978; Kernell and Hibbs, 1981), but our approach is somewhat novel in execution. In particular, by incorporating independent measurements made by five survey organizations, we are able to assess the relative sensitivity (and error) of each organization's measurements within the context of a substantive model of the dynamics of presidential popularity. The latter exercise provides us with a second and substantively grounded assessment of the relative accuracy of the different measurements of presidential popularity.

Description of the Data

Publicly available measurements of presidential popularity were collected from the following:[3]

1. Gallup: 313 measurements beginning in 1963
2. Harris: 116 measurements beginning in 1963
3. CBS/*NYT*: 23 measurements beginning in 1977
4. NBC/AP: 34 measurements beginning in 1977
5. Roper: 27 measurements beginning in 1973

Survey measurements made by these organizations used three basic question forms. The form used by both Gallup and CBS/*NYT* asked:

Do you approve or disapprove of the way [name] is handling his job as president?

Louis Harris and Associates and NBC/AP used roughly similar question forms, which asked respondents to rate the job the president was doing. In the Harris version respondents were asked:

> How would you rate the job President [name] is doing as president—excellent, pretty good, only fair, or poor?

and NBC/AP asked

> What kind of job do you think [name] is doing as president—do you think he is doing an excellent job, a good job, only a fair job, or do you think he is doing a poor job?

Finally, the Roper organization used a third form of the question, which asked respondents:

> How do you feel about President [name] at the present time, would you describe yourself as a strong [name] supporter, a moderate [name] supporter, a moderate critic of [name], or a strong critic of [name]?

While the wording of each organization's question was meant to be invariant over time, our review of questionnaires filed at the Harris archive indicated that minor and apparently inadvertent alterations sometimes occurred. For example, the Harris item sometimes dropped the "as President" tag from the question (see Martin, McDuffee, and Presser, 1981:148-169).

While there is variation between survey organizations in the question posed (and minor variation within organizations), these presidential-popularity series are commonly thought to tap the same general phenomenon: public approval of the president's performance. It is thus reasonable to ask about the degree to which these five series produce comparable readings.

The dependent variable we have focused upon in our analyses is the (adjusted) proportion of respondents who approve of the president's performance. (In our contingency tables we use a dichotomy of approve versus disapprove, excluding all cases in which the respondent replied "don't know" or did not answer the question.) For each survey, the (adjusted) proportion approving (A) is:

$$A = \frac{\text{(Number approving)}}{\text{(Number approving + Number disapproving)}}$$

For the Harris and NBC/AP questions, the categories "excellent" and "(pretty) good" were called approval, and "fair" and "poor" were treated as disapproval. For the Roper question, "strong" and "moderate supporter" were called approval and "strong" and "moderate critic" were treated as disapproval.

Our adjusted approval measure excludes "don't know" and "no answer" responses, because Sigelman (1981) has shown that the placement of presidential approval questions within the questionnaire (at least for Gallup's surveys) can alter the proportions of "don't know" (DK) and "no answer" (NA) responses. Sigelman reports, however, that question placement did not alter the ratio of approvals to disapprovals (when DK and NA responses were excluded). Since the placement of the popularity question within survey questionnaires has varied across time and organizations, our use of this adjusted rating should diminish the impact of any such artifacts.

Reliability Analyses

Initially we attempted to assess the extent to which the five time-series agreed with each other. This agreement might be termed the interseries reliability of the measurements. Agreement between the time-series produced by the five survey organizations can be understood in at least two senses. We can ask:

1. To what extent do organizations asking the same (or seemingly equivalent) questions obtain the same distribution of responses?

and we can also ask

2. To what extent do the various series of measurements (whether asking the same or only similar questions) obtain similar readings of the *changes over time* in public opinion? For example, when Organization 1's measurements of presidential popularity rise, do Organization 2's measurements rise in a similar manner?

Both of these questions are treated in this section.

Since presidential popularity changes with time, it would be of little use to compare measurements made in the spring by Organization 1 to those made in the summer by Organization 2. Of course, it is never possible to provide precisely overlapping measurement periods, but any reasonable analysis must come to grips with the need to ensure that variations in the timing of measurements are not overly large (or else one may risk mistaking the sensitivity of a series to the flow of events in time for simple measurement unreliability). In this reliability analysis, the criterion for temporal equivalence used a period of one-twentieth of a year in length (that is, about two-and-a-half weeks). We assume two measurements made during the same one-twentieth of a year period to be made at the same time. This assumption, of course, distorts reality to some extent. Dramatic events may sometimes alter the public's regard for the performance of the president in a single day; the impact of such events will not be well represented by our procedures. It is nonetheless useful to remember in this regard that surveys themselves are not instantaneous. Telephone surveys are commonly conducted over a period of several days, and personal interview surveys often have field periods of more than a week. Hence, the surveys we discuss do not provide a fine-grained picture of public opinion; they too will mask the variations caused by such dramatic events. (This occurs because, for example, measurements made in interviews on the first of April will be included with those made in interviews conducted on the sixth of April.)[4]

DATA DESCRIPTION

We constructed a special dataset that included all instances in which two or more organizations made measurements at (approximately) the same time. We found 100 time periods during which two (or more) organizations asked the national population to evaluate their approval of the current president. We excluded all time periods in which only a single organization reported a measurement and all surveys of other than the national adult population (for example, samples of registered voters).

As noted, the 100 time periods were one-twentieth of a year in length.[5] The date of a survey was taken to be the midpoint of the sampling period. If two surveys were made by a single organization during the same time period, the results of the two surveys were aggregated.

Approval ratings were constructed from tabulation summaries provided by the Roper Public Opinion Research Center, the Louis Harris Data Center, and Louis Harris and Associates, Inc. Frequency counts of the numbers "approving" and "disapproving" were reconstructed using the percentage distributions and sample sizes provided by these archives. (Since these percentage distributions were reported in only two digits, a small amount of imprecision due to rounding errors was introduced into our reconstructed frequency counts.)

The reconstructed frequency counts are the basic data for the following reliability analyses.

COMPARING MEASUREMENTS MADE USING SIMILAR QUESTION WORDINGS

Identical Wording. The least-complicated reliability analysis involves measurements that were made using identically worded questions. The CBS/NYT survey has since its inception in 1977 used the Gallup wording of the presidential-popularity question. Thus, the comparison of these two series is not vulnerable to any (simple or interactive) effects attributable to differences in question wording.

Accuracy of Presidential Ratings, 1963–80

In Figure 16.1 we trace the path of the Gallup (adjusted) approval rating during the years 1977–80 and insert points representing the 23 survey measurements made by the CBS/NYT poll. It quickly will be seen that the agreement between these two series is remarkably close. The product-moment correlation between the measurements made by the two organizations was 0.975 (for the 19 time periods in which both organizations made measurements). This correlation is comfortingly high, but it should be remembered that it reflects two factors: (1) the relatively large fluctuations evidenced by the underlying phenomenon, and (2) the relatively low level of disagreement between the series. Thus, although there is a very substantial agreement between the series about the large variations that occur in presidential popularity, it is still possible that at any given time the two series may give significantly discrepant readings of the level or the variation across time in the popularity of the president.

To study this possibility in greater depth, we fit five models to the 3-way table of frequency counts for the Gallup and CBS/NYT popularity measure-

FIGURE 16.1

Presidential Approval Measurements Made by Gallup (line) and CBS/NYT (dots), 1977-80.

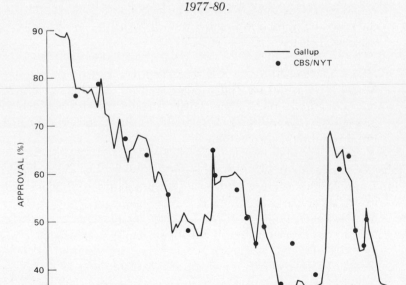

NOTE: The time period of this plot is restricted to years in which CBS/NYT made survey measurements.

ments (that is, 19 time periods [T] by 2 survey houses [H] by 2 response categories [A: approve or disapprove]). These models were:

- Model 1: *No Change and Consistent Indicators.* Model 1 posits that the two organizations obtained identical estimates of a phenomenon that did not change over time. (Model constrained to fit {A} and {HT} marginals.)

- Model 2: *No Change and Constant Bias in Measurements.* Model 2 posits that the two organizations differed by a fixed amount between themselves in measuring a phenomenon that did not change over time. (Model constrained to fit {AH} and {HT} marginals.)

- Model 3: *Reliable Indicators of Change.* Model 3 posits that the two organizations obtained identical estimates of a phenomenon that changed over time. (Model constrained to fit {AT} and {HT} marginals.)

- Model 4: *Constant Bias in Measurements of a Changing Phenomenon.* Model 4 posits that the two organizations tracked the same variations across time, but their measurements differed by a constant amount at each time point. (Model constrained to fit all 2-way marginals, that is, {AT}, {AH}, {HT}).

- Model 5: *Variable Bias in Measurement of Changing Phenomenon.* Model 5 posits a 3-way interaction, that is, that the two organizations measured a phenomenon that changed with time, and that the bias in each organization's measurements also varied over time. (Entire 3-way {AHT} distribution fit.)

Table 16.1 presents the fit of each of these models to the data from the Gallup and CBS/*NYT* surveys. Since the wording of the questions used by these two organizations was identical, one would hope to fit Model 3 to these data. However, neither Model 3 nor the simpler models provide an adequate fit to the data collected by these two survey organizations. Moreover, somewhat different variations across time are observed in the two series. Hence, Model 4 does not provide an adequate fit ($L^2 = 52.6$, d.f. = 18, p < .0001). We are thus forced to accept a model that postulates a modest confounding of variations over time with those induced by survey-specific measurement biases.

We do note, however, that a model incorporating a parameter representing a *constant* house effect provides an insignificant improvement in the fit to the observed data (Model 1 minus Model 2: $L^2 = 3.5$, d.f. = 1, p =

TABLE 16.1

*Test of Fit of Alternative Models for Behavior of Measurements
of Presidential Popularity Made Using Identical Question
Wordings: Gallup Versus CBS/NYT*

Model for Behavior of Series	Mean Absolute[a] Discrepancy from Model	Test of Fit[b] L^2	d.f.
1. No temporal change and no difference between organizations: {A}, {HT}	10.10	4,026.5	37
2. No temporal change, only difference between organizations: {AH}, {HT}	10.07	4,023.0	36
3. No difference between organizations, only temporal change: {AT}, {HT}	1.23	58.7	19
4. Temporal change and *constant* difference between organizations: {AT}, {AH}, {HT}	1.15	52.6	18
5. 3-way interaction (differences between organizations vary with time): {AHT}	0.0	0.0	0
Total N: 61,415			

NOTES: Gallup and the CBS/NYT surveys use identically worded questions. Measurements have been aggregated into approximately biweekly time periods (i.e., we have added together frequency counts for all measurements made in the same time period; each year was divided into 20 time periods).

A = Approval; H = Survey House; T = Time

L^2 = Likelihood-ratio chi-square.

[a]Mean absolute discrepancy between observed frequency count and those expected under the model. This statistic (sometimes called the index of inconsistency) indicates the percentage of observations that would have to change (from approve to disapprove, or vice versa) in order to bring them into complete agreement with the values expected under the model.

[b]Except for Model 5, all tests of fit have $p < .0001$.

.061). Moreover, we note that the relative improvement in fit that is obtained by fitting the 18 parameters representing all possible 3-way interactions of Approval by Time by Organization {AHT} is relatively small (L^2 = 52.6) given the enormous size of our sample. Finally, we note that the discrepancies (between the actual measurements made by the two survey organizations and those measurements expected under Model 4) are sufficiently small that only 1.15 percent of the measurements would have to change (from approval to disapproval, or vice versa) in order to bring the observed and expected measurements into complete agreement.

To provide a further understanding of the magnitude of the effects in-

TABLE 16.2

Estimates of Lambda Parameters Representing Effects of Time, House, and Time-by-House Interactions on Measurements of Presidential Popularity by Gallup and CBS/NYT

Lambda Parameters for		Estimate (and SE)		Standardized Value
House Effect (λ^{AH})		−.008	(.005)	−1.76
Time Effects (λ^{AT})				
1:	1977 − 06	.610	(.030)	20.32
2:	− 11	.552	(.033)	16.70
3:	− 17	.283	(.018)	16.03
4:	1978 − 01	.288	(.020)	14.08
5:	− 06	.038	(.017)	2.18
6:	− 10	− .050	(.020)	− 2.55
7:	− 15	.171	(.014)	12.01
8:	1979 − 02	− .019	(.017)	− 1.11
9:	− 04	− .133	(.019)	− 7.02
10:	− 05	− .025	(.018)	− 1.41
11:	− 09	− .333	(.021)	− 16.14
12:	− 11	− .339	(.016)	− 21.05
13:	− 16	− .304	(.018)	− 17.21
14:	− 17	− .295	(.021)	− 14.33
15:	1980 − 01	.208	(.020)	10.55
16:	− 05	− .122	(.019)	− 6.31
17:	− 06	− .149	(.019)	− 7.99
18:	− 07	− .042	(.020)	− 2.14
19:	− 10	− .339	(.017)	− 19.66
Time-by-House Interactions (λ^{AHT})				
1:	1977 − 06 by Gallup	.068	(.030)	2.27
2:	− 11 by Gallup	− .056	(.033)	− 1.70
3:	− 17 by Gallup	− .034	(.018)	− 1.94
4:	1978 − 01 by Gallup	.046	(.020)	2.22
5:	− 06 by Gallup	− .031	(.017)	− 1.79
6:	− 10 by Gallup	.028	(.020)	1.40
7:	− 15 by Gallup	− .022	(.014)	− 1.52
8:	1979 − 02 by Gallup	.008	(.017)	0.48
9:	− 04 by Gallup	.004	(.019)	0.22
10:	− 05 by Gallup	.039	(.018)	2.16
11:	− 09 by Gallup	− .019	(.021)	− 0.92
12:	− 11 by Gallup	− .043	(.016)	− 2.67
13:	− 16 by Gallup	− .036	(.018)	− 2.01
14:	− 17 by Gallup	.001	(.021)	0.05
15:	1980 − 01 by Gallup	.034	(.020)	1.73
16:	− 05 by Gallup	− .035	(.019)	− 1.80
17:	− 06 by Gallup	.003	(.019)	0.14
18:	− 07 by Gallup	− .003	(.020)	− 0.15
19:	− 10 by Gallup	.048	(.017)	2.78

NOTES: Estimates derived from fitting of saturated model (No. 5). House effect shown is for Gallup. Time effects and House-by-Time interactions are differences between effect for indicated level and average effect for all levels. Time periods were one-twentieth of a year in length, so, for example, 1979–01 indicates the first twentieth of 1979 (approximately the first 18 days).

volved in producing these results, Table 16.2 presents estimates for the lambda parameters representing the effects of Time, House, and Time-by-House interactions on Approval. Lambda parameters were estimated using the saturated log-linear model (No. 5) for the 3-way table $A \times H \times T$. Following Goodman (1970:Sec. 3.1) we use P_{ijk} to denote the probability (in a population table) that an observation will fall in cell (i,j,k) ($i = 1, 2$ [approve, disapprove]; $j = 1, 2$ [Gallup, CBS/NYT]; $k = 1, 19$ [for time periods]), and $v_{ijk} = \log P_{ijk}$ (where log refers to the natural logarithm). The v_{ijk} are decomposed as follows:

$$v_{ijk} = \mu + \lambda_i^A + \lambda_j^H + \lambda_k^T + \lambda_{ij}^{AH} + \lambda_{ik}^{AT} + \lambda_{jk}^{HT} + \lambda_{ijk}^{AHT}$$

The lambdas represent the possible effects of variables A, H, T on v_{ijk}. For sample data, maximum-likelihood estimates of the lambdas can be obtained using procedures described by Goodman (1970). Viewing A as the dependent variable, the parameters that are of particular interest are the λ^{AH} and λ^{AT} parameters, which represent the 2-way interactions of Approval by House and Approval by Time, and the λ^{AHT} parameters, representing the 3-way interaction. The first two represent the "true" change that is occurring over time (λ^{AT}) and any constant difference that exists between the survey houses (λ^{AH}). In the present analysis, the last set of parameters (λ^{AHT}) represents effects that might be thought of as noise, that is, deviations induced by sampling variation *plus* other factors that have not been specified in our analysis, such as differences in sample design and execution, in the precise timing of surveys, in measurement procedures, and so forth.[6]

It can be readily seen from the estimates presented in Table 16.2 that

1. Notable House-by-Time interaction effects (estimated magnitudes exceeding twice their standard errors) occurred in 6 of the 19 time periods, and hence the inadequate fit of Model 4 shown in Table 16.1 is not due to a rare "odd" measurement.
2. However, the Time-by-House interaction effects, while significant, are of much smaller magnitude than the effects induced by Time.

Almost Identical Questions. Since its inception in 1977, the NBC/AP poll has used a question that parallels the question used by the Harris organization. Both ask respondents to rate the job the incumbent is doing as president, and both provide four categories for response. The categories vary in one case:

Harris categories:	excellent	pretty good	only fair	poor
NBC/AP categories:	excellent	good	only fair	poor

We note too that the Harris question refers to the incumbent as "President" (for example, President Carter), while the NBC/AP question refers to him by name only (for example, Jimmy Carter). Such differences in the wording of the two questions might lead one to expect minor variations in the response distributions obtained by Harris and NBC/AP. Notwithstanding these differences, one certainly would expect them to track parallel changes across time.

There were 17 biweekly time periods in which both Harris and NBC/AP made measurements. The product-moment correlation between the approval ratings obtained by the two organizations in those 17 time periods was 0.955.

Table 16.3 fits the five models described previously to the 3-way table of Approval *by* Organization *by* Time. It can be seen from these results that there is a substantial difference between the two organizations in their results—suggestive of a wording effect (or other house effect). Inclusion of a model parameter to allow a constant difference between organizations (that is, constraining the model to fit the $\{AH\}$ marginals) produces a substantial improvement in model fit (Model 4 minus Model 3: $L^2 = 164.7$, d.f. $= 1$, $p < .0001$).

As with the CBS/NYT and Gallup comparison, a model incorporating both true change and survey-specific measurement biases is required, since Model 4 provides an inadequate fit to these data ($L^2 = 96.4$, d.f. $= 16$, $p < .0001$). We note also that the fit of Model 4 (true change plus constant bias) is poorer for these two series than for the Gallup-CBS/NYT comparison ($L^2 = 96.4$, and mean absolute discrepancy of 1.67 versus 52.6 and 1.15, respectively). This occurs despite the fact that the Gallup-CBS/NYT comparison included more time periods (that is, d.f. for the test of fit is 18 versus 16 for Harris-NBC/AP).

Table 16.4 presents estimates of the lambda coefficients representing the effects of House, Time, and Time-by-House interactions on Approval. It will be seen, as with the preceding comparisons, that there are many notable interaction effects; these effects are significant, but considerably smaller in magnitude than the effects induced by Time. Here, however, unlike the preceding comparison, we do find a notable constant effect of House on Approval (the lambda parameter for this effect has an estimated magnitude of 0.063, $SE = 0.005$). This suggests that in any naive comparison of two measurements made in different time periods by these organizations, the magnitude of any temporal change may be masked (or accentuated) by a noteworthy House effect (or wording effect)—as well as by significant House-by-Time interactions.

In considering this result (and those in Table 16.2), we might conceive of the "true" time-induced changes in presidential popularity as the "signal" that analysts are attempting to monitor. Survey measurements reproduce

TABLE 16.3

Test of Fit of Alternative Models for Behavior of Measurements
of Presidential Popularity Made Using Similar Question
Wordings: Harris Versus NBC/AP

Model for Behavior of Series	Mean Absolute[a] Discrepancy from Model	Test of Fit[b]	
		L^2	d.f.
1. No temporal change and no difference between organizations: {A}, {HT}	10.10	3,604.1	33
2. No temporal change, only difference between organizations: {AH}, {HT}	9.99	3,533.6	32
3. No difference between organizations, only temporal change: {AT}, {HT}	2.78	261.1	17
4. Temporal change and *constant* difference between organizations: {AT}, {AH}, {HT}	1.67	96.4	16
5. 3-way interaction (differences between organizations vary with time): {AHT}	0.0	0.0	0
Total N: 52,481			

NOTES: The Harris Survey and the NBC/AP surveys used very similar question wordings. See text for exact wordings. Measurements have been aggregated into approximately biweekly time periods (i.e., we have added together frequency counts for all measurements made in the same time period; each year was divided into 20 time periods).

A = Approval; H = Survey House; T = Time

L^2 = Likelihood ratio chi-square.

[a] Mean absolute discrepancy between observed frequency count and those expected under the model. This statistic (sometimes called the index of dissimilarity) indicates the percentage of observations that would have to change (from approve to disapprove, or vice versa) in order to bring them into complete agreement with the values expected under the model.

[b] Except for Model 5, all tests of fit have $p < .0001$.

this signal with less than perfect fidelity. (Sampling fluctuations, of course, provide one component of "noise," but it is a component for which we have a well-developed theoretical framework to use in deciding when measurement variations are large enough to be attributed to variations in the signal.) Other (largely unknown) measurement factors also introduce a component of noise. Tables 16.2 and 16.4 present estimates of the magnitude of both the true variations that occurred in the signal (that is, the Time "effects") and estimates of the noise introduced by constant and time-variant

TABLE 16.4
Estimates of Lambda Parameters Representing Effects of Time, House, and Time-by-House Interactions on Measurements of Presidential Popularity by Harris and NBC/AP

Lambda Parameters for	Estimate (and *SE*)		Standardized Value
House Effect (λ^{AH})	.063	(.005)	13.28
Time Effects (λ^{AT})			
1: 1977 – 03	.769	(.025)	30.61
2: – 10	.392	(.018)	21.75
3: – 13	.272	(.018)	15.15
4: – 16	.127	(.018)	7.19
5: – 18	.075	(.018)	4.20
6: 1978 – 01	.070	(.019)	3.73
7: – 03	– .078	(.018)	– 4.27
8: – 05	– .064	(.018)	– 3.54
9: – 07	– .220	(.020)	– 10.97
10: – 10	– .214	(.017)	– 12.74
11: – 15	.015	(.019)	0.79
12: – 20	.001	(.018)	0.04
13: 1979 – 03	– .206	(.020)	– 10.36
14: – 05	– .244	(.019)	– 12.92
15: – 12	– .380	(.018)	– 21.45
16: – 14	– .422	(.021)	– 20.35
17: – 20	.107	(.019)	5.71
Time-by-House Interactions (λ^{AHT})			
1: 1977 – 03 by Harris	.105	(.025)	4.19
2: – 10 by Harris	– .001	(.018)	– 0.03
3: – 13 by Harris	– .088	(.018)	– 4.92
4: – 16 by Harris	– .047	(.018)	– 2.67
5: – 18 by Harris	– .037	(.018)	– 2.08
6: 1978 – 01 by Harris	.010	(.019)	0.54
7: – 03 by Harris	.004	(.018)	0.20
8: – 05 by Harris	.041	(.018)	2.27
9: – 07 by Harris	– .013	(.020)	– 0.63
10: – 10 by Harris	.039	(.017)	2.30
11: – 15 by Harris	– .058	(.019)	– 3.08
12: – 20 by Harris	.048	(.018)	2.69
13: 1979 – 03 by Harris	.027	(.020)	1.33
14: – 05 by Harris	– .043	(.019)	– 2.29
15: – 12 by Harris	– .014	(.018)	– 0.81
16: – 14 by Harris	.065	(.021)	3.12
17: – 20 by Harris	– .037	(.019)	– 1.97

NOTES: Estimates derived from fitting of saturated model (No. 5). House effect shown is for Harris. Time effects and House by Time interactions are differences between effect for indicated level and average effect for all levels. Time periods were one-twentieth of a year in length, so, for example, 1979 – 01 indicates the first twentieth of 1979 (approximately the first 18 days).

artifacts in our measuring instruments (that is, the House effect and the Time-by-House interaction effects).

Both Table 16.4 and Table 16.2 indicate that the signal-to-noise ratio in our measuring systems is quite favorable: the signal the survey organizations are monitoring shows fluctuations that are considerably larger, in general, than the noise introduced by our measuring instruments. Nonetheless, since there are detectable noises that distort our readings, it follows that comparisons of measurements that use (only) sampling error as a criterion for inferring changes in the signal must produce more errors of inference than would otherwise be expected.

Comparing Measurements Made Using Different Questions. Up to this point, our analysis has focused on differences between pairs of organizations that used (virtually) identical question wordings. This strategy ignores the rest of the presidential-popularity measurements and thereby makes it impossible to answer many questions of interest to us, for example, whether any one organization's measurements are widely discrepant from those made by other organizations. In the following section we treat these questions by analyzing the entire set of measurements for the 100 time periods.

As a first step in our analysis we computed the product-moment correlations[7] between the five measurement series. These results are presented in Table 16.5. It will be noted from this analysis that while the general level of the correlations is high, there is some variation between organizations. Measurements made by the Harris organization have the lowest mean correlation, although this correlation is still reasonably large (+0.879).

As noted previously, these correlations can obscure substantial discrepancies between the series, and so we undertook further analyses. To assess the reliability of these data, we fit models of the sort previously described

TABLE 16.5

Product Moment Correlations for Five Presidential-Popularity Time Series

	Gallup	Harris	CBS	NBC	Roper	Mean
Gallup	—	.928 (61)	.975 (19)	.939 (26)	.961 (22)	.951
Harris		—	.737 (7)	.955 (17)	.897 (11)	.879
CBS			—	.968 (10)	.986 (6)	.917
NBC				—	.937 (7)	.950
Roper					—	.945

NOTES: Approval rates obtained by each organization were aggregated into approximately biweekly time periods (1/20th of a year). Entries in parentheses show the number of time periods for which there are estimates by both organizations. (Coefficients derived from a weighted analysis, in which weights were proportional to survey sample sizes, produced virtually identical results; see note 7.)

to the full 3-way table representing the responses (that is, approve versus disapprove) obtained by the five survey organizations for all 100 time periods. This table, of course, is not complete, since all organizations did not make measurements in every time period. Indeed, of the 1,000 cells in the 3-way table, only 476 contain nonzero entries. Most of the missing data are concentrated in the period 1963–76; during that period only two organizations, Gallup and Harris, made regular measurements. Using the procedures of Goodman (1968; 1978:Chapters 4 and 5) we fit the hierarchy of models shown in Table 16.6 to the full 3-way table. Zeros were fit in all instances where observations were missing from the table.[8]

Table 16.6 provides strong evidence of the effects of time and organizational factors upon measurements of presidential popularity. Since question wording differs between organizations, we do expect to find differences in the levels of approval obtained by the different organizations. We would, nonetheless, hope to observe parallel changes across time in the data produced by each organization. Model 4, which fits the Approval-by-House {AH} marginals (in addition to the {AT} and {HT} marginals), postulates the appropriate set of constraints. We observe two things about the fit of Model 4 to these data:

1. Tests of fit for Model 4 provide evidence of the constant effects of wording (and/or other organizational factors) on response. The existence of these effects can be tested by contrasting the fit of Model 3, which does not constrain the {AH} marginals and Model 4, which does. The effects are substantial and statistically reliable (Model 3 minus Model 4: $L^2 = 6,478$, d.f. $= 4$, $p < .0001$; mean absolute discrepancy: 5.57 versus 2.21).

2. And, we note that Model 4 does not provide an adequate fit to the observed data ($L^2 = 1,452$, d.f. $= 134$, $p < .0001$). Despite the lack of a fully acceptable fit, we do note that the mean absolute discrepancy[9] between Model 4 and the observed data declined to the point where only 2.21 percent of the sample would have to change in order for the observed frequency counts and the counts expected under the model to be in perfect agreement. [When wording (plus organization) effects are excluded from the model, the corresponding percentage rises to 5.57.]

Our failure to obtain a satisfactory fit of Model 4 to the pooled set of measurements naturally raises questions about the relative contributions of each organization's measurements to this lack of fit. One may wish to know whether the measurements made by one (or more) organizations are consistent outliers. To assess this, we partitioned the L^2 statistic for the fit of Model 4 into components contributed by each organization.[10] Table 16.7 displays the results of this analysis.

It will be seen from Table 16.7 that one organization (CBS/NYT) shows a

TABLE 16.6

*Test of Fit of Alternative Models for Measurements
of Presidential Popularity Made by Five
Survey Organizations*

Model for Behavior of Series	Mean Absolute[a] Discrepancy from Model	Test of Fit[b]	
		L^2	d.f.
1. No differences across time or organizations: {A}, {HT}	13.21	40,655.4	237
2. Only differences between organizations: {AH}, {HT}	11.73	33,906.0	233
3. Only differences across time: {AT}, {HT}	5.57	7,930.4	138
4. Parallel changes across time (but *constant* differences between organizations): {AT}, {AH}, {HT}	2.21	1,452.3	134
5. 3-way interaction (differences in approval between organizations vary with time): {AHT}	0.0	0.0	0
Total N: 378,043			

NOTES: Measurements have been aggregated into approximately biweekly time periods (i.e., we have added together frequency counts for all measurements made in the same time period; each year was divided into 20 time periods).

A = Approval; H = Survey House; T = Time

L^2 = Likelihood ratio chi-square.

[a] Mean absolute discrepancy between observed frequency count and those expected under the model. This statistic (sometimes called the index of dissimilarity) indicates the percentage of observations that would have to change (from approve to disapprove, or vice versa) in order to bring them into complete agreement with the values expected under the model.

[b] Except for Model 5, all tests of fit have $p < .0001$.

deviation from model expectations that is about as large as would be expected on the basis of sampling fluctuations alone. The 21 CBS/*NYT* measurements contribute just $L^2 = 32.4$, and only 1.36 percent of the CBS/*NYT* observations would have to change to bring them into complete agreement with the expectations derived under Model 4. In contrast, the 68 measurements of the Harris organization are most discrepant (mean absolute discrepancy = 2.77 percent; contribution to $L^2 = 538.4$).

In interpreting the results shown in Table 16.7, it should be kept in mind that the expected value for an observation is a function of the central tendency of the entire body of observations at any given time point. When there are only two organizations making measurements in a time period, it is theoretically impossible to distinguish the instability of one set of measurements from the rectitude of the other. Since only two organizations

TABLE 16.7

*Deviations of Five Survey Organizations' Measurements
from Values Expected Under Model 4*

Time Period and Organization	Mean Absolute[a] Discrepancy from Model	L^2	N Measurements	Respondents
1966 – 80				
1. CBS	1.36	32.4	21	24,478
2. Roper	1.74	95.7	26	46,937
3. NBC	2.09	167.7	31	49,632
4. Gallup	2.15	618.1	92	156,910
5. Harris	2.77	538.4	68	100,086
All Organizations	2.21	1452.3	238	378,043
1977 – 80				
1. CBS	1.36	32.4	21	24,478
2. Roper	1.60	57.7	18	33,052
3. Gallup	1.77	215.2	51	96,565
4. NBC	2.09	167.7	31	49,632
5. Harris	2.53	194.8	32	48,166
All Organizations	1.92	667.8	153	251,893

NOTES: Discrepancies are differences between expected values under Model 4 (see Table 16.6) and observed values for each organization.

L^2 values show each organization's contribution to likelihood-ratio chi-square statistics for deviation of observations from expectations under Model 4 (see Table 16.6)

[a] Mean absolute discrepancy between observed measurement and that expected under Model 4. This statistic (sometimes called the index of dissimilarity) indicates the percentage of observations that would have to change (from approve to disapprove, or vice versa) in order to bring them into complete agreement with the values expected under the model.

(Gallup and Harris) were active during the period 1962–76, the inconsistency between these organizations affects both of them equally.

To provide more useful information on the relative performance of the five survey organizations, we separately analyzed the residuals for the 1977–80 period. During this period the pooled data from the other three organizations can be used to adjudicate disagreements between Harris and Gallup. (This approach is roughly equivalent to asking which organization best matches the measurements made by the other three.)

Using the 1977–80 results, we note that the Gallup organization improves its relative ranking, while Harris remains the most discrepant of the five organizations (mean absolute discrepancy from model = 2.53 percent). Indeed, we note that the Gallup and Harris organizations contribute almost equally to our failure to fit Model 4 during this time period (L^2 = 215.2 and 194.8), even though Gallup made 50 measurements (N = 96,565) compared to 30 for Harris (N = 48,166).

Overall, the average magnitude of the observed discrepancies in the entire set of measurements is 1.92 percentage points for the years 1977 through 1980. Three organizations (CBS/NYT, Roper, and Gallup) have average discrepancies that are smaller than this, ranging from 1.36 to 1.78 percentage points. The remaining organizations (NBC/AP and Harris) show larger discrepancies. In the case of the Harris organization, its average discrepancy is almost twice that of the organization with the least discrepant measurements, CBS/NYT (2.53 versus 1.26 percentage points).

Fitting a Substantive Model

The direct comparison of popularity measurements generates a precise test of survey-house variability. The only difficulty stems from the arbitrariness of the central tendency for each time point against which each house's measurement is compared. In theory, that comparison point is determined by the "true" popularity at the moment of the simultaneous measurements; in practice, it is determined endogenously, which is to say, by the measurements themselves. The test does not explicitly take into account the fact that presidential popularity ought to be generated by the political and economic environment at any time point, and that an exogenously determined "popularity" may be arrived at. Such a comparison point for the house measures can provide an additional standard for comparison. That is, an external-construct validity test may be added to the reliability test for cross-house comparisons.

The strategy used in this section introduces a substantive causal element by modeling presidential popularity as a dynamic function of the political environment. A cross-house difference can then be tested as a direct, but separable, effect. The idea is to first develop a full model of presidential popularity as a response to the conditions of the economy, external warfare, and ordinary political events, and then to compare instrument differences which cannot be attributed to variations in the contemporaneous environment. Finally, a further assessment of measurement reliability may be added to the direct comparison by analyzing the residual variation left after the substantive and (constant) house effects have been estimated.

CONSTRUCT VALIDITY

The substantive model of popularity used here is one which is about as simple as possible and which yet can capture the flavor of the short-term dynamics found in these data. For each variable in the model, popularity is taken to be a reflection of the current level of that variable and, with decreasing weight, its past levels. For example, support for the president is assumed to be (partially) due to today's inflation rate, to a lesser extent due to last month's inflation rate, and to an even lesser extent due to the previous month's, and so on. A simple way to write such a function is

$$P^{(i)}_t = bI_t + dP^{(i)}_{t-1}$$

where $P^{(i)}$ is the component of popularity attributable to inflation; I_t is the level of inflation in the tth time period. This equation represents a familiar partial-equilibration process in which the effect of any shock (in this case the level of inflation) will persist into the future as an exponential function of the passage of time (bd^t) as the population's judgment of the president slowly returns (equilibrates) to a level determined by the rest of the system. This first-order model represents a process in which the rate of reequilibration is a simple linear function ($1 - d$) of the extent to which the system is out of equilibrium at any moment. This model yields a response pattern that begins at its maximum and then gently, exponentially, approaches the equilibrium level as an asymptote.

By assuming that popularity is an additive function of the factors in the model, estimates for the scalar transforms (the b's) and the dynamic coefficients (the d's) may be obtained for each variable. The straightforward Koyck transform (Koyck, 1954; Theil, 1971) cannot be used for these estimation purposes because (1) the previous popularity level, P_{t-1}, is not uniformly available for each reading; (2) using it would introduce the effect of previous, unspecified disturbance terms into the dynamic coefficients; and (3) the simple model assumes equal equilibration rates for all forms of system shock. The first problem is a practical one and might otherwise be circumvented by collapsing the series into a monthly one (although this would limit the analysis to periods of frequent measurements). The second problem is a standard estimation bias and needs attention; the procedure here solves the problem only in part. More important, the third problem is that a simple Koyck transform depends on an assumption that is theoretically unsatisfactory. We might naturally expect the effect of, say, a presidential speech to be more transitory than that of, say, an election campaign, simply because the latter is likely to generate a complex attitude change, more resistant to subsequent reequilibration forces. This is not to say that the immediate impact will be greater (though it might be), but that its observable duration will be longer.

With this in mind we obtained the current results by directly estimating the model's dynamic parameters with a nonlinear procedure coupling a grid search and Marquardt's iterative gradient compromise. In practice this amounted to setting initial conditions for 1961 and dynamically generating the estimated popularity path for subsequent time points as the specified function of the previously estimated popularity and contemporaneous input.[11] The lay reader will note that the observed values of popularity (for example, P_{t-1}) never appear on the right-hand side of the estimation equation as they are replaced by values estimated from previous shocks to the system. A further advantage of this estimation strategy lies in the fact that modeling presidential popularity on exogenous sources allows estimates to be obtained for all data points,[12] not just those for which another house made a coincident reading (as was the case in our previous analyses).

Substantively there is nothing remarkable about the underlying model: it is a linear combination of four sets of dynamic components plus a dummy variable for each presidential administration.[13] The economic variables, unemployment and inflation, were introduced additively[14] (experimentation with interactive components did not compel a more complex specification). The Vietnam War variable represents the number of troops (in tens of thousands) in Vietnam and thus provides an indicator of ordinary citizens' personal involvement with the war effort. This variable was set to zero after the inauguration of Nixon in the belief that Vietnam was not viewed as his war and because, empirically, these data did not show a relation between troop levels and Nixon's popularity. In addition, one other variable was employed. It represents the ephemeral glow that surrounds each new president as he takes office and citizens (appear to) give him the benefit of the doubt (followed by the subsequent gradual decline as doubts become justified). In practice this variable is simply a unit spike placed at inauguration day with its magnitude and decay rate left to be estimated from the data. Finally, in order to capture the short-term dynamics, two variables representing events of transitory and then of more long-lasting impacts were introduced.[15]

Table 16.8 displays the results from estimating this model,[16] assuming that the differences between each organization's measurements could be represented as a constant bias. The expected value at any time might vary by a constant effect if the the organization's survey procedures were constantly different with respect to wording, sampling frame, and so forth. In terms of wording, the effect might be due to the various probes and response categories given the respondent, or to an organization's interviewer training, that gave different instructions on the tone in which the question was to be read. In terms of the sampling frame, such a difference might obtain if the houses incorporated a constant bias in drawing their initial sample (say, picking more middle-class or better-educated respondents) or in their call-back procedures (which might overweight the sample with accessible respondents). The house coefficients in the estimation equation are dummy variables comparing each condition with Gallup sampling, wording, and interview procedures.

By far the most important result is that the CBS/NYT replication of the Gallup approval wording produces almost exactly the same estimates obtained by Gallup. This is to say that for any given reading of popularity, their *expected value* would be almost identical. (These estimates do not assess their relative precision; the matter of reliability requires analysis of variation, not expected value, as will be discussed below.) Here the data

TABLE 16.8

Presidential Popularity and Constant House Effects
(Modeled as a Function of Political Climate, Administration,
and Survey House)

Coefficients for		B	SE(B)	D	SE(D)
Intercept		72.53*	2.79		
House effects:	CBS	− 0.05	1.25		
	Roper	0.52	1.05		
	Harris	− 11.85*	0.67		
	NBC	− 18.62*	1.02		
Substantive Model					
Presidential Administration:	Johnson	5.51*	2.56		
	Nixon	− 9.70*	1.72		
	Ford	− 6.56*	2.14		
	Carter	− 17.26*	2.33		
Presidential glow:	Johnson	21.95*	3.82	.96	.32
	Nixon	37.09*	2.06	.96	.06
	Ford	53.17*	2.89	.85	.07
	Carter	53.77*	2.21	.97	.07
Political climate:	Short Events	1.09*	.05	.83	.07
	Long Events	1.06*	.09	.94	.11
	War	− 0.12*	.01	.69	.07
	Inflation	− 0.35*	.02	.84	1.40
	Unemployment	− 0.65	.52	.00	—

NOTES: This model predicts all observations (except for voter samples), 1963 – 80. Variables were entered as shown, with the Constant House Effects introduced as dummy variables contrasted with Gallup as the baseline. Administration coefficients mark the president's equilibrium value that is not determined by the rest of the equation; they are contrasted with Kennedy's equilibrium popularity represented in the constant term. The fit may be indicated by: R − square = 0.91; F − ratio = 261.08; d.f. = (17/419), mean squared error = 24.29.
*Probability that parameter is equal to zero is less than .01.

provide a good experiment on the comparability of survey methodologies in that the question wordings are identical and any difference in readings could be attributable to constant house-induced effects. The fact that two houses (CBS/NYT and Gallup) produce indistinguishable readings suggests that houses can eliminate biases in measurement, and this reinforces the contention that these measurements can be taken seriously. This conclusion must be taken all the more seriously because the similarity in readings may not be ascribed to each house's being aware of an experimental comparison, and thus paying particular care to its procedures; instead, the readings were produced by the houses' everyday practice.

More surprising, although more of a curiosity, is the inability to distinguish statistically the Roper results from those of Gallup and CBS/*NYT*. Both measures do emphasize a "pass the mark" frame of reference rather than a graded form of evaluation, and in doing so may produce similar readings. However, given the two very different sets of words used to elicit a response, we can only suggest that the correspondence be seen as a happy coincidence for the organizations and that it provides a puzzle for more elaborate questionnaire research.

We may not conclude that the idea of presidential approval is insensitive to measurement technique. This can easily be seen by inspecting the large differences in Table 16.8 for the Harris and NBC/AP measurements, which ask for a graded job rating, not support or approval. Clearly far fewer citizens are willing to judge the president's performance as excellent or (pretty) good than are willing to approve or support him, and the difference is statistically reliable. (The further distinction $[(-11.85) - (-18.62) = 6.77]$ between the very similar Harris and NBC/AP probes is troubling, but no firm conclusion is possible about its source, given the present data.)

The foregoing results are based on the assumption that the inconsistencies in measurement can be expressed as a constant bias. There is no reason to exclude a priori the possibility that the observed differences are due to time-variant survey procedures. For example, if an organization should have oversampled the highly educated or attentive public, then it may also oversample responsiveness to changes in the political climate. Alternatively, the different question formats may elicit a sentiment that is peculiarly sensitive to elements in the political and economic environment. Thus further examination is called for. In particular, the contrast between responses to the Gallup-CBS question and the Harris-NBC question may be due to a number of respondents who are willing to approve of a president whose job they rate "fair." (A presidential job rating of "only fair" is counted as not approving of his performance. See previous discussion.) If this were so, there would be a number of Gallup "approvers" whose support would be tentative in that they rate job performance as "only fair." These soft supporters might thus be more easily moved in and out by shifts in the political climate.

This notion of a proportion of Harris "only fair" raters also approving of the president has been studied. Sussman (1978) and Orren (1978) report a *Washington Post* survey in January 1978 directly comparing respondents' answers to both the Gallup and Harris questions. The *Post* found that 46 percent of those rating Carter's job as "only fair" also "approved" of his handling of the job. This same proportion may be estimated from our data across all the Gallup and Harris samples. The difference between the Harris and Gallup readings may be expressed as a proportion of those saying "only fair" to Harris who would "approve" in the Gallup format. Performing the proper analysis on the *Post* data, which is to say excluding the "don't know" categories and working from the marginals, yields an estimate of 46.06 percent.[17] A similar procedure for all the Gallup-Harris direct comparisons for the 1969–80 period yields the estimates shown in Table 16.9, which are slightly smaller than the *Post*'s 1978 figure. Either the proportion was high for that reading or, more likely, the aggregate estimates suffer from some underspecification and thus are modestly depressed toward zero. Of some interest is the low estimate for the Watergate period, because it suggests that at that time only the president's hard-core supporters were willing to give Gallup an "approval" response. The overall pattern indicates that the difference in wording may have something to do with the different levels of popularity readings for the two questions, and it suggests that this difference may be due to a portion of presidential supporters whose support may be more susceptible to influence.

This possibility may be formally assessed by modeling the Gallup and Harris popularity measures with the coefficients free to pick up a unique sensitivity to the political-economic environment. The coefficients displayed in Table 16.10 are produced by a test of such a less restricted model of Gallup approval and Harris rating results for the Nixon, Ford, and Carter years.[18] Dummy variables (for Harris) were introduced to allow the substantive model to have distinct effects for each organization's measures of support. The first column presents the coefficients for the Gallup popularity readings. The second column of figures is the crucial set because it presents the magnitude of the *difference* in Gallup-Harris readings due to variable sensitivity to the model's substantive components.

Of those substantive coefficients, the only one that seems significantly different for the Harris readings is the one due to inflation. As expected, Harris's evaluative rating measure is less sensitive. Lukewarm supporters included by the Gallup question do seem more sensitive to fluctuations in

TABLE 16.9

*Estimates of Proportion Rating President's Job "Only Fair" (Harris)
Who "Approve" (Gallup)*

Administration	Number of Comparisons	Proportion "Fair" Who "Approve"	Standard Error of Estimate
Nixon (before Watergate)[a]	13	.46	.08
Nixon (during Watergate)[b]	8	.05	.03
Ford	12	.38	.04
Carter	25	.37	.02

NOTES: These estimates derive from separate mappings of the Harris "only fair" sample proportion to the difference between Gallup and Harris approval ratings. Numbers are rough due to likely underspecification.
[a]I.e., prior to 15 March 1973.
[b]I.e., from 15 March 1973, to Nixon's resignation.

Accuracy of Presidential Ratings, 1963–80

TABLE 16.10

Presidential Popularity and House/Substance Interaction
Modeled on Political Climate, Administration, and Survey House
(Gallup and Harris)

Coefficients for		Gallup: B	Harris Difference: B	SE: Difference
Intercept:		59.80*		
Presidential administration:	Nixon	—a	−16.69*	4.60
	Ford	2.06	−12.45*	3.38
	Carter	−5.31*	−13.34*	2.07
Presidential glow:	Nixon	43.49*	−14.10*	1.51
	Ford	63.30*	−11.46*	4.46
	Carter	52.87*	2.84	3.79
Political climate:	Short Event	1.12*	0.00	0.08
	Long Event	1.16*	0.03	0.15
	Inflation	−0.41*	0.18*	0.03
	Unemployment	0.37	1.30	1.08

NOTES: These estimates are for the Nixon, Ford, and Carter administrations only. Column 1 (Gallup) gives the baseline substantive model. Column 2 (Harris Difference) presents an estimate of the difference in the sensitivity of the Harris measure to the particular variable. The standard error of the estimate of the difference is presented in column 3. The analysis uses the same dynamics as those generated in the analysis reported in table 16.8. The fit may be indicated by: R−square = 0.97; F−ratio = 412.86; d.f. = (19/244); mean squared error = 8.01.
aThe Nixon administration was the residual category for the comparison.
*Probability that parameter is equal to zero is less than .01.

the Consumer Price Index than do the relative stalwarts Harris picks up. Surprisingly, though, this differential sensitivity cannot be identified for the political event series or for unemployment (though the estimates of the latter are very imprecise). In any case, the differences here, though reliable, are very small.

Overall, however, the contrast between Gallup and Harris does not reflect unique sensitivities to the immediate environment, but instead is best represented as a simple function of the presidential equilibrium level and the glow for each administration. Gallup's question seems to capture consistently more approvers whose support is not affected by short-term changes in political climate and whose support erodes as the glow vanishes.

This form of comparison may be expanded to include all organizations, but only for the 1977–80 period. For this purpose, a separate model was "custom-fitted" to the popularity readings of each house (the collinearity in a full house/substance interaction model is overwhelming). Coefficient estimates, displayed in Table 16.11, are a little uncertain because Carter's readings moved so as to confound the contributions of the unemployment and glow variables. Nevertheless, the different questions' responsiveness may be compared for the event and inflation variables. The same pattern is observed in that the Harris, and now the NBC/AP, questions seem less sensitive to inflation, but the statistical test of that difference is a little more murky. Their susceptibility to the impact of political events seems much the same as that for the other houses. In addition, it is evident that the Roper question (about presidential "supporters") is mildly less responsive to the event data. This is not surprising, given the loyalty implications of the response categories, but this difference is only on the edge of statistical significance.

This further work underscores the apparent distinction in Table 16.8 between Harris on the one hand and NBC/AP on the other. Estimated equilibrium levels for Carter seem noticeably different for those two houses, although the estimates are imprecise. A more explicit comparison in which the two organizations' readings for the Carter period are estimated together (thus constraining the model somewhat) yields an estimate of 6.49 for a constant difference[19] in their readings, with a standard error of 0.75. The probability that this difference is actually zero is considerably less than .01. Thus it is likely that there remains a distinction between the organizations' readings which cannot be attributed to their questions being differentially sensitive to the substantive determinants of popularity.[20]

TABLE 16.11

Presidential Popularity and House/Substance Interaction Custom Fitted to the Political Climate (Carter administration only—all houses)

		Coefficients for				
Organization	Intercept	Presidential Glow	Short Event	Long Event	Inflation	Unemployment
Gallup	53.73	55.15	1.09	1.06	−0.36	−0.26
	(3.24)	(2.20)	(0.05)	(0.13)	(0.03)	(0.54)
Harris	7.51	54.39	1.00	1.08	−0.10	4.17
	(19.03)	(12.59)	(0.15)	(0.26)	(0.07)	(5.41)
CBS/NYT	46.64	66.34	1.00	1.03	−0.22	−1.23
	(16.18)	(17.29)	(0.09)	(0.37)	(0.14)	(1.28)
NBC/AP	19.29	53.23	0.82	1.04	−0.16	0.94
	(7.36)	(4.94)	(0.12)	(0.24)	(0.08)	(1.49)
Roper	50.12	41.52	0.79	0.78	−0.34	1.96
	(13.11)	(9.11)	(0.09)	(0.18)	(0.06)	(3.91)

NOTES: These coefficients derive from a separate, custom-fitted model for each house for the Carter years. Intercept (equilibrium), glow, and unemployment coefficients are very imprecisely estimated due to their marked collinearity. More reliable are the estimates for the event series and for inflation. The standard errors of the coefficients' estimates are included in parentheses under each estimate. The model uses the same dynamics as that reported in table 16.8.
R^2 values were: .97 (Gallup), .95 (Harris), .93 (CBS/NYT), .95 (NBC/AP), and .98 (Roper).

A SECOND TEST OF RELIABILITY

The equations represented in Tables 16.8, 16.10, and 16.11 attempt to establish the fact that popularity measures do in fact covary with the external environment and that they do so in sensible and predictable ways. They do not assess how accurately these organizations measure popularity.

Another measure of the variability of these measurements, in addition to the direct test presented in our first set of reliability analyses, may be derived from analyzing the deviations of each organization's measurements from the score predicted by the substantive model. The utility of this effort depends on the predictions being meaningfully related to theoretical expectations; the foregoing analysis of construct validity seems to suggest that this is so.

A simple comparison of residual deviations is presented in Table 16.12, in which the predicted scores are manufactured by the constant-effects model of Table 16.8. The first column of numbers is the set of mean absolute values of the residuals associated with each survey house.[21] A first glance indicates that the most reliable organizations, that is, those whose average deviation was smallest, were CBS/NYT, Gallup, and Roper, while falling somewhat behind were NBC/AP and Harris. Comparing across houses, however, is a difficult problem, because the houses attempted to measure popularity during somewhat different periods. In particular, only Gallup and Harris generated frequent measures for any but the Carter years. Thus the second array of numbers displays the mean absolute deviations for each house from the constant-effects models reestimated for the 1977–80 period. The same classification of relative precision holds, though the scores look more accurate than before because of the model's superior prediction of the Georgian's popularity.[22] Differences within each clustering are not statistically significant, but the wide gap between Gallup, CBS, and Roper on the one hand and NBC and Harris on the other is large and statistically reliable. These results mimic the direct comparisons of the first section, and they add an extra weight to those findings because these are differences due not to an endogenously determined "true" value, but to one that has some substantive interpretability.

There is one potential source of error in this analysis, however. The constant-effects model does not take into account the minor question/substance interaction displayed in Table 16.10 for Harris and in Table 16.11 for Harris and NBC. Finding that both Harris and NBC fall toward the bottom suggests that the model may attribute to unreliability, error due to model underspecification. The predictive model is dominated (in terms of sample points) by the Gallup series, and thus the other house measures may be slighted by the fact that they may respond differently to environmental stimuli. Thus, an examination of the custom-fitted models represented in Table 16.11 is necessary in order to eliminate this possibility. Table 16.13

TABLE 16.12

Analysis of Residual Deviations from Constant-House-Effects Model:
Popularity Modeled on Political Climate, Administration,
and Survey House

Time Period	Organization	Mean Absolute Deviation	Standard Error of Mean	L^2	Number of Readings
1963 – 80	1. CBS	2.11	.45	87.0	20
	2. Gallup	2.33	.10	1905.4	270
	3. Roper	2.59	.44	311.4	27
	4. NBC	3.34	.47	458.1	31
	5. Harris	3.87	.34	1312.4	76
	All	2.69	.19	4074.3	424
1977 – 80	1. Roper	2.07	.41	108.4	18
	2. CBS	2.09	.45	86.5	20
	3. Gallup	2.38	.20	533.8	70
	4. NBC	2.66	.46	365.8	31
	5. Harris	3.10	.41	341.9	32
	All	2.53	.29	1436.5	171

NOTES: Entries in column 1 represent the absolute value of the residual deviations from the substantive predictive model. Models here represent the Constant-Effects model of the political climate, administration, and house shown in table 16.8. The difference between these tests and those of table 16.7 lies in the estimated polularity being derived from the substantive model. The second column presents the standard error of the mean estimates, and the third gives the likelihood-ratio chi-square. The last column shows the number of presidential-popularity readings taken by each house during the period. (Model parameters were separately estimated for the entire period, 1963–80, and for the years 1977–80.)

presents the residual analysis. Clearly, the same clustering of houses is manifest and the same statistical conclusion must be made. Whatever its source, both Harris and NBC consistently display significantly greater variation in their measurements.[23]

(Plots of these observed and expected presidential-popularity ratings for 1977 through 1980 are shown in Figures 16.2 and 16.3; in these figures the custom-fitted model was used to provide the predicted values for the measurements made by the five survey organizations. Figure 16.4 presents similar plots for the Gallup and Harris measurements during 1963 through 1976 using the constant-effects model.)

While the gap between the two reliability clusters may be identified, in absolute terms it is not large. After all, popularity ratings move over a range of about 60 points. However, in terms of a total-error model (see Volume 1, Chapter 4) the proportion of variability added on top of a theoretical sampling error is important. The expected deviation due to sampling runs from 0.88 to 1.05 for the organizations' Carter ratings, but the observed deviations range from 1.29 to 2.55.[24] And we note that Harris and NBC/AP add

TABLE 16.13

*Analysis of Residual Deviations from Models Custom-Fitted for
Each Survey House: Popularity Modeled on Political Climate
(Carter administration only)*

Time Period	Organization	Mean Absolute Deviation	Standard Error of Mean	L^2	Number of Readings
1977–80	1. Roper	1.29	.27	42.3	18
	2. CBS	1.80	.46	73.9	20
	3. Gallup	2.19	.18	456.9	70
	4. Harris	2.68	.34	246.0	32
	5. NBC	2.55	.41	265.0	31
	All	2.20	.25	1084.2	171

NOTES: Entries in column one are the absolute value of the residual deviations from the substantive predictive model. Here, a separate model was fitted for each house on the political climate (all for the Carter administration). The second column presents the standard error of the mean estimates, and the third the likelihood-ratio chi-square. The last column shows the number of popularity readings taken by each house during the period.

(very roughly) about 1.5 to 2 times the amount of measurement error that Gallup and CBS/*NYT* introduce.

The source of the latter difference and its implications for development are not clear. It could be that both NBC and Harris use survey practices that are noticeably less precise than those used by other organizations. This might be the result of less rigorous procedures for sampling, call-backs, and interviewer training. (The one available comparison in this regard [see Figure 3.1 in Volume 1] does indicate that the Harris samples substantially overrepresent the college-educated; no systematic evidence is available to us concerning the NBC/AP surveys.) However, finding that it is the houses with a particular question format that produce the greater variance suggests that the source may lie in the nature of their questions. Simply increasing the number of options presented to the respondent might be expected to increase test-retest reliability if there is any randomness in response. Furthermore, presentation of the "only fair" option may introduce an ambiguous response category that makes the division between, say, "pretty good" and "only fair" an easy line for uncertain respondents to slip over.[25] If the analyst were certain that respondents have a dichotomous attitude (approve or disapprove), the fine-grained response format may build in a measurement error. However, if respondents' attitudes genuinely fall along a continuum, the increased variability may be due to the respondents' uncertainty about how their feelings can be translated into simple approval or disapproval. If this were the case, the Gallup-CBS approval-disapproval forced choice may introduce reliability where it should not exist. (We note,

FIGURE 16.2

Presidential Approval Measurements Expected Under Custom-Fitted Model (see Table 16.11) and Actual Measurements Made by CBS/NYT, Gallup, and Roper, 1977-80.

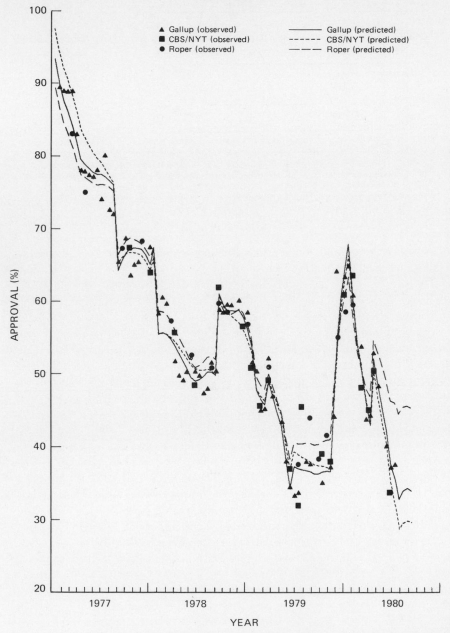

NOTE: The time period of this plot is restricted to years in which CBS/NYT made survey measurements.

FIGURE 16.3

Presidential Approval Measurements Expected Under Custom-Fitted Model (see Table 16.11) and Actual Measurements Made by Harris and NBC/AP, 1977-80.

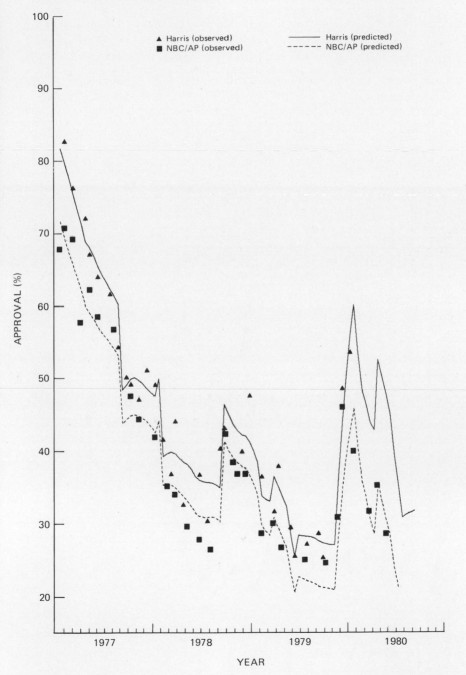

NOTE: The time period of this plot is restricted to years in which NBC/AP made survey measurements.

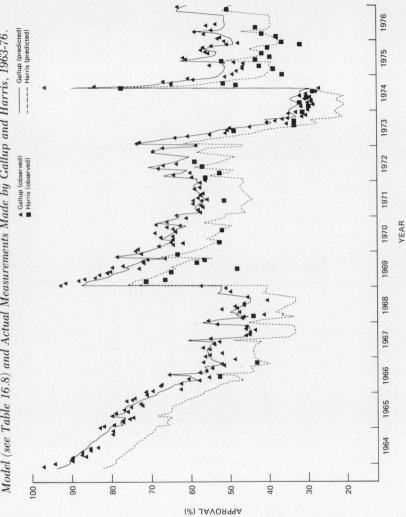

FIGURE 16.4

Presidential Approval Measurements Expected Under Constant-House-Effects Model (see Table 16.8) and Actual Measurements Made by Gallup and Harris, 1963-76.

▲ Gallup (observed) ——— Gallup (predicted)
■ Harris (observed) - - - - - Harris (predicted)

APPROVAL (%)

YEAR

nonetheless, that one organization [Roper] using a four-category response scale evidenced reliabilities at the same level as those of CBS/*NYT* and Gallup.)

Conclusions

The results of this analysis address two matters: (1) whether the different house/instrument combinations do in fact measure the same thing and thus whether the construct of popularity may be validated in substantive terms, and (2) whether there exist statistically discernible differences between the organizations' precision in measuring popularity.

If survey measurements are to be taken seriously, they must be subjected to external validation (see the panel's recommendations: Volume 1, Chapter 10). Assessing survey organizations' ability to monitor a subjective state, which is in principle unobservable, requires that their measurements be identical, or at least that they diverge in an explicable manner, and that those measurements be related to theoretically motivated observables.

The resolution of the first set of concerns is clear. The variation in all the organizations' measures of presidential popularity may be successfully accounted for with a fairly simple model. It includes economic performance, political events, and a gradual diminishing of each president's inaugural glow. While small distinctions may be discerned in each measure's sensitivity to the political climate, they are all in accord with an expectation based on the nature of the question format. For the most part, however, the readings move in concert. The main dissimilarities between any two organizations' measures seem to be adequately expressed as a constant. The gap between the Gallup-CBS/*NYT* and the Harris-NBC/AP levels appears to be consistent with an explanation centering around the nature of the latter's "only fair" response option. The clearest, and the most heartening, result is that the exact coincidence of the Gallup and CBS/*NYT* questions produces almost identical readings. More troubling is the persistent contrast between the Harris and NBC/AP readings, which are based on very similar (though not identical) question formats. The summary view, though, is one of a set of measures that track a substantively justified presidential popularity in a remarkably coherent fashion.

The concern about instrument precision is a little less easily resolved. It is clear that the Gallup, CBS/*NYT*, and Roper instruments show greater reliability then do the Harris and NBC/AP measures. This divergence was shown both in terms of a direct, substance-free comparison of variability and also in terms of deviations from the predictions of our substantive models. These separate assessments supplement each other because the first derives from a straightforward statistical test that does not rely on an intricate model specification, while the second takes into account the information produced in the validity test.

The implications of this finding, however, are not self-evident. Should the unreliability of the Harris and NBC/AP readings be due to the organizations' internal practices,[26] a call for firmer operational standards must be heeded if the survey task is to be taken seriously. The same message must be read if the imprecision is due to an undesirable ambiguity in response options; less reliable question formats should give way to more reliable ones. However, if the increased variability reflects a substantive phenomenon, here an attitude uncertainty, which is masked by a simpler format, the tables are turned. Making a judgment about the sources of this difference in instrument reliability requires a more extensive examination of organizational procedures and of individuals' attitudes than can be attempted here. Nonetheless, if Harris and NBC/AP are to avoid being tarred with the brush of unreliability, then further and more extensive research would seem in order.

On a broad scale the picture looks fairly good, at least with regard to assessing presidential popularity using the techniques of survey research. Aside from an obvious constant difference in levels, the instrument distinctions are not large. The differences in the organizations' precision, while requiring action, are of relatively small magnitude compared to the large variations occuring in presidential popularity over time. While measuring popularity requires caution in interpreting the details of the results, our findings do not support claims that such survey measurements are either invalid or entirely unreliable. Rather our analysis suggests two, more specific conclusions.

First, given a large body of data containing frequent measurements of a phenomenon that varies considerably over time, such as presidential popularity, common survey measurement procedures do seem to provide a generally consistent portrayal of the fluctuations that occur in the national population. Survey estimates of these fluctuations, moreover, are systematically related to exogenous variables that are (theoretically) likely causes of shifts in the popularity of presidents. A general claim to reliability and validity for these measurements is thus sustainable.

Second, our analyses also indicate that the range of inconsistencies existing in these survey measurements is sufficiently large that comparison of two measurements made at different times may yield erroneous conclusions about changes in the national population's approval of a president if sampling error is the only source of variance taken into account in making inferences. (This appears to be particularly problematic when the measurements are made by different survey organizations.) Inconsistencies evident in the series we examined suggest that the nonsampling components of variance in these measurements are sometimes as large as are the components attributable to sampling variance. Thus, a cautious analyst may wish to allow correspondingly larger margins of error around point estimates of presidential popularity.

APPENDIX TABLE 16.A
Estimates of Event Impacts

Administration & Event	Date	Estimated Impact
Johnson		
Election 1964	64092 – 64102	0.22
Bomb Vietnam	65021	– 3.24
Dominican Republic	65051	4.25
Watts	65082	– 0.11
Escalate war	66021	0.70
Demonstrations	66041	1.15
Demonstrations	66051	– 4.12
Escalate war	66071	4.91
Urban riots	66072	– 7.73*
Election 1966	66101 – 66102	– 2.74*
Glassboro Summit	67062	7.60**
Newark-Detroit riots	67071 – 67072	– 5.52**
Nonproliferation announcement	67121	7.88*
Christmas message	67122	5.29
Tet Offensive	68021 – 68022	– 2.89
New Hampshire primary	68031	3.44
Abdication	68041	2.41
Czechoslovakia invasion	68082	0.08
Election 1968	68092 – 68102	3.10*
Nixon		
Nixon world tour	69022	1.77
Moon walk	69072	1.88
Anti-war moratorium	69102	– 4.41
Silent majority speech	69111	13.07**
Cambodian invasion	70051	3.74
State of Union Speech	70012	0.62
Election 1970	70101 – 70102	4.47**
Laotian invasion	71021	– 5.04*
Pentagon Papers	71062	– 0.90
China visit	72021	5.13**
ITT scandal	72032	– 2.17
Mine Haiphong	72051	7.57*
Moscow trip	72052	4.46
Election 1972	72092 – 72102	3.95**
Rebomb Hanoi	72122	– 7.79
Peace announcement	73012	15.72**
POW return	73021	2.96
Watergate	73032 – 74081	– 1.31**
Brezhnev visit	73062	– 2.63
Agnew resignation	73101	– 5.60**
John Dean's testimony	73071	– 5.38
TV Watergate speech	73082	0.78
Saturday Night Massacre	73102	– 2.82
Impeachment hearings	74052	– 1.16

Administration & Event	Date	Estimated Impact
Ford		
Nixon pardon	74091	−8.79**
"WIN" speech[a]	74101	1.15
Vladivostok Summit	74112	−3.00
Tax cut	75041	0.81
Mayaguez rescue	75052	12.24**
Assassination attempts	75091−75092	2.56*
Fire Nixon cabinet	75111	−4.04*
New Hampshire primary win	76031	0.83
Florida primary win	76032	6.02*
Republican nomination	76081	−26.47
Election 1976	76092−76102	6.87
Carter		
MEOW speech[b]	77042	−0.89
Lance hearings	77091	−10.29**
Carter world tour	77122	−0.06
State of Union speech	78012	2.99
Panama Canal Treaty	78021	−9.38**
Camp David Peace Treaty	78092	11.11**
Election 1978	78101−78102	−0.16
Deng visit	79021	−3.04
Three Mile Island	79032	3.87**
Gas lines	79052−79061	−2.84**
Salt signing	79062	5.44*
Iran Embassy takeover, etc.	79112−80012	9.65**
Rescue mission	80042	10.49**
Credit controls	80031	2.14
Billy-gate	80062	−4.24

NOTES: Dates are given in terms of year, month, and whether scored as in the first or second half of month. For example, 79052 indicates the second half of May 1979.

Impact coefficients are in pure percentage points—which is to say that Ford's pardon of Nixon (impact coefficient = −8.79) is estimated to have hurt his standing by about 8.79 points. Most estimates have a standard error of 2 to 4 points and the exact impact is only roughly indicated. In particular, the estimate for Ford's nomination seems overly large and imprecise; its standard error is 75.01. Those events which are individually distinct from zero are so marked. For events taking place over a period of time, the impact was estimated for all included time points and subsequently applied to all. For example, the impact of the Newark-Detroit riots was applied to both the first and second halves of July 1967. Importantly, Nixon seems to have lost about 1.31 points for each half-month of the Watergate period, aside from adjustments for discrete identifiable events.

[a]WIN: Whip Inflation Now.
[b]MEOW: (Energy crisis is) moral equivalent of war
*Probability that coefficient is actually zero is less than .10.
**Probability that coefficient is actually zero is less than .05.

Notes

1. Two decades earlier, Neustadt (1960:224) noted that presidential-popularity ratings "are very widely read in Washington. Despite disclaimers, they are widely taken to approximate reality."

2. This figure is derived from a review of abstracts of the evening news for the month of June in the years 1973 through 1975 and 1977 through 1979. The abstracts were prepared by the Vanderbilt University Television News Archives (1973–79). A single month was used to make the sampling of stories practical (given our limited resources). For the 6 months in question, we found 13 stories that seemed definitely to include poll data on the president's "popularity" or "job rating," for example, where the abstract read "CBS/NYT poll re. Carter popularity." In addition to these stories, we found five more dubious instances, for example, an abstract showing "ABC/Harris poll re. inflation and Carter," and two news reports of poll measurements that might be dubbed "unpopularity" measurements. The latter two stories (CBS and NBC News on June 13, 1974) reported poll findings on public support for the impeachment of President Nixon.

If the five dubious and two "unpopularity" stories were included in our count, we would obtain an average of 3.3 stories per month; if these stories were excluded, the average would be 2.2.

We should also note the conclusions of Paletz et al. (1980:499), who independently coded the CBS and NBC evening news and stories in the *New York Times* for the entire years of 1973, 1975, and 1977. They observed that

> . . . the most frequent [subject for news stories using poll data] we dubbed "presidency"; this category contains assessments and evaluations of the president's job performance and of members of his family. These popularity polls were prominent on television, encompassing almost a quarter of all poll stories, somewhat fewer for the [*New York*] *Times*. At times the pollsters' desire to measure, and the passion of the press to publish, presidential approval ratings appear to be fetishistic. During the first few months of the Carter administration, the *Times* printed three such polls in 24 days . . . .

3. Marginals and survey dates for the Gallup, Roper, CBS/NYT, and NBC/AP measurements were obtained from the Roper Center. Marginals and survey dates for the Harris measurements were obtained from the Louis Harris Data Center (University of North Carolina) for the years 1963 to November 4, 1978. Later dates were supplied by Louis Harris and Associates' New York office.

Surveys were assigned a date corresponding to the midpoint of their field period. For some survey measurements, the archives did not supply precise information on the starting date of the survey or the length of the field period. Often the archival records contain vague notations (for example, early May 1966). We used all available data to estimate midpoints. Where a precise starting date and field period were supplied, the midpoint was computed arithmetically. Where a precise start-date was not known, the following rules were followed: (1) if the "early" part of the month was specified in the archives records, the seventh of the month was coded as the midpoint date; (2) if only the month was specified or if the records specified "middle" of month, the fifteenth of the month was coded as the midpoint; (3) if the "late" part of the month was specified, the twenty-first was coded as the midpoint; (4) if the survey was said to span 2 months, but no precise dates were given, the last day of the first month was called the midpoint; (5) if the survey occurred in January of a year in which a new president was inaugurated, a survey measuring approval of the new president was assumed to have a midpoint of January 25.

4. We do note, nonetheless, that if Organization 1 consistently had longer field periods (than Organizations 2 and 3) during times when public opinion was shifting rapidly, the agreement between Organizations 1 and 2 and 1 and 3 would be expected to be less than that between Organizations 2 and 3.

The length of field periods for the surveys in our database averaged 4.4 days for Gallup, 5.4 days for Harris, 3.8 days for CBS/NYT, 2.1 days for NBC/AP, and 8.7 days for Roper. In our analysis we found (see Table 16.5) that the highest correlation (+0.986) occurred between the organization with the longest field period and that with the second shortest—suggesting that similarity in field periods is probably not a dominant factor in explaining the patterns of agreement between these measurement series.

5. The time periods were constructed by beginning from January 1 of each year and dividing a decimal representation of the year into 20 equally spaced units. Time periods were subdivided into separate periods if there was a change of administrations.

6. Specifying the factors that produce this noise and estimating their effects remains a challenging task for future analysts. To facilitate their work we have deposited a copy of our dataset with the Roper Public Opinion Research Center (P.O. Box 1732, Yale Station, New Haven, CT 06520).

7. A weighted analysis of these approval ratings produced coefficients that varied by no more then 0.01 from the (unweighted) coefficients shown in Table 16.5. The weighted analysis was designed to place more weight upon comparisons involving large samples. Weights were calculated for every pair of organizations in each time period. (Thus there were 61 separate weights for the Gallup-Harris comparison—one for each time period in which both organizations made measurements.) Each weight was the reciprocal of a (upper bound on the) standard error for the expected difference between estimates of proportions based upon samples of the size (N_1, N_2) used by the organizations in that particular time period $[(.25/N_1) + (.25/N_2)]^{0.5}$. (It should be noted that samples in question may sometimes be the sum of the samples in two surveys conducted by an organization in the same time period.)

8. The incompleteness of our 3-way table introduces difficulties in the computation of the degrees of freedom for the chi-square statistics. As Haberman (1979:469) notes in his text: "Unfortunately, no simple rules for degrees of freedom appear to be entirely adequate when the generating class of the hierarchical model has at least three members."

Because of this difficulty, we note explicitly the algorithm we used to calculate the degrees of freedom in Table 16.6. Let $M_{ij} = 1$ if organization i made a popularity measurement in time period j; otherwise $M_{ij} = 0$. (Remember that our 100 time periods include only instances in which two or more organizations made measurements.) We calculated the degrees of freedom for each model as:

$$\text{Model 1: } d.f._1 = \left(\sum_{j=1}^{100} \sum_{i=1}^{5} M_{ij} \right) - 1$$

$$\text{Model 2: } d.f._2 = \sum_{j=1}^{100} \left(\sum_{i=1}^{5} M_{ij} - 1 \right)$$

$$\text{Model 3: } d.f._3 = \sum_{i=1}^{5} \left(\sum_{j=1}^{100} M_{ij} - 1 \right)$$

$$\text{Model 4: } d.f._4 = d.f._3 - 5 + 1$$

Allowing for some uncertainty in the calculation of d.f., we observe that the L^2 values in

Table 16.6 are so large that an error in the reported d.f. would not have a meaningful impact on our inferences about the fit of Models 1 through 4.

9. The mean absolute discrepancy was computed as:

$$\left(\sum_{i=1}^{N} |O_i - E_i| \right)/2N,$$

where O_i is the observed frequency count at time i, and E_i is the count expected under the model. N is the total number of residuals (which is equal to the number of nonempty cells in the table of observations). This measure has sometimes been termed the index of dissimilarity. It indicates the percentage of observations that would have to be changed to bring the observed data into perfect agreement with the values expected under the model.

10. To perform these analyses, we altered the normal execution of the ECTA program (Goodman and Fay, 1973) in order to write the table of observed and expected values for our models onto a reusable storage medium. The resultant dataset was then reanalyzed using a special-purpose program designed to provide the measures of residual dispersion presented in Table 16.7. (The residuals from the fitting of the various substantive models (see below) were subject to a similar reanalysis to provide the measures of residual dispersion shown in Tables 16.12 and 16.13.)

It should be recognized that the decomposition presented in Table 16.7 was obtained by computing the *actual* contribution of the measurements made by each organization to the likelihood-ratio chi-square for Model 4 of Table 16.6. This is an exact arithmetic decomposition, i.e., the sum of each organization's contributions equals the total chi-square for Model 4. A somewhat different procedure might also be applied to these data; this procedure requires us to compute models constrained to fit all data points except those produced by organization 1 (then 2, etc.). The difference between the fit obtained in the overall analysis and that obtained when the measurements produced by organization 1 are "blanked out" can be taken as another indicator of the contribution of that organization's measurements to the poorness of fit of the overall model. This method does not, however, provide an exact decomposition (i.e., the sum of each organizations "contributions" does not equal the chi-square for the overall test). This occurs because slightly different models are being used in each case (due to the fact that a slightly different set of data points is being fit in each instance). For the present data, such an analysis yields likelihood-ratio chi-squares of: 1,452.1 (overall), 302.7 (without Gallup), 443.7 (without Harris), 1,407.8 (without CBS/NYT), 1,209.4 (without NBC/AP), and 1,283.8 (without Roper). Subtracting, we would obtain estimated contributions under this procedure of: 1,149.4 (Gallup), 1,008.4 (Harris), 44.3 (CBS/NYT), 242.7 (NBC/AP), and 168.3 (Roper).

11. Setting the initial conditions normally would have a noticeable effect on subsequent values. However, by setting the starting point as though the process were in equilibrium in January 1961, and by running the process for two years before any estimate was made, the effects of the starting conditions virtually wash out. The only relevant impact of the initializing input was that due to inflation, and its weight by January of 1963 was only 0.000409. All other components have a natural starting point at a subsequent time.

12. The time-stream was divided into half-months (beginning on the first and the sixteenth of each month). Thus the time scale is roughly comparable to that of the first set of analyses (one-twenty-fourth rather than one-twentieth of a year); a very minor imprecision is introduced for February. As before, coincident readings by the same house were given a weighted average for that half-month.

13. This substantive model is based on earlier work by Mueller (1970, 1973), Kernell (1978), Kernell and Hibbs (1981), Stimson (1976), and Monroe (1978). The examination of movement in presidential popularity is now a bit of a cottage industry. The war and economic variables are nothing new at all. Allowing the "glow" or honeymoon decay to be estimated is slightly novel, and the results suggest that this effect persists somewhat longer than was previously thought. The event series are a substantive addition. They were found to be necessary to obtain stable estimates for the other elements, a finding that suggests their place in a full specification. Response to the economic variables here are modeled as a constant process across all administrations. Some experimentation suggests that this might be an oversimplification, as might be expected if presidents are differentially judged by the emphasis they give to different national problems.

14. The actual level of unemployment was used here rather than a change rate because (1) that is the common reference point in popular discussion, and (2) experiments with other formulations suggested no stark differences. Furthermore, the measure of unemployment focused on adult males so as to control for seasonal and long-term changes in labor force composition. (Finding such a low and imprecise parameter for unemployment suggests that more substantive work may be useful here. See previous note.) The inflation rate used is the percentage change from the previous time point's Consumer Price Index and thus is not seasonally adjusted. Because the time-series is defined in terms of half-months, both economic series represent linear interpolations for the rate on the seventh and twenty-first days of each month. The actual number for inflation is multiplied by 24 so as to produce an approximation of the familiar annualized metric for each half-month.

15. At first a sequence of 69 variables was generated (see Appendix 16.A for details), all zero except for a unit spike to mark the fortnight during which a significant event occurred that was thought to bear on presidential popularity. (The inclusion of particular events is a matter of judgment, and the strategy adopted here was to be liberal in allowance. *The New York Times Index* and *The World Almanac* provided the dates of the relevant events.) Then, given a single dynamic parameter (which was determined by iterating on this process), the magnitude and a sign for each event was estimated with OLS (ordinary least-squares). Inspection of the time paths suggested that some especially significant events had a longer-lasting impact— the Newark-Detroit riots, the Saturday Night Massacre, John Dean's testimony on Watergate, Camp David, and the several presidential election campaigns—and so another event series with a larger d (a longer lag structure) was designed for them.

It should be noted that some error variance might be mistakenly attributed to the occurrence of specific events, but worries about merely matching up "white noise" ought to be alleviated in that (1) the estimate for each event is constrained because a single reequilibration parameter was used for all events, and (2) of the events whose individual impacts were statistically discernible from zero, every one has the correct sign (something definitely not expected if those terms mostly represented sampling error). In any case, our purpose was to eliminate from the error term any movement that might plausibly be attributed to real change rather than to measurement error.

The event magnitudes estimated by this procedure are presented in Appendix Table 16.A. After the rough magnitude of the event impacts was estimated, a single pair of series of political events was created, for the reevaluation of the dynamic parameters and the house/ question differences, by simply replacing each of the unit spikes with its estimated magnitude. The dynamic parameters were then estimated using a nonlinear procedure. Then the entire process was repeated until reasonable convergence was obtained. (This back-and-forth process could have been accomplished in one large, nolinear-equation estimation, but the cost was practically prohibitive.)

16. A model, transforming the popularity proportions into logits, produces a similar (though slightly less satisfactory) fit and pattern of results. Using a linear scale for popularity makes it difficult to predict the initial, high values of popularity in each administration; the logit transformation exacerbates that problem. More elaborate transformations might improve the precision of the model and reduce the estimated error components, but given the relatively small number of bad misses, should not change the substantive conclusions much. The nominal scale of percentages is here maintained to ease interpretation.

17. This procedure depends on the assumption that the additional Gallup "approvers" come only from the Harris "only fair" category and that all Harris approvers are also Gallup approvers. The *Post* data suggest this is only slightly unrealistic. The percentages giving a Gallup "approve" coming from each of the Harris categories are: "excellent," 7.45; "pretty good," 61.37; "only fair," 29.18; "poor," 0.6; "don't know" 1.4. The size of the "only fair" contribution suggests the possible importance of the difference between Gallup and Harris "approvers." Only 3.7 percent of Harris "excellent" and "pretty good" group did not also say "approve" to the Gallup question.

18. The Gallup-Harris comparison used here takes advantage of the greater range of change covered by those two houses' time spans. The analysis is limited to the last three administrations because Harris provided too few Johnson administration readings ($N = 3$) for precise measurement. Other Harris samples during the Kennedy and Johnson years were of special (voter) samples, and they were dropped from the analysis because such samples might manifest different responsiveness that was due to the intentionally special character of their respondents rather than to the survey procedure.

19. Allowing the variables' effects to be different for each house, as was done for the equation in Table 16.10, indicates that the NBC/AP and Harris measures are not significantly different in their substantive responses. This is in accord with the results of Table 16.11. However, the constant effect (of NBC/AP's rating being lower) persists.

20. Finding that the NBC/AP readings were lower is not altogether surprising. Their question refers to the president by name only, not as "President Carter." In addition, the response category of a "good job" may be more difficult for uncertain supporters to choose compared with Harris's "pretty good." The magnitude of this difference, however, is troubling: the wording dissimilarities are fairly minor. Moreover, whether the constant divergence in measurement level is due to the differences in question wording, or to the organizations' internal sampling and interview procedures, cannot be determined from these data.

21. The mean absolute value of the residuals was chosen rather than, say, the standard deviation, because the inability of a house to match the prediction may be as much due to the model's inadequacy as to the house's shortcomings. This consideration suggests that large deviations should be weighted proportionally to their absolute value rather than to their squared value, so as not to unduly penalize a set of predictions as a consequence of a single, large miss.

22. The slight reduction of the Gallup accuracy reflects the diminished proportion of Gallup readings represented in the number of readings to be estimated. Thus, the estimation equation has fewer Gallup errors to be minimized.

23. The parameters for each substantive variable are mostly statistically undifferentiable across houses, though they do wobble about a little so as to maximize the fit for each particular series. On the one hand, finding differences is not troublesome because the purpose is to

measure deviations off some (not precisely specified) function of the external environment, and no single house has a claim on validity (as the Gallup series would have to in order to rely on Table 16.12's Gallup-dominated numbers). The problem lies in each separate model's exhausting 6 degrees of freedom, a substantial portion of the CBS (20) and Roper (18) observations. Making the theoretical statistical correction, however, yields the same rough rank-order, though CBS falls closer to the Harris-NBC end of the spectrum. The mean squared error (a variance rather than absolute deviation measure) for the houses read 6.64, 12.73, 10.42, 13.18, and 4.07 for Gallup, Harris, CBS/NYT, NBC/AP, and Roper, respectively.

24. An expectation may be derived by taking the standard sampling error for *random* samples ($[pq/(n-k)]^{.5}$) of a dichotomy and multiplying it by the expected value of (twice) the right-hand side of the normal distribution. This, of course, assumes that the errors cumulate a number of small disturbances and thus are distributed approximately normally. Mechanically, this estimation took the sample for each survey and the observed approval as the true proportion, calculated the expected deviation due to sampling, and then averaged across all observations. The expectations estimated by this procedure for the Carter years are as follows: Gallup, 0.91; Harris, 0.96; CBS/NYT, 1.05; NBC/AP, 0.92; and Roper, 0.88. The differences are due to some distinctions in the times when ratings were taken (the estimated proportion differed) and variability in the sample sizes of each house.

To be sure, these organizations do not take simple random samples, and the true error must be somewhat larger, but this number provides a theoretically motivated benchmark. Differences between the average absolute deviation expected by random sampling and the observed absolute deviations from the estimated model are these: Gallup, 1.28; Harris, 1.72; CBS/NYT, 0.75; NBC/AP, 1.63; and Roper, 0.41. Understanding that the actual sampling error is somewhat larger suggests that relative differences in the magnitudes of these "measurement errors" may be even larger.

25. The slight reliability advantage NBC/AP has over Harris may be due to the wider semantic gap between "good" and "only fair" as opposed to "pretty good" and "only fair."

26. O. D. Duncan suggested to us another source for cross-house differences—one that is distinct from the quality of instrumentation. It may be that the timing of the surveys is itself a function of matters that may generate measurement variance. For example, some houses may deliberately attempt to catch turning points in popularity (which are presumably newsworthy), and thus find they are trying to measure public opinion when it is unusually and genuinely unstable. For this possibility to account for the observed pattern of measurement variance, it would have to be the case that NBC/AP and Harris were more inclined (than CBS, Gallup, and Roper) to send their interviewers out in stormy times.

References

Brody, R. A. and Page, B. I. (1975) The impact of events on presidential popularity: the Johnson and Nixon administrations. In A. Wildavsky, ed., *Perspectives on the Presidency*. Boston: Little, Brown.

Converse, P. E. (1979) The Impact of Polls on National Leadership. Paper presented at Symposium on the Fiftieth Anniversary of the Social Sciences Research Building at the University of Chicago, Dec. 16-17.

Drew, E. (1979) Reporter at large: phase in search of a definition. *New Yorker* (Aug. 27):45-73.

Goodman, L. A. (1968) The analysis of cross-classified data: independence, quasi-independence, and interactions in contingency tables with or without missing entries. *Journal of the American Statistical Association* 63:1091-1131.

Goodman, L. A. (1970) The multivariate analysis of qualitative data: interations among multiple classifications. *Journal of the American Statistical Association* 65:226-256.

Goodman L. A. (1971) The analysis of multidimensional contingency tables: stepwise procedures and direct estimation methods for building models for multiple classifications. *Technometrics* 13:33-61.

Goodman, L. A. (1978) *Analyzing Qualitative/Categorical Data*. Cambridge, Mass.: Abt Books.

Goodman, L. A., and Fay, R. (1973) ECTA program: description for users. Unpublished ms., Department of Statistics, University of Chicago.

Haberman, S. J. (1978/1979) *Analysis of Qualitative Data*. Two volumes. New York: Academic Press. (Volume 1, 1978; Volume 2, 1979).

Kernell, S. (1978) Explaining presidential popularity. *American Political Science Review* 72:506-522.

Kernell, S., and Hibbs, D. (1981) A critical threshold model of presidential popularity. In D. Hibbs and H. Gassbender, eds., *Contemporary Political Economy*. Amsterdam: North Holland.

Koyck, L. M. (1954) *Distributed Lags and Investment Analysis*. Amsterdam: North Holland.

Martin, E., McDuffee, D., and Presser, S. (1981) *Sourcebook of Harris National Surveys: Repeated Questions, 1963-1976*. Chapel Hill, N.C.: Institute for Research in the Social Sciences (University of North Carolina).

Monroe, K. (1978) Economic influences on presidential popularity. *Public Opinion Quarterly* 42:360-369.

Mueller, J. (1970) Presidential popularity from Truman to Johnson. *American Political Science Review* 64:18-34.

Mueller, J. (1973) *War, Presidents and Public Opinion*. New York: Wiley.

Neustadt, R. E. (1960) *Presidential Power: The Politics of Leadership*. New York: Wiley.

Orren, G. (1978) Presidential popularity ratings: another view. *Public Opinion* May:35.

Paletz, D. L., Short, J. Y., Baker, H., Campbell, B. C., Cooper, R. J., and Oeslander, R. M. (1980) Polls in the media: content, credibility and consequences. *Public Opinion Quarterly* 44:495-513.

Sigelman, L. (1981) Question order effects on presidential popularity. *Public Opinion Quarterly* 55:199-207.

Stimson, J. A. (1976) Public support for American presidents. *Public Opinion Quarterly* 40:1-21.

Sussman, B. (1978) Jury is still out on Carter: distortion in popularity polls. *Washington Post* Feb. 12:A1.

Theil, H. (1971) *Principles of Economics*. New York: Wiley.

Vanderbilt University Television News Archives. (1973-79) *Television News Index and Archive*. Nashville, Tenn.: Vanderbilt University Television News Archives-Joint Universities Library.

Von Hoffman, N. (1979/1980) Public opinion polls: newspapers making their own news? Syndicated by King Features, Inc., July 30, 1979 (Reprinted in *Public Opinion Quarterly* 44:572-573).

Acknowledgments

We are grateful to Theresa DeMaio who collaborated with us at the outset of this work. We also wish to thank Clifford Clogg, Otis Dudley Duncan, Robert Fay, Stanely Presser, and Tom Smith for their helpful advice. (The order of authorship is alphabetical.)

17

Cultural Indicators and the Analysis of Public Opinion

Elizabeth Martin

The premise of this chapter is that participation in popular culture is an important vehicle by which beliefs, attitudes, and commitments held by members of a collectivity are created and communicated. Cultural symbolism represents a language in whose terms members of a culture may debate and affirm abstract issues of value and commitment. Often, the significance of seemingly mundane activities as a means of affirming common value orientations is not fully appreciated by either participants or observers. As Wittgenstein (1953: No. 129) notes, "The aspects of things that are most important for us are hidden because of their simplicity and familiarity. (One is unable to notice something because it is always before one's eyes.)"

The values and beliefs of a culture may not be expressly articulated by members of the society; rather, they may be represented in a symbolic form whose meaning is not, for a variety of reasons, fully acknowledged by them. The fact that members of society are likely to appreciate the meaning of cultural symbols only partially implies that value conflict and value change may be submerged and disguised in cultural symbolism, and that we cannot rely solely upon explicit statements of values, norms, and attitudes, either by elites or masses, in drawing inferences about cultural values.

547

Therefore, explicit statements obtained from respondents in surveys can provide only a partial reading of collective values and beliefs. Survey data can usefully be supplemented by analysis of symbolic meanings expressed through participation in a common culture in order to arrive at a more complete understanding of collective values and the process by which they change.

From this point of view, Americans' fears, desires, values, and beliefs are expressed in and shaped by the ordinary activities and artifacts of their lives—the things they buy, the movies they attend, the sports they watch, the way they dress, and so on. Such expressions are not individualistic phenomena with idiosyncratic meaning for each person; rather, styles and customs emerge and acquire symbolic meaning through a process of communication within specific social contexts.

This perspective is of course familiar to anthropologists, who are accustomed to finding significance and meaning in mundane cultural customs and artifacts. Sports, an example to be discussed in more detail, has been analyzed by anthropologists such as Roberts, Arth, and Bush (1959), who find that games and sports reflect the structure and values of the larger society. Public opinion researchers have also recently begun to pay more attention to the cultural context in which public opinion is formed. MacKuen (1979) and Beniger, Watkins, and Ruz (1978) have analyzed the influence of the mass media on public opinion formation. (See also early discussions by Lasswell and associates [1949].)

The reverse is also true, that is, survey-based analysis of public opinion can augment our understanding of the process of culture creation, since subcultures are often defined, implicitly or explicitly, in terms of political commitments and issues. Some sociologists have rejected surveys as an appropriate tool for the analysis of subcultures, in part because surveys rely upon "publicly expressed value statements" and tend to "overlook elements that are particularly distinctive about cultures—customs, behaviors, shared understandings, and artifacts" (Fine and Kleinman, 1979:5). However, surveys can be used to collect information with which to analyze patterns of subcultural participation and symbolism. We will consider several hypotheses about the social consequences of symbolic culture, and for each, provide illustrative analyses using survey data.

The first idea to be explored is that cultural activities serve to integrate and differentiate the members of society into subcultures which participate (directly or vicariously) in the symbolic activity, and which share its language and affirm (and perhaps debate) a characteristic set of values, norms, and symbolic attachments. We may define a subculture as a group of people who are identified by themselves and others as participants or audience for a particular symbolic activity; who share attachments to a particular set of symbols and the values they represent; and who share the language and knowledge permitting them to communicate about those symbolic attachments.

By this broad definition, then, such diverse groups as football fans, followers of rock music, Catholics, Americans, or feminists might be considered subcultures. Subcultures may represent well-defined social groups, with members linked by direct interaction, or they may be quite broad and diffuse, with membership defined in terms of common interest in the symbolic activity, such as football.

The boundaries of the subculture define a group of people engaged in symbolic discourse about a characteristic set of values and norms. Subcultural participation may be restricted by formal or informal discrimination, differential access to knowledge and skill in the symbolic activity, and by properties of the symbolism itself. Subcultural boundaries may thus be narrowly defined or may be so broad they include virtually all members of society. Depending on the society and an individual's place in it, a person may have access to few or many symbolic activities (either supporting or contradicting dominant social values), or to none. This suggests that patterns of individual attachment, indifference, and alienation from society and its values are influenced by the structure and extent of subcultural participation.

Subcultural boundaries may or may not be coterminous with boundaries defined by race, religion, occupation, and so forth. Hence, subcultural differentiation may act either to reinforce or to break down barriers between social groups, thus enhancing or reducing potential for group conflict. As suggested in the following section, football represents a cultural activity that crosscuts group boundaries and hence facilitates symbolic attachment to the nation as a whole.

Football and National Allegiance

Several characteristics of American sports make them a uniquely suitable vehicle for creating symbolic allegiance to the nation. First, patriotism is expressed in symbolic and ritual form in the sports arena; the flag is flown and the national anthem is sung at many sports events. Sports nomenclature symbolizes and reinforces a national identity; there are the American and National leagues in football and in baseball; one of the highest honors a collegiate football player can receive is to be chosen as "all-American," and so on. The salience of one's identity as an American is further heightened when the competition is international rather than national, as in the Olympics. Sports also foster loyalty to and pride in one's school, city, or region, although that function is not discussed here.

Sports participation may be particularly significant for ethnic and minority groups. Winning at sports has long represented a symbolic achievement for immigrant groups in America and provided symbolic entry into mainstream American society. In this fashion, sports sustain the myth, and perhaps the reality, of democratic participation and equal opportunity in America.

Second, sports symbolize and have traditionally been intended to foster the American ideal of winning by tough, fair competition, in which teammates cooperate to achieve corporate success. Traditionally, American sports were extravagantly promoted as character-building training to prepare young men for democratic participation and capitalist competition (Lipsky, 1978). Even now, it is significant that throughout the 1960s and 1970s Americans' idealism about and interest in sports was apparently undiminished. Americans lost faith in their presidents, perhaps, but not in their football players. Indeed, we might speculate that during and after a decade of national defeat, scandal, and disillusionment, American idealism and pride found refuge in the symbolic realm of sports.

A third factor is the inclusiveness of the audience of sports fans and the intensity and frequency of their participation. Of the respondents in a 1969 Harris Survey (N = 1,457), 43 percent reported that they or a household member watched televised sports "nearly every weekend." 27 percent watched "some weekends," while 29 percent watched "hardly ever" or not at all. It is likely that participating as one member of the vast television audience of American sports fans helps to create a bond of sentiment with other Americans and with the collectivity as a whole.

Table 17.1 presents trends in the percentage of Americans involved in different sports during the 1970s. Respondents in six cross-sectional Harris surveys conducted between 1969 and 1978 were asked, "Which of these sports do you follow?" and were given a card listing eleven (in early surveys) or thirteen sports (in later surveys). ("None" was accepted as a response if volunteered by the respondent, but was not listed on the card.) "Following" a sport implies that one pays attention to it over some period of time, usually over the course of the sports season.[1]

Results in Table 17.1 suggest that sports differ in their intrinsic appeal to fans, with football (closely followed by baseball) generally dominating all other sports in popularity. This pattern of sports preferences is exclusively American, particularly the intense interest in football. American football is played nowhere else in the world except Canada (with considerable variation in rules). In addition, American sports preferences, while subject to seasonal fluctuations, were relatively stable from 1969 through 1976. (An exception is tennis, which grew in popularity in the early 1970s.) From 1976 to 1978, all sports showed an increase in the proportion of Americans following them, and the proportion who followed no sport dropped to its lowest level. The reliability of this trend is suspect. In 1978, data were

TABLE 17.1

Trends in Percent of Americans
Who Follow Selected Sports

	March 1969	Sept. 1969	March 1974	Feb. 1976	Nov. 1976	July 1978
Football	50	49	54	53	51	64
Baseball	45	47	52	47	49	55
Basketball	37	30	43	34	32	42
Boxing	n.a.	n.a.	21	22	21	36
Tennis	7	11	21	26	20	45
No sports	25	23	16	15	24	9
N	1,457	1,913	1,495	1,512	1,482	1,150

NOTE: Data from six Harris Surveys (Nos. 1905, 1969, 7483, 2621, 7688, 3844T). All data archived at Louis Harris Data Center, Institute for Research in Social Science, University of North Carolina at Chapel Hill. March 1969 survey included persons 21 years of age and older; September 1969 survey included persons 16 and older; and the remaining surveys included persons 18 and older.
n.a.: Question not asked.

obtained in telephone interviews, while personal interviews were used in the preceding surveys. This means that the showcard used in the five earlier surveys was not used in 1978, and, in addition, "none" was not an explicit code category for the interviewer to check in 1978. These procedural differences may well account for the increase in reporting.

By several criteria, then, football is the national sport: it is consistently followed by more Americans than any other sport, it is unique to this country, and, in addition, it is the sport most often given by Americans as their favorite (Harris, 1978). An active, common interest in football characterizes a large segment of the American population, particularly men, two-thirds of whom said they followed football in 1976.

Our analysis is guided by the hypothesis that involvement in sports, especially football, encourages fans to feel they are part of the larger collectivity. The integrative function of sports may be especially important for groups not otherwise well integrated in society. The emergence of minority champions represents a vicarious success for the group, which enhances racial, ethnic, or gender pride.

Some evidence that the athlete is a symbol of group success is provided in Table 17.2. Overall, blacks were more likely than whites were to root for Hank Aaron, the black baseball player who broke Babe Ruth's home run record in 1974. It is noteworthy that fans of each race were more likely to root for Aaron than were nonfans, and this difference exceeds the race difference. In a certain sense, loyalty to the sport and its heroes transcends racial loyalty.[2] Fans of different races have more in common with each other, in terms of these particular sentiments, than they do with nonfans of the same race. Symbolic participation may pave the way for real minority participation in two different ways. Members of the minority acquire loyalty to the larger collectivity via their sense of identification with athletes who are like them. Conversely, members of the majority acquire a sense of identification with minority athletes via their loyalty to the sport and the athletes who excel at it. Findings in Table 17.2 suggest that sports can create a bond of shared sentiment and interest that transcends racial barriers.

In the next set of analyses, we present evidence suggesting that football is a source of symbolic identification with the nation for Americans who participate as fans, particularly black men and less-educated white men. We rely upon a variety of indicators of symbolic national attachment, including the use of the American flag decal as a personal emblem, sentiments of personal and political alienation, and voting in a national election. Throughout this chapter, log-linear analysis is used to test hypotheses about relationships among variables.

In 1969, involvement in football was associated with the symbolic patriotic act of displaying an American flag decal, as shown in Table 17.3. Except for black women, football fans were nearly twice as likely as nonfans to display a flag. Whites were also more likely than blacks to display flags. (The effects of following football and of race upon flag display are statistically significant at the .05 level.)

Table 17.4 presents the results of an analysis of several measures of respondents' cynicism about and sense of isolation from national political leaders and people in general. Football fans were less likely to express such

TABLE 17.2

Rooting for Hank Aaron, by Race and Baseball Involvement

	Percent distribution				
	Rooting for Aaron	Hope he falls short	Don't care (vol.)	Total	N
Black People:					
Follow baseball	89	1	10	100	105
Don't follow	61	6	33	100	54
White People:					
Follow baseball	76	6	18	100	649
Don't follow	50	5	45	100	593

SOURCE: March 1974 Harris Survey (No. 7483).
ITEM: Hank Aaron of the Atlanta Braves is very close to breaking Babe Ruth's record of 714 lifetime home runs. Are you rooting for Hank Aaron to break Babe Ruth's record, or do you hope he will fall short of it?

TABLE 17.3

Flag Display among Fans and Nonfans,
by Race and Sex

	Percent displaying flags	
Race and Sex	Football Fans	Nonfans
White male	30	19
	(435)	(251)
Black male	18	7
	(60)	(45)
White female	33	23
	(239)	(482)
Black female	7	10
	(28)	(86)

SOURCE: September 1969 Harris Survey (No. 1969).
NOTE: Respondents younger than eighteen, and those who were "not sure" about flag display, are excluded. Ns are shown in parentheses.
ITEM: Do you have an American flag pasted on your auto or home window or not?

sentiments in 1976, but this relationship held only for black men and not for other groups.[3] Data presented in Table 17.4 show that black men who did not follow football were significantly more alienated than those who did, for five of the six measures of alienation.

It is plausible that the lower level of alienation among black male football fans might be due to the indirect effect of educational differences between those who follow football and those who do not, or it might be a spurious result of the fact that interest in football is a surrogate for involvement and participation in national affairs generally. The 1976 data permit indirect tests of these hypotheses, using the respondent's report that he voted in the 1976 presidential election as a proxy measure of participation in national affairs. The four-way cross-classification of education × vote × alienation × football is analyzed separately for black and white men; only item 1 is used in these analyses (see Table 17.4).

Using four categories of education, we find that the data for black men are described by a model that includes two-way associations between alienation and football, alienation and voting, and football and education (likelihood-ratio chi-square: $L^2 = 9.28$, d.f. = 14). These results (not shown here) imply that the association between football involvement and alienation is not due to the indirect effects of education, nor is it attenuated when voting participation is introduced as a proxy measure of involvement in national affairs.

TABLE 17.4

Alienation Among Fans and Nonfans (Black Men)

		Percent "Agree"			
Item		Football Fans (N = 35)	Nonfans (N = 34)	L^2	p (d.f. = 1)
1.	The people running the country don't really care what happens to you.	69	94	7.69	.01
2.	The rich get richer and the poor get poorer.	85	100	7.02	.01
3.	What you think doesn't count much anymore.	68	100	13.96	.001
4.	You feel left out of things.	69	94	7.37	.01
5.	Most people with power try to take advantage of you.	76	94	4.48	.05
6.	The people in Washington, D.C., are out of touch with the rest of the country.	77	93	2.69	n.s.

SOURCE: November 1976 Harris Survey (No. 7688).
NOTE: For each item, "not sure" excluded.

As noted, involvement in football is unrelated to alienation for white men, and this negative result holds when voting participation and education (six categories) are introduced in the analysis. However, we find that white men who did not graduate from high school are more likely to vote if they follow football; this relationship does not hold for those who graduated from high school. These results are summarized in Table 17.5. The interaction between education (fewer than 12 versus 12 or more years), football, and voting is statistically significant at the .05 level.[4]

These results, though fragmentary, suggest that involvement in football is associated with a sense of national identification, and that the nature of this effect varies among social groups. The various analyses draw upon surveys spanning a considerable time and are based upon diverse measures of national attachment (displaying a flag, voting, and voicing alienation). Thus, we may have some confidence that the link between football involvement and national attachment is not a fluke produced by a single set of data or at a single point in time. These findings are consistent with the hypothesis that American football fosters a symbolic identification with the nation among spectators, especially men, who are more extensively and intensely

TABLE 17.5

Voting Among Fans and Nonfans,
by Education (White Men)

	Percent Voting in 1976 Presidential Election	
Educational Level	Football Fans	Nonfans
Fewer than 12 years	76	52
	(113)	(87)
12 or more years	78	80
	(303)	(127)

SOURCE: November 1976 Harris Survey (No. 7688).
NOTE: Ns are shown in parentheses.

involved as fans. This hypothesis suggests an interpretation of the striking associations between football and alienation for black men, and football and voting for poorly educated white men. We would expect the influence of vicarious participation in football to be less important for people who are exposed to allegiant values in many settings, and more important for people who have fewer symbolic links to the nation as a whole. Black men and uneducated white men are not otherwise well integrated in society; in fact, society discriminates against them. The symbolic attachment provided by football may be particularly important for them, since the sports arena may be the only setting in which they can participate as full members of the collectivity, and thereby acquire a sense of allegiance to it. Experimental evidence presented by Cialdini et al. (1976) is consistent with this hypothesis. They find that, following a victory by their football team, university students are more likely to wear school-identifying apparel and to refer to their school as "we". Moreover, a student's symbolic identification with the school's winning team was enhanced if the student had experienced a personal failure. A sense of personal failure may intensify the need to identify with a "winner" in the symbolic realm of sports.

In general, differences among race or education groups are attenuated among fans. Data presented in Table 17.2 suggest that sports can provide a common ground for fans of different races. Table 17.5 shows that less-educated white men who follow football vote at the same rate as their more-educated counterparts. In effect, fans are more homogeneous, in terms of their voting behavior, than are nonfans. Table 17.4 shows that black men who follow football are less alienated than are those who do not. As a consequence, in terms of these particular sentiments, black male football fans are more similar to their white counterparts than they are to black men who do not follow football. This can be seen in Table 17.6, which compares alienation among black and white men for one of the items in Table 17.4. For all six items, the tendency for black men to be more alienated than white men is attenuated among fans. In other words, greater racial homogeneity is associated with a shared interest in football. (The three-way interaction between race, football, and alienation is statistically significant for five of the six items.)

The greater homogeneity among football fans could occur because the sport itself acts as a direct socializing influence on fans and athletes. Although our data do not permit any conclusions about causality, a number of analysts have proposed that cultural values and norms—particularly those concerning success and competition—are acquired and reinforced through involvement in sports. (See Lipsky [1978] and Weinberg and Arond [1952] for discussions of the values represented in sports symbolism.) It has also been suggested that the symbolism of sports represents a metaphor that adapts to other competitive situations, such as war. If so, we might hypothesize that involvement in competitive sports would encourage a more "tough-minded" attitude toward national "enemies" and a greater concern with winning and domination of them.

In fact, there is evidence of a link between involvement in football and "tough-mindedness" about the war in Vietnam. Table 17.7 shows a significant positive association between "hawkish" opinions on Vietnam and following football, but only among white respondents with some college education.[5] (The three-way interaction between education, football, and opinion is significant; $L^2 = 10.94$, d.f. $= 2$, $p < .004$.) Again, we find that football fans are more homogeneous in opinion than are nonfans. Among the

TABLE 17.6

Alienation Among Fans and
Nonfans, by Race (Men Only)

Race	Percent agreeing that "The people running the country don't really care what happens to you"	
	Football Fans	Nonfans
Black	69	94
	(35)	(33)
White	57	57
	(406)	(216)

SOURCE: November 1976 Harris Survey (No. 7688).
NOTE: Ns are shown in parenthe-ses. Respondents who were "not sure" are excluded.

latter there is a sharp division of opinion according to educational level, with more-educated respondents more "dovish" on the bombing question. There are no significant education differences among football fans, although the college educated are slightly more conservative than others. It is noteworthy that football was "politicized" (in terms of the war issue) only for the college educated. We will find this pattern repeated in the next section.

The analysis thus far suggests that participation in a common symbolic activity which is widely shared and understood can facilitate normative consensus. However, this is not necessarily the case. If groups impute different meanings to common symbols, group polarization and conflict may be exacerbated and the problems of communication between groups may be severe. The evolution of distinctive subcultural symbolism and some of the implications for social conflict are analyzed in a second example.

The Symbolism of the American Flag

Since the American flag is a national symbol and an article of mass culture, we might expect uniformity in the meaning attributed to it. In fact, Americans in 1969 did not agree on what the American flag stood for; the attitude correlates of flag display vary among groups in ways that suggest that their perceptions of meaning reflect their various concerns.

TABLE 17.7

Opinions on Vietnam Among Fans and
Nonfans, by Education
(White Respondents)

| | Percent saying bombing helped | |
Educational Level	Football Fans	Nonfans
Fewer than 12 years	73	74
	(154)	(204)
High school graduate	75	67
	(241)	(147)
Some college or more	80	58
	(240)	(137)

SOURCE: November 1972 Harris Survey (No. P007).
NOTE: Ns are shown in parentheses. Respondents who were "not sure" about bombing Vietnam are excluded.
ITEM: Do you feel the bombing of Vietnam by the U.S. helped or hindered both sides finally arriving at a peace agreement?

During the 1960s there was a proliferation of symbols and signs proclaiming, among other things, one's stand on the war in Vietnam. Peace symbols were scrawled on walls and displayed at antiwar rallies. Replicas of the American flag, stuck on car windshields and construction workers' hardhats, proclaimed loyalty to the country. In the liberal college population at least, displaying an American flag implied support for the war in Vietnam and opposition to the antiwar movement.

Data on respondents' opinions on whether particular groups were "helpful" or "harmful" to the country were used to investigate the hostilities and sympathies of those who displayed flag emblems and those who did not in 1969. The initial hypothesis was that flag display would be associated with hostility toward antiwar protesters. The relevant data, presented separately for sex-race groups, are shown in Table 17.8.

Only among black men do we find a statistically significant relationship between flag display and attitudes toward antiwar protesters, and the direction of the relationship is opposite from that predicted. Thirty percent of black men who viewed antiwar protesters as helpful displayed a flag, compared with 6 percent of those with negative or neutral views. (The four-way interaction between flag display, attitude toward protesters, race, and sex is not quite statistically significant; $L^2 = 3.04$, d.f. $= 1$, $p = .08$.)

Results presented in Table 17.9 show that among black respondents generally, displaying an American flag is associated with the view that civil

TABLE 17.8

Flag Display, by Opinions About Antiwar Picketers,
for Race-Sex Groups

Race and Sex	Percent displaying flags among those who say picketers are		
	More Helpful	More Harmful	Neither
White male	22	28	27
	(126)	(422)	(100)
Black male	30	6	7
	(30)	(49)	(14)
White female	24	27	26
	(84)	(451)	(119)
Black female	8	12	22
	(38)	(52)	(9)

SOURCE: September 1969 Harris Survey (No. 1969).
NOTE: Ns are shown in parentheses.
ITEM: America has many different types of people in it. But we would like to know whether you think each of these different types of people is more helpful or harmful to the country, or don't they help or harm things much one way or the other?—*People who picket against the war in Vietnam.*

rights demonstrators, antiwar picketers, or both, are "helpful to American life." In contrast, not one of the black respondents who viewed civil rights and antiwar activists as harmful to American life displayed a flag. Among white respondents, we find a weak relationship in the opposite direction. (The three-way interaction is statistically significant; $L^2 = 9.45$, d.f. = 1, $p < .003$.)

Clearly the symbol of the flag meant something different to the black and white Americans who used it as a personal emblem in 1969. Based upon results presented in Tables 17.8 and 17.9, it might be inferred that black respondents who were sympathetic to civil rights or antiwar activism had a stronger sense of national identity than did those who were not sympathetic. This interpretation may be correct, but does not follow with certainty from these data, since we cannot assume that black respondents who viewed picketers and demonstrators as "harmful to American life" were necessarily unsympathetic to them. Black respondents who regarded "American life" as inherently racist probably rejected national symbols such as the flag and may have sympathized with protests viewed as harmful to that way of life. Thus the meaning of the American flag as a symbol for black people is somewhat obscured by the ambiguity of the questions used to tap their attitudes.

Among white Americans, there is no apparent connection between symbolic attachment to the flag and the divisive issues of the decade— civil rights and the war in Vietnam. This may surprise those who were exposed to the polarized campus environment of the 1960s, and for whom the memory of the opposing symbols of nation and peace is vivid. Perhaps the flag symbolized support for the war and hostility toward the protesters only in

TABLE 17.9

Flag Display, by Race and Opinions
About Activists

	Percent displaying flags	
Opinions about activists	Blacks	Whites
Activists Helpful: Civil rights demonstrators and/or antiwar picketers help American life	16 (129)	24 (332)
Activists Harmful: Civil rights demonstrators and antiwar picketers harm American life	0 (31)	28 (698)

SOURCE: September 1969 Harris Survey (No. 1969).

the campus milieu. This hypothesis may be tested by identifying respondents who were college students during the period of the antiwar protests and who therefore were likely to have been exposed to the polarized political symbolism of the college campus. Since the antiwar protests first occurred in 1964 and continued throughout the war, the potentially "polarized" cohort includes respondents with at least some college experience who were 18 to 23 in 1969. Unfortunately, imprecise age categories and a flawed measure of education were used in Harris Survey No. 1969.[6] Nevertheless, Table 17.10 presents data comparing respondents 18 to 29 with older respondents; because of an ambiguity in the measure of education, the analysis is restricted to white male heads of households.

Despite the fact that the data are not perfectly suited to test the polarizing effect of exposure to the campus culture of the 1960s, the hypothesis is strongly supported. As we would expect, sympathy with antiwar protesters is greater among the young and among college-educated respondents. However, only among the young, college-educated cohort do we find that the flag symbol clearly signifies antiprotester sentiment. In this group, 54 percent of those hostile to protesters display a flag, while only 4 percent of those who are sympathetic or neutral display flags. The four-way interaction between flag display, attitude toward protesters, age, and education is statistically significant ($L^2 = 5.65$, d.f. $= 1$, $p < .02$). We also find evidence of symbolic polarity among young (18- to 20-year-old) white men who were

TABLE 17.10

Flag Display, by Opinions About Antiwar Picketers,
by Age and Education
(White Male Heads of Households)

	Percent displaying flags		
Age and Education	Picketers Harmful	Picketers Helpful or Neither	Total
18-29 years old:			
High school grad or less	7 (27)	16 (19)	11 (46)
Some college or more	54 (13)	4 (23)	22 (36)
30 and older:			
High school grad or less	28 (241)	35 (63)	29 (304)
Some college or more	29 (80)	24 (62)	27 (142)

SOURCE: September 1969 Harris Survey (No. 1969).
NOTE: Ns are shown in parentheses.

not household heads, and who presumably include some number of students and people at risk of induction or already in the armed forces. In this group (N = 69), 38 percent of those hostile versus 16 percent of those sympathetic or neutral to antiwar protesters displayed flags (L^2 = 4.19, d.f. = 1, $p <$ .04). In contrast, the use of the flag as a symbol apparently had no war-related significance for older or less-educated white men. These results are consistent with Schuman's finding that "broad sentiment against the war was not coupled, *as it was on campus*, with criticism of the United States . . ." (1976:289; emphasis added).

It is initially surprising that a national symbol, such as the flag, in 1969 carried diverse meanings in different subgroups in American society. On reflection, however, it is reasonable to suppose that different Americans have different ideas about what America stands for, and that these diverse ideas find concrete expression in the way they use the flag as a personal emblem. It seems clear that the symbolic meanings attributed to the flag reflect the dominant concerns of different groups.

The flag carried a clear and strong meaning to the cohort of young men who were in college during the period of antiwar protests. The flag was linked in a simple, direct way to opinions about the antiwar movement. In this group, for example, we find that people who sympathize with antiwar picketers also tend to sympathize with civil rights demonstrators, but the use of the flag emblem is strongly associated with the former and not at all with the latter set of attitudes. (Twenty-two percent of those sympathetic to civil rights demonstrators, versus 25 percent of those unsympathetic, displayed a flag.)

We must carefully distinguish between the source or agent that transmits a cultural symbol, and the social context in which it is actually expressed and acquires meaning. The mass media represented a cultural agent that transmitted the flag as a symbol to the American people in a fashion, via football, that encouraged them to use it.[7] Despite the fact that the flag as a symbol was produced on a mass basis and consumed relatively uniformly (except for the race difference), its meaning was not homogeneous or universal. Rather, the symbolism of the flag was modified and embellished in each particular cultural milieu in which it was adopted. The evidence suggests that the process by which a symbol acquires meaning may be separate and distinct in character from the process of cultural transmission. Symbolic meanings, even when the symbol is a national one, may be highly differentiated depending upon the social context.

If different groups use the same symbol to say different things, what happens when they come into contact with one another? The potential for group conflict and misunderstanding arising from conflicting symbolism seems great, in part because subcultures may be ignorant of the extent to which common symbols carry heterogeneous meaning. For example, the fact that the flag symbolized attitudes toward the war for college students, but did not have this meaning for other Americans, implies that ritualistic acts involving the flag would not be understood in the same way by the two subcultures. Intentional destruction of the flag, for instance, probably carried a specific, issue-related meaning to student activists, but most Americans undoubtedly did not understand it that way at all. Differences in the meaning attributed to such symbolic acts may have contributed considerably to the polarization and intergroup hostility of the 1960s. (See Schuman [1972] for a related discussion of polarization on the Vietnam war issue.)

Further evidence that conflicting symbolism derives from and contributes to intergroup conflict is provided by Aberbach and Walker (1970), who in 1967 surveyed Detroit area residents' interpretations of the slogan "black power." They found an enormous gulf between black and white respondents' interpretations of the slogan. Among black people, 40 percent (versus 11 percent of whites) interpreted "black power" to mean a fair share for black people, or solidarity among them. About 40 percent of whites (versus 8 percent of blacks) interpreted black power to mean that blacks wanted to take over and rule white people. Aberbach and Walker conclude that "the overwhelming majority of whites are frightened and bewildered by the words black power," and that their fear represents "an almost hysterical response to the symbolism of the slogan" (1970:373, 371). It is clear that the emotionally potent and conflicting meanings attributed to the phrase "black power" could effectively prevent communication between the races about black goals and aims.

Conclusions

Although the data presented here are fragmentary, they strongly suggest that participation in mass culture is significant in ways that have not been fully appreciated by social scientists. Empirical analysis shows that such diverse aspects of the culture as football and displaying the American flag as a personal emblem may be implicated in the process by which Americans' attitudes and commitments are shaped and expressed. Although the findings presented here do not permit strong conclusions, they certainly suggest that an investigation of cultural symbolism may provide important insights in analyses of public opinion. Understanding the process of public opinion formation requires an understanding of the symbolism in terms of which public attitudes are expressed and communicated. People are seldom able to articulate fully the meaning of cultural symbols; indeed, symbolic meaning may be denied if the symbolism is unacceptable. To the extent that this is true, it becomes essential to augment respondents' explicit statements of values and beliefs with other, more indirect measures.

Surveys can, and should, include other measurements in addition to the traditional attitude and belief questions. Results presented here suggest that it is feasible to collect information on cultural customs, practices, and artifacts. Public opinion surveys have neglected such topics, perhaps because they were not considered important. To the extent that mundane particulars of the culture have social significance, certain data considered trivial will become scientifically interesting. I refer to marketing studies. Marketing research firms have long collected data on what Americans buy (cultural artifacts) and how they spend their time (cultural customs) and may thus represent an unexploited source of information for public opinion analysts and anthropologists alike.

Notes

1. It might be objected that the meaning of "following" a sport is vague, and that the absence of an explicit "none" category encourages overreporting. A more precise question appeared in an April 1967 Harris Survey. Respondents (voters in previous elections) were asked, "Do you follow sports as a spectator, such as going out to games, watching them on television, listening to them on the radio, or reading about them in newspapers or magazines or don't you follow sports?" Sixty percent reported that they followed sports.

2. It is quite probable that many people, both black and white, who do not follow baseball do not know that Aaron is black and Ruth was white. If these people could be excluded from the analysis, we would have a more meaningful test of the relative strength of racial loyalty among fans and nonfans.

3. The four-way interaction between race, sex, football, and alienation is statistically significant at the .05 level only for items 2 and 3 in Table 17.4. For item 1, black women who follow football are also significantly less cynical than those who do not. The negative association between alienation and football holds for black men at all income levels.

4. White men at all six levels of education are less likely to vote if they are alienated. Education is an important predictor of voting rates among men who graduated from high school, but is insignificant for those who did not graduate.

5. For the small sample of black respondents, neither football nor education is significantly related to opinions on bombing in Vietnam. The relationship presented in Table 17.7 holds for both white men and women when analyzed separately.

6. It is unclear whether the interviewer was to ask for the respondent's education or the education of the household head. This ambiguity is only resolved when the respondent is the head of household.

7. Although football transmitted the symbol itself, it evidently did not transmit a particular meaning. Thus far, I can detect no evidence that the flag symbolized something different to fans and nonfans.

References

Aberbach, J.D., and Walker, J.L. (1970) The meanings of black power: a comparison of white and black interpretations of a political slogan. *American Political Science Review* 64:367-388.

Beniger, J.R., Watkins, S., and Ruz, J.E. (1978) Trends in the abortion issue as measured by events, media coverage and public opinion indicators. *Proceedings of the American Statistical Association (Social Statistics Section)* 1978:118-123.

Cialdini, R.B., Borden, R.J., Thorne, A., Walker, M.R., Freeman, S., and Sloan, L.R. (1976) Basking in reflected glory: three (football) field studies. *Journal of Personality and Social Psychology* 34:366-375.

Fine, G.A., and Kleinman, S. (1979) Rethinking subculture: an interactionist analysis. *American Journal of Sociology* 85:1-20.

Harris, L. (1978) Football is tops. *The Harris Survey* January 19.

Lasswell, H.D., Leites, N., and Associates (1949) *Language of Politics*. New York: George W. Stewart.

Lipsky, R. (1978) Toward a political theory of American sports symbolism. *American Behavioral Scientist* 21:345-360.

MacKuen, M.B. (1979) Social communication and the mass policy agenda. Ph.D. dissertation. University of Michigan, Ann Arbor.

Roberts, J.M., Arth, M.J., and Bush, R.R. (1959) Games in culture. *American Anthropologist* 61:597-605.

Schuman, H. (1972) Two sources of antiwar sentiment in America. *American Journal of Sociology* 78:513-536.

Schuman, H. (1976) Personal origins of "Two sources of antiwar sentiment in America." Pp. 287-291 in M. Patricia Golden, ed., *The Research Experience*. Itasca, Ill.: Peacock.

Weinberg, S., and Arond, H. (1952) The occupational culture of the boxer. *American Journal of Sociology* 57:460-469.

Wittgenstein, L. (1953) *Philosophical Investigations*, Vol. I. Translated by G.E.M. Anscombe. New York: Macmillan.

Acknowledgments

I would like to thank Diana McDuffee and Josephine Marsh for their help in providing data from the Louis Harris Data Center of the Institute for Research in Social Science, The University of North Carolina, Chapel Hill. My thanks also to James Beniger, Howard Schuman, Charles Turner, Robert Abelson, and other members of the Panel on Survey Measurement of Subjective Phenomena, National Academy of Sciences, for helpful comments on earlier drafts. Neither they, nor the panel, are responsible for any errors.

18

Do Polls Affect What People Think?

Catherine Marsh

The idea that public opinion itself might affect what people think is not new. In their different ways, Rousseau's notion of a general will and Durkheim's conception of a "conscience collective" were both intended to sum up a force in society that was outside of and a constraint upon the individual members of the society. However, this conception of public opinion as the property of a society rather than of individuals within society proved rather difficult to measure, and the flowering of empirical social science in the twentieth century brought about an atomization of this concept, as it did so many others. Gradually the meaning of the concept has shifted, and we are now left with a concept of public opinion that amounts to the aggregation of individual opinions expressed privately. " 'Public opinion,' whatever that phrase once meant, now is taken by most people most of the time to mean poll findings." (Gollin, 1980:448).

The idea that public opinion *polls* might affect what people think is threatening to this individuated notion of public opinion, and is threatening to the claim of pollsters that the opinion polls *reflect* public opinion and should therefore be considered part of the working apparatus of a modern democracy. The claims that polls could be a "creative arm of government" (Gallup, 1972:151) would be compromised if it could be shown that the poll results themselves help shape as well as reflect public opinion, as the classical sociological tradition suggests they should.

The question posed in the title of this chapter raises very broad issues of the dynamics of public opinion formation. The small amount of empirical research that exists on this topic has, however, concentrated on a narrow range of issues within the general question—in particular, on the existence of "bandwagon" or "underdog" effects on the general public during election campaigns.

This chapter first explores the concept of an "opinion bandwagon" and briefly considers some hypothetical attempts to model varieties of bandwagon situations. The rather scanty empirical evidence derived from both experimental and nonexperimental studies is then reviewed. This review constitutes the bulk of the chapter, even though it addresses only a tiny part of the question. As will be seen, our perspective is limited by the fact that only a very restricted set of hypotheses has ever been submitted to empirical test. The bandwagon literature is almost exclusively about election polls, ignoring the possible effects of issue polls. It is concerned with net effects rather than with gross effects of polls, whereas it is possible that poll results may cause some people to switch their vote in one direction and others in the opposite direction. The literature is concerned with effects on an undifferentiated electorate, whereas there may well be subpopulations of particular importance—opinion leaders, people whose views have not yet crystallized, and so on. It has concentrated on bandwagon effects (often neglecting underdog effects). It has looked for effects from the publication of a single poll result, whereas it is reasonable to believe that the slow buildup of results over an extended period has the most social influence. Rarely are attempts made to control for individuals' prior beliefs about majority views, whereas there is reason to think that surprising information (so long as it is plausible) may have the most impact. And, finally, the literature reviewed here has sought to test only the "persuasion" hypothesis, that is, that the publication of a majority view helps persuade the individual to adopt that view, rather than to test the agenda-setting hypothesis, namely, that the effect of publication of an issue poll is to alter the individual's conception of what is on the current political agenda. (See MacKuen, Chapter 14 of this volume for a discussion of agenda-setting.)

In light of these shortcomings, at the end of this chapter, we consider new directions in which research might proceed in order to provide a fuller understanding of the impact of public opinion polls.

Hypothetical Models for Bandwagon Effects

The bandwagon literature relates almost exclusively to voting and to candidate and party preference studies. The simple thesis is that some people decide how to vote by conforming (bandwagon) or going against (underdog) the perceived majority opinion. Before considering attempts that have been made to model this idea, we should consider some of its conceptual implications. There are three things to note. First, the thesis stated does not presuppose reasons for bandwagon or underdog behavior; the reasons could be rational, for example, not wanting the party to win by too big a majority for fear of what overconfident parties are likely to do, or the reasons could be psychological, for example, stemming from a desire to be identified with the winner. The convention is to label as rational those explanations that are intended to affect the outcome of the election, and as irrational those that posit individual psychological benefits. (There is no reason, however, why psychological benefits could not also be considered as utilities that the rational individual tries to maximize.) Second, this formulation fails to capture an important aspect of the popular idea of a bandwagon, namely, of a movement that is growing in popularity. A party or candidate need not be ahead at the start of an electoral contest to be considered a winning bandwagon, but people must believe that the party or candidate will increase its popularity over the course of the campaign to the point where it can win the election. Third, complications will arise whenever more than two candidates or parties are running, and whenever electors have the choice not only of changing their vote but also of deciding whether or not to vote. It is common to hear the claim that a natural science of society is impossible because all science involves accurate prediction and because predictions in the social arena may themselves alter outcomes (see, for example, Brown, 1963). Bandwagon voting on the basis of electoral forecasts is a good example; if the poll projections themselves make people change their minds, then the predictions are bound to be fundamentally unstable.

Simon (1957) takes up this issue because of its theoretical importance for social science. He shows that stable predictions are still possible in bandwagon situations, and suggests the outcomes that could arise from various attempts to correct for this effect. Simon argues that if the outcome was a continuous function of the prediction, and if the pollster knew both what the outcome would have been in the absence of a prediction and also the shape of the function, there would always be at least one point at which a correct prediction could be made (see Figure 18.1).

The straight 45° line in Figure 18.1 is the line where prediction equals outcome. The bandwagon curve shows V (percentage of people actually voting for a candidate) as a function of P (percentage predicted for the candidate). It is more properly a function of both I and P, where I is the

FIGURE 18.1

Simon's Bandwagon Curve (Actual percentage of votes for a candidate (V) is plotted against predicted percentage of votes (P) for that candidate)

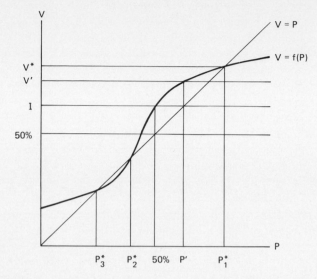

percentage of votes that would have been cast anyway, but, for the purposes of this exercise, Simon considers I as "given" and depicts it as a percentage above 50 percent. He constructed this model on the assumption that I is the value of V arising when $P = 50$ percent; that is, that a prediction of an evenly split vote would have no effect. The curve in Figure 18.1 is a bandwagon curve because it lies below I when $P < 50$ percent and above I when $P > 50$ percent. Simon assumes that the effect will be most changeable around $P = 0.5$, so the curve is steepest here.

There are three points on this graph where prediction is safe, P^*_1, which does not change the outcome of the election, and P^*_2 and P^*_3. (This just happens to be true with this particular curve; a bandwagon curve only has to cross the line once.) Usually pollsters can only make unadjusted predictions such as P'. If they knew enough to draw the graph, they could adjust their prediction to P^*_1 (although they would have a difficult time justifying their action before a professional ethics committee). But note that they could also predict P^*_2, or P^*_3 (whereupon they would surely be summarily dismissed from their professional association!). So long as P' is a reasonably good estimate of I, they cannot, by predicting P^*_1, alter the outcome of the election. But, in the case of an underdog curve (which would slope in the other direction), precisely the converse is true: failure to adjust the prediction could change the outcome of an election if the underdog effect was strong enough. Simon's argument is important theoretically. It demon-

FIGURE 18.2

Gartner's Model of Differential Turnout in One Election (Actual percentage of votes for party X and party Y (V_X and V_Y) is plotted against expected percentage of votes (P) for party Y)

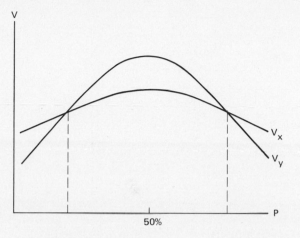

strates that accurate prediction is possible in principle. It also reminds us of the asymmetry between positive and negative feedback—the bandwagon curve can cross the $V = P$ line several times, whereas the underdog curve can only cross it once. However, it is erected on a set of quite unattainable assumptions: that I is a quantity that is fixed and knowable, that it represents the votes cast when $P = 50$ percent, and that the shape of the bandwagon/underdog function is known and independent of I. In reality, it does not help us much. In the absence of knowledge of I, if we find that $V > P$, we cannot know if it is the result of a bandwagon process or of inaccurate prediction.

Gartner (1976) proposes a dynamic model for bandwagons in repeated elections, based on the assumption that the effect is likely to operate on turnout rather than by making people change their vote. He asks us to consider a situation in which party X's supporters are much less discouraged from voting by expectations that the result is a foregone conclusion than are party Y's supporters, who are more likely to vote if they perceive a closely fought result.

The model shown in Figure 18.2 has been drawn up on the assumption that everything apart from voters' expectations of the likely result is fixed. For this reason it is highly artificial; in a situation where the electorate's prior preferences for a candidate (I, in Simon's terminology) are fixed, it is hard to imagine expectations actually varying between 0 and 100. This model shows a situation where the two turnout curves are symmetrical, i.e., party Y's supporters are equally discouraged by an expectation that Y

FIGURE 18.3

Gartner's Bandwagon Curve (Actual percentage of votes (V) is plotted against predicted votes (P) for a candidate)

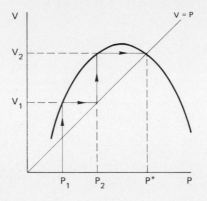

will definitely win as by an expectation that X will definitely win. (This, of course, need not be the case for a turnout effect to occur.) It also shows a situation where prior preferences for X and Y are so finely balanced that the differential turnout effect means that the curves cross, and the result of the election is in the balance. The resulting bandwagon curve where X is expressed as a percentage of the total votes cast $(X + Y)$ is shown in Figure 18.3. The situation modeled here is a dynamic process occurring gradually, where the results of an election at time $t-1$ are used as the basis for predictions at time t. Gartner argues that the result would converge on the equilibrium point P^*. This can be verified by tracing through the effect of an arbitrary prediction P_1; it would result in V_1, which would act as the prediction P_2; this would lead to V_2, and so on until P^* was reached. However, this conclusion is valid only if the sole thing changing over these elections is the value of P; however, I would change too, and, moreover, we have already noted that it is possible that $V = f(P)$ might change with changing values of I.

The value of these theoretical exercises is to allow researchers to follow through the effect of making different assumptions about how bandwagons might operate. They produce artificial results, such as Gartner's model which suggests that if expectations that Y will win get too high, it is possible to imagine a situation where this allows X in. Their value would be greatly enhanced if an attempt were then made to fit them to empirical results. In the only attempt to test a hypothetical dynamic model of bandwagon behavior, the information about the likely winner is provided not by opinion polls but by knowing how other states have committed their votes in a presidential nomination contest.

Brams and Riker (1972) propose a model of two blocs vying for an uncommitted middle group of voters. They suggest that an uncommitted voter should join bloc X if the increment of power he or she would add to X was larger than the power that he or she would have alone. This model is not very suitable for national elections, in which the concept of the power of the unaligned voter makes little sense, but it can be generalized effectively to conventions.

The concept of power that is used in this application is derived from game theory and presumes that in a coalition there is one voter (or bloc) who is pivotal to the formation of a coalition. Imagine a legislature in which there are nine votes, divided into one bloc casting three votes, one casting two, and four single voters. On any one issue, the blocs might be arranged in the order 3 2 1 1 1 1 in terms of their favorability toward the issue. In this instance, the bloc of two is pivotal since it determines the outcome of the vote. It can be shown that there are 30 possible orderings in which a coalition might form, and the bloc of three is pivotal 40 percent of the time; the bloc of two, 20 percent of the time; and each block of one is pivotal 10 percent of the time.

Straffin (1977) generalizes this idea to a hypothetical situation with an infinitely large number of voters, and he draws the path of the bandwagon curves for two candidates, X and Y (the outside curves on Figure 18.4). (It should be noted that it is beyond the scope of this chapter to explain how the curves were derived; interested readers are referred to Straffin's original article.)

The results of the 1976 contest for the Republican presidential nomination are also plotted in Figure 18.4, showing support for Ford (who finally wins) and Reagan; the small numerals represent the time in weeks from the beginning of the campaign. The bandwagon curves are constructed by calculating, according to the rules of game theory, what sort of split is necessary to start a bandwagon for the stronger bloc when only 10 percent of the total percentage of delegates are committed, when 20 percent are committed, when 30 percent are committed and so on. At no point until the very end does the actual split cross the bandwagon curve, although Ford came quite near to it in week 4, after the Illinois primary, when newspapers actually started to speculate about bandwagons. In short, the bandwagon did not develop until Ford actually won. (No one has ever investigated whether results in the bandwagon area tend to be followed by the predicted result in presidential nomination contests.)

This illustration of three very different approaches toward modeling a hypothetical idea of a bandwagon serve to illustrate the variety of mechanisms that the seemingly simple notion can in principle represent. However, our central concern, the effects of polls on opinions and behavior, is not addressed. Indeed, the concept of a bandwagon employed in the examples discussed could easily be generalized to cover any interaction effects in

FIGURE 18.4

Straffin's Bandwagon Curve for Presidential Nomination in 1976

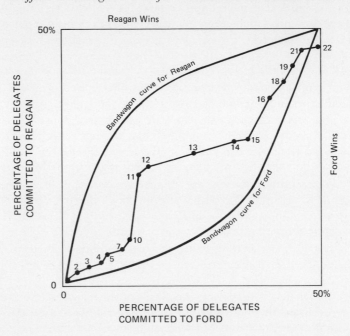

opinion formation where individuals consider the news of a reference group when forming their own views (see May and Martin [1975] for an explicit example of this type).

Moreover, the models have not readily lent themselves to empirical test. Straffin's game-theoretic ideas in bandwagon formation are very elegant, but have hardly been tested against reality. We must therefore turn now to the rather dreary data analysis of the researchers who have attempted to test the existence of bandwagon effects.

Empirical Evidence

What evidence could there be that the publication of a poll or a series of polls has any effect? It is hard to imagine how we could design a really convincing test, especially if we suspect effects that accrete slowly. Other than opinion polls, people have many sources of information about what people think. The only completely satisfactory way to isolate the effects of correlated variables is, of course, to perform an experiment on randomized groups; ideally we would need to control people's sources of information about majority views over an extended period of time. We first consider the experimental and quasi-experimental evidence, and then we look at the correlational studies that have attempted to provide this kind of evidence and attempt to substantiate the criticisms made of this literature at the beginning of this chapter.

EXPERIMENTAL EVIDENCE

A frequent by-product of achieving the enhanced analytical power of the randomized experiment is that one loses out on realism. Experiments that attempt to model elections and electoral behavior fare quite badly in this respect.

Consider, for example, two rather similar experiments that constructed mock elections in which a series of votes were taken. Information about the results of a first vote was experimentally varied and presented to the respondents before they voted a second time. The experimental control was only achieved because this was a situation of minimal information—the voters could know nothing else about the candidates because there was nothing else to know; it was therefore unlike real-life situations of minimal information in which it is reasonable to suppose that others might have more information than you. This is important, because it means that any insights gained from such studies are likely only to reveal psychological rather than rational motivations for vote switching. Nor can these studies reveal anything important about turnout behavior.

Both these experiments suggest support for the underdog hypothesis. Fleitas (1971) conducted a study in which 625 students were told they were to play the part of voters in a mayoral election; they indicated their choice of mayor in four separate ballots. They were told experimentally varied results before the last three ballots. Two of the treatment conditions involved information about the last ballot only, and one involved giving more qualitative information designed to convey the idea either of a successful frontrunner or of a worthy underdog. (The frontrunner was described as having a good family, financial security, and the support of the capable, outgoing mayor. The underdog was described as being an outsider, active in the United Fund, and forced to conduct a personal, door-to-door campaign to win voters.) Announcing that one candidate was ahead, regardless of the point at which this information was given, produced no effect on its own. But substantial sympathy for the underdog was evoked by the qualitative information; indeed it was more important than was subsequent information about the candidate's party.

Laponce (1966) produced both strong and consistent underdog effects by the release of information about which candidate was ahead. In a series of four experiments, involving a total of 2,160 students, there was a consistent tendency for votes to be switched to the underdog once the results had been announced. Moreover, the more hopeless the chances of the losing candidate seemed, the more people switched their votes. Laponce concluded that people were obeying the rules of games rather than the rules of warfare, operating to keep candidates in the game as long as possible; in a three-cornered fight there was also movement toward giving equal votes to all three candidates. Even when party identification was revealed in a later ballot, not all underdog sympathizers moved away from the losing candidate, even when he was of the opposite party; 12 of the 45 Republicans, for example, continued to support a Democratic loser. Laponce calls those voters for whom the urge to protect the underdog is stronger than party affiliation the "Red Cross voters," noting that in games, as on the battlefield, only a minority join the Red Cross.

It is hard to evaluate this type of evidence because of the artificiality of mock elections. Let us simply advance a cautious hypothesis: to the extent that elections have the characteristics of a game, a psychological underdog effect will operate on candidate preference.

An alternative to setting up mock elections is to feed the subjects with experimentally varied results of opinion polls and to look for intergroup differences in stated opinions as a result. To be sensitive enough to pick up differences in opinions about real objects (when the respondent probably has already formed personal preferences), an experimental study should be more complex than the mock elections just discussed. It should be a before-after design, as the literature in artificial elections suggests that some switching takes place in both directions. (Understanding bidirectional switching is clearly an important part of the psychology of poll effects, but even in applied research, compensating switches are of concern, because circumstances could arise that would shift the balance of switching in one direction or another.) There should also be some measurement of the crystallization and strength of people's existing views, to investigate whether effects are stronger among those with weak or uncrystallized views.

More important, people should be asked for their perception of majority opinion before the treatment. One fairly well-established finding in the psychological literature is that surprising information has a more powerful impact than information that confirms what one already knew (so long as it remains plausible), (see, for example, Gollob, Rossman, and Abelson, 1973). This could be a psychological mechanism of profound importance when studying poll effects, and research designs should take it into account.

Only one study has employed a before-after design, and it is one of the rare exceptions to the rule that all bandwagon research is about candidates and elections. Unfortunately, little reliance can be placed on this old study, since it is based on 26 subjects, albeit responding to 50 opinion items. Wheeler and Jordan (1929) repeated their 50 items 1 week after the initial measurement to measure "chance changes." Selecting only those questions that received at least a two-thirds majority in the first measurement, the authors then repeated them a third time, preceding them with information on the marginal responses. Their results suggest an interesting mixture of bandwagon effect and a yea-saying response set; people moved toward the majority, but also toward any agreement position.

The more recent versions of this research have been cruder, simply inserting a sentence before the final opinion question to inform respondents of the state of majority opinion. Most of the American studies of this kind have yielded rather inconclusive results. Dizney and Roskens (1962) rigged a college straw contest of the Nixon-Kennedy election. They randomly assigned a sample of 1,419 into three conditions, one which was told that Kennedy was ahead 55-45, one which was told that Nixon was ahead by that amount, and one which was given no information; no significant differences were produced.

Navazio (1977) asked people to rate Nixon's performance as president, the confidence he inspired, his honesty, and the way in which he was governing. The experimental group was additionally given the details of the most recent Gallup and Harris polls on these questions, which were heavily anti-Nixon. In 1974 most respondents probably not only had highly crystallized views already, but also did not need telling that a majority of the American public had clear anti-Nixon views as well. The study is further compromised by a low response rate (42 percent) and by clear evidence of an interaction between response rate and variables in the study; the experimental version of the questionnaire discouraged blue-collar response and encouraged white-collar response (compared with the proportions expected from the city directory). Navazio found no significant differences between the groups, except for the question on Nixon's ability to command confidence, which barely achieved significance ($p = .05$, $N = 201$). Since the information contained in the poll result was hardly irrelevant to an individual's assessment of Nixon's ability to command confidence, it is not surprising that the experimental group was more critical of Nixon; this cannot be interpreted as a bandwagon result. The most interesting result is apparent when the information is disaggregated; it appears that the experimental treatment produced underdog effects in blue-collar workers and bandwagon effects in clerical and white-collar workers. However, given the problems with the response rate, these results must be treated as tentative.

One recent study tried a more interesting experimental manipulation, which better captures the sense of a bandwagon. Roper performed a split-ballot trial with the presidential approval ratings by introducing the "approval" question to half the sample with the preamble, "As you know, all the polls have been showing support for Carter going down. We'd like to get your opinion about him." Roper reports (although without giving any of the technical details) that the experimental version produced a 1 percent movement away from Carter (Cantril, 1980:53), but this result is almost certainly statistically insignificant.

What could explain the discrepancy between these rather inconclusive results and the underdog effects found in artificial elections? One obvious possibility is the greater sensitivity of the artificial situations. But another explanation could lie in the group being identified as "the majority." In the contrived ballots, the majority is clearly "people like me" (students), whereas in the studies just discussed, the majority is an undefined general public. To the extent that we are dealing with psychological rather than with rational bandwagon effects, it is reasonable to suppose that the social and spatial distance of the majority could attenuate any bandwagon or underdog processes.

The only American study that contradicts this conclusion is an experiment by Tyson and Kaplowitz (1977). They "informed" groups of students of the views of the student majority on draft evasion, wage and price controls, prohibition of smoking tobacco, marijuana use, and premarital sex. Like the other study on nonelection opinion, the sample size of this experiment is extremely small (15 in each of 4 treatment groups). The results were therefore almost bound to be nonsignificant, but, more important, the direction of the results was not consistent either. So, it cannot really call into question the previous conclusion.

There are, however, two British studies that contradict these null findings. They both suggest that there may exist an underdog effect operating on voter turnout. After the Orpington by-election in 1962, many people were convinced that the Liberal landslide had been due to the projected narrow lead of the third-party candidate. In the 1964 general election, therefore, pollsters and the media were watching for effects of this kind.

Rothman of Sales Research Services varied information given to three treatment groups of 400 voters before the election. The first group was told that the Labour Party was in the lead, the second that the Conservative Party was in the lead, and the third was given no information. There was no effect on switching of preferences, but the supporters of the party behind at the polls said that they were more likely to turn out to vote (cited in Teer and Spence, 1973:131).

The second study comes to similar conclusions. In the last three days before the February 1974 general election, at a time when the polls were not predicting a clear-cut winner, Gaskell (1974) experimentally varied the information he gave to 395 people about who was ahead at the polls. Instead of a no-information condition as a control, he said that the polls were close. Fewer supporters of both parties said that they would vote if a clear-cut victory was predicted, but the effect was stronger on the supporters of the party predicted to win. Contrary to the hypothesized effect in the Orpington by-election, the Liberals were not less likely to vote as the lead narrowed. The group for whom the effect was stronger consisted of people who had not yet decided which way to vote.

We cannot, however, conclude that people will behave as they say they will. Thus, while there is a widespread belief in the effect of opinion polls upon rating behavior, the problems of interpreting the available experimental evidence preclude any firm conclusions about the validity of this belief.

In summary then: studies of artificial elections seem to produce support for the underdog thesis, while studies that use simple poll information on real issues do not seem to produce systematic intergroup differences in stated preference, but suggest a possible effect on the turnout in elections (at least in the United Kingdom). However, these latter studies are poorly designed and are probably insensitive to the kind of effects that we are looking for.

QUASI-EXPERIMENTAL EVIDENCE

I argued earlier that most of the experiments were flawed by their failure to use a before-after design to gauge the effect of surprising poll information. The same point could be made with natural experiments: ideally we want to find an election in which poll announcements surprised the electorate. Operationally this probably means an election in which the poll predictions were changing and, ideally, crossing the 50-50 mark, but not so close to it that a winner was never predicted. (This idea could suggest that information about trends in polls would have more effect than static information; a trend represents a change from a base level, and reported trends in poll results might therefore have an impact because they are by nature surprising.) An interesting natural experiment, or quasi-experiment, is possible in the United States, where the time zone differences between the West and East coasts are sufficient to allow the late voters on the West Coast to hear the voting results on the East Coast before they go to the ballot box.

The studies that have examined effects of this time difference have been widely cited (for example, Hodder-Williams, 1970:49) as refuting the bandwagon thesis about the effect of poll information in elections, but it is important to realize that they do not address this topic. Rather, they consider only the effect of early election returns on late voters. Since most people have made up their mind which way to vote by election day, such studies test the bandwagon thesis at a time when opinion has, for the most part, crystallized.

There are four such studies: Lang and Lang (1968); Mendelsohn (1966); Fuchs (1966); and Tuchman and Coffin (1972). None of the elections studied meets the desired criteria just mentioned. The first three relate to the 1964 presidential election, which, as the authors admit, was a particularly clear-cut contest, and opinion presumably crystallized early in the campaign. Since the Johnson landslide was predicted so early and so consistently, the information that confirmed the predictions on election day can have come as a surprise to nobody, and, indeed, no effects of exposure to early election returns were found on West Coast voting.

The only study that is important for our purposes is therefore the study by Tuchman and Coffin (1972) of the 1968 election. This election was much more closely contested and was, moreover, a three-cornered fight between Nixon, Humphrey, and Wallace. We have noted from the Orpington by-election in the United Kingdom that polling effects are believed to be more prevalent when there are three blocs vying for votes. But this election was such a closely fought contest that the early returns available to California voters 5 hours before the ballot boxes closed simply served to indicate that it was still a very close contest. The only likely effects in this election were therefore the effects of this knowledge on turnout, since there was no clear bandwagon or underdog for the electors to rally to.

The study consisted of two waves of interviews with a sample of 1,455 registered voters in the Pacific time zone and 547 registered voters in the Eastern time zone. Of the 1,455 voters in the West, only 6 percent were exposed to broadcasts before casting their vote; this figure is low, because only 38 percent of the voters went to the ballot box after 3:00 P.M. Of the 1,368 unexposed western voters, 3 percent changed their turnout plans, whereas 4.3 percent (4/94) of the exposed voters changed their turnout plans. This difference is too small to be significant with samples of this size, but we should note that its direction is consistent with the suggestion from the British experiments that turnout behavior could be affected by the prediction of a close election.

It was not possible to look separately at those who were undecided about their turnout plans, since none of the undecided western voters watched a broadcast before voting or deciding not to vote. The only statistically significant finding was a difference between the West and the East; voters in the East were more likely than were voters in the West to change their turnout plans.

There is one final caveat to sound with respect to these quasi-experiments. They all rely on panel designs, and it is well known that subjects of a longitudinal election study behave differently than the population from which they were sampled: the very act of being interviewed about voting intentions and political views sensitizes subjects to the issues and produces higher levels of turnout (Yalch, 1976; Kraut and McConahay, 1973). It may also produce in respondents a desire to appear consistent to the interviewer, and therefore encourage them to vote for the party they said they would vote for, even if they had changed their minds.

Let us summarize the main criticisms of these widely quoted quasi-experiments. They do not look at the effect of information about likely election outcomes at the time when voting decisions are being made. Moreover, these studies are not very sensitive to any effect that may exist because of the small size of the relative samples; few people vote late, and of those who do, very few watch broadcasts. This is very different from election polls in general, where the majority of people claim to have heard at least one poll result before election day (National Opinion Polls, 1974:7).

NONEXPERIMENTAL EVIDENCE

Bandwagon (or underdog) effects of the polls must be shown to stem from the publication of the information per se. The minute we leave the laboratory, or those situations in which there is quasi-experimental control, a whole universe of variables that have an impact on voter decisions is brought into play. While time series or panel data could provide refutations of simple theses about the effects of the polls, they do not permit convincing positive demonstrations. It becomes essential to control for other sources of information about majority opinion and strength of commitment, but this is not done in the handful of existing studies.

One of the earliest discussions of bandwagon effects in voting is found in *The People's Choice* (Lazarsfeld, Berelson, and Gaudet, 1944). Members of their panel sample who were undecided about which way to vote said expectations of who would win an election affected them. Some respondents explicitly stated that they were trying to vote for the winner:

> Just before the election it looked like Roosevelt would win so I went with the crowd. Didn't make any difference to me who won, but I wanted to vote for the winner. [p. 108]

Fully 75 percent of this sample of 600 people changed their expectation of who would win the election during the course of the campaign, and 42 of them (around 10 percent) said that the source of their changed expectations was an opinion poll. However, these explanations of how the decision to vote was made are the result of respondent introspection (with all the concomitant dangers; see Nisbett and Wilson, 1977) and not inferences derived by the investigator from the evidence of systematically patterned variation.

In a later study, *Voting*, Berelson, Lazarsfeld, and McPhee (1954) use their panel data to disentangle the complex causal relationship between expectations and preferences. In the earlier study it had been assumed that expectations led to preferences and not vice versa, whereas it is also plausible that voters would expect that the person whom they and their friends favored would win. By investigating which changes first, they conclude that the bandwagon effect (expectations altering preferences) and what they call the "projection effect" (preferences altering expectations) are about equal in strength (Berelson, Lazarsfeld, and McPhee, 1954:289).

These two studies introduced the idea of bandwagons into the literature;

the latter also shows a way of untangling various effects. (It is regrettable that later studies do not also carefully document changes in both expectations and preferences.) These voting studies do not, however, really address the question of the effects of the polls.

The most extensive and scholarly study of the trends in poll predictions examines the possibility of bandwagon effects in presidential primaries (Beniger, 1976). Primaries have been the arena of electoral behavior where the discussion of polling effects has been dominant (see, for example, Davis, 1967), and where the largest body of circumstantial evidence has built up (see, for example, Wheeler, 1976). It seems plausible to suggest that if bandwagon effects were to occur anywhere, they should occur here; the primary is used by candidates "as a weapon to force the national convention to nominate the 'popular' candidate" (Davis, 1967:3), and as a context in which candidates can demonstrate their ability to win. It would be perfectly rational behavior on the part of the voters to use information about a candidate's potential to win before voting in a primary.

Beniger collected data from Gallup candidate preference polls, recording carefully both the date of fieldwork and the date of publication, and compared them with the outcomes of state primary elections from 1936 to 1972. This allowed him to discover whether poll results change more immediately after primaries than primaries do after poll results are published. Beniger found that winning a primary consistently gave the victor a boost at the polls in the period immediately following. He looked for a bandwagon effect by examining all the polls to see whether the leading candidate rose or declined in the following poll. Of the 183 Gallup preference polls that were followed by a subsequent poll, in 83 cases the rating of the leading candidate rose in the next poll, in 81 cases it fell, and in 19 cases it remained the same. This means that we must rule out simple bandwagon effects of polls; it would appear that in the short run, primaries affect polls and not vice versa.

But it would be striking indeed if the effect of the poll was to produce a large enough change in preferences to be detected in net changes over time. The number of people who hear any particular poll result is very small. If only 5 percent of the voters, say, know the most recent poll result, and 2.5 percent intend to vote for the winner anyway, it would probably take the remaining 2.5 percent changing their minds to register a net effect that could be detected. It is much more plausible to imagine that poll results contribute slowly to a general picture of who is to win.

The strongest relationship in Beniger's data is the correlation between the standing in the initial poll and the final outcome. Over half of the variance in candidates' primary performances can be accounted for by the percentage of people favoring them at the outset of the contest. Moreover, the strength of the relationship increases gradually as the convention approaches, although this probably reflects only gradual opinion crystallization. There are many explanations that could be put forward for this continuity in the predicted winner, but it is consistent with the idea of a slower-moving, glacial bandwagon effect. Polls do not in themselves seem to influence subsequent polls, but we cannot rule out the possibility that they could have an increasingly important impact on winning the presidential nomination.

There is no other study comparable to Beniger's. There are countless stories told of situations in which the polls either produced a bandwagon or underdog effect (the accusation often being made by the party that loses the election; see, for example, the complaints by Carter's campaign aides that CBS News cost him the Maine caucuses by predicting a big Carter win hours before the caususes were over [*Washington Post*, February 12, 1980]). The well-known phenomenon of poll results overestimating support for a third party in an election is also often interpreted in this light; supporters of the third party blame their poor performance on poll predictions which suggest that certain votes will be wasted in the election.

However, there does seem to be a *prima facie* case for the opposite, underdog effects to operate in general elections in the United Kingdom. In every postwar election (with the possible exception of October 1974), the party that has been leading in the polls at the dissolution of Parliament has lost support by election day. It would take a careful study such as Beniger's to clinch the argument, but, as can be seen from Figure 18.5, there does seem to be a similar pattern in the preelection polls. In all the most recent elections except the last, the poll soundings are consistently above the final result. If this is an underdog effect, it operates only on the vote itself, not on stated party preference: the results do not show declining support for the predicted winner, except in 1979 (we shall return to that election shortly).

This pattern in the poll results has led one of the pollsters to commit public "hari-kari" (Wybrow, 1974:234). Thompson, chairman of Opinion Research Centre (ORC), claimed that the reason the predictions were wrong was because the polls themselves affected the outcome (Thompson, 1974a). After the October 1974 election, he called for an inquiry, and suggested in an article in the London *Evening Standard* that one could have predicted the true outcome by making a correction for the polling effect (Thompson, 1974b). Retrospective prediction is an easy game to play, of course.

However, Harris and ORC did carry out re-interviews with respondents after the October 1974 election to investigate reasons for last-minute changes of voting plans; these produced qualitative evidence in support of the underdog hypothesis (Louis Harris International, 1974).

In 1970, Britain's equivalent of the 1948 U.S. polling fiasco occurred.

FIGURE 18.5

Polling in Recent United Kingdom Elections
(dashed line indicates election results)

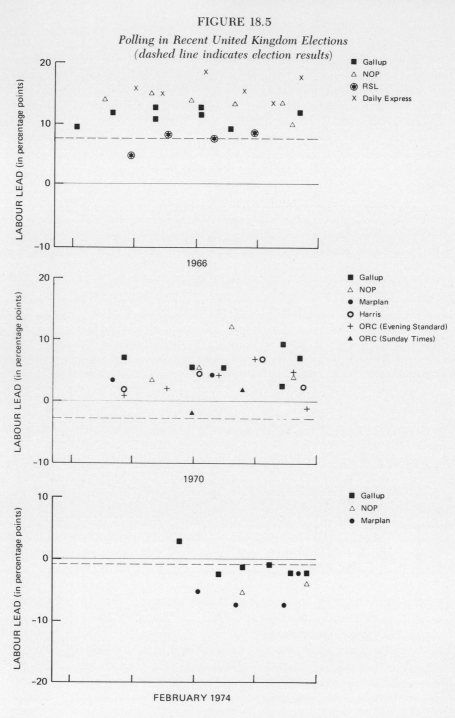

Do Polls Affect What People Think?

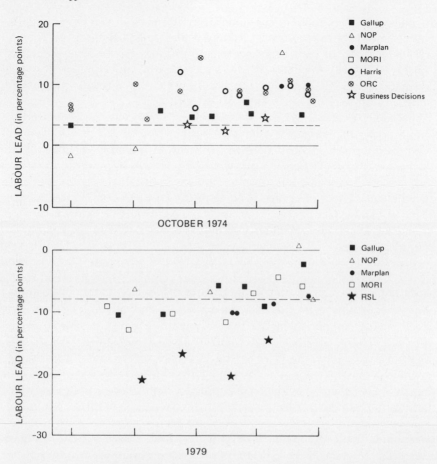

SOURCES: For 1966 and 1970 elections, Teer and Spence (1973:70); for February 1974, directly from polling companies; for October 1974, National Opinion Polls (1974); for 1979, MORI (1979).

The predictions of all the polling companies were wrong, and a committee of inquiry was established afterward to investigate what had gone wrong and to make recommendations for the future. Examination of Figure 18.5 shows that the 1970 election conforms to a pattern found in the other elections as well—an overestimation of the winning party's majority; the problem in 1970 stemmed from the fact that this constant error included the zero point, and so the wrong winner was called, but the basic problem is visible in all these poll results.

The 1979 election might seem at first glance to undermine this pattern; out of the 26 results in the 40 days prior to the election, 15 were above the final result and 11 were below. But by election time there was widespread speculation about the possibility that the outcome could be influenced by the polls. A well-publicized, last-minute result from National Opinion Polls, which showed the Labour Party leading at the polls, led the press to suggest that a replay of 1970 might occur, and this may have reversed flagging Conservative Party fortunes; Worcester of Market and Opinion Research International (MORI) has called the pattern of these poll results the "boomerang-backlash-bandwagon" effect (MORI, 1979:ii).

This ad hoc evidence is unsatisfactory. The eye can easily be deceived by simple graphs, and many a tale can be spun from them; the movement might be interpreted as being antigovernment, for example, since in all the elections except 1979 the party ahead at the polls was in power at the time. Only a more systematic study would end the contradictory arguments adduced about British elections. (The Orpington by-election is cited as evidence of bandwagon effects [Teer and Spence, 1973:133] and the Leyton by-election as evidence of underdog effects [Hodder-Williams, 1970:50], for example.)

One other type of nonexperimental evidence is sometimes cited in support of the idea that people get pleasure out of climbing on successful bandwagons. In many (but by no means all) postelection periods, the winning party or candidate enjoys what is known as a "honeymoon period" during which popular support is higher than at any other time (see, for example, Mueller, 1970). Cigler and Getter (1977) used a panel study, interviewing both before and after the 1972 presidential election, to investigate the extent of this phenomenon and to explore possible reasons for it. Although they found widespread evidence of people switching support after the election, there was no net effect in favor of the winning candidate, Nixon.

Sometimes the postelectoral swings are seen to operate differently on subgroups. Noelle-Neumann (1977:152) observes that after the German Bundestag election of 1972 there was no general bandwagon shift to be observed, but if the analysis was broken down into subgroups a different picture emerged; young workers, who had voted heavily for the Social Democratic Party, showed a shift toward the Social Democrats, while older, upper-class people, who had voted for the Christian Democratic Party, showed a movement toward the Christian Democrats. This suggests that it is the views of an appropriate reference group that may provide the basis for bandwagon shifts. If this is true, then poll results are unlikely to produce bandwagon effects because they are not regularly disaggregated into appropriate reference groups.

One final way in which poll results might influence the political process should be mentioned. Polls can create levels of expectation about the success of particular candidates against which their subsequent performance can be compared. The newspapers may feature a story stating "Johnson will carry New Hampshire by 60% +." In this way, a candidate who is only a runner-up can be declared a winner when he or she does "better than expected," as Eugene McCarthy did in New Hampshire in 1968.

News items like this are particularly common in presidential primaries, but they occur in other situations where attention focuses on trends in opinion on the ability of a candidate or a party to win. Roy Jenkins, co-founder of the new British Social Democratic Party, did not win the Warrington by-election in 1981 (the first parliamentary by-election that the Social Democrats contested), but by exceeding the polling expectations for him, he was pronounced a "success" by the press.

Summary and Conclusions

There is a persistent suggestion in the results discussed in this chapter that underdog effects may exist in some electoral situations. The clearest results come from artificial elections, in which subjects are asked to take part in repeated ballots, and in which the information about the ballot results is experimentally varied; candidate preferences subsequently change toward favoring the underdog. But there is suggestive nonexperimental evidence from the United Kingdom suggesting that there may also be underdog effects in real elections. Moreover, varying the poll results presented to individuals in two British experiments produces differences in the proportions who say they intend to vote. It is hard to say whether this is a characteristic peculiar to the British, since similar studies have not been undertaken in the United States.

There is no experimental evidence in favor of a bandwagon hypothesis, that is, that people switch preferences for candidates in line with the majority view, although there is an interesting suggestion that a bandwagon may operate when a view is perceived as *growing* in strength, rather than necessarily being the majority view already. The pattern of poll results in American presidential primaries is compatible with the idea that information from polls about majority views has a glacial effect in presidential nomination contests.

Many legislative bodies in different countries have not awaited the results of studies of this kind before concluding that the polls are likely to have some effect on the electoral process. Brazil bans the publication of polls immediately before an election, although this ban is very hard to enforce (Webb, 1980). In France, a law was passed in 1978 making polling illegal in the period immediately before an election. In the Federal Republic of Germany, the polling companies organize a voluntary restriction on polling in the week prior to elections. In Canada, the broadcasting of either poll projections or early results is forbidden while any polling booths remain open. The protestations of the pollsters that experimental evidence runs to the contrary have been ignored.

Some investigators have expressed surprise when their simple experiments on poll effects produced null results (for example, Tyson and Kaplowitz [1977] who claim that theirs is the first conformity study ever to produce null results). I argue that the reason for this is that the design of these experiments is simply not sufficiently sensitive to pick up any effects; perception of majority views must build from several sources of evidence, and one piece of new information inserted in a questionnaire directly before the opinion question may not be sufficient to shift already existing ideas of the majority view. Since the early 1950s no one has seriously investigated the relationship between expectations and preferences, and no control for expectations has been introduced into any of these experimental studies.

Underdog effects should not cause surprise. To be sure, there is a stable paradigm of conformity experiments, which shows, for example, that one-third of individuals will deny the evidence of their eyes rather than disagree with a unanimous majority about the length of a line (Asch, 1951). This paradigm has been, however, subject to reinterpretation and qualification in recent years. The case for conformity effects has often been overstated. Moscovici and Faucheux (1972), for example, have shown that if you present a majority of naive subjects with two stooges who stick to their guns in an implausible case (the reversal of the Asch experiment), a robust influence of minorities can be demonstrated. Moreover, several attitude comparison studies have shown that by changing people's perception of the majority opinion, people's views can be shifted away from the majority opinion; studies of mock jury deliberations and experimental studies of shifts of opinion in small communities suggest that individuals do not wish merely to conform to the majority but wish to be closer to the perceived ideal than to the majority (Myers, Bach, and Schreiber, 1977; Myers, Wojcicki, and Aardema 1974; McGuire and Bermant, 1977). When the majority is as removed and undefined as the general public, it might be predicted that underdog effects are more likely than are bandwagon effects.

The underdog effect is by no means proved; there is merely some evidence suggesting that this is an area in which more careful research should be conducted. But the importance of conducting that research with respect to elections was noted earlier; predictions that are not adjusted for a real underdog effect could change the outcomes of elections if they were strong enough.

In conclusion, we must ask whether the literature examined has answered the question posed in the title of this chapter. The answer must be that it has not. The evidence just examined relates to an extremely circumscribed area: the effects of information about the voting intentions of others on the behavior of individual voters. Concentration on this aspect of the question has diverted attention about other social effects of polling; the straw man of bandwagon effects can then be pooh-poohed (for example, Gallup, 1966:546; Durant, cited in Hodder-Williams, 1970:47) and the other possible effects ignored.

The defense for concentrating research on electoral polling is that it is the most distinctive subject matter of the pollster's work. However, it is an atypical area of political life in a way that tends to obscure the agenda-setting potential of polls; in elections there is a consensus about the terms and rules of the game. No one objects that the following question: If there was an election tomorrow, who would you vote for? is biased in favor of one candidate rather than another, whereas on most controversial political issues there is no consensus about the appropriate terms in which to frame the debate. Claims of bias in wording abound in these other arenas of opinion polling (for example, North American Newspaper Alliance, 1980, Volume 1, Chapter 3). Moreover, there is no consensus about which issues are the most important ones to ask questions about.

The news media supply information, first and foremost. The power they have derives from their ability to select the information they present, and thus help to determine what it is that people know; their power to persuade people to a particular point of view by a direct communication has always been questionable (Pool, 1963). Media research in recent years has moved away from the "persuasion paradigm" and toward a concern with "agenda-setting" (Westergaard, 1977).

Opinion polls are, after all, the progeny of the news media. Once we leave the arena of election polls, the case for opinion polls being influential in agenda-setting is more plausible. We noted at the outset of this chapter that opinion poll results are often treated as coextensive with public opinion; thus, the group that can produce an opinion poll to favor its position can seemingly claim that public opinion is on its side. The survey researcher knows that responses to many opinion questions cannot be taken as evidence of the existence of public opinion: the mass of people may never normally discuss the topic that they are asked to pronounce on. In Britain, a clipping study (see Volume 1, Chapter 2) showed that there is a heavy imbalance in poll topics; British trade union policy and wage negotiation—a subject that the public does not place high on its list of important issues facing the country—was the most frequent subject of polls. If the agenda-setting function of the polls also works in a glacial way (as MacKuen [1979] suggests it might), the impact of this kind of polling on public views of current topics of discussion could be profound. The survey researcher also knows that finding opinion statements that reflect all sides of an issue is a difficult, and sometimes impossible, task; the very terminology used can betray a partisan position. Yet the public is assailed with claims that the majority believes that workers should accept wage restraint to combat inflation, or that gene-splicing research should continue, and so on, with no caveats of this kind.

In short, issue polls present topics as objects of current public concern, and suggest that the majority is debating a particular issue in a particular way. If the results of these issue polls are then treated as proof that public opinion exists, they could be an important part of the process of creating a climate of opinion.

Postscript

Since this chapter reviewing the bandwagon literature was written, I have conducted an experiment into poll effects on abortion attitudes (Marsh, 1984). From this research it does seem that there is indeed a bandwagon effect from telling people that the trend in recent polls has been in a particular direction. We drew an interlocking quota sample of parents in three British towns, with controls set on age, sex, and employment status. In one experiment we told a random half of the respondents that the trend in recent polls had been toward making abortion easier to get, and the other half, toward making it more difficult to get. Respondents were then asked their own views, using the following question: "In general, do you think the law should be left as it is, or should abortion be made easier to get, or should it be made more difficult to get?" The results are shown in Table 18.1. A similar experiment manipulating information about *current* public opinion rather than about *trends* replicated the null findings reported in the section on Experimental Evidence in this chapter.

TABLE 18.1

Effect of Trend Information on Attitudes toward Abortion

Information Provided	Attitude toward Abortion Law			
	Make easier	Leave as it is	Make more difficult	N
Trend to easier	34.5%	39.6%	25.9%	255
Trend to more difficult	25.4	37.1	37.5	256
d =	+9.1	+2.5	−11.6	

NOTE: X^2 = 9.2, d.f. = 2, p = 0.01

References

Asch, S.E. (1951) Effects of group pressure upon the modification and distortion of judgments. In H. Guetzkow, ed., *Groups, Leadership and Men.* Pittsburgh: Carnegie Press.

Beniger, J.R. (1976) Winning the presidential nomination: national polls and state primary elections, 1936-1972. *Public Opinion Quarterly* 40:22-38.

Berelson, B.R., Lazarsfeld, P.F., and McPhee, W.N. (1954) *Voting.* Chicago: University of Chicago Press.

Brams, S., and Riker, W.H. (1972) Models of coalition forming in voting bodies. In J.F. Herndon, and J.L. Bernd, eds., *Mathematical Applications in Political Science VI.* Charlottesville, Va.: University of Virginia Press.

Brown, R. (1963) *Explanation in Social Science.* London: Routledge and Kegan Paul.

Cantril, A.H., ed. (1980) *Polling on the Issues.* Cabin John, Md.: Seven Locks Press.

Cigler, A.J., and Getter, R. (1977) Conflict reduction in the post-election period: a test of the depolarization thesis. *Western Political Quarterly* 30:363-376.

Davis, J.W. (1967) *Presidential Primaries: Road to the White House.* New York: Crowell.

Dizney, H.F., and Roskens, R.W. (1962) An investigation of the "bandwagon effect" in a college straw election. *Journal of Educational Sociology* 36:108-114.

Downs, A. (1957) *An Economic Theory of Democracy.* New York: Harper and Row.

Fleitas, D.W. (1971) Bandwagon and underdog effects in minimal information elections. *American Political Science Review* 65:434-438.

Fuchs, D. (1966) Election-day radio-television and Western voting. *Public Opinion Quarterly* 30:226-236.

Gallup, G. (1966) Polls and the political process—past, present and future. *Public Opinion Quarterly* 29:544-549.

Gallup, G. (1972) Opinion polling in a democracy. In J. Tanur et al., eds., *Statistics: A Guide to the Unknown.* San Francisco: Holden-Day.

Gartner, M. (1976) Endogenous bandwagon and underdog effects. *Public Choice* 25:83-89.

Gaskell, G. (1974) Polls and the voters. *New Society*, 4 April, 28(600):23-24.

Gollin, A. (1980) Exploring the liaison between polling and the press. *Public Opinion Quarterly* 44(4):445-461.

Gollob, H.R., Rossman, B.B., and Abelson, R.P. (1973) Social inference as a function of the number of instances and consistency of information presented. *Journal of Personality and Social Psychology* 27:19-33.

Hodder-Williams, R. (1970) *Public Opinion Polls and British Politics.* London: Routledge and Kegan Paul.

Kraut, R.E., and McConahay, J.B. (1973) How being interviewed affects voting: an experiment. *Public Opinion Quarterly* 37:398-406.

Lang, K., and Lang, G. (1968) *Voting and Non-voting: Implications of Broadcasting Returns Before Polls Are Closed.* Waltham, Mass.: Blaisdell.

Laponce, J.A. (1966) An experimental method to measure the tendency to equibalance in a political system. *American Political Science Review* 60:982-993.

Lazarsfeld, P.F., Berelson, B.R., and Gaudet, H. (1944) *The People's Choice*. New York: Duell, Sloan and Pearce.

Louis Harris International (1974) *Harris and ORC Election Surveys, October 1974*. London: Louis Harris International Inc.

MacKuen, M.B. (1979) Social Communication and the Mass Policy Agenda. Ph.D. dissertation. University of Michigan.

Marsh, C. (1984) Back onto the bandwagon. *British Journal of Political Science*, 15:113-136.

May, R.M., and Martin, B. (1975) Voting models incorporating interactions between voters. *Public Choice* 22:37-53.

McGuire, M.V., and Bermant, G. (1977) Individual and group decisions in response to a mock trial: a methodological note. *Journal of Applied Social Psychology* 7:220-226.

Mendelsohn, H. (1966) Election-day broadcasts and terminal voting decisions. *Public Opinion Quarterly* 30:212-225.

MORI (1979) *Public Opinion Polls and the 1979 Election*. London: Market and Opinion Research International.

Moscovici, S., and Faucheux, C. (1972) Social influence, conformity bias, and the study of active minorities. In L. Berkowitz, ed., *Advances in Experimental Social Psychology*, Vol. 6. New York: Academic Press.

Mueller, J.E. (1970) Presidential popularity from Truman to Johnson. *American Political Science Review* 64:18-34.

Myers, D.G., Bach, P.H., and Schreiber, B.S. (1974) Normative and informational influence in group discussion. *Sociometry* 37:275-286.

Myers, D.G., Wojcicki, S.B., and Aardema, B.S. (1977) Attitude comparison: Is there ever a bandwagon effect? *Journal of Applied Social Psychology* 7:341-347.

North American Newspaper Alliance (NANA) (1978) Press release: Survey of New Right poorly worded and meaningless: NANA poll. By R. J. Wagman and S. D. Engelmayer. New York: NANA

National Opinion Polls (1974) *NOP Political Bulletin*, Vol. 131, November.

Navazio, R. (1977) An experimental approach to bandwagon research. *Public Opinion Quarterly* 41:217-225.

Nisbett, R.E., and Wilson, T.D.W. (1977) Telling more than we can know. *Psychological Review* 84:231-259.

Noelle-Neumann, E. (1977) Turbulences in the climate of opinion: methodological applications of the spiral of silence theory. *Public Opinion Quarterly* 41:143-158.

Pool, I. de S. (1963) The effect of communication on voting behavior. In W. Schramm, ed., *The Science of Human Communication*. New York: Basic Books.

Simon, H.A. (1957) Bandwagon and underdog effects in election prediction. In *Models of Man: Social and Rational*. New York: Wiley.

Straffin, P.D. (1977) The bandwagon curve. *American Journal of Political Science* 21:695-709.

Teer, F., and Spence, J.D. (1973) *Political Opinion Polls*. London: Hutchinson University Library.

Thompson, T.F. (1974a) Why the opinion polls were wrong . . . *The Times*, London: March 4.

Thompson, T.F. (1974b) Don't be beastly to the pollsters. *Evening Standard*, London: October 14.

Tuchman, S., and Coffin, T.E. (1972) The influence of election night television broadcasts in a close election. *Public Opinion Quarterly* 35:315-326.

Tyson, J.L., Jr., and Kaplowitz, S.A. (1977) Attitudinal conformity and anonymity. *Public Opinion Quarterly* 41:226-234.

Webb, N. (1980) The democracy of opinion polls. Paper presented at 63rd European Society of Opinion and Marketing Research seminar on opinion polls, Bonn, Federal Republic of Germany.

Westergaard, J. (1977) Power, class and the media. In J. Curran et al., eds., *Mass Communication and Society*. London: Edward Arnold.

Wheeler, M. (1976) *Lies, Damned Lies and Statistics: The Manipulation of Public Opinion in America*. New York: Liveright.

Wheeler, D., and Jordan, H. (1929) Changes of individual opinion to accord with group opinion. *Journal of Abnormal and Social Psychology* 24:203-215.

Wybrow, R.J. (1974) Foreword. *Gallup Political Index*, Vol. 163, February.

Yalch, R.F. (1976) Pre-election interview effects on voter turnout. *Public Opinion Quarterly* 40:331-336.

Acknowledgments

I am indebted to Charles Turner, Bob Abelson, and Tom Smith for the careful reading they gave an earlier draft of this chapter, and for the painstaking advice over both structure and detail they gave me.

Name Index

Note. The *name* index lists all individuals and organizations referred to in this volume. References to some individuals and organizations have also been included in the *subject* index when the reference extends beyond the citation of an individual's published work or the data produced by an organization (e.g., if the organization, its procedures, or interviewing staff was discussed).

593

Subject Index

Abortion attitudes and contraceptive behaviors, 477, 494–498

Academic survey research: central place of attitude studies, 100; similarity to commercial survey research of question formats used by, 295–296, 309

Accuracy of presidential ratings. *See* Presidential popularity measurements

Acquiescence response set, 260, 262

Advertising, early uses of survey research in, 24

Agenda-setting hypothesis, 443–474, 566; polls and, 587, 588

Allport, Floyd H., 10, 28

Allport scale, 11–15

Ambivalent attitudes and responses, 228–230, 249n11

American Economic Review, 94–114

American Journal of Political Science, 94–114

American Journal of Sociology, 10, 13, 94–114

American Political Science Review, 94–114

American Sociological Review, 94–114

Annual Housing Survey, 147, 148. *See also* Housing measurements

Arrow's impossibility theorem, 443

Associated Press/NBC News Poll, measurements of presidential popularity by, 501–545

Atoms of pleasure, 48

Attitude concept, 219–220, 399; definition of, 2, 3, 4, 29n19

Attitude consistency, 215–255; correlates of, 217, 235

Attitude constraint, 238, 247n1

Attitudes and behavior, 6, 9–10, 17, 30n6, 100–101, 494–497; LaPiere studies of, 30n6; use of behavior to infer attitudes, 18, 51

Authoritarianism, 13

Bandwagon effects, 565–591; experimental evidence of, 573–577, 588; hypothetical models for, 567–571; in 1980 Maine primary, 581; nonexperimental evidence of, 579; quasi-experimental evidence of, 577–579; West Coast voting and, 577. *See also* Underdog effects

Bans on publication of polls before election, 585–586

Bias, 413–424; adjusting for effects of, 422–424; in variance estimates when measurement error present, 431–432, 434; models for constant and variable, 508. *See also* Mean square error of survey estimates; Measurement error; Nonsampling variance; Response variance

Black-and-white model and alternatives, 216, 220, 230, 231, 235. *See also* Nonattitudes

Black power, 562

Note. References to some individuals and organizations have been included in the *subject* index when the reference extends beyond the citation of an individual's published work or the data produced by an organization (e.g., if the organization, its procedures, or interviewing staff was discussed). The *name* index contains a comprehensive listing of individuals and organizations referred to in this volume.

If a person spoke openly and clearly against the faith, offering the arguments and authorities upon which heretics usually rely, it would be very easy for the faithful learned of the Church to convict him of heresy. . . . But since present day heretics attempt and seek to conceal their errors rather than to avow them openly, men trained in the learning of the Scriptures cannot convict them, because they escape in verbal trickery and wily thinking. Learned men are even apt to be confounded by them, and the heretics congratulate themselves and are all the stronger therefore, seeing that they can thus delude the learned to the point of escaping artfully by the twists and turns of their crafty, cheating and underhanded replies.

BERNARD GUI, circa A.D. 1321
Manual of the Inquisitor